The 100 Most
Influential Books
Ever Written

The 100 Most Influential Books Ever Written

The History of Thought From Ancient Times to Today

Martin Seymour-Smith

CITADEL PRESS
Kensington Publishing Corp.
www.kensingtonbooks.com

CITADEL PRESS books are published by

Kensington Publishing Corp.
850 Third Avenue
New York, NY 10022

All Kensington titles, imprints, and distributed lines are available at special quantity discounts for bulk purchases for sales promotions, premiums, fund raising, educational, or institutional use. Special book excerpts or customized printings can also be created to fit specific needs. For details, write or phone the office of the Kensington special sales manager: Kensington Publishing Corp., 850 Third Avenue, New York, NY 10022, attn: Special Sales Department, phone 1-800-221-2647.

Citadel Press logo Reg. U.S. Patent and Trademark Office
Citadel Press is a trademark of Kensington Publishing Corp.

First printing: March 2001

10 9 8 7 6 5 4 3 2 1

Printed in the United States of America

Library of Congress Cataloging-in-Publication Data

Seymour-Smith, Martin.
    The 100 most influential books ever written : the history of thought from ancient times to today / Martin Seymour-Smith.
        p.   cm.
    "A Citadel Press book."
    Includes index.
    ISBN 0-8065-2192-9
    1. Books and reading—History. 2. Intellectual life—History. I. Title.
Z1003.S495 1998
028′.9—dc21   98-10027
                                                                 CIP

To James Hodgson

THIS WORLD IS NOT CONCLUSION

Emily Dickinson

This world is not conclusion;
   A sequel stands beyond,
Invisible, as music,
   But positive, as sound.
It beckons and it baffles;
   Philosophies don't know,
And through a riddle, at the last,
   Sagacity must go.
To guess it puzzles scholars;
   To gain it, men have shown
Contempt of generations,
   And crucifixion known.

CONTENTS

ACKNOWLEDGMENTS

I have to thank, first, Gary Fitzgerald: for thinking of this book and then for so strenuously bearing with me and for his suggestions, editing, and advice.

For more suggestions and advice I am grateful to Nick Jacobs, Cressida Bastinado, and my wife. My greatest debt in this respect is expressed in my dedication (and for much else besides).

I am also glad to thank Margaret Wolf for her sensible and sensitive editing.

My debt to Mark McConville cannot be expressed in words, but his kindness could be said to be in part the subject of this book.

PHOTO CREDITS

INTRODUCTION

This book does not provide a list of the one hundred most famous, or the most exciting, or even the "best," books. As for the "greatest" books: I have frequently questioned, throughout the essays, the very concept of "greatness." What do we really mean by this term when we use it? It is accepted easily and willingly enough—especially by some apparently cold-blooded, but really sentimental, academics who ought to know better—but is it not really just a catch-all for "what excites and pleases *me*," "what *I* think is the best"? A means by which the drier kind of person can release feelings the raw emotional crudity of which his intellect can hardly properly admit to possessing? Is it worth creating a whole new category of meaning in order to define this vague and vexing concept "greatness" more precisely? On the principle implied by the English philosopher William of Ockham (whose works are a very near-miss in terms of this selection), that entities should not be multiplied—that we should not create unnecessary complications by introducing hypotheses that, upon reflection, we can do without—evidently it is not. Some of course might conceivably define "greatness" as simply "the most influential," but this is not widespread.

Some major thinkers did not even *want* to be influential, or at least they did not initially proceed as if they did. They needed to express the truth as it presented itself to them, and be damned to its influence or otherwise. After they had finished their work, they might then have started to think about greatness, but their first inspiration had not been polemical. Plato was possibly one of those, although he became increasingly polemical as he went along.

Did the Czech writer Franz Kafka (included here because he defined the nature of bureaucracy, which is, in his gnostic—if also richly comic—terms, an expression of the Demiurge, the evil principle) want to exercise influence? It would be rather disturbing if he had. Perhaps this was what he was worrying about when he left a note decreeing that his works should be destroyed after his death. Nonetheless, my guess would be that he has had a beneficial influence: one tragicomically *against* bureaucracy as this century has practiced it. The nature of it is well summed up in the characteristically twentieth-century saying that runs something like: *We can do all this without killing or torturing so many people.* Nothing so well as this (and Kafka's fiction) epitomizes the grand and self-destructive malice at the heart of what may at first sight seem to be perfectly beneficent activities such as collecting taxes or blandly collating private information.

Perhaps it is a reaction to Hegelian (and then Nazi) stresses and strains: Why put people in concentration camps or other unpleasant places when they can quite as easily be controlled, along "democratic" lines, in their own homes—and be entertained at a profit to boot? In Great Britain it is now sometimes called "Blairism," but it is not essentially different from what was never called "Majorism" but was called "Toryism," "socialism," "Thatcherism," and so on and so forth. The little differences of emphasis here and there do not really betoken much. Perhaps it is only the mere *spirit* of Kafka's Josef K. that dies at the hands of those knife-wielding assassins. But there is always plenty of religious writ to support this new concept of everything-being-for-the-best-really. The American philosopher Noam Chomsky (included here), who might be taken to dissociate himself from all such beneficence, does not—whatever he may feel about God—look to that kind of support. But for right-minded people God is always there, at least officially.

As for the real God: Such an influence, as I have no doubt controversially tried to show, persists in what may be called the gnostical and anarchistic strand of thought, from *The Gospel of Truth* through Godwin, Thoreau, and even Jean-Paul Sartre, to Martin Buber and Noam Chomsky himself.

Nor is this book a list of literary masterpieces, although many of the works (for example, Plato's *Republic*) included certainly qualify on that score. Some (for example, *Das Kapital*), though, quite as certainly, do not. That book remains, after all, although important and unduly maligned because of what has (so far) been made of it in practice, notoriously *unreadable* for the most part; when we know of people who *enjoy* all of it we know we are dealing with a sort of obsessiveness that has little to do with it. They might thus consult it to discover in what place it deals with the matter of the right action to take if one's five-year-old son makes a remark against the Party. Not that, of course, it does have such a place—it is far better than that. Such obsessed readers, though, believe it must, that it does *really*. But in this instance we are spared *Das Kapital* because we can substitute the more lucid and simple *Communist Manifesto,* although that is not a *literary* masterpiece either.

The same kind of reader can find everything dealt with in the tawdry "philosophy" of Ayn Rand, who is not in this selection because ultimately, and always much sooner than might be expected, the fifth-rate is eclipsed. But works such as *Das Kapital,* which lie somewhere between first- and second-rate (and that is high in the order of things), are none the worse for not being literary masterpieces. For that matter, you might find Plotinus (who is nobler than Marx, and unequivocally first-rate—for all that this matters or does not matter) hard to read through at a sitting, just as Pareto (who is neither nice nor noble) surely is.

Enjoyment, though, (some) professors (and many other overintellectually endowed people) apart, is not necessarily a bad thing. It can help. Then again, *famous* is not necessarily the same as *influential*. Everyone has heard of Lewis Carroll's *Alice in Wonderland,* but has it been influential? On the way writers compose "nonsense," perhaps. But otherwise? Has it changed lives? Has it even the potential to change lives?

Nor, emphatically, is this a list of the one hundred books that I believe—or anyone else believes—*ought* to have influenced the people of the world. I might have included *Alice in Wonderland* had that been the case. I should certainly have included Sherwood Anderson's *Winesburg, Ohio*. But, instead, I have given a substantially annotated list of the one hundred books that *actually* have exercised, if sometimes in devious and very subterranean ways, the most decisive influence upon the course of human thought—and therefore, of course, upon various kinds of conduct, too.

I could not rank these books in any sort of order. Tempting as that prospect might have been, it would have been too frivolous and would have begged far too many questions. It would have called for too unreasonable speculation. For example, we know by now that Plato's *Republic* and even the New Testament are going to continue to be influential. But how can we say that of Marx, let alone of Norbert Wiener or Noam Chomsky. There are no machines for measuring influence, and one's preferences have a way of creeping in unnoticed. So my selection can do no more than speak for itself. About seventy of the books selected are obvious choices; the remainder must in the very nature of things be controversial.

On the matter of "influence" itself, many difficult problems naturally arise. For example, how much has the Sermon on the Mount, included in the New Testament—with the majority of whose precepts, at least, humanity as a whole (say, any pragmatic director of public services), likes to proclaim its sincere agreement—*really* much influenced behavior? Or have, on the whole and as a general rule, the Moneychangers always expelled Christ from the Temple, and have most civilizations been *business as usual* ones? There was plenty of profitable banking going on among not only the damned but also the elect of Calvin's merry Geneva. Enoch Powell, the politician who tried (but failed) to make race a major issue in British politics in order to gain power, used to say words to the effect that things would be different in the Kingdom of God. He presumably meant that Sambo would be all right there: in Great Britain, he warned, borrowing from other rhetoricians, there would be "rivers of blood." His ambitious project looked to become influential in its time, and liberals were afraid; but ultimately it amounted to no more than an unpleasant minor episode in British history.

There are more problems than just those. What is the difference, if any,

between a very wealthy and powerful businessman, and Christ—and why are
such questions considered to be vulgar and irrelevant? Why could Christ not
achieve the same sort of clear-cut and obviously virtuous success as those of
Rupert Murdoch and his kind? What would Machiavelli, safe in the Elysian
Fields (if indeed he is), have now to say about the relationship between
Christian precepts and practical policy? Would he recant his view—regarded
as from Satan by many of those who tried to employ his methods in the centuries immediately after him—or would he stick to his guns? The same ques-
tion might be asked of his latter-day successor, the wine-bibbing Vilfredo
Pareto who, on hearing of Mussolini's march on Rome, exclaimed, *"I told
you so!"* And what do the two Germans, the clever and not sufficiently wise
Hegel and the Nazi charlatan Martin Heidegger, safely in Hell (as surely they
must be), have to say about their contributions (and about the Gospel of
Christ, or Martin Buber)? What does the profound and poetic ironist,
Thomas Hobbes, who seems to have some attitudes in common with Machi-
avelli, think about morality now?

    It would have been much nicer to include books by the essentially reli-
gious philosopher Alfred North Whitehead, or even by his pupil, and coau-
thor of *Principia Mathematica,* the atheist Bertrand Russell, rather than the
one by Hegel; but the measurement of real influence has had to be observed.
And what is evil has on the whole, though by no means always or unequivocally—a balance is somehow achieved—been more influential than what is,
shall we say, better. And what does Russell now say about Christianity or any
other of the religions that he believed were the result of delusion? Was he
right and can he say nothing, or is in some way the quality of his sincere
good wishes for humanity still somehow, somewhere, by means incomprehensible to "science" as it is practiced, preserved? And is all true *quality* thus
preserved? Plato would have answered in the affirmative. And if *lack of quality* is somehow preserved, too, then in what kind of unspeakable place can
that of the most unequivocally vile man represented here, John Calvin, be?
In the Hell he planned for the majority of humanity with only the apology
that this was terrible but that it was so?

    My principle of selection has meant that many of the writers of litera-
ture of astonishingly high quality, such as Goethe, Dickens, and Dostoyevsky,
as well as many purveyors of highly successful and not necessarily unintelligent entertainment such as Margaret Mitchell (whose name is rather less
well known that that of her long-lasting title, *Gone With the Wind*), have
been omitted in favor of certain philosophers not only less well known today,
but largely unread outside universities. Even inside the universities scholars
all too often only pretend to have read them. There is nothing like being an
expert in a subject to conceal ignorance of its essence. Look at politicians.

    Plotinus comes to mind in this connection. Yet—as you will, I hope, dis-
cover in the section devoted to him—his *influence* on Christianity as well as on
the development of his own Neoplatonism was enormous, even incalculable,
and far greater than that of *The Pickwick Papers,* let alone *Gone With the Wind*

could ever have been. The same could be said of the skeptic Pyrrho; but since he left no writings that we know of, we have had to have recourse to Sextus Empiricus in this important connection. Now how many of those who have heard of Margaret Mitchell (or of *Gone With the Wind*), or of Ernest Hemingway or John Steinbeck—let alone the Beatles or Bob Dylan—have heard of Sextus Empiricus? Yet there is a very strong sense in which Sextus Empiricus is far more important than Margaret Mitchell, who *entertained* readers but did not in the least influence them, and far more important, too, than Hemingway and other more famous names—even than the Beatles. If some women thought they modeled themselves on Scarlett O'Hara ("I'll think about it tomorrow") then, since Scarlett O'Hara was herself based (though ably based) on a stereotype rather than on a real character, those women would have modeled themselves on another version of that stereotype. No woman changed her character because of *Gone With the Wind*, or, indeed, could have done so. But to be influenced to become a skeptic, or even a partial skeptic, after Pyrrho and Sextus Empiricus, can (arguably) change the course of character, and certainly does change behavior. This last point is nicely illustrated by the comic tales told of Pyrrho: that disciples walked before him to test that the crust of the earth was thick enough to take his next step safely, and so on. Untrue as these stories were, a point was being made.

But a few true literary classics (*Gone With the Wind* is a popular classic: It is in no way a literary one) have nevertheless forced their way in, even if never for strictly literary reasons. Thus Dante's *Divine Comedy*, Rabelais's works, Miguel Cervantes's *Don Quixote,* and Tolstoy's *War and Peace* are all here, because they have changed or colored the way in which people, even whole nations—as well as individuals—think of themselves. George Orwell's *Nineteen Eighty-Four* is nothing like as great an imaginative achievement as its model, the little-known Russian writer Evgeny Zamyatin's *We* (although it is much better than Aldous Huxley's *Brave New World*); nor for that matter is it as good as several novels, to take names at random, by Fielding, George Eliot, Dostoyevsky, or Ford Madox Ford, or very many others not included here; but this particular book did change our habits of thinking in ways that those—and many other novels superior in terms of imaginative literature— did not. Even George Eliot's majestic and subtle *Middlemarch* did not have quite that effect. John Milton's long epic poem *Paradise Lost*—to defend another omission—has been much more *admired* throughout its history than influential, or even much liked. Perhaps this is fortunate.

The books selected here, then, are those of fundamental influence. The emphasis therefore falls more upon philosophy, on thinking, than upon literature. Works of literature certainly have influenced readers, and the ones that have done so really decisively are here. It could be argued that Goethe's novel *The Sorrows of Young Werther* was influential because it caused a number of young men to kill themselves. But then so did the now completely forgotten novel *Sanin* (by Mikhail Artsybashev) when it was published in 1907. In both cases the phenomenon was merely temporary—and those young men would have committed suicide anyway. The respective novels did not actually cause suicides: The reading of them just acted as triggers for depressed people. Had they not been written, then something else would have done it. Goethe himself came to despise *Werther,* and he wrote a comic and rude verse about it and its short-lived influence—which he regretted. Goethe's more substantial novel *Wilhelm Meister's Apprenticeship* seems to have been influential; but it was far less influential than it was taken to be, because no one (least of all Goethe), really knew what it was all about. Double-entry bookkeeping? Some asserted that this was the case. As for his shorter and superior novel *Elective Affinities:* That is no more than a literary masterpiece, and so cannot qualify.

Writers of imaginative literature are themselves, in any case, inevitably, initially influenced by a certain sort of predecessor. Such predecessors, however—the ones more likely to be on my list here—have, like Plato and Aristotle and then later Hume and Kant, made it their first purpose not to express their personal vision but to determine what kind of world it is that we live in, and then whether it can be known at all, and how, if indeed it is knowable, or partly knowable, mankind would be best off looking at it. Thus the holy books of most religions prescribe what kind of world it is, and how we *must* live in it (the Buddhist scriptures offer a partial exception). The philosophers have tried to look at the problem without religious assumptions but were for long threatened, like Descartes and then the cowardly Locke, with various more or less drastic forms of persecution. Both religious and philosophical thinkers were influential in the true and fundamental sense, even if the books were sometimes written by less than admirable people (an example is the shifty and emotionally indecisive, but gifted, English philosopher John Locke, to whose thinking America owes its constitution).

First, though, as to why certain books that might well be expected by some to be here, are not. Adolf Hitler's *Mein Kampf?* Surely he did much of what he said, there, that he intended to do? Yes indeed. But few took note of his stated intentions. Had they done so, and had the Second World War been averted—but could it have been?—then *Mein Kampf* would be here. As it is, while *Mein Kampf* has some historical value, it is of no true interest or quality whatsoever—unless one takes the extreme view that it gives a record of what some Germans will always want. But Hegel's more sinister contributions does a far better job in that regard. *Mein Kampf* is a psychopath's crude version of Heidegger's contemporaneous *Being and Time* (a dishonorable near miss), in which a charlatanic sense of puzzlement is created in order to make egoism, indifference, and brutality seem respectable. The legacy of Heidegger's odious work is to be seen in contemporary nihilism: If and where this temporarily prevails, then it is entirely because of its essential incomprehensibility.

Another kind of book that a few readers may miss lies in the by no means contemptible category of popular science: books such as E. O. Wilson's *Sociobiology: The New Synthesis* or, far below that in quality,

Richard Dawkins's ludicrous *The Selfish Gene*. These two books are quite different, and the reasons for the rejection of both from this selection must be treated separately. One reason for rejecting both, however, is common: They cannot have permanent influence. There are too many books of fundamental influence for books of merely temporary influence even to be considered here.

In the case of *Sociobiology* we had a true scientist, a zoologist whose work on ants is both fascinating and authoritative, branching out into what he took to be *the* general synthesis. As such, although astute, he was intolerable. In brief, he tended—as we might expect—to treat human beings as ants. In fact human beings are far more complex than even ants. The result was third-rate. That no doubt is quite high up in the scale, but *Sociobiology* and Wilson's other books on this subject will not contribute to the formation of a new scientific paradigm—that, after all, is being really influential. But they are worth reading because he has made his own contribution to science.

The case of Dawkins is more dire. A professor, he has—unlike Wilson—made little or no contribution to his subject. Like the somewhat less undignified theorist of history Arnold Toynbee (not included here, either), he has no distinction in his subject. But Toynbee's project dated from his days as a senior schoolboy; Dawkins's dates from that period during which he took his first tentative steps against total illiteracy. Shortly after that time, perhaps, he gained a facility for a style of writing which, like that of the tabloid press, conceals its confusions beneath a mask of almost bewildering facility:

> The argument of this book is that we, and all other animals, are machines created by our genes. Like successful Chicago gangsters, our genes have survived, in some cases for millions of years, in a highly competitive world. This entitles us to expect a certain quality in our genes. I shall argue that a predominant quality to be expected in a successful gene is a ruthless selfishness. . . . If you wish . . . to build a society in which individuals cooperate generously towards a common good, you can expect little help from biological nature. Let us try to teach generosity and altruism, because we are born selfish.

This astonishingly confused rubbish, in which the complex and essentially interactive gene is individualized, simplified, and personalized and then taken quite illogically to resemble a whole human being, had and still has some popularity among certain sorts of reader. But its influence cannot last because, as the persistent noninclusion of Dawkins in any dictionary of thought suggests, it is even more philosophically intolerable than Robert Ardrey's crude overemphasis on territoriality had been in his now forgotten but similarly popular books of an era ago. In another book Dawkins took a good deal of trouble to try to refute the "argument from design" which William Paley had used to "prove" the existence of God. Apparently he was unaware that this argument had long before been properly demolished by David Hume. But since Paley's *Natural Theology* does not get in, either—despite the fact that it was popular for more than half a century (and was used by the father of Percy Bysshe Shelley to refute his son's youthful atheism), there is certainly no room here for the archdunce Dawkins. A selection of great *temporarily* popular works would no doubt be a fascinating one; but this is not that selection.

England, November 1997

The 100 Most
Influential Books
Ever Written

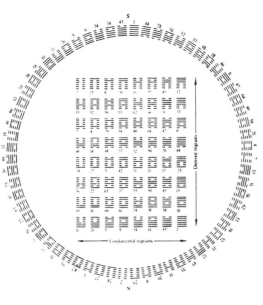

The I Ching

c. 1500 B.C.E.

The I Ching (pronounced "Yee Jing," and usually translated as *Book of Changes*) is almost as old, or even as old, as China itself. In various versions, it asserted itself sufficiently to become the foundation of both the Confucian and the Taoist way of life, and it was through an aspect of it (the Taoist "Dark Learning") that Buddhism gained its hold on China. In the eighteenth and nineteenth centuries the West gradually became aware of it (LEIBNIZ was fascinated by it), and it may have had more influence here than is generally accepted. More people in the West practice divination (ranging from purely superstitious fortunetelling—for which the I Ching offers a convenient framework—to more or less profound meditation) by means of it than one suspects; some admit to it, many more do not. The *New York Times* once commented that "on the face of it the *Book of Changes* seems about as unlikely a candidate for a mass-cult following as the *Summa Theologica*"—but conceded that such was the case. It seems just as unlikely a candidate for

3

"mass-cult following" in Chinese history itself; yet it has survived every change (including that of Maoist Marxism) over the past three thousand years. Is it endemic to China?

The slow but sure post–World War II shift among large numbers of Western peoples from respect for politicians and the externals of life to some sort of consideration of the inner life continues, although it takes many different forms. The influence of the I Ching on this shift has been indisputable: It has played an incalculably important part in the way that the Chinese themselves made their decisions, both cultural and political, and has thus affected the West in that way; but it has influenced individual decisions, at least since around 1950, to an equally incalculable degree. That it may, particularly in the latter case, only have seemed to be the agent of making choices, is neither here nor there: It has, over the past half century, been present—in the Legge or Wilhelm-Baynes version—and has been regarded as, and employed as, an oracle. Indeed, its purely oracular influence in Western societies, unless the confessional functions in an oracular fashion, has been greater than anything since Roman times.

The importance—and influence—of the I Ching, whose true origins remain shrouded in mystery, stems from its being one of the earliest efforts of the human mind to find its place in the universe. That much is still clearly apparent. The general notions behind it thus seem, in a pragmatic sense, to "work." It was preceded—and generated—in China by the very early theory of *yang* and *yin*. *Yang* originally meant sunshine, whereas *yin* implied the absence of heat and light. The two antithetical principles came to be regarded as cosmic forces: masculinity/femininity, heat/cold, brightness/darkness, dryness/wetness, hardness/softness, and so forth. The Chinese saw the tension set up by two phenomena as having brought forth the universe itself. The legendary Fu Hsi, emperor of China, is supposed to have invented the eight basic trigrams—sets of three lines, broken and unbroken—which form the basis of the I Ching. Any two of these trigrams will combine into sixty-four hexagrams. The original text of the I Ching consisted of accounts of the symbolic meanings of each of these hexagrams. Even as we know them they are still cryptic and laconic.

Traditionally it is believed that the twelfth-century King Wen invented the sixty-four combinations while he was in prison. His son, the duke of Chou, is supposed to have added the commentaries on the single lines of each hexagram (the *hsiao*); but the version of the I Ching that has, although modified in 1715, come down to modern times is, officially, that of CONFUCIUS—or, rather, it was, like the *Analects* and his other "writings," put into what is roughly its present form by people who described themselves as Confucian scholars. It is unlikely, though, that Confucius himself was much interested in divination, even if students can point to remarks supposed to have made by him. This book still bears a religious sort of authority; Confucianism is not a religion, but a (failed) code of ethics. It is inconceivable, however, that Confucius would not have had something to say about the book; what it might have been we do not know. There are countless and very widely differing speculations.

The I Ching, whoever wrote it, has been held to contain, in the words of a Western devotee, "the reasons for everything." Less hyperbolically, it may be that it can be of much value for those who wish, along Jungian or even strictly non-Jungian lines, to explore their own unconscious minds, or, to "find out who they are." On the other hand, such an idea may be the foundation of much harmful or at least self-indulgently wishful thinking. Probably it is both. It would be odd, though, since the Chinese have always attached so much importance to it, if the book itself contained no wisdom at all.

The I Ching really originated in the second millennium B.C.E., when the Shang and Chou peoples used turtle shells for divination. Heat was applied to the shells until they cracked, and the lines thus formed were "read." Fu Hsi himself is supposed by the legend to have said that he first saw his eight trigrams on a turtle shell. By 213 B.C.E., when the tyrant Shih Huang-ti, first emperor of the Chin Dynasty—one of the earliest of those monsters who, like Stalin and Hitler in our own times, try to alter the past in the interests of power—ordered the notorious Burning of the Books, the I Ching had reached something perhaps resembling its present form. It was the one book of the so-called historical records—music, rituals, poetry, and old songs—that openly survived. It was not considered a threat because it was a book of divination. After that it soon came to be regarded as an essential part of every scholar's training, providing the framework within which everything was discussed. Eventually the I Ching was used, much like the Bible, for every purpose under the sun. Alchemists used it, but so did promulgators of ethical systems and sadists. So far as we in the West are concerned, the most influential versions of the book are the ones given in English by the scholar and missionary James Legge, a Protestant who became the first professor of Chinese at Oxford, and the later German one made by Richard Wilhelm—the latter (and a rather less good one) is famous in the translation made by Cary Baynes (1951) and introduced by JUNG.

All this obscurity about our most frequently consulted private oracle might seem distinctly unpromising. It is not only a muddled record in itself but also, as we in the West know it, translated by men with an inevitable bias—Legge's toward Christianity, Wilhelm's toward Teutonic system making. There could be a dozen different and in their own way valid versions made by those with a good knowledge of Chinese. But underlying the book there remains its original wisdom, which thrusts itself forward as possessing a quality as formidable as that of any other such work, even though it usually seems cryptic and strange. For all but strict atheists its thesis is unexceptional: Life is centered upon cosmic order, and that itself is subject to change—therefore human beings should learn to adapt themselves to what is inevitable. Probably many Western users of it have looked at the concept of *fate* from the commonly held Western point of view: A "fatalist" is regarded as one who is convinced that everything, including his own destiny, is already determined.

This attitude is often taken by intelligent psychopaths: It removes any need for personal responsibility.

The Chinese concept of fate, *ming,* is not the same—and is, in fact, echoed in many less crude Western attitudes. *Ming* is no less than "the total existent conditions and forces of the whole universe." If we are to undertake successful activities, then we need to cooperate with those conditions, over which we exercise no control whatever. Thus Confucius said, or is supposed to have said, "He who does not know *ming* cannot be a superior man." The "superior man" is a phrase that crops up again and again in our texts of the I Ching. This superior man is not "superior" in the usual sense; he is simply superior to his circumstances because he possesses wisdom. Thus, while we cannot control our fates, we can decide how we should live: We can choose to go along with the prevailing cosmic conditions.

Confucius himself did not, apparently, consult the oracular book. He tried to reform the world instead, and he failed. He did add however, that "if my ideas are to prevail, it is *ming,* if they are not, it is *ming.*" The basis of the I Ching then, could be looked upon as *nonmoral:* as having no connection with morality or virtue whatsoever. The man who learns to consult the oracle may thus benefit whether he is "good" or "bad." That it lends itself to this interpretation in the hands of shrewd rather than virtuous men may very well account for some of its sheer popularity. The Christian has always asked the question: "How can a good God allow evil?" The Chinese "God," though, is more impersonal and is not to be questioned like that. It is not a matter of being "good," but of being in touch with reality. Why was Hitler so "lucky"? Not, of course, because he had heard of the I Ching; but in some way such men (like most of the millionaires and billionaires of today, indifferent to virtue, although they may profess a religion) are in touch with the realities of their times. How else can we explain what we call the "instinct" and "luck" of such people?

The I Ching itself, though, is open to virtuous as well as opportunistic consultation. However, it by no means contains the "reasons for everything." It is any case far too vague and cryptic for that. Perhaps it once did? But its general principle, the recognition that everything is in a process of change, still manages to cast a spell of authority. It can, as has often been observed, seem to reprimand those who consult it—unless they are simply fortune-telling. It cannot be said to have exercised any more of a "good" influence than it has "bad"—we do not know.

Its true status here is that, while it can act as a tool for genuine meditation, its origins are too shrouded in mystery—and in addition to that, it was conceived in a predominantly agricultural civilization—for it to be of more than private use. It does convey, for those who have worked with it, some sense of being *alive*; unfortunately, it is as obscure a guide to conduct as it is authentic—unless the Western user interprets it through some system of his own.

Jung's recommendation of it as a key to the unconscious was influential; but his attitude to it was, in a historical sense, totally uncritical. Jung was after all, as has emerged in the years since his death, gallantly unscrupulous in regard to facts, if only in the interests of his beliefs. The other oracle that many people in the West like to consult is the Tarot, and that, significantly, is also as obscure in the answers it gives as it may (or may not) be as profound. They are in the hands of the consultant, so that Tarot experts are as numerous in the West as I Ching experts are in the East. But the Tarot is a comparative newcomer—and in any case when Count Antoine de Gébelin pronounced in 1781 that the picture cards had been invented by ancient Egyptians as symbols of their esoteric doctrine, he may have been mistaken, although they are clearly symbols of something coherent. Thus, we have a newfangled oracle serving quite well as a vehicle of prediction; but one which lacks the hallowed authority of age.

Lastly, we must consider the kind of philosophy that the I Ching embodies. As Jung so influentially and in this case rightly pointed out, this involves an "acausal connecting principle." In 1931 at the time of Wilhelm's death, Jung gave this the name of *synchronicity*. Instead of the familiar scientific cause-and-effect argument, we are here presented with what the Greek pre-Socratic philosopher Heraclitus called an "unapparent connection"—which he said was more interesting than an "apparent" one.

In consulting the I Ching one uses coins to determine the hexagrams (the Chinese employ a different method involving yarrow stalks, but this too depends entirely on chance). The way these coins fall *is* random, but, as SCHOPENHAUER (quoted by Jung) put it, the result expresses a "subjective connection which exists only in relation to the individual who experiences it:" In other words, there is a "meaningful coincidence" between the throw of the coins at that moment and the simultaneous play between *yin* and *yang*. There is no doubt that this can be used as an excuse for coming to any decision. The meanings of the hexagrams that we have are not at all clear-cut. However, when consulted in a spirit of true sincerity, the connections do seem meaningful. The question that the sympathetic skeptic would immediately ask is, Would anything else do as well? The answer, strangely enough, seems to be no!

The Old Testament

c. 1500 B.C.E.

The Old Testament and the NEW TESTAMENT—what we have known since William Tyndale published his English versions, and, more certainly, since Elizabethan times (1611), in a single book as the English Holy Bible—are two quite separate books in a series of fundamental scriptures of faiths, such as the KORAN, the AVESTA and the DHAMMAPADA. The Old Testament leads into, or is assumed by the Christian Church to lead into, the New. The two works, bound together, are still held, by biblical fundamentalists—in the teeth, it must unequivocally be stated, of overwhelming evidence to the contrary—to represent a single volume containing the message of God, and a *literally* truthful account of the Creation. That is a part of the history of belief but not of scholarship.

The word *bible* is derived, by way of Latin and French, from the Greek *biblia,* "books," which is itself a translation from the Hebrew *sepharim,* of the same meaning. The Hebrew word is the oldest of all terms for biblical literature. These *sepharim* are most usually called, in Hebrew, *Tanakh,* a consonantal acronym (written Hebrew is consonantal) which is helpful in reminding us of its contents: **T**orah (law—better rendered as "guidance"), **N**eviim (prophets), **K**etuvim (writings—hagiography). This, only a fragment of the literature of the ancient Israelites, is the "Old Testament" only to Christians. It was compiled by the Jews over a period of about one thousand years, and contains legend, history, poetry, anecdote, prayer, law, statistics, and prophecy; it is by far the best known book in the Western world, and it has inspired deeds both brightly heroic and darkly horrific. It was mainly the Dutch-Portuguese Jewish philosopher BARUCH DE SPINOZA—to a certain but definite extent a Kabbalist, although this is seldom acknowledged—in the seventeenth century, who was instrumental in subjecting this collection or anthology of texts to historical and other proper criticism. He was, of course, excommunicated by his fellow Jews.

The history of the formation of the texts of the Bible—all in Hebrew except for a few passages in Aramaic in Genesis and elsewhere—is highly complex, and still controversial. Before the Christian Era this anthology had been translated into Greek (the Septuagint), specifically for the use of Greek-speaking Jews. Then, because of certain events in Palestine at the beginning of our era (probably occurring about 30 C.E.), the Christians were led to appropriate it as their own. By the second century C.E. its only rival among Christians were the writings of the great "heretic" Marcion, from Sinope, who died in 160, and whose gnostic-type writings have all been suppressed or lost.

An invaluable aid to historians are the extant works of the remarkable Josephus, a first-century Jew, a Pharisee, who became a Roman citizen (as Flavius Josephus), but never abandoned his Jewish faith (it was not luck but cunning that enabled him to survive: He prophesied that Vespasian would become Roman emperor, and Vespasian obliged). He was allowed to live and write in Rome, where he completed his *Jewish Wars* (as a Jew he had taken part in them, but had been captured by the Romans at Jotopata) in 77 and his indispensable *Antiquities of the Jews* in 94. Here is Josephus (in the translation of the industrious William Whiston, a nineteenth-century professor of mathematics from Cambridge University) beginning a well-known tale, and one which would have grim consequences for some:

> About this time the Sodomites grew proud, on account of their riches and great wealth: they became unjust toward men, and impious toward God, inasmuch as they did not call to mind the advantages they received from him: they hated strangers, and abused themselves with Sodomitical practices. God was therefore much displeased at them. . . .

Confusions and controversies made it necessary, by the last decade of the fourth century C.E., for Saint Jerome (342–420) to make, or in some cases supervise, a Latin translation—it included Jerome's own versions of the four

Gospels. This was called the Vulgate, and was first collected together into a single volume in the sixth century; but the oldest known manuscript text of the Vulgate, named the *Codex Amiatinus* (because it ended up in the library at Monte Amiata—this was suppressed in 1782, and it is now at Florence, in the Laurentian Library), was written at Jarrow by monks under Abbot Ceolfrith between 690 and 700. There were three copies, which are said to have needed the skins of fifteen hundred calves—so much for animal-lovers and vegetarians. Ceolfrith was on his way in 716 to present the codex to Pope Gregory II at Rome but died before he got there.

The first translations of the Bible into English (discouraged by the Church of the time, which believed that the poor and humble should not be allowed to read it, lest, not having the wit to understand the Latin which they had never been taught, they should form their own ideas about it) were made in Anglo-Saxon times, but there is no complete Anglo-Saxon Bible. The earliest complete or nearly complete versions are known as "Wycliffite," after the fourteenth-century English philosopher and leader of the Lollards (probably from the Dutch word *lullen,* "to sing"), John Wycliffe, who inspired them, and who thus gained a bad name as an anticipator of Protestantism (which he was). The Lollards were the earliest coherent English group to question the Catholic Church. The very great and poetic, but hardly yet fully appreciated, prose writer William Tyndale (1494–1536) made much of the translation that still forms the firm basis of the well-known Authorized Version of 1611. He was strangled and burnt at the stake at Vilvorde near Brussels, in the name of the God of the Bible that he had dared to translate. The people who carried out this murder, servants of ferocious and backward persons who were sure of their righteousness—they have their defenders today—were the equivalent of today's servile bureaucrats.

The Bible is still best known and best loved, in English-speaking lands, in the majestic Authorized Version; so far as readers are concerned, the modern New "English" Bible—known among many in England as the "Inland Revenue Version" because of its pitiful, uninspired English, approved by a "styling committee" composed of ambitious nonentities—is not just an unworthy successor, but an insult to all that religion represents.

Emily Dickinson, the wise old maid of Amherst, Massachusetts, whose poetry was not reckoned quite suitable for publication in her own time, but which is now regarded as towering above that of most of her contemporaries, wrote a (perhaps unfinished) poem in about 1882 which tersely sums up one way in which people have thought of the Christian Bible:

> The Bible is an antique volume—
> Written by faded Men
> At the suggestion of Holy Spectres—
> Subjects—Bethlehem—
> Eden—the ancient Homestead—
> Satan—the Brigadier—

Judas—The Great Defaulter—
Sin—a distinguished Precipice
Others must resist—
Boys that "believe" are very lonesome—
Other boys are "lost"—
Had but the Tale a warbling Teller—
All the boys would come—
Orpheus' Sermon captivated—
It did not condemn.

Orpheus of course is the legendary pagan, the Greek singer who was able to charm beasts and even stones with his lyre, and whose head, even after it had been torn off by the maenads, still sang—it certainly did not "sermonise," and that is what Dickinson meant, ironically, to convey—as it drifted away to Lesbos. The poem implicitly criticizes the Bible for expressing the merciless tone of the Jewish rather than the Christian God toward sinners and idolaters. Emily Dickinson was lamenting the fact that the Holy Book was not written in a "captivating," but rather in a frequently condemnatory manner—she was sorry that the thundering, Jewish Jehovah of the Old Testament could not be more like the gentler Orpheus.

It is, indeed, an anomaly, especially in our age of more exact and scrupulous scholarship, that the Christian religion should be an offshoot of the Jewish one—to the extent that the original, Roman Catholic, Church, in an abandonment of its real principles, forgave the Jews (in very recent times) for executing Jesus, who was in fact crucified by the Romans. But that, somewhat grotesquely, is how it has turned out.

The whole affair now causes the modern churches to seem increasingly anachronistic—and to have to rely on unreason far more than is convenient in our positivistic age. It has led to a bitter quarrel between traditionalists and those who want to pay heed to fact, or perhaps just to seem "contemporary"—the latter are often unjustly, but sometimes justly, accused of being unbelievers, pallid liberal rationalists or, worse, reedy-voiced men who received education but have not a thought (but to be modish) in their heads.

The controversy has usually been conducted in tired clichés at a low intellectual level. The danger is that the Church, supposed to be otherworldly, will become secularized; but then it has been pretty secular throughout history, although with notable exceptions. What is called religion has always been an uneasy mixture of reverence for God and politics.

The facts so far as they can be known should not deter those who are religious (which I take to mean, here, those who acknowledge an authority greater than mankind's), because religion must imply pursuit of truth and because no one ought to be afraid of the truth. But they are, nevertheless, if it interferes with their plans.

It is unsafe and unwise to argue with those who prefer not to be critical; but it is appropriate to argue with those who pretend that they are being critical when they ignore facts. Mere facts remain important until they have been unignored. The true value of the Bible now, for Christians, ought to lie in its inspirational and literary qualities—not in any "authority" that they believe this Jewish anthology might possess for them. It is not the less holy for that—the word *holy* derives ultimately from words meaning "good omen" and "whole."

Jesus Christ, one of a few extraordinary men, all shocking and uncomfortable to their neighbors (Zarathustra, Gautama the Buddha, and Mohammed are among others), is by no means dead. Christianity, as it has been practiced for two thousand years, is. More precisely, it is alive only in certain phases of its past and in certain individuals (often Jews, such as MARTIN BUBER). A severe distinction must be made between Jesus Christ and the religion practiced in his name: He was not only, embarrassingly, a Jew, but also, in all probability, what is known as a gnostic. It was gnosticism, in particular the gnosticism of Marcion, that forced the Christian Church—from too early on a power-seeking body, intent on worldly success—most decisively into its antignostic positions. It drew, ruthlessly, upon the monotheism of the Jewish religion as expressed in the Old Testament, and, cleverly (as one might say) on astralist tendencies in the very Greek world which it sought to convert. By the time of Marcion's challenge, there were few true Christians left: "the true fiend," to adapt (slightly) a poem by Robert Graves, ruled "in Christ's name."

What we call the Old Testament—most particularly the first five books, the Pentateuch—is, however, the cornerstone of the Jewish religion. The claim of the Christian Church to be the legitimate heir of Israel, the true Israel, is unhistorical and perverse. (The New Testament is a partly different matter.) There is an emphasis on the Pentateuch because this contains the most direct revelation the Jewish God made, through Moses, on Mount Sinai. But the fact that it is really an address to a particular people, and of the false but eventually more universal Christian claim otherwise, have created enormous difficulties, which have led to, among other regrettable and irreligious results, anti-Semitism: The worst sort of Christian or person brought up in the Christian faith has continued to try to appropriate a Jewish God whom they were taught to worship as a non-(even specifically anti-) Jewish one. On the other hand, less offensively, there has been this understandable feeling among Christians: "How odd/Of God/To choose/The Jews." Gnosticism alone within the Christian Church made religion an inner matter, and was ruthlessly suppressed; in the Middle Ages, when people started to try to interpret the Jewish religion, the KABBALAH—which is also gnostic—more realistic, more erotic, made the salvation of God by man, the *tikkun*, as vital a matter as its contrary. That, too, was eventually dismissed as superstitious by modern rationalistic Jews. But both alarming doctrines persist—to trouble those in authority, and to keep them on the rack of their ignorance.

The Iliad and *The Odyssey*

HOMER

c. 9th century B.C.E.

Homer's *Odyssey* and *Iliad,* of which the earliest extant manuscripts date from, at the very least, seventeen hundred years after his lifetime, had become classics in ancient Greece by the time of PLATO (who admiringly disapproved of them) and ARISTOTLE (who did not disapprove of them). Yet we know nothing whatever, for certain, about Homer (Homeros). His name has been variously translated to mean "one who does not see," "hostage," "comrade," "one who puts matters in order." His very existence cannot be proved, and some scholars have doubted it. Even if he did exist, did he write both of these epic poems? Few problems have been so vexing, or have had so changing a history—or have generated, at various times, such rage.

For the Greeks there were few problems. A poet called Homer—whose dates and origins, however, were very variously given—had written these two epics, just as SHAKESPEARE wrote his plays or Milton his *Paradise Lost.* This is what many today are content to believe—and there is no harm in that, because the two poems are there, and, what is by far the most important thing, they may be read. Their high quality, the unifying factor in both poems (the anger of Achilles in the *Iliad* and the contrast between the pre-Trojan War Ithaca and the one to which Odysseus returns in the *Odyssey*), has helped, in very large part, to define to our civilization what the very word *quality* means. VOLTAIRE's description of Homer as a "sublime painter" is one from which only an eccentric would dissent. The superiority of the Homeric poems over the many examples we have of other such epics is very marked indeed.

However, a reaction arose. The idea was advanced that Homer did not exist, or was at best just an anthologist. The two epics were put forward as narrative folk poems that reached, very approximately, their present form by about the ninth or eighth century B.C.E. In 1795 the German scholar F. A. Wolff published a book advancing the theory that both *The Iliad* and *The Odyssey* were compilations from the works of many poets. He himself had misgivings, and simply presented the arguments in favor of the hypothesis (it was not an altogether weak one, but it tended to attract those who hate poetry at heart and therefore like to see it demoted in the public estimation—just as the "deconstructionists" of today are motivated by their envy of people who can write, and therefore like to cut out "the author" as an entirely irrelevant factor); but those who followed Wolff were more confident. They were called "analysts." Those who believed in Homer the poet were called "unitarians." Neither party was wholly wrong, since there are undoubtedly passages in Homer that were originally composed by "other poets." There are also obvious interpolations: There is no question whatsoever of our having the text as the poet composed it. The twentieth-century scholar who finally, and brilliantly, synthesized the "analytic" approach was the American Millman Parry (who died at only thirty-three because of his carelessness with a loaded revolver). To Parry we owe the powerfully made suggestion that Homer composed orally and not by means of writing. But that is by no means established.

Indeed, it now seems more likely that *The Iliad* and *The Odyssey* are the first substantial products of the collision between a newly literate and an old illiterate culture—hence their extraordinary nervous power and subtlety. There is no question of either culture being sovereign in the author's mind: He fully recognized the terrors of the new, and he loved and was attached to the old. In the two poems some readers have felt a creative joy at what can be done in the written form, at what it can achieve—a realization of what can be done outside recitation. The art of writing with some unknown reader in mind, and not a live audience out there *here* and *now*, was in its infancy; nor, then, had writing been semidestroyed by bureaucrats, one of whose triumphs may be seen in the recent "internal revenue style" versions of the Bible. *Gilgamesh*, the epic of the first Babylonian dynasty (from which the Jews drew their flood story), was synthesized about a millennium before Homer. It is a wonderful work, but it wholly lacks the far subtler qualities that we find in Homer. However, there could not, at around 1750 B.C.E., have arisen such a poet.

The Iliad, rather more often the preferred poem, tells the story of a brief and late stage in the siege of Troy. The events of the Trojan War live and glow in the imagination of every reader who has ever heard of them. Some contemporary Greek scholars—just a very few of them triumphalist whiz kids who resent poetry and who miss the point (however, the nature of their material tends to keep most scholars of Greek, as distinct from Roman, culture, in decent human order)—believe that this war never took place. Certainly it did not take place as Homer described it, just as his two poems are in no way properly historical descriptions of the Mycenaean civilization. He has been solemnly reproved for this—but does it matter?

Not in the least! This is poetry, not historiography. Then why does it seem to us as though this war had taken place? First, because the Greeks themselves believed in the Trojan War (that this was partly because of Homer himself is irrelevant); secondly, because it captures the *essence* of whatever that history really was—just as Aristotle said poetry should. In a certain very important, phenomenological, sense that War *did* take place and is taking place now in the sense that it is still an incomparable metaphor for what causes men to quarrel. However "inaccurate" *The Iliad* may turn out to have been about events, however unreliable a guide it may be to the Dark Age, it remains what Aristotle—still a supreme literary critic—called it (I have very slightly adapted the text of the *Poetics,* but have in no way departed from what Aristotle meant):

Homer is divinely inspired beyond all the other poets in that, although the Trojan War had a beginning and an end, he didn't try to put the whole of it into his poem: it was too large a subject to be taken in all at once. Had he limited its length the diversity of incident in it would have made it too complicated. As it is, he selected one part of it and introduced many incidents from other parts as episodes.

Earlier in the *Poetics* Aristotle had written that the poet's function was not to describe what actually happened *"but the kind of things that might happen"* (my italics, for there is a wealth of meaning in the phrase): "For this reason poetry is something more philosophical and more worthy of serious attention than history, for while poetry is concerned with universal truths, history treats of particular facts."

This still holds absolutely good, provided always that we respect that "particular facts" are supremely important *at their own level*—which is a lower one. But we need lack no confidence in Homer's ability to express what he understood as particular events as a universal truth, despite the huge number of inconsistencies and anachronisms in the text as we have it.

No, it does not quite cohere. Yes, its division into twenty-four books— one for each letter of the Greek alphabet—is unlikely to have taken place before about the third century B.C.E., long after Homer lived. But in both poems we are confronted by an integrity and, above all, by a grandly imaginative and humane wisdom. Here is a poet, of lower social rank than his wealthy patrons, who beautifully draws his similes from his knowledge of ordinary people and their lives, and thus appeals, not to the bearer of rank or fame or a fortune, but to the common man.

The consensus, whiz kids apart (they come and go), is as follows: that a poet called Homer, from Ionia (Ionic is the predominant dialect in the language of the poems) put a folklore epic, or two such epics, into a poetic form. The poet is most likely to have lived in the eighth century, and he may well have been blind because bards often were blind (bards in *The Odyssey* itself are blind). Those who believe—more do than do not—that both poems come from the same hand are on slightly weaker ground, because the spirit of the two is undoubtedly different, and *The Odyssey* is certainly a little later. However, Homer was a supreme poet, and just as Shakespeare developed, so may he, from a peerless epic celebrating courage to another, this time celebrating endurance and a beneficent kind of cunning; he may well have been in far better control of his art than modern scholars have liked to think possible, since so many like to believe in the myth of "human progress," rather than change—thus there is a kind of concealed snobbery about the fitness of even the most eminent people of the past to get things right.

Both Shakespeare and Homer drew upon often fanciful accounts of a past long distance from themselves, and, if we believe that Shakespeare, for all his multitudinous "factual errors," gives us the essence of English history—knew something more about his country than its mere rulers ever did or could—then why should not Homer have done exactly the same for the archaic, letterless Greece that was *his* past?

The features of the Homeric poems that led some to believe that they were simply folk epics is the presence of what are called *formulae*: themes, groups of words, phrases such as "rosy fingered dawn," "wine-dark sea," "much-enduring Odysseus," and so on. In the twenty-eight thousand lines of the two poems there are no less than twenty-five thousand such repeated phrases. Of course Homer did not invent all of these—though he artfully used them for his own stylistic purposes. Their original function, in a letterless age, had been to provide mnemonic aids for reciters and bards as they improved their recitations. It might be that Homer as we have it is simply the record of one such performance—but that is unlikely.

The city of Troy (the site is in present-day Turkey), was destroyed in about 1200 B.C.E., and it is likely but not provable that this was at the hands of Mycenaean invaders from the mainland. The Mycenaean civilization itself was then destroyed by Dorian invaders from the north (but that, too, has been challenged). The civilization of what we know as ancient Greece—the Greece of Aeschylus, Sophocles, Euripides, Plato, and Aristotle—began to take shape. Politics (wonderfully ingenious and, like most human enterprises at their inception, such as money, a good idea—but now at their last gasp, and practiced only by polite psychopaths and their too willing victims) were,

Circe and Odysseus

alas, invented. The bards of the centuries between 1200 and 800 B.C.E., the Dark Age, were of course unlettered. The Phoenician alphabet was being adapted by the Greeks, as inscriptions show, during the course of the eighth century. So, even in the unlikely event that Homer himself composed orally, it was not long after his death that his two epics (the so-called *Hymns of Homer* are not by him) found written form. They became the property of a group of bards, the Homeridae, who had exclusive reciting rights.

Then, during the reign (560–527) of the ruler of Athens, the tyrant Pisistratus, it was arranged that they be put into a "final" form (we can note the changes made from the poems' basic Ionic to the Athenian Attic). It is possible that another poetic genius performed that task. This would explain much. After all, we have before us another sublime example: that of the Verdi who understood Shakespeare so well that he transformed an English poetic masterpiece, *Othello,* into an Italian musical one *Otello,* that is as nearly—as has ever humanly been possible—exempt from criticism. The Pisistratan Homer might have had a similar sympathy with his predecessor—but might well have been, as Shakespeare always was, under such pressure that he did not have time to put the material into the apple-pie order demanded by twentieth-century academics. Thus sometimes do tyrants and oppressors defeat their own ends: Homer is no friend to men of rank and power, although the reading of him may well have influenced a few of their lackeys to abandon their horrible callings.

As we shall see, the much- or possibly even the overcelebrated *literary* quality of the KORAN was challenged by certain free-thinking Muslims (to be free-thinking is to be a *heretic*) of the Middle Ages, who suggested that the mindless assumption that it was a masterpiece of literature was not altogether justified. Undoubtedly, too, about almost every human phenomenon widely regarded as perfect or near perfect, *and* successful, a type of mindless idol-atry does exist: this is demonstrated in the ephemerality of certain books, "acclaimed" for a few months or years and then entirely forgotten. There are those who admire mechanically, thus vicariously rewarding their own vanities in the process known (since FREUD) as projection. The breathless admira-tion of "groupies" for this or that tedious phenomenon, whether it be Madonna or Salman Rushdie, is simply self-admiration. However, manifesta-tions of inferior quality have been relatively short-lived—even the sales of *Gone With the Wind,* which is not a good novel—no serious-minded person has suggested that it is—but which does possess certain qualities (a keen eye for types, if not for character), have gradually diminished.

The author of *The Iliad* was quite as sophisticated as any more modern writer has been—and he had an astonishing eye for character, let alone types. He did not want his readers casting about trying to identify particular islands, landscapes, and places. He was very well aware that he was creating a legend. His genius has transcended that of even his best critics. His account of the Trojan War is a far more convincing account of war itself than a record of the "particular facts" of any single war could possibly be. It has lasted over millennia. The Odysseus of the second epic—this describes the last six weeks of his ten-year return from the Trojan War: skillfully placed flashbacks tell the tale of his earlier adventures—has become the paradigm of the ferocious, undeflectable, sly man who endures and emerges in victorious possession of his integrity. The portrait of Ulysses in Shakespeare's *Troilus and Cressida,* although the product of another age, owes almost everything to Homer (indi-rectly, and even though Shakespeare, like most of us, was not good at Latin and had even less Greek).

Homer, who if he was blind at all must have gone blind in middle age, had an extraordinary vivid visual sense, and his metaphors and similes, whether borrowed or not, always suit their subject. Many of the passages in the poems—Ulysses' old dog awaiting his return before dying, all those deal-ing with the anger of Achilles, Hector's last encounter with his wife, countless others—have to be the work of a single genius, reshaping older material. Woman is a chattel, as she seemed to be in the Homeric world—yet she is given her true place. Helen caused the war—or did, rather, male foolishness cause it? (The latter of course).

The Greeks built up their culture on these poems, and thus ours, too, is built up from it. No poet, not even VIRGIL or DANTE, has nearly equaled these epics; those who have had the opportunity to read them (in transla-tions) and have not done so, are not complete human beings—as some dis-cover as soon as they are fortunate enough to stumble upon them. But ours is an age in which training in the arts of greed and lying has replaced mere education, and already the robot-clerks who, with plastic identification but-tons on their lapels, plan curricula, have no place for them. Only when it is pointed out to them that sales of Homer have made money for hundreds of years do their dead eyes seem to glint.

4

The Upanishads

c. 700 B.C.E.–400 B.C.E.

The history of the origins of the first Indian religion—although some deny that it is a religion at all—Hinduism (the Persian word for "Indian," first used in the West in 1829)—has been somewhat complicated by comparatively recent discoveries about the Indus Valley civilization, which—we now know—sprang up more or less contemporaneously with those, the earliest known, of Mesopotamia, China, and Egypt.

This civilization (c. 4000–c. 2200 B.C.E.), which had one of its chief centers at the city of Harappa, had contacts with at least the Mesopotamian, and probably others, too. Excavations at Harappa did not begin until the 1920s and are still uncompleted. The script found on the seals and statuettes there has not yet been fully deciphered, although active attempts are now being made. Some call what little is known of its religion "protohistoric Hinduism."

Certainly most of what we know of Harappa's religious characteristics, particularly those of ritual bathing and the worship of a god remarkably similar to Shiva, reappear in later Hinduism. Harappa seems, too, to have been highly patriarchal, although there was a mother-goddess cult, as well. Nor did the Aryans, Indo-European tribes who had reached Iran and Afghanistan, and who later poured into India, put an end to this Indus Valley civilization. It seems to have perished through lack of water and through other natural causes.

The history of the extraordinarily diverse Hindu religious tradition, as it is best called (more than five hundred million people, probably close to seven hundred million, now embrace forms of it—reliable figures are hard to come by, and vary wildly from authority to authority), is immensely complicated and beset by controversy at almost all points. But simple outlines may be traced. Out of the original Hinduism have emerged three main "heresies": Jainism, Buddhism, and Sikhism. All of these have much in common. Buddhists now vastly outnumber Hindus.

By about 900 B.C.E. the Rig Veda had reached what is probably its final form. *Veda* is a Sanskrit word meaning "knowledge," and in particular the sacred knowledge of the Hindus. There are four collections of Veda (which is a single entity), the most vital of which is the Rig Veda, which collects 1,028 hymns. One of the other, later, collections, the Atharva Veda, of spells and charms, must have originated among the indigenous population of India.

There is no doubt a technical case for selecting the Rig Veda above the Upanishads for inclusion in this volume. But it was composed long before writing was known in India, and its later hymns tend to take up a monotheistic attitude (that is, belief in a single god, as distinct from belief in many, as in polytheism); this notion is expressed in its most brilliant and refined form in the Upanishads, which are really a later, and more philosophical and (perhaps most important) poetic offshoot of the Rig Veda. The earlier ones are in poetic prose; some of the later are in verse.

These Upanishads have been the prime influence on Hindu thought— and on Buddhist and Western thought, the latter through SCHOPENHAUER, and in more modern times WITTGENSTEIN (surprisingly no doubt) and others. When Wittgenstein wrote, "the spirit of the snake . . . is *your* spirit, for it is only from yourself that you are acquainted with spirit at all," he revealed much of his true inspiration, revealed perhaps whatever is consistent in him and at the heart of his project; he had gotten to the Upanishads through his love of Schopenhauer, that philosopher whom, really—despite a few rather desperate disclaimers—he loved most of all, and who was most congenial to his unhappy temperament.

Few outside India now read translations of hymns of the Rig Veda (though millions of Indians say in the mornings, "Let our meditation be directed to the glorious light of Savitri [the life-giver], and may his light illuminate our minds") but most educated people have some knowledge of the Upanishads. They are so called because the pupils had to sit (*shad*) down (*ni*) close (*upa*) to the teacher.

There are over one hundred Upanishads, but many of these are afterthoughts. The really vital ones are fewer than twenty in number. We know next to nothing about their authors. Although the Babylonian *Gilgamesh* and, possibly, the earliest layers of HOMER predate them, it is in the Upanishads that mankind is first seen consciously to think as well as to tell stories and praise the gods and express sexual love. They have been interpreted in various ways, but the disagreements, though sometimes vehement, have never been as vicious as those between various Christians, who have all too often been more concerned to obtain power and suppress alternative opinion than to think.

The essence of the Upanishads is that *Brahman* and *Atman* are one and the same thing. Brahman is the truth of the universe. Atman (like the "Thou" of BUBER) is individual inner truth. This can be put in many ways, more often than not, in the Upanishads, paradoxically. It has thus deeply irritated many of those Christians who dislike mysticism and take their religion as simply given, as the literal truth. They have called Hinduism (and Buddhism, too) atheistic.

The Upanishads are humbler (and more tolerant) than most of the materially successful systems of Christian doctrine. There is less in them about obedience to an external power, and far less—in early as in later Hinduism—about inflicting death upon so-called "heretics." (This does not mean that disagreements were not extreme.) That gnosticism of which the early Christians were so fearful is far less uncongenial to them. They begin, one might say, in the mind of the child, a mind that can accept paradox more easily than that of the adult thirsty for sensation and worldly success (called sometimes in the Upanishads "what is adored here"—i.e., in the material world, or ordinary life). Thus, in the Mandukya Upanishad we find Brahman defined, or, rather, not defined, as both "everything" or "all," and as "nothing" and "no thing."

This might seem ridiculous, but is it any more ridiculous than our contemplation of the "nothing" or "no thing" that existed before the universe was created (if indeed it was created)? We cannot understand nothingness. Is it the absence of "something," or is that notion merely foolish in a context of "nothing"?

From the same Upanishad comes the famous tale of the two birds (this passage is translated by the Irish poet W. B. Yeats with the help of a Sanskrit scholar):

Two birds, bound to one another in friendship, have made their homes on the same tree. One stares about him, one pecks at the sweet fruit.

The personal self, weary of picking here and there, sinks into dejection; but when he understands through meditation that the other—the impersonal self—is indeed spirit, dejection disappears.

He who has found spirit, is spirit.

Another Upanishad, the Brihadaranyaka, says "He who knows that he is spirit, becomes spirit, becomes everything":

For as long as there is duality, one sees the other, one smells the other, one hears the other, one speaks to the other, one knows the other; but when everything is one self, who can see another, how can he see another; who can smell another, how can he smell another; who can hear another, how can he hear another; who can speak to another; how can he speak to another; who can think of another, how can he think of another; who can know another, how can he know another? . . . How can the knower be known?

Juan Mascaró, a distinguished translator of some of the more important Upanishads, quotes SPINOZA: "Blessedness is not the reward of virtue: it is virtue itself. We do not find joy in virtue because we control our lusts: but, contrariwise, because we find joy in virtue we are able to control our lusts."

The thinking in the Upanishads is not puritanical in the familiar Christian manner (insofar as external Christianity fell at the milestone of sexual activity, finding it absolutely sinful). Can one imagine a Christian Kama Sutra? The target of Hinduism is not just sexual activity, but, rather, selfishness within sexual activity (which in the Kama Sutra of the sage Vatsyayana is highly prized); really the target is the tiny personality, the ego that seems all-encompassing, the bird on the branch that is dejected. But that the personality is in reality tiny and insignificant, and that its pleasures are largely illusory, does not mean (as it so often does in Christianity) that what it "adores" is *evil;* it is merely *mistaken* in not being able to see that it itself, when it is dejected because its quest for pleasure and sensation fails—as it is bound to fail—is the chief obstacle to the truth that all is one, and that the key to the prison of suffering lies in the understanding of that part of the self that is, in fact, identical with Brahman.

The whole cast of the thinking here, even if it cannot appeal to those who have not experienced glimpses of the sort of release from suffering that can come from such insights, is unarguably far less "moral" than we are used to in the Christian or post-Christian West. Here, Hell is simply the daily round of existence from which, so long as this is believed in as the only good, it is impossible to escape. The writers of the Upanishads separated *pleasure,* the restless endless search for pleasure that cannot ever be fully gratified, from *good*. There was only one true pleasure for them: self-knowledge; this was the ultimate good. Their psychological analysis was acute and more realistic than that of the sex-fixated orthodox Christian establishment (of the rest, of course, one cannot thus speak). As a modern Indian philosopher has put it, "True self-knowledge is attained by philosophical reflection supported by greedless performance of social duties"—he could have added, too, "supported by the type of sexual activity that is also greedless and centered in the beloved." The real is what remains the same through change and "cannot be thought away." Indian philosophy is full of Berkeleyan attempts to demonstrate that matter is unreal. This is because such a notion is naturally congenial to such a philosophy. But it is not important whether we believe matter is real or otherwise. The spirit of the Upanishads and so much that followed them (and the Rig Veda was going in the same direction) does not depend on such distinctions. Once (and, of course, if) we can grasp *through our own experience* that all is one, that there is a place in the universe beyond time ("Fear and constraint arise from a second, therefore to understand that the self alone is real without a second, is to be fearless and free"), then we can be free. It is never pretended that the process is an easy one, or that life does not have to be lived through. A development of a way to it, one of the most remarkable, is to be found in the DHAMMAPADA.

5

東王公

The Eastern Royal Duke, a Taoist saint

The Way and Its Power

LAO-TZU

3rd century B.C.E.

Traditionally Lao-tzu ("Master Lao" or "Old Master")—the central figure in the Taoist religion, but, appropriately, not a real person—was an older contemporary of CONFUCIUS, whom he is supposed to have instructed in matters pertaining to rituals; he was born in the sixth century B.C.E. in the state of Chu, and wrote *The Way* (*Tao-te Ching*) as the first book of philosophy in Chinese. There is even a legend that Lao grew so disgusted with conditions in China that he left it, after handing in the *Tao-te Ching*—and that he then turned up in India as no less than the Buddha himself! But none of these tales, interesting though they are, accord with the facts as modern scholarship has revealed them; they are certainly untrue.

There probably was a sixth-century B.C.E. sage called Lao-tzu, and a few of his sayings may be in the book (of, in Chinese, just 5,250 words), *The Way and its Power* which was sometimes called by his name. But *The Way*, which criticizes Confucian values and is not mentioned by the Confucian Mencius (371–289 B.C.E.), must be later than Confucius; it is in all probability a compilation made some time during the period known as that of the Warring States (403–221 B.C.E.). The word *Taoism* itself was not coined until the second century B.C.E.. There is an accompanying text, the *Chuang Tzu*, also named after its author or part-author, probably of the same period; this functions as a kind of more detailed commentary on similar concepts, and differs in a few respects—but it need not be considered here, since it is *The Way* that is central, and far better known outside China. *Chuang Tzu* was compiled to persuade the warring rulers to cease their furious and harmful activity in the interests of the *wu-wei*, the principle of "creative nonaction," to which Taoists adhered—but its purpose may also have been the somewhat pessimistic one of confirming that those who had given up hope in the world had been justified, by supplying them with religious and philosophical solace.

Some of the differences (and similarities) between Confucianism and Taoism are discussed here in the essay on the *Analects* of Confucius. A number of them are obvious, too, from the *Analects*, in which we are told that some people who wished to hide themselves from the world—i.e., were Taoist-style recluses—ridiculed the sage while he was on his travels, for trying to save the world from itself; Confucius was, one of them said, a man who knew he could not succeed, but nonetheless kept on trying. The fundamental difference between the two attitudes could not be better summed up: Confucius told the recluses off by remarking that theirs was indeed a selfish desire for purity, since they neglected the most important aspect of human existence, namely, the place of man in society. But chapter 3 of *The Way* asserts that, on the contrary, "If we stop looking for 'superior men' to put in power, there will be no more jealousies among people."

Just as *Ju*, now taken as "Confucianism," was in existence before Confucius, so what we call Taoism was in existence before the traditional "time" of the mythical Lao-tzu. The Confucian strand in Chinese philosophy expresses its ethical and sociological concerns, the Taoist its individualistic—

and mystical and humorous—ones. There is more humor in the latter, and it has on the whole been more of an inspiration to artists and poets. The early Taoists, comments Chinese philosophy's leading twentieth-century interpreter Fung Lu-lan, were "selfish." But soon, the Chinese being a practical people, this selfishness or hedonism—a feature of which is its reliance on old magical beliefs, something that Confucius broke with—gave way to a more political concern (expressed in yet another important Taoist book of uncertain date, the *Lieh Tzu*).

Confucianism attributed the troubles of the times to lack of an ethical approach, and to neglect of the rules of an ordered past which Confucius believed had existed in China. The Taoists attributed them to too much striving after "worldly goals," to an adherence to old conventions which prevented people from functioning *naturally*—in accordance with the natural order. This, from our Western point of view, is the anarchic or at least "Rousseauist" aspect of Taoism, which, quite unlike Confucianism, had its origins in ancient Chinese magic and shamanism.

The Way itself has had far wider currency, though, than has any knowledge of the history of developments in Chinese philosophy—bedeviled as this is by disagreements between the scholars and the upholders of tradition. *The Way* is quite certainly a mystical text, and is so in a spirit wholly absent from the *Analects*. It is obscure and aphoristic in style, and it can be and has been translated in a variety of different ways.

It is also a mixture of highly sophisticated philosophical argument revolving on old magic and the puzzle of the creation of something from nothing. Thus while chapter 1 gives us the doctrine that it was "from the Nameless that Heaven and Earth sprang," and that only he who has rid himself forever from desire can "see the Secret essences," chapter 6 (obviously a quotation from a poem belonging to an earlier period) goes back to the time before thought as such developed: it identifies the origin of life in a much less philosophico-mystical manner: "The Valley Spirit never dies. It is called the dark female, and from her doorway Heaven and Earth sprang." One can fruitfully compare some of its speculations about being and not-being to those of the KABBALAH, and, as fruitfully, the attitude it cultivates to the skeptical one of Pyrrho (dealt with here under SEXTUS EMPIRICUS), who also recommended quietism—a refusal to take action. It is probably the most famous of all mystical texts, and, while this may be so in part because any construction may be put upon it, it is also so because it represents a compromise between ancient popular magic and advanced philosophical speculation. It might even have been thus designed.

We may see, too, the roots of Confucianism as having been in a desire to eliminate quietist attitudes—even in, although it would be heresy to many to suggest it, a desire to weaken the worst effects of the I CHING. For the basic philosophy of *The Way* is quietist, or at least leads to quietism. Insofar as Taoism became political it relied, on the whole—with intermittent appeals to *The Way*—on other and later texts. Political conclusions may be drawn from chapter 34, which recommends, in effect, that the person who "never at any time makes a show of greatness in fact achieves greatness." Thus the state that is noncompetitive with other states is assured that it will prevail—because of the phenomenon of *reversal,* by which everything turns into its opposite (see GURDJIEFF, *Beelzebub's Tales to His Grandson*). The ideal Taoist government would not be obtrusive: it would not impose anything at all on the people, even conventional morality—thus everything would be allowed to take its *natural* course. Thus chapter 30: "He who by Tao [the Way] wishes to help a ruler will oppose all armed conquest, for matters are subject to reversal. What is against Tao will soon die." That is at least one of the elements in the continuously persistent if also continuously failing cause of Western anarchism (see WILLIAM GODWIN), which in its turn has a connection with gnosticism (see THE GOSPEL OF TRUTH).

Western philosophers, even those most interested in religion, have shirked the question of how the universe came into being. There is now nothing within Western philosophy which could deal with such a question. *The Way* fulfills a need that philosophies—not even those, like DESCARTES's or LEIBNIZ's, that were obliged to offer a "proof of God"—never have, and it also especially satisfies those of a religious disposition who want to exercise it but feel offended or confused by dogma: Without appeal to any particular God, it accounts or attempts to account for the creation in a manner that suggests that the supernatural is always at work.

We can incidentally see why China offered so fertile a ground for Buddhism in the first century C.E. Buddhism cannot really be whatever you want it to be—but it can, again, provide refuge for those who reject dogma. The concept of the Tao itself owes much to the ancient *yin-yang* principle; one might even call it a kind of dualism, for so it could become. The *yin* is nonbeing, the *yang* is being. There cannot be *being* without *nonbeing*. There is purposeful action and there is nonaction, passivity. Not a few commentators have been reminded of HEGEL and his thesis-antithesis process.

Chapter 25 begins (the italics are mine, to emphasize the contradictions) "There was something *formless* yet *perfect* that existed before heaven and earth . . . we do not know its real name but we call it *Tao;*" and the poem states that going-away means returning. One of the few simplicities of *The Way* is its delight in paradox, which is based on the premise that what creates cannot itself be created, and that whatever causes change cannot itself be changeable. The wise ruler must attain a perfect state of not-doing because that will generate correct rule.

The Confucian wise ruler attends to a recommended system of ethics, the Taoist wise ruler will be inspired by his seeking out of the natural in himself. The two attitudes could not be further apart, yet Taoists were able to work with Confucianists just because of that. The Chinese character does not admit of permanence, unless it be the somewhat evasive permanence of the Tao itself, which is together emptiness, nonaction, and nonbeing, and yet also possessed of *te,* virtue, which gives it the *potentiality of being*. Only from the position of being are we led into the illusion that Tao is not-being!

Throughout its history Taoism has in fact favored either the *yin* or the *yang*, and under the influence of the Manichean religion in the fourth century the latter was given decided preference. Doctors of medicine put emphasis on the one or the other principle. The greatest commentator on *The Way* was the short-lived Wang-pi (226–249 C.E.), who believed Confucius to have been a more advanced adept that even Lao (because, in fact, he was not foolish enough to have attempted to speak about nonbeing!). He taught that nonbeing was the "substance" of the Tao, the source of all things, but that its function could only be manifested through being, and thus created a metaphysics as formidable as most Western systems.

The *Tao-te Ching* is reconcilable with the *Analects* because the one could hardly have done without the other; both together have helped to give China whatever equilibrium she has possessed. The influence of both has been, of course, mainly upon China. But by means of that they have influenced the world. MARX, through MAO, will have left his mark on tomorrow's China, but neither mark will fade either. Indeed, without too much ingenuity, a case could be made out by which the Chinese fate of Marxism, and of Marx, was really determined by the tension between Confucianism and Taoism, or at least of versions of them. And what will be the influence of the China of tomorrow on the world?

6

The Avesta

c. 500 B.C.E.

On today's datings, accepted by the majority of scholars, the Iranian religion Zoroastrianism is the oldest of the monotheistic religions. Certainly Zoroastrianism deeply influenced its successor religions: Judaism; Judaism's offshoot Christianity; the Dead Sea Scrolls community (probably the Essenes); Mahayana Buddhism; Manicheanism, the dualistic religion of the great Mani (c. 216–77)—often thought of as a dead faith, but in fact still vital and flourishing in many forms, existentialism, nihilism, and anarchism among them—and Islam. Zoroaster is the Greek name used by Western writers for the prophet Zarathustra, also later known as Zardust. *Thus Spake Zarathustra,* by FRIEDRICH NIETZSCHE, although highly influential, and a masterpiece, has no bearing whatsoever on Zoroaster or Zoroastrianism. The seventh-century B.C.E. date until recently most commonly assigned to Zarathustra's lifetime was invented by the Greeks (as was an even earlier one, of five thousand years before the Trojan Wars).

Zoroaster, of the Spitama family—legendarily the only infant ever to have laughed at birth—might very well have lived as early as 2000 B.C.E., but the most likely date is now taken to be around 1400–1200 B.C.E.. The problem of dating is complicated because Zoroaster lived before the art of writing reached Iran; after it did, Zoroastrians in any case for a long while refused to employ it for holy purposes. Thus the first Zoroastrian writings were not set down until 500–400 C.E., toward the end of the religion's thousand-year sway in the world (its decline was prophesied). Furthermore, the language in which these texts were written, Avestan (later called Zend), closely related to ancient Persian, has been extinct for almost fifteen hundred years.

Interpretations and therefore translations vary wildly and have further been distorted by scholars' and specialists' fear of dualism—meaning in this case, not that there is a decisive split between flesh and spirit, but that evil is co-eternal with good in the universe. We know that some texts date from around 1200 B.C.E.—some elements in them are pre-Zoroastrian—and others from between 800 and 600 B.C.E. Zoroastrianism was the state religion of two great empires: the Achaemenian (559–323 B.C.E.), ended by the vainglorious Alexander the Great, and the Sasanian (226 B.C.E.–c. 650 C.E.), finally destroyed by the advance of Islam.

Zoroastrianism's great "heresy," Zurvanism, whose adherents worshipped Zurvan, the god of time, also flourished at various periods, as did the form of the religion that is more dualist than Zoroaster would (probably) have approved—for it makes the evil god Angra Mainyu even more independent, and therefore more heretical, i.e., "Satanic." The oldest extant manuscript was written in 1323 C.E. Only the hymns, the *Gathas*, which are genuine poetry, were written by Zoroaster himself. The Avestan texts have greater theological authority, but there is much that derives from Sasanian times written in Pahlavi, a middle-Persian language; the latter writings (they reached their final form in the ninth and tenth centuries C.E.) are invaluable for the light they cast on the earlier, and on the manner in which the religion developed; the *Dinkard*, for example, is a summary of the Avesta; the *Bundahishn* tells the story of the creation. The scriptures consist of the purely religious Avesta, the Gathas (Zoroaster's poems, or "hymns"), the prayerbook known as the Khorda Avesta, the *Visperad* (extensions to the liturgy, called the *Yasna*), and the legal and medical *Vendidad*, which also contains some legends.

This profound and complex set of beliefs did not die out, although the number of Zoroastrians dwindled to a tiny minority, which fell upon desperately hard times in Iran under Islam, until the noble Persian Zoroastrian, Manekji Limji Hataria, pleaded, with some success, in the mid-nineteenth century, for the amelioration of the lives of his coreligionists in Iran. The main body of modern Zoroastrians consists of the Parsees (Persians), most of whom live in Bombay, where they are much respected—but some twelve thousand are in Iraq, and there are others in Persia (more, it is claimed, than before the revolution that deposed the Shah).

There are now less than 150,000 Parsees in all, and their form of Zoroastrianism has been thoroughly purged of every hint of the dreaded dualism. But Zoroaster still works his way in Judaism (as a dualist heresy, e.g., the insistence of the KABBALAH upon *sitra ahra,* the "other side," the eternally demonic) and in Christianity—and in particular, here, in those magnificent and so discredited gnostic "heresies" of whose uncomfortable, too "otherwordly," doctrines it has been so afraid that it hysterically suppressed them, and then vainly appointed the Inquisition (offically dated from 1232) to root them out by such especially orthodox Christian methods as burning.

Zoroaster, priest, poet, seer, and prophet, of the steppes of eastern Iran, was a reformer of the polytheistic religion into which he was brought up. This so-called Old Iranian religion is obscure, and can only be reconstructed hypothetically, although the Indian Rig Veda offers an invaluable guide to it. Zoroaster's own theology is properly called Zarathustrianism, to distinguish it from Zoroastrianism, the religion that was actually taken up by politicians for a thousand years—after being rendered suitable to serve their purposes. This involved the reintroduction of elements of the Old Iranian religion convenient to the process. Religions begin to turn into their opposites as soon as they achieve political *success.*

Zoroaster's theology is (very briefly) thus: The god Ahura Mazda ("Lord Wisdom"—the name does not occur in any Vedic texts, but is probably a conversion of the Vedic god Varuna) is an eternal uncreated (i.e., has always been in existence) being of the utmost good, who created the universe, which is also good. Opposing him, and also uncreated and original—in other words, until then and indeed now in human time, co-eternal—is the unequivocally evil Angra Mainyu (later called Ahriman). The duty of humanity, but a duty which each person must choose in heart—*not* by rote—is to aid Ahura Mazda against Angra Mainyu. This belief, containing much exquisite detail, expressed in moving prose, and with accompanying ethical ideas hitherto unknown (although perhaps nascent in the contemporary Egyptian and Babylonian religions), was by far the most powerful in the world at the time of Christ, and was known to PLATO and ARISTOTLE almost five hundred years before that—disconcerting to those who still put their faith in the old-fashioned dating.

Zoroaster himself gained a legendary reputation as a mage and sage (often described as Persian), was identified with Baruch and other Jewish figures—and was even said to have studied with Pythagoras. Despite the enormous gap of some one-and-a-half thousand years between Zoroaster's proclamation and the written record, it is generally agreed that his message has been preserved with an astonishing authenticity—and that until his time no god in the world, not even Jehovah or the savage Indian gods, had been invested with the powers that he ascribed to Ahura Mazda—thus, the prophet rhetorically asks: "Who supports the earth below and keeps the heavens from falling down?" "What artificer created days and nights?" Yet after Zoroaster's death various of the old Iranian gods reappeared—not, to be sure, with the powers of Ahura Mazda, but as formidable *yazatas,* the first angels to be encountered in world religion.

The community of this trainee-priest—for such Zoroaster almost certainly was—took no notice of him. Christ went similarly unheeded. He traveled and preached—there are many legends in the often attractive wonder literature that has gathered around his name—and finally found a prince, Vishtapsa (Hystapses in Greek), in another Iranian kingdom, who did notice him—the legend has it that he was able to cure Vishtapsa's favorite horse after everyone else had failed. Zoroaster's monotheistic religion was, after vicissitudes, soon made that of the realm, and spread from then onward.

Zoroaster, who claimed to have received his teaching directly from Ahura Mazda, his personal friend (recalling DANTE's poignant line lamenting that the king of the universe is not "our friend"), optimistically preached that time would end with the victory of good. He thus first contributed the notion of *eschatology*—last things, the end of the world—to religious thought. But in the meantime, men were free to choose between good and evil, and it was on the precise internal nature—we might call it the phenomenological nature—of their choice that they would be meticulously judged. (In fact this "end" is a beginning: The world is at last cleansed of evil, or, as a Kabbalist might have put it, *tikkun* will have been achieved.) Great emphasis is put upon freedom of the will, and indeed Ahura Mazda himself made the initial free choice: To follow the righteous path of *Asha,* which is the all-pervasive idea in Zoroastrianism.

The *daevas,* the gods of the Indo-Iranians, who also featured in the Old Iranian religion in which he had been brought up, Zoroaster opposed as violent and without morality: In them he saw—and those whom he converted saw—the destructive powers of the invaders who were always threatening the peaceful pastoral life of his people. Horses and cows are therefore important, and the lament of a cow, one of the Gathas, is a famous passage in the Zoroastrian canon. The cow cries out that she is suffering from the forces of the Lie (i.e., will either be sacrificed, or carried off in a raid by people who worship daevas, or both), and Ahura Mazda and his assistants (the Amesha Spentas) assign Zarathustra to protect her. But she is not pleased with this: she thinks him a weakling. ("Must I endure a keeper without power, the talk of a man without strength, when I need a powerful ruler?")

Essentially, though, this is an allegory of the sufferings of the soul in quest of righteousness, with some attention to the soul's weakness, most notorious among those who have tried to follow such a path as Zoroaster was perhaps the first to recommend. This and the other Gathas come several hundred years before HOMER, and are thus all the more remarkable in their psychological and metaphysical sophistication—although never in any heart-withering or overintellectualizing sense.

Zoroaster's teachings do reflect his society, that of herdsmen trying to lead a settled life against the maraudings of ruthless and lawless nomads (the impact of such invaders can never be underestimated); but they also contain an ethical and mystical element that stands apart from historical considerations. He did not want only to preserve the values of his time and place and tribe. He was peaceful and against blood sacrifice. In his system a person is

A Zoroastrian fire temple

judged, at death, at the Chinvat Bridge, the Bridge of the Separator, by the three yazatas, Mithra (from the old pantheon), Sraosha, and Rashnu. Good and bad acts, *and* thoughts and desires—there is no doubt that "good works" in proper Zoroastrianism, really Zarathustrianism, are not sufficient—are weighed in a balance. If good predominates then the soul is led across the bridge to Heaven, if bad then a vile old hag leads it across the gradually narrowing pathway of the bridge until it slips down into a Hades of bad food and misery.

But when the time for the great cleansing of evil from the world comes the *whole person* is judged at *Frashokereti* ("making wonderful"). The world and men pass through a great river of white-hot metal in final purification (thus the Zoroastrians worship fire, upon which of course the early ones greatly depended in the cold winters on the steppes), and "literally the best of both worlds" becomes true. In later, and authentic, elaborations it was said that when Ahura Mazda created the world he actually consulted the *fravashis*, the eternal spirits, of all people, as to whether they wished to take material form: They *chose* (this theme of choice is sovereign) to assume material form in the battle with evil, rather than to stand aside.

Thus the Jews, Christians, and Muslims all gained their various notions: of Heaven and Hell, death and resurrection, and doctrines of the nature of evil. The *Saoshyant,* the fortune-bringing savior to be born of a virgin at some future time, of the prophet's own seed (preserved miraculously in a lake, wherein it glows even now), is the origin, of course, of both the Jewish Messiah and of Jesus Christ. The nature of the judgment at the Chinvat Bridge is based, essentially, on Asha, an elaboration of the Vedic Indian Rita (with which the earlier Egyptian *Ma'at* or *Mayet*—truth, justice, order— should be compared). "Asha" cannot be translated by a single word: An approximation would be "the way things are naturally," a concept that embraces compassion, kindness, world-order, fitness, and much else, above all perhaps inner knowledge (not of the exclusively intellectual kind), and of the good-in-evil and evil-in-good: The "loving-kindness" of the Psalms, which so appealed to Thomas Hardy. The diametrical opposite of "Asha" is "Druj," the principle of disorder, which often, as in today's "democracies," poses as order—this "order" is comically revealed in *The Trial* and in *The Castle,* novels by the twentieth century's Jewish gnostic, FRANZ KAFKA: In the latter the mayor, in a mundane aping of mysticism, insists that the utterly irreme-diable chaos of the files is underlain by a certain order. The same scene takes place in every town hall all over the world today: The clerks "have it under control." *Money,* too, in the "democracies," poses as *justice*—just as *usury* poses as *helping people* ("social work"). Yet helping people is a vital and majestic notion in the thinking of this Zoroaster.

Eventually Zarathustrianism turned, as all religions have, into its own opposite: witness the corrupt priests who made it suitable to serve as a state religion, and thus to shore up the worldly glory of rulers. But there is no doubt that its founder was possessed of humanity and wisdom—as were a few of those who succeeded him. By Pahlavi times (in the Dinkard), in agree-ment with the spirit of the prophet himself, Ahura Mazda desires to be *un*known: "If they know me no one will follow me." This God—a realist—is already anticipating the unknown gnostic God, who is *not* to be equated with the Creator.

Analects

CONFUCIUS

c. 5th–4th century B.C.E.

Confucius (Venerable Master Kung, 551–479 B.C.E.)—his name was Latinized in the seventeenth century by Jesuit missionaries to China—so far as is known, wrote nothing down. He was solely an educator—a private teacher, with many pupils—and one, moreover, who made no overt appeal to supernatural authority. He called himself a transmitter of knowledge. But he is the best-known and the most influential thinker in Chinese history, and has thus been interpreted in diverse and contradictory ways. The man must be separated from the legend; but this is not easy—not even possible beyond a certain degree.

That Confucianism is not a religion, and that Confucius was not what we call "religious," must be taken against the background of the generally humanist nature of Chinese religion as a whole. In this the figure of God does not loom very large, and is not much appealed to—even Taoism is not reverent toward God—who is in any case equivalent to Nature. Compared with a Jewish sage, for example, Confucius has no reverence whatsoever: He appeals to a virtue natural to man but in need of being brought out by a distinctly unmystical kind of self-scrutiny. Nor does Chinese humanism resemble that of the Renaissance: It puts less emphasis on the individual, and much more on the individual as a unit in society. The notion of an *Almighty* is endemic to Chinese thought; but the notion of the universe momently in process of profound change is not.

The man, the first biography of whom was not published until almost four hundred years after his death, was born in the state of Lu into an impoverished aristocratic family. He held a minor (some claim major) post in the government of Lu for a time, but then resigned in 496 B.C.E. and took to traveling about in search of a ruler whom he could persuade to follow his ideas, which are perhaps as clearly admirable and rational as those of any such thinker.

Unlike PLATO, Confucius had no one even prepared to offer him a chance at trying out his political hand. Eventually, in 476, he returned to his native state to die, as a disappointed but still wise failure, who might have been aware that the details of this failure would, in a comparatively short time, permeate the society of his country from the top to the bottom. China's educational system was built around his ideas until the advent of communism; exactly how much Confucianism affected communist rule is a vexing question, but is certain that it did to some degree. Much in Maoism is Confucianist in spirit.

It is universally agreed that the best guide to what Confucius actually thought and said is to be found in the *Analects*. These, in the form of aphorisms or short narratives and dialogues, were collected by a disciple (or disciple of a disciple). To what exact extent they reflected the thoughts of Confucius himself has never been fully revealed.

It is impossible to give precedence to either of the two great philosophies of China. They reflect, very approximately, the opposition between romanticism and classicism in the west. If Taoism is the religion of *yin*, femininity, pantheism, innocence, anarchism, the inner world, and emotion, then Confucianism is that of *yang*, masculinity, morality, justice, organization, the outer world, and the intellect. Thus LAO-TZU is appropriately a mythical personage (there is no evidence of his existence, although someone of that name probably lived in the sixth century B.C.E., or a century or two later), but Confucius is human.

Both philosophies stem from a single source: agriculture. The scholars in China were usually landlords who depended as much upon successful farming as the farmers themselves. Taoism is concerned with nature, intuition, and spontaneity, Confucianism with nurture, logic, and social responsibility. Taoism is what you yearn for, Confucianism is what you must have. The latter was generated by a need to justify and then rethink and codify the complex system of family relationships and government that had grown up over the years. Both philosophies, however, shared one outlook: They accepted that the ceaseless interplay between *yin* and *yang* involved what they called *reversal*:

That process by which each event or thing involves its own reversal—at its simplest, that the dawn follows the night, and at its less obvious, that one emotion involves its opposite. Youth involves old age and vice versa. Both schools therefore revered, if for different reasons, the *Book of Changes,* the I CHING (the section devoted to this explains both *yin* and *yang*).

Throughout their long history both philosophies drifted apart and then came together: Taoists of the third century tried to bring themselves closer to Confucianism, and Confucianists of the twelfth century tried to bring themselves closer to Taoism. There were Taoists such as Wang-Pi (third century C.E.) who regarded Confucius as having attained a state beyond Being (*Yu*), but Lao-tzu himself as having remained just within it! The two attitudes have offered a useful balance to the Chinese people, and have gave them a foothold in the two available worlds, the "other" (Taoism), and this one.

That this should be so offers powerful witness to the existence of the "other," impossible to the positivist though such an existence is. Western positivism in its crudest form would grasp eagerly at Confucianism, as offering a useful code of ethics; Taoism, insofar as it has heard of this, it would dismiss as the product of sentimental superstition.

The Taoist looks at the color red and is immediately put into that "meaningful" subjective state acknowledged by SCHOPENHAUER (quoted in the discussion of *I Ching*); it does not do any injustice to the Confucianist to say that when he sees the color red he tends to reject "subjectivity" in favor of a quantitative measurement—wavelength. But that is an over-simplification, since Confucius was not insensitive to poetry, although he regarded it as morally helpful rather than simply delightful—he is supposed to have viewed love songs as valuable illustrations of how a wise ruler would act; whether that is true or not, it indicated what kind of man he was.

To what extent we have to distinguish Confucius from Confucianism (in Chinese parlance *Ju,*) is not quite clear. He did not do even a tenth of the things that have been attributed to him: did not even edit, let alone write, the so-called *Six Classics* (or *Liu Yi:* the *Changes,* and books of poetry, history, music, and ritual), although, a conservative, he upheld their authority. He was idealistically inclined, and he insisted that a well-ordered society must be clear about the names of everything: "The thing needed first," states the *Analects,* "is the rectification of names." Thus a son must be a son, a ruler must be a ruler. The bad ruler is not a ruler, because, although he is called a ruler, his actions in that capacity do not accord with the essence of what the word *ruler* implies.

Confucius lived at a time when many warlords were struggling with one another to share out the by then almost exhausted power of the Chou Dynasty. He sought to inject moral and humanitarian principles into politics. By cultivating the essence contained in the word *human* (*jen*)—that essence combines consideration for others with a specific admonition not to treat others as one would not like to treated oneself (compare "Love thy neighbor as thyself")—a person becomes "great" in both personal and public life. By cultivating virtue in himself a person may learn how to cultivate it in others. The concept of *li* (propriety, conduct) also plays an important part in Confucius's philosophy; this is an innately conservative element. In Confucianism virtue was its own reward; and the *Analects* state that "the superior man" will go into politics because it is the right thing, even though he may know that he cannot succeed.

Of all those considered to be major thinkers of the world, Confucius is probably the most aphoristic, the least original, and the least profound. But he was by no means empty in spite of that, since he was the very opposite of a charlatan; and he was original inasmuch as he elaborated the concern of the *Ju* school,° of which he was a member, into a wider one: He wanted to bring back the system of traditional ethics of the past, and was therefore fierce in his justification of them. He is probably the least profound (for obvious reasons Western romantics have preferred Lao-tzu) because he was—whether he was much interested in religion or not: an unanswered question—by far the most secular of the great thinkers until the eighteenth century and VOLTAIRE, and after him COMTE and MARX in the nineteenth.

The pragmatism of Confucius was also accompanied by an emphasis on self-reflectiveness that eventually led to much metaphysical speculation. Modern ethics can find much to draw upon in the implications of the *Analects,* although more in Confucia*nism* and what is known as neo-Confucianism (of the eleventh and twelfth centuries of our era). Much in KANT would have seemed wholly irrelevant to Confucius, most particularly Kant's concern with epistemological questions (questions dealing with the nature of knowledge and how it is gained), since Chinese philosophers, all pragmatists, have taken little notice of the problems presented by knowledge; he would, however, have accepted at least the principle of Kant's categorical imperative—it would have harmonized with his assumptions. Above all, though, he is relevant today because he was concerned with *how to live through and survive disorder,* and because he had a contempt for one of the driving-forces of our era: *profit.*

Our own age of global technology instantly reveals the disorder in which we live; and those who profit from it are above all interested in providing *instant information* which will stifle and suppress just what Confucius emphasised: *reflectiveness.*

An important developer of the ideas of Confucius, as well as thinker in his own right, is Mencius (the Latin form of Meng-ko), who lived between about 371 and 289 B.C.E. There is no doubt that Mencius received the teaching at fairly close hand—probably from a disciple of Confucius's own grandson. He put the stress on the essential goodness of man, which had been challenged from within Confucianism itself; he also did what Confucius failed

---

°*Ju* may originally, and curiously, have meant *weakling,* but it came to denote *teacher of ritual* and finally *literatus,* in that a bit reminiscent of our *professor;* although often translated as "Confucianism" the meaning is really quite distinct.

to do—give an explanation of why men should behave charitably toward others. The later (third century B.C.E.) Hsun-tzu, another important Confucianist, was more cynical, and pushed one wing of Confucianism into a more realistic mode.

Confucianism would not be what it has become—now flourishing in the countries immediately outside China, and beginning to spread to the mainland in the wake of the death of the himself partially Confucianist MAO ZEDONG—without Confucius; Taoism does not really have Lao-tzu at all. But then it would reject such vulgarities. Confucius's influence has been so very great, perhaps, just because he lacked the profundity of a Plato. He may well have had a total scorn for the world of the spirit, for what the Taoist valued in poetry, for that paradoxical yearning for a knowledge of the unknowable that we meet, for example, in the KABBALAH. He wanted rulers to be wise and virtuous men, but never questioned the system of hereditary rule. But he may well have contributed something even to our Western notion of a *gentleman* ("superior man"), and it is not uninteresting, even if it is startling, to compare his definitions of proper behavior with those of the Renaissance Italian writer Baldassare Castiglione in his *Il Cortegiano* (*The Courtier,* 1528).

What is the difference between the Confucian *Chun Tzu*—who was supposed to cultivate integrity, righteousness, loyalty, reciprocity, and kindness—and the possessor of the Italian *virtù*? More to the point, what do they have in common?

Undoubtedly the Confucian "superior man" is more innately moral and less individualistic, but there is more in common than is at first apparent. However, Confucius has been a more unequivocally good influence, not only than the man who cultivated the notion of *virtù* (Benvenuto Cellini—whose memoirs are a near miss in this context—is a good example, as he was sure he possessed it) but also than many profounder thinkers, or than "thinkers" such as Martin Heidegger, who vainly fiddled about with the profound.

What is missing in Confucius is a philosophical (or religious) basis for wishing to achieve what Plato called "the good." Yet his teaching of the necessity for benevolence and consideration of others, whether he gave it a base or not, is still of pressing relevance. Bureaucrats are unpopular in the West on account of what we call their "facelessness": Only a minority of them are considerate of individuals, and yet they do not themselves like to be treated inconsiderately. Confucianism is much, much less demanding than Christianity, with its more intense admonition to *love* our neighbors. Neither Confucius nor Confucianism ever dreamed that the world was about to come to an end. Perhaps its appeal has all the more force for its existing, at least in the thinking of Confucius himself, as just a fair assumption? We know as Confucius knew that admonitions to decency fail; but how much worse would the world be if they were never made?

8

History of the Peloponnesian War

THUCYDIDES

5th Century B.C.E.

Herodotus is not quite a "historian's historian": He was too full of interest in matters not strictly historical. It is to his and our literary benefit. But Thucydides, born some twenty years after him, is quintessentially the historian's historian. He is explicitly interested in method and interpretation, and he sets himself up as a rival to his great Halicarnassian predecessor.

The long Greco-Persian War, the main subject of Herodotus's *History*, ended in 448 B.C.E. with the Peace of Callias. But at least since 478 there had been fierce rivalry between Sparta and Athens, especially on account of Athens's increasingly autocratic leadership of the Delian League, originally formed to combat the Persians. A paradoxical rivalry grew up: Democratic Athens sought to suppress the freedom of all its allies, Sparta in particular, while the militaristic dictatorship of Sparta—held by the Athenians to exhibit the extremes of wrongheaded politics—became the champion of self-determination.

In 460 the Athenians went to war, really on account of trade, with Corinth and other states in the Peloponnese, including Aegina. Aegina was besieged and captured in 457. At this point Sparta reneged on her old ally, and defeated an Athenian army at the Battle of Tanagra, near Thebes. But under the leadership of Pericles, Athens continued to achieve success over the next few years.

In 446 Sparta and other states pushed Athens back, so that even her powerful navy was hard put to retain control. Pericles saw that Athens must cease aggressive policies and become, rather, a self-contained trading country with a strong army and navy. He built the defensive Long Walls between Athens and her seaport of Piraeus. He concluded what was called the Thirty Years Peace in 445. Thus ended the First Peloponnesian War. This peace lasted a decade. In 432, after Athens had loftily intervened in another conflict between two states, Sparta declared war. Her reason was the Athenian breach of the Thirty Years Peace. Thus began the Second Peloponnesian War, the subject of Thucydides' work.

Thucydides was born between 460 and 465 into an aristocratic family with Thracian connections. He was probably related by blood to Cimon, the son of the Athenian general Miltiades (550–489), who received more of the glory of the great victory over the Persians at Marathon than he perhaps deserved. Thucydides caught the plague of 429 in Athens (later terrifyingly described by LUCRETIUS) but survived it. He was as a young man devoted to the cause of Pericles (who died in 429 of the plague), whose famous funeral oration for the dead of the first phase of the Second War we have only in his words. This ensured Pericles' enduring fame as a public speaker.

In 424 Thucydides was elected, as were nine others, as general. He was given command of the northern fleet (we should call him an admiral). In that same year he failed to prevent the important Macedonian city of Amphipolis from being captured by the Spartan Brasidas. In Book IV of his *History* Thucydides gives a detailed account of the affair, in which he praises Brasidas for his moderation and "gentleness." But it was the end of the war for him personally—except as its historian. He was sent home, tried, and sentenced to twenty years of exile from Athens for his failure. As he himself put it, with an objectivity in no way false, in Book V (I quote from Richard Crawley's 1876 translation, still unbettered and still available):

> The history of the period has also been written by . . . Thucydides,
> an Athenian, in the chronological order of events by summers and

winters, to the time when the Lacedaemonians and their allies put an end to the Athenian Empire, and took the Long Walls and Piraeus. . . . I certainly all along remember from the beginning to the end of the war. . . . I lived through the whole of it, being of an age to comprehend events, and giving my attention to them in order to know the exact truth about them. It was also my fate to be exiled from my country for twenty years [he traveled extensively during the years of his exile, and returned to Athens to die within a few years, his *History* unfinished] after my command at Amphipolis; and being present with both parties, and more especially with the Peloponnesians by reason of my exile, I had reason to observe affairs somewhat particularly.

In this passage, much of Thucydides' then unique methodology as a historian was laid out. He sets himself up—not without hauteur—to be an exact recorder of contemporary events, and he emphasizes that he has been conscientiously objective in this. He set himself up, too, against Herodotus, and is determined to demonstrate that the Peloponnesian War was more important than the Persian. He was justified at least inasmuch as this war did herald the end of Greek civilization. A network of states failed to function together and was thus eventually destroyed. Of course his own feelings about his exile sharpened his objectivity: He had not been a bad commander and was perhaps more unlucky than negligent. His exile, unjust or not, was in any case a great piece of good fortune for the art of history.

In certain respects Thucydides is the precursor of MACHIAVELLI. The bleak message of his record is that men will always pursue the course of expedience rather than that of virtue. In view of the fact that PLATO, who preached the Good, was born in the year after the Athenian plague struck, this is depressing. It is even more depressing that Machiavelli was born (approximately) 1,469 years after Jesus Christ—who rejected violence (except in an increasing number of special cases, including those of heresy, which Christians have always been eager to point out). But children are never taught this at school.

Thucydides' prose is dense, his chronicling of events admirably fast, his characterization usually shrewd and to the purpose. He has a far better sense of character, within his admittedly narrower range, than did PLUTARCH, who wrote so much later than he did. Rivalry with Herodotus caused him to underestimate Persian influence throughout, and occasionally his judgment, like that of all historians, is at fault. But in general he was astonishingly accurate. He was the first substantial author to write history to be read—not recited—and he wrote with the humane purpose of instructing his readers in the likely patterns of future human behavior. He does not gloat over his sad version of reality (as Machiavelli might be accused of doing).

The accuracy of the speeches he inserts—after the manner of HOMER—has of course been the subject of much debate, since he admits both that his powers of recall are imperfect and that he has (therefore) been forced to have recourse to the use of his imagination, something that in general he wished to avoid, in the interests of exactitude. Certainly he conscientiously took notes or sought the accounts of listeners; as certainly he dramatized his material. In this he was both artistic and, for the most part, successful. His re-creation of some events is brilliant and brilliantly judged. What is fictional in him is to good purpose—there is more of it than he would have preferred to admit, but we are grateful. His blending of tragic art and factual reportage has seldom been equaled, since, with Herodotus, he has been the most potent influence upon history ever since his work saw the light of day. Most blamed the loss of Amphipolis (whose citizens gave themselves up to Brasidas only because they were ignorant of the proximity of Thucydides) on the Athenians rather than on him in particular. It was in any case a failure and an injustice that proved a remarkable gain for history.

9

Works

HIPPOCRATES

c. 400 B.C.E.

The semilegendary figure of PLATO's older contemporary Hippocrates (c. 469–399 B.C.E.) was, to the ancient Greeks, to the Arabs, to medieval men of learning throughout Europe and elsewhere—to all ages, as to our own—the embodiment of the ideal physician. We cannot be quite sure, but he may deserve this; in any case, in a Platonic sense (and Plato thought highly of him), he is. However, he did not write the so-called *Hippocratic Writings,* although he may have written bits of them or inspired some of those that do not postdate his lifetime. Some claim that Greek medicine was as high and original a creative achievement as Greek drama.

First, though, who was Hippocrates, and what are the writings?

That so many legends have gathered around the man should not suggest that he did not exist, a thesis that has—if only occasionally—been advanced; in this case the very number of legends attest to his importance and his reputation as teacher and healer in his own time. But, his medical eminence apart, there are few certain facts: He was a native of the Greek island of Cos, off the west coast of Asia minor; he was of diminutive stature; he traveled much in his capacity as teacher of medicine. The son of Heraclides, also a physician, he was a member of a medical guild called the Asclepiadae (named after Asclepius, the Greek god of healing). Another medical school, just as important, existed across the sea, on the mainland at Cnidus.

That Hippocrates became a very famous and revered physician is undoubted; but we have to rely on sources near to his own time to discover the measure of his individual achievement, and these are few. Throughout the centuries that followed him his reputation tended to eclipse that of countless other doctors, so that the *Writings* contain works written after he died—few of them, however, date from after about 330 B.C.E. All the efforts to ascribe definitively to him, and to him only, various works among them have been unsuccessful—but not necessarily wrong. Two that stand out are a treatise on epilepsy, the main purpose of which is to take a sternly empirical look at an illness that was widely believed to be "holy," and the so-called "On Environment," which gives an account of various "local" diseases, i.e. diseases caused by conditions such as climate, soil, and demographic situation.

The *Writings* are invaluable for the account they give us of the history of medicine and of medical thought, and they have been edited in modern times. They consist of fifty-eight works arranged into seventy-three books. Their approach is, allowing for their period, resolutely empirical, and lays much emphasis on observation. They indicate an awareness that injuries to either side of the head manifest in effects on the other side of the body. They influenced both PLATO and ARISTOTLE. They went as far as they could against superstitious interpretations. From them it is quite clear that a scientific outlook already coexisted with a folkloristic one.

Platonic idealism, whatever its value, was not found suitable in a medical context. However, unless his Hippocrates is partially a fictional device (as his Socrates might be) Plato gives us valuable information about him in his *Phaedrus.* There he presents him as asserting that nothing can be understood about parts of the body unless the body is understood as a whole—this means that one cannot fully know about an important part, say the liver, unless one can understand its function in terms of the whole.

Hippocrates himself may have believed (or so a pupil of Aristotle, Meno, related) the assumption, now peculiar, that disease is caused by incomplete digestion: Undigested air is expelled along with the remnants of a meal, and then invades the body. Yet such a conception of illness is not in the *Writings* themselves, which are of course inconsistent. Well informed doctors who are not classical scholars tend to believe that about six of the books are by Hippocrates. One of these states that the "wealth of original observation, the unerring sense of what is relevant, would set them [the best works in the corpus] among the great works of genius." One very famous passage reads:

Life is short and the Art long; the occasion fleeting; experience fallacious, and judgment difficult. The doctor must not only be prepared to do what is right himself, but must also make the patient, the assistants, and the externals cooperate.

It is the *Prognostics*, however, that contain the most famous passage of all. It concerns the appearance of dying people: "a sharp nose, hollow eyes, collapsed temples. . . ." But the author tells doctors to beware—there may be others causes of this appearance. The description is still a classic one.

Hippocrates was idealized by medical men of most cultures, and not least by the Greek Galen (130–200 C.E.), "the Prince of physicians," whose writings, like those of Hippocrates, were regarded as almost scriptural—but only for fifteen hundred years after his death. More is known about him than about his great predecessor, and not all of it is pleasant: Galen

Galen

was arrogant, weak in theory, and immensely self-satisfied. He had the unpleasant duty of being entrusted with the task of looking after, by special request, the health of the repulsive and awful son and heir of MARCUS AURELIUS, Commodus. Furthermore, had he had a successor of equal or nearly equal eminence then his lack of self-criticism might not have been so damaging.

Probably the work of two physicians of the third century B.C.E., Herophilus and Eristratus, was even more important than his; but he did draw attention to them. He also drew attention to Hippocrates. Sometimes he criticized them on poor theoretical grounds, and that was unfortunate for the progress of medicine. But his reputation paid a price: In the sixteenth century it began to decline, while that of Hippocrates grew.

Forms of the famous Hippocratic Oath existed before Hippocrates, but the name is not felt to be inappropriate. Indian doctors had a similar version of it, and the Greek may well have been Pythagorean or Egyptian or, of course, both. By taking it the physician promises, among other things, to devote himself to his patients, to not enter into sexual relations with them, to never give a poisonous drug, to never help to cause an abortion, and to always maintain confidentiality.

10

Works

ARISTOTLE

4th century B.C.E.

Even today, and even among those who have never heard the name, the "inspired common sense"—as Michael Grant has called it—of Aristotle, philosopher, scientist, and general-purpose thinker, has "percolated so thoroughly into our inherited ways of thinking that we adhere to them automatically and without recalling their source." If we exclude religious figures, Aristotle's influence on the world must have been greater than that of any other single individual. But, since he was a pupil of PLATO, we must, for all that he disagreed with him on certain subjects—chiefly, he did not believe in the separate existence of Plato's Forms, or Ideas—give the older man precedence. However, Aristotle amounts to more than just a mere "footnote to Plato," however tempting it may be to so describe him. If what has survived of his work is on the dull side, we have the Roman Cicero's word for it that in the lost works there was a "golden stream" of eloquence—it may therefore be that we hardly know him!

Aristotle was born in 384 B.C.E. in Stagira (now Stavros), a small town on the Thracian seacoast, the son of Nichomachus, a physician who had connections with the Macedonian court. At the age of eighteen he entered the Academy, Plato's school in Athens. There for twenty years, he became a lecturer on his own account. Plato called him both "the intelligence of the school" and "the reader"—he also said, however, that he needed "the curb rather than the spur." He figures in Plato's *Parmenides*. After Plato's death (347 B.C.E.) Aristotle became dissatisfied with the Academy, because he believed that it was now set on "turning philosophy into mathematics." He joined a group of Plato's disciples who were living with Hermeias, a former student of the Academy who had become the tyrant of the coastal town of Atarneus, in northwestern Asia Minor. During the three years he spent there, Aristotle married Hermeias's niece and adopted daughter Pythias, who became the mother of a daughter—whether she or his second wife (or concubine), Herpyllis, was also the mother of his son, whom he named after his own father, is not known.

In 342 Philip II of Macedonia invited Aristotle to supervise the education of his thirteen-year-old son Alexander at Mieza, near the Macedonian capital of Pella. This he did for two years, until about 340, when the boy became regent for his father (who was assassinated four years later). Aristotle was richly rewarded for his tutoring services, but the tales of his being supplied with thousands of slaves for the purpose of collecting specimens for studies in natural science are perhaps exaggerated. However, he may well have been a man who wanted to get on with exploring human knowledge to its uttermost limits, at whatever costs.

We should consider just what influence Aristotle had on his vainglorious pupil, called—and often thought of as—Alexander the "Great." Having put down revolts in Greece and Macedonia, the young Alexander conquered Syria and Egypt (where he found no opposition). In 331 he was pronounced a god in Libya, and in the same year he completed his conquest of Persia. Now ruler of Asia, he set out in 327 for India, but failed to penetrate it. In 324 his exhausted armies demanded that he return, and they arrived at Susa after a terrible march. He died of fever at Babylon at the age of thirty-two. He is generally regarded, rather weakly, as (for example) "a great military leader who almost accomplished his aim: to create and rule a world empire." The notion that the creation of a "world empire" is anything other than desirable usually goes unquestioned—and it is always pointed out that Alexander ended the autonomy of the Greek city-states forever and spread the benefits of Greek culture. Did Aristotle's teachings affect Alexander's ambitions?

As the poet W. B. Yeats fancifully put it, Aristotle really did "play the tawse/Across the bottom of a king of kings." A few have discounted PLUTARCH's evidence to this effect, but for no good reason. Therefore we ought to ask the question. And an answer may be inferred: Aristotle, whatever he may have thought about war or peace or the benefits of Greek culture or about the convenience of hundreds of thousands of people, was quite powerless, and could not possibly—anyway—have done anything but supported what may be called a nationalist program. Besides which, notoriously—and this is relevant—his work contains no objection to the practice of slavery, which meant that—rather like those who believe that Jesus Christ spoke English—he assumed the natural superiority of Greeks (he had the disadvantage of not having heard of the superiority of England, just as, although to become the chief inspiration to the most pious of Christian philosophers, he was denied the benefits of paradise on the grounds that he made the seriously rational error of being born before Christ—and not in England to boot). To point this out is not, however, to point any triumphalist and "politically correct" finger at Aristotle. Political correctness is the sullen revenge of the spiteful, intolerant, and ill-willed dunce upon all the liveliness in this world. It is no more than the humorlessly insincere resort of minds so mediocre that, for them, a revival of Stalinism is preferable to the pain of a glimpse of self—it is the last sigh of the beast that NIETZSCHE identified as *ressentiment*. Such minds take their grim notion of pleasure—like the fantasised erections of centenarian eunuchs—in combing what little they wish to know of history for figures who seem not to conform to the artificial standards of twentieth-century government at its most inept.

But whereas Aristotle thought the Orientals "slaves by nature"—just as Kipling and many others felt about the non-British in the 1900s—and would have had Alexander so taught, the playwright Euripides, almost exactly one hundred years older, questioned the institution of slavery—as had the sophist philosophers, one of whom, Protagoras, had been his friend. Aristotle thought Euripides the most tragic of the poets. That difference between them remains.

To balance this undoubted flaw in his notions of humanity and justice (there were of course notable exceptions to the British colonial idea, too), it is more than likely that Alexander owed his famous magnanimity in victory to Aristotle, so that, since the former would have become a conqueror anyway, the influence—in consequentialist terms—must be counted as ultimately a beneficial one. Alexander's excuse for his invasions was that he wished to save his victims: for that, a good philosophy was necessary. Aristotle provided it. Besides, it is not safe to ignore one of the enormous number of legends about him: that he freed his own slaves. He saw (what some Athenians never did) that there was nothing anti-Athenian about Philip or Alexander; that for them the barbaric Persians were the first enemy. Alexander (according to Plutarch) wrote to Aristotle:

> Alexander to Aristotle, greeting. You have not done well to publish your books on oral doctrine: What is there now that we excel others in, if those things which we have been particularly instructed in be laid open to all? For my part, I assure you, I had rather excel others in the knowledge of what is excellent, than in the extent of my power and dominion. Farewell.

Alexander at the battle of Issus

Alexander hardly meant this, but it tells us something about Aristotle's effect on him.

Aristotle was below average height, a lisping dandy with tiny eyes, bald, with thin legs, who when asked why he liked pretty women replied that only the blind would ask. Despite being quite kindhearted, he was ruthlessly efficient in everything he did—and there is really little reason to challenge the predominant view that he was an ethical man whose standards of behavior were far above those common in his day. An intelligent layman's view—laymen are not in quite every respect inferior to philosophers—of Aristotle's *Ethics* would certainly be that, while it was a bit boring, it was also eminently sensible and had to be written. What we have of his *Poetics* (students' notes) is truly admirable and still seminal; but, while it accepts the notion of inspiration, it lacks real attention to or interest in it. He has thus in this respect always been a model for university professors, who (generally) do not believe in inspiration.

In 334 Aristotle, taking advantage of the pro-Macedonian government then in power, returned to Athens and founded the Lyceum. He gained the name of a peripatetic (Greek: "walking about") philosopher because he taught while strolling with his pupils. Eleven years later, after Alexander had died and the Athenian government had changed to an anti-Macedonian one, he was charged with "impiety." After commenting that he did not want another Athenian government to disgrace itself as it had over Socrates, he fled to Chalcis where, a year later, in 322, he died.

Aristotle's writings are usually divided into three groups. First there are what he called his exoteric writings, all lost (but surviving in quotation form). He called them *exoteric* (Greek: *exo*, "outside") because, written while he was at the Academy, they were not for its members, but for an audience outside. Second, there were the memoranda, written for information at the Lyceum for information for scholars—these, too, are almost all lost. Third, the bulk of his extant writings: the treatises, lecture notes, and textbooks written for students at the Lyceum and therefore *esoteric* (Greek, *eso*, "inside")—but not in our newer sense of "secret."

It is clear that Aristotle, even though the status of his texts is highly uncertain and although so much is lost, was an archsystematizer—and a scientist before he was a philosopher—and probably the first popularizer. It can hardly be just an accident that such a mind has been so influential. A pagan Greek, his philosophy became the pillar of Christian doctrine (but LUTHER called him "stinking"); before that he had been a master of the thought of the Islamic world; English scholars of the seventeenth century were actually obliged by statute to recognize him as "paramount"—earning the comment from HOBBES that he had been a prime source of nonsense. He became, inevitably, much that he had not been: his authority was appealed to in matters which he could not have anticipated. He regarded God as uncreated, endless, and as endowing the world (in the largest sense) with purpose. "Every serious intellectual advance," wrote Bertrand Russell, "has had to begin with an attack on some Aristotelian doctrine." The legend that he threw himself into the sea because he could not explain the tides is apt, and was hardly intended literally.

Whether the German scholar Werner Jaeger was right (as most believe) or not in discerning in Aristotle three phases—acceptance of Plato's theory of Forms, rejection of this, and a last one tending toward empiricism (the quest for knowledge based on the traditional five senses)—he differed from his master in substituting scientific inquiry for the tendency to idealize the world. "There is nothing in the intellect that was not first in the senses," he said, and the medieval schoolmen philosophers followed him in this. A born categorizer, we owe to him the very way we classify knowledge: With his huge library, collection of the one hundred and fifty-eight constitutions of Greek states, his scientific specimens, he introduced logic, metaphysics, biology, meteorology, politics, ethics, rhetoric, psychology, and physics to the world. It is here above all that he is not just a footnote to Plato.

We owe to him, too, the distinctions between the glutton and the mean man, the lover and the friend, the buffoon and the wit; our notion of moderation begins with what he said. Could anyone have done it better? The syllogism—and many of the subtleties associated with it—is his: the argument that runs, so familiarly to us, in the form of, "All men are mortal, Socrates is a man, therefore Socrates is mortal." It is from Aristotle, originally, that we get the realization that the assumption implicit in *I saw a policeman calling at number six this morning, I wonder what she has done wrong* is false and malicious. That all the known political parties of the world proceed by these methods, treating those they aim to rule as mindless scum—a source of cash with which they may take the world to the brink of disaster—is no tribute to their respect for Aristotle.

Lastly, on a subject that has proved inexhaustible, a brief history of *Aristotelianism,* by no means whatever always to be identified with Aristotle. Some of the terms he left with us are *syllogism, substance, conclusion, dialectic*—there are perhaps a dozen others. But he has been used by various factions to prove very different points. In the last century before our era, his works were translated into Latin. This ushered in the first period of his influence, only brought to an end when Justinian forbade the teaching of philosophy in Athens in 529. Now it was the turn of the Arabs: Both Avicenna (Ibn Cina) and Averroes (Ibn Rushd) treated him as sovereign, and it was largely by way of their commentaries that new Latin versions of his works reached Europe again, this time via Spain. AQUINAS, as may later be seen, more or less reinvented him, influentially squaring his doctrines with those of the Christian Church. DANTE pronounced him "master of those who know." And, whereas Aristotle himself would have taken one peep through the telescope of GALILEO (in which he would have delighted) and acceded to what he saw, the conformist Cremonini, a leading Aristotelian, refused to do this lest he see something that denied the current paradigm. So when Hobbes attacked the *Metaphysics* and the *Ethics* for their absurdity, he was not so much attacking Aristotle as Aristotelianism. Modern philosophy, properly, tries to reconstruct what Aristotle actually thought. He justifies the oft-made remark that he is the last man to have "known everything that was to be known in his time."

11

History

HERODOTUS

4th century B.C.E.

History is a cross between an exact and a speculative science, and was thus early forced to become an art form. It is easy to list external events; much less than easy to select what is significant from them, and then to try to discern the human motivations or patterns in them. Many quite exact, but imaginatively impoverished, historians have been unable to write in an interesting way; the great ones, such as EDWARD GIBBON, always do so. Herodotus (c. 480–425 B.C.E.), rightly called (by the Roman lawyer, philosopher, and orator Marcus Tullius Cicero) the "father of history," wrote outstandingly well and set a standard for all his successors—a standard that has been acknowledged by almost all of them.

As we have recently noted, the extent to which the epic poet HOMER gives us history as well as legend and custom is a very vexing question. It will remain so. With Herodotus—a sort of prose Homer to the Greeks, since he was the first Greek to write truly majestic prose—the question is still vexing, but to a far smaller degree.

All societies, with their religions, customs, traditions, and laws, have had their professional chroniclers or remembrancers. Many of those have been, and still are, professional liars, obedient bureaucrats, or "statisticians"—while others, mostly as ungifted, have done and still do their honest best. In Greece, as elsewhere, this was so even before the advent of writing—the Greeks adapted their alphabet (in all essentials our own) from the Phoenicians in the course of the eighth century. Before that they kept oral records, which were remembered by officials and priests just as their bards remembered the narrative poems such as the *Iliad*.

History as we now understand it—as an attempt to uncover the truth and the reasons for it—developed independently of external influences in only three societies: the Chinese, the Hebrew, and the Greek. But Herodotus is the first individual historian we know of. He invented the form. He transformed himself, in all probability, from an inveterate note taker into a historian proper, whose great work may have involved the complete rewriting of an earlier composition—or notes for lectures and recitations—from scratch.

However, there is a legitimate "grandfather of history," whom Herodotus affected to disdain but of whom he made much use. This was the geographer Hecateus of Miletus, who lived from the sixth and into the fifth century B.C.E. He was less lucky than Herodotus because we have only fragments (about three hundred) from his *Circuit of the World* (*Periegesis*), written around 500 B.C.E. It is unlikely, though, that we should find the *Circuit* readable from cover to cover, as Herodotus so eminently is. Hecateus was a pupil of Anaximander, also of Miletus, often and justly called the first real philosopher. The map with which he illustrated his *Circuit* reflected Anaximander's ideas.

This map shows the world as a disk neatly divided into four sections, with the ocean flowing around it. Herodotus dismissed it, but this did not stop him from drawing on Hecateus's books whenever he felt like it. Many historians have been like this, although nowadays they put their rivals down not only by failing to mention them—Herodotus hardly mentions Hecateus unless he wishes to criticize him—but also by savaging them in obscure and often coded footnotes. (Then these historians may have to meet one another at conferences and so have to pretend that they were paying compliments: "I didn't mention you because your work is so fundamental" or "You misread that note" and suchlike.) But Herodotus had no rivals, since, for all his now obvious failings, he invented history. Nor can we blame him for thinking of Hecateus as dull.

One interesting fact about Hecateus, though, which justifies our high valuation of him as a technical predecessor, is that he prefaced a later work with the following remark: "What I write here is what I believe to be the truth. The Greeks tell many tales, which are in my opinion absurd." This is a real historian, a writer with a critical mind, speaking. But, alas, he was not immune from credulousness himself. His contemporary, the philosopher Heraclitus (a supercilious man, however, who applied the same judgment to Pythagoras), offered Hecateus as an example of one who demonstrated that great learning by no means presupposes intelligence. However unkind and superior he liked to be, Heraclitus would never have been able to say this of Herodotus.

Herodotus was an Asian Greek born in about 484 B.C.E. (he himself wrote "just before the Persian War") at Halicarnassus (modern Bodrum, in Turkey), in Caria in Ionia, into a good family. His uncle was the epic poet Panyassis, whose (lost) poem *Heraclea* was once compared, not unfavorably, to Homer. Herodotus may have inherited some of his ideas from his uncle. Halicarnassus stood near the border between Greece and the Persian empire, and was a part of the latter when Herodotus was born. He was thus a young witness to some of the events he relates—certainly he would have seen a Persian ("enemy") fleet depart and return. He begins his *History* (more strictly translated as *Researches,* since that is what the word really means) thus:

> This is an account of the researches of Herodotus of Halicar-
> nassus. It has been undertaken so that the achievements of men
> should not be forgotten, so that the great and wonderful deeds of
> Greeks and barbarians [any non-Greek to a Greek was a barbarian]
> should not go uncelebrated, and, not the least, to explain the rea-
> sons why these two peoples fought each other.

Panyassis was murdered, during an uprising, by the tyrant of Halicar-nassus, Lygdamis, who ruled the city for the Persians. Herodotus himself had to withdraw to the nearby island of Samos. He could have returned in 354, when Lygdamis was overthrown and Halicarnassus became Greek again—a member of the Delian League, and thus ultimately dependent on Athens. He could not have remained there long, though, because after about ten years, when he settled at the newly founded Greek colony, Athens-inspired, of Thurii in Italy (near Tarantum), he had already become a famous traveler. He may well have traveled widely before 354. He probably began the *History* in about 443, at Thurii; it was finished—if it is finished, for some maintain that it is not—within twenty years, and he died either at Pella or, more likely, in Thurii in or just before 420. In 425 he was ridiculed by the satirical playwright Aristo-phanes; but then absolutely everyone, including Socrates, was ridiculed by Aristophanes, who made it his business—more thoroughly than anyone before or after him—to mock everything. Such people as Socrates were not, of course, really ridiculous. But every reputation can do with taking down a peg, and it pleases theatergoers anyway, so Aristophanes fulfilled a useful function. There is no one like him today because so-called "eminent men" are no longer like Socrates or Herodotus: they are, increasingly, mediocrities.

By 443, then—as well as lecturing and reciting in Athens—Herodotus had seen Egypt, Palestine, Syria, Babylon, Macedonia, and, probably, the island of Crete. The *History,* which was written to be recited, and divided into two parts, was later further divided, by a scholar at Alexandria, into nine books. Since the object of the work as a whole is to trace the origins of the Greco-Persian conflict, it takes five books to reach the Battle of Marathon (490)—Marathon was an unimportant village near Athens where the forces engaged—in which the Greeks defeated a far greater Persian force.

Herodotus begins with the semimythical Trojan War, the subject of Homer's *Iliad,* and then goes on to trace in more detail the story of Croesus, the king of Lydia between about 560 and 546; Marathon does not come until Book VI. The culmination is reached in Books VII–IX, when Xerxes of Persia makes his great expedition (480) in order to subdue the Greeks once and for all. Herodotus exaggerates the size of Cyrus's army and navy—he maintains that they consisted of 1,250,000 men and 1,200 ships—but these were nonetheless gigantic compared to the resources of the Greeks (about 40,000 men and fewer than 400 ships). In his view the making of Greece was Persia's contribution to history: By wishing to subdue the Greeks the Persians brought them together, under the leadership of Athens, to whose ideals Herodotus was devoted.

Since the Greeks started fighting among themselves (in the Peloponnesian War between Athens and Sparta in particular) even in his lifetime, however, his viewpoint very soon came to seem old-fashioned. There was never much notion of real unity among the Greeks after the Persian Wars in any case. So it was not until Alexandrian times that Herodotus came back into his own.

He has been criticized as failing to distinguish history from geography—as if he could have done otherwise, or as if this mattered. Ought they, in any case, to be distinguished? He gave us the first complete picture of the world as it could then be known, and he was so objective about the Persians that PLUTARCH called him "friend to the barbarians." He was among the first writers to understand that points of view differ and that what is bad in one society's eyes is not necessarily bad in a universal sense—he quotes the Greek poet Pindar (518–430 B.C.E.) approvingly, to the effect that "custom rules all."

Herodotus also demonstrated, for the first time, what prose can do. He reconciled his two main influences, Homer and the very Hecateus whom he so derided. The Homeric speeches he inserts in the course of the *History* are candidly fictional, artistic, fitted to provide background and good sense. He is also stimulated by the admirable sense of curiosity seen in Hecateus—than whom he was undoubtedly more intelligent and understanding.

Like all indisputably major writers, he has been subjected to varying interpretations by his successors. The stricter Athenian admiral, THUCYDIDES, did greatly improve on him as a historian; but he set himself up as an explicit rival, and could not possibly have done without his example. Plutarch thought him disrespectful of tradition and believed that he was unfair—but he was fairer and less hidebound in his views than Plutarch, who, though important, is a mere gossip beside him; Plutarch had the advantage of writing half a millennium after him. The spendidly intelligent and skeptical first-century C.E. Greek comic writer Lucian thought him a liar—but he has proved, rather, to be one who genuinely sought the truth, even if he had a writer's eye for a poetic story. Thus he introduced the Phoenix—which dies in its own ashes and then rises from them—into Western lore. Yet he added, "I have not myself seen this bird except in a picture." Did he believe in its literal existence? In general he works first from observation, then from oral sources, of which he is highly critical. In telling of Cyrus of Persia he writes: "I could have given three versions . . . but I choose to base my account on those Persian books which seem to give the whole truth without exaggeration."

Herodotus did believe, though, in *nemesis* and in *hubris*. He has been criticized, as a historian, for this. Thus King Croesus of Lydia is his hero, but is also seen—after the manner of Sophocles, the great Athenian tragedian who was Herodotus's friend and who wrote a poem in his honor—as the victim of his hubris: of his insolence, his excessiveness, his provocation of the gods by trying to take on powers that only they possess. But is this so unhistorical and so wrongheaded, after all? Or were the Greeks right in their view of the role of fate in human life? Herodotus's bequest to biography, that history has been made by individuals who were under certain divine laws, has not yet been discredited, although it has been ignored.

How many times has Herodotus been bettered, in the prose of the world, than in his laconic, somber and genuinely tragic telling of the tale of Harpagus and Astyages, who fed Harpagus his own son for dinner because the former had had his daughter killed?

But where Herodotus is most exemplary for us today—and we can buy decent translations of him just around any corner—is in his humanity, his tolerance, and his freedom from prejudice. The worst error made by both his ancient and his modern readers has been to find him lacking in power, tragic sense, and that "high seriousness" that Matthew Arnold found lacking in the poet Geoffrey Chaucer. On that account he has rightly been compared to Mozart. Mozart, it has been well suggested, had so much charm and grace that his profoundly melancholy view of life was for long neglected. Herodotus is similar: The *History* as whole sounds a sad—and profound—note. He was never at heart a *mere* patriot. He knew that the Greek way of life had much in it that would be precious to posterity, but he could also praise "barbarians," and knew too, just as well as Sophocles and Aeschylus, that human aspirations are ruled by a type of fate of which human beings only very occasionally display even a glimmer of understanding. He is still as fresh on the page as he was in 425 B.C.E.

12

The Republic

PLATO

c. 380 B.C.E.

The philosopher Alfred North Whitehead declared that philosophy was no more than a series of "footnotes to Plato" (c. 429–347 B.C.E.). This is not quite true; but it cannot easily be argued against, especially in view of the chronology involved. But Heraclitus (who lived earlier and who, along with the semilegendary Pythagoras, most influenced Plato from among the earliest Greek philosophers), ARISTOTLE, HUME, and KANT (to say the very least) would, from the safety of the Elysian Fields, vigorously assert otherwise.

Plato, more than any other philosopher, has been all things to all men. He comes first, being universally regarded as the first rational philosopher, although the thinking of Socrates (469–399), who wrote nothing, has usually been thought of as the source of Plato's. In Plato's dialogues Socrates is always used to express Plato's point of view—and, equally certainly, the philosophers who came before Plato are called, not "pre-Platonic," but, rather, "pre-Socratic." But that is just a misleading habit. Plato learned much from many of the philosophers—Thales, Parmenides, and Heraclitus in particular—who came before him. The largest part of their influence is enshrined in Plato (they are the only known influences of his literary style) and Aristotle.

Of those two, Plato, although a rational philosopher (meaning no more than that he appealed to reason and to logic to prove his points—the earlier Greek thinkers did not proceed in this way), was at heart a mystic; Aristotle was not.

Plato preceded Aristotle and was his teacher. Of all Plato's books *The Republic* has been by far the most influential, although much else has been, too, especially his ideas about how poetry gets written—nor are these ideas necessarily inconsistent with his apparent condemnation of poetry in his *Republic*.

The Socrates we meet in Plato's work is a fictional figure—ugly, captivating, erotic, a wonderful talker—the chief character in a set of plays or dramas (called "dialogues") written by Plato. To what extent Plato's Socrates resembled the real Socrates has been the subject of fierce controversy; it is, however, reasonable to believe that the resemblance is close. The comic playwright Aristophanes (c. 457–380), in *The Clouds*, mocked Socrates as a corrupt teacher of rhetoric, and severely misrepresented him. We don't know if this caricature was inspired by personal dislike or what has been called "artistic necessity" (i.e., having some irreverent fun against a celebrated man who was—after all—there to answer back). All that can safely be said here is that Aristophanes liked to exaggerate to the point of wild fantasy; nor is scrupulosity likely to have been one of his virtues. However, it is possible that his target was not Socrates but, rather, mindless adulation of him, the equivalent of today's pop-star worship.

Plato has been in trouble with many twentieth-century thinkers because of his bias against "democracy" (Greek democracy had no place for slaves or women). He disliked democracy, probably, because he had seen at first hand what went on: was a man who "had seen too much." He did not like Pericles, either; no doubt, again, he knew too much about what went on behind the scenes during Pericles' long rule of Athens. In any case, Plato did condemn out of hand the government of the Thirty, the tyrants who ruled Athens in 404 B.C.E. His disillusion was complete when Socrates, his revered older friend, was executed for "irreligion" and for "corrupting the young" (whereas in fact he had enlightened them by making them aware of their own ignorance), under a democratic government, in 399. Plato went off with other disappointed and angry supporters of Socrates to Megara for a time and then traveled to Italy and Sicily; but, in about 385, at the age of forty-five, he began to teach at what came to be known as the Academy, a grove on the outskirts of Athens sacred to the hero Academus (hence the word). This was the world's first university.

But Plato's life was not going to be the outwardly uneventful one of a mere teacher. He was to have a further adventure. This has been held against him. Back in 387 he had made friends not only with the mystical Pythagorean

Archytas of Tarentum (in southern Italy) but also with Dion of Syracuse, the brother-in-law and son-in-law of King Dionysius I of Syracuse.

Plato's political position, as chief teacher at the Academy, was well known: The future of cities would be doomed until rulers became philosophers—or, of course, philosophers rulers. That is what *The Republic* is about: the proper rule of a philosopher-king. But Plato made an exception in the case of Syracuse—and his reputation has suffered for it. Some in this century have even referred to him as the "first Fascist." The most effective modern attack on him is contained in Karl Popper's *The Open Society and Its Enemies*. It should be said in this connection that Popper was a humorless man—whereas Plato, like Socrates, was a bitter and ironic humorist. Still, whatever a writer may have meant by his book, we have to take into account how it has been understood by its readers. Popper's attack on Plato was influential for a time.

Dion had been decisively captivated (in 389 or thereabouts) by Plato's notion of the "philosopher-king." As admiral and trusted statesman, Dion had influence at the court of his father-in-law Dionysius I, who is still regarded as a "great" ruler. When his feebler and more irresolute son, Dionysius II, succeeded in 367, Dion might have tried to push him aside; instead of that, however—although, like most politicians, he was an educated psychopath who keeps to the smaller rules and regulations only to flout them on an enormous scale—he made a serious attempt to establish a republic according to Plato's ideals. We do not know the date of Plato's *Republic* (between 380 and 370 is the best guess), only that it belongs to what is known as Plato's "middle period." Clearly, though, we can relate it to this episode in his life.

For it is the first—and possibly the last—historical example of a practical experiment, in which the loftiest ideals of philosophy were actually put to the political test. It was a dismal shambles. Dion, like Plato, loathed the Greek version of democracy: He planned to institute at Syracuse a Platonic constitution instead. We can be quite sure that he would have read *The Republic*. He knew that the citizens of Syracuse would never have elected such a constitution. So, he decided, he must impose it for the citizens' own good, since he and Plato knew better than the citizens. Possibly they did, but peoples do not like it to be suggested that they do not know best what is good for them, even if most of them don't. I think that Plato knew this perfectly well.

It is here necessary to insert a warning. Plato was not an enemy of the treasured one-person-one-vote democracies of the modern Western world, this utopia in which we are now privileged to live, in which governments are "fairly" elected (but elections, said Jean-Paul Sartre, are *pièges à cons* [traps for idiots]). Plato and his student Dion knew only of Greek "democratic" governments such as the one which had executed Socrates. Confronted with a modern democracy, Plato would have been surprised: He would have criticized a system in which governments are afraid to do the right thing because they might incur unpopularity and get thrown out. He had not recognized that everyone is equally wise at all times.

Dion sincerely felt that the young King ought to meet the man who could tell him, as a tyrant, how to limit his own power in the people's interests. And Plato, in journeying to Syracuse in 367, at the age of about sixty-two, can hardly be faulted: Here was a king who wanted to become a philosopher. What, he must shudderingly have asked himself (he was no fool), was the Academy for? It was actually teaching men how to become philosopher-kings!

Yet was Plato less wise than crudely ambitious? He had many misgivings. It is likely that Diony-sius I had, twenty years back, had

Socrates

him kidnapped and handed over to a Spartan admiral, who put him up for sale at Aegina—he was spared only because a friend from Cyrene ransomed him. Ought he to have been forewarned? Was the excitement of the opportunity to create a philosopher-king too much for his sense of caution? Yet it was tempting because Dionysius II's education had been neglected—perhaps he would prove as wax in Plato's hands. That is what he may have told himself—but did he also ache for the chance to exert political power?

Plato's great defender in all matters (even to the fantastic extent of declaring that he was not interested in homosexuality), the scholar A. E. Taylor, dismissed the idea that he wanted to set up "a pinchbeck imitation of the imaginary city of *The Republic* ". . . in the most luxurious of Greek cities" (Syracuse) as "ridiculous." It is not, however, quite such a stupid notion as Taylor believed. Even a man such as Plato may well have had some fatal flaw. The Greek poet-tragedians—Aeschylus, Sophocles, Euripides—all of whom just preceded him in time, explored human character in terms of such a flaw, a "tragic error," *hamartia*. However, as we shall soon see, all poetry was resolutely banned from Plato's ideal city.

Plato started to teach Dionysius geometry, and for a brief period geometry became fashionable at his court (it is not hard to see just how false all this was, and how embarrassing to Plato—imagine modern culture-gush to consist not even of pretentious nonsense about writers and artists, or, more likely, people who are imitating them, but about the elegance of hypotenuses and circumferences of circles: "I saw ever such a lovely little circle this morning!"). But the young king, a cruel fop who was himself a would-be poet and philosopher, soon became jealous of the friendship between Dion and Plato.

The Athenian Stoa

So he virtually banished Dion. He tried vainly to retain Plato, but the latter returned to Athens.

Dion now came to the Academy. Plato tried to reconcile the ex-minister and his monarch. This did not work: Dionysius confiscated all the money Dion had in Syracuse, and even forced his wife, Arete, to marry someone else. Yet, despite this pettiness, Plato was tempted back to Syracuse in 361. It was his third visit. But the king, or his bodyguards, became so hostile to Plato that he was only able to get back to Athens by the help of his old friend, the Pythagorean Archytas. So his role in this sorry story almost ended. But it has been suggested that he just might have been a party to Dion's death: "Dion was assassinated by persons," writes a scholar, "who seem to have had something to do with Plato."

In 357 Dion captured Syracuse and declared it free. Plato (if certain letters are his, rather than forgeries) congratulated him but warned him of his haughtiness. Dion proceeded to make himself unpopular: He would have nothing to do, on Platonic grounds, with democracy. Then he was party to the murder of a former ally. He was himself done away with by the treachery—this seems to have been a peculiarly nasty affair—of yet another member of the Academy, Callippus. The eventual fate of Dionysius II was to be put into exile at Corinth, "as a lesson to would-be tyrants."

This adventure forms the background to *The Republic*. And in the adventure, would-be philosophers are seen as just ordinary politicians and murderers; the paradigmatically wise man himself as a dupe. Are the sour ashes of that calamitous affair contained in *The Republic* itself—for all that it was written previously—as Popper and others believed? Was Plato guilty, like HEGEL and MARX, of stifling the individual in the interests of the state? Is *The Republic* an enemy of the "open society"?

Plato takes the collective, the people as a whole, the state, as more important than the individual, who must treat its ends as ultimate. His pupil Aristotle took this as an error: He pointed out that it is meaningless to talk of the well-being of a community quite apart from the well-being of its members. One remembers the "values" of the Third Reich and of Stalinist Russia. That Plato did some harm by thus arguing seems undoubted. But did he do it wittingly?

The Republic is a misleading translation of the Greek title, *Politea*, which may best be rendered, for these purposes, as "The Proper Public and Political Life of Communities." It is a massive work, bulging at the seams. If it wanders, then it does so because it is written in imitation of conversation between enlightened people. Like many other readers, I take it to be as more of an ironic and discursive play (though not drama) than a solemn treatise. There are many "characters." In ten books, it is as long (in English) as about three average-size novels—and it touches on most subjects that were under the sun in the fifth and fourth centuries B.C.E., and still are now. It is probably "set," as we say of a play, in about 420—but Plato never worried about being completely accurate in these circumstances, and he was happy to be anachronistic if he wanted to be.

The argument does not get going until the second book; but the opening is nonetheless typical of the work as a whole. Socrates, Glaucus, Polemarchus, and others have gone to a festival in honor of the goddess Bendis, in Piraeus (the seaport of Athens). They start to discuss the meaning of justice, and Polemarchus comes up with a definition of it which he attributes to the sixth-century poet and sage Simonides: that it consists of giving everyone their due, of paying back what is owed, telling the truth, harming wrongdoers. . . . Socrates soon demolishes this, showing it to be conventional and thoughtless.

The Republic as a whole is too complex to summarize here. Many books have been devoted to it, and most differ wildly in their conclusions. Let us concentrate on the main and most famous arguments. The ideal city-state, Plato says, must be in the charge of specially educated people called Guardians. The two other classes are Auxiliaries, who aid the Guardians in their work, and Farmers and Craftsmen. Guardians and their assistants, and soldiers, should live in camps.

The Guardians are those who understand the Forms. The notion of the Forms, which was so influential upon all succeeding philosophy, is introduced by Plato's famous analogy of the Cave. We are asked to imagine men living in a cave, chained with their backs to the entrance. Behind them a fire is burning. A wall built along the road outside hides the people passing by. However, the firelight casts a shadow of the objects the passers-by carry on their heads.

These shadows provide, for us living in the cave (Plato means us to take this as our own, and also as *his* own, situation) the only view of reality. Freed from the cave to see things as they really are, we should experience pain and shock—and when we returned to the cave everyone would laugh at us and fail to believe our story. This is equivalent to asserting that objective standards do exist. For example, no completely genuine circle exists to the senses: There is only the perfect circle, "the idea of the circle," which can appeal only to the mind. Thus nothing can be arbitrary: There is a reality to which we can appeal—Plato thus, and famously, dismisses the notion of "relative truth."

Plato's Guardians have been properly educated, and so they know what reality is, so they will rule correctly. However, in a democracy—Plato argues—in which all kinds of people take part in government, there will be incorrect rule, since many of them do not understand reality.

Basing himself on this notion of the "Forms" (sometimes called "Ideas") Plato also (in Book II and Book X) forbade "all imitative poetry," which included Homer. "Socrates" admitted to a personal reverence for Homer, but dismissed his (and the tragic playwrights') value as a truth-teller. Plato gives the example that there are three sorts of beds: God's bed, the perfect bed, the one true bed; the craftsman's particular bed in imitation of it; and the painter's imitation of that latter bed. On the same grounds, "poetic truth" is misleading and false: It is but a copy of a copy of a copy!

Moreover, the poet's inferior representation of reality is not only false but harmful. Solon (an early ruler of Athens) was a good lawgiver, but has any poet been such? "Now if Homer had really been able to help men to be virtuous, then would his contemporaries have allowed him . . . to wander around singing his songs? Wouldn't they have treated [him] like precious gold, and asked [him] to live at home with them? . . . . No, poets are imitators of virtue . . . they do not tell the truth." The stuff they write, continues "Socrates" (the real one, of course, would never have made such a revolutionary assertion), is like an aged face, without real beauty."

All this has done Plato much harm. His Guardians seem like gloomy, despotic men, knowing better than everyone else, favoring the abstract notion of the state over the individual—and daring to forbid us the pleasures of poetry and even those of music, too.

But Plato has been misunderstood. What he was talking about in his play was the perfect state: *The Republic* is the first of all the Utopias. Now in a Utopia, a perfect kingdom, there would, after all, be no need for poetry—or at least, no need for the poetry of the sort Plato is talking about in *The Republic.* This is because the greatest poetry, from Homer onward, is generated by the presence of evil in the world—as well as by the joy to be found in it. Plato, himself a victim of untruthfulness just as we all are, had his tongue partly in his cheek when he proposed that only a few heavily censored arts would be permitted in his republic. The whole scheme, *as a practical scheme,* was naive—just as Dion found when he realized that he would have to force a Platonic constitution upon Syracuse. People are not going to wear that kind of thing. If we take *The Republic* as a marvelous and stimulating game, then we make the best possible use of it.

Our awe at its lofty position in the world's books ought not to blind us to its lack of practical value. If, though, we want to consider what paradise-on-earth might be like—and few of us in fact really do, since we are so absorbed in our own pleasures—then we have to look at some of the ideas in *The Republic*. This was what Plato meant. He could not in this book be concerned with the fact that the Craftsman would soon rise up against the Guardians and their assistants. A paradise on earth would only be possible if everyone agreed, if everyone were enlightened.

As for what actual influence *The Republic* has had: Its first influence was of course on its own author, who made a fool of himself in Syracuse. This brings to mind the advice of Hilaire Belloc to would-be electricians: "Lord Finchley tried to mend the Electric Light / Himself. It struck him dead: And serve him right! / It is the business of the wealthy man / To give employment to the artisan." That means: leave politics to politicians. But stop a minute!

That's wrong, surely! No, Plato is right after all. Yet think of his fate at Syracuse, of that of the philosophical and spiritualistic President Madera of Mexico (murdered), of any intellectual who has tried to rule a country. Disastrous! Stalin, Hitler, and other repulsive tyrants didn't have the wit to understand Plato. Yet Trotsky, who was a literary man, an intellectual, as well as a mass murderer, did. . . . Can we say that behind him stood Plato? I doubt this. Politicians are seekers after power, and (as perhaps in the case of Trotsky himself), a little power (as Lord Acton remarked), tends to corrupt—by the time they have become busy in the practice of "the art of the possible" they have eschewed mere philosophy, wisdom, and they think more of what happened to Dion, who was foolish enough to dabble in it. . . .

As for Plato, he had second thoughts. In his later writings on politics he makes it clear that he thinks the quest for a Utopia is a doomed one. We must be fair to him and read all he wrote on this subject—not just *The Republic*. Meanwhile, that muddled, entertaining book has sparked some excellent defenses of democracy, and also some excellent defenses of poetry and the arts, which describe our imperfect world and sometimes inspire us to better things—such as that our rulers ought to be better than they are. And it is more than likely that this was just what Plato wanted to do when he wrote *The Republic*. That he went on the Syracuse adventure, after all, may have been a demonstration that telling people what is good for them, even when it is true, is just not enough.

13

Elements

EUCLID

c. 280 B.C.E.

Euclid's origins are unknown; nor is much else known beyond the fact that he lived and taught at Alexandria—at the Museum—during the reign of King Ptolemy I (306–283 B.C.E.). He was, it is plausibly said, kindly, genial, and forthright, and is supposed to have had great scorn for the practical value of the geometry he taught. The most famous and important of his works, some of which are lost, was the *Elements* (*Stoicheia*) in thirteen books: Books 1–6 deal with plane geometry, 7–9 with number theory, 11–13 with irrational numbers (the last two were likely not written by Euclid). Proclus, who wrote a much valued commentary on the first book, states that he was "of the persuasion of Plato," but this has been doubted. However, if the story about his scorn for the practical side of his work is true, then that is no more, after all, than a Platonic scorn for the vulgarly useful—it may remind us of the poet Samuel Taylor Coleridge's remark to the effect that there is something inherently mean about *matter.*

Euclid's influence has been enormous, and not the least, no doubt, in the matter of the painful inconvenience of youngsters of the last century who failed to master his proofs—and for whom geometry was not "geometry," but, quite simply, "Euclid." He *was* his subject! Until quite recently there were not many who were unfamiliar with the QED—"quod erat demonstrandum"—with which the theorems end. Even now the geometry taught in schools is based squarely on the *Elements* because, although (as will become clear) there are other geometries, Euclid's is the most obviously useful one, the easiest one to believe in—especially in land surveying—even despite the fact that it is true only on a perfect plane, something which must be created artificially. When King Ptolemy I, just like any boy or girl bad at math, protested about the great length and difficulty of the *Elements,* Euclid is supposed to have replied that although there could be a royal road in Egypt, there could be none in geometry. This not-so-funny anecdote, once beloved of schoolteachers trying to be "interesting" and humorous, but not very good at it, has, alas, been told of other kings and their tutors, Alexander the Great and ARISTOTLE among them.

Ironically, Euclid was not a first-class or even an original mathematician; he was nowhere near the equal of his near-contemporary Archimedes. He was, as has often been remarked, only as good as his sources, which were numerous: Theaetetus, Hippocrates of Chios, Eudoxus, and many others. Most of the theorems in the *Elements* were already known. One was the famous one attributed to Pythagoras—who is supposed (against his vegetarian principles) to have sacrificed an ox when he discovered it—on the right-angled triangle. In essence, then, Euclid was an inspired compiler; he was also one of the most persistent logic-choppers ever to have lived. But he was a supreme teacher and systematizer, and there is no doubt that the organization of what is known about plane geometry is due to him. Bertrand Russell, one of the great mathematicians of the twentieth century, wrote: "The more one studies geometry, the more admirable this order is 'seen to be' "; and he called the *Elements* "one of the greatest books ever written." He pointed out that Euclid's work on conic projections, not thought of as being of any practical use in his own times, suddenly became, in the seventeenth century, "the key to warfare and astronomy."

The *Elements* were translated into Arabic in about 800 C.E., lost sight of for hundreds of years in the Western world—although there was a Latin translation extant around 400, now lost—but then put from Arabic back into Latin by Adelard of Bath (1120—then from the original Greek into Latin, then into Hebrew, then into Italian and German. The authoritative modern text comes from a manuscript discovered by F. Peyrard in the Vatican Library in 1814. There have been more than a thousand editions of the *Elements.* Adelard of Bath had to go to Spain disguised as an Islamic scholar in order to get the job done. Always, then as now, there were bureaucrats eager to sniff out ways of persecuting seekers of knowledge, of preventing the dissemination of the truth. Was there anything heretical, these pitiful clerks hoped, or offensive to the orthodox God, in those celebrated lines that never met, of which (despite their efforts) we all learned at school?

Euclid has seemed so impressive because of his doggedly axiomatic method: The way in which he built up an edifice of proof has impressed people, even to the extent that some have believed that such a method could lead to a calm and orderly demonstration of the basic truths about the universe, the absence of any authority in it, why and how it was created, what our duties (or otherwise) are, and how we tick. A crass dunce of the type of Richard Dawkins—who has demonstrated on British television, in some fifteen minutes, the great ease and self-evident simplicity with which the universe was created—may still be called "Euclidean" in his simplistic, narrow, wooden, triumphalist "reasoning." But this vain crudity, although a disgrace to humanity and to its aspirations—if by no means to its capacity for self-destruction—is no discredit to Euclid himself, who was simply using the invaluable hypothetico-deductive method within the limits of two-dimensional flat space. He starts from unproved assumptions which he simply—and surely rightly in those circumstances—takes to be the case. It is ironic that his assumptions were in fact wrong—but, we might fairly suggest, wrong in a right way. It should be noted that Pyrrho (see SEXTUS EMPIRICUS), the skeptic, insisted—in Euclid's own lifetime—with an irritating confidence, that such "self-evident truths" were invalid. Pyrrho was awkward—but that he was after all right shows how important skepticism always is. But Euclid's impressive achievement has stood, for emotionally stunted dolts, as the paradigm of rational certainty in *all matters*. It is far from just to blame Euclid for this.

Euclid is thus not important just because he has been taught in schools all over the world for well over two thousand years. However, the fact that his work is the most suitable for its purpose, of teaching plane geometry, is doubtless claim enough to fame in itself. The *Elements* seem so exceptionally neat, satisfying and, above all, legitimate. Their reliance on pure abstract reason appealed deeply to the boys and girls who were forced to study them—when we are young they leave us feeling satisfied with our own capacity for reason. And always, even to such as the medieval writer Robert Grosseteste, who was determined to elevate experimental science to as high a status as mathematics, Euclid provided a model of logical analysis. Indeed, his influence on philosophy and therefore on attitudes-toward-the-world-in-general has far outweighed even his influence on mathematics.

Mathematics is important to philosophy not only for its own sake but also for its ability to demonstrate the nature of knowledge (epistemology): It provides a clear case of purely rational, nonexperimental, a priori knowledge. Experience prompts us to infer that two and three make five, but we do not need to experiment—to set up a test in a laboratory—to confirm this. Then again, while two and three do make five, so that a group of two cats and another of three cats in a room will mean that five cats are in the room, the numbers two, and three, and five, are not *just* cats, or apples, or fingers, or whatever. They are *numbers*—but what exactly are numbers, and do they have an *existence* or not—and if they do, what sort of existence is it? The questions have not been answered, but PLATO used this philosophically odd, and still highly disputable, property of numbers to support his notion of a suprasensible world accessible only to reason, and from there argued for the actual existence of his Forms or Ideas, of the perfect bed or the perfect cat, and, from that, of the perfect quality.

Empiricists, who believe that the world can only be known by the senses, were made unhappy by this. Reasonably to them, it threatened common sense. There is now a theory, called the logistic theory—associated with Russell, Whitehead, and Frege—which, while it goes well beyond Euclid in its details, insists that mathematics is indeed no more than a set of axioms, each one deriving from its predecessors.

On a more mundane level—for the above account is only an extreme oversimplification—one sort of person likes logic-chopping without mysticism, while another distrusts it and likes Plato's "heaven" of the Forms. It is more a matter of temperament than most philosophers like to admit. But for all this there is no reason to disbelieve in the Platonism that Proclus ascribed to Euclid, for Plato would not have objected to what he did. Euclid might even have been cleverer—and more humorously Platonic—than anyone has given him credit for, in the following way: Euclid "proves" his postulates by the *reductio ad absurdum* method. Beginning by blockheadlike assuming the opposite of that he wants to prove, he then demonstrates that it is an impossibility. Hence the appealing simplicity of his famous five postulates as he put them:

1. To draw a straight line from any point to another; 2. To produce a finite straight line continuously in a straight line; 3. To describe a circle with any center and distance; 4. That all right angles are equal to each other—and the difficult one, peculiarly stated—5. "That, if a straight line falling on two straight lines make the interior angles on the same side less than two right angles, if produced infinitely, meet on that side on which are the angles less than the two right angles." This fifth postulate is a curious way of stating that two parallel lines will never meet, and was thus put in order to avoid a negative. The most acceptable way of stating it is now John Playfair's eighteenth-century axiom: "Through a point not on a given line, there passes not more than one parallel to the line." This so-called "parallel postulate" was worrying to many Greek mathematicians, who tried to prove it—all failed miserably. Nor was it the case.

Later, the Arabic mathematicians, who succeeded the Greeks in mathematical study after geometry had gone into eclipse under the Romans, also examined it. All ended up without success—and found themselves trapped in circular reasoning. (SCHOPENHAUER, at heart a romantic philosopher, even despised Euclid's theorems, calling them "mousetraps.")

During the eighteenth century an Italian mathematician called Saccheri suggested that there could be certain geometries in which the parallel postulate did not hold. In 1868 Beltrami proved that it could not be proved! Three other mathematicians, Johann Bolyai, Karl Friedrich Gauss, and Nikolai Lobachevsky, working independently, devised geometries in which parallels do not exist, and in all of which space is curved—these are not "truer" than Euclid's, since no geometry can be truer than another, but they demonstrated the limitations of the earlier one. Later Bernhard Reimann further refined this work. Now there may be said to be three geometries: Euclidean, in which the angles of a triangle add up to 180-degrees; Riemann's geometry, in which the angles add up to *more* than 180 degrees; and the hyperbolic geometry of Gauss, in which the angles add up to *less* than 180 degrees. It should be noted that the Euclidean triangle, although it works in practice, is a fiction in terms of the earth's surface, since the earth is a sphere.

Staunch defense of Euclid came from a very unexpected source: An Oxford mathematician whom one would supposed to have loved such affairs as the "negative space" geometry of Gauss and his successors, wrote a book called *Euclid and His Modern Rivals* (1879). The real literary career of this clergyman, who loved to photograph naked young girls and was something of a reactionary imperialist, was long over; and this series of dialogues—in which the ghost of Euclid pleads his case—was far less effective or funny than an earlier fiction from the same pen, *Alice in Wonderland;* but the Rev. C. L. Dodgson's work did go into one more edition.

Euclid himself had, in one sense that I have suggested might have been clever, the last laugh: He left this problem serenely alone. Was he well aware that his assumptions were unprovable?

The Dhammapada

c. 252 B.C.E.

The Buddha ("one who has awakened up" [to reality]), a princeling whose given name was Siddhārtha ("he whose purpose in life has been attained"), was born into the Guatama clan in a part of India near the present-day Nepal, probably in the second quarter of the sixth century B.C.E.; he lived well into the fifth century B.C.E. He was the least dogmatic—indeed, he was positively antidogmatic—of all the great founders of religions. His "Way" of enlightenment was a pragmatic one, deliberately rooted, initially, in what we call ordinary life; it is usually known as the Middle Way, a way between "too much and too little"—the strings of an instrument such as the harp must be neither too slack nor too tight in order for it to be effectively played.

Guatama opposed excessive ritual and superstition; but he also opposed what is today called scienticism, which could be defined as the mistaken (and unscientific) notion that what cannot be measured does not exist or, rather more persuasively, is irrelevant *because* it is not amenable to scientific method (a perfectly proper and valid, but limited, mode of enquiry). On the scientistic or positivist view, our inner experience, so precious to us, and yet so confused, and largely secret, is malevolently rejected as so much trash.

The Buddha was also against the sort of overintellectual metaphysical speculation that did not help people to attain the Way—thus it is hardly appropriate to describe him as a philosopher, except in an older sense of that word, i.e., "friend of wisdom."

The events in his life, or what we know of it, are quickly told. After receiving a good education he devoted himself to the luxurious and lazy life of a prince of his kind; but he then began to question the purpose of his own and all other forms of life. He thought, with a gloom that was tinged with despair, that everything consisted of unhappy change, and asked himself if there were nothing but decline and extinction.

He left his father's palace and studied meditation in the forest with whatever teachers he could find. He starved himself; but he found that self-starvation, too extreme, was not a way to peace of mind. Famously, he sat beneath a sacred fig tree and said to himself, "I will not get up from here until I have found a way beyond decay and death." Like Christ, he was tempted by a devil (Mara the tempter); but he would not even argue with him. When he ceased his trance he found that he had been reborn: He was the Buddha, the awakened one; he had attained *Nirvana* (in Pali *Nibbana*), a state of complete inner freedom. The word derives from a verb, *nibbati,* "to cool by blowing," and thus means "cooled from the fires of delusion, lust, greed, egoism." Whether this involves complete extinction, or an understanding of the meaning of *nothing,* has been much debated. Certainly *Nirvana* is a far more sophisticated and less "unscientific" goal than the orthodox Christian Heaven, although it can be and has been called vague; as certainly it indicates a state of freedom from *Samsara,* the wheel of unhappy existence, of one rebirth after another. In any case the Buddha out of his compassion decided to stay on the earth and devote himself to helping others to attain what he had attained.

Since that now uncapturable and mythical moment—of which we have only this legend and its details—Buddha's message, like all else on earth except lust and greed for power, has lost its original force. Buddhism has split up into various paths. There is Theravada (Southern) Buddhism, Eastern Buddhism, and Northern Buddhism. These traditions, unlike the Christian ones, can and do happily and unjealously coexist with others (Zen Buddhism with Shinto in Japan, with Taoism and Confucianism in China, and so on). Early Buddhists and undoubtedly the Buddha himself enjoined followers to speak modestly of Buddhist teachers but enthusiastically of those of other religions. What would the savage and neurotic African early Christian Tertullian, or the Puritan persecutor John Calvin, have made of that kind of tolerance?

There are millions of words of Buddhist texts, some of them not yet published, belonging to different languages and traditions. Of all these, the Dhammapada (Verses on Dharma)—423 pithy verses—is one of the most beautiful, brief, and complete. It is carried around by Buddhists and non-Buddhists, and its wisdom would be hard to refute. One of its translators, Eknath Easwaren, claims that it must contain a record of what Buddha's own followers recollected. It is said to have been complete by 252 B.C.E. But there were no texts in those days, and the first version we have of this work is in a Pali form—Pali is a descendent of Sanskrit. There are other versions, longer and shorter, in other Indian languages. In the Dhammapada things are put in a simple form. The idea of karma is dealt with thus:

> Safely returned from distant lands a man
> With joy is welcomed by his friends and kin.
> So too, a good man who has left this world,
> By his good deeds is welcomed in the next.

But these "good deeds" do not consist of giving to charity, as arms manufacturers (the Buddha expressly warned against helping them) usually do. They are, rather, actions stemming from good intentions, actions responsible in the profoundest sense—"We are what we think."

It should be mentioned that an influential group of scholars think the twenty or so more important UPANISHADS are in part post-Buddhist. This is possible. But the early Upanishads are certainly pre-Buddhist, and the Buddha himself was, as certainly, influenced by Vedic thinking—for all that some scholars have tried to separate him, often by no more than verbal prestidigitation, from Hinduism.

There were two kinds of religious influence in Buddha's time, apart from the powerful hereditary caste of Brahman priests—no better than most powerful priests ever are—who preserved and no doubt where they could enforced the more conventional sorts of the Vedic tradition. (They disliked the Upanishads and so, very cleverly, appropriated them, only to castrate them and rob them of their power to provoke any thinking independent of their own authority, which had become more important to them than truth.) The two other influences were the naked ascetics among whom the religion of Jainism emanated (it was founded by Vardhamana around the same time as Buddhism) and the more thoughtful and on the whole less fanatic and neurotic, and clothed, forest wanderers, among whom were many adherents of the old Vedic tradition. These latter influenced Buddha in the independent conclusions to which he eventually came.

Those sorts of people who, over many years, wrote the Upanishads, had gone to forest retreats to examine the contents of their minds as closely and as scientifically as they could. The Buddha himself did this. The Upanishads (or at least, if we are being absolutely scrupulous about the uncertain chronology of the Buddha himself vis-à-vis the Upanishads, then that strand of Vedic thinking which led to their composition) establish, so to say, that karma, the law that everything you do will come back to you ("as ye sow, so shall ye reap"), is a purely natural affair of cause and effect, and not at all a religious tenet. Philosophically it is far more sophisticated than anything outside the thinking of the pre-Socratic philosophers—and as it happens it just preceded them. But India was known to the early Greeks.

The writers of the earliest of the Upanishads were the direct antecedents of the Buddha, for he and then his followers set out to devise a practical Way by which the basic precepts in them could be elaborated and upheld. It was for them a matter of common sense, or, more precisely, of "spiritual common sense." There was no savage external God who was going to punish people because they disobeyed "him." (True, there were, quite prominently around, cynical hedonists, who argued with great humor for taking whatever pleasure you wanted and be damned; and there were those of opposite persuasion who were said to, by storing up what was called *tapas,* i.e., by gathering up the power bestowed by sexual abstention—what FREUD called "sublimation"—rivaled and even threatened the gods themselves; there were many other kinds of thinkers, too.) In Vedic doctrine, as in Buddhist, when we are punished, we punish ourselves. If your mother-in-law beats you and is a horrible person, you are not "unlucky" but paying a karmic debt—and this you have to pay before you can escape from the prison of existence. This is another way of saying that the state of our being attracts the nature of our lives—"Seymour-Smith's women always beat him up" might mean that Seymour-Smith both wants and needs and arranges for his women to beat him up, whether he knows it or not. When Seymour-Smith learns and fully understands why this is the case, that particular misfortune peculiar to him—at least—stops.

But there are more obvious and easier examples, operating within our single lives. Say, for example, that we are particularly heedless of others' feelings. Eventually that heedlessness is going to provoke others to anger or to revenge or to hatred toward us—then we shall be harmed. (So will they: Actions are "bad" not in the familiar "moral" sense, i.e., what society deems as bad, but because of the more or less subtle damage they do in the ceaseless cause-effect-cause cycle of existence.) The notion of karma later became more complex and longlasting, and it was seen to operate endlessly, throughout many existences. The more subtle forms of Buddhism do not assume the continuation of a "soul" through many lives, but, rather, an energy pattern left by a dead person which, when the circumstances are ripe, repeats itself in essence—it is not the "same life," but a life exactly equivalent, parallel, in the spiritual sense. It might be said that there are many ways in which the essence of a life may be lived. And that life may be lived in good or in bad circumstances. Thus, the Buddha himself probably did not teach literal "reincarnation," but a far more complicated process. The dying person's thoughts must be the sum of his or her entire existence, in particular of the quality of his or her intentions. This it is that is continually "reborn" until egoistic craving and ignorance—called altogether forms of *graspingness*—are destroyed. The "new life" bore the same relation to the old life as the new flame to the old one from which it was lit. However, there is little doubt that the vast majority of Buddhists, as also Hindus, do believe in literal reincarnation—or that they fear it greatly, in a manner which we in the West find quite incomprehensible. We, on the other hand, or some of us, are fascinated by the crude notion that there is a chance of the survival of our egos. Yet in Buddhist thinking memory of previous incarnations is acknowledged to be possible among adepts—perhaps this is of a certain kind of "pattern of graspingness."

It is not hard to accept Buddha's initial argument or postulation: that all existence is suffering. Fear of death, old age, illness, the very fact that we can never have *all* that we wish for—all that and more is suffering. There is no question that bliss does exist; but it is almost defined by its transitoriness.

For some, death—feared or not—provides the ultimate release. It is oblivion, no thing, nothing, the utter end. But here Buddhism differs—and, because it differs, it may be called rather more of a religion than otherwise. Bodily death is not the end. The law of karma operates. What a person truly intends, how he is truly motivated, determines—in some way or another—his future existence. And this endless chain is kept alive by two things: *craving* (including even craving for Nirvana) and ignorance. To overcome all this the Buddha offered the Eightfold Way.

Guatama's eight recommendations for ending the mechanical operation of the law of karma are as follows. Right View: understanding of the origin of suffering and how it may be ended. Right Resolve: consciously choosing to refrain from self-indulgence. Right Speech: refraining from trivial chatter and gossip. Right Action: refraining from all forms of murder (arms-manufacturing, soldiering) or theft. Right Livelihood: avoiding making money from harmful activities. Right Effort: striving to induce wholesomeness of thought and to avoid unwholesomeness. Right Mindfulness: attempting to gain conscious control of inner states. Right Concentration: achievement of an inner serenity in which one is able to receive true insight. The Dhammapada puts it thus:

> To refrain from all evil and to develop the wholesome,
> To purify one's mind, is what Buddhas teach.

There is no doubt that the sincere consultation of the Dhammapada—in which all this and much more is presented in lucid if brief and simplified form—would tend to improve both an individual and his society. But what many in the West find hard to accept are the natures of both the Law of Karma, and of Nirvana. In the philosophy of the Upanishads the soul can become united with the All-Soul of *Brahman*. But Guatama, in a new departure, denied the existence of an immortal soul. A person is only (recall HUME) a bundle of phenomena; there is no true self. The dissolution of this bundle marks the end of suffering, the attainment of Nirvana. The latter can only be defined (and here some Jewish thinking, and gnosticism, are relevant) by negatives. Happiness is when there is no happiness: when there are no more sensations. Thus Buddhism is both the most rationalistic and at the same time the most mystical of all religions.

15

The Aeneid

VIRGIL

70–19 B.C.E.

The Emperor Augustus (as he called himself from 27 B.C.E.), that conscientiously republican architect of imperial Rome (meaning no more than that he presided over a republican constitution), possessed—in this like Mussolini (novelist), Goebbels (novelist) and Hitler (painter)—markedly artistic leanings. To judge from what Virgil wrote or dared to write, the true greatness of Augustus was unquestionable.

Augustus's *Res Gestre* (Acts—*his* acts: there were no other), a justification of himself, survives, and is probably the most historically important Roman document that we possess. Augustus founded imperial Rome and is fully characteristic of it. This book, a supreme example of effective triumphalist propaganda if there ever was one—his successor Tiberius had it inscribed at various places throughout the Empire—explains that his powers and respect for republican liberty entitle him to his special position, which is supported (he says) by his tremendous personal wealth; all of his conquests have been for Rome's sake. He found the city of Rome brick, he boasted, but left it marble.

Augustus was a master of craft, duplicity, and hypocrisy, especially in his strict moral reforms. The great conqueror Alexander, drunken and debauched, died half mad. Yet he was supposed by most nineteenth-century historians to have been responsible for "a vast impulse" which, wrote one, "first taught civilized man to . . . embrace at one view of the universal brotherhood of man." Augustus, to the contrary, was supposed to have been "essentially reactionary" and especially so in his determination to impose the Roman religion—such as that feeble imitation of the Greek religion was—on his empire: He was thus inspired by "an apprehension for his own safety."

It is a pity that Augustus is so relevant to the poetic achievement of Virgil. The former wrote other (lost) literary works, including a poem in hexameters about Sicily and a tragedy which he himself, not believing it to be good enough, destroyed.

Publius Vergilius Maro (70–19 B.C.E.), Virgil to us, was born near Mantua into the family of a landowner of Etruscan family, described variously as a "potter" and a "courier." Virgil grew up into a big-boned countryman of dark complexion and of chronic ill health (bleeding piles, stomach ulcers, headaches). He received a good education and studied rhetoric in Rome under the best teachers. He entered literary circles as an "Alexandrian," the name given to a group of poets who sought inspiration in the sophisticated and cosmopolitan work of third-century Greek poets also known as Alexandrians. The Romans aimed at technical perfection, "art for art's sake"; but they also wished to demonstrate that Latin poetry could be as good as Greek. At their worst they were precious and mannered; we see them at their incomparable best in the poetry of Catullus.

Virgil soon gave up the idea of a career, and, at the start of the Civil War of 49 B.C.E. (between Julius Caesar and Pompey), retired to Naples to study the Epicurean philosophy (see LUCRETIUS) under the sage Siro, whose villa he subsequently inherited. Then, in the years following the assassination of Julius Caesar, Augustus managed to win power for himself. In 41 (when he was still allied with Mark Antony) he took over privately owned property to redistribute it to war veterans. The property of Virgil's father was thus expropriated, and he took refuge with his son in Naples. Nor is it likely in fact, although it was for long so supposed, that this property was ever restored. One of his son's early poems is on this subject. However, later, when Virgil had become Rome's most illustrious poet, he enjoyed—although he lived mostly at Campania—a house at Nola by favor of Augustus.

Augustus developed his interest in Virgil by way of his close and trusted friend Maecenas, a wealthy homosexual poetaster and patron of writers (the poet Horace is the most famous of those he patronized) who was also extremely able politically, and who was twice left in virtual control of Rome when Augustus was away. Their relationship became strained only when the author of the new strict laws against adultery committed it with Maecenas's wife—Maecenas, unlike Virgil (who could not stomach it), married. But long before that Maecenas had introduced Virgil to Augustus. The subject of a great Roman epic was soon being discussed between ruler and subject. Its hero was to be Rome, but Augustus identified Rome with Augustus. How Virgil felt about this is not known; but one part of him must have held back, since on his deathbed he asked that his poem be destroyed.

Virgil's two earlier sets of poems, the *Bucolics* or *Eclogues* (meaning, respectively, "rustic poems" and "selections"; but these titles are not his own) and *The Georgics* (literally, "pertaining to agriculture"), made him famous. The first is a set of ten poems, not in the poet's order, and includes the homosexual second eclogue, in which the shepherd Corydon (the French writer André Gide chose the title *Corydon* for his very influential major essay about homosexuality—I shall be blamed for not including it here) laments the fact that his fellow-shepherd Alexis cannot return his love. This and the other poems are Alexandrian in that they are deeply influenced by the Greek third-century poet Theocritus, author of elegant, superbly skillful, ornate, and artificial pastorals. *The Georgics,* which followed *The Eclogues,* is a long poem divided into four books, on farming: It is a townsman's sophisticated view of the country. Much of it is carefully based on a rather technical and even boring prose treatise on this subject. It is dedicated to Maecenas—who was, as a politically incorrect person might (alas) say, as politically dangerous as he was fluttering as a pansy—and it forecasts that Octavian (the name of Augustus before 29) will bring peace to the world. He did, but in his peace lay the seeds of eventual war, for his respect for democracy was that of a master illusionist.

In 31 B.C.E. Augustus won the Battle of Actium against his former ally Mark Antony. By 29 the way was open for him. He it was who conceived the notion that Rome's best poet should write of the glory of Rome under his sway. Despite his own literary efforts, he knew he was not capable of it himself. He pressed "his" poet, but we do not know for sure just how hard. Probably very hard indeed. Clearly Virgil, although ambitious, was never really happy about it. In 26 Augustus wrote from Spain complaining that he had not seen any of it. Virgil refused to show it, complaining in his turn that he must have embarked on the project "in a moment of aberration" and that he would have to study much more profoundly before he could show it. But in the same year the poet Propertius spoke of *The Aeneid* as greater than Homer's *Iliad*.

In 23 Virgil read the second and the fourth books to Augustus personally. In 19 he left for a planned three-year trip to Greece and Asia. He would, he said, polish the poem—but would thereafter devote himself to philosophy. He got to Greece, and there met Augustus, at Megara. Augustus "persuaded" him to return to Italy with him. But he fell seriously ill in Greece, and, when they arrived at Brundisium (modern Brindisi), Virgil died, having instructed his executor Varius to destroy the poem. Thus he seems to have repudiated, not the excellencies of what was his own in *The Aeneid,* but, rather, what was *not* really his own in it: fear, falsehood, bad motives, lack of independence. Augustus ordered Varius to ignore this dying request, and the poem was published.

It very soon became a classic, and Virgil (absurdly) became a Christian hero. A legend grew up around him: He had been the first Christian, he had been a magician, a prophet, a great orator, and much else. More recently he has become a sort of homosexual saint—although his Christian admirers still deny that he could possibly be guilty of such a "hideous crime" as homosexuality. DANTE made him a hero in his poem *The Divine Comedy*—but cut him out of Paradise because he had died in 19 B.C.E.

It was well understood in Virgil's own time that *The Aeneid* was in its first half an *Odyssey* and in its second an *Iliad*. But Virgil looked back, too, at the first Latin writers of epics, and in particular to the *Annals* of Ennius (239–169 B.C.E.). We have only about half of this poem of twelve hundred lines (*The Aeneid* has almost thirteen thousand); it was a chronicle of Rome, and at its beginning Ennius declared himself as Homer reincarnated as a Roman.

There is little or no humor in Virgil, and it is "with heartfelt earnestness," as a scholar has said, that he glorifies Rome as the supreme and enlightened ruler of the known world. In Homer's *Iliad* the Trojan Aeneas was alluded to as a man destined to found a kingdom. Early poets writing in Latin had treated him as a Trojan who came to Italy.

Virgil starts with his arrival at Carthage. Then there is a flashback to the sacking of the city of Troy. Then comes the most famous passage of all: The love affair in Carthage between Aeneas and Dido, his cruel desertion of her, and her curse upon him before she kills herself for love. Then Aeneas descends into the infernal regions.

The second half of the poem, with its elaborate tributes to Augustus, who is carefully associated with Aeneas, is devoted to the wars between the Trojans and the Latins, whose leader, Turnus, is supposed to recall Homer's Achilles. The Romans at this time looked down with derision at mere *Italians,* for whom Roman citizenship was the highest honor they could attain. Aeneas is made by Virgil into the chief ancestor of the founder of Rome, the hub of the world. The God Vulcan forges a special shield for Aeneas: In the middle of this shield is a depiction of the Battle of Actium, won of course by Augustus. Rome is ready to be founded by the descendant of Aeneas— Augustus claimed such descent.

Virgil's handling of the theme of what he knew Augustus wished for is masterly. But it lacks a certain quality, something between humor and humanity. Parts, in particular the Dido and Aeneas episode, have genuine high pathos. The poem is held by academics (and those now few politicians who have been educated in the arts) as well-nigh perfect. It is, too—although unfinished and condemned by its author—in one sense, perfect. It is too perfect. It was produced for an unscrupulous, cunning, cultured ruler—a great ruler, and a morally disgusting man. The conscience of the poet was aware of this.

What kind of poem would Virgil have written about the monster Augustus if he had dared? Or did he just not have it in him?

On the Nature of Reality

LUCRETIUS

c. 55 B.C.E.

About Titus Lucretius Carus (c. 99 or 94–55 B.C.E.), now regarded as one of the greatest of Latin poets—a few good critics have preferred him even to Virgil—we know hardly anything. The chief record is contained in the Christian scholar Saint Jerome's translation into Latin of Eusebius's Greek *Chronicle;* Cicero mentioned him favorably—and has even been supposed to have corrected his poem, which is in vigorous hexameters. He was probably of an aristocratic family, and may have been the owner of property near Pompeii, and thus have learned the Epicurean philosophy—it is the subject of his only (known) poem, *On the Nature of Things* (usually translated as *On the Nature of the Universe,* but best of all rendered as *On the Nature of Reality*)—at a long-established center of Epicurean studies near Naples.

Jerome states that Lucretius was poisoned by a "love-philtre" (or an aphrodisiac—if there is really such a substance), went mad as a result, wrote his poem in his lucid intervals, and then killed himself. Some have taken the unmistakably bitter attack on romantic love in Book IV to confirm this; but, at least as the prurient Jerome tells it, it is an unlikely tale. Part of the famous passage goes:

> In love there is the hope that passion may be quenched by the body that aroused it. But that hope is against nature. Sexual pleasure is the one thing that, the more we have of it, the more our breasts burn with the ache to possess. When we take in food and drink these fill up spaces in our bodies—hunger and thirst are thus easily appeased. But a lovely face or a sweet complexion gives our bodies nothing to enjoy: only fantasies, which hope scatters to the four winds.

Later he asks, "Have you noticed how those couples linked to each other by mutual rapture are often tormented by their common bondage?"

On the Nature of Reality is dedicated to C. Memmius, an aristocrat who was patron to another famous (and even superior) Latin poet, Catullus. Unfortunately this does not tell us much more about Lucretius, except that it suggests that he might have depended for money on Memmius.

Epicureanism was and, in its modernized—post–splitting of the atom—form, still is an influential philosophy. Why not then represent it with the writings of Epicurus (341–270 B.C.E.) himself? The reasons are simple: Very little of Epicurus's major work, *On Nature,* survived—some other writings have but they hardly match those of Lucretius—whereas Lucretius's poem, although written more than two hundred years after the Greek's death, is by far the most faithful, vivid, and dramatic account of the Epicurean philosophy. Moreover, the energetic nature of the poetry challenges the very purpose of the philosophy, which is specifically designed to ensure peace, pleasure, and deliverance from fear. *On the Nature of Reality* therefore expresses a tension that is psychologically much more real than anything in the somewhat facile philosophy itself.

As Henri Patin in a French study of Lucretius (1883) suggested, there is in Lucretius an "anti-Lucretius," that is to say, an anti-Epicurean. Lucretius says that passion and controversy are pointless, but his rival sets out to prove otherwise in a highly passionate and controversial manner. Albert Camus, who was devoted to the poem, said that it was the first "attack on divinity in the name of human suffering."

Epicurus established his school in 306 just outside Athens. The property he bought, and its garden, lasted for almost five hundred years. The teaching spread widely throughout civilized Europe, and only in the course of the second century C.E. did it yield to Stoicism (dealt with in the work of its last great expositor, MARCUS AURELIUS), which, for all it had in common with it—but its materialism was of a different kind—had always opposed it, even to the extent of gross libel. Epictetus, one of the gentler Stoics, went so far as to characterize its goal as "eating, drinking, copulation, shitting, and snoring." The Christians were understandably opposed to Epicureanism, and it remained submerged until well into the Renaissance.

Epicureanism recommended people to "live unnoticed," and taught what was, in our terms, a kind of rational humanism. Whether it is the shallowest of all the great philosophies that have influenced mankind is perhaps a matter for debate; but Lucretius's rather violent expression of it is certainly not shallow, and amounts to something far greater than it, in itself, is or ever was.

Epicurus and his successors (Hemarchus, Polystratus, and others) did not, contrary to popular belief, preach that people ought to lead voluptuous lives devoted to culinary and sexual pleasures. *Hedonism,* the name properly given to an essential part of this philosophy, does not imply this, and the word *hedonist*'s meaning of "pleasure-seeker" has not been gained legitimately. Epicurus himself led a fairly ascetic life, although he liked to enjoy a bit of cheese—this kind of modest enjoyment, he believed, was just about all life offered. He preached *against* sexual as well as other excesses: because of the inevitably unpleasant reaction suffered by those who thus indulged themselves. The charge of voluptuousness was a deliberate slander on the part of the Stoics who opposed him.

The Epicurean philosophy, probably a reaction against Platonism, is firmly rooted, technically, in the *atomism* of Leucippus and Democritus, both of whom lived in the fifth century B.C.E. This, a materialistic philosophy notably rejected by PLATO, taught that the world consists of an infinite number of indivisible atoms and an infinite void in which they move at a velocity faster than that of light. Everything in our experience is to be regarded as the result of a collision of atoms. The soul itself consists of very fine atoms, and at death it will dissolve. There is no afterlife.

Epicurus added the explanation of the *clinamen,* a slight (and random) divergence of the course of just a few of the atoms, which accounts for the formation of universes and the rest. Lucretius expresses it thus:

> When the atoms are falling straight down through the void by reason of their own weight, they swerve very slightly—and entirely randomly—from their course, by only just so much that you could call it a change of direction. If it weren't for this swerve, everything would fall down from space like vertical rain. Then no collisions could take place between atom and atom: there would be nothing at all.

Epicurus accepted, as an empirical fact, the existence of the pantheon of gods; but these gods have no theological status, and thus Epicurus, although not technically an atheist, is one to all true intents and purposes. His gods are aloof. It is unlikely that he believed in them.

ARISTOTLE rejected atomism itself, which only triumphed in the seventeenth century after it was taken up (via Lucretius) by the French Catholic priest Pierre Gassendi, whose ideas—too often neglected by modern historians—provided some of the bases of modern scientific enquiry. Gassendi built on Epicureanism when he explained mental events as physical distortions in the brain. He, and therefore Epicurus, had a profound effect on the thinking of ISAAC NEWTON. Atomism, at least by analogy, influenced Bertrand Russell, whose *Logical Atomism* influentially asserted that all complex entities can be reduced to simple particulars.

But, while the Epicurean account of the world did indeed contribute to modern science, few modern thinkers have been comfortable with the philosophy. This is, just possibly, more of an "atheist religion" than a philosophy proper. Certainly it is morally admirable, unless of course it is immoral to deprive people of whatever may be the consolations of religion. The Epicurean goal was *ataraxia,* or peace of mind.

Epicurus

Epicurus thought it pleasant to be free of the idea that the gods might torment him in an afterlife, which he rejected on the grounds that, since all experience consists of sensation: "Death can be nothing, for that which is absent cannot cause sensation." Lucretius has it:

> You must admit that when the body has perished there is an end to the spirit that is diffused through it. It is not short of mad to couple a finite with an eternal object and suppose that there could be harmony between them. What could be more incongruous, more repulsive, more discordant, than that a mortal and an immortal object should join up and weather the raging storm?

This has not been very influential even on those who do not believe in the afterlife.

Aristotle believed thinking to be the natural function of man, but Epicurus—perhaps rather dumbly and overliterally—narrowed this down to the contemplation of pleasure or pain. Thus poetry meant little to him, since there can hardly be any real value in the contemplation of the truths inherent in various situations if those truths have not already been very comfortably defined: "It doesn't matter, I'll be dead soon and out of it."

In place of the search for truth, Epicurus put friendship. More influentially, and perhaps more seriously, he admitted into his ideal communities both slaves and women. He saw no reason to omit them.

Epicureanism is an antisuperstitious philosophy. It is thus appropriate that it should have been so influential on modern scientific method, which proceeds in part by cutting out any reality that makes it "feel" uncomfortable about its own completely unscientific atheistic assumptions. One might say that the Epicurean approach is "nice" but, like modern science, spiritually feeble and inadequate. How can it deal with the problem of creation (it does not seriously try to do this) or with the apparently supernatural or at least transrational?

Lucretius gives us the fullest account of the system. But what takes him above it is his poetry, and this is in part generated by his fear. Here we have a man who is himself very far from tranquil preaching a lesson in tranquillity. Not only is he overwhelmed by sexual misery, but he chooses to end his poem with such alarming accounts of catastrophe—for example, the plague in Athens in 430 B.C.E.—that the philosophy of Epicurus is rendered almost meaningless, despite his recommendation of it. Thus he ends with an account of an epidemic whose horror is in no way mitigated by any kinds of musings on friendship:

> Here, crammed between stifling walls, death piles his heap of victims high. Along the roads by the drinking fountains lay the bodies of those who died of thirst or of a glut of water. The city teemed with the wasted frames, covered by no flesh, but only stretched skin, of those who lay dying in filth and rags virtually already buried in by their loathsome sores. Death had filled, too, every holy shrine with corpses—yes, those heavenly temples once filled with worshippers now lay waste with dead bodies. Reverence had no further place: all that was banished in the immediacy of agony. Proper burial was no longer possible, the nation was in terror, each family abandoned its dead, amidst shrieks of fear, as best it might: people flung their spouses, children, parents on pyres built by others for their own. Sometimes they fought rather than leave their dead.

Death no doubt is, as Lucretius was so anxious to prove, the end of the personality. But there is nothing in his poem about what is called, variously, the soul, spirit, or essence.

17

Allegorical Expositions of the Holy Laws

PHILO OF ALEXANDRIA

1st century C.E.

Philo of Alexandria, often known as Philo Judaeus (Philo the Jew), Greek writer on the Jewish religion and Greek philosophy—that variety of it known as "Middle Platonism"—was a contemporary of Jesus Christ and Paul the Apostle, born about 30 B.C.E.; he probably died some time in the 40s of the first century C.E. He is most usually, and quite properly, regarded as the first theologian (of a type that studied Christianity). Yet he was a Jew, and there is no reason to suppose (although it used to be claimed that he had it in mind) that he ever mentioned Christianity.

Indeed, there is not even agreement about the audience for which he wrote. Was it for his fellow Jews, for the Gentiles, or for both? The best guess is that, since he was a prolific writer (his extant works—some are lost—in parallel translation run to ten volumes), he wrote for anyone who would read him. Many, throughout the ages, did read him, and the *City of God* of

AUGUSTINE is much influenced by him, as are the *Enneads* of PLOTINUS. He is thus of very great importance, although for rather strange reasons. Few of us are likely to read him at any great length; yet we have to know who he was if we want to know about the history of just that matter he does not mention: Christianity. He wrote in Greek, but some of his works survive only in Latin (and in one case, Armenian) versions.

Of his life we have scant details, except that he was born in Alexandria into an important Jewish family. His brother, Alexander, was a tax official, and he himself eventually became head of the large Jewish community in Alexandria. Although he may have had some private views about the true nature of religion—he seems to have been an independent and eclectic, although not himself original, thinker—he was, as citizen, a loyal and even inflexible Jew, devoted to the interests of his own community.

This was certainly the case in the single event of his life of which anything is known in detail. In 37 C.E. Gaius Julius Caesar Germanicus, the son of Germanicus and Agrippina (12–41 C.E.), became Roman emperor. Because at the age of about four, when he was on the Rhine with his parents, he was paraded in military boots, he became known as Baby Boots, or Bootikins, i.e., in Latin, Caligula—best known to most of us, no doubt, for having made one of his horses consul, or perhaps for planning an invasion of Britain but at the last moment ordering his soldiers to collect sea shells instead.

Some of the information we have about him comes from Philo himself, who maintains that his mind became unhinged as a result of an illness he suffered in October 37, just after he became emperor. He was among the most autocratic as well as maddest of the Roman emperors, and he caused serious unrest among all the Jews under Roman rule. Philo and others went to Rome in 39–40 in order to try to persuade him to withdraw his insistence that the Jews at Alexandria should worship him as a god. This mission failed, but in 41 Caligula was assassinated.

Philo's books as we have them, possibly fragments of larger works, include *On the Creation of the Universe, On the Embassy of Gaius,* an account of the mission to Caligula (but the bit of it describing the downfall of the emperor is missing), and *On the Contemplative Life.*

But what is most important about him is his approach to the Jewish OLD TESTAMENT. In this he discovered what, strictly speaking, was not there: Greek Platonic philosophy. (It may, though, of course, be there in a philosophical, if not historical, sense.) His allegorical pursuit of the meaning of his Scriptures became the accepted manner of biblical exegesis among the Christian Church Fathers. In the second century Philo's emphasis on the Logos, the second person of the trinity, the word of God (a term going back to the pre-Socratic Greek philosopher Heraclitus, who took it to be the universal reason governing the world), was taken up by such as Clement of Alexandria, on behalf of the writings of the John who wrote the fourth gospel and who was the traditional author of the *Book of Revelation.*

Philo's belief was that Greek philosophy, especially PLATO, had been anticipated in the first five books of the Old Testament, whose authors (he maintained) had been used by God to communicate his will. Allegorical exegesis, the procedure of discovering hidden meanings, was not new in Philo's time. It had been used by commentators on HOMER. By means of it, at worst, you could "discover" your own metaphysical system in whatever text or texts you liked. The later Stoics used the method on the myths of

the Greeks, and another Alexandrian Jew, Aristobulus, who lived between the third and the second centuries B.C.E., had interpreted the Old Testament along Greek philosophical lines.

Philo recommended that people should obey Mosaic Law but employ allegory to divine its deeper meaning. The Law is sacred and must be followed: It is sanctioned by God. But, in a truly Platonic spirit, it is but a shadow: That which casts the shadow is the deeper truth. This proved of great use to Christians when they came to reconcile their faith with Hellenistic thought. Philo was the first writer to take the step of trying to integrate Greek philosophy with the Old Testament, or, rather, to see this as a Platonic allegory:

> For God is the maker of time also, for he is the father of time's father. . . . Thus he stands in relation to God in the relation of a grandson. . . . To the elder son, the intelligible universe, he assigned the place of the firstborn.

It is ironic that it was, initially, the Christians and not the Jews who took up Philo. But his impact on both Jews and Moslems was eventually great, as it was on the scholastic philosophy of the Middle Ages. It was necessary to the last-named that philosophy be the "handmaid" to theology.

Philo's revisions of Greek notions of the nature of God became the foundation of the common philosophy of Judaism, Christianity, and Islam. In this respect he exerted enormous influence on the development of world religions.

18

The New Testament

c. 64–110 C.E.

The prophet Jeremiah (Jer. 31:31) announced: "Behold the days come, saith the Lord, that I will make a new covenant with the House of Israel and the House of Judah." The Christians seized upon this as the main OLD TESTAMENT passage to justify their belief that the Law would be abrogated in the person of Jesus the Messiah. But the Jews, when it came to it, did not accept Jesus as their Messiah, and he has had no influence on the development of their religion. It needs to be stated, therefore, that—without any prejudice whatsoever to the value of Jesus and of the drama in which he played a part—the New Testament is an historically unreliable, and above all an incomplete, set of documents; it may well, too, distort and mislead us in its account of what Jesus really intended. If people wanted real religion, religion that was not secular but religious, then they would recognize this. As it is, we have to gather, piecemeal, the true facts. The full picture in all its detail is impossible to establish—it has been too well suppressed in the name of the true God—but its outlines are clear enough.

In the KORAN, which drew mostly from material in gnostic or apocryphal gospels excluded from the canon by the Church Fathers, Jesus is seen as a prophet; his Christian status as the Son of God is totally denied; but Muslims in general believe that, as a model for individual mystics, he will return at the end of time to sit alongside God; he figures in the Muslim *Stories of the Prophets*. The more exclusive Christians have not returned this compliment. It is still a minority who look upon all the religions as ways to the same goal; the various Christian churches remain the most cruelly savage exclusionists of all.

The amount we actually know about the man Jesus (the Greek form of the Hebrew Joshua) remains small. Josephus (see the Old Testament) seems to have referred to him in the *Antiquities;* but that is a forgery by a Christian, although it is usually called an "interpolation." Jesus was a Gallilean Jew who came under the influence of the ascetic John the Baptist. John preached, in common with many others at that turbulent time, the imminent coming of the end of the world and the foundation of the Kingdom of Heaven. It is possible, probably likely, that Jesus lived with the Essenes, the sect now associated, almost certainly rightly, with the recently discovered Dead Sea Scrolls. The more orthodox a Christian, however, the more likely he is to deny this speculation: The early Christian Church, in its struggle to gain secular power and influence, and regardless of the psychological fact that nothing that has not been thought through by an individual can really mean anything to that individual, relied greatly on the notion of *orthodoxy*—which means, simply, "believing in what is currently held to be right in opinion." The values of a church, if not of its individual members, that is uncritical—to say the least— of its sources, must be held in question.

Certainly Jesus wandered, gained followers, and preached that the coming of the Kingdom of God was at hand. His clashes with the Pharisees— the third, with the Saducees and the Essenes, of three sects of the Jews, and the most observant of the Law, and the most subsequently influential—were exaggerated in the Christian gospels. He gained the notion that in order to fulfill his messianic mission he must suffer and die, and it is likely that he arranged with Judas Iscariot, his favorite disciple, to appear to betray him. Judas is thus in all probability the opposite of what history—though not the gnostic sect of the Cainites, which revered him and had a gospel according to him—has taken him to be. Judas might thus be an interesting example of one who took what is in Sufism called "the way of blame," or "way of Malamat." Irenaeus, the gentlest of the great heresy-hunters of the second century, says that the Cainites held that he "was thoroughly acquainted with these things, and he alone was acquainted with the truth as no others were, and so accomplished the mystery of the betrayal." Judas's motives are not otherwise consistently or convincingly explained in the four canonic gospels.

In all probability Pilate, the Roman procurator, had Jesus crucified at the insistence of certain Jews who feared that his claims might disturb the peace. His followers then claimed to have met him after he had died (but some have claimed that he survived the crucifixion, which is medically possible—he does so in both George Moore's novel *The Brook Kerith* and in Robert Graves's and Joshua Podro's *The Nazarene Gospel Restored,* an account regarded as reasonable by the American Christian theologian Rheinhold Niebuhr). His first followers formed a sect within Jewry (there is still a minority Jewish cult which recognizes him as the son of God); but the new Christianity ("a local cult called Christianity," wrote Thomas Hardy—echoing EDWARD GIBBON—famously, in *The Dynasts*) began to spread among Gentiles, especially after the catastrophe, the Destruction of the Temple, in 70 C.E. The establishment of the New Testament scriptures (the letters of Paul, for example) as authoritative was a haphazard, even largely accidental, process—and not always even an honest one. The words of Jesus, or what people reported as his words, were not much quoted in writing until well into the second century, although the gospels (Mark 64–65, Matthew, Luke, and John 80–110) already existed.

There were two tendencies that the much persecuted new Christian sect members had to guard themselves against. The first was the Judaizing habit of drifting into calling Jesus merely a good rabbi, and thus detracting from his true, unique status as Son of God. But the other was a much more serious one.

The first person to try to create a canonical New Testament—a "fixed list"—was Marcion (usually pronounced with a hard *c*), a wealthy shipowner from Sinope in Pontus (Cappadocia) who was excommunicated from his home church as a heretic, traveled about Asia Minor in search of followers, came to Rome in about 140, and was active there until his death in about 160. He was in Rome at the same time as the Samaritan Christian Justin, and the admirable Egyptian "heretic" Valentinus—and he surely must have known both, although Justin pointedly does not mention him. Marcion donated a large sum of money to the Christian cause there, but was rejected again, so in 144 separated himself from the official church, being finally persuaded that the Christian method of interpreting the Old Testament by means of allegory was unsatisfactory.

Marcion took the Old Testament as true, but saw Christ's coming as a redemption from it: There were two Gods, one the demiurge of the Old Testament, the other the charitable and merciful one of the New. Marcion is a figure of immense significance, who, although he has been put forward as both a nongnostic and the prime anticipator of Protestantism (by the great nineteenth-century scholar Adolf von Harnack), was undoubtedly a gnostic, although we do not know his exact views. He taught that there was a radical opposition between the Law of the Old Testament and the mercy of the New, and he set forth these contrasts in his suppressed *Antitheses,* a pared-down New Testament, consisting of an edited Luke and certain Pauline epistles— all purged of Judaic matter. Marcion's Old Testament demiurge was an inept troublemaker, and Emily Dickinson (see Old Testament), had she known of him, would have liked his God better than she liked Jehovah.

A contemporary Christian apologist has written that "if gnosticism had prevailed it would have destroyed Christianity: by absorbing Christ into the system of 'knowledge'"; and because "the only escape from flesh to spirit was through secret 'knowledge' known only to a few." But such "knowledge" was then quite open, as Marcion's life and work demonstrates—the writer (Frederick Norwood, of the Garrett Theological Seminary) is applying the standards of later centuries, when "heresy" was persecuted and driven underground, and Christianity had established itself as a secular power very much "of this world." The same writer adds, rather naively, that "something had to be done if the Christian movement was to be kept on the main track." And he records how, after cruel persecutions from the emperors Decius and Diocletian, the faith triumphed when Constantine ascended the throne in 312: He had been promised victory under the sign of the Cross in a vision at the Battle of Milvian Bridge. Thus, for this-worldly reasons, Christianity triumphed: "Now finally the upper classes entered in large numbers." "No longer was the faith disdained by supercilious pagans," continues Norwood. By the time of the reign of Theodosius (379–395) the Christians were tolerantly able (391) to get all other faiths proscribed. The way was set for Gibbon's "history of crime." This of course is to speak of the Christian *Church,* the institution, and of its other-wordly record—not of what individual Christians found in the often gnostic traditions of the mysticism that quickly grew up within it. Whatever Christ's message exactly was—it was certainly not warlike—it had by then turned into its opposite.

By the time of Theodosius's edict, the New Testament canon had been closed, or semi-closed, for almost two hundred years. Flush with success, the Carthaginian Council of 419 finally ratified the list. The earlier Christians had preferred the tradition by which what they believed to be the sayings and doings of Jesus had been handed down by word of mouth, but, largely owing to the efforts of the Samaritan Gentile Justin (c. 100–165, when he was denounced and executed in Rome, hence Justin Martyr), the written material began to gain respectability. The heresy-hunter Iraeneus helped to develop it still further by means of numerology. The four canonical gospels and the other material was, he wrote, "inspired," but the heretical gospels and other similar material were "uninspired."

But were the "pagans" really just "supercilious"—and were those gospels now known as gnostic, such as that of Thomas, really uninspired? And what of Jesus Christ? Was his real message heeded? Did he mean something else by the coming Kingdom of God? The inclusion of the oft-fought-over Gospel of John, gnostically and magically tinged as it is, helped some of the literal-minded to find an understanding of the problem of the reluctance of the world to come to an end; but for the most part the church happily adapted itself to the delay.

19

Lives

PLUTARCH

c. 50–120 C.E.

By 264 B.C.E. the Romans controlled all of Italy except for the Po Valley. Eleven years before that their success over King Pyrrhus of Epirus, when they forced him to retreat back over the Adriatic after the drawn Battle of Beneventum, had attracted the interested attention of the Greeks. In 146 B.C.E., Scipio Aemilianus burned Carthage and plowed salt into its ashes, thus ending the three Punic Wars.

In the lifetime of the Greek moralist, biographer, and priest L. Mestrius Plutarchus (to give him his full Roman name), or Plutarch (c. 50–120 C.E.), Rome, under the successors of Augustus (Octavian), first Roman emperor, was supreme. Or was it quite? The work of this agreeable busybody—indispensable to us for his information, dubious though much of this is—tells us a great deal about Rome's idea of itself at its peak.

The Romans showed more skill, and much more cunning, in keeping their vast empire together than the Greeks ever had bothered to exercise. The chronically ill Augustus (63 B.C.E.–14 C.E.), whose climb to power and eventual godhood was so assured and masterful as to lead us to wonder how fully aware he was that, as adopted son of Julius Caesar, he held a hand of cards such that he had only to play it to win, was overtly worshipped as divine not only by plebians but by such men as the poets Horace and VIRGIL.

Yet it is ironic—or is it?—that the so-called Principate, the firm and enduring form of government that the seventy-six year-old god bequeathed to Rome and its empire as he lay dying in 14 C.E., should lack any spiritual dimension whatever. Or was that all there is to success and greatness in the Roman world? Those times resemble our own in many respects.

The great success began in earnest in 43 B.C.E.—just after the assassination of Julius Caesar—in a bloodbath: the killing, by "proscription," of some twenty-five hundred men. Nor did Augustus ever practice mercy for its own sake—only for its expediency. Those murdered in 43 included the greatest Roman orator of all: the manipulative, ambitious, astonishingly boastful, ultimately ineffective, hugely talented, amoral moralist Marcus Tullius Cicero. The killers of Julius Caesar had not trusted him enough to let him into their plot. But in one of his rare moments of courage he launched writings against Mark Antony, one of the triumvirate (the others were Lepidus and Octavian, the future emperor) formed just after the assassination. He was condemned for these—his severed hands and head were put on public display by the vengeful future lover of Cleopatra. Yet, as Plutarch tells us, "the glory of [Cicero's] rhetoric still remains."

As one of the "greatest" of all the Romans, it is worth looking briefly at Cicero's achievement—hollow in the light of what he had been given. He is the subject, after all, as is Antony, of one of Plutarch's famous *Lives*, in which he is paired with *the* Greek orator Demosthenes. If this Cicero—orator, lawyer, politician, critic, notoriously bad but technically able poet, letter writer, philosopher—had any aim beyond self-glorification, it was to make Rome great. But Rome, while it thrived, thrived in the shadow of the Greece of the past, of which it was both adoringly imitative and jealous. Like brutal Rome itself—one refined woman's idea of torture, Plutarch informs us, was to force a man to cut off his own flesh, roast it, and then eat it—Cicero was timid and insecure, and so he practiced aggression. He made himself peculiarly vicious in court. This (Plutarch again), "gave him the repute of ill nature." Like Mussolini, whose model was always Imperial Rome, "he was always excessively pleased"—"nauseous and irksome"—"with his own praise, and continued to the very last to be passionately fond of glory, which often interfered with the prosecution of his wisest resolution." This fault neither excuses nor is justified by Cicero's achievements; but it does coexist with them; and the same applies to the republican Rome of which he was so much a child, and to its imperial successor.

Plutarch was a Greek born, during the reign of Claudius, in the old and by that time decayed town of Chaeronea near Thebes in Boetia, into an old family of the middle class. He went to Athens to learn philosophy. He kept a school in his own town, and there taught philosophy in his turn. By the time he was forty he had been sent to Rome on some business probably connected with Chaeronea. He gave lectures there, on ethics, during the reign of Domitian; these attracted some favorable attention. But his lecturing was not quite sufficient to give him substantial fame, which he got from his writings.

He spent the latter part of his life at home, serving his town. For his final thirty years he officiated as priest of Apollo at the oracle of Delphi. Despite his priestly duties, however, he lived the peaceful life of a scholarly sage, much consulted and much visited—and feeling important. He was a prolific writer, the author of some two hundred books. We have about half of his writings (twenty-three of the pairs of *Lives* survive, each pair contrasting a Greek with a Roman hero, and four single lives). The miscellaneous writings and dialogues left over from the *Lives* have been rather misleadingly given the title of the *Moralia;* these were popular in the Elizabethan version of Philemon Holland. Plutarch appropriately received great honors—or so we are led to believe—from the emperors Trajan and Hadrian.

In the *Lives* Plutarch did not set out to write history, but biography, a poor form of which he almost invented. His method—not new—was to set the life of an illustrious Greek by the side of that of an illustrious Roman, and then make a moralistic comparison between them. His aim is part psychological and part superstitious: to show a man placed under the various stresses of circumstance and to display how he dealt with the problems these caused him.

But Plutarch is a great writer in neither the *Lives* nor the nowadays preferred *Moralia*. He is a pleasant minor gossip for whom we must be intensely grateful. Here we have one whose extrinsic value, far outweighs his intrinsic value. His style is undistinguished: heavy and diffuse. He lacks wisdom. The regulation Platonism and Pythagoreanism he learned from his Athens teacher Ammonius is compromised by his subservient and shallow belief in the Greek pantheon of gods, which the Romans took over and altered only in trivial ways. His characterization is poor. He is sometimes good at noting the revealing detail, but all is vitiated by his conviction that character is an unchanging thing, fixed at birth. He can never see it as developing or changing—as, in fact, it does—whether it improves or otherwise—under external circumstance. He is, most typically, an antiquarian, who likes to give his leisured and conservative readers a series of quaint details—rather like your interesting grandfather who soon, though, can become tedious. But he can always just about hold the interest by means of his anecdotes, which are as often significant as they are simply frivolous. No one is likely to forget his story of Crassus, the wealthy member of the triumvirate of 60 B.C.E., with Julius Caesar and Pompey: Roman houses burned down very easily, and so Crassus formed the habit of presenting himself early at the scene of house fires, full of sympathy and offering to buy the ground upon which the house had stood. He bought cheaply and thus acquired much of Rome.

Plutarch is the perfect product of the Pax Romana. He has no concept of historical change and is thus entirely bound in by his own time and place. He is driven by petty pride in his own family. He is superstitious rather than religious. He is naive about his sources. His method of paralleling lives—an old device—did not bear fruit, since its purpose was to express loyalty to Rome while demonstrating that the Greeks had been as noble and as heroic. He is an authoritarian to whom psychologically more astute readers go, not to approve his rather stiff rhetoric, but to gather whatever information they can. Character is for Plutarch less individual than simply geared to the service of an orthodox and guaranteed notion of the state. He is a hero worshipper— never a useful or profound thing to be—and even when he throws in a person he considers to be really bad, such as Demetrius or Mark Antony, it is to utter a moral warning.

Plutarch, with his wide and shallow learning, was popular in his own time because he provided good Romans with what, besides amusing anec- dotes, they wanted to hear: that their culture was a worthy successor and continuation of that of Greece. They had little culture of their own, after all. After the decline of the Roman empire, Plutarch's work fell into neglect. But he later became immensely influential, first when his books were published in Byzantium and then, as educational tools, in medieval times. He finally came into his own with the Renaissance, with the French humanist Jacques Amyot's versions of the *Lives* (1559) and the *Moralia* (1572). Amyot popu- larized a somewhat falsified notion of the "wisdom of the ancients," which achieved increased currency in the essays of MONTAIGNE. (This view has had to be gradually dismantled over the course of four centuries.) His impact on the Renaissance, in some ways an accident because of the wealth of facts that he seemed to offer, was enormous. Those in debt to him include SHAKESPEARE in *Julius Caesar, Antony and Cleopatra,* and *Coriolanus* (this through Sir Thomas North's English version of Amyot's translation) as well as the far more profound Montaigne, Dryden (whose translation of him is still in print in its revision by the Victorian poet and critic Arthur Hugh Clough) and ROUSSEAU. A few of the lives, such as "Brutus," helped to inspire the spirit of revolution in France.

Plutarch is talented, charming, and about as harmless as a writer can be—all such, after all, are at the mercy of ruthless appropriation by extrem- ists. Of real intrinsic importance, however, he possesses little.

20

Annals, From the Death of the Divine Augustus

CORNELIUS TACITUS

c. 120 C.E.

Most histories of Rome, from which we might have learned so much more, failed to survive the decline and destruction of its empire so eloquently described by EDWARD GIBBON in his *Decline and Fall of the Roman Empire*. To speak only of the two most celebrated of all the Roman historians, we have less than a quarter of the works of Livy, thirty-five from 142 books—and only about half of those of Publius (or Gaius: one manuscript is thus signed, but the other is signed Publius) Cornelius Tacitus.

We know, however, from Tacitus himself that the duties of the Roman historian were similar to those of such Greeks as THUCYDIDES: It was to record the history of their own country above all—"vast wars," wrote Tacitus, "the sack of cities, the defeat and capture of kings, or in domestic history conflicts between consuls and tribunes, legislation about land and grain-distribution, the struggles of the aristocracy and plebs." The purpose of *Annals,* he wrote, was to preserve acts of virtue, but to disgrace those who did wrong actions. There was not yet any conception of writing with a show of complete objectivity, of writing what we now fondly think of as "history," of giving an unbiased account of "what happened." But Tacitus comes nearest to doing this.

The first Roman historians wrote in Greek, to commemorate the triumph over the countries of the Mediterranean Sea. They also kept records, which go back to the foundation of their republic at about the beginning of the fifth century B.C.E. A good deal of legend got mixed up with fact, so that Romulus and Remus were given an elaborate and wholly false genealogy. The first Roman historian of any account was a Greek, Polybius (c. 202–120 B.C.E.), from Megalopolis, who set out to explain the reasons for the triumph of Rome. Simple and direct in style, his *History,* of which the first five (of forty) books have survived, is useful, but overdidactic and without literary significance. But the account of his own exploits by Julius Caesar, orator as well as soldier and dictator, born exactly one hundred years after Polybius, in his *Gallic Wars,* has been much admired by historians, from Cicero onward. Caesar's purpose is to glorify himself, but he does this in forceful, unadorned prose, and his attitude is at times detached.

However, it was Caesar's partisan Gaius Sallustius Crispus, known as Sallust (86–35 B.C.E.), from a plebeian family, who was the first truly scientific Roman historian. It is unfortunate that so little of his work survives: We have his remarkable history of Cataline's conspiracy to seize power, in which he gives so vivid and convincing a portrait of Cataline (gratefully used by the Elizabethan playwright and poet Ben Jonson in his powerful play on the subject); but only fragments of his *History,* which dealt with Rome between the years 78 and 67 B.C.E. His method was based upon that of THUCYDIDES, and he thus invented appropriate speeches for his chief players. He has something of the drama, the moral objectivity, and the genuine indignation of Tacitus, and he might well be even more highly valued had more of his work survived.

But it was left to the Paduan, Livy (Titus Livius, 59 B.C.E.–17 C.E.), to write the history of the Republic. A few believe him to be a greater historian than Tacitus, although schoolchildren who have studied Latin have always shown a marked preference for the latter. As already mentioned, of his *Ab Urbe Condite (From the Foundation of the City)*, only thirty-five of 142 books have survived. These books describe Rome's original subjugation of Italy; the (mostly) lost books took the story up to 9 B.C.E., and thus dealt with part of the reign of the Emperor Augustus, with whom Livy formed a comparatively close friendship. His history is frankly "Augustan": designed to please Augustus, to establish Rome as the grandest of all nations; it is not easy to conceive of it in any other way. He was much admired by Tacitus, and was again widely influential during the Renaissance because of the translation into English by Philemon Holland (1600). He is not particularly accurate—sometimes not as accurate as the sources available to him—but, like Tacitus, he had marked literary gifts, notably his capacity for vivid and sympathetic descriptions.

One of the human disadvantages of the glory imparted to Rome by Augustus was that, although the latter pretended to honor the conception of it, in effect he completely ignored it; decisions were made in secret by him and by his cronies. Thus Tacitus, Rome's greatest historian, was conscious of working in what a commentator has called "a narrow and inglorious field."

Tacitus was born in about C.E. 57; he died about 117. Not much is known about his early life. He married the daughter of the governor of Britain, Julius Agricola, in 78, and thus achieved a distinguished political career in Rome; in 112–13 he was proconsul of Asia. He wrote mainly during the rule of the Emperor Trajan. His earliest known work is a eulogy of his father-in-law. His *Histories* covered the years 69–96, the *Annals*, written later, cover the period preceding, from the death of Augustus. Of the latter, only the parts dealing with Tiberius (successor to Augustus) and parts of the reigns of Claudius and Nero survive.

His aim, or so he claims, is to write *sine ira et studio* (without passion or bias—the "customary incentives to these were lacking" he dryly adds); but in fact he writes high tragedy, rebelling against the elaborate style of Cicero and taking up instead that of Sallust. He reveled in his role of ironic moralist, and is more artistically detached than any writer of history before him. It was during the nineteenth century taken to be an achievement that his dark view of the history of the Romans had been discredited; but in the twentieth century he came into his own. To him above all (and perhaps equally to the satirical poet Juvenal) belongs the credit of showing just how degraded Roman life and morals became. Robert Graves drew eagerly upon him for his modern account of this degradation in his two Claudius novels—so that his influence upon our view of the Romans has extended into the twentieth (and the twenty-first) centuries.

Tacitus was subtle, dramatic, morally disgusted, and ironic. No historian has been nearer to poetry in his deliberately rugged and uneven style, abounding in archaisms and biting epigrams. "The age was not so barren of virtue," he says, "that it did not produce some fine examples of conduct." He was not too scrupulous about detail if this might interfere with a good and shocking story. Although he is grand, not stopping to record the trivial, and although he knows that history is a noble theme, he is not really as earnest as Livy about Rome's greatness, and one suspects that in himself he may well have had reservations and have transcended such glories in the interests of a greater truth.

It has been observed that his elaborate (and ironic) circumlocutions in order to avoid mentioning the petty anticipated the dry grandeur of the great French tragedians such as Racine. His portrait of Tiberius is, so far as we can tell, a true one, and modern historians have tried to mitigate it in vain: suspicious, hypocritical, intelligent, and enlightened but malevolent at the core. For Tacitus, it has been well said, destiny might well *explain* human conduct—but it did not excuse it!

Many modern classicists, though they admire Tacitus, also passionately dislike him. He is too pessimistic, they feel, and "unfair." Thus doubtless would historians of two thousand years in the future (should this much time be granted to the world) dismiss accounts too "gloomy" of such as Hitler and the Holocaust. The truth is that Tacitus is far more than a historian, and in his underlying insistence that rule by one man is intrinsically evil he even anticipates the twentieth century. No wonder the nineteenth century liked to discredit his view of history and failed to discern his essential humanism.

The fate of Tacitus's reputation is hardly surprising. The last great writer in Latin until AUGUSTINE, he was virtually ignored for centuries, both in antiquity and then in medieval times. Then he awakened the consciences of sixteenth-century thinkers, not least among them MACHIAVELLI and ERASMUS. And he was, significantly, by far the favorite historian of that remarkable and unusual politician Thomas Jefferson. Above all, it has been hard for the majority of historians—but there are notable exceptions—to forgive him for being so readable and true to reality. Thus it has been the intention of many to rob him of his due; but that due is too powerful and too tragic to be forgotten. No wonder Gibbon admired him.

21

The Gospel of Truth

c. 1st Century C.E.

This gospel is noncanonical: missing from the NEW TESTAMENT. It is known by its opening: "The Gospel of Truth is joy." It is also known as the *The Valentinian Speculation* and *Evangelium Veritatis*. The Latin name was (probably) coined by the zealous heresiologist—or hunter-out of heresies—the Christian bishop, Irenaeus. "Gospel" here means, simply, "good news": This book, unlike the canonical gospels, does not purport to give a complete life of Christ.

It has been plausibly suggested that *The Gospel of Truth* was written by Valentinus himself, although that cannot be proved. It hardly matters, because it is a Christian work of the Valentinian, gnostic, type. We have it in a Coptic version (Coptic—from the Arabic *Kibt, Egyptian,* the ancient Egyptian language spoken by the Egyptians, the "Copts," until about the tenth century C.E., when it was supplanted by Arabic—was written in characters very closely akin to those of the Greek alphabet) but the language of its (lost) original composition was Greek. It dates from the middle of the first century C.E.

Since few readers could reasonably be expected to have heard of this, and since it was only discovered (by two of the murderous sons of a recently murdered man) just before the Christmas of 1945, and not published until some years after that, how can I possibly justify including it among the world's most influential books? Who was Valentinus, and why is what he, or one of his close followers, wrote so important?

In fact this is only an aptly typical one of many books containing such precious material; hundreds or perhaps thousands like it were destroyed by zealous orthodox Christians bent on denying them to humanity. However, the type of gnostic thinking that *The Gospel of Truth* contains has persisted, has survived Christianity—and it still persists. Being so close to so many "forbidden" notions, including that of anarchy—used here in the broad sense of the idea that human beings could get on better without such things as flags (TOLSTOY called a flag a "dirty piece of rag on a stick"), the media, central governments of polite psychopaths pretending to be "for the people and of the people," large-scale wars, laws framed to be privately broken by the "initiated" (the word was thus used by Lord Milner, one of the architects of the Boer War), and a few men so rich that they have lost sight of the reason for which money was invented—the gnostic strand of thought and feeling has never prospered officially. We do not know much about how it fared when, for a limited period of time, it was a state religion (as Manicheanism); but its rival Zoroastrianism (see THE AVESTA) was not persecuted—and it was an ambitious and evil Zoroastrian priest, Kirder, who saw to it that Mani was tortured and murdered. Orthodox Christians would of course have needed to kill Kirder (himself an adherent of a "heresy," Zurvanism) as a heretic. Yet they would have been as grateful to him—prior to their happy certainty in dispatching him—for this piece of exemplarily murderous zeal and charity; as grateful as they had been to the Zoroastrian, Jewish, and Neoplatonic heresies from which they had stolen so much. These gentle men never agreed with Manes, who had mercifully, realistically, and openmindedly written: "The countries and the tongues to which they [Manes's own predecessors] [were] sent differ from one another; the one is unlike the other."

Valentinus, founder of the heretical Christian sect called, after him, the Valentinians, was born in Egypt. Although his ideas are more reminiscent of those of the gnostically tinged Saint John (of the Gospel, and, traditionally, of Revelations), his disciples claimed that he had been taught by Theodas, a pupil of Saint Paul. He was in Rome between about 136 and 165 (at the same time as Marcion), and hoped to be elected bishop. But he was passed over, and withdrew, probably to Cyprus, where he died in about 175. He was among the most influential of the gnostic Christians and, if only we knew more about him (until recent finds of writings we knew about him almost exclusively from his enemies, the heresiologists), then we should know more, too, about the second-century struggles between Christians over the form their creed should take. A few writers believe that such Church Fathers as Irenaeus and the other heresiologists and apologists for what became orthodox Christianity entered into a conscious conspiracy to excise from the religion—at first only for Jews, then, later, for Gentiles—all the mystery elements. This seems to be what happened, although it is considerably oversimplifying matters to assume that the orthodoxists knew that what they were doing was wrong. What was important to them and to their lackeys was that they could prepare for a secular hell on earth in the religious name of the greatest heretic of all, the gnostic originator of all the trouble: Jesus Christ, who himself protested (if we are to believe the gnostic *Apocalypse of Peter*—and we have as much reason to do so as we have to believe in, say, Luke) thus: "They will cleave to the name of a dead man, thinking that they will become pure. But they will become greatly defiled. . . . These people are dry canals."

Certainly the Fathers arbitrarily selected from the available literature in order to establish an artificial canon. Within that canon no mention must be made of Christ's early years among gnostics. The Church itself, although some of its members have undoubtedly been responsible for much good in the world, and for many heroic individual lives (many of which, though, the Church and its cruel clerks set out to reduce to silence), soon turned Christ's message into a means of oppression. (One of the teachings of modern gnosticism is that projects end up by changing into their opposites.) The Inquisition proper, of 1232, was specifically founded (by Emperor Frederick III) to hunt out gnostics (particularly Mani's successors, the exemplary Cathars, who lived in France). The secular and papal authorities quarreled about exactly who was to conduct the Inquisition (it is after all good fun to be right); by only 1252 the "dry canal" Pope Innocent III (very much in the spirit of his Savior) had decreed torture permissible (by his bull *ad extirpanda*). Thus was Christianity turned into its opposite (for more details of this process, see GURDJIEFF's *All and Everything*).

Therefore one of the key documents, and one of the most lucid, in the history of what had so offended the Church that it used torture and execution to rid itself of it—but was nevertheless so fearlessly persistent—is bound, to say the least, now to be, and to have been from the time of Christ, both important and influential.

On the night of May 7, 1945, a night watchman (over irrigation equipment) in the fields of an area of upper Egypt called Jabal al-Tarif killed a marauder. Doubtless this was no more than in accordance with his duties, but by the midmorning of the following day he had himself been killed—if with less slow delicacy than an employee of the Inquisition might have used—as an act of blood vengeance. I give these details because, as I have already asked elsewhere, "What could be more appropriate—in its mixture of chance, fraud, lying, theft, murder, and objective and scholarly curiosity—to the very nature of gnosticism, its alien spirit, than [this] climax of some hundreds of years' research into it?"

This climax is the discovery of the Nag Hammadi texts, which included *The Gospel of Truth,* in a steep cliff honeycombed with caves, many of which had been used as grave sites more than four millennia earlier.

In December 1945 a son of the slain watchman, Muhammad Ali al-Samman—thirty years later he would take part, for money, in television interviews, although he would not return to the site of his find until suitably bribed and in disguise—was digging with his brother Kalifah in the area for nitrates: Like the other peasants of the area, he was used, at the end of the year, to gathering and then carrying this fertilizer to his fields near his home at Al-Qasr (the site of the ancient Chenoboskia) in the saddlebags of his camel. They came across a jar, sealed with bitumen.

The lonely caves of the area were exceptionally suitable for meditation as well as burial, and they had undoubtedly been used as such, especially by Saint Pachomius (290–346), who had lived near there and had founded a series of monastic communities which became of great importance to the Coptic church and to other churches as well. Jeremiah 32 quotes the God of the Jews as pronouncing that books, in order to be preserved, should be "put into an earthen vessel, that they may continue many days"; chapter 36, though, alludes to the practice of burning as the proper fate of undesirable literature. So those who hid the Nag Hammadi texts in a jar wanted them preserved. We cannot say for certain what community hid them thus, or why; but it is possible or even likely that, since possession of such books had by then been made into a criminal offense, some monk—between about 350 and 400 C.E., the date of the making of the books—hid them from the marauding soldiers of the Church Triumphant.

Ali and his brother were afraid to open the jar in case it contained a jinn. In a very substantial sense it did indeed contain one, although not of the sort of which they were superstitiously frightened. Greed for possible gold overcame their caution, and they smashed it open with their mattocks. No money poured out—but a cloud of papyrus fragments rose into the air.

Ali and Kalifah wrapped the books they had found deep down in the jar into their tunics, and carried them home—a hovel—in their saddlebags. For a time they served good use as fuel for their mother's oven; others were bartered or sold for a pittance. Ali, for his own part, might just as well have left them in the jar—they became a positive nuisance to him.

For in very early 1946 Ali was told that his father's alleged killer, a peasant called Ahmad, was taking a midday snooze on the road near their home. Ali ran home to alert all six of his brothers who—Ali with the very mattock with which he had smashed the jar—murdered Ahmad (who was innocent) by cutting him up into pieces. The family then cut out Ahmad's heart, took it home, and devoured it as part of a ritual revenge feast.

Ahmad's father was an influential man, a much hated sheriff from another part of Egypt, who caused Ali's house to be searched, nightly, for arms—so Ali hastily got rid of whatever he thought could incriminate him. The story after that—of European professors disguised as smugglers, one-eyed crooks, shady dealers, and all varieties of academic greed and chicanery—has not yet been fully told. When it is, and if it ever is, it will be a bestseller. Nor will it strengthen the orthodox Christian case that God does not of himself permit evil. The wonder is that in the end what remained of these precious finds was collected and published at all (1972–84). Professor James T. Robinson, who edited the one-volume edition of 1978 (which contains *The Gospel of Truth*), wrote: "With the publication . . . the work has only just begun, for it marks a new beginning in the study of Gnosticism."

At first scholars wanted to understand what was so worrying to the heresiologists; then, between the wars, Hans Jonas presented in *The Gnostic Religion* an interpretation "that for the first time made sense of it as a possible way to understand existence." The eminent theologian Rudolph Bultmann reinterpreted the construction of the NEW TESTAMENT in the light of the struggle between gnosticism and orthodoxy in the first centuries C.E. when Christianity was no more than a loose conglomeration of various sects—gnostic and otherwise. "Now the time has come," concluded Robinson, "for a concentrated effort, with the whole *Nag Hammadi in English* available, to rewrite the history of Gnosticism."

The thinking of Valentinus, the culmination of what Hans Jonas called the Syrian-Egyptian type of gnostic speculation, is, initially, forbiddingly complex. Yet once his use of symbols and allegories (unlike Marcion, but like the Jewish PHILO, he did not reject allegory) has been understood, so his system falls into place as one of the more profound and good-willed speculations about the mysteries of our human existence. It was, after all, potent enough to be responsible (to some extent) for the formation of the less profound

The Nag Hammadi Codices

opposition to it: orthodox Christianity, which has served well as a means of oppression for fourteen centuries of criminal history. Attempts to discuss the details of *The Valentinian Speculation* are, as Jonas himself wrote, out of place in all but very highly specialized works. Had it not been for the suppression of this system (there is no record of Valentinus, essentially a reformer, having advocated the cowardly and reprehensible destruction of the work of others) by orthodoxists, it would be regarded as a noble forerunner to that of the non-Christian PLOTINUS.

Valentinus's presentation of the cosmic drama involves the intertwining of two worlds: the Platonic one, of Ideas or Forms, and the material one. The first world he named the *Pleroma*, the second the *Kenoma*. Existence came about through an error of curiosity within, although not of, the godhead itself ("Oblivion did not come into existence close to the Father, although it came into existence because of him.") that is not identical to, but may fruitfully be compared with, the profundity of that suggested in the KABBALAH.

The God of ARISTOTLE was a Prime Mover in an uncreated, eternal universe (Aristotle needed to appeal to such an entity in order to explain motion); but Aristotle showed little true curiosity in, and no emotion about, creation. The supreme God of Valentinus is itself uncreated, eternal (outside time—"the moving image of eternity," wrote Plato in a passage known to Valentinus—and thus untainted by it), and ineffable. But the error that led to the eventual creation meant that the Pleroma had to be restored (compare the Kabbalistic *tikkun*). Salvation could only be achieved by acquaintance with God—and that is *gnosis*. When this special knowledge has been achieved or even partly achieved it is understood that Jesus, *Christos,* was produced—even before the creation of matter—in order to provide salvation. He enlightened the Aeons (higher beings) by bringing them the *gnosis* (really best translated as "insight" or "intuition"), the gist of which was, paradoxically, *the very unknowability of the Supreme Being.* (In Homeric thought the attempt to be like a god was called *hubris*—these ideas are connected.) "Since Oblivion [the originally lower world] did not know the father," states *The Gospel of Truth,* "therefore if they attain to a knowledge of the Father, Oblivion becomes at that very instant nonexistent. That, then, is the Gospel of Him whom they seek and which Jesus revealed to the Perfect."

The Jesus who came to earth and died was not, however, in Valentinian speculation, real—the Valentinians were therefore "guilty" of the *docetic* "heresy," which was utterly intolerable to those determined to force through a literal-minded orthodoxy, and who were blind to the powers of symbol and metaphor. All other kinds of thinking must be *suppressed* at all costs—and soon, with armies at their command, these authorities were able to carry out their wishes. Their own emotionally mean version of the Christ-myth, "well-attested," must—they believed, for the sake of the world—prevail.

It is important to note that, as a result of some complicated mythologizing, the true suffering in *The Valentinian Speculation* is not that of Christ so much as of Sophia, Wisdom—it is a *feminine* suffering. It was Wisdom herself who lapsed. It is here that true "feminists," men and women, should look. But that involves an examination of the whole complex Valentinian myth.

Were those scared Christian monks really so evil and heretical when they hid these words, again from *The Gospel of Truth,* in that jar some time in the late fifth century of our era? The gist of it, when the message has been unscrambled (as I have tried to do in this adaptation of the text for the modern age), is stated in the book as follows:

> Help those dead to reality who want to awaken, to wake up, feed those hungry for knowledge of truth, for you [those awakened by *gnosis*] are the intelligent ones. Do not return to the old chattering parts of yourself. Do not go back to your old vomit. You have destroyed evil in you—do not fall into it again. Do the will of God for you come from God.

Meditations

MARCUS AURELIUS

167 C.E.

The Roman emperor Marcus Aurelius was not an original expositor of Stoic philosophy, but he was one of the last and one of the clearest. Moreover, unlike his more subtle and philosophically qualified predecessors, he had an empire to rule and much national misfortune to contend with. It was during his reign (161–180 C.E.) that the celebrated Pax Romana collapsed and that "barbarians," men untainted with the vices of "civilization," began to knock at the door of the Roman Empire. These facts have made Marcus Aurelius the most impressive of all the Stoics: For here, after all, we have a man of action actually utilizing a philosophy—and not, initially, for the public view! Ironically, had Marcus Aurelius not been a Stoic, he might have been a more effective emperor. But the odds were against him in any case—a fact he fully appreciated.

The Stoic philosophy gets its name from the painted colonnade in Athens, the *Stoa poikile,* where the Stoics taught. For some two thousand years a "stoic" has been understood as one who accepts misfortune without complaint. Nor is this, for once, an inappropriate association. An important feature of the Stoic system was that everything will recur: The whole universe becomes fire and then repeats itself.

The philosophy was founded by Zeno of Citium (335–263 B.C.E.), whose writings are all lost. It was developed by Cleanthes (331–232) and Chrysippus (280–207), who organized it into a system; then later by Posidonius (135–50 C.E.), whose version of it, through the freed slave Epictetus (55–135), Marcus Aurelius expresses.

Stoicism has not been found to be a more consistent philosophy than any other; but it was a remarkably complete one, and its influence upon both Neoplatonism and Christianity, as well as upon countless individuals who became acquainted with the *Meditations,* was profound. Its essence is that to be virtuous, and thus wise, a person must live in conformity to nature. To understand nature the Stoics divided their philosophy into three parts: a *physics* to deal with the universe and its laws, a *logic* to learn to distinguish true from false statements, and an *ethics* derived from these two enquiries to apply to conduct. The first two parts are still technically influential, but, in a more general sense, it is the ethics which is relevant to our own times.

Stoicism is religious in spirit, but, unlike PLATO—who believed that only the Ideas were real—regards everything as material. The Stoics were the first thoroughgoing pantheists: God is the universe, the universe is God; the wise and virtuous man learns his place in the scheme. In each individual there is a soul, a divine spark, which comes from the universe—and which will be reabsorbed by it.

Posidonius worked out in detail a theory by which all the forces in the universe worked together; individual conduct, however icily cold it might seem, must be directed to an understanding of this. Man was above all a citizen of the world. The affinities between this view of existence and the philosophy of SPINOZA, or with Spinozism (since he has been so varyingly interpreted), are obvious. The Stoics, too, like Spinoza and others, evolved a "compatibilist theory." This is to say that they found ways of reconciling determinism (the notion that everything is predetermined) with free will— these complex arguments all depend, in fact, on how freedom is defined. In the case of the Stoics, whose ethics is their most important legacy, it amounts to the view that the wise man should be satisfied if he has done his sincere best without harming anyone else. Our actions may be predetermined, but we are still responsible for them.

The idea that the virtuous man is above misfortune, above poverty, above despair (in particular) has been found to be both sublime—a reflection of the serenity of God himself—and deeply repulsive. ADAM SMITH has been appropriately quoted as in common-sense support of the latter view: "By Nature the events which immediately affect that little department in which we ourselves have some little management . . . are the events which interest us the most, and which chiefly excite our desires and aversions, our hopes and fears, our joys and sorrows."

But the Stoic would have replied that this is neither inhuman nor heartless: This is the truth of things, and can only help men to create, by means of the divine spark within them, a social mirror of the universe as it really is. Moreover, the truly wise man is as rare as gold. Thus the Stoics recognized a class of people who, while not yet truly virtuous, were "making progress," and who possessed some insight into the true universal morality underlying the many false moralities that cause evil in the world.

Marcus Aurelius, of Spanish origins, attracted the attention of the Emperor Hadrian—a pedophile—when only a small child. At the age of eight he was thus made a priest in an ancient order. Hadrian referred to him as more truthful even than his own original name, which was Marcus Annius Verus [Truth]. The Emperor Antoninus, who succeeded Hadrian, adopted Marcus Aurelius as his son, and he succeeded him in 161, together with his other adopted son, whom he called Lucius Aurelius Verus. The latter, useless and lazy, was, by Marcus's own ill-advised wish, regarded as a kind of junior emperor, and supposedly trained to succeed him—fortunately he died in 169.

Marcus spent his entire reign fighting—at one point he had to sell the imperial jewels to raise cash—and toward the end faced a revolt by Avidius Cassius, whom (unusually in those times) he praised and attempted to accommodate (but Avidius was assassinated in any case). Faustina, Marcus's wife, may have been involved in this conspiracy, or may not; but, among the children she bore him was his successor Commodus, of whose total unfitness to rule he was well aware when he died in 180. As an emperor he was conservative and just (by Roman standards); but under him, for reasons still not fully understood, persecution of the Christians markedly increased. His obvious virtues still prove a great embarrassment to many modern Christians, as these find it hard to grant any kind of real virtues to one not himself officially of the faith. But, while upbraiding him for his cruelty to their own, the demonic Church Fathers—and betrayers of the man in whose name they seized power—soon absorbed and took over the virtues of Stoicism.

The Latin writings of Marcus Aurelius, letters to a teacher, Fronto, are dull. But the "Writings to Himself," later collected from notebooks in Greek, and called *Meditations,* are remarkable—and all the more so for having been private and unintended for an audience. Here are the living thoughts of a man with huge responsibilities. In that sense these *Meditations* are unique. Their value, a modern philosopher has justly written, is

> to show us what it would be for a man at the apex of human power to live honorably, deliberately, and sensitively in accordance with the world-view and moral principles of Stoicism: that the All is one great natural system having order and excellence as a whole; that man should seek to understand this order, should accept what is inevitable for himself, and should act with understanding and integrity toward others.

The book itself, for the arrangement of which the author was not responsible, is entirely unsystematic except for the least important of its twelve books, the first, which simply acknowledges those to whom he is grateful.

The rest consists of always readable and often irrefutable reflections. It is frequently almost astonishing to recall that Marcus Aurelius, while by no means perfect, did try to put many of his precepts into practice. He was certainly an exception to the general run of Roman emperors, and he is thus remembered. At his death, true, he was planning further European acquisitions for the empire, and his wisdom, apparently, did not discern that in any great things lie the seeds of its decay; but even in this he can be defended—papers can hardly be found on the emperor which betray his indifference to his empire!

A few of the more famous quotations verge on the trite, if not in their context: "If it is wrong, do not do it; if it is not true, do not say it." Others do not, and of these many recollect Buddhist doctrine. For example: "Such as are your habitual thoughts, so will be your character"; "The best kind of revenge is, not to be like unto them."

The work is not at all insincere or cliché-ridden, and it is convincing almost throughout. Although Marcus was not an original philosopher, he certainly understood, absorbed, and believed what he was taught. One suspects that he has been called overaustere or even cold because his doctrine provides little comfort. Yet surely his notion, in part carried out, that we must treat our fellows with unselfishness and decency offers some comfort at the end of a century of "progress." Of those whose manifestations we cannot abide, he writes:

> Be not angry neither with him whose breath, neither with him whose armholes, are offensive. What can he do? Such is his breath naturally, and such are his armholes; and from such, such an effect, and such a smell must of necessity proceed. "O but the man [sayest thou] hath understanding in him, and might of himself know, that he by standing near, cannot choose but offend!" And thou also (God bless thee!) hast understanding. Let thy reasonable

faculty, work upon his reasonable faculty; show him his fault, admonish him. If he hearken unto thee, thou hast cured him, and there will be no more occasion of anger.

Above all, though, Marcus Aurelius suggested that people should cast all "opinion" ("point of view") from themselves:

> Cast away from thee opinion, and thou art safe. And what is it that hinders thee from casting of it away? When thou art grieved at anything, hast thou forgotten that all things happen according to the nature of the universe; and that him only it concerns, who is in fault; and moreover, that what is now done, is that which from ever hath been done in the world, and will ever be done, and is now done everywhere. . . .

The distance between the point of view expressed here to the one expressed in the Dhammapada is not far. Yet within a few years the West was engulfed in superstition or in the savagery of the "Christian" conquest.

23

Outlines of Pyrrhonism

SEXTUS EMPIRICUS

c. 150–210 C.E.

The writings of Sextus Empiricus—a Greek physician and philosopher whose birthplace is unknown but who probably lived for a time in both Rome and Alexandria—are of prime value, and crucial influence, just because of his lack of interest in philosophical originality. Sextus's name puts him among the "empirical" school of doctors; nothing more is known of him. His (usually) prolix summaries of invaluable material became suddenly influential when they were republished in Latin translations in 1569, about a quarter of a century before the birth of DESCARTES, and ready for MONTAIGNE to read them. His most famous metaphor reminds us that he was a practicing doctor, the "trickster reason," he wrote, in purging the mind, is itself vomited up with whatever it has purged. Not only was Montaigne familiar with his material; much later, DAVID HUME, to whose skeptical mind he greatly appealed.

Sextus provides us with the fullest account of the philosophy of skepticism, not only in his volumes devoted to Pyrrho of Elia or Elis (365–275 B.C.E.), *Outlines of Pyrrhonism,* but also in his salutarily entitled *Against the Professors* (*Adversus Mathematicos*), in eleven books, of which Books VII–XI, against dogmatism in the sciences, are of particular importance. Greek skepticism effectively begins with Pyrrho. Pyrrho is of greater importance than Sextus, and so was Pierre Bayle (see below) but skepticism would not have reached Europe when it did had it not been for Sextus.

Only through Sextus did the sixteenth century obtain a thorough codification of Greek skepticism. It is Pyrrho whose philosophy Sextus is most concerned to defend—and to recommend. Pyrrho wrote nothing, and only a few fragments written by his disciple Timon of Philius survive. His critics created a portrait of him as one who had to be helped from falling over precipices and from all the other hazards of being a skeptic; but that, while comic, was just a caricature as irresponsible as it was irresistible. Pyrrho began as a painter; then he went to India in the wake of Alexander the Great. There, from "magi," he is supposed by legend to have picked up his ideas. This is likely, since it is not hard—as will be seen—to equate his goal, which he regarded not so much as a means to philosophy but as a way of life, with those of the Indian religions, particularly Buddhism. That makes more sense of the man than the apocryphal stories. He settled back in his hometown and was so admired that he was made high priest—and a decree was passed exempting philosophers from tax. (Surely his greatest achievement—how skeptical was he about that?) A statue of him was put up after his death.

Philosophically, and enormously influentially ever after, Pyrrho was the first (although he owed much to Socrates' example and practice, and Bertrand Russell, who believed that Socrates' profession to know nothing might not have been ironic "but could be taken seriously," wrote that "there was not much that was new in his doctrine"—alluding, unfairly, to ideas held by the Sophists) to hold that no positive knowledge is possible, and that the only reasonable procedure therefore is to suspend judgment upon all matters. Thus the true skeptic must be careful to say, not "The sun will rise tomorrow," but "The sun has seemed to rise on all the days of my life so far as I am aware, and it therefore may do so tomorrow." This may seem frivolous, but not only does it aptly sum up an oft encountered "cautious" approach to life, but also gives the kernel of a very important starting point in philosophy. Some later skeptics were more polemical in their attitudes and wished to undermine dogmatists of both the Epicurean and the Stoic schools (but EPICURUS himself admired Pyrrho while not agreeing with him).

Pyrrho's main purpose may well be called psychological, since it was in the interests of achieving a state called *ataraxia,* tranquillity of mind: imperturbability, no striving for what Keats called "irritable reaching after fact and reason," no anxiety. Pyrrho was not in fact frivolous in recommending a skeptical attitude. He sensibly confined his attention to the world beyond immediate experience and to the annoyances (and worse) that too much attention

Pierre Bayle, chief inheritor
of ancient skepticism

to it may cause. It is a little ironic that *ataraxia,* also the goal of both the Stoics and the Epicureans (but to be reached in different ways), was transformed, in the form of *abulia* into a serious disease from which the Spanish accused themselves (with great bitterness) of suffering. But that in itself points to what is at least a practical difficulty: when do tranquillity and apathy turn into complacency—and the kind of lack of care that would make a doctor (Sextus, for example) into a charlatan? But passive conformity accompanied by inner suspension of judgment in all matters outside commonsense experience was recommended by Pyrrho.

There is not much that can be done with skepticism except argue about its proper extent, although more can be done with it than with pure solipsism, the view that only oneself exists (there is a "softer" version, again without much potential, that entails taking only one's own experience as certain—a danger that Descartes almost fell into), which is its most extreme form. Discussion of this fundamental difficulty alone would hardly have provided philosophers with an occupation, let alone a salary, for over four hundred years. Therefore, one might say, how can its main historian Sextus Empiricus be regarded as highly influential?

That republication of his works in mid-sixteenth century was absolutely crucial—at just the time when the Christian religion and all the philosophies which took it for granted were falling into such doubt that even Christians or professed Christians were having to reinvent it—because it proved to be the starting-off-point for Descartes (who had to refute it by means of a "natural light" in the mind), for ERASMUS in his refutation of LUTHER, and, most important of all, for David Hume, who may at least fairly be claimed as the most consistent Pyrrhonist of all time. Could he have been that without Sextus? True, Hume depended on the *Historical and Critical Dictionary*—it has long been evident that this was the primary source of his skepticism—the masterpiece of the French philosophical commentator Pierre Bayle (1647–1706), the man who has been persecuted as a Calvinist *and* as a Roman Catholic, and who is quoted by the historian EDWARD GIBBON as having said, "I am most truly a Protestant; for I protest indifferently against all systems and sects." Bayle did influence people more crucially (e.g., Hume), despite Montaigne, than did Sextus—but Bayle, who held the chair of philosophy at the University of Sedan (1675–1681) until it was itself suppressed, had himself obtained his knowledge of Pyrrho and his various descendants from Sextus, who thus did the world, and philosophy, a great service. Sextus is, as Russell wrote, "the only Skeptic philosopher of antiquity whose works survive."

Sextus gave accounts of the other skeptics, including the most brilliant of the later ones, Carneades (214–129 B.C.E.), the founder of the Third Academy in Athens, yet another who wrote nothing down, but whose ideas were transmitted by others. Carneades made two impressive speeches, both for and against "just behavior," in 155 B.C.E.—and gained the later grateful admiration of Cicero (and, hopefully, ourselves) for demonstrating so eloquently that there are two sides to any question. Carneades is most important, however, for his theory of probability—ancient skepticism's most positive contribution to philosophy. All this is from Sextus, who enabled Bayle to write many of the articles in his witty and priceless dictionary (published in Holland in 1696), as well as ones on Adam, Eve, Manicheans, various popes, Cain, Abel, HOBBES, SPINOZA (by whom he could not but be influenced—and who, knowing him, has not?) EUCLID, KEPLER, and many others, including obscure libertines.

So, although Pyrrho, Carneades, Montaigne, Bayle (an honorable miss in this context), and many others in the history of skepticism are much more important thinkers than Sextus, he gave an opportunity that no one else did, and he thus changed the course of European thought.

24

Enneads

PLOTINUS

3rd century C.E.

Plotinus, the hugely influential mystic who would neither have liked nor used the word *mystic,* was the greatest of all the Platonists. In the Middle Ages it was mainly through his writings that people got to know about the philosopher PLATO, the master who, for Plotinus, could never be wrong. In the *Enneads* Plotinus combined the ideas of Plato with those of Greek religion and of ARISTOTLE to form the philosophy now known as Neoplatonism (at the time it was called Platonism). This is by no means even now a dead philosophy, and Plotinus's ideas are eminently capable of further development.

Not much is known about Plotinus himself. Even his race is in question, although most believe him to have been, despite his Latin name, of a Greek family. He was, at least according to an unreliable fourth-century writer called Eunapius, born in Lycopolis in upper Egypt in about 205 C.E. and studied in Alexandria under the Pythagorean teacher Ammonius Saccus, a shadowy figure who also taught Tertullian and the Christian theologian Origen—who enraged his fellow Christians by holding the uncharitable notion, peculiarly horrible to the tolerant AUGUSTINE, that *all might be saved,* and who also emasculated himself ("if God had wanted eunuchs," snarled Tertullian, "would he not have made them?") Plotinus himself, possibly at first a gnostic, never mentioned Christianity—although no pagan ever influenced Christianity more; but eventually he violently attacked the gnostics for both their pessimism and their hatred of matter. However, in other respects his own teaching very closely resembled that of the gnostics, and he himself, just like Plato, did not really value matter and regarded the form of it below the moon as deficient and evil (that above the moon was still celestial)—but he also saw it, somewhat paradoxically, as beautiful in its arrangement—it was not to be degraded, in any case, *because* it came forth from the *One.*

Plotinus wanted to travel in search of new, Eastern ideas—unlike the Christians, he fell into the error of having an open mind—and in 242 he joined the military expedition of the Emperor Gordian III against the Persians. But he did not get to Persia: Gordian was assassinated in Mesopotamia in 244, and so in that year Plotinus moved to Rome, where he soon became famous as an intellectual leader and teacher—and gained a useful ally in the philosophical emperor, Gallenius. His attempt to establish a Platonic community foundered, and he died in 270 after a painful illness (probably leprosy) which he bore with great fortitude. He was widely known, says his Greek disciple Porphyry (c. 232–305), who wrote his biography (said to be an unusually accurate one for its time), as a kind man in a practical sense (nor did he go on about executioners, just wars and heresies).

In about 301 Porphyry rearranged all Plotinus's lectures into six books of nine sections each (*ennea* is the Greek word for nine). The arrangement is often criticized as an odd and fanciful one, but it is the form in which the writings have come down to us; we cannot be sure that Plotinus himself did not recommend it. At one point in the Middle Ages a book called *The Theology of Aristotle,* really a series of extracts from the *Enneads,* was read by— and deeply influenced—a Spaniard called Moses de Leon, the author of the Zohar, the chief text of the KABBALAH.

The thought of Plotinus is difficult, initially, to understand. He was the leading member of a movement that fought for intellectual paganism on two fronts: against the dogmatic Christians on the one hand, and against the dualistic element in gnosticism on the other. It is hard for us, in a post-Christian era in which we are free to think for ourselves, to see how objectionable Neoplatonism seemed to the Christians. Certainly it was a great embarrassment to them; they were, after all, in considerable debt to it. As we shall see, the good Augustine—sensual, reluctantly cruel—could rejoice at the destruction of pagan temples and approve of the execution of pagans (as he all-knowingly wrote in *The City of God,* there "are some whose killing God orders": like B. F. SKINNER, Augustine needs to be in charge of his own Utopia), even presumably ones of the Neoplatonic variety to whom he owed so much. But that is one means of expressing gratitude: There's no good turn, as the Irish say, that does not deserve punishment. In fact Augustine, who found him difficult and loved him as he loved Plato, called Plotinus "the great Platonist," and kept his wrath for Porphyry who, unlike his master, was aggressively anti-Christian in his own writings: Porphyry was, pronounced Augustine, subject to "envious powers" and was wrong in failing to accept Christ as the principle. In fact Porphyry was skeptical of all the popular religions, and his treatise in fifteen books *Against the Christians* was effective enough to be burned (448); but he greatly admired Christ, even while believing him not to have been divine. His views on these subjects almost certainly coincided with those of Plotinus, who—after all—did trust him enough to make him his executor. That we do not have Porphyry's exposure of the inconsistencies in the Gospels is a loss to scholarship, and shows that his methods and accuracy greatly worried the Church Fathers, who acted in the only manner (learned, presumably, from their own equally unwise persecutors) that institutional Christians have ever been able to understand. Porphyry's chief value, though, is his putting of what is often obscure in Plotinus into a more lucid and readily understandable form. (Some have asserted that at one time Porphyry was himself, for a time, a Christian; perhaps his dislike of the Church was a form of self-hatred.)

Plotinus saw the universe as in itself a living thing. Like the Kabbalists after him, he thought of it in terms of a series of *emanations* from the One God, the First Principle—sometimes called the Absolute. If we look at the illustration of the Kabbalistic *Sefiroth* then, although (it must be noted) this is *not* identical to Plotinus's Absolute, the concept is of the same type. This Absolute, for Plotinus, is beyond human understanding, and cannot be thought of in such merely human terms as space, time, or number. Nor—while it would strain things much too far to refer to it as feminine—is it in any way masculine, even though he does tend to use the masculine form of *One* or *Good.* For Augustine, it may be well noted, God was more resolutely *male:* an image made by Augustine into something as savagely perfect as it needed to be, to defend him from his own natural doubts, from his skepticism, and from his puritanical fear and hatred of what he most loved doing and made him feel most guilty: indulging in sexual activity. For Augustine stopping sexual activity meant finding God. Like Paul before him, he hardly considered that love might be found within sexual activity—women Augustine saw in the image of his own mother: only wrongly ravishable.

Plotinus's Absolute or One Principle is external to all reality. Reality exists simply by virtue of the power and energy the Absolute emits. When we compare his thinking to Buddhism the doubts about its influence on him may well seem rather petifoggingly academic and foolish. It would be impressive indeed if he had he reached his conclusions in ignorance of it! We shall meet something very like it in the cosmology of GURDJIEFF, who agrees with Plotinus that evil is really owing to a gradually increasing density—an increasing coarseness, an increasing *lack of quality*—of matter as it proceeds downward from the Absolute or *One* or *Good*.

Here, though, in Western terms, we have a God who seems to be imperfect inasmuch as he is not entirely in control of creation, even a God (it has been suggested) who sees himself mirrored in the murk of creation, and cannot but love what it sees.

This is not such a God as that of the Jews, or of Augustine after he had concluded that he could not transform his lust into love (that he gave up trying to do this is the true key to his desperate theology): This God is not called God and does not know when every sparrow falls or how many hairs are on each person's head—and, perhaps significantly, it does not command that those who deny it be condemned, tortured, or murdered for "heresy." It could be regarded as tragic, for the world, that Augustine and a few other zealous men so disingenuously absorbed, into their Christianity, just what was useful to them in Neoplatonic thinking—and thus, having appropriated it, brutally cut off its disturbing mercy. Can one seriously imagine Neoplatonists torturing and burning people? No doubt their distance from such self-confidence was what helped them to fail: By all means, the Christians reasoned, steal their wisdom—but should such pagans really be allowed to exist? And since Porphyry had such regard for Christ, probably Plotinus did, too: Perhaps he believed, as did his executor, that the Apostles had poisoned Christ's message—and then released it in a distorting stream. . . . That is what the Jesus Christ of George Moore's novel *The Brook Kerith* tells Paul, long after he has survived the cross.

From Plotinus's *Good* streams forth an ever-multiplying series of entities. Just as in the very influential philosophy of the great Jewish Frenchman Henri Bergson (1859–1941), there are two movements in the universe: the one is downward from the Absolute, but the other is upward and toward it, aspiring to it. Plotinus held, with the Stoics—and perhaps with NIETZSCHE—that history exactly repeats itself, in every minute detail, after very long periods. He saw life as being present in everything, including what most of us think of as inanimate objects. The downward movement, "Nature," is not "bad"—it is simply devoid of the better qualities.

Plotinus, too, did acknowledge that the miraculous existed; but he had little use for it because he felt that human beings must attain union with the One (present in all of us, along with every one of the hierarchies of being) by their own efforts. For Plotinus human beings choose at what level they wish to live, but then they take the consequences, which may involve being reborn at a lower level (Plotinus drew this from pre-Socratic philosophers). Some souls are actually dead. He himself claimed (Porphyry tells us), but in no way immodestly, to have occasionally attained union with the One—but this union was not lasting, nor does he ever suggest that the achievement of such a union is anything but an immensely difficult process.

It is right to regard Plotinus as an essentially intellectual mystic, just as it is right to ascribe to Augustine qualities both intellectual and then—after his lusts caused him to sell out—fiercely anti-intellectual. But Plotinus was not excessively intellectual: There are passages of great beauty in the *Enneads,* and we may see that their author was a man quite as troubled by the erotic as was Augustine. Some say that for Plotinus spiritual ecstasy—such that for the soul, as he wrote, "all things are transparent, and there is nothing dark and impenetrable"—did involve asceticism as well as a striving for moral purity. Yet this may be a misreading. He allowed that low levels of understanding (what else have we got?) could offer what he called appropriate instantiations of higher ones—and may therefore not have excluded sexual experiences. For him the One, of course, came first. Then came Intellect. Only then came Soul. But the Intellect of Plotinus is not just rationalistic. It could be called *Understanding*—Understanding which contains Love without sentimentalizing it, and incorporates gratitude for existence. Much is difficult in Plotinus; but nothing jars and jangles, there are no executioners or self-emasculations or false arguments; he is in quest of an exquisite and modest sweetness, a decency in the profoundest sense of that word. The Fathers plundered it, often praised it; they were not going to allow it to persist unhindered.

25

Confessions

AUGUSTINE OF HIPPO

c. 400 C.E.

After Jesus Christ and the Apostles, no human being influenced the course of Christianity, and therefore of an unhappy world, more than Augustine of Hippo. Although he lived for only seventy-five years, his mighty presence managed to bridge the gap between pagan Rome and the Middle Ages. Whether we feel at ease with him or otherwise, he compels a response. His abilities and his insights were perhaps, originally, as full as almost any man's have been; few can read the *Confessions* and remain unaffected by their persuasive candor and self-knowledge. Augustine lived between two poles: those of narcissism and God. *"Noverim te, noverim me"* he wrote: "I want to know you [God], I want to know myself!"

But is his actual legacy, his solution to the problems set to sensitive people by their very existence, really as rich and fruitful as the theologians tell us? Or was he, together with his mother, the insistent Christian Monica, a misguided puritan who, despite himself, chose the dogma of universal damnation (but for the grace of God) in favor of a ripe, kindly, but less certain wisdom? And did he not end up by equating sensuality, the expression of sexuality, with what we should call simple narcissism? Could he have known what real love is, or of the possibility of the physical expression of it? The language modern Christians use when they write of him tends to resemble that of Edward Pusey in his Victorian version of the *Confessions:* gushing, false, resting on many unexplained assumptions.

Is Augustine's "God" no more than the hysterical projection of a passionately intelligent man who has finally given up on making sense of his life? What should he mean to those who cannot be orthodox Christians—those who mistrust the Christian *Church* because of its history of smug exclusiveness, its patronizing intolerance, its cruelty, its violence, its too often worldly rejection of the teachings of its founder, its hatred and envy of mysticism, its pretence that its arguments are reasonable when they are not even plausible?

Augustine, for whom God's absolute goodness and omniscience were *the* great inescapable facts, came to believe that all human beings were eternally damned but for his grace. We have, in trying to decide upon the real worth of Augustine's decisive final Christian phase, to recognize that the alarming nature of his doctrine is in itself no argument against its possible truth. He did not seek to make matters easy—and he was a bit too wise to want to change the face of the world. However, that he might have reached his doctrine for a personal—indeed, for a "psychological"—rather than for a philosophical reason is at least relevant: He did after all present his belief as philosophically justified, and much of his voluminous writing is given up to the condemnation of "heresy" or, if we dare to look at it otherwise, the frequently good-willed beliefs of others. Was he just a gifted bully who sold out when his sense of personal guilt became too much for him? Has he not had a far too adulatory press? Is his perfect virtue not too much taken for granted?

If we are convinced that it was only a "conspiracy of circumstances" that led to the rise of Christianity in the West—an accident—then, even if we do acknowledge some kind of authority in Christ, we are not Christians in an institutional sense. We might even in that case think that it is in the very nature of all institutions to betray their founders. "If you believe in God, keep away from priests" is, after all, a widespread saying.

But if we believe that Christianity "succeeded" because God revealed that all other religions were false and misguided, we are Christians in every sense and we must decide which of the thousand or more contemporary Christian churches are "true," and swiftly join it—or, one must suppose, join the "ecumenical" bureaucracy. It has been a source of great dismay to everyone that the history of Christianity has been so like the history of everything else, and that such even as the mystics Meister Eckhardt and Jacob Boehme were in continuous trouble with the conformist clerks of their time—the first condemned as a heretic and the second forced for a time to stop writing altogether. The Christian bureaucrat—petty, jealous, mean-minded, obstructive, cruel, at very best insensitive—has an uncanny resemblance to all other joyless officials. It seems almost as if the light of truth has done no more for him than the outer darkness has done for those, like PLATO, not born into the right circumstances, before the Common Era, or for the heathenish Hindu or mere popeless fuzzy-wuzzy with his disgusting convictions.

In the first centuries after Christ, when the Church was busy establishing itself, there were two sorts of Christian leadership. The first and by far the more common sort, like Tertullian and Jerome (himself intellectually gifted), presented Christianity as a matter of the heart. The excitable Tertullian (accidentally anticipating KIERKEGAARD), although later himself to become a heretic of the overenthusiastic sect of Montanus—who threatened to put the cat among the pigeons by reverting to Christ's own teaching that the end of the world *was* after all at hand—pronounced that orthodoxy, the decisions of various councils, must be accepted just because they were "ridiculous." The appeal of this kind of early Christianity has been summed up as "God has revealed himself and so now it is not necessary, it is even *wrong*, for *you* to think."

That argument was of no intellectual value whatever; but it was badly needed then because the vast majority of those who were pouring—innocently enough—into a Christian Church ripening itself for secular power would not have understood intellectual persuasion anyway.

The other sort of Christian, of whom Augustine is the prime exemplar, were until his day more obscure figures—indeed, ironically and possibly even significantly, these "intellectuals" were not Christians at all, but Neoplatonists. Augustine came to Christianity not through any Church Fathers but through the "heretical" prophet Mani and the Neoplatonists PLOTINUS and his anti-Christian follower Porphyry.

Since he probably knew little more than the Greek alphabet—he did not like Greek—it is unclear how Augustine gained his knowledge of these thinkers; but he mentions and quotes them, and it is universally agreed that he was very well acquainted with what they believed. Although himself an intellectual, he ended as a vehement antiintellectual. He had done the thinking for everyone else. They now need not do it for themselves.

He was born at Tagaste, a smallish town, now Souk Ahras in Algeria on the border with Tunisia, the son of a pagan father and a Christian mother, Monica. His father, Patricius, a municipal official, was converted on his deathbed—but probably had no option. Augustine, whose language was Latin, was brought up as a Christian (by then the religion of Roman Africa) but, when he started to study law at the University of Carthage, he cast it aside. He had already taken a mistress (he never divulged her name), and he lived with her for fifteen years and had a son by her. His reading of the now lost *Hortensius* of the Roman lawyer and politician Marcus Tullius Cicero (106–43 B.C.E.) not only gave him his literary style but turned him into a serious philosophical inquirer. When young he was, essentially, intensely curious. Not long afterward he became a Manichean, an episode he treats in lurid detail in the *Confessions*.

St. Augustine by Gozzoli

Modern commentators refer to the gnostic Manes as both philosophically contemptible and wicked, and they do so largely in Augustine's voice— although he himself stopped short of the unscrupulous Christian habit of piously and falsely impugning Manichean morality.

The teaching of Manes, while certainly as alarming as Augustine's in due time became, was in fact, whether mistaken or not, profound; but it has always been hard to understand because almost all accounts of it have been written by its enemies. It was the very highly systematized outcome of several apparently different strands of thinking and belief. These we need to trace, for it was above all Augustine's anxiety about dualism that rushed him, at thirty-two, into his mother's camp.

First, there was the dualism of Zoroaster (see the AVESTA): From the beginning of time two gods, one evil, one good, have fought it out, and still are fighting it out—only at the end of time are we promised that the good will triumph. Later there is the philosophical dualism of Plato. For Plato eternal spiritual ideas have only ephemeral material counterparts; in the *Laws* there is, if controversially, even a hint of an inferior soul (or souls) which causes (or cause) "disorderly motion" (the source of evil). This is what would now be called entropy: Victorians who assumed that the universe was a closed system called it "the heat death of the universe." In fact there is no such guarantee.

Then in Buddhism (Manes himself turned to India when expelled from Persia by jealous neo-Zoroastrian priests) there is a parallel type of dualism between *Being* and *Appearance* (or *Becoming*). There were also the gnosticisms that preceded Manes (216–77 C.E.) himself, in which, as in the system of Valentinus (see THE GOSPEL OF TRUTH), matter was finally and emphatically identified as *evil*—just as it was in certain Orphic teachings which influenced Valentinus and his fellow speculators.

Manes, born into a Persian gnostic baptizing sect whose teachings he elaborated and refined, founded his own group at the age of twenty-four after receiving instructions from his Divine Twin and "companion." He was as sincere as Augustine in his own teaching that a Kingdom of Darkness coexists, eternally, with a Kingdom of Light. This is peculiar to the Manichean expression of gnosticism, since in others—and in the KABBALAH—a process of declination is traced in the godhead itself. Matter in these systems is a kind of flaw or accident. In the system of Manes the Buddha and Jesus Christ are redeemers; he himself claimed to be another. Publication of what fragments of his own writings (some discovered in this century) have survived is even now incomplete. His system is immensely complicated, almost mathematical in its exactitude, and would take much explication here (which it has not in any case yet had); but, brought to its essence, it consists of means by which the dispersed light (good) in the world (it is trapped in the brains of human beings as in every other living thing) may be tended and rescued.

The Manichean communities, like those of their medieval successors the Cathar, were divided into two: the elect or perfect, and the more numerous "hearers" who have not yet reached the higher level. There were ten commandments: monogamy, the duty to care for the elect, and renunciation of the following—killing of animals, fornication, lying, hypocrisy, doubt, idolatry, theft, and the practice of magic. Augustine—once a hearer—speaks in the *Confessions* of the light of God in a fig being released by going through the belly of an elected one.

Augustine did not leave this sect for nine years, although he had doubts about it for the last few of those. Perhaps disingenuously, he accepted an appointment in Rome as head of a school of rhetoric that a pagan had arranged for him. Disgusted with his students, who tried to cheat him, he went to Milan and became a skeptic—in other words, he temporarily took refuge in the belief that there was no sure way to truth. Then, in a Milanese garden, he found himself on his knees before a text of Paul the Apostle that contained the phrase "make no provision for the flesh."

The fact is that Augustine had never been at ease with the sexual pleasure he so valued. He was a puritan who could not wholeheartedly enjoy bodily pleasure. He found it "distracting." So far, so good. Many have been or are in a similar fix. Now influenced by Bishop Ambrose of Milan, he heard an unlikely but modish tale of how two bureaucrats had become monks upon reading a life of Saint Antony (famously tempted by the Devil in the desert). Augustine was baptized in 385, and became bishop of Hippo in 389. The rest of his life was spent in the battle against heresy—against the Manicheans and then against the Donatists, who believed that the efficacy of the sacraments depended upon the worthiness of the priest, and finally against Pelagianism, which believed that human beings could be good without the grace of God. This latter, the grace of God, became a sort of blunt instrument in the hands of this saint.

He wrote the *Confessions* between 397 and 401, and this is undoubtedly his most widely read book. His polemic and fiercely dogmatic work, of which there is a vast amount extant (he claimed in 427 that he had written ninety-three works of literature and two hundred thirty-two books), are not much read except by Christian theologians. He was a master rhetorician even in these, however, and, because he was so convinced—or just possibly because he was not—he did not hesitate to employ every trick of his trade. His other great, and still much read, work is the huge *The City of God* (written in installments between 413 and 426). This, upon which Church policy in the Middle Ages was based, was originally undertaken to answer the charge—made after Alaric sacked Rome in 410—that Christianity had been responsible for the empire's decline. It is an eloquent attack on paganism, although, because its author had himself come to Christianity through paganism, it allows the latter some virtues.

Augustine is the key figure in the transition from pagan to Christian philosophy, but is nonetheless more a theologian than a philosopher proper because his philosophy is always the handmaiden of his theology. Everyone can find something that is psychologically true in him, particularly in the *Confessions*. But he prepared the way for Calvinism, since he argued that election (to heaven) is by God's grace and therefore predestined; it was left to CALVIN (whose theology is peculiarly weak) to invent eternal and arbitrary hellfire.

We cannot judge Augustine by modern standards, even if his times were, in some ways, quite like ours. But his prophecy (in *The City of God* in particular) of a viable and a Christian world has not come true: We have entered what is now, quite undoubtedly, a post-Christian era. Christian pretensions, if not Christ himself, are dead. The churches have failed and now consist of clubs for liberals, homosexuals—and other less wholesome groups. History is written by the victorious for their own purposes. But the Christ of that institution called the Christian Church, often creeping, often cruel, always sure of itself and its holiness, is now dead. After the Apostles Augustine is the prime apologist of that Church or those churches. History may now be more truthfully and less neurotically written.

Admirable and insightful though Augustine is, and always to be valued, he could be said not, ultimately, to have been on the humane side: The perfection of *his* God too often came first. He celebrated, even gloated over, the execution of those who indulged in pagan practices, and he absolved executioners and soldiers who fought in the cause he thought right. Clearly he thought sexual desire under any circumstances was a part of original sin, and in this did not perhaps solve the problem of sex any better than he solved the problem of evil. Intolerance, it is true, must have bridled at having so delicate a man on its side. But on its side he firmly was.

26

Decorative page from a copy of The Koran (1313 C.E.)

The Koran

7th century C.E.

Even before the Koran much—if not the essential part—of the Islamic religion, in common with all the others, was already in place. But Islam (in Arabic, "submission to God") differs from all other religions inasmuch as it is much more than just a religion in the usual Western sense. It is "a total way of life," a surrender to the Will of God as revealed to the Prophet. The Prophet, though, is a human being with fully admitted faults who did not claim divine powers: Any worship of him is a serious heresy, but one that has proved hard to resist, simply on the grounds that an ordinary human being could hardly be expected to bear so heavy a weight of revelation.

The adherents of this religion are called *Muslims* (Arabic *Muslimun*), believers. Our distinction between "religious" and "secular" is unknown—inconceivable—in Islam, a way of life, a type of civilization, rapidly spread by the sensational seventh- and eighth-century Arab conquests of North Africa, western and central Asia, Sind, and Spain (whence Islam was ultimately ejected). In later centuries it spread farther: to southern Russia, India, Asia Minor, then to the Balkans (hence the current problems in Bosnia)—and to Indonesia and China.

Its prime source and authority is the Koran, in Arabic *al-qu-ran*, "the recitation." This recitation of the Word of God was given to Mohammed by, according to Muslim tradition, an archangel of mercy with a long Jewish—and before that Zoroastrian—history, but one now usually understood as Christian: Gabriel, in Hebrew "Man of God," who in the New Testament foretold the birth of John the Baptist, and also announced the miraculous conception of Jesus to his mother.

Angels, it should be explained, of whom there are innumerable multitudes, are mediators between God (a vision of whose magnificence in Heaven they perpetually enjoy) and human beings; the great monotheisms can hardly do without them, since they keep their worshippers happy. Lucifer himself, of course, had once been an angel. Angels are beings not destined to have a body. AQUINAS put it thus: They are immaterial and cannot be in a place, but they can act on a place if they wish to be at it. Discussion of angels, *angelology*, by the schoolmen philosophers is often interesting (for example, in the famous conundrum about how many angels can dance on the head of a pin something less religious than interestingly philosophical is being discussed), just as are the angels in the twentieth-century poetry of the German Rainer Maria Rilke; ultimately, though, such discussion became overintellectual and therefore sterile. Protestants have kept fairly quiet about angels, and there are some who regard excessive attention to them as tending to the idolatrous. Anyhow, owing to the will of the Archangel Gabriel—who also appeared to Mohammed immediately before he died—there are something like four hundred million Muslims (probably about equal to the number of Hindus). The Jewish and the Christian faiths were both taken by Muslims to have failed.

Mohammed (often now spelled Muhammed) was born in about 570 C.E., in Mecca. The sources for his biography include oral records of those who knew him, but they did not reach written form until the eighth century. He was of the Quraysh tribe. Mecca was already a center for both religious pilgrimage and commerce—it was on the busy caravan route, which Mohammed came to know well, between southern Arabia and the Mediterranean countries. Orphaned at an early age, he was brought up successively by his grandfather and an uncle, Abu Talib. At the age of twenty-five he made a financially advantageous marriage to a widow, Khadija, older than himself, by whom he had three daughters. He was successfully engaged in the caravan trade when, in his late thirties, he began to develop contemplative habits and to experience visions. At forty he announced in the streets of Mecca that he had been called upon to proclaim the worship of the single God (Allah), against the many gods worshipped by his fellow-citizens and by most Arabs.

Any suggestion that the tradesmen and worshippers at Mecca's shrine, the Kabah, were idolaters was alarming news to the leading families of the city, simply on economic grounds: They expelled Mohammed and his clan. Over the next decade he gained the support of two leading citizens, Abu Bakr and Umar, who after his death became his successors and the launchers of the military expeditions that expanded the new religion.

In 622 Mohammed and his followers made the celebrated Hegira, "Emigration," *hijira,* to Yathrib (later Medina), a mixed settlement of Jews and Arabs which had invited him. This marks the first year of the Islamic calendar. He then became militant: He organized the community into a political unit, expelled the Jews (who opposed him), and harassed the caravans and Mecca itself. In 624, by maintaining a unified command and by better tactics, he won the Battle of Badr against a numerically superior force of Meccan merchants.

In 630 Mecca peacefully surrendered. It was purged of its polytheism, the Kabah was made into a Muslim shrine, and it rapidly became the center of the new religion. In 632 Mohammed died, and Abu Bakr was elected as his successor, the *caliph*. He died two years later, and was succeeded by Umar, who was in turn succeeded by Uthman.

It was the very military success of Islam, together with commercial rivalries, that led to civil war within thirty years of Mohammed's death. This was won by a faction in Damascus, who inaugurated a new dynasty of caliphs. One group of Arabs, the largest, putting the survival of the community first, recognized this new dynasty. These are the *Sunis* or followers of *Suni* (practice). The *Shiite* ("partisans of Ali"), however, held that a mistake had been made back in 632, and that Mohammed's cousin and son-in-law Ali, the fourth caliph, ought then to have become caliph. A third and much smaller group, *Kharijites* ("seceders"), rejected both the other factions. This last form of Islam survives as *Ibadi* in Oman, Zanzibar, and southern Algeria. The success of the Ayatollah Khomeni in the 1979 revolution against the Shah in Iran rekindled the Shiite faction.

Mohammed was undoubtedly a true mystic, a man who underwent periods of ecstasy in which his normal external personality was absent. Maxime Rodinson, the French Marxist who wrote such a just and engaging book on Mohammed, aptly quotes the tenth-century poet Husyan ibn Mansur al-Hallaj's description of this state:

I have become the one I love and he whom I love has become me.
We are two spirits, compounded in a single body;
When you saw me you saw him
And when you saw him you saw us,
And so to see me is to see him, and to see him is to see you.

Mohammed certainly felt himself to be separate from God except on these occasions, and not on any account to be confused with him. But he had a message to convey, and he seems to have done so with extraordinary sincerity and consistency.

At some unknown point of time he started to make a habit of retreating to a cave in the bare hill of Hira, a few miles from Mecca, where he engaged himself in contemplation. One morning the Angel of God said to him: "You are the messenger of God!" He was devastated with terror (in part, lest he be mistaken), and even thought of throwing himself off a crag. After a while the Angel said, "Recite!" He asked, "What shall I recite?" And there followed the first words of the Koran. This was in 610, during the already established feast of Ramadan, when Arabs fast by day.

Over the next twenty years Mohammed continued with his revelation, mainly an exhortation to lead a moral life. His words were written down on scraps of leather, bits of broken pots, camel bones, palm leaves; a little later Muslims made collections of all these, and in about 651 the third caliph, Uthman, issued an official version. It is generally agreed that the contents of the Koran as we know it date back to the Prophet—but not its arrangement. There is not yet a truly critical edition—nor is there likely to be—and the final recension was not made until 1924, in Cairo. (One other set of writings has almost—but by no means quite—the authority of the Koran. This is the Hadith (in Arabic "tradition"), which consists of various works and reports of the sayings and doings of the Prophet.)

The Koran, except for the first *sura* (chapter), is divided into one hundred and fourteen units, in (approximate) order of descending length. There are in our time arrangements of the Koran in chronological order; the best-known one now, in the Penguin edition, is not recommended by all scholars. The parts written earlier contain no statements that can properly be called monotheistic—indeed, at a certain point they seem to acknowledge three goddesses known in the Meccan area, but these, in the passages received at Medina, are transformed into angels; it is only at Medina that the Prophet's monotheism becomes really apparent, as his confidence in the authenticity of his source grows.

Literary quality is not a thing in itself, for at the level that matters it depends on factors outside mere literature; that of the Koran is high, and Mohammed was a gifted poet of a certain sort (the Koran is incantatory poetry, not prose). Any non-Muslim can appreciate the work as mystical poetry of a high order—even if parts seem to be repetitive—and as a reflection of the development of Islam during the Prophet's lifetime. He became, in fact, the mouthpiece of the currents of monotheistic thinking that were sweeping over the Arab world in his time. However, the "perfection" of the Koran as an act of faith has been challenged—from among Muslims themselves, some of whom in the Middle Ages wrote what they considered to be better books, one saying of his text, when challenged as to its quality: "Read it out in mosques for centuries and you will see!"

Muslims point to Mohammed's receipt of the Koran as an undoubted miracle because, they say, there was absolutely nothing in the man to suggest the presence of literary genius. It has been argued, though, that this is not peculiar because the quality of the Koran is not in fact strictly literary (it has of course since then become a classic of literature) but rather "surrealistic": "beyond the Christian speakers with tongues," Rodinson thought, Mohammed "rediscovered the tradition of the great prophets of Israel"—his "style" was "aesthetically striking." The speaker is in a trance, and the effect is to put the listener into a trance. Who is to say that, "literary" or otherwise, this is not close to the truth of mystical experience?

The idea, much canvassed in the past, that Mohammed was a fraud who released the message in a cunning and contrived way, in accordance with a careful and preconceived plan, has nothing whatsoever to recommend it. The mystical strand in Mohammed's thought was taken up by the Sufis (whose name seems not, after all, to be as certainly derived from the Arabic word for wool as is so often stated), who came under the well-acknowledged influence of gnostic thought. *Dikhr,* a Koranic term meaning "remembrance of God" alludes not to some sterile or mechanical exercise but to a special kind of self-consciousness. The dance of the famous "whirling dervishes," imitating the movement of the planets around the sun, of the Turkish Sufic order called Mevlevi is a type of *dikhr.*

For many outside the faith the spiritual authenticity of Islam—made less credible by examples of what has looked to the West like fanaticism and incitement to violence—is guaranteed by the poetry of the thirteenth-century Persian Jalal ad-Din ar-Rum (usually known simply as Rumi), the founder of the Mevlevi order. He was not an orthodox man (he believed in many lives and was religiously eclectic in a manner disliked by conventional Muslims) but he influenced Muslim and non-Muslim alike. His tomb at Konya in Turkey (to which he was invited by the Seljuk ruler, under whose protection he came) is a place of pilgrimage.

Rumi, whose poems are in the collection *Divan-I Shams-I-Tabriz,* and whose long mystical poem the *Mathnavi* he himself described (blasphemously) as the "Persian Koran," was far more innovative than he has been given credit for; he was quite undoubtedly one of the six or seven supreme poets of all time, ranking with HOMER, SHAKESPEARE and DANTE. It was Rumi who brought the art of writing the erotic but simultaneously devotional poem to its height (outstripping, if that is the right word here, even the author of the *Song of Solomon*), and if a man of his genius could acknowledge Mohammed as an authentic prophet, then so can and should we. In the *Mathnavi* Rumi wrote, "Everything apart from love of the most beautiful God is anguish of spirit, even if it is sugar-eating. What is anguish of spirit? To go toward the grave without seizing the Water of Life"; his love poetry ("I do not get tired of You./Don't get tired of being compassionate to me!/All this thirst-equipment/must surely be tired of me,/the water jar, the water-carrier" one poem begins) is irresistible and immortal and has never failed to give hope to lovers of tolerance and justice.

27

Guide for the Perplexed

MOSES MAIMONIDES

1190

A politically correct person of our unhappy times would have to call Maimonides (or RamBam, another name by which he is often known) an "elitist." But his *Guide for the Perplexed* (*Dalahat-al-Havin*) was not written for readers stupid, tyrannical, and mediocre enough to take up such a position; besides, such people are far from regarding themselves as "perplexed."

There is a rabbinical tradition that the faith of uninstructed people ought not to be disturbed by the discussion of matters which they do not understand—and, while the philosophically uninstructed Jews of the twelfth century were certainly, like everyone else, more intelligent than the neo-Stalinist politically correct of today, there is common sense in the notion if it is not strained, if access to books is not denied, and if simplicity of faith is respected.

Maimonides was born in Cordoba, in the Muslim (Almohovid) part of Spain, in 1135. But when he was thirteen he and his family were driven out of their home by the Almohad conquest. By 1165, after a sojourn in North Africa, he was settled in Old Cairo as a court physician. Eventually he became leader of the Jews in Egypt.

He is important as an influence on his people not only on account of the *Guide for the Perplexed* but also for his heroic work on Jewish law, the whole corpus of which he reinterpreted in a fourteen-volume code. This latter is written in a type of Hebrew, but most of his other books, including the *Guide*, are in Arabic. The main influence exerted by the *Guide*, though, was in its Jewish and, in particular, its Latin versions.

Maimonides was a precursor of the great European classical rationalists—DESCARTES, SPINOZA and LEIBNIZ—in the sense that he believed knowledge could be discovered by the use of reason. However, this was all in the interests of faith. The *Guide* is deliberately written in an enigmatic manner, containing inconsistencies and downright contradictions—of most (or possibly all) of which he was perfectly well aware. He was much opposed in his own time by pious and literal-minded Jews, who suffered, he believed, from an oversuperstitious outlook. In his work of codifying Jewish law he adhered to his motto: "Man should never cast his sound reason behind him, for the eyes are in front and not in the back." Always he relied on the plainest meaning obtainable.

The *Guide* was written for those who were confused between the teachings of the faith and those of philosophy: "The object of this treatise is to enlighten a religious man who has been trained to believe in the truth of our holy law . . . and at the same time has been successful in his philosophical studies."

Maimonides was an antifundamentalist: He deprecated the anthropomorphic interpretation of scriptural texts on the grounds that God, being wholly beyond human understanding, could not possess human attributes—could not "love" or "walk" or "have vengeance." In his view all these attributes were human metaphors for the actions of a transcendent being. Fundamentalists of all persuasions in our contemporary world would of course condemn him out of hand—and a few of those who have heard of him.

Maimonides drew extensively upon earlier Arabic philosophy for many of his arguments. He drew most from Avicenna (Ibn Sina, 980–1037) and Averroes (Ibn Rushd, 1126–98), and there is therefore more than a trace of PLOTINUS in his thinking. Avicenna, a Persian poet, reconciled Aristotelian thought with Islam by means of Neoplatonism. Averroes was above all the interpreter of ARISTOTLE, translations of whose works into Arabic date from about 800 C.E. However, unlike (of course) these *Falasifa* (Islamic philosophers), Maimonides saw both Christianity and Islam as arising exclusively from Judaism. He regarded pagan thought as shallow and worthless.

Maimonides substantially agreed with his Arabic predecessors that the philosophy of Aristotle, if suitably modified in certain respects, represented the truth. He saw faith and philosophy as two completely separate but complementary things. It was the task of philosophy to confirm the truth of faith—and, in particular, to disprove anything to the contrary. He compiled what has become known as the Thirteen Principles of Faith, a complete formulation of the dogmas of the Judaic faith.

Maimonides modifies Aristotle's philosophy in one important respect. Aristotle interpreted the world as having an eternal existence: It never *had not been:* God did create form in it, but not matter. Maimonides postulated a creation of matter *ab nihilo,* from nothing, by a God whose true attributes cannot be known to human beings, and who therefore can be known only negatively—by what he is *not.* This is a peculiarly Jewish (as well as gnostic) manner of thinking, and is found in many different forms in Kabbalistic speculation. We must not, for example, say, "God is alive." We can only begin to understand God by saying, *"God is not dead."* Modern positivists prefer to pretend that *God is not, does not exist,* because they are too arrogant to admit that anything could exist which they cannot understand either immediately or in the near future. When therefore it comes to the questions of how matter arose in the first place, and of the status of *nothing* (paradoxically *something,* and, for the mystic, an attribute of God), they come almost comically adrift, and make meaningless remarks (usually on television, their preferred medium) such as "Before the Big Bang the laws of physics were a whisper." The essence of this attitude is fear of the unknown: They are unable to respect or even to consider what makes them afraid.

Most might understandably assume that Maimonides was an archenemy of mysticism. This is not the case. The true case is that much mysticism—of the nonvulgar, popularly "occult" type—itself is, somewhat paradoxically, sturdily rationalistic so far as rationalism can take it. The thirteenth-century prophet, who went to Rome with the object of converting the pope to Judaism, Abraham ben Samuel Abulafia, another Spanish Jew and an ecstatic who influenced the later Kabbalists, believed that his teaching was nothing more than the logical outcome of the teachings of the *Guide for the Perplexed.* Nor can he be faulted on that score.

Even more surprisingly, the Dominican mystic Meister Eckhardt (1260–1327) recognized Maimonides as second only to AUGUSTINE. But he had influence in a somewhat more conventional domain: AQUINAS studied him, and so did Spinoza; Leibniz admired him; Moses Mendelssohn (1729–1786), the German pioneer of Enlightenment Judaism, author of *Jerusalem,* and regarded by many in his time as superior to KANT, was more influenced by Maimonides than by any other writer. He, too, insisted that Jewish teachings arose from reason. But, as we have seen, such reason does not preclude intelligent speculation.

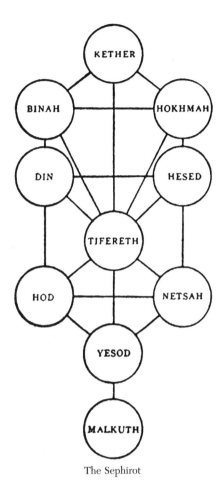

The Sephirot

The Kabbalah

12th century C.E.

This is often spelled in its Spanish form: as *Cabala* or *Cabbala*. It may also be encountered as *Quabala*. Nor, in a book devoted to books, is it by any means a book! However, the vast majority of people who have been influenced by it—although they are unlikely to be aware of it—think of it, when they think of it at all, as a book. I am therefore going along with them, and will also, although I offer an immediate and vital correction—initially call it a book. (After all, had I listed it here under *Zohar*—or under the names of one of the even more obscure books, such as the crucial Book *Bahir*, which are considered to form that aspect of the Kabbalah that is in written form—then hardly anyone could have been expected to know to what I was referring.) In fact, although unknown except to devotees—or, paradoxically, to those who have not understood what it is—it has exercised an incalculable

135

and special influence upon us all, because such concentrated thinking and feeling has lain behind so many efforts made in the world. It may even be that much that remains good in a world now generally taken to be corrupt and greedy is owed to the Kabbalah! Such an assertion is not, though, open to proof—nor, curiously, would anyone making it with any seriousness be interested in proof, since it is essential to kabbalistic thinking that nothing whatsoever be taken simply on trust: Everything must be a matter of inner conviction.

The word *Kabbalah* means, literally, "that which is received" and therefore, also, *tradition*. By the end of the twelfth century there had developed, in the south of France, a Jewish mystical tradition, a body of doctrine, ambiguous and complex, that existed outside the Pentateuch, the Jewish written law. Since it developed alongside the gnostic "heresy" of Catharism, there is every reason to believe that there were connections between Christian and Jewish scholars—but there is little evidence of this now. All the religions, major and minor, have their mystical form. The word *mysticism* itself has two implications: first, an urge to know the Divine "from inside," to have intimate knowledge of it, to be aware of it on the level of personal experience, to know God *directly;* second, to pass on the information thus gained only to initiates.

The single man responsible for our present understanding of this vastly complex and apparently cryptic phenomenon is the Israeli (Berlin born) scholar Gershom Scholem (1897–1982). He, almost alone, created the modern field of academic study of Jewish mysticism, and by doing so he changed our perception of the essence of Judaism. In the nineteenth century Judaism was considered by its leaders to be a rationalistic and legalistic religion. Scholem, however, although not himself a mystic—a conscientious pacifist who broke with MARTIN BUBER on account of his beliefs, he was, for himself, chary of mysticism—showed that mysticism had been, and still was, a vital force in Jewish history. All the vitality—he demonstrated—would have gone out of Judaic philosophy and public doctrine without its challenging energy and its often ecstatic irrationality. He believed that the false messiahs, the most famous of these being the tragic Sabbatai Sevi (1626–1676), offered Kabbalist challenges. Scholem's *Sabbatai Sevi* (1973) is one of the most exciting and crucial books of this century—and, it could be claimed, it in its way, too, derives from that extraordinary phenomenon, the Kabbalah.

Scholem went on to explain that the book *(Sefer) Bahir,* and the *Sefer Yetsirah,* although they purported to be the products of the years between 200 B.C.E. and 200 C.E.—pretended, in other words, to be very ancient and therefore of great authority—were in fact *pseudepigraphic:* that is, far from having been written in ancient times, they had been written much later. The *Yetsirah,* the earliest, however, was first written not later than the sixth century of our era. Scholem gave proof that while *Bahir* (in Hebrew, "shining") had indeed been written in the twelfth century, it did contain ancient and Oriental ideas that came directly from gnosticism. It is in *Bahir* that we find the first reference in Jewish literature to the doctrine of the transmigration of souls. There is, too, a hint of the *Sephirot,* the all-important notion which lies at the very heart of Kabbalism, and which is somewhat elaborated in the *Yetsirah.* In his *Major Trends in Jewish Mysticism* (first published in 1941, and subsequently revised) Scholem began by pointing out that while Kabbalism had been closed to the rationalistic Jews of the previous century, various Christians such as A. E. Waite had tried to interpret it correctly, but that their insights had been inhibited by their lack of "all critical sense as to historical . . . data." They had therefore "failed completely" when they "had to handle problems bearing on the facts." Yet their books are still in print and are still taken as authoritative by far more readers than are aware of Scholem's work!

There is thus, because of the stream of trash (or at best, as in Waite, historically false speculation) that has emanated from the initial, well-meant but doomed, turn-of-the-century studies—culminating, no doubt, in what Scholem called the "highly colored humbug" of the foolish and boastful pseudomagician Aleister Crowley—a serious confusion as to what the word *Kabbalah* means. For too many it is, at best, a sort of ceremonial magic (sometimes, as with Crowley, of a dark and unpleasant, if also silly, kind); only for a small minority, outside certain small inner circles, is it one of the most complex but beautiful searches for true mystical experience, for self-perfection, for a direct knowledge of the creator that does not imply superiority (but rather the contrary); it also has its own unique cosmology.

The Kabbalah is the Jewish version of gnosticism, represented here by the GOSPEL OF TRUTH. And Kabbalah, the secret and ecstatic inner speculation of a mostly oppressed people, has given much to modern forms of gnosticism (such as Sartrian existentialism). The system of GURDJIEFF differs from that of Rudolf Steiner by virtue of what it owes to Kabbalah. Here it need only be added, in fairness, that while such organizations as the Hermetic Order of the Golden Dawn (of which not only Waite but also the poet W. B. Yeats was a member) were in no true sense Kabbalistic, they were not as vulgar, boastful, and nasty as the rubbish later dreamed up by the not untalented but finally pathetic Crowley, who wanted to be a "black" magician—he even claimed to have turned a bookseller into a camel.

The most important of the Kabbalistic books is the *Zohar* (in Hebrew *Zohar* means "splendor"). For a time this ranked with the Bible and the Talmud. Scholem proved both that it was written by a Spanish Kabbalist called Moses de Leon (1250–1305), who lived in Guadalajara and, from 1290, in Avila, and that in itself it contained, despite its pretensions, no ancient writing at all. Indeed, Kabbalism itself has its origins, not only in mystical hints in the truly ancient Jewish writings (to what extent we cannot be absolutely sure), but in the formulations of Jews living in Provence in the century previous to that of Moses de Leon, who evolved what was, literally, a new way of thinking about life and its meaning. The *Zohar*—written in an artificial and literary Aramaic that apes what the author believed was the living language of the people of the second century C.E.—can only be described as a sort of mystical fiction whose purpose is to give commentary on the Bible. It is in itself a mixed bag, ranging from passages of great brilliance to those of unutterable tedium. Set in the Palestine of the second century of our era, it gives a record of the wanderings of the Rabbi Simeon ben Yohai and his son Eleazar as they discuss the meanings of life and death. The text betrays the influences of the Neoplatonism of PLOTINUS as well as of the kabbalistic thinking of his age.

Central to all kabbalistic thinking is the notion of the *sefiroth* (numbers). This is the kabbalistic representation of the creation; essential to it, though, is the fact of the unknowableness of God. Many readers will have come across diagrams of the *sefiroth,* as a symbolic tree showing the hidden Faces of God, and showing, too, that the divine lives in man. According to the Palestinian Kabbalist Isaac Luria (1534–1572), creation became possible only because an ineffable creator, in an act called *Tzimtzum,* withdrew from himself, thus causing a catastrophe known as the *breaking of the vessels;* this allowed the light of creation to spill over, so that its sparks fell into increasingly lower realms, and evil as well as life was created. We find something very similar in the Manichean "heresy" of much earlier times. In Luria's Kabbalism the purpose of existence is that of *tikkun* (restoration): all the fallen sparks, the souls, must be returned to their original place. This in turn involved the notion of *gilgul,* the transmigration of souls—and even of a doctrine curiously akin to the Eastern one of *karma.* By each human act man can fulfill a redemptive role. The complexities and obscurities of Kabbalism at first seem immense, but, viewed emotionally as well as intellectually, and in the light of many other doctrines, they can be simplified. A nineteenth-century scholar rightly pointed out that *Tzimtzum* is the only serious attempt to account for the creation of something out of nothing—a subject generally avoided by even Christian philosophers. That, in all its ramifications and in the way subsequent Kabbalists have treated it, it is a profound conception there is no doubt.

One could write infinitely about the Kabbalah, which is a living thing. I have been justified in calling it a book—although really it is a series of books, the most important of which I have listed here—because outsiders cannot come into contact with it without reading at least exegeses of it. It is not irrelevant that it has been the subject of a movie, Sidney Lumet's *A Stranger Among Us* (1992): this in itself offers a dubious guide—but it might have sent someone to a study of the real Kabbalah. And, after all, Kabbalah is taught on the Internet, and not just by a single set of people. It thus remains to summarize what, in its contemporary and accessible form, it could tell us if we would allow it to.

The cosmology contained in the symbols of the *sefiroth* and of Luria's *Tzimtzum* anticipate all the "discoveries" of modern physics, and the rest still to come. They do so, however, in an emotional way. Whereas modern atheist-scientists—tend to treat of such matters as the creation of life itself, or the "laws of nature," as if they were only to be apprehended in an intellectual manner. Surely, too, the intellect does play its part in our understanding—but, approached by reason alone, our view of our own existence becomes warped and impoverished. The impulses behind great religions themselves, too, have become stultified: have often crystallized into their very opposites, so that Christians have burned people in the name of their faith, and Muslims even now go against the precepts of theirs—in the name of it. Such behavior is hardly, of course, unknown among Jews, either; Scholem, not a Kabbalist, but the impeccable and always conscientious scholar of Kabbalism, was himself desperately unhappy about Israel's attitude to the Arabs. Kabbalists themselves have erred: in being overintellectual, overtortuous, arrogant. . . . But Kabbalism itself remains alive and resistant. It teaches that Man can perfect himself, or at least that there is a path toward perfection. The universe as a whole, and all parts of it, are permeated with the energy of its creator; but all we as ordinary human beings really know is what our own reactions to reality are—we do not know reality itself. We do not feel objects, or entities—such as love—themselves, only our reactions to them. The affinity with various forms of Buddhism is obvious.

Modern Kabbalists tell an exemplary fable. A good man is hit by misfortune, his wife dies, his children die, he loses the little property he had, he himself dies—of grief. His case is in the highest court: What can be given to such a long-suffering soul? The court decides to give him this: the feeling that he is alive and can enjoy whatever he has. The zealous and diligent functionaries who torment us, the unjust lawyers, the overrigorous bureaucrats, the abusers of the religions they profess, the usurers, the oppressors of people: All these, and more, do not feel alive, do not feel their part in creation—and are not grateful for their existence. The Kabbalist, however, feels that he or she can rise above this and see things as they are. He or she must have, though, above all, humility and a passion for the truth.

29

Summa Theologiae

Thomas Aquinas

1266–1273

The *Summa Theologiae* (often rendered *Summa Theologica*) of Thomas Aquinas, begun in 1266 and left unfinished at its author's death, is the crowning achievement of medieval theology; it is also the most impressive, meticulous, and convincing summation *(Summa)* of a vast body of knowledge (or what was then taken to be knowledge) ever made.

And Thomas was by far the busiest of all philosophers: During his short life, which included only sixteen years of writing time, he wrote some eight million carefully considered words. The Latin he used is "dense, lucid, and passionless"; it was perfect for his ruthlessly logical purposes. DANTE regarded his theological system as well-nigh perfect, and for centuries he was the leading authority in Christendom (his work underpins the faith of the contemporary Roman Catholic Church). Of his own good faith it is quite impossible to doubt; indeed, it is hard to reconcile the sheer amount he achieved with an ordinary "common-sense" view of what is possible for a single human being. His path in life, just like that of Mozart, seems to have been in some way innate to him.

One of his most extraordinary achievements was to reconcile Christianity with the *Physics* of ARISTOTLE, then regarded as the scientific paradigm; within his lifetime this *Physics* had not long been available to Christians in complete translation. That is another way of saying that, for his own time, he seemed to have successfully reconciled science, as this was then understood, with the Christian religion. No modern philosopher has come near to such an achievement. Other works besides the *Summa* include commentaries on books of the Bible, works of Aristotle, and another huge *Summa* against infidels; there are ninety-two works in all.

It is hard, now, for us to recognize that he was, through and through, a *rebel*—and one of the most persistent ones of all time. He opposed his family, he opposed his colleagues, and he opposed the entrenched ideas of his own church. He called the standard textbook of his age, the *Sentences* of Peter Lombard, a "multiplication, questions and arguments." Nor did he live to see his work immediately accepted; in 1277, three years after his death at the age of not more than fifty, there was a concerted effort to crush all of it. Two archbishops of Canterbury denounced the whole of Thomism (as it is called). Yet by 1323 he was canonized. Though he had not performed the necessary miracles to qualify for this, the pope simply pronounced that the answers he had given to each of the vexing questions was in itself a miracle. . . .

It is hard, too, to reconcile what we know of Thomas's tough and no-nonsense persistence with the "rotund" "angelic doctor," the large quiet man liked even by his enemies, of the painting by Piero della Francesca (and we see exactly the same face in Raphael's *La Disputá* and not too different a one in Zurbaran's *Apotheosis of Saint Thomas*. In the scientific sense we now know that he was on very many points (for example, and most obviously, in his belief that the sun revolved around the earth) plain wrong, and that he could not help this any more than could any of his contemporaries. Yet in much of twentieth-century theology and even philosophy his insights are still invaluable and widely discussed.

He was born near Naples in 1224 or 1225, into a noble family whose power was on the decline. His father, Count Landulf of Aquino, was a vassal of (indeed, was distantly kin to) that remarkable poet, man of learning, soldier, king of Sicily and Holy Roman emperor, Frederick II (1194–1250), who in 1228 pronounced himself the instrument of God—the so-called *Stupor Mundi* (astonishment of the world) who was the scourge and the rival of the popes of his time. At the age of five Thomas was sent to the Benedictine school at Monte Cassino, of which his mother wished him to become abbot. In 1243 he wanted to enter the Dominican order, but his ferocious mother had his elder brothers imprison him (for fifteen months) in his own home. They are said to have tempted him with a woman, but he repulsed her with a burning brand. Such was his determination that his mother was forced to relent: He joined the order in 1244. He went to Paris, the center of Catholic learning, and then came under the decisive influence of the German

Albertus Magnus, Albert the Great (c. 1200–1280), whose aims he—as the superior systematizer—set out to realize.

Thomas went to Germany with Albert, and then returned to Paris as a Dominican lecturer. He taught throughout Italy, and then, from 1269 until 1272, at Paris again. His final year was spent in Naples, at whose university he had been a student. One day at mass shortly before his death he had an "ecstasy" (such as Saint Francis was wont to experience), and said, "All that I have written seems to me like straw compared with what has now been revealed to me." He wrote not a word more and died soon afterward on his way from Naples to Lyons to take part in a church council there.

Albertus Magnus is almost as important as Thomas himself (for some, because of his eclecticism, his greater interest in "heresy"—the gnostical tinge to his adventurous mind, which gave rise to the later legend of his "magic"—and his lack of fear of being personal, he is more important): He gave the latter his direction in life, and he defended him after his death. He had learned about Aristotle from the great Arabic philosophers—he was among the first Christians to understand that neither the Greek nor his great Arab interpreters (in particular Avicenna and Averroes) could possibly be ignored, "infidels" though they were (this did not worry him as unduly as many of his conventional contemporaries would have liked). His greatest legacy to his pupil, though, was his insistence that problems of philosophy (as distinct from theology) must be resolved by means of philosophy. He inspired Thomas with the notion that Christianity could be reconciled with the Aristotelian corpus (some parts of which were in fact not by Aristotle), in other words, that religion could be reconciled with remorseless logic.

Thomas allowed that certain matters could only be known to us by revelation, but he nevertheless believed that reason—philosophical and *not* theological reason—could lead us to as much truth as was accessible to us. He admitted, as perhaps every seriously religious person has admitted, that we cannot have an insight into the nature of God. But he was adamant in wishing to demonstrate that God did exist, and he adduced five famous proofs. All of these proofs begin from a divine phenomenon, a "knowable fact of the world," and then argue back to its cause. He was one of those honest enough to insist that all arguments must proceed from the knowable facts of the world, and was sufficiently empiricist to start, therefore, from sense-perception. Of the *quinque viae* (five ways), three come from MAIMONIDES.

Briefly and baldly stated they are: the argument from motion (since some things are in motion, so there must be a prime mover); that there must be an uncaused first cause; that the existence of some things not self-explanatory imply a necessary being; that comparisons imply the existence of a perfection; that there has to be something that guides natural things to their end, an end which is evident to us but not necessarily to them. These arguments have been dismissed; but they have also been found to be still relevant.

Thomas dealt with the matter of free will by means of a metaphor. How can human beings be free if God is omniscient? God sees all as a man looking down from the top of a hill sees all the many travelers walking along a path winding up to it, although these travelers cannot see much of one another. God's knowledge is always *present* and does not mean that the travelers are unfree. This argument depends on subtleties on the subjects of time and eternity that have vexed many, who have very strongly objected to it; but, particularly as we have little idea of what time really is, it still has much life in it—and is relevant to the *compatibilist* position (held by HOBBES, LEIBNIZ, LOCKE and HUME), in which free will may be reconciled with determinism.

Despite Thomas Aquinas's canonization in 1323 (Albertus Magnus was not canonized until 604 years later, Thomism was not as properly respected in centuries that intervened between his and the nineteenth as much as it is now. His philosophy was not studied but simply accepted by Catholics; and Protestants and others assumed that it was merely special pleading (which it is not, and almost certainly the rebel Thomas would at a certain time in history—perhaps when Pope Leo XIII inaugurated modern Thomism, in 1879—ceased to have been a Roman Catholic). Only in the twentieth century is he coming into his own as a true philosopher, and one who was by no means the hardened dogmatist presented by the official side of his church. There is now no more reason for non-Catholics to ignore him than there is for non-Christians to ignore BERKELEY.

Furthermore, he fruitfully developed Aristotle's distinction between potentiality and actuality, no mere technical achievement. And it may even be argued that he preserved the best in PLATO from Aristotle's critique of him. It seems certain that his stock as a philosopher—he never wished to make philosophy just fit theology—will go up and up. The atheist criticism that his proofs of God's existence appeal to an "antiquated physics" are cogent enough to be taken seriously, but are largely disingenuous. His solution to the eternal question about the nature of universals—to put it shortly, do *doghoodedness* or *human* exist independently of all the dogs and men in the world, or are those terms extracted *after* the fact of observing so many dogs, man, and, of course what have you?—is one of the most profound of all. The Neoplatonists—misleadingly but accurately called "realists" (i.e., universals were *real*)—such as the followers of AUGUSTINE (a disingenuous man by the side of Thomas) argued that faith would be undermined if people did not withdraw from materialism and rely on the existence of a Platonic kind of heaven where all the qualities existed. Their opponents (called *nominalists*) denied the reality of universals, but gave these a status. Thomas's argument depended on our acknowledgment that matter could not be excluded from the world; i.e. must exist. Thomas reconciled the two opposing views: He ascribed to the human intellect a power of creating (his God, too, is a creative God) unchanging truths, but from changing perceptions.

30

The Divine Comedy

DANTE ALIGHIERI

1321

Dante's poem, unlike certain classics, has never for very long been without sincerely devoted and nonacademic readers, even if it has not been read as widely as, for example, CERVANTES's *Don Quixote*—which is (in various adapted versions), quite apart from anything else, a children's classic. But *The Divine Comedy* is after all in a verse which, although amazingly lucid and concise, is usually not immediately accessible to modern readers. Readers have certainly loved it more than one of its chief rivals, John Milton's epic *Paradise Lost,* which is on the whole more revered and respected than warmly loved. Milton is forbidding. Dante is severe, but much more "human." Puritanism had not been invented in the fourteenth century.

Dante's *Commedia* (he called it that, not because it is a comedy in our sense, but for technical reasons to do with genres: he meant that it was not a tragic work in Latin) is more user-friendly than *Paradise Lost* and is much more full of home truths (two examples: the marvelous line, "If only the king of the universe were our friend"; "How bitter another's bread is, thou shalt know / By tasting it; and how hard to the feet / Another's stairs are, up and down to go"). The *Commedia* (the adjective *Divine* was added by a grateful posterity) does immediately appeal to everyone with a taste for poetry, even if it is more enjoyable read with the aid of at least a few introductory notes to put it in its context (T. S. Eliot said that this did not matter, but that was a disingenuous plea on the part of a disingenuous man, who came to believe that high poetry ought to be kept out of the hands of mere plebeians). The *Commedia*'s enormous influence is beyond doubt, if only because the famous description of Dante (by, as it happens, FREDERICK ENGELS!) as "the first universal mind of our era" is so apt; and because it is a careful allegory of man's difficult ascent to the Heaven of the God so successfully postulated in the theology of THOMAS AQUINAS.

Yet many have disliked Dante, and VOLTAIRE wrote in his *Philosophical Dictionary* (1764): "The Italians call him divine; but it is a hidden divinity—few people understand his oracles. He has commentators, which, perhaps is another reason for his not being understood. His reputation will go on increasing, because scarce anybody reads him."

But Voltaire, though he would like to have been a good poet himself, was immune to that sort of poetry, and in the Augustan "age of prose," the eighteenth century, Dante often really was despised, even as "extravagant, absurd, disgusting . . . a Methodist parson in Bedlam"—that, though, was said by Horace Walpole, a "frigid Frenchified coxcomb" (said William Wordsworth). But Dante was not despised by everyone, and he soon became a major hero of the nineteenth and twentieth centuries.

T. S. Eliot did not like to say so, but it is quite clear that he preferred Dante to SHAKESPEARE (*Hamlet* being, for him, notoriously, "a failure"). However, influential though Eliot's championship of him has been, it is to be doubted whether Dante's true worth lies in any anticipation of the frigid, elitist, and Jew-free cryptofascism that was the naive and emotionally under-developed American Eliot's prescription for Europe. True, Dante, torn out of his context, can be made to seem like that, especially by those who yearn for certainty at all costs, and by those who have no taint of liberalism in their makeup. But Dante's age was a very different one from ours, and it does not do to try to go back to it. In any case, that would not be possible.

For Dante the truth had been laid out by AUGUSTINE and Aquinas (and a few others such as PLATO, whose example he did not mind admiring), and he set out to describe it: to make the world of his poem a mirror of the world of the Christian God of his era. He was already nine years old when Aquinas died. He assumed that Aquinas had effected the final reconciliation between ARISTOTLE's philosophy and Christian belief; that the last stone of the Christian edifice had been put into its place; that further change was neither needed nor possible. All he now wanted was a Holy Roman emperor who would make the corrupt state reflect a Church purified along the lines prescribed by Aquinas, and who would be superior to the pope. He thought he had found the man to achieve this in the high-minded, unrealistic Henry

VII (1274–1313), but Henry failed—and died of malaria in a swamp near Siena.

In his masterwork, probably begun in about 1307, Dante therefore set out to enshrine this notion in an ideal form. There was no trace of skepticism in his nature: That habit of mind was never treated as amounting to more than the work of the Prince of Darkness. But Dante was not unsympathetic to sin, much as he deplored it. Much of the *Commedia* is about its inevitability.

Nothing good, ever, can come from orthodoxy—static, anodyne, inert, contrary to human feeling—though of course all that is socially good must come from the natural order that orthodoxy, by mimicking it, seeks to subvert in the interests of power, lust, wealth, and (above all) spiritual sloth; nevertheless, the *Commedia* could be called a tribute to orthodoxy. However, it was then a very new orthodoxy, and, as it is in the poem, it was not politically realized. The system had been set out, but it was not yet followed. Henry VII was dead; Florence was in the hands of a godless faction. And the *Commedia* is by one who, himself, cannot be orthodox enough to gain salvation easily, or without the help of a superior guide—his Beatrice. The spell of Aquinas had only just then been cast. In that sense Dante is rightly taken to be the medieval poet *par excellence*, despite the fanciful efforts that have been made to present him as in some way "pre-Renaissance." He was, yes, the first "universal man"—but he was not a Renaissance man. His beliefs were medieval! His poem really is, therefore, one of a bygone era. Our age has no series of such fixed beliefs, and Eliot's authoritarian wishes for this (he was prepared to embrace Hitler in the interests of crushing Russia, and he never protested against the Final Solution) are just now beginning to be seen for what they really were. We can today see that, among his many other grave shortcomings and dishonesties, Eliot was never able to come to terms with what the Copernican system implied. Dante of course knew none other than the "perfect" system of Ptolemy; and so that was perfect, at least to the second decimal point. It got in the way of the sort of medieval culture that Eliot would have liked to prescribe for the rest of us. Hence his lack of interest in science.

But human nature itself, if not human thinking, remains in certain essential features the same, and, since Dante never suggested that salvation within the framework of the system he accepted was an easy matter, and since Dante (unlike his dubious twentieth-century champion), had robust sexual appetites, he has of course very much more to say to us today than Eliot ever did. The significance of the light that suffuses the *Paradiso* has not been wiped out by COPERNICUS or NEWTON or even EINSTEIN. Dante's great love Beatrice Portinari, died; Eliot's first wife, once the source of the poetry in him, the key to his appreciation of ordinary people and their extraordinary use of language, had to be locked away on the pretext that she was mad; and so Eliot guiltily destroyed his muse so that he should become official great poet. Also, because Dante really did unquestioningly accept the truth of the system—it is no longer possible to do this, of any system whatever—he was able to see himself as only a small part in it: He recognized, as well as anyone, just how full of fault he was (too). At the beginning of his poem he says that he does not know how he has lost the true way. For, essentially, he is the pilgrim in the poem. Divided into the *Inferno* (Hell), *Purgatorio* (Purgatory), and *Paradiso* (Paradise), *The Divine Comedy* famously begins:

> Midway life's journey I was made aware
> That I had strayed into a dark forest,
> And the right path appeared not anywhere.
> Ah, tongue cannot describe how it oppressed,
> That wood, so harsh, dismal and wild, that fear
> At thought of it strikes now into my breast.

The *Commedia* is quite untranslatable, because it does not work in English without rhyme, and English just is not rich enough in this. Bits of it have been done brilliantly; but the most consistent complete translation is the one by the English poet Lawrence Binyon (from which I quote here), and most people without Italian read it, initially, in that excellent and painstaking version.

Little detail is known of Dante's life. He was born of impoverished nobility in the city of Florence, and was educated by Franciscans. His family, and he after them, was of the Guelph faction. That is to say, they supported the papacy in its battle with the imperial powers (which was supported by the Ghibelline faction). Imperial power over Italy was broken at the Battle of Benevento in 1266, just a few months after Dante's birth in 1265 (and only thirty-nine years after the death of Saint Francis of Assisi, whose sincerity and freshness orthodoxy had barely, but had just about, endured; it was now preparing to disperse and trivialize Saint Francis's too truthfully dramatic, and therefore alarming, teaching).

Florence—to oversimplify a highly complex situation—was divided between two Guelph factions: the Whites and the Blacks. The Whites, and Dante with them, favored Florentine independence of both papacy and imperial forces; the Blacks were more happy to collaborate with the Church. Dante in his earlier years held high office in Florence, and he was even a party to the exile of his friend the poet Guido Cavalcanti. This has been put forward as an example of how Dante could put personal matters aside in the interests of state; equally, however, he might have been envious and glad to be rid of his old friend. It is a mistake to overvalue Dante the man. However, if he did err in this and other matters, then he would have made himself suffer for it.

Dante had turned to the consolations of philosophy after the death of Beatrice Portinari, wife to the painter Simone de Bardi, in 1290. Dante's famous love for Beatrice was a chaste, ideal, and Platonic one, and his own marriage (arranged by his father) was hardly relevant to it (we do not even know whether his wife accompanied him in his later exile). The nature of his love for Beatrice has its roots in the medieval concept of "courtly love," although it was not itself an example of this. It is a high point in the medieval and then Renaissance habit of idealizing women, and it has important Platonic elements.

In 1302 the Blacks seized power while Dante was on a diplomatic visit to the pope (who had deliberately kept him hanging around); he never saw Florence again. He was fined and banished, but he refused to appear before the magistrates. He was therefore condemned to be burned alive should he be caught in Florentine territory. Later he was invited back on the condition that he recanted his "treason," but he would never do so. Because of his fame, he did not lack patrons, and he spent time in various places in Italy. He died in Ravenna. Scholars have often regarded Dante as having been politically in the right, but the matter is not as simple: He seems to have behaved just as any other scholar-politician might have behaved. However, his love for Florence, in whose army her served, is not in question.

In about 1292 Dante wrote his first major book, a miscellany of prose and verse called *La vita nuova (The New Life)*. This deals, explicitly, with his experience of Beatrice. The version of it by the Italian-English poet Dante Gabriel Rossetti is the best of all Dante translations. When Dante first saw Beatrice, when she was nine years old, he tells us that his body said: "Here is a deity stronger than I; who, coming, shall rule over me." And Beatrice it is who shows him heaven in the *Paradiso*. Among his other writings are a treatise on philosophy, *Convivio (Banquet)* (unfinished), and a book of political theory, *De Monarchia* (c. 1313). But it is the *Commedia* by which he is remembered. He is said to have completed it just before he died.

The Divine Comedy is the embodiment of the religious and moral ideals of its age. But there is much in it that is original to Dante, such as (notably) the details of the punishments, which so exactly and subtly reflect the sins, handed out to sinners in Hell. Dante could do nothing but exclude VIRGIL, his guide in the Inferno, from bliss or the prelude to bliss—because there simply was no room for him in the system, and for Dante the system was true. For him therefore this exclusion was a tragedy—but a tragedy that he had to accept.

It is often asked whether Dante's Catholicism is an obstacle, to the non-Catholic, to the complete enjoyment of the *Commedia*. The question ought to be: Are the (as it happens) wrong scientific assumptions of the poem an obstacle to its complete enjoyment? Of course they are not. Or is the Copernican system an obstacle to navigation?

31

In Praise of Folly

DESIDERIUS ERASMUS

1509

The Dutch name of Erasmus was Gerhard, which in Latin means "beloved," hence the name Desiderius (chosen by himself, because this was what he called his father) by which he is known to us. He was born illegitimate in about 1466 in Rotterdam, the son of a priest probably called Roger Gerard, and his mistress, the daughter of a physician; she had already borne Gerard another son, Peter. Erasmus went to school in Holland, at Deventer, and then became a choirboy at Utrecht. At school he had a good grounding in Latin, the language he used in his writing and tried, just too late, to turn into a *lingua franca* for the use of enlightened people. No one wrote better Latin during the Renaissance.

After the deaths of his parents he was put into the charge of guardians whom he represented as villainous—and if he said so, then they probably were, although they have been defended as having done nothing unconventional. . . . The truth is, they had stolen his money and therefore did not know what to do with him, so they put him into a monastery.

Of all the great men who have been monks and then priests, Erasmus had the least inclination for that kind of life. His guardians forced him, however—as they had his older brother—to take vows as an Augustinian canon in 1488, at the age of twenty-two. Four years later he was ordained as a priest. From then onward his life was characterized, not by piety—he was the least pious of all religious thinkers, being a religious man rather than an observer of prescribed rituals—but by the desire to get to any place where he could find contact with the best minds of his age, preferably people with a sense of humor.

He was opportunistic in this respect, although he did no one any harm. He got a bishop to finance a period of study at the University of Paris, where he soon aligned himself with the humanists—this is to say, with humanism, the Renaissance movement that, while not atheistic, directed attention away from the status of God toward that of his creature, Man—of whom he eventually became the greatest of all. He was one of the most learned men of the entire Renaissance—learned to a much greater degree than, for example, his friend Sir Thomas More, to whom *In Praise of Folly* is dedicated, and whose Latin title, *Encomium Moriae* is a pun on More's name.

Erasmus did more than any single man of his time to prepare the way for the Reformation, and the German Protestant artist Albrecht Dürer confided to his diary, when he heard false news of the death of LUTHER, that he expected Erasmus to come out against the church that he had so savagely, so justly, and so effectively criticized. He was expected to do so by many others. But Erasmus would not change sides: He saw that the consequences would become as disastrous as their causes—as they very soon did in the person of the demonic CALVIN, the most odious man (not clinically insane or psychopathic) ever to have lived, the first edition of whose horrific and vindictive *Institutes* appeared in the very year of Erasmus's death.

Although he had a full understanding of it, Erasmus did not care much more for philosophy, particularly in its metaphysical aspects, than he did for the priesthood. The sort of metaphysics he did not care for is the sort that (and he heard arguments on these very points learnedly discussed at the University of Paris) disputed as to whether Jesus Christ could have appeared as a gourd, or as to which sin is the larger, working on a Sunday or killing a thousand people. Erasmus is not, indeed—and quite properly—regarded as a philosopher. If the Church was too full of hypocritical, dull, or corrupt ritualists, then much of philosophy was to him a too cold discipline.

Erasmus was essentially an imaginative writer—he began by trying to write poetry, but found he could not do so to his own satisfaction—a writer who wanted, by his works, to make the world into a kinder and gentler place. He became frustrated by stupidity, folly, and thus a satirist of it. He was, perhaps most noticeably of all, an opponent of war, and his work is full of arguments against it and ridicule of it as a means of settling affairs. He thus failed to suit most of the really powerful official Christians of his time, whose encouragement of fighting (by others) in behalf of their various truthful points of view was seen as a sacred duty. As Alastor (the Greek Destroyer) tells Charon the Ferryman in one of Erasmus's *Colloquies*, "War breeds a great many bishops who were not thought good for anything in time of peace." Erasmus was angered and repelled by this so-called Christian attitude.

But he has not received, in general, a good press from historians and scholars: He has been seen as a gifted but hardly admirable character who became ineffective through his lack of realism ("inability to grasp that factors other than reason might influence a man's course of action"). He was a satirist with a peculiarly "modern" and sophisticated view of existence—one which did not care at all for forms and conventions—and such men, especially if they are complex ironists, tend to be misunderstood, often as themselves hypocritically irrational. Erasmus was indeed guilty of some of the practices (absentee priesthood was one of them) that he condemned; but he could not otherwise have existed as a free thinker. He turned down brilliant posts for the sake of his freedom of mind. He was, too, beset until middle age by financial problems—a difficulty often ignored by well-salaried theologians and historians.

Furthermore, he must have felt, deeply, the absurdity and injustice of the fact that his illegitimacy imposed a bar on his progress—he could not get this ban lifted until he was over fifty years old. In his letters he often takes up the attitude of a whining valetudinarian, although he seldom declares that his trouble is the colic from the kidney stones that plagued him throughout his life; but this is obviously a self-critical mask.

Erasmus was popular in his own time. He wrote, essentially, for enlightened men like himself who felt themselves powerless to prevent the folly perpetrated by those with more direct influence upon events; this has been grudgingly acknowledged, but commentators, often unable themselves to handle the sting and sharpness of his satire (in particular of mechanical overobservance of religious rites instead of independent thinking) have tended to judge him too much in the terms of his classical models (the Greek satirist Lucian in particular) rather than in those of his originality, which was more considerable than they will admit. They have called him overintellectual when a form of intellectuality, superior learning, was his only weapon in a world which not only banned (all Erasmus's works were several times banned by the Church he refused to leave) but burned. The spirit of the age was that of Luther and Calvin rather than of humane letters, and he wrote to bring into focus what resistance there was to their violent dogmatism. There was much of this resistance, but it had little effect at the time.

Erasmus went to England in 1500 and made friends with More and other humanists such as the great poet John Skelton (tutor to the children of Henry VIII) and Colet. He returned in 1505, when he taught at the University of Cambridge, and again in 1509, when he wrote *In Praise of Folly*. He mastered Greek, which had defeated many of those who wanted to know it (a century or so later the best version of HOMER, by George Chapman, would be largely done from a Latin crib), and produced a translation of the Greek

NEW TESTAMENT into Latin which he intended, against the wishes of his church, for the common reader.

He supported Luther's complaints against the Church, but could not enter into the spirit of his hysterical dogmatism. He spent the last years of his life traveling about Europe, translating the classics (Lucian, Ambrose, AUGUSTINE, and many other Church Fathers), but living mostly at Basle in Switzerland, where he died in 1536.

Erasmus's two most accessible works are the *Colloquies* and *In Praise of Folly*. In the former, to which he continually added (and which at one point were pirated, so popular were they), until there were sixty-three in all (1534) he used the familiar classical form of the dialogue to convey supposedly didactic material, which—together with the types who perpetrated it—he sends up. Many have taken Erasmus's own purpose to be didactic, but the degree of this didacticism has been vastly exaggerated; his chief intention, rather, was ironic.

If Erasmus had a fault, then this certainly consisted of taking undue pleasure in the discomfort of his conservatively minded adversaries. How likely was the man who wrote, in a letter, of how he amused himself by "making game of some pseudotheologians of our time, whose brains are rotten, their language barbarous, their intellects dull, their learning a bed of thorns, their manners rough, their life hypocritical, their talk full of venom, and their hearts as black as ink," to be truly revered by the establishment of any party. Luther himself, who owed so much to him, ended by insulting him and calling him an Epicurean.

Erasmus is misunderstood mainly because he was an imaginative writer who has been judged as a failed reformer, a man who believed in human progress but failed in his duty to it: the man who was largely responsible for engineering the Reformation but who could not decide what to do when it came, and so turned himself at last into an insignificant and impotent figure. In other words, his chief book, *In Praise of Folly*, has been taken as a political rather than a poetic work. Of its subversive influence there need be no doubt. But is it the sort of political masterpiece it is taken to be, or is it a more enduring and altogether more literary book? For Erasmus did not believe in history, in progress, at all; but he was not, for all that, a pessimist.

The real subjects of *In Praise of Folly*, as well as the weaknesses which Erasmus so eloquently exposed, are human diversity and vitality. He needed a figure which stood for several things at once—this book is the most famous of all examples of sustained paradox. A paradox is a form of oxymoron (from the Greek for, be it noted, "pointedly foolish"—i.e., an example of *folly*) that yokes together, with the utmost daring, two opposites; in doing so it hopes to demonstrate an unexpected truth which could not, less daringly, be reached.

Erasmus was a complex ironist who, like most such, was in search of some satisfying and heartfelt simplicity in face of all the issues that troubled him; he was aware that human beings are never consistent, being compounded of many different selves, some of whom scarcely even know of one another. He was also aware that history, the "current affairs" of the past—as Henry Ford long after him said with unwitting truth—is largely "bunk," being a matter of judging people and events as if they made sense, or as if it could be satisfactorily explained by a reasonable man as consisting of reasonable and consistent actions. It is in fact a record of greed, crime, confusion, and delusion. Erasmus's was, after all, the age of Calvin! The picture of him as a man lacking in reality is therefore mistaken: he saw that reality as we know it did not make sense, and yet he longed to make some valid affirmation of so difficult a state of affairs.

The figure of Folly, or the Fool, was directly to hand. The German writer Sebastian Brant's *Ship of Fools* of 1594 was read and discussed by everyone. This is a well executed but conservative and highly moralistic collection of aphorisms drawn up to demonstrate that conformity is the only way to wisdom. Erasmus, using the example of Lucian, but going far beyond him, turned this on its head. In the first place he had Folly herself speak: the book is a praise of Folly by Folly herself. Such a title would have been taken to be ironic. So in part it was. But Folly's praise of Folly is also true praise. It is tribute to vitality, to honest and natural feeling, to instinct, to energy, to simplicity, to—above all—Christ as Fool. It is even a tribute to irresponsibility. As Erasmus writes in it, "This much is certain: without a little folly, no party is any fun." As a commentator wrote, in *In Praise of Folly* Erasmus "by virtue of his faith in man . . . united the old feeling of mystery and freedom connected with the wanton folk fool to his picture of erring fools in society; he censured earthly morality in the double name of earthly and spiritual vitality."

The best and most lively biography of Erasmus, as is usually conceded, is that by the Dutch historian Johan Huizinga, whose most famous book, *Homo Ludens: A Study of the Play Element in Culture* (1938), regarded by many as very unduly neglected (though it is hardly surprising that this is so), is about an element in life more often than not entirely ignored: play. Its thesis is that both seriousness and play are necessary to all cultures. Demonstrating the nature of the relationship between seriousness and play, in particular in *In Praise of Folly*, was Erasmus's greatest contribution of all.

32

The Prince

Niccolò Machiavelli

1532

Niccolò Machiavelli, diplomat, poet, playwright, political theorist, and military planner, was born in Florence in 1469 into an impoverished family of good, but not aristocratic, descent. Although he always thought of his native state as *the* nation, by the time he had grown up the true greatness of Florence had vanished: Even within Italy it was, by comparison with, say, Venice, a second-rate power. Two events helped to shape Machiavelli's indignant thinking. The first was the invasion of Italy by the armies of Charles VIII of France in 1494, which horrified him: The rulers of the Italian principalities, for all their arrogance, proved to be useless. The second was the downfall and execution by burning, in Florence itself, of the great Giralomo Savanarola. "Unarmed prophets have always been destroyed," Savanarola remarked grimly, "whereas armed prophets have always succeeded." This may seem unexceptionable enough to us; it was not the language of the late fifteenth century.

"We doubt," wrote Lord Macaulay of Machiavelli, "whether any name in literary history be so generally odious." By the middle of the sixteenth century *The Prince* (*Il principe*) was supposed by many to have been written by the Devil Himself. The name "Machiavelli" was synonymous, for Elizabethan Englishmen, with "atheist." A familiar term for the devil, "Old Nick," gained a new credibility because of Machiavelli's first name.

Machiavelli himself did learn, from experience, about how even a badly weakened republic could survive: He worked from 1498 until 1512 for the Florentine government as an assistant secretary of state and second chancellor—a fairly but not very senior civil servant. His own greatest concern during these years was to build up an efficient militia, one that would consist not of mercenaries but of loyal citizens—one that would be a people's army.

Then, in 1512, this republican government to which he had given such conscientious service came to an abrupt end. Machiavelli was dismissed, put into prison, questioned, tortured, and sent away into exile to his small country farm at San Casciano—from which he could just glimpse, no doubt with frustrated wistfulness, the buildings of his beloved Florence. He was thus—apart from a commission to write a history of Florence—effectively disgraced, at least in a political sense; certainly he died a broken man. Yet, had he not suffered this reverse of fortune he would have been no more than a footnote in history. Whether he would have had the time to write the literary works that gave him fame is a moot point. They are, after all, the product of some bitterness at his fate, as well as of his undoubtedly well-relished knowledge of the nastier side of human nature.

Historical scholars rate Machiavelli's *Discourses* (*Discorsi*) as his most important work—and so, if we need to know the details of what his position as a political thinker really was, it surely is; but few are aware of this and far fewer have read it. Literary critics, though, would rate his major work as the brilliant play *The Mandrake Root* (*La mandragola*). Sociologists of sex, for their part, might well reckon that his famous letter to his friend Francesco Vettori, describing a meeting with a prostitute, is by far his most interesting work. (More recently this candid and exemplary document has become, not unamusingly, prey to enraged and humorless pseudofeminists, and has thus given a new, and alas utterly frivolous, dimension to Machiavelli, as a "sexist pig"—this is about on the same level as "Socrates as black genius.") Not much is known about his life, except that he married at the age of about thirty-two, one Marietta Corsini, with whom he had six children. He had many love affairs, but so did many popes.

But it is for a relatively small spinoff from the *Discourses* that he is famous. In the course of writing the *Discourses* he came across a special case, one which he felt he needed to deal with separately. What could be done, he asked himself, if the stability of a republic were threatened by the violent seizure of power by an individual? He had a single practical purpose in mind: to persuade the Medici family—although it had been an enemy of the government he had served—to conduct a crusade against foreign usurpers. There was then hope that such a project might succeed. Giovanni de' Medici was pope, and his brother Giuliano (the duke of Nemours) seemed to be in a powerful position. Machiavelli hoped to be taken into their service, and he even said that he would work for them "even if they start me off by rolling stones." He finished the first version of *The Prince* at the end of 1513; it had reached its final form in 1516, when he dedicated it to Lorenzo de' Medici. *The Prince* was published in 1532, five years after his death, and it began a debate that has been raging ever since. The first translation into English appeared in 1640.

Some keywords of *The Prince* occur in chapter 15: "I radically depart from the procedures of others. . . . My aim is to write something that is useful . . . [so] it seemed to me to be right *to search for the real and not the imaginary truth of affairs. . . . Hence it is necessary for a prince who wishes to maintain his position to learn how not to be good. . . .*" The italics type are my own, but Machiavelli, an extremely passionate man and superbly lucid stylist, would not have been averse to such italicization. Pasquale Vitale, who wrote the fullest and best documented biography (in the late 1870s), found good historical grounds to describe Machiavelli thus: "Of middle height, slender . . . sparkling eyes . . . a tightly closed mouth; all about him bore the impression of a very acute observer and thinker, but not that of one able to wield much influence over others. He could not easily rid himself of the sarcastic expression continually playing round his mouth . . . which gave him the air of a cold . . . calculator. . . ." Although, as so often—as, even, always, perhaps?— we find upon close scrutiny that Machiavelli himself does not much resemble his popular reputation, he was, as we see from this reconstruction, "sarcastic": He wouldn't be altogether averse to the sinister effect that his work, minor in scope for him—just a treatise on monarchy, aimed to get him credit with the Medici family—has achieved. Nor is it unfair that he should be judged by *The Prince*. "I have composed," he told his confidant Vettori in a letter of December 1513, "a little work . . . there I plunge as deeply as I can into a consideration of this subject." In its pages we encounter, for the first time, the New Man, the ruthless and immoral autocrat, the prince unfettered by the rules of traditional morality. Or is he really? Might not he be a strict moralist using the only means open to him to enforce morality? Or is Machiavelli's prince more like a description of any ruler?

There is no doubt that, as well as influencing both Christopher Marlowe and SHAKESPEARE (could Richard III or Iago have existed, we ask ourselves, without Machiavelli?), this "master of evil" also influenced not only the science, if such it must be called, of modern dictatorship, but also KARL MARX—and many of the much nicer sounding tricks of modern "democracy." Does he deserve his bad reputation, especially among rulers, or did he just acquire it–as VOLTAIRE claimed—because he "gave away their trade secrets"? The enlightened despot Frederick the Great of Prussia, Voltaire's erstwhile friend, attacked Machiavelli for his immorality. But supporters of the value of his analysis of affairs include FRANCIS BACON, ROUSSEAU, and, perhaps above all, DAVID HUME. Did Machiavelli in other words, and indeed does he, give a truer picture of reality than rulers—and those who are in the business of defending their "morality"—found (and find) at all comfortable?

Certainly his subtle and ironic view of morality has made him both famous and execrated. Did he believe in evil? Are we justified in our pejorative use of the word *Machiavellian* to describe nasty office intriguers? It has taken centuries to give fair and reasonable answers to these questions—and few are in much agreement about them. But no: He did not believe in evil; he was in his way as much of a moralist as any of his pious critics; and, no, it is not fair, at least to Machiavelli, to describe any nasty and manipulative person by recourse to his name. Some modern commentators agree that he was a shrewd prophet; almost all agree that there is a peculiarly "modern" flavor to his thinking: Machiavelli, although he had a vivid and poetic imagination, was also a scientific—a "tough-minded," "operationist"—type. He saw that it was the possession of power, rather than of the moral high ground (he noted that Savanarola fastidiously refused to incite the mob when he might have been saved by it), that got results; he was (quite apart from being ambitious) fascinated by this; and so he set out to examine how in fact, rather than in the politer terms of "ought"—power worked. But he did not publish *The Prince* in his lifetime because a successful realization of its immediate aim was made impossible by the deaths of the duke of Nemours in 1516 and that of Lorenzo de' Medici in 1519.

It was no intellectual theorist or academic, but, of all men, Thomas Cromwell (1485–1540)—Henry VIII of England's agent, called "the Hammer of the Monks" because he so brutally presided over the dissolution of the monasteries—one of the founders of the modern centralized state, who brought the first manuscript copy of *The Prince* to England. Christopher Marlowe wrote his tragic farce *The Jew of Malta* in 1589; when at last the text was published in 1633, long after his death at the hands of an assassin, the prologue announced that there was a story of a "rich and famous Jew. . . . You shall find him still. / In all his projects, a sound Machiavill'." And the play begins with an address to the audience from Old Nick himself:

> Albeit the world thinks Machiavel is dead.
> Yet was his soul but flown beyond the Alps. . . .
> I count religion but a childish toy,
> And hold there is no sin but ignorance.
> Birds of the air will tell of murders past;
> I am ashamed to hear such foolishness. . . .

But is this sort of villainy what Machiavelli actually advocated, even in *The Prince* (let alone in the longer and more detailed *Discourses*)? The answer is, plainly and unequivocally, no: This is to say that he did not at all *intend* to advocate it. He is actually a stern moralist; but—it is the crucial difference between him and the other more conventional theorists of his time—in terms of the state alone, whose interests are the only ones he is here prepared to consider: "For when a decision to be taken depends on the survival of one's country," he writes, "no consideration may be given to justice or injustice, to kindness or cruelty, to actions being laudable or ignominious. . . . That course must be followed which will save its existence and preserve its freedom." This seems to throw morality out of the window; but, after all, it is based on the practice of all (or most—but look at the fate of the moralist Savanarola!) political practitioners. But this does not mean that in effect it does not throw morality away.

Of the man Machiavelli himself, then, it may be said that he was candid, a bold and salutary realist, a man (so far as we can tell) who refused to put his own cynical precepts into practice when he might have furthered his career by doing so, and a sincere patriot. But he cannot, for all that, and for all his honesty and realism, be entirely acquitted of exercising a "bad influence." Firstly, because a cynic like him ought to have known that honesty never pays, and, secondly and far more gravely, he was one of the anticipators of modern scientism, of the erroneous notion that Christianity—and by implication all other religions—cannot work because it wishfully denies the laws of nature: "Thus the world has fallen prey to villains, who can rule it without fear of punishment because their subjects, in order to go to heaven, prefer to bear . . . abuses rather than punish them." We meet this in Marx, too. And what is said is true. But this truth, although the indignation that promotes it is urgent and valid, is not a really profound one. For it is not even logical to assume, because religious feeling is thus abused—and because, no doubt, too, the magnificent and truly human beginnings of all the great religions fade away into merely trivial observances, which aids the corrupting process—that the supernatural does not exist.

Machiavelli, like HOBBES, Hume, and Marx, saw the problem and wished, with more or less ingenuity and subtlety, to sweep it away. In clearing up a dishonest confusion between *is* and *ought* Machiavelli played, and still plays, his highly intelligent role. He knew, as *The Mandrake Root* demonstrates, much about the disingenuous side of human nature; but his views of reality, while shockingly well educated, lack a sense of God—and, moreover, like all such views, fail to account for this major dimension of human experience. That religion is often a delusion does not mean that it *is* a delusion.

33

On the Babylonian Captivity of the Church

MARTIN LUTHER

1520

Great movements such as the Reformation, or the recognition of the essential irrationality of human motives (FREUD, PARETO, KUHN), are never the work of a single man or woman. Nor, of course, except in purely scientific terms—as in the case of the heliocentric hypothesis—do they represent the sudden emergence of the whole truth. Even the theory of COPERNICUS had to await further clarification, and some smaller details about the sun and its satellites are still unknown. John Wycliffe, William Tyndale, ERASMUS, countless others, played as great if sometimes less willing part in the emergence of Protestantism as did Luther. But Martin Luther (1483–1546) was chosen by fate to precipitate it.

He was born in Eisleben in Saxony, the son of a peasant miner, Hans, who was able to pay for his son's education. The boy had an unhappy childhood at the hands of parents as irascible as he was himself to become. His childhood was so harsh that he found it hard to express pleasure, although he was able to feel it. On one occasion at school he was punished no less than fifteen times in one day. He attended the University of Erfurt, and was about to take up a legal career when, presumably, he remembered—in the course of a violent storm—the role he had to play in history. At the age of twenty-two he entered a hermit order of Augustinian monks. Ordained in 1507, he was by 1511 a doctor of theology at the University of Wittenberg, and might well have risen rapidly in his church.

But this church was already in a state of turmoil, even to the extent that the papacy itself was, at that time, ready and willing to give serious consideration to reform. Christian humanists such as Erasmus and his friend Thomas More were advocating changes from within. The *Devotio Moderna* ("Modern Devotion"), at first an amorphous movement of the Netherlands dedicated to overhauling both religious and lay life, gathered force throughout the latter half of the fifteenth century. It included such men as Erasmus. These "modernists" attacked heartlessly observed ritual, foolish superstition in the devotion to saints, and the sale of indulgences, and they advocated fresh and more lively translations of the Scriptures. They advocated, too, a striving for "true goodness," in the place of a by then largely stultified theology that was far too much the province of "experts": men who were usually no more than scholastic bureaucrats. In September 1517 the ever-prescient Erasmus exclaimed: "I am afraid that a great revolution is impending." In the following month it exploded into life because of the action of the Wittenberg monk Martin Luther.

At first sight Luther was not too different from many other German monks of his time. He was shocked by the laxity of the clergy (he had visited Rome and been horrified by it) and by the free sale of indulgences. These offered remission from the temporal penalties for sin, but had long been sold in order to raise money. Chaucer in England had earlier satirized this misuse in his *Canterbury Tales;* and so had many other writers. When a cardinal came to Germany to try to sell more, Luther was not the only monk or priest to object. He was already an admirer of the monastic houses set up by men of the *Devotio Moderna:* "Brothers and Sisters of the Common Life," in which monks, nuns, and laity alike submitted themselves to simple rules of decent conduct. . . .

But he was more pugnacious than most of those dissatisfied with the state of affairs—unusually so, indeed, by any standards, past or present—and he was even more deeply troubled about his own salvation. He was in a state of deep depression about this. His own indignation, as well as his grievances against the Church, happened to fit in with those of a majority of the populations of many of the states of which Germany was then composed.

In November 1517 he chose a not unusual method for the demanding of an open dispute: He nailed his famous *Ninety-Five Theses* to the door of the Castle Church in Wittenberg. These reflected a crisis he had undergone two years earlier, often called the *Turmerlebnis* or "Tower Experience," during which he believed, with a fervor not less than mystical, that God had imparted to him the nature of the essence of the Gospels: that faith alone—regardless of "works," mere deeds—can ensure salvation.

Within a month the *Theses* had traveled far and wide and were soon printed. The Church, now alarmed, hoped to settle the matter by disciplining Luther; but he refused to obey its authority. He converted some like-minded eager men to his point of view, and he put himself under the protection of the elector of his native state, Saxony, who, mainly for political reasons, was ready to accede. When a papal Bull, condemning his actions and his writings, arrived from the Vatican, Luther angrily tore it up.

In 1520 Luther issued three documents that became decisive in the break with the Church. Among these, the *Babylonian Captivity* (the title, *von der Babylonische Gegenschaft* in German, refers to the Babylonian captivity under Nebuchadnezzar recorded in the OLD TESTAMENT) is as representative and as eloquent of his views as any other single document. Originally written in Latin (unusual for Luther) it was soon translated into German. Other works such as the *Catechism* deal with different theological details, and it could be argued that his translation of the NEW TESTAMENT (based on the revised text of Erasmus of 1518), and above all his hymns, exercised a wider influence. (The famous *Confession* of Augsburg of 1530 was approved but not written by him; besides which it is more conciliatory than Luther really felt.)

Against this, however, it must be said that after about 1524–25, with the eruption of the Peasants' War, Luther's influence on the course of the Reformation began to fade. A political conservative at heart, he quickly grew afraid of the disorder he had helped to provoke, and he vehemently opposed the peasants—thus losing many friends. He found himself regarded as noisy and arrogant by those of the Catholic Church, such as Erasmus, who had no wish to leave it, but who did understand and accept many if not all of his complaints. From the other side—from, as we should now say, the left of him—he was seen as a dangerous conservative.

At the heart of Luther's protest lay his personal conviction that human beings were helplessly predisposed to sin and depravity and could be saved by God's grace alone. Man is wholly in the power of evil and can do nothing but sin (Luther, a strongly sexed man, certainly equated sexual desire with sin); but God, owing to the merits of Jesus his son, still regards man as sinless. Thus it is only by a kind of merciful fiction that a man or woman can attain justification by faith alone. Later Thomas Cranmer, burned by Queen Mary for not recanting his "heresy," would talk—in the English Book of Common Prayer—of a "quick lively faith"; certainly the far from complacent Luther meant just that, something alive at every possible moment.

In the *Babylonian Captivity* Luther denied the traditional seven Sacraments (outward signs of inward spiritual grace, which had been boiled down by the Church from many more):

> I must deny that there are seven Sacraments [baptism, con-
> firmation, eucharist, penance, extreme unction, holy orders, mar-
> riage] and must lay it down, for the time being, that there are only
> three, baptism, penance, and the bread [in Catholic ritual the laity
> received only the bread, the priest alone partaking of the
> wine]. . . . I should hold that there was only one Sacrament, and
> three sacramental signs. . . .

Luther insisted that communion in both kinds (i.e., the laity partake of
both bread and wine) alone had scriptural authority. On the subject of the
controversy over whether Christ's actual blood and flesh were on the altar, as
distinct from various theologically determined metaphors for it, Luther
declared himself in favor of the real presence, but added "whoever chooses
to hold either opinion should do so." He attacked the priesthood, saying that
"every man . . . who has learned that he is a Christian recognizes that we are
all equally priests. . . ."

In 1524 Luther finally resigned his order and married an ex-nun. His
family recorded his *Table Talk,* which, although it can hardly be said to have
been influential in the sense demanded by this book, is essential for those
who wish to understand him. At a less informal level, his own philosophy is
perhaps best encapsulated in the famous hymn which, translated by Thomas
Carlyle, is almost as famous in English as "A Safe Stronghold Our God Is
Still." (Americans know it in another version as, "A Mighty Fortress Is Our
God.") Here occur the telling lines which mean, literally, "All we do is in
vain, even in the best life."

It may be that Luther, a man of violent temper—as his father had been
before him—tended even more than most of us to judge other people in the
light of his own obvious failings, which for him included lustfulness and,
although he may not have been able to discern this fault, vituperativeness—
but there is no doubt that his personal pessimism, even depressed mentality,
struck a chord among other equally gloomy Germans, many of whom eventually carried his reforms much further than he himself would have wished.
He struck an even more certain chord among the poorer people with his
message to the complacent that the matter of their salvation was *not* already
settled, and that the carefully graded hierarchy of penance laid down by the
Church, and mediated by priests, was *not* adequate.

Luther's hatred, and he did not lack it, was a very potent factor in his
success; it often came out in his superb and very highly effective oratory. But
he hardly fell into the logical trap which caught the French priest JOHN
CALVIN: He could easily answer the questions (much pondered upon by
the Russian novelist Dostoyevsky, and always far too lightly dismissed by
twentieth-century atheist humanists, often resentfully lacking in the robust-
ness required to commit really decent sins), *"Why if I am already damned
should I behave well in this life?"* or, as it is often stated, and as Dostoyevsky
stated it, *"Why is not everything permitted?"* Good works, Luther never

denied, helped faith. But faith alone counted.

But of course Luther was inconsistent, as have been almost all those whose thinking has had so decisively immediate an effect on the course of history. He could, too, be intolerably dogmatic and cruel, as when, in a pamphlet of 1525 (not actually circulated until hostilities had ceased), he urged the rulers to

> go on unconcerned, and with a good conscience lay about them as long as their hearts still beat. It is to their advantage that the peasants have a bad conscience and an unjust cause. . . . These peasants have deserved death many times over. . . .

The Papal Bull excommunicating Luther

The Reformation was inevitable, for political as well as for doctrinal reasons. Luther was not the kind of man that gentler Christians might have chosen to precipitate it. He never learned, despite the excellent intellect with which he had been endowed, to control his emotions for long. But he thus gave men a sense of comfort about their sins. He called Reason "the Devil's whore"—a silly thing to say, in fact, even if one knows what he meant, which was that the faculty of reason had been corrupted by original sin and was therefore in itself unfit to judge how men should think of God.

Luther is, alas, unlovable and even somewhat worthy of the intolerance that he ultimately bred: He was not scrupulous in argument, and he could even be quite deliberately obtuse if it so suited him. The "gracious" God to whom he appealed as sole justification was not merciful in an ordinarily Christian sense. Yet he is fairly described as "the pivotal point in the tradition from Paul's doctrine of justification through faith . . . to the [modern Calvinist theologian] Karl Barth." His last work (1545), does him little credit: A violent and unbalanced attack on the papacy, *Against the Papacy Established by the Devil* all too clearly shows signs of the bad health from which he was suffering; it is by turns sexually obscene, scatological, and abusive.

Luther's theology is weak when he deals with the matter of secular justice, which he only very uneasily leaves to the secular authorities. No man until the advent of Hitler had such charisma for the German peoples.

34

Gargantua and *Pantagruel*

FRANÇOIS RABELAIS

1534 and 1532

Most often known in English as *The Adventures of Gargantua and Pantagruel*, François Rabelais's work—more variously interpreted, perhaps, than any other of similar stature—lacks a collective title. It appeared in four parts, as follows: *Pantagruel* (1532), *Gargantua* (1534), *Tiers Livre* (*Third Book;* 1546), and *Quart Livre* (*Fourth Book;* 1549, expanded 1552). A *Cinquiesme Livre* (*Fifth Book*) of 1562 is only partly, or just possibly not at all, by Rabelais and has posed a problem for scholars.

In the seventeenth century Rabelais was most often seen as primarily a humorist; that was the view of MONTAIGNE ("simply amusing") and then of Sir Thomas Urquhart, whose famous English version of the first four books (1653, 1693) remains the most lively as well as the least accurate and most misleading. In the eighteenth century the work was often interpreted as allegorical or esoteric, or both; the nineteenth and twentieth centuries have seen him most variously, as smutty mocking rationalist, Stoic, "naturist," libertarian, and—most recently—devoutly religious man, and thus (again) as allegorist. Apart from the fact that Rabelais wrote at a time when the Puritans were only just in the process of inventing "smut"—his celebrated obscenity was not unusual in its own time, though the envious CALVIN knew and of course condemned his work—there is a degree of truth in all these interpretations. But it is a mistake to view the work as a carefully planned whole. It built upon itself as it was written, and was never revised or given any sort of consistency. It has, however, remained important enough for every age, even every decently read individual, to have to come to terms with it.

Most of the books about Rabelais have been scholarly, so that to an extent, and ironically, the reputation of a humorist has become entangled in and engulfed by a thick web of meticulous and invaluable, but obscuring overearnestness—for Rabelais after all does have a genuinely popular appeal. Actually, he is the first of all truly popular writers—and his is the first substantial book in French Renaissance literature. Its influence is inestimable. It was inestimable even while the myth of the drunken and irresponsible buffoon, the "jolly winebibber of Chinon," lived on—it was perpetrated until quite recently in the tiresome and "smutty" novels of the American *pasticheur* James Branch Cabell, and still is now in similar but happily less well known practitioners. Yet VOLTAIRE resembled Montaigne at least in rejecting him altogether, as a "drunkard" whose writings were done only while he was drunk. For the novelist Balzac, however, his was "the greatest mind." And the modernists, such as Proust and Joyce, rediscovered his essential seriousness long before the critics did.

Not much is certainly known about him. He was born, the son of a lawyer, near Chinon in the Touraine. He spent his early years as a Franciscan friar and was ordained a priest. His interest in the new humanism and therefore in the Greek language led to persecution by his obscurantist superiors—he never forgot this, and he satirizes them mercilessly throughout the whole of his work. In 1524, clearly a resourceful man, he got permission to transfer to the rather more lax Benedictine Order. He had by this time gained the protection of important people. By 1528 he was able to abandon the priesthood. Rabelais studied medicine in Paris and later became famous as a leading physician of his time; he may even have made some contributions to anatomical knowledge. His "lost years," 1526–1530, must have been spent in travel, and not only in absorbing learning but also the ways and means of the common people, for it was to them above all—while the scholars of the Sorbonne thirsted in their turn for his blood, doubtless particularly provoked by a pun he made on *soul* and *asshole* (in French *âme, âne*)—that he appealed.

In Montpellier in 1530 he lectured on Galen and HIPPOCRATES, using the Greek texts, thus causing a sensation. It is pretty clear that he turned to romance writing for money ("lack of money—there's no affliction like it"). He became physician to the hospital at Lyons. Three times he went to Rome in the company of his protector, Jean du Bellay (not to be confused with his younger cousin, Joachim du Bellay, one of France's greatest poets). Until his death (before May, 1554) he remained the bane of the ecclesiastical authorities, always their own worst enemies.

For the first book (now always printed as the *Second Book*), *Pantagruel*, Rabelais took his inspiration from a popular work of the time relating the exploits of a giant, Gargantua; this was a not particularly distinguished example of by then debased Arthurian romance—it would not be worth reading now. He was also impelled to write it by the still famous drought of the summer of 1532, one of the worst in history. Pantagruel, the demon of thirst (symbolizing, no doubt, Renaissance thirst for new knowledge), another giant, is Gargantua's son. Another main character in this first book is Panurge. Just as ERASMUS did, Rabelais owes much to the Greek satirist Lucian. Another influence is Erasmus's *In Praise of Folly* itself. There is here, in what is in some respects a brilliant ragbag, much fun with language itself, and the satirical expression of many points of view—Rabelais always emphasized, in an age when dogma and scholasticism still dominated, that truth can speak with several voices. It is already clear not only that he is a serious humorist who can never be pinned down, but also a remarkable polymath.

Gargantua, although composed later, and now presented as the *First Book,* is set chronologically earlier. Here Rabelais introduces his "anti-monastery," the Abbaye de Thélème (*thelemus* is Greek for "will"), which makes it perfectly clear that Rabelais is a humorist with a serious religious and educational purpose—not the purveyor of mere nonsense as he has so often taken to have been. He saw, like Erasmus and a few other humanists, that one of the keys to a better life lay in educational method (Rabelais also resembled Erasmus in that, although passionately reformist, he did not wish to rock the boat). Two sorts of people are not allowed in his Abbaye: monks and hypocrites. Humanists, however, are welcome:

> You hypocrites and two-faced, please stay out:
> Grinning old apes, potbellied snivelbeaks,
> Stiffnecks and blockheads. Worse than Goths, no doubt. . . .
>
> Stay out, usurers and misers all, . . .
> But welcome here, and very welcome be,
> And doubly welcome, all noble gentlemen,
> This is the place where taxes all are free,
> And incomes plenty. . . .

The *Third Book,* at the beginning of which Rabelais begs his readers to withhold laughter until the seventy-eighth book, has little in common with its two predecessors. There had been a twelve-year gap. Pantagruel's hugeness is almost forgotten. Here is essentially an uproarious send-up of the dispute then raging in France called the *Querelle des femmes,"* what we might call "the Woman Question." This had been going on, at a variety of levels from the comic and vulgar to the exceedingly overlearned, for almost a hundred years. It often became as ridiculous as modern pseudofeminism can now become—a Stalinist exercise—but was as often serious and considered, and frequently a sincere attempt to deal with the differences between the sexes. Rabelais brings back his character Panurge and makes the subject of the whole work the question of whether he should get married.

The general conclusion was for long that Rabelais had ranged himself firmly on the side of the "woman-haters"; and "Pantagruelist" became a synonym for "woman-hater." That is indeed the position which he appears to take up. But, as Samuel Putnam, the best of Rabelais's modern translators, wrote, it is not as simple as that. It is not possible to go into the question in a short space, but is at least worth pointing out that this very book is dedicated to the Neoplatonist Margaret, Queen of Navarre (author of a series of stories, the *Heptameron*), who was foremost among the many feminists of her time. Like Cervantes soon after him, Rabelais was criticizing the *false* chivalry of the times, which tended to diminish and patronize women, and not at all to honor them.

The *Fourth Book* (we can omit here the dubious *Fifth*) describes the voyages of Pantagruel, now again differently conceived, and is really concerned with sixteenth-century geographical (and, by implication, inner) exploration and its consequences. Voltaire, despite his own anticlericalism, hated Rabelais, but he did make one insightful remark about this book: "It has never been forbidden in France [in fact it was] because everything in it is hidden under a mass of extravagances which never give one time to disentangle the true aim of the author."

There is a very famous passage in Rabelais at the beginning of his own *First Book:*

> Following the dog's example, you will have to be wise in sniffing, smelling, and estimating these fine and meaty books; swiftness in the chase and boldness in the attack are what is called for; after which, by careful reading and frequent meditation, you should break the bone and suck the substantific marrow—that is to say, the meaning of the Pythagorean symbols which I employ—in the certain hope that you will be rendered prudent and valorous by such a reading; for in the course of it you will find things of quite a different taste and a doctrine more abstruse which shall reveal to you most high sacraments and horrific mysteries in what concerns our religion, as well as the state and our political and economic life.

Now this means *exactly what it says.* But, unlike most other mystics, Rabelais's method was laughter. There is no laughter, there would be no reason for laughter, if life were reasonable and just. His work needs to be looked at, not as a single book, but as four interconnected books, all on the serious subject of what life actually is, and what the difference is between our illusions and the reality in which we have them. He is far closer, not in spite of but because of his laughter, to Plato, Buber, Bunyan, the Dhammapada, than he is to the political or rationalist writers discussed in this book. In laughing he explores the meaning of seriousness.

35

Institutes of the Christian Religion

JOHN CALVIN

1536

Calvin concedes that it is "awful," but declares that there is no help for it: "Some men are born devoted from the womb to certain death [to eternal suffering and damnation, not to mere oblivion], that God's name be glorified in their destruction."

God is clearly understood, by Calvin, to have decreed, before the beginning of time, that certain of his creatures should be eternally damned: "If there were no one to punish, then God would be incapable of demonstrating that he was a mysteriously vindictive God." Ironically, this view of God has even influenced recent Catholic educational practice, as James Joyce indignantly made clear.

Those arbitrarily elected by God to salvation and eternal life (their exact number was always a matter of dispute, but was invariably taken as being smaller than the number of permanently damned) had done nothing whatsoever to merit this gift; not to be reprobate is impossible in Calvinism; but the elect do possess one (sort of) consolatory virtue—they are "assured" that they are elected. It is perfectly clear that Calvin himself believed that he was thus elected. Only a very few of those who believed in his theology thought that they were *not* elected—but these unfortunate people did exist. The case of the Englishman Francis Spira, who believed himself damned, is the most famous of them. In England, when that country came under Calvinist influence, there was a spate of publications, with titles such as *A Case of Conscience . . . How a Man May Know Whether He Be a Child of God, or No* (1592) and with subtitles such as *Wherein every man may clearly see, whether he shall be saved or damned. Set forth dialogue wise for the understanding of the simple* (1601).

"In man," wrote Calvin in the *Institutes*, "all which had reference to the blessed life of the soul is extinct." The Church, he said, was full of reprobates of "apparent faith": They were hypocrites "into whose mind God insinuates himself, so that . . . they may yet taste the goodness of the spirit." The rejected, he said, "are raised up by God's inscrutable judgment to illustrate his glory by their condemnation."

Does this most decisive theological book (after that of LUTHER, who never met Calvin) of the sixteenth century stem from a profoundly neurotic hatred of life, or from a sincere "assurance" (such assurance *is*, for Calvin, faith) of his own salvation? Either way, the world is viewed as an implacably hostile one, and its God as a vindictive monster, glorious in his cruelty. Luther, for all his roughness and rudeness, seems positively genial by contrast; nor did he revel in the damnation of millions. Calvin felt "reasonably sure" of his own salvation, since he passed his own "tests": sincere belief, an upright life, attendance upon the sacrament of the Lord's supper. Luther denied that there were such tests—and so, more honestly, could not form a "community of the elect" such as the state he ruled, Geneva, was supposed to be.

But the repulsiveness of Calvinism, of the odiously cruel God it presents to us, is not in itself a valid argument against it. The horrible nature of this God is at least in part (even if it took a peculiarly vindictive man to invent such a God) owed to the purely philosophical difficulties encountered by the early Christians. Theology, as KARL POPPER once wrote, is only lack of faith; and the anthropomorphic God invented by the Church Fathers presented intellectual problems for them. AUGUSTINE in particular, as an ex-"heretic," became exasperated with Pelagianism, a "heresy" named after Pelagius, who taught that men could achieve their own salvation apart from God's grace (the existence of which he did not deny).

This led Augustine—for whom God was, to an almost hysterical extent, omnipotent—to a position very close to that so gleefully taken up by Calvin. But he did try to preserve free will, and he was eager, if he could, to distinguish between God's foreknowledge and his will. The mercilessness of God was not something he wanted to over advertise.

Both Augustine and Calvin relied upon Saint Paul rather than Jesus Christ for their views, and both were hidebound by dogma. The trouble with both was that they regarded *concupiscence*, literally "desire for the things of this world," but, for them, mainly sexual desire, as absolutely wicked, and as the mark of original sin. Adam and Eve had dwelled "without sin" in the Garden of Eden until Eve ate the apple offered to her by Satan: Sex, in other words, *is* sin. The great Polish anthropologist Bronislaw Malinowski wisely wrote that sex causes so much anxiety and has so many taboos placed around it, because *"it really is dangerous"!* No one has been able to solve the problems set up by it (let alone by the necessary "regulation" of it).

Both Augustine and Calvin (whose mind was a markedly inferior one), were made anxious by their sexual appetite—hence their construction of an artificial God who, even if he "created" sexual appetite, somehow simultaneously transcended it. Calvin is an Augustine (who could be genial and friendly) gone rancid. Because his doctrine is nominally at the heart of every church that calls itself "reformed," he has been accorded (except by a few) an intellectual standing far higher than the quality of his mind deserves. He wrote clear French, but his stylistic achievements have nonetheless been exaggerated.

Unlike Luther, son of a miner, Calvin (1509–1564) came of the middle classes. He was born in Noyon in Picardy, France, the son of an attorney. He was trained in law, and, although brought up by his mother as a good Catholic, was never ordained. After an education at the University of Paris, he underwent, at the age of twenty, a "conversion" in the course of which he not only went over to Protestantism but also was convinced that he had been entrusted by God with a mission to restore the church to its original purity. It might well be asked, at this juncture, why, since God had planned everything in advance, before the beginning of time, Calvin thought that this could make any difference. The answer is that he was not a philosopher, let alone a logician: He was a cruel and anxious man hankering after earthly power—which he obtained.

He first published the *Institutes* in March 1536, after which he soon became well known and had to flee from persecution by Francis I of France. Passing through the Swiss city of Geneva he was persuaded by the equally cruel reformer Guillaume Farel to stay there and help to establish the Reformation. It is said that Farel threatened him with the pains of Hell—but that, again, was scarcely to the point since the matter had been decided before the beginning of time.

Calvin was appointed professor of theology at Geneva, and, apart from a two-year absence when the opposition gained the upper hand, remained there until the end of his life. During the period of his exile (1538–1541), at Strasbourg, he married the widow of an Anabaptist, Idellette de Bure; their son died at birth (1541), and Idellette died in 1549.

In due course Calvin established a reign of silent terror in Geneva. As an economic unit the city flourished, but there was strict control of morals and no toleration. Spies were set upon "delinquents," and the "unruly" were excommunicated. The details of everyone's lives were known and scrutinized, and in 1552 the *Institutes* was declared by the Council of Geneva as "holy doctrine which none may speak against." Already, in 1547, one Jacques Gouet had been tortured and then beheaded for "impiety." There were more tortures and executions. EDWARD GIBBON was even more shocked by Calvin's personal sadism than he was by the dreaded Catholic Inquisition.

Calvin's malice, envy, and undoubted sadism are best seen in his treatment of the physician and "heretic" Michael Servetus (1511–1553). In 1531 Servetus had published a tract denying the trinity—in other words an early Unitarian opinion. Calvin had disputed with him by correspondence and had felt himself outdone in controversy by him. He swore that if he could get Servetus into Geneva, the physician would not escape with his life.

First, Calvin had him denounced to the Catholic Inquisition. But Servetus escaped. Some fascination drew him to Geneva; perhaps he thought that he could enlist the considerable, but gagged, opposition to Calvin there. Calvin had him tortured, engaged him in dispute even on the day of his execution (at some advantage, one might say), and then gloated as he watched him being burned alive. "Tomorrow he dies," he had just written to his fellow-torturer, Farel.

It is now quite commonly conceded that what we call Christianity stems not from the teachings of Jesus Christ (who may well have been a gnostic), but from Paul's interpretation of him. All the churches, but Calvin especially, relied on Paul. Philosophically and historically neither the early church nor Luther or Calvin had a leg to stand on. But the twisted religion that stemmed from these confusions did retain, of course, much truth and profundity, even though Marcion and the later gnostics were so savagely excluded from it. No one would want to be without Augustine just because he was misled by his failure to be able to maintain an open mind.

To recapture the essence of Christianity it is necessary to go back, earlier than the demonic Saul of Tarsus. But even Luther, like the gentler ERASMUS, had at least wished to cleanse the Church of its corruption—to return it to what he believed to be its original purity. When Calvin erupted on the scene, the betrayal of decency and mercy was almost as drastic and devilish as what occurred when Paul took over the teachings of Jesus Christ in order to launch his own life-denying movement. It is ironic indeed that the twentieth-century theologian Karl Barth should have needed to call upon the spirit of Calvinism to restore his church to seriousness. But he saw that any church would have to oppose Nazism, whereas Calvin's Geneva was one of the blueprints for the Third Reich.

36

On the Revolution of the Celestial Orbs

NICOLAUS COPERNICUS

1543

The influence of the Polish canon and astronomer Copernicus (1473–1543) has been crucial and fundamental, but from the start it has been poorly understood. Copernicus was not the first to put the sun at the center of the solar system, and his reasons for doing so were in many respects mistaken. Yet of course his achievement was immense. His famous book, published as he lay dying, was not put on the index (list of forbidden books) of the Roman

Church at the time of his death, as so many suppose, but only in 1616. It was quietly removed long after his theory had been accepted—as late as 1757.

Copernicus studied at Cracow in Poland and then at Bologna in Italy. He then took up the position of canon of Fruenberg in East Prussia. His duties included looking after the properties of the Church there, and he carried them out conscientiously; but he spent much of his time in a little observation tower he had built in 1513.

ARISTOTLE had criticized the Pythagoreans for holding that the most precious thing in the universe, fire, lay at the center of the universe, and for believing that a "counter-earth" (invisible to us), as well as a rotating earth, revolved about this celestial fire; the sun as well as the earth also orbited this celestial fire. But, despite the heliocentric views of Aristarchus of Samos (about 200 B.C.E.), who had the support of others, the hypothesis that the earth was at the center of the universe prevailed. And we do, after all, for ourselves, seem to live at the center—just by virtue of the fact that we are where we are. We navigate on such a thus not quite false assumption.

The system of Claudius Ptolemy (second century C.E.) perfected this fiction: In it, the perfect circles of planetary motion around the earth, upon which PLATO, heir to the Pythagoreans, had insisted, are preserved by means of "epicycles," an ingenious but wholly untrue means of "saving the phenomena" (as ancient astronomers called it). The most perfect motion was circular, and Ptolemy's theory accounted for this.

Copernicus, too, firmly believed in the perfection of circular motion, and the old notion of a central fire was not far from his mind. He pleaded thus:

> At rest, however, in the middle of everything is the sun. For in this most beautiful temple, who would place this lamp in another or better position than that from which it can light up the whole thing at the same time? For the sun is not inappropriately called by some people the lantern of the universe, its mind by others, and its ruler by others. Hermes the thrice Great [this is none other than Hermes Trismegistus] labels it a visible God, and Sophocles's Electra, the all-seeing.

It is thus a supreme irony that Copernicus arrived at his revolutionary theory for what historians of science grudgingly call "reasons of hermeticism." Hermeticism, mysticism—whatever people prefer to call it—need not in fact rule out scientific truth; on the contrary, it can and should encourage it, as Abulafia and Meister Eckhardt recognized when they embraced the works of MAIMONIDES. Indeed, it was just such a hermeticism that caused the English magician John Dee, and the Italian philosopher Giordano Bruno, to take up the heliocentric theory so eagerly and so early. (Dee, it is true, kept quiet about it and left it to his pupil Thomas Digges to publicize it.)

Copernicus, who, like KEPLER, only wanted to demonstrate the harmony of the universe, made no contribution to the science of celestial motion. He relied, he declared, on the fact that the sun was "the lantern of the universe." Nor could he conceive of bodies moving around the sun at anything but a constant speed—for God himself was constant, was he not? He was therefore never able to patch up his theory to fit his observations, and he thus retained Ptolemy's epicycles.

Afraid of ridicule or worse, Copernicus circulated *A Little Commentary,* and this was even approved by a pope of the time, who wanted the theory published. In 1539 Copernicus began to work on the theory in earnest, in collaboration with the professor of mathematics at the University of Wittenberg, George Joachim (known as Rheticus). By the time his book was published, Copernicus was on his deathbed. Certainly he did not know about—or at the very least was unable to prevent—an unsigned preface written by a Protestant cleric called Osiander, which stated that the theory was only offered as a hypothesis and not as the truth. While it was *only* a hypothesis, it seems, it was safe enough.

Copernicus was unable to complete his work, and it remained for Danish astronomer Tycho Brahe, the Pythagorean Johannes Kepler, and the Italian GALILEO GALILEI—and finally ISAAC NEWTON—to do this. It is often—almost always—stated, and not unreasonably, that Copernicus began the process of casting man from the center of the universe, and thus of undermining religion. This may be so in some minds; according to most historians it is even true. But the matter is more complicated than this.

What Copernicus in fact started was the undermining of a false Christianity, a Christianity that had become tired, that had become so rotten within itself that it could no longer recognize the truth but might tolerate it—if it were wrapped up in a "harmless" hypothetical form. The Protestant authorities were as guilty in this as were the Roman Catholic.

At first, for reasons by no means fully understood, the heliocentric theory met with little opposition. LUTHER, Brahe, MONTAIGNE, BACON, and most others rejected it out of hand. Luther, with his usual violence, referred to Copernicus as a madman and traducer of the Scriptures. It was only gradually that opposition to the theory grew up; eventually Galileo was forced to deny it to the Inquisition. Meanwhile, the great mystic Giordano Bruno (1542–1600) took it up as a fact central to his gnostic philosophy. Bruno, like many modern mystics, believed in a purely material universe, but one imbued at all points by God. For him as for many others the universe was itself a great intelligence. He was burned for his beliefs, about which (however) he was not tactful. It is not clear how much his adherence to Copernicus's theory counted against him; nor did he in certain details fully understand the mathematics of it. But such a good man—such was the state of the Roman Church at that time—a man dedicated to scientific as well as religious truth, could not be allowed to live unless he made a full recantation. That he would not undertake. A wealthy young man, a Venetian, led him to return to Rome but, on discovering that Bruno would not teach him black magic, denounced his presence to the Inquisition. "Greater perhaps is your fear in pronouncing my sentence than mine in hearing it," he told his pious murderers. One of these, the Jesuit Cardinal Bellarmine, was canonized as a saint by a grateful Church as late as 1930. But Bruno's influence lives on, particularly in SPINOZA. He lives on, too, in James Joyce's *Finnegans Wake,* as "Mr. Brown," "Bruno Nolan," and other names. Copernicus himself, a more timid man, would have been appalled; nevertheless, it was in that religious direction, rather than that of scientific positivism, which he himself would have preferred to go.

Answering the Inquisition, Bruno said, "I hold that the universe is infinite . . . a finite world would be unworthy of God. Hence I have declared infinite worlds to exist beyond this earth; I hold with Pythagoras that the earth is a star like all the others. . . . God is present in all . . . in a way that is beyond words."

It was Galileo who became the first real victim of the Church's rather sudden hatred of Copernican theory, possibly a matter of intrigue between jealous priests. But Galileo escaped with his life. It had been fear of Bruno, though, certainly, which decisively turned the Church against the truth.

37

Essays

MICHEL EYQUEM DE MONTAIGNE

1580

At first it may seem odd that Michel de Montaigne (1533–1592)—such a fountain of decisive influence on seventeenth-century thinking, and therefore on ourselves too—was so casual about his own work that he could immediately describe it as "frivolous." But Montaigne the essayist is a kind of prose SHAKESPEARE, and he has been almost as influential. This is a startling comparison; but it does allow for the fact that, as an essayist, as a commentator on life in all its manifestations, Montaigne deliberately lacks passion, is always temperate, and above all never lets his imagination run away with him. He does not allow his manner to be indignant, even if he himself is. However, he is almost all that Shakespeare might have been—had the latter continually poured oil over the troubled waters of his own fancies, dreams, and nightmares. For, like Shakespeare, he does cover every field of life; he is not, for all his cautious conservatism (and Shakespeare himself was rather like that, too) to be prevented from speculation; and he is constitutionally unable to follow convention (although he was not persuaded by COPERNICUS).

Montaigne's appreciation of poetry is very considerable—he quotes nearly nine hundred passages—and, paradoxically, he takes the Platonic view that it is at its best when it is at its most intense (at its most "mad"); but all this is from the point of view of a nonpoet, of a *reader*, which is really what Montaigne above all was: he is the very paradigm of that elusive but vital character—he comes as near to it as any individual writer has ever come—to a *common reader*. That is why he is not *too* learned: both Julius Caesar Scaliger and his son Joseph Justus, the most sheerly learned scholars of the sixteenth century, murdered the spirit, with the letter as well, with their vanity and their arrogance: In "On the Vanity of Words" Montaigne wrote of professional jargon as "trickery," and complained that such "rare and exotic" forms of language were "no more than housemaid's chatter." This will not have pleased Scaliger or his vain kind; nor should it please contemporary advocates of postmodernism. . . .

Montaigne took up his skeptical position because his contemporaries or near-contemporaries were so theoretical and dogmatic (especially, for example, in the realm of the theater). It was also a piece of disrespect: Up to that time the authors of autobiographical works had had something to boast about: Caesar, Cicero, AUGUSTINE. Montaigne had no power or glory to boast about—he was just a man—and literary tradition did not allow the "unqualified" man to indulge in commentary on life. Until Montaigne, that is.

His method of writing is unassuming (we would say "laid back"—he is one of the first of all the laid-back writers in literature), casual and relaxed (just, of course, as the good familiar essay—the genre he virtually invented—ought to be); but he was a serious, not to say deliberative man, whose intelligent and well-informed opinions on everything under the sun—how to converse properly, how to endure pain, how to prepare for death, what were the virtues of the "new" American subcontinent, how to read well, how to bring up children, the "cannibals" of Brazil, how to deal with the sexual urge, how to be virtuous, and a very great deal else that concerns us all—influenced educated men all over the world. He became the most widely read prose writer of the Renaissance; he still is. That Shakespeare read and noted him, knowing him from the famous 1603 translation by John Florio, is certain; some have even seen the character of Hamlet as a reflection of Montaigne—not of his personal life, but of the especially skeptical way in which he thought. And even if that isn't strictly true—there has been debate about it—then there is still merit in the suggestion. *Hamlet* takes place in a world of ideas that is Montaigne-influenced. And it was written only some quarter of a century after the first *Essays* appeared—and only a decade after Montaigne's own death.

Michel, who became Seigneur de Montaigne in 1568, was the eldest son of a venerable country gentleman of Périgord, near Bordeaux in Gascony. But, as the aristocratic Joseph Scaliger—more learned than Montaigne or anyone else of his time (1540–1609), but at the same time less understanding—jealous of his fame, later sneeringly declared, his forebears had sold salted herrings. Montaigne's grandfather, Ramon Eyquem, bought the estate of Montaigne in 1477, and thus gained the right to its name. His son Pierre, soldier and lawyer, raised in the family tradition as a Roman Catholic, married Antoniette de Lopez, who came from a Spanish Jewish family converted to Protestantism.

Two of the nine or so children born to this couple adopted their mother's faith, but Michel—brought up to speak Latin before French—remained a nominal Catholic to the end. He attended the humanist Collège de Guyenne, where he learned of the Stoicism to which he was always devoted. At twenty-one he began a legal career. He became a close friend to, and colleague of, another young lawyer, Etienne de la Boëtie. La Boëtie, a gifted writer, described him as, at this time, lazy—but vehement, and (as a commentator from a more polite era than our own put it) "somewhat prone to the gratification of his passions." When la Boëtie died at only thirty-two, in 1563, of dysentery—leaving Montaigne his library—Montaigne suffered the most severe emotional experience of his life: One of his key essays, "On Friendship," deals with it. He wrote: "In the friendship I speak of, our souls blend and melt so entirely, that there is no more sign of the seam that joins them. If I am pressed to say why I loved him, I feel that I can only express myself by answering, 'Because it was he, because it was I." Thus, although in part imitating a classical pattern of ideal friendship that he had learned about back at the Collège de Guyenne, but also with genuine and sincere feeling, he continued to love his friend in death just as he had loved him in life. Some contemporary homosexuals have found no difficulty in claiming Montaigne as one of their own; but they probably misunderstand: Montaigne of course discussed homosexuality (just as Shakespeare did in his own way, in inventing Iago and others), and he did state in "On Friendship" that friendship is to be preferred to the "impetuous and fickle love for women"—but he was talking about *friendship,* not *romantic homosexual love* (just as "fickle" as romantic heterosexual love?), and there is no reason to doubt that he meant it when he also said that physical intimacy among males is "justly abhorred." But any discussion about whether such friendship as he advocates has an element of homosexuality in it would have to refer to his essay—just as much as to Freud—and we have to refer to it, too, when we discuss the matter of whether Shakespeare's Sonnets contain an element of homosexuality. If we take Montaigne at face value, then he seems to be saying that he is not homosexual.

Thereafter he never had as close a relationship, even with the woman he married in 1565, and with whom he had several children; only one of these, a daughter for whom he had scant liking, survived infancy. From the time of la Boëtie's death he withdrew into himself and conscientiously carried out, but was not seriously interested in, his duties. Or perhaps he hoped to receive a major post, and, too impatient for it, allowed his zeal to dim prematurely. He took part at a high level in the diplomatic negotiations during the years of the French Wars of Religion (wryly aware, no doubt, that he himself was a mixture of Spanish Jew, Roman Catholic, and Protestant). He was liked and valued at court; but, for some unknown reason, in 1571 he abruptly retired to his estate.

Montaigne now dropped the style "Eyquem" altogether—and even pretended that the "de Montaigne" was an originally authentic title (which it was not). He had published a translation—first undertaken to please his father—from a Catalan theologian in 1569, and had written a travel journal (not published until the eighteenth century); he had also issued the translations and other writings of Boëtie; but even then he showed little interest in writing on his own account. The rest of his life, travels apart, he spent in his library tower, which may be visited today. On the walls of its small study he had engraved (in Latin), "In the year of Christ 1571 . . . Michel de Montaigne, long wearied of the courts and of public functions, while still in health, retires to the bosom of the learned Virgins, where in quiet and security he hopes, if the fates allow, to pass what may be left him of a life already half spent, consecrating this ancestral dwelling and sweet retreat to his liberty and tranquillity and leisure." But there is nothing about becoming a writer in that bitter and modest declaration.

It was only after the Massacre of Saint Bartholomew's Day (1572), when leading members of the Protestant Huguenot faction were murdered at the orders of Catherine de Médicis, that Montaigne began to jot down little notes about matters that interested him—at first, we may be sure, for his own edification. But the habit grew upon him as he continued with it. By the time he published the first two volumes he had developed a part-truthful, part-ironic mask. His famous preface of 1580 runs, "This is a sincere book, Reader. It forewarns you at the outset that in writing it I had no other but a private . . . end in view." The thought of being "serviceable" to the reader or even to himself had never occurred to him, he continues: "My powers are not equal to such a design. I intended it solely for my . . . friends. . . . I am myself the subject of my book; it is not reasonable to expect you to waste your leisure on a matter so frivolous and empty."

Of course he did not mean this. And yet he did. It was his way of pointing out that he was just an ordinary person, even if also a bit learned and a bit of a snob. It was, too, a mask, a device by which to present himself to the world. His older contemporary RABELAIS used the mask of a drunkard; Montaigne used that of a man eating humble pie, one who, above all, is not instructing anyone in how to be glorious. He even referred to his work as that of the excrement of a man in his dotage. The keynote of his essays is that of the danger of vanity, as the long essay in the second book on presumption, or vainglory, makes clear. He meant it when he wrote, in Florio's translation, "What I doe, it is but bunglingly, and wants both polishing and beauty." As well as being bitingly ironic, he was saying that this new kind of writing he was doing ought to be essentially unpretentious, however pretentious or cautiously conservative or indolent the writer himself might happen to be. He was in the process of inventing a new literary form—and no one has yet bettered him in it.

He suffered from gallstones and went in search of curative waters in a series of European journeys he undertook just after 1580, the year of publication of the *Essays*. He passed through all of France, Italy, and Germany—

but perhaps that was just an excuse to satisfy his huge and never fully satisfied curiosity. Under royal pressure he had to be mayor of Bordeaux (as his
father had been) from 1581 until 1585. (He has been much criticized for
absenting himself from his duties there at a time of plague.) After 1586 he
stayed at home, working at and improving his essays.

Montaigne thought of the essay as an *assay,* that is to say, as a *trial:* of
an idea, of himself, of the quality of his judgment, of his own experience and
of its extent—a skeptical test of, in fact, everything. Thus he could explore his
own psychology in a way that no prose writer had before him. André Gide,
whose *Journals* follow the tradition he set, wrote: "I ought never to travel
without a Montaigne." He was the first writer openly to abandon the notion
of the human being as a consistent entity: He examines his moods, his habits,
his emotions while they change; but he wants to discover more about consistency, too—he pursues the nature of what is permanent in him. There is
no dogmatic certainty about anything in Montaigne. Indeed, in 1586 he had
a medallion struck, with *Que sçay-je?* on it—"*What do I know?*" Thus he is
one of the first writers to stand firmly behind *modernism:* the attempt, conducted in a spirit of inquiry, by twentieth-century thinkers such as FREUD,
and by writers such as Joyce, Proust, Virginia Woolf, Joseph Conrad, and
many others, to present themselves and other people *as they really are* and
not as the various theologians, philosophers—and of course, above all, the
holders of power (whom they sometimes advise), who are devoted to the
ethics of obedience for fully understandable reasons—tell them they *ought* to
be. Thus, while he takes the orthodox side—is that another piece of ironic
comment?—he undermines its very existence by his style and method.

Montaigne himself took the (moderately) conservative and Catholic
point of view, so that commentators have tried to prove that he was a conservative Catholic—others, however, have put him forward as an atheist and
a liberal. They are all missing the point: He employed a skeptical method of
looking at the world—and was thus, ultimately, skeptical, even about his own
viewpoint. It is a salutary form of modesty. He explicitly refused to equate
self-examination (Socrates became his greatest hero) with narcissism; ultimately he is telling us that *self-knowledge* is more important than *self.* He is
thus an apt pupil of Socrates. Such an attitude points toward tolerance, the
lack of which turned his country in his lifetime into a hotbed of war and dispute. The Stoicism that he learned when he studied the Roman world was
personal to him, and he liked to practice it; the skepticism was less personal,
more objective, a matter of inner discipline; at bottom, it subscribed to a certain philosophy—that of Pyrrho (via SEXTUS EMPIRICUS), whose attitude has
been as, or even more, influential than that of many much greater names,
and by no means the least so because of Montaigne's interest in him. Montaigne is the first man in literature to confess to boredom, and the first man,
too, to express fear of it. He was, as well, a *nonprofessional,* a man who loved
literature but also distrusted the overliterary. Virginia Woolf said of him that
his self-portrait becomes, for the reader, a mirror.

38

Don Quixote

MIGUEL DE CERVANTES

Part I, 1605; Part II, 1615

Spain's greatest literary critic of the twentieth century, José Ortega y Gasset, honored *Don Quixote* thus:

> Cervantes—a patient gentleman who wrote a book—has been seated in the Elysian Fields for three centuries now, from which he casts melancholy glances about him as he awaits for a descendant to be born who shall be capable of understanding him

Like his contemporary WILLIAM SHAKESPEARE, the Spaniard Miguel Cervantes, far too serene and wise in his greatest writings ever to have deliberately planned them, left few clues about his life. In his two-part novel *Don Quixote*, usually (and reasonably) called "the greatest book in the world," is to be found almost every so-called modernist device of the twentieth century. That is not, of course, to try to diminish modernist writers, the responsible ones of whom extended literary conventions in order to accommodate new things that they felt ought to be said: things that had either been forbidden or even that had not been thought of (such as the different rates of time in subjective experience, and the shortcomings of the powers-that-be). *Modernism* as a term was unknown until long after Cervantes's time, but in fact, insofar as all literature is a struggle against the disingenuous lies of the orthodox, he was one of the most "modern" of all writers of any time. But then so were Sophocles and Aeschylus.

So to say that within *Don Quixote* are to be found most modernist devices, or anticipations of them, is not to say that other later writers are inferior in that sense. But it is to say that Cervantes, in this single astonishing work, initially designed by him, in the despair of poverty, to have as wide as possible a popular appeal, seems—with a humorous effortlessness that must have been born of acute suffering—to have understood pretty well all of the problems set by the writing of fiction, which is after all in large part a matter of "telling lies like truth" (as Daniel Defoe put it).

To a certain extent, as we may see it in retrospect, he carried on where RABELAIS left off; and, like Rabelais, his grand essence has become engulfed in the excellent and invaluable but often dubious exegeses of frigid professors, too frightened of the fires of life to want to stretch out their hands to be warmed by them. Cervantes triumphantly belongs, even more than Rabelais (if only because we do need some guidance to the topicalities of Rabelais's four works), to the common reader—that common reader who is all too often absent from the hearts of scholars who, profitably thriving on their intellects, have not experienced an emotional development. Like Rabelais yet again, Cervantes draws upon the lives and ways of "ordinary people." He sees what is most precious in their experience.

Cervantes was born in Alcalá de Henares, some twenty miles from Madrid, in 1547. His father was an obscure surgeon, not of the best qualifications, and possibly even a "ne'er-do-well," although of his real nature we have no inkling. We know nothing whatever of Miguel's childhood, except that there is no serious evidence (alas for the professors!) of his ever having attended a university. In 1568 he was a student—probably having already seen army service in Flanders—at the City School of Madrid.

After some now obscure trouble over a duel, which forced him to flee Spain, he joined the Spanish legion in Italy; in 1571 he found himself at the Battle of Lepanto, a showdown between Christians and Turkish "infidels." During this he (quite undoubtedly—it is not mere legendary lore) showed a thoroughly quixotic (to employ the word that he gave so generously to the world) bravery. He was twice wounded in the chest—and permanently lost the use of his left hand.

He remained a soldier for a time, serving in Tunis, and then, the time of his service up, in 1575, was on his way back to Spain from Naples when he was captured by pirates. He was not ransomed until 1580, but, apparently always resourceful, he made several attempts to escape from his captivity in Algiers before that.

Of the stories or novels embedded in *Don Quixote* the captive's tale is relevant here: This has always been taken as highly "romantic," yet it is based squarely on his own experience. It gives us cause to wonder at just how great is the human capacity for making the best of misfortunes—although it seems that Cervantes's Moorish master treated him exceptionally well.

He started to write during those dreary five years of imprisonment, mainly plays to entertain his fellow captives. A couple of these, out of many he wrote, have survived and were published long after his death. They are quite unremarkable—as unremarkable as the poetry he tried but always failed to write throughout his life. Perhaps it was his lack of capacity to write great poetry, his frustrated yearning to discover the magical language in which to do so (such frustration should never be underestimated, although it is not the desire for fame as a poet that is important here—it is the need to have the vision and understanding of a poet, and then to be able to express this), that contributed to the astonishing universality—indeed, to the undeniable poetry—of *Don Quixote*. Most of those who feel rejected by poetry but do not try to manufacture it, become the most invaluable readers of it; Cervantes took a different course.

Cervantes after 1580 tried but failed to make money from writing plays. His pastoral work *Galatea*, a miscellany of prose and verse along then familiar lines, and hardly original, made him next to nothing. He had an illegitimate daughter named Isabel (we know nothing of her mother), and then in 1584 married Catalina, whose father was a well-off peasant. The marriage is said to have been unhappy, but there is no real evidence for this—it may have been unhappy and tempestuous sometimes, but based in affection.

From 1588 he showed at least one subsiduary qualification for genius: He failed as a government official. Given the task of collecting money from cunning Andalusians (at first for the purposes of the Armada about to be launched against England), he was cheated by them, and on a number of occasions slung into prison because he could not balance his books—no doubt, then as now, such bureaucratic tasks were in any case beyond common sense or decency, for all the dully correct intentions of their perpetrators. It is said that he started *Don Quixote* in prison, where he must have learned much more about lowlife than he already knew.

Cervantes, like the French poet François Villon and many other writers (the same liking is present in Shakespeare, Ben Jonson, Hardy, Kipling, and Whitman—to mention just four more major writers) was attracted, if not by crime itself, then by the liveliness, energy, and self-honesty of criminals. He saw clearly that the world of good manners and good breeding was but a bizarre and hypocritical reflection of the world of lowlife; and that education is very useful, but not everything. He saw, too, that many sow's ears, in the "upper" world, were going around dressed as silk purses.

But a man who saw such things so easily, a tough ex-soldier of an extraordinarily penetrating intelligence and wit, had to be careful. It was the age of the Inquisition, that misguided recourse to violence in the interests of keeping religion going which thus undermined its own reasons. In England at that time, in particular—we have only to think of Ben Jonson, Thomas Middleton, and William Shakespeare—similar exposés of the pretensions of the rich and in particular the powerful were being undertaken in the field of drama.

So it came to be that Cervantes wrote his greatest works in his final years—between the ages of fifty-eight and sixty-nine. He would be remembered if he had only written the *Exemplary Novels* (1613), a form of short fiction which he more or less invented and then introduced to Spain. In 1605 he published the first part of *Don Quixote,* and, although he never made much money himself from it, it quickly became famous all over the known world. Badly printed by a Madrid bookseller named Francisco de Robles, who did not bother to protect what then passed for the copyright, it became a runaway bestseller.

The first translation into English, by Thomas Shelton, was on sale by 1612 (the book has by now been translated into almost every language, even into Tibetan—thus Shakespeare could have read part of it in English, although it is unlikely that he did so). There were many pirated editions, and then there appeared in 1614 a "continuation": wretched trash signed with the false name of "Alonso Fernandéz de Avellaneda," that also insulted Cervantes personally—on the grounds of his mutilated hand and of his poverty. No one knows who was responsible for this monstrosity. It might well be that Cervantes did not value his own success much at an artistic level, and that he did not therefore much wish to carry on with his work. But this wretched imitation of it, a travesty by a person of no comic or other talent whatsoever, stirred him into action. He made sure that no one else could profit from his novel by allowing Don Quixote himself to die, and, what was more, die sane and "cured" of his affliction—which was, of course, mainly, an obsession with chivalry and all that chivalry implies. The second part of *Don Quixote* was published just one year before Cervantes's own death, which took place within a few days of that of Shakespeare.

The story is too well known to require repeating here. Quixote is a little country squire who has lost his mind through his obsession with chivalric romances. Sancho Panza is a none too scrupulous and greedy peasant. The mad knight errant Don Quixote has, at least since the nineteenth century, been taken as mistakenly but nonetheless admirably engaged in righting wrongs. The theme appears to be that of the noble or holy fool, the person whose essential purity goes to the heart of things and does eventually right wrongs. But in his madness Don Quixote does *not* right wrongs. His madness is a separate matter, caused by reading romances (just as Madame Bovary in Flaubert's masterpiece of that name is driven into folly by reading similar material of her own time: love fantasies).

Don Quixote's wisdom and his intelligence, which are considerable, exist side by side with his distinctly harmful madness. The wisdom does *not* spring from the madness.

Thus *Don Quixote* is an accurate study of a case of actual madness. Spanish literature is uniquely strong in this, and at the end of the nineteenth century we find the novelist Benito Peréz Galdós writing detailed psychiatric studies, case histories, whose analytic powers have not been surpassed even in text books of psychiatry.

But madness has not been irrelevant at any time in our world: Alexander the Great was mad, Hitler was mad, and, at a somewhat lower level of disaster, the long-ruling prime minister Margaret Thatcher of Great Britain had a decidedly quixotic *idée fixe* on what she called "wealth"—when she was thrown out, it was with the firm popular notion that she had, as everyone said at the time, "gone off her trolley."

The message of Cervantes's book is much harsher than the rosy notion that in madness lies sanity. No doubt in a certain limited sense it does. But not in this wide-ranging book. It is true that Quixote comes across as a sympathetic figure, but that is only because the reader of his adventures also lives a life—although less disastrously and, of course, less obviously—based on illusion, a life that engages reality at no point. The play *Hamlet*, written at about the same time, also has a central character who attracts high romantic sympathy—although he is in fact quite as deplorable as ourselves. This is the nature of our "private," erotic lives. For *Don Quixote* is a critique of the romantic ideal written long before the advent of romanticism. It has taken upon itself a life of its own, so that the romantic interpretation of it cannot be dismissed out of hand. It has been all things for all men. But its ending makes its message perfectly clear:

> "The mercy [of God] I speak of," replied Don Quixote, "is that which God is showing me at this moment—in spite of my sins, as I have said. My mind is now clear, unencumbered by those misty shadows of ignorance that were cast over it by my bitter and continual reading of those hateful books of chivalry. I see through all the nonsense and fraud contained in them, and my only regret is that my disillusionment has come so late, leaving me no time to make any sort of amends by reading those that are the light of the soul. . . ."

And the narrator adds that he had always been "of a pleasant and kindly disposition" so that he was beloved of all who knew him.

39

The Harmony of the World

Johannes Kepler

1619

Johannes Kepler (1571–1630), born in a small town in Swabia in southern Germany, was the son of a Lutheran pastor. LUTHER himself had angrily remarked of COPERNICUS that he was an "ass who wants to pervert the whole art of astronomy and deny what is said in the Book of Joshua." But Kepler, a more selfless man than the irascible, constipated, fervent founder of the church in which he was brought up, could not live with so thoughtless and then conventional a notion: A Pythagorean mystic who (like GALILEO) believed that the universe could be explained in terms of mathematics, he also believed in the truth, made a virtue of holding a scientific attitude—and was able to demonstrate the way in which the heliocentric theory worked. But later scientists have seldom lauded mysticism.

Historians of science to this day try to separate Kepler's mysticism from his science, but in vain: The two are as inseparable from each other as all the scientific advances of the sixteenth and seventeenth centuries are inseparable from religion. They were not made despite religion, but because of it. However, they were made despite religious orthodoxy—not the same thing at all. Kepler was persecuted and inconvenienced by bureaucrats and sickly clerks, of both religions. These were men no better than atheists, although perhaps sincere; but, having nothing substantial to be sincere about, they could only be sincere about being bureaucrats, about upholding whatever they were told was the status quo. All those mysterious and heartily irrational compulsions that make human beings what they are, they did their best to pretend did not exist. Their weapon, then as now, was torture. But in these days subtler, mental torments have been substituted for the medieval rack and thumbscrew.

The perfecting of Copernicus's work started with the observations of the Danish astronomer Tycho Brahe (1546–1601). In early life Brahe had part of his nose sliced off in a duel at Rostock, and ever afterward he wore a metal substitute which, perhaps surprisingly, is shown in all the portraits of him. That he allowed or encouraged this tells us something about his bold sincerity.

Tycho, astronomer and hermeticist, built instruments of then astonishing precision to survey the sky (one of them was accurate to .0014 of a degree), and he was able to tell from the observations he made with them that the old Aristotelian universe was a false one. This universe—apparently confirmed by the truly impressive arithmetic of Ptolemy—was the one in which a stationary earth stood at a center orbited in perfect circles by the planets and the sun; beyond it and limiting it lay a sphere of perfection which rotated once a day.

But Brahe just could not accept the Copernican view that the sun lay at the center. He therefore devised his own, now almost forgotten, but once quite widely accepted, model of the solar system: The motionless earth was still at the center, as required by the old theory, and the sun and moon revolved around it; but the other (then known) planets were allowed to orbit the sun. It was a curious and interesting compromise, and one which satisfied the uncomprehending clerk-torturers of his day.

Kepler, already persecuted for his Copernicanism by Protestants and Jesuits alike (the latter because he would not convert to their beliefs) met Brahe in Prague and became his assistant. Brahe had noticed, from Kepler's *Mystery of the Universe* (1597), what a good mathematician his assistant was. The *Mystery of the Universe* in fact proved to be based upon an error: A mistake had led Kepler into believing that he had discovered a clue to the nature of the universe. He had written, with a typically Pythagorean fervor:

> I undertake to prove that God, in creating the universe and regulating the order of the cosmos, had in view the five regular bodies of geometry as known since the days of Pythagoras and Plato, and that he has fixed according to these dimensions, the number of heavens, their proportions, and the relations of their movements.

But when he saw that he had been wrong, and after desperate efforts to fit the dimensions to his observations, he changed his mind.

Tycho, who had had a long and difficult correspondence with Kepler, but who ultimately treated him with great generosity, died in 1601, and Kepler succeeded him as imperial mathematician at the court of Rudolph II. He worked heroically, and against the ordinary Aristotelian intuition of the time (for how could the earth move if objects fell back into it?) on Tycho's observations of the planet Mars, and adding more of his own (made despite wretched eyesight). In 1609, the year in which a crooked publisher issued a pirated edition of the *Sonnets* of SHAKESPEARE, Kepler published *The New Astronomy*. In it he proved two things: that Mars moved around the sun not in a circle but in an ellipse (a figure regarded at that time as imperfect and inappropriate because it has two foci—instead of one center—one of which can, inelegantly and unworthily of God, be empty); and that the planet moved at varying speeds, but that the line connecting the planet and the sun always sweeps out an equal area of the ellipse in the same period of time.

By 1619 in *The Harmony of the World*, Kepler could clearly enunciate all three of his laws: The last was that the square of a planet's year (the time it takes to orbit the sun) is proportional to the cube of its mean distance from the sun. Thus he introduced not only mathematics but physics to the heavens, the explanation of whose manifestations had until then been left to theologians who, all too often knowing little mathematics, adhered to Aristotelian notions and relegated inconvenient phenomena to "sublunar" invisibility.

It needs to be understood that in certain respects the heliocentric theory did then seem unreasonable, not only because of entrenched beliefs but also because of the difficulties raised by the fact of the earth's motion. Not until Newton explained gravity as a force did this become completely clear. Before that, things were said to return to their proper place (a far less accurate and vaguer, if not entirely incorrect, explanation). Kepler, like Brahe, recognized that some phenomena were not "sublunar"—and it was left to the former to provide the first proper explanation of the apparently retrograde motion of the planets.

Kepler was the most remarkable of all the great scientific innovators of the sixteenth and seventeenth centuries. His mysticism or Pythagoreanism was far more clearly and unequivocally expressed than was that of, say, Galileo, which may for all we know have been held just as strongly. Bertrand Russell was so irritated by Kepler's religious beliefs that he called him "persistent" rather than possessed of "much genius"—a biased view, but one not untypical of an archpositivist.

Kepler was first turned toward the Copernican theory by Michael Maestlin (1580–1635) at the University of Tübingen. Maestlin taught Ptolemy's system publicly, but in private, to his graduate students, recommended the Copernican. Kepler, a man of subtle and ironic mind—as secure, with such works as *Somnium* (first written in 1611), in the history of German mysticism as he is in the annals of science—later said that he had been led to

Copernicus for "physical or, if you prefer, metaphysical reasons"—an ironic remark that still enrages many modern scientists, who rejoice in his discoveries but are too mean to allow him his thirst for spiritual truth. He was the greatest pioneer of scientific astrology since the ancients; his work in this—which included many remarkably accurate predictions about wars and weather—was rediscovered by the French statistician Michel Gauquelin in the twentieth century. Gauquelin's own work led to one of that century's bleakest scandals, in which scientists displayed their lack of scientific objectivity in a spectacular manner. They behaved so abominably that one of them, who by no means could accept Gauquelin's conclusion, resigned from the committee that was supposedly "investigating" Gauquelin's work.

Besides inventing a type of thermometer and doing innovative work in optics and the workings of the eye, Kepler was a gifted creative writer whose mysticism is firmly in the line of other mystics who wrote in his language: Paracelsus, Böhme, Franck. In the *Somnium,* which has been translated, he wrote an ironic allegory which has been persistently ignored and underrated. He saved himself from anti-Copernican censure by writing as though from the moon, whose motion was not denied by the orthodoxists. He was thus able to demonstrate that the motion of the "fixed" stars was only apparent. The book only requires to be better known to become an established classic.

The *Harmony of the World* itself was inspired by his revival of the Pythagorean notion of the music of the spheres. He related his findings to the "archetype of the world," the musical scale. It has been grudgingly written that "no scientific value can be attached to this," but, its possible intrinsic value apart (the significance of the octave figures powerfully in some modern spiritual systems, and in no way fancifully), surely it has value if it inspired such astronomy! Talk of Kepler's "romantic confusions," then, or Russell's petulant denial to him of genius, is mere impertinence. Few scientists have bothered to investigate the relationship between Kepler's science and his religious imagination. For them, only established "scientific method" can yield results, and those results have to conform to a certain fashionable paradigm. When Michel Gauquelin, an at first skeptical investigator, published his results confirming that Kepler had been right in his views about "planetary heredity," the scientific establishment not only rejected the figures, but condemned them out of hand.

40

Novum Organum

FRANCIS BACON

1620

The "brightest, wisest, meanest of mankind"? So wrote Alexander Pope of Francis Bacon, in his conventional but epigrammatically neat summary of eighteenth-century complacency, *An Essay on Man*. And that is how most people think of Bacon today.

But among specialists, historians of science, and historians of politics, there is still debate about both Bacon's character, and, more important, the nature and quality of his influence. His greatest and most generally appealing book, surely, is his *Essays* (he began to publish these in 1597; the final edition of 1625 contains fifty-eight essays); but his most directly influential book is the Latin treatise *Novum Organum,* the second volume of his *Instauratio Magna,* which is the name he gave to his great program of scientific reform: the Great Instauration ("Restoration"). An earlier work of 1605, *The Advancement of Learning,* written in English, of which *Novum Organum* is in many respects an elaboration, has been called by a few "more important" (by, for example, Bertrand Russell, who much admired Bacon); but the later work in Latin, arranged in two books as two sets of aphorisms (130 and 52), was the more influential.

Bacon was born into a ranking family; both his parents were gifted and highly thought of. His father, Nicholas, was the queen's keeper of the Great Seal, while his mother was the sister of William Cecil, Lord Burleigh, Queen Elizabeth's chief secretary of state and one of the two or three most powerful men in the land. Francis did not receive the preferment he expected from Burleigh, who did, however, secure him a seat in Parliament. Queen Elizabeth, who knew him from boyhood, seems never to have trusted or liked him, despite his loyalty to her. There may very well have been something distinctly unlikeable in his manner—something that did not, however, creep into the *Essays.* He entered Parliament at twenty-three and turned to the Earl of Essex, who helped him considerably. But when Essex fell foul of the Queen, Bacon prosecuted him with an ambitiously great zeal—and saw him to his death. A hint of what Pope called his "meanness," as of his overweening pride, is given in the famous portrait by J. Vanderbank in the National Portrait Gallery in London; he was anything, it seems, but generous in spirit. True nobility was beyond him.

From the time of the accession to the throne of James I (1603), Bacon prospered and was knighted. In 1618, upon attaining the highest legal office of the land, lord chancellor, he was created Lord Verulam. In 1621 he became viscount of St. Albans. But in that year his career was abruptly terminated: he was accused of taking bribes and immediately admitted it—defending himself on the grounds that his judgment in the case had not been affected! It was a usual practice of the time but still meant that Bacon had to retire in disgrace. He went on working assiduously at his scientific projects until his death in 1626.

As an essayist Bacon possesses wisdom and a marvelous turn of phrase. But the *Essays,* though prized and loved, have exercised little influence. As a philosopher, though, Bacon's discovery of a method (or an alleged method) of overcoming all obstacles to the acquisition of certain knowledge has, despite its flaws, been exceedingly influential, especially upon JOHN STUART MILL and then on KARL POPPER.

Interpretation of the two technical terms *deduction* and *induction* differs among logicians. Approximately, however, the deductive method (*not* that of Sherlock Holmes, despite what his creator believed), depends upon the type of argument in which, if its premise is true, then its conclusion must be true. In inductive arguments the premise may be true but the conclusion false.

Bacon is most famous for his belief that scientific discovery depends upon a new type of induction: huge amounts of data are amassed and then judiciously interpreted. This amounted to a rejection of ARISTOTLE's view, which was highly influential in itself; Bacon respected Aristotle well enough, but he deplored the "fruitlessness of the way" (method).

Induction was not in itself new. It is obvious that, all philosophical considerations apart, people are going to generalize from a series of particulars. But Bacon's method involved more rigor and, specifically, attention to negative instances (here lie some of the seeds of Popper's falsification principle). Bacon wrote:

> After the rejection and exclusion has duly been made [from "tables" of facts] there will remain at bottom, all light opinions vanishing into smoke, a Firm affirmative, solid and true and well-defined . . . the way to come to it is winding and intricate.

There have been two major criticisms of Bacon's idea of proper scientific method. First, his so-called inductive procedure, whatever its practical or inspirational value, has convincingly been shown to have serious flaws. Second, Bacon was as profoundly as he was surprisingly ignorant of mathematics, in which he was clearly a man of the past rather than of the future: He rejected COPERNICUS and had no time for KEPLER or GALILEO. In that way he failed to see the use of the deductive method, which is sometimes possible by use of mathematics. He also failed to grasp the importance of the work of his own doctor, William Hervey, on the circulation of the blood. But for all that his emphasis on observation, and the general spirit of his scientific quest, have been inspiring.

Bacon's enumeration of the obstacles to scientific progress that reside in the human mind is often on surer ground, and, while not a complete catalog of human frailty (he was, despite gestures toward conformity, an almost positively *irreligious* man), are remarkably shrewd. He listed four, which he called Idols of, respectively, the Tribe, the Cave, the Market Place, and the Theater.

The Idols of the Tribe are fundamental: Human beings have a dull and distorting perceptual apparatus. The Idols of the Cave, more controversial, are generated by individual idiosyncrasies—mainly innate prejudices. Idols of the Market Place could now be called "Idols of the Media": People are led, through "daily intercourse and association," into "numberless empty controversies and idle fancies." Today these would include "discussion" of movies, the lives of movie or pop stars, and what the papers have to "say" about new novels or "revelations." ("To know nothing," wrote the twentieth-century Aus-

trian satirist Karl Kraus of newspaper writers, *"and be able to express it!"*)
Idols of the Theater are equally useless theories and philosophical systems
(especially, for Bacon, a rationalist—used here in its older sense). Among
such theories useless to Bacon would have been, of course, Kepler's laws!

Bacon's motive for his political behavior was, he explained, to achieve
good. He is thus in one sense, and not an unimportant one, a forerunner of
the utilitarianism of Bentham and MILL. His scientific curiosity was without
bounds and is his most impressive feature. The strange mixture in him, of
medievalism and modernity, has made him look both extremely subtle (and
thus really at his best, as a writer, in the essay, to which form he is an important contributor) and at the same time extremely disordered. He is not quite
lovable, although we can admire and even wonder at him; of his huge influence there can be no doubt. If he was a genius but with something wrong
with him—a meanness of spirit brought on by vanity—that prevented him
from quite realizing himself, then the genius that was given him was one of
very high magnitude. Writers will continue to debate about his strange
nature, because it was indeed a fascinating one: on the one side his avid
curiosity and humility in pursuit of truth, and his skill and sometimes even
warmth as an essayist—and on the other his cruelty (he seems to have
observed men being tortured), his ambition, and his blindness to the genius
of others.

41

The First Folio

WILLIAM SHAKESPEARE

1623

The First Folio, published in 1623, contains all of Shakespeare's plays—thirty-six, of which exactly half had not previously been published as single quarto texts—except for *Pericles,* which we will nonetheless understand as included here. The poems (the sonnets in particular) appeared in quarto editions during Shakespeare's lifetime, but we will include them, too. (If we did not sometimes cheat a little, we would have far fewer influential books.) If it so happened that Shakespeare had not really influenced anyone much at all—if he had done no more than merely entertain—I should still have had to include him in this book, and advance some false or specious reason as to why he was influential. But I do not need to invent anything. Yet it is not easy to discover, with any degree of precision, what Shakespeare's influence, upon either human behavior or thought, has been. However, one thing is obvious and certain: He has caused an enormous number of people to spend an enormous amount of money. There is a Shakespeare industry. But, too, as the editor of the *Shakespeare Encyclopedia,* Oscar James Campbell, wrote, "No other author . . . has stimulated so much thought among the best minds of each generation."

T. S. Eliot once pertinently remarked that every book about Shakespeare reflected its writer more than its subject. "Others abide thy question, thou art free," wrote Matthew Arnold. We all understand what Arnold meant—that Shakespeare is "good" or "better than anyone else" is such a ubiquitous opinion—but can that *really* be right? That Shakespeare cannot be questioned!

The eminent Shakespearean actor Henry Irving, in introducing a popular edition of his works, thought him superior to Socrates and Christ. Only George Bernard Shaw and Colin Wilson—and a few schoolboys and girls, and even then only temporarily, for they eventually bow to opinion—have thought him no good; but that has gotten them nowhere. All this in itself: The sheer amount of attention Shakespeare has had, from audiences and investors alike, not to speak of literary critics—who are supposed to have influential minds—could account for his inevitable presence here. But let us take it a bit further and try to discover more about the nature of his influence on humanity.

The BIBLE and the KORAN, as well as other religious texts, have influenced mankind in two opposite directions. On the one hand they have inspired virtuous behavior; on the other they have inspired wars, torture, and lives of misery for billions of children and adults. But has any nation gone to war over Shakespeare? The "Crusades"—yes; even the "Children's Crusade." But the "Shakespeare Wars?" And have not children suffered floggings and moral torment far less over failing to memorize lines from Shakespeare than they have for sinning against what their masters have taken to be the precepts of Jesus Christ, Mohammed, or Zoroaster? Such are the distortions of which the human mind is capable.

One of the passages from Shakespeare that children seldom have to learn, though, one of the passages that is not remembered when the "authorities" decide to put at best dubious representations of Shakespeare's head upon postage stamps, is Sonnet 66:

> Tir'd with all these, for restful death I cry:
> As, to behold desert a beggar born,
> And needy nothing trimm'd in jollity,
> And purest faith unhappily forsworn,
> And gilded honour shamefully misplac'd,
> And maiden virtue rudely strumpeted,
> And right perfection wrongfully disgrac'd,

> And strength by limping sway disabled,
> And art made tongue-tied by authority,
> And folly (doctor-like) controlling skill,
> And simple truth miscall'd simplicity,
> And captive good attending captain ill.
> Tir'd with all these, from these would I be gone,
> Save that, to die, I leave my love alone.

How is it, then, and why is it, that the authorities—who put Shakespeare's head on postage stamps when their cultural advisers think it will be beneficial to us—can bring themselves to ignore such subversive grumbling? Life is so rotten, Shakespeare is unequivocally saying here, that only being in love makes it tolerable. And King Lear says,

> Thou rascal beadle, hold thy bloody hand!
> Why dost thou lash that whore? Strip thine own back.
> Thou hotly lusts to use her in that wise
> For which thou whipst her

And when, a line or two later, he speaks of politicians—*politicians*, surely, after bureaucrats and usurers, the wisest, most honest, just, and self-sacrificing people in the world!—as "scurvy" and as having "glass eyes"? Well, it is not *Shakespeare* that is being so subversive, a cultural bureaucrat would try to instruct you, not at all—he is simply portraying the mad Lear! Only a madman could talk like that! As for the sonnet, well, it can be no more than a "literary exercise"! But such arguments are nonsense, of course, and cultural officials in fact just will not discuss such questions. They are too busy organizing Shakespeare festivals; and in any case they can point out that governments were very poor then, and do not at all resemble our own near-perfect ones. (An incidental question may trouble some: Why is *Macbeth: A Tragedy* highly credible, but *Clinton: A Tragedy* or *Reagan: A Comedy*—somehow not?)

The truth is that Shakespeare could not possess his unique and consistently enduring popularity if he had been a supporter of any faction—ruling, rebellious, critical, conformist, or anything else. Books have been written to prove that he was a Marxist (before MARX), an authoritarian, a Roman Catholic, a Puritan, a Freudian (before FREUD)—and, naturally, that he did not write the plays attributed to him in his lifetime by everyone, including by his friend Ben Jonson, whose own collection of his works inspired the publication of the First Folio. (It is sufficient to state here that the "village-idiot Shakespeare-did-not-write-Shakespeare" amusement is a harmless form of minor mental illness, or perhaps just snobbery: There is no evidence whatsoever that Shakespeare did not write the plays that were attributed to him.)

Therefore Arnold was, at least in part, right. While of course Shakespeare can and should be questioned on various grounds—his friend Ben Jonson foresaw snobbish Shakespeare-worship, and therefore Shakespeare-tyranny, and so cannily warned that he must be appreciated "this side of idolatry," and that some of his plays are much better than others—he does also belong to everyone in a unique manner. Of all writers he was the least "literary," and he does not "belong to the critics" in a way that Proust and even Jonson himself sometimes threaten to do.

Academic criticism is a two-faced monster. On the one hand it preserves the excellencies, the subtleties, the essential truths, about such works of art as Shakespeare above all produced. It puts literary works in their proper contexts, saves us from misinterpreting them or misunderstanding them, draws attention to the means by which they illuminate and enrich the lives of individuals, saves them from vulgarization. It is in this way absolutely precious and absolutely necessary.

On the other and far less attractive and even sinister hand, academic criticism can rob literature of its vitality and force, overwhelm it with technicalities at the expense of its content, mute it, cause it to become attenuated: bring it into the pseudopossession of a dry, thin-blooded, self-appointed elite. The critic who wishes to be useful must tread a delicate and humble path, and, above all, must not subordinate the power that experience confers to mere book-learning. Nowhere is it more appropriate to raise this significant matter than in the case of Shakespeare. A "common reader" can indeed understand plays of Shakespeare better than a professor. However, he may, too, gain further illumination of his understanding from a professor. Alas: The process all too often does not work the other way. But Shakespeare above all is the writer who takes true literature back into the ownership of the people to whom it ultimately belongs: to this elusive common reader. His plays tend to "play themselves;" his work as a whole, the poetry (in particular the sonnets, an intense record of a ubiquitous personal experience, that of being in love) and the plays together, illuminate what is often called "ordinary" experience. But "ordinary" ought to be, and is, *extraordinary*—and that is what Shakespeare, perhaps above all other human beings—though HOMER, too, right back at the beginning of literature, comes to mind—demonstrates. An *ordinary* situation or person or thing is a *common* one, as in that vital phrase *common reader*. There are as many histories of the world as there are realities. One is the false, selected, arranged-to-taste *history* of the professional historians, who believe, or believed, that the most significant aspect of history is political. Another and very much larger and truer sort of history is what the Spanish philosopher and novelist Miguel de Unamuno (1846–1936) called *intrahistoria*—the largely unrecorded and submerged traditions of the common people, their sayings, their songs, those places never visited by tourists, the places never even heard of by tourists, those events *unimportant to professional historians,* or beneath their contempt. That, *intrahistoria*—but we shall call it *real history*—is Shakespeare's subject. It is my life, your life, and the life of everyone else. That Shakespeare was able to do this is something of a miracle, or at least seems to be so. And so it has been thought that he must have been a self-conscious philosopher carefully planning and then composing his works, all intended to display the meaning of life. I was myself given this view by, as it happens, an important cultural official (a member of the British Council, who helped to present the British Shakespeare to various Europeans); he was incredulous that there could be any other view, especially mine, which he clearly believed was scandalous. For I had suggested that no one, no writer, could possibly be so illuminating of, and eloquent about, almost every subject by conscious intent.

My own Shakespeare—for we all have one, as Eliot rightly said—is a man of little learning (in the academic sense of learning) who initially wanted to be a gentleman, a poet of rank. His ambition was to retire as a gentleman (which he did). He was himself a bit of a snob, but he could see through this and mock it in himself as in others.

He was disappointed, however. His ambitious, "literary" poetry, as in *Venus and Adonis* and *The Rape of Lucrece,* was only middling good: Better poetry had been written by a few of his contemporaries, such as Christopher Marlowe and George Chapman. He had to survive, and so, as he had already discovered that he had a small talent for acting and a huge gift for writing plays—and for pulling in audiences—he relied upon these means to get back home, eventually, to his native Stratford-on-Avon. Thus, that he was what he was, was in a superficial sense the result of a mere accident: He was conscientious, there was always pressure on him to deliver the goods, and so— never, as Jonson observed, having the time to blot a line—he was able to demonstrate exactly what has been seen in him by scholars and readers alike, a development into an astonishing maturity. He did it because he was so ordinary, not special, so faulty, not faultless, so like everyone else.

42

Dialogue Concerning Two New Chief World Systems

Galileo Galilei

1632

Galileo (1564–1642)—he preferred to be known by his first name—was an experimental scientist and mathematician before he was a philosopher, and what he did in philosophy was in the interests of science; but his influence upon philosophy, as upon science, was very great. Of all the scientific revolutionaries of the sixteenth and seventeenth centuries, from COPERNICUS onward, he seems to have been the least concerned with religious belief or with mysticism. But the orientation toward science of this remarkably industrious, curious, and dedicated man has been somewhat exaggerated.

Like HOBBES, BERKELEY, and HUME in England, and quite unlike KANT in Germany, he was a great stylist in his native Italian. He has been called, and this sheerly on literary grounds, a "great shaper and modernizer of linguistic usage—one whose style is characterized by vigor, clarity, and elegance." He wrote competent minor verse, and his commentaries on DANTE, Tasso, Ariosto, and other important Italian poets have always been valued. One of Italy's greatest literary critics, Federico de Sanctis, declared that Tasso had been illuminated for him by Galileo.

He found time to devote himself to this literary work despite (or because of?) his scientific interests. He wrote, too, in Italian instead of in the learned Latin preferred by most scholars. Although not a philosopher, his grasp of the subject (he studied it, as he studied physics and mathematics and medicine) was secure and even profound. He saw clearly, but without hostility to ARISTOTLE himself, that the Aristotelianism practiced by the medieval schoolmen was quite inadequate to deal with the advances in mathematics and physics of his own time, and his were the courageous steps that led to the eventually universal acceptance of the Copernican hypothesis. An admirer of his near-contemporary JOHANNES KEPLER (they corresponded but never met), he was overtly less mystical; but neither that fact, nor that he was (of course) persecuted by his church, means that in him we have an atheist-in-the-bud.

However, what Galileo actually believed about God and the universe cannot be wholly recovered. Unlike Kepler, he was a conventionally accomplished stylist who was also a biting ironist, and he well knew (sometimes) how to keep his mouth shut. We might put it that he was more "modern" in spirit than Kepler, that he was more of a "man of the world." But that does not mean that he was just a man of the world. Unfortunately there is as yet no biography of him in English that treats him as both scientist and thinker. In all probability he was, just like Kepler, a Pythagorean—inasmuch as he wished, and said he wished, to explain the universe in terms of numbers—who wanted above all to save the Church from its atrophied and cruel bureaucracy by firmly separating its out-of-date cosmology from its theology. Among his most famous words are these—pure Pythagoreanism—from his *Assayer* (1623):

> Philosophy is written in this grand book, the universe, which stands continuously open to our gaze [but doubters, terrified of what they might see with their own eyes, refused to look through his telescope]. But the book cannot be understood unless one first learns to comprehend the language and read the letters in which it is composed. It is written in the language of mathematics, and its characters are triangles, circles, and other geometric figures without which it is humanly impossible to understand a single word of it: without those one wanders about in the dark labyrinth.

Galileo was born in Pisa into an old Florentine family. His father, Vincenzo, an "all-around" man with an interest in science and literature, was primarily a musicologist. Galileo was educated at the University of Pisa, at which he became professor of mathematics at an early age. Later (1592), already in trouble over his bold views, he went to the University of Padua in the same capacity. His early treatise *On Motion* (*Du Motu*, 1590), is sometimes said to be as important as anything he did in astronomy. In it he revolutionized the concept of the motion of bodies, and so initiated the modern science of dynamics. Later, in his last work, *Two New Sciences*, he reiterated all this work. That he dropped weights from the Leaning Tower of Pisa is, alas, apocryphal; but he did demonstrate that the thinking of his time about falling bodies was all wrong.

Careful observation may well have prompted him to this innovation. It was supposed that a heavier object would take less time to fall to earth than a lighter one. Galileo showed that this was untrue. He rolled balls of different weights down wooden channels which rang bells as they passed various points. It remained for NEWTON to show that there was a force of gravity, but Galileo demonstrated that bodies, as they fall, accelerate at a rate of thirty-two feet per second. He went further in showing that the path of a projectile, far from being a horizontal one followed by a sudden reversion to the vertical, is parabolic. Thus men learned that the way to calculate the paths of such objects as arrows from bows or shells from guns was to combine two forces together and take account of both. So far as he could he always made his postulations observable by people of good faith who could believe what their own eyes told them. But he failed to realize, at least at first, that bureaucrats do not like that kind of thing.

Such proofs did away at a stroke with the basis of the old Aristotelian physics. To the zealous clerks of the Inquisition this could not be made to seem quite intolerable, especially as artillery, the stuff (operated by someone else) of their wilder dreams, was affected. However, even the odious Bellarmine, chief murderer of Bruno—his conscience by then blackened by guilt, his future sainthood perhaps dimly in his twisted mind, his faith in his church to put wrong things right reviving—displayed (while he lived) some sympathy for him.

The publication of Galileo's *Starry Messenger (Nuncius siderum)* in 1610, on his telescopic observations, did not please the more orthodox scientists, while the Inquisition could smell burning flesh. Like the politically correct of today, although more powerful, they ached to kill so that they could assert their pitiful mediocrity.

Galileo had managed to get hold of the design of a Dutch refracting telescope, and, inspired by this, made an improved one in 1609. He was able to see the craters on the moon, and some satellites of the planet Jupiter. This was grist to his heliocentric mill, since here were several objects orbiting a much larger one. With great courage Galileo decided to try to force the Church to accept the heliocentric hypothesis; his correspondence of the years 1610–1616 makes this clear. His 1613 book on the sunspots he had observed, which gave an account of the earth's journey around the sun, alarmed his opponents. A Dominican called Thomas Cassini preached a sermon against him, but Galileo managed to avert the crisis this prompted. The sly Bellarmine then advised him to adopt the "hypothesis strategy"—i.e., to pretend that he was only offering a hypothesis.

In 1616, at which time Copernicus was declared a heretic, Galileo was forbidden to advance the *heliocentric* system. One scholar has convincingly suggested, however, that his real crime in the eyes of the Church was his adoption of Democritus's atomist theory of matter: This would have interfered with the doctrine of transubstantiation (what happens to the bread and the wine at the mass of the Eucharist). What is clear is that there was much more at stake than just the Copernican theory, and that Galileo's enemies fully recognized the international consequences of accusing so eminent and admired a scientist of heresy.

Galileo continued to write, still insisting that nothing that could be seen with the eye (miraculous change of bread to flesh and blood to wine of course cannot be seen) could be regarded as untrue on the grounds of scriptural statements that were capable of two or even more interpretations. He veered between caution and boldness, and has even been rebuked by contemporary Roman Catholic commentators—the sanctity of the murderous Bellarmine fragrant in their nostrils—for not being "circumspect" enough!

In *The Assayer* Galileo gave new impetus to Democritus's notion of the "primary" and "secondary" qualities of objects. This was possibly a strategic move on his part, since arguments not going against the Church's views about transubstantiation might be derived from its application. However that may be, the difficulty over primary and secondary qualities was to bedevil philosophy until Berkeley, and then Hume, demolished it. Before that it was taken up by DESCARTES and enshrined in LOCKE. "I conclude," wrote Galileo, "that if the ear, tongue, and nose were removed, shape, quality, and motion would remain, but there would be no odors, tastes, or sounds, which apart from living creatures I believe to be mere words."

After Maffeo Barberini, once a friend, ascended the papal throne in 1623 as Urban VIII, Galileo may have felt himself safer. In 1632, midway through this papal reign, he published his masterpiece, the *Dialogue*. It purported to "compare" the geocentric and heliocentric hypotheses, but made Galileo's preference for the latter witheringly obvious—and painfully so for those who suspected him of having viler tendencies, connected with the eucharist. They wanted him burnt or at the least forced to recant. At seventy he presented a more vulnerable target. Pope Urban was persuaded that he was himself characterized in the book as Simplicio. The *Dialogue* was seized and Galileo taken to Rome. There the correct of their era showed him their instruments of torture (the rack and thumbscrew then taking the place of today's "exposure" and dismissal; the petty details of faith in "relativist" nihilism); probably they did not use them. There, despite his recantation, he was sentenced to infinite imprisonment, later commuted to permanent house arrest at his home near Florence. Like some Soviet dissident, he lived and worked there. He lost his daughter, went blind (1637), but wrote *Two New Sciences (Dialoghe delle nuove scienze)*, which he had to publish (1638) outside Italy, at Leiden.

Galileo's persecution by the Church, for reasons by no means yet fully clear—he wanted only to save it from fatal errors bound to be put right sooner or later—led to a speedier acceptance of the heliocentric theory: In 1600 the heliocentric hypothesis was a dangerous novelty; but by 1700 few educated people believed in a geocentric universe.

Discourse on Method

René Descartes

1637

René Descartes (1596–1650), deservedly known as the father of modern philosophy, was one of the most influential men—in both the direct and the indirect senses—who ever lived. That is a heavy burden to carry; nor did he measure up to the responsibilities that his momentous significance entailed. But then, could anybody except Zoroaster, Christ, or Mohammed (and did they?), and a very few others of that unfamiliar kind, have done so? And did the foolish and obstinate intolerance of his times cripple his self-expression, as it did that of Galileo?

When we read the millions of words that have been expended upon Descartes, we do not gain much sense of the man himself; we do not feel an immediate warmth for him—awe and respect, of course, but not warmth— as we do for, say, Shakespeare or, in particular among philosophers, Spinoza. But Descartes kept his private life very dark, and among the only things

203

known for certain about him is that the death of an illegitimate daughter, Francine, when he was forty-four, was a severe blow to him. In the portrait by Franz Hals, or even more in the one given in his *Philosophy of Words,* he could almost be an anticipation by a few years of a D'Artagnan turned to philosophy in middle age; after all, he had been an army man, even if only, as he put it, for "educational" purposes. But he also looks just a little like his own "malicious demon." It may not be without significance that he served in two armies: the first Protestant, the second Catholic.

Another of the few things we know about him has been inferred from the manner of his death of pneumonia in Sweden while he was visiting the court of Queen Kristina: The illness was contracted through his being forced to break his usual habit of late rising, as he was required to give lessons at five in the morning. He is supposed to have observed, when the time came, *"Ça, mon âme, il faut partir"* [So, my soul, it is time to part], which was of course too astonishingly appropriate for the man who so (as it turned out) spectacularly "split" the soul from the body. He occasionally seems to us—when we are simply being literal-minded—actually, in some kind of anguish, to have done exactly that. But whether—the late rising apart—he was able to have, or allowed himself to have, an adequate *emotional* apprehension of what he had done ("the Cartesian split") is to be doubted.

He was secretive, although perhaps not excessively so when one realizes that he had been educated by Jesuits and lived at a time when advocacy of free thought could be punished by death, torture, or both (they burned you to help you, but "they" were no more than the equivalent of today's assiduous middle-rank bureaucrats, who are under orders not to resort to physical measures). It is hard to know for sure about the degree of his sincerity, or how much his famous proof of the existence of God really meant to him. It has even been postulated that Descartes was a member of a Rosicrucian sect, a suggestion that, although it has attracted the timid scorn of conventional philosophers, is in its way plausible; but if he was a member of some secret order—and no trace of any type of occult organization has ever been discovered—then it is only fair to say that there is no tangible evidence of it. It is mentioned here because historians of philosophy have conspired to keep their histories remarkably free from matters that they do not consider philosophical—and have therefore, unquestionably, omitted a great deal that is humanly relevant. Philosophy tends to stray too far, by humorless hair-splitting and by dishonest omission of frightening—emotionally disturbing, unrespectably "occult"—material, from the humanity and the humaneness that it is supposed to serve. Descartes's work is just his work, and it has to be considered in isolation from him; but it is also, in another aspect, the product of a character in adversity—of a genius short of cash who had to serve in two armies in order to think, and who felt frustrated that all European minds wouldn't instantly accept what he stated—and thus a part of something larger than the history of philosophy as it has been written down by mere philosophers. To whom, if to anyone, did he feel close? The mother of his daughter? Who knows? When he begat that daughter, just how "split" did he feel?

Descartes overcame everyone else's severe doubts about the validity of his own knowledge by telling himself *Cogito, ergo sum*—"I think, therefore I am," or "Je pense, donc je suis." There is very much a sense, in his philosophy, of the first person. The *Cogito* was one of the first of his statements to be criticized as lacking in explanatory potential—philosophy undergraduates delight in learnedly refuting its validity, just as first-year medical students like to say, "I don't like the sound of that cough." But its fame is still warranted, because, however unsatisfactory it may in fact be, it gave Descartes the impetus to continue with his work—or so we believe. That work, riddled as it is with scholastic terminology ("substance," "extension") reinvented the way men did philosophy, and so did help to dismantle the medieval—and the Renaissance—apparatus for it. Descartes said that when he was young it had occurred to him that although the discipline had been observed by "the best minds" for a long time, and although its status was high, "it contained no point which was not disputed and hence doubtful."

Being primarily a mathematician and therefore used to mathematical logic—his contribution to modern mathematics is beyond question—Descartes decided to apply the so certain-seeming methods of mathematical reasoning to the more disputed areas of philosophy: "[I supposed] that all the things that fall within the scope of human knowledge are interconnected in the same way [as in mathematics]." A poet, even a writer of fiction, a Thomas Nashe, not to speak of a follower of the *Tao-te Ching*, or a Kabbalistic practitioner, could hardly have agreed; yet had not the legendary mystic Pythagoras suggested that everything could be explained in terms of number?

Looking at this from the standpoint of the positivistic twentieth century—in which Pythagoras is all too often resented as a crazy and mythical sage lacking in atheistic insights—in which men who should know better (and others who could not) announce that all the secrets of life will shortly be unraveled, we tend to see the age of Descartes as having resembled it; the fact that, for example, the writings of Paracelsus on alchemy were not as ridiculed and misunderstood by such as Descartes, Spinoza, and LEIBNIZ as they are today is hard for us to understand. We cannot know how seriously this philosopher took such then heretical subjects—what he would have said about them privately—and modern philosophers tend to ignore them if they can. Was not the astrologer, poet, and philosopher Giordano Bruno, a very great (and inconsistent) mind, as well as an "anticipator of Leibniz, burned by the Inquisition in 1600 in the interests of God? Men such as Descartes must have felt those flames licking at the very hems of their robes. But someone in any case was going to have to fall into this utterly necessary error, this dividing of reality, this rough dismissal of Horatio's statement in *Hamlet* (written when Descartes was about seven years old), that there is more in heaven and earth than is dreamed of in mere "philosophy"; and this person was

Descartes, as well known for his fruitful mistakes as for his triumphs. He wanted above all a mathematical kind of certainty. It is of incidental interest that an Indian philosopher's reaction to the *Cogito* might have been a relaxed question: "Why can't I argue that 'I think, therefore thinking exists'?" which is both less dramatic and less egoistic. But this has never been raised by a Western philosopher, and Western philosophers, with the exception of SCHOPENHAUER, have taken Indian philosophy to be unphilosophical— actually, it is just different.

Descartes was born in La Haye (now La Haye-Descartes) near Tours and was educated at the newly founded and rigorous Jesuit College at La Flèche, in Anjou, where he gained a thorough knowledge of the very scholastic philosophy that his influence would later challenge and devastate. He also formed a distaste for ARISTOTLE, or at least for the Aristotle of the schools, the Aristotle whom AQUINAS had turned into a sort of honorary practicing Catholic. He went on to read law at Poitiers and graduated in 1616; but at the age of twenty-two, wishing to have "time to think," he thanked his Jesuit educators by enrolling in the protestant Dutch army of Maurice of Nassau. While on duty at Ulm (and there is no reason to doubt the story, for people's lifework does often appear before them in a flash—a memory of what they have done before, and more than once?) he experienced, in a "stove-heated room," a dream in which he devised a methodology for the unification of the sciences.

Descartes eventually settled (1628) in Holland, where he remained for the next twenty years. He soon wrote his first work, *Rules for the Direction of the Understanding;* but this is unfinished and was not published until the beginning of the eighteenth century. By 1634 he had completed his *Le Monde (The World)*; he was going to publish it, but when he heard that GALILEO had just recanted, under threat of torture, his teaching of the Copernican system, which Descartes, too, accepted—along with, to "save the phenomena," (i.e., to preserve certain ancient assumptions) its fantastical elaborations of Ptolemy's epicycles—he withdrew it.

Descartes's *Discourse on Method* appeared in 1637, as a preface to three short scientific treatises. In 1641 his *Discourses on the First Philosophy* appeared, together with a series of *Objections* by noted thinkers (HOBBES and Gassendi among them). *The Principles of Philosophy* was published in 1644; his last publication, an excessively intellectual dissection of the emotions, in which he influentially robbed animals of a soul and pronounced them utterly mechanical (did he have a mechanical cat he loved?), all in the interests of being right, was *The Passions of the Soul.*

Descartes is perhaps almost too well known, at least popularly, as an epistemologist—that is to say, one who fruitlessly, but not unsalaried, seeks to establish the grounds for our knowledge to make sure that it is impeccably held. He is still too little known as the propounder of what was, from the point of view of those Jesuits who had delightingly flogged him into his advanced knowledge, a revolutionary system so cunningly devised that his

Descartes in his study

church would not burn him for having invented it. The system was what he was really interested in, but he was forced by the circumstances of his age to explain, first, why he thought he could overcome the skepticism in which everyone had been so interested since the works of SEXTUS EMPIRICUS were republished. His arguments against such propositions as that he was dreaming, or that a malignant demon (the *malin génie*) was purposely misleading him, were mainly rhetorical in purpose, but by invoking this "malicious demon of the utmost power and cunning" only to dismiss him on the grounds that "I am, I exist," he demonstrated that he was aware of the sorts of phenomena that fascinate poets, Kabbalists, and even nonphilosophers. Whether this malevolent demon had "esoteric connections" or not, he has a long and sinister psychological history—in Descartes and in all of us, for is he not (among so much else) the Tempter, the agent of deadly sexual error, the Devil, the thing that takes us consciously against the real certainties contained in our unconscious minds? Did Descartes, as I suggest Leibniz did, suppress his awareness of the direction in which his efforts were leading him in the interests of his quest for the limited knowledge that mere intellectual "certainty" could allow—and could his work be analyzed along those lines, and is his "split" actually the work of such a "demon"? Was he, after all, *misled?*

Such questions should not be asked—and there is little doubt that the suggestion that he was, in particular, a Rosicrucian, is misdirected. But it is not to be wondered at that Descartes, in separating mind and matter in the drastic way he did, disturbed (and stimulated) everyone. He did say (in the *Meditations*) that "No one has ever seriously doubted" that there really was a world (BERKELEY, the empiricist who very influentially really did doubt if the external world existed at all, was born just thirty-six years after Descartes's death); his mapping out of what he took to be reality along the lines of mathematics, or physics, which was his main concern—he was led to go too far, almost desperately, by actually limiting reality to what could be described mathematically, as if he was frightened of the rest—has tended to take second place to his excuse for venturing to do so. We can safely say that the skeptical doubt with which he struggled in public (he anticipated the modern "celebrity," and would have contributed a popular newspaper column: DON'T WORRY ABOUT THE SPLIT, SPLIT WILL NOT AFFECT SPICE GIRLS' PROFITS RENÉ ASSURES) was never, for him, a genuine doubt—he did it all for the sake of argumentation, as has to be done in philosophy, a pursuit often paid for by the state, if the philosophers will just be seen to be working.

The *Cogito* may be expressed in another form: If there is doubt, then at least, whatever else holds or does not hold, there has to be a doub*ter,* for otherwise doubt itself could not exist! That was, Descartes thought, a demon-proof point of certainty. Is this so-called "method of doubt" a good argument? He himself thought it so "firm and sure" that it was quite beyond doubt. It has great appeal as a proof, and it had occurred to others, notably to SAINT AUGUSTINE, who wrote in *The City of God*: "The certainty that I exist, that I know it, and that I am glad of it, is independent of any imaginary and deceptive fantasies."

But Descartes then used his point of certainty to leap to a further conclusion: He found that if he possessed the notion of a perfect God (or being), which he did, then, so must this perfect being exist; the very idea of a perfect thing could not exist unless a perfect thing existed. Alas, one of the many problems with the *Cogito* is that it only proves that Descartes exists *while he is thinking.* And to get over this, Descartes cheated: he (still partially trapped in medieval terminology) claimed that he was a thinking or enduring and therefore permanent *substance.*

From this he developed what is known as the Cartesian system; possibly he did a great deal of unwitting harm by propounding a new kind of fictional dualism, and by foisting upon the world the wrongheaded notion that a valid philosophy that went beyond skepticism could exist. He put post-scholastic philosophy into business, and he made sure that it survived in the face of the new positivistic "science" (another bleak fiction, although one based not on false propositions but on a deliberate exclusion of the inconvenient from its considerations—a perfect system for emotional dolts) improperly stripped of the magic that belongs to true science. No wonder that philosophers are grateful to him!

In religion dualism implied that the Devil was co-eternal with God, or that *yin* co-existed with *yang*. Other sorts of dualism imply other fundamental polarities. But Descartes split the soul itself—which he said resided in the pineal gland (for long thought of as atrophied, but in fact vitally important)—from the body. Like FRANCIS BACON and Thomas Hobbes, he rejected the Aristotelian theso-willed (teleological) view of nature as consisting of a large number of different entities all striving, through their essences, toward their special ends. Unlike PLATO, who saw matter as a gross obstacle to the truth of the "Forms," Descartes regarded the essence of matter as an infinite extension in space of mathematically quantifiable substance. But his own *thoughts,* those things of which he was so aware that they had proved to him that he existed at all, could in no way thus be quantified. He cleverly conceded this, and, so to speak, invented another, *un*quantifiable "substance": mind. His solutions to all the problems he then encountered were—had to be—although he was antischolastic, permeated by scholastic language and scholastic concepts. His theory represents a compromise between, on the one hand, positivistic science (in fact a pseudo-science except in its own terms), and, on the other, the Roman Catholic religion as it then stood with its panoply of torture for thinking—perhaps he really wanted to "save" this from science, on account of his emotional beliefs.

Descartes seems to have been sincere, but he may have been forced by the kind of intolerance that Bruno and Galileo met from an Inquisition that was as savage as it was closed-minded and afraid, into something that fell rather short of what he truly believed. More likely, he dared not pursue his studies to their conclusion because he was himself afraid not only of flames but also of what he might find. His very insistence on God's being real and perfect and offering a counter to the deceptive demon by his nondeceiving nature does not conceal serious doubts about his existence.

It would have been easier for Descartes if he could have been a materialist. But he felt he could not then have demonstrated his rightness about everything—such as that, because matter is "extension," there can be no vacuum—with the proper religious certainty. One might say that Descartes's perfect and undeceiving God was none other than the strong individualist Descartes (compare the self-effacing Spinoza); but that would involve applying to philosophy matters not proper to the study of it as this has been decreed by the philosophers (who else?), and so would be unfair.

But mind, or consciousness (some say that Descartes's *pensée* ought to be rendered as "consciousness"), remains a problem, simply because, unlike matter, you cannot touch it—and yet you know that it is there. For some modern materialist philosophers, "mind" is just a series of physically definable states in the brain—but that is unsatisfactory because no one has succeeded in defining them. For Hobbes, similarly, mind was just "matter in motion," but he was not really a man for the scholastic niceties into which, ironically, Descartes got himself sunk when he was forced to defend his *Cogito*.

Philosophy is a dignified occupation, or thinks itself to be so; it is certainly a necessary one in a world that is now materialist in the worse sense. But it can become as ridiculous as tabloid newspapers—as the philosophers of common sense and "ordinary language" have seen but only tried to remedy—even in the hands of a Descartes, when a proper balance between emotion and intellect has not been observed, and when "uncertainty" has arrogantly been rejected. Kabbalistic studies are not as respectable or as widely quoted as those of Descartes; but there is more wisdom in the KABBALAH's virtue of the "unknowable" nature of the *Ein Sof*—and by simple meditation upon what we simply cannot know, we learn more than those who seek a certainty narrowed into paltry geometry. It should not be heresy to say so.

Yet Descartes's work, with its unintentional hints of solipsism (in him just vanity), led not only to the idealism of Berkeley, but to NEWTON's *Principia* and to Kantian metaphysics (which, by the mysterious ways and means that fundamental thoughts possess, themselves affected the pastoral comedies and tragedies, and the consoling poetry, of the so-called "pessimist" Thomas Hardy).

Descartes could have outwitted those who held the power of life and death over free thinkers only by being an imaginative writer, a creator, one who could employ irony (as I think, or prefer to think, the poetic Hobbes did). But there is no irony in him: He steered an icy way between the flames that devoured the braver, greater, openly hermetic Bruno; of the many complex engines that drove Descartes's genius, two unacknowledged ones were among the simplest and most powerful—vanity and fear. Nor was the man who tried to invent certainty on the grounds of doubt unhaunted by doubt. He was so "eminently learned" that, says John Aubrey in his *Brief Lives*, many came to visit him—he was a tourist attraction for rich, self-styled intellectuals—and would want to see his "instruments" (they needed to because they could not *really* think of mind as just "stuff"); and, rather as Pirandello typed the word B-U-F-F-O-O-N-E-R-Y with one finger on a typewriter while journalists quizzed him about his Nobel Prize, so Descartes would "draw out a little Drawer under his table and shew them a paire of Compasses with one of the legges broken." But in his case this was a serious piece of stage business. Pirandello, who had made a special (and notably scholarly) study of skepticism, knew better.

44

Leviathan

Thomas Hobbes

1651

The very long-lived (1588–1679) Thomas Hobbes, founder of English political (and moral) philosophy, wrote on almost every subject—not only philosophy, but also religion, mathematics, logic, psychology, language, and optics. He was tutor to the future Charles II in Paris (1646), when he, like the future king, was in exile from the Commonwealth. He knew or corresponded with almost every great mind of his time: GALILEO, to whom he owed the most, DESCARTES, BACON, LEIBNIZ. . . . No philosopher of any nationality has surpassed him in the writing of prose (only a very few, such as SCHOPENHAUER, have equaled him). He was even something of a poet, and his understanding of life was not only that of a philosopher and psychologist but also that of an ironic poet, only a little *manqué*.

Yet *Leviathan*, by far his most famous work, and one of the undoubted classics of world literature, is much misunderstood. For although he liked to present himself as of timid disposition because he had been born prematurely as a result of his mother's fear over the coming of the Spanish Armada, his writings are really very bold and courageous—so much so that he became known as "the beast of Malmesbury," an atheist forbidden (after 1666) to publish certain works. He always knew when he was being offensive—to the king's party because he denied the Divine Right of Kings, to the Puritans, to the Roman Catholics in particular, and to all moralists of whatever hue. There were many who wanted not just his works burned, but also his person. The true key to Hobbes is that, despite his passion for the deductive method that he learned from Galileo, he was an ironist well aware of his ability to provoke.

Hobbes was born in Malmesbury, on the border between the western counties of Gloucestershire and Wiltshire, the son of an ignorant, gambling, and impetuous vicar who was forced to vanish into obscurity when he struck a fellow-priest. For most although not quite all of his life he was, after a brilliant career at Oxford, in the service of the Devonshire family. Visits to the continent as tutor-companion enabled him to learn about MACHIAVELLI as well as about the latest European thinking. Although Hobbes rejected Francis Bacon's inductive method, his personal friendship with the aged Bacon helped him in his decisive repudiation of Aristotelian scholasticism and its by then overabstract manner of reasoning. He was certainly influenced, too, by Bacon's notion of the "Idols of the Market Place": the absurd carelessness with which words were used. There is no reason to suppose that Hobbes disliked religion itself, but he did greatly dislike the uses to which it was put. He spoke of death, at his own end, as a "great leap into the dark." When Hobbes wrote

> Put thousands together
> Less bad,
> But the cage less gay

or (in *Leviathan*), "The secret thoughts of a man run over all things, holy, profane, clean, obscene, grave, and light, without shame or blame," he was being a poet rather than a philosopher. But he has been judged only as a philosopher and political theorist. It has not been fully enough understood that he wished to give such a rigorously scientific account of the world as could legitimately be made—thus he left out much to do with "secret thoughts" (introspection), just because they were not open to strictly scientific inquiry. He saw the practice of religion of his day as a system of law, not of truth. But he loved God's question to Job: "Where wast thou when I laid the foundations of the earth?"

Although he has been compared to B. F. SKINNER, he was in fact no Skinner: He was not eager to exclude from human consideration all that pained him because he had been disappointed. But he was one of the inventors of the behaviorist method, which tries to describe the scientifically describable. He was no more of a behaviorist, though, than WILLIAM JAMES. The majesty and resonance of Hobbes's prose, with its unmistakable appeal to the emotions, amply demonstrates this. Besides, he explains psychology by reference to introspection: "Whosoever looketh into himself, and considereth what he doth, when he doth *think, opine, reason, hope, fear, &c,* and upon what grounds, he shall thereby reason and know, what are the thoughts and passions of all other men upon the like occasions."

Besides *Leviathan* Hobbes wrote, most notably, a philosophical trilogy in Latin—he published an English translation of its middle book as *Philosophical Rudiments of Government and Society* in 1651—and autobiographies in Latin and in English. He translated THUCYDIDES in 1628, and both the *Iliad* and the *Odyssey* of HOMER in his old age. His English works run to eleven volumes; the Latin to five.

The aim of *Leviathan* (the reference is to Job 41, to the awesome power of the great sea monster, a metaphor for Hobbes for the horrifying power of the sovereign state of his thesis, which he has too carelessly been taken as himself liking or relishing), is to describe the price of individual human convenience, security, and peace. Hobbes, inspired by Galileo's deductive exploration of the physical universe, wishes to analyze human activity in similarly incontrovertible terms. (It should be remembered that the deductive method involves drawing incontrovertible conclusions from true premises; the inductive method deals only with probabilities.) Everything, Hobbes believed, could be explained by "matter in motion." "Only one thing is real," he wrote: "But it forms the basis of the things we falsely claim to be something. . . . The only inner reality . . . is motion."

Hobbes's universe, like SPINOZA's, is material. Our thoughts and our passions are all caused by matter in motion. Chapter 6 of *Leviathan* is entitled "Of the Interior Beginnings of Voluntary Motions; commonly called the PASSIONS. And the Speeches by which they are expressed." Hobbes uses what he purports to demonstrate in this chapter as a basis, a true premise, from which he then deduces his idea of the state, the "Leviathan," which is necessary to impose in order that human beings may coexist in peace. He never implies *harmony,* because he is at heart a poet in whom utopian notions inspire what has been called "a nostalgia for evil." Human beings, he says, are not like the cooperative ants or bees: they compete, and they use "reason." (Is he being ironic? Most would say not, doubtless.) The ants and the bees agree naturally; human beings can only agree *artificially.* The "covenant" is not made between people and sovereign (as it is in ROUSSEAU or LOCKE), but between the people themselves. It could be seen this way: They agree (they are forced to agree by the selfishness in their natures) to become slaves. Hobbes's sovereign is an artificial God, and, he makes sure we know, a terrifying one. Is this political theory, or political description?

But from the point of view of serious, straightforward political theory, Hobbes put himself into difficulties. His answers to the related questions, What if the sovereign is a tyrant, what if he takes away far more freedom than he needs, what if he is greedy and what if he becomes, or is, mad, have been found to be unsatisfactory. True, he was writing about his times, just as Locke, who stated that peoples have the right to remove their sovereign, was writing about his (the removal of James II in 1688, which he supported). But Hobbes will only say that the worst despotism is better than anarchy (he means by this word total disorder, not what anarchists mean).

However, I think that Hobbes here is being descriptive, ironic, and pessimistic. One of the happiest states in the world is, all other things being equal, the pessimist's happiness in his message of gloom (one thinks of Thomas Hardy, Schopenhauer, and many others). Hobbes takes delight in depicting his state, in which men agree to give a sovereign absolute power because they fear death and want security. It may well be that he was, in his ironic way, *criticizing* human nature for being so selfish and mechanical—far from being agnostic about God's attributes, he may have been genuinely unhappy about human beings' capacity for understanding them. He is not saying, perhaps, that his sovereign *does* preserve peace and order (indeed, he may be silently pointing at political reality). The fact is that *Leviathan,* as philosophers do concede, and often say, is an "extraordinary book." Its prose appeals to the imagination in a particular way that Locke's and Rousseau's do not. One of its concluding passages is:

> In what shop, or Operatory the Fairies made their indictment, the old wives have not determined. But the Operatories of the *Clergy,* are well known to be the Universities, that received their Disciplines from Authority Pontifical. When the Fairies are displeased with any body, they are said to send their elves, to punish them. The *Ecclesiastics,* when they are displeased with any Civil State, make also their elves, that is, Superstition, Enchanted Subjects, to pinch their Princes, by preaching Sedition; or one Prince enchanted with promises, to pinch another.

45

Works

GOTTFRIED WILHELM LEIBNIZ

1663–1716

When we assert that a man or a woman is "great" we are guilty of an imprecision that is as extreme as it is ubiquitous—unless we admit at the outset that we mean no more than that this person, for some reason or another (perhaps unknown to us), arouses our personal enthusiasm. It does not matter if we are a professor of philosophy or a jobbing gardener—except that few jobbing gardeners, less vain and self-important than professors, would employ the term at all. The word *great* when applied to people has no meaning except in a subjective sense; yet gallons of ink have been wasted in attempts to prove that various persons, such as the vainglorious if well-tutored thug Alexander the Great, are indeed "great" in some morally superior manner that goes well beyond their impact on history—a history that is, as wrote EDWARD GIBBON, largely one of crime. It would be different if we could agree on a definition of the morality implied in the word; but, since we cannot agree, and since, on the principle of Ockham's Razor (that we should not introduce anything into a discussion if it isn't necessary: "entities should not be multiplied"), we ought not to, we should abandon it altogether. But we shan't, because we are all, even "objective" professors, too much in love with our own opinions; therefore our differing conceptions of "greatness" incorporate, as well as sincere devotion, a tyrannically moral dimension. (The only satisfying definition of greatness that I know is to be inferred from private jottings of Thomas Hardy, who clearly believed that "greatness" involved doing the right and gracious thing even in small matters. That, *pace* admirers of Alexander, is not a popular view.)

There is no one who would not, hearing the name of Gottfried Wilhelm Leibniz (1646–1716), instantly accede, although with a degree of timidity and confession of ignorance—and almost certainly without the usual enthusiasm—that he was "great." Bertrand Russell hated him but conceded that he was "great." It is true that, unlike Alexander, Leibniz did not introduce any huge misery into the world, or make much unnecessary trouble for those unconcerned with his ambitions—he lacks that sort of indubitable greatness admired by professors of history when they fantasize themselves into the position of world conquerors, or, more probably, as trusted advisers to world conquerors, as Aristotles to Alexanders. But there can be no doubt that Leibniz's influence has been large, practical, and enduring. There is scarcely an area of learning to which he did not contribute. For example (others equally pertinent can be given) he was the first writer to introduce the notion of the *unconscious*: He pointed out, with the great precision characteristic of him, that we can perceive something and not be aware of it at the time.

Yet we are in severe difficulties with him from the outset. He is, as he is invariably called, *strange*. The ordinary educated man or woman is perhaps less likely to be able to say anything much about him—except that he discovered the calculus at about the same time as NEWTON, and had a quarrel about priority; that VOLTAIRE ridiculed him in *Candide*; and "something about *windowless monads*"—than about any other figure of a similar degree of eminence. If we cannot put a too firm finger on those monads, well, nor (dignity apart) can anyone else, either. The philosophers are usually as lost as we are. We may, however, recollect what Bertrand Russell wrote of Leibniz, to whom he devoted an early book, in his *History of Western Philosophy:* "one of the supreme intellects of all time . . . as a human being he was not

admirable . . . there are two systems of philosophy. . . . One, which he pro-
claimed, was optimistic, orthodox, fantastic, and shallow; the other . . . was
profound, coherent, largely Spinozistic, and amazingly logical." Not everyone agrees with Russell, who was often careless in his judgments (as of
SCHOPENHAUER)and the matter can hardly be quite as simple; but something
like it remains true.

Leibniz's influence was spread by means of the written word, but can
any single book he wrote be selected as paramount? By no means! Much of
what is vital in him was not published in his lifetime, but, as Russell said,
had to be "unearthed from his manuscripts." Thus his work in symbolic logic
was not resurrected until the twentieth century. That he was important is
demonstrated by Voltaire's mockery of the popular side of him as Dr.
Pangloss. A German, he wrote mostly in Latin and French (although one of
his books, in German, advocates the wider use of German; but that, *Unvor-
greiffliche Gedanken betreffend die Ausübung und Verbesserung der
deutschen Sprache,* did not appear until the year after his death, and who
reads it now?), and much that has been influential on individuals and thereafter in thought is to be found in his correspondence. So we are stuck with
his *Works* or *Werke.* . . . Yet there is something artificial about that: Not only
do these works not yet exist in quite complete form, but also, in all probability, no single person has read them in their entirety—or ever will. We will
therefore be realistic, and state that most of what we need here is contained
in P. P. Weiner's *Leibniz Selections* (1951) or in one or two other, similar projects. A brief account of his life, though, will immediately bring out his significance and may help us to answer the question of what the world would be
like had he not existed.

Gottfried Wilhelm Leibniz was born in Leipzig, the son of a Professor
of moral philosophy at Leipzig University. Leibniz was perhaps the last "Universal Man" of the Renaissance type. A supreme polymath, he was a mathematician, scientist, lawyer, diplomat, engineer, historian, courtier, librarian,
and inventor (of the first calculation machine that could extract roots, a great
improvement on that of PASCAL). He was also a poet, but a bad and exceptionally conventional one—a significant but neglected topic to which I shall
return. He was a very public figure, described by George I of England as a
"walking encyclopedia." He was a prodigy who attended college at fourteen.
In 1669 he entered into the service of the elector of Mainz, then, in 1672,
always devoted (again unlike Alexander) to the notion of international peace,
he traveled to Paris to try to persuade Louis XIV to expel the Turks from
Egypt in order to distract his attention from marching on Holland (this ploy
did not work). He went to England twice: in 1673 and again three years later.
But when George of Hanover, his employer from 1676, became king of England, he would not allow him to come there.

In 1676 Leibniz spent four days with SPINOZA making notes on the
latter's *Ethics*—and completed his work on the calculus. Many mathematicians were working on allied problems, Newton among them, and, while the

latter used friends, unscrupulously, to accuse him of plagiarism (of which he was not guilty), Leibniz had to stoop to putting his case anonymously—this was soon discovered, and he was made to look a fool. Yet his system of notation is superior to that of Newton, and is still in use today. Essentially, insofar as credit is important, they share the honors. The consequences of this discovery of a new means of solving problems, many of them practical, do not require enumeration.

Yet, like Newton, Leibniz did not observe the modern practice of drawing a line between the unknown (or, as it is often misleadingly called, the "occult") and the rather more easily verifiable (and understandable), and is thus as great an embarrassment to modern atheist commentators, as is Newton, too, the discoverer of the laws of motion and gravity. Leibniz had a lifelong interest in alchemy, and it is in no way unexpected to those who know something about him that he should have been among the few people in the West to investigate, in his own peculiar manner, the I CHING.

When Leibniz died, feeling miserable and unfulfilled, plagued with gout, and under secret surveillance, not a single person from the court of Hanover was present at his funeral. He had been avaricious, multifariously active, accessible, power-loving—and the greatest intellect of his time with the exception of Newton. He never married, (did he have recourse to women of pleasure?—it is a formidable thought), and it is said that after he proposed at the age of fifty he withdrew his proposal "before it was too late." He was not "smooth," charming, or "nice," but relied on his eminence and indeed on his "greatness" to get by socially. Had it not been for his irresistible influence he would hardly have attracted the attention of posterity; no historical novel or even "psychic biography" (beloved of certain Germans or Austrians such as Feuchtwanger or Stefan Zweig) has been written about him. He died lonely, and he is neglected as a person even today. Biographies of him are grim affairs.

The rigorous manner in which Leibniz worked at his general philosophy of mind has been crucially influential, as has his "law of indiscernibles" (that if two things are identical then anything that applies to the one must apply to the other, which looks like common sense, but which raises philosophical difficulties that he went some way toward solving), the philosophy itself less so after the end of the seventeenth century. KANT, who used Leibnizian textbooks in his lectures, and whose philosophy took some time to supplant that of Leibniz in his native Germany, went to a great deal of trouble to refute the notion that his position was that of Leibniz, whom he bitterly criticized—yet he may well have accepted the Leibnizian notions of space and time as fundamentally true. He could not have proceeded without him.

Leibniz's metaphysical system, which he saw as underpinning all his work, is now as inaccessible—even to his fellow-philosophers—as he was ambitiously accessible in his own time. What can we say about it today?

Leibniz's definition of reality—that it consists of a number of nonmaterial monads (this meant to him: the smallest possible entity that is a unity, the simplest possible unit of energy), absolutely independent of one another—is one of the three important accounts of reality of the seventeenth century; that it is by far the oddest should not deter us from acknowledging this. DESCARTES argued for two substances, Spinoza for one, and Leibniz for an infinite number, of which God is the most intelligent one. His system, complex and forbidding—often described as "fantastic"—in some ways resembles mystical or Kabbalistic accounts of reality, and, given his interest in alchemy, one is entitled to wonder how influenced he had been by such matters. (KEPLER and Newton were so influenced, and they have never been forgiven for it; their biographers have had to make a false, indeed a brutishly wooden and closed-minded, distinction between what they call "superstition" and what they think of as science, when in fact the more sensible of them know very well that the scientific achievements would have been impossible without the "superstitious beliefs.") Alfred North Whitehead, who with Russell made great use of Leibniz's mathematics in *Principia Mathematica,* declared that Leibniz was outstanding because he had "answered another question" beyond those posed by Descartes and Newton; he "explained what it must be like to be an atom." That is perhaps the essence of his monadology.

But what was perhaps most important of all about Leibniz's ideas as they struck his learned contemporaries was that they boldly challenged long-accepted assumptions about beliefs held by most philosophers. He seemed to imply, for example, that human beings are incapable of free choice. Antoine Arnauld (1612–1694), the French theologian, himself bold enough to attract persecution for his anti-Jesuit and Jansenist views, wrote to a friend that he saw in Leibniz's meditations so many things that frightened him "and ought to frighten the whole of mankind" that he could not see what purpose they could serve—since mankind would reject them. For Leibniz had defined an individual as, among other things (this individual was also a congregation of monads), all that happened to him. This is in its way quite close to gnostic doctrine, for it implies that God himself, although the creator, is not free to undo his own work. So is his assertion, made in a letter to Queen Sophie Charlotte of Prussia, that "since the senses and inductions could never teach us truths which are thoroughly universal, nor that which is absolutely necessary" so there must be *a light born within us.*"

For a nonphilosopher to deal with Leibniz would be difficult, since he is so desperately technical as well as so, as we would now say, quaint. Yet to deal adequately with him one needs a wider grasp of the world than that of a regular philosopher. After all, his mathematics alone have had far-reaching and practical consequences: he invented the binary system, a general method of integrating rational functions, the signs for similarity and congruence. . . . Boole's work in algebra could not have been done without him. All this in a light born within him, which he was thus just able to acknowledge—in a letter. It was in letters that he expressed himself most vitally. This can be said of no other philosopher of his weight.

I mentioned above that Leibniz wrote bad poetry, although lip service was paid to it in its time. It was formalistic, a little skillful in that sense—but inert. His failure in that form reflects his own failure: He was emotionally deficient, clumsy as a person, "not quite of this world," lacking in the "common touch." He was lopsided, his life was led in his intellect, while his emotions starved. He was thus not in a good position to fulfill his ambitions, and so seemed to be arrogant and vain. Brought up a strict Protestant by his mother, his father's third wife, he had a vision that, in the light of strict Protestantism, was gnostic dynamite: So he early learned to contain it in intellectual gymnastics (which were awesome). However, all phenomena, to be viewed completely need to be viewed in an emotional as well as an intellectual light. Leibniz canalized his, initially, intensely emotional search for truth into a pursuit of the cause of peace, and thus could protect himself from the blasphemous and even revolutionary implications of his concept of a God who was limited in power. In thus suppressing his emotional nature he robbed his system of much of the real poetry and Blakean grandeur that it might have possessed. It thus exists as a vision *manqué,* lacking in the sinister beauty that he himself, as well as Arnauld, feared. But he offered more than the majority of his fellow-scientists, who still reject the validity of taking an emotional view at all.

46

Pensées

BLAISE PASCAL

1670

I will forgive Descartes. In all his philosophy he would have been quite willing to dispense with God. But he could not help granting him a flick of the forefinger to start the world in motion; beyond this, he has no further need of God.

Thus the mathematician, scientist, and Jansenist theologian Blaise Pascal, who also took his stand on the following famous saying (acknowledged by many modern philosophers with the greatest difficulty): "The heart has its reasons which reason knows nothing of."

What he was saying was that DESCARTES had ignored very pressing psychological problems in his philosophy. But the problem here for the professional philosophers, especially for the authors of ambitious systems of truth—if not for the rest of us, provided we do not seek to provide such systems—is that this is all too obviously true. But how—it is a fair question in every sense—can philosophers, how can logic, how can followers of pure reason, accommodate it? Philosophers are not poets or novelists, and the positivistic doctrines of some of the most conscientious and eminent of them would make nonsense of poetry if they chose to press them thus (they usually don't, because some of them like poetry, even though as philosophers they would be unable to give an official answer as to why). When the important Austrian mathematician and philosopher Edmund Husserl (who is discussed here in the sections on William James and Jean-Paul Sartre) decided to treat the question of the contents of consciousness in a purely scientific manner, his own austere and strikingly nonemotional treatment soon became one of the bases of existentialism, the name given to one of the most emotionally directed (and politically rebellious) systems ever known in the history of philosophy. So much was this so that many people refused it the status of a philosophy at all. Pascal was an early anticipator of the manner in which Husserl's philosophy of phenomenology would be taken up.

Yet, existentialism aside (and this, as in the hands of SARTRE, was mostly atheist, and even used atheism as a prop), in the twentieth century only the philosophies of WILLIAM JAMES and Alfred North Whitehead, and a few others of similar type and nature, have made any serious attempt to deal with what poetry (and therefore faith, or "the will to believe") represents.

Of course, reason itself does have its reasons, too; but, as things are in the world today, is the heart quite so ignorant of these, as reason is of the heart's? If we were balanced creatures, then all could be well. But in general we are not, and our scientific enterprises, wonderful and wonderfully ingenious though they are, are by no means in balance with our vague and diffuse religious feelings, which, however, are quite as irresistible to our sensibilities as they are irrational to pure logic. The great world outside—which, the KABBALAH and many other similar traditions, as well as some important philosophies, teach, is little more than the world we choose in our laziness or stupidity, to perceive—is all too often discerned, by the person who wants to know before he conforms, to run on principles just as irrational. Hence no doubt arises the facile proposition, by more than a few popular scientists of today, that we and the universe we live in came about by pure chance—it is interesting that these people should advance their hypothesis with such irritated fervor, or that some of them have actually said that, "we ought to be more moral"—as if that, from them, had any force behind it; but the Russian novelist Dostoyevsky's realization that *if God does not exist then anything is permitted* does have a true and terrifying force, for it means that, strictly speaking, there is nothing at all morally wrong with, say, Hitler, or Stalin: Humanism on its own has no emotional driving force, and it willfully ignores the clearly supernatural origins of *conscience* as distinct from seeing conscience as an essential part of maintaining social order.

Pascal was not so foolish, knew more about chance and its nature than most men have known (he is one of the founders of probability theory), and he did not feel that "everything should be permitted." Those ideas, essentially, drove his project in life. As the *Pensées* demonstrate, his peculiarities did not make him into any kind of fanatic or lead him into any kind of mad denial of inner reality such as drives today's triumphalist atheists.

The heart—even of a dedicated positivist—knows of all sorts of pain (and of Kierkegaardian "dread" or "anxiety"); but reason does not know how to deal with pain, or, worst of all, how to explain it. People have expected that any God they are prepared to worship (or even just to appease) would be "fair-minded"; but it is, again painfully, much more complicated a question than that. So Blaise Pascal's "Thoughts" have been much attended to. Many of them appeal—indeed, they do not even have to appeal—to the inner experience of us all.

The general tendency of philosophy from PLATO and ARISTOTLE, both of whom could accommodate poetry, with later serious resistance only from SPINOZA ("I believe in Spinoza's God," stated ALBERT EINSTEIN, when he was challenged), has been to ignore religion, and therefore whatever it is that most poetry (too)—the product of the intelligent heart, "the true voice of feeling" and not of reason alone—stands for, and so to imply, often unhappily, that it stands for nothing. At least Pascal, like William James after him, takes the bull by the horns. And, like James, he is a precursor of the post–World War II existentialist movement—of immense importance as a phenomenon, however unconvincing Sartrian existentialism may be as a philosophy—who is not always acknowledged as such. Himself a scientist, one of the most accomplished mathematicians of all time, one of the greatest of investigators of the meaning of *chance* (of randomness, of processes now often called stochastic), and therefore extra well endowed with the faculty of reason, he also denied reason supremacy. He was studied in depth by the most important of the pre-existentialists, SØREN KIERKEGAARD, and is held in high respect by all philosophers.

Pascal was born in 1623 at Clermont. His father Etienne had unusual ideas about education, and taught his son himself. He withdrew all mathematical books from him, but then discovered that the boy (at about twelve) had started to work out mathematics for himself. He relented and gave him a copy of EUCLID. Before 1654 and the religious experience which caused him to dedicate himself to Christianity, Pascal made many achievements in science and mathematics. He produced what was only the second calculating machine ever to be invented. He did invaluable work on conic sections. His experiments led to the invention of the barometer. With the mathematician Fermat he laid the basis for the all-important science of probability as we know it today. He didn't, in that matter, allow reasons of the heart to distract him. What is sometimes called his "first conversion" took place in 1646 at the age of twenty-three, when he came into contact with the Jansenists.

The Jansenists, who took their doctrine from the *Augustinus* of Cornelius Otto Jansen (1585–1638), have been and often still are called "Calvinist Catholics." This is a justified but misleading description. The Jansenist movement, which caused extreme and indeed almost hysterical alarm in the orthodox Catholic Church for a time, had died out by about 1800 except among a few secretly convinced. When Jansenism was at its peak as a religious movement it centered upon the convent of Cistercian nuns at Port-Royal, near Paris. After 1664 this community was persecuted. One of Pascal's two sisters, Jacqueline, entered it in 1652. In November 1654 Pascal announced his "definitive conversion," his "ecstasy," an account of which he always carried with him until his death eight years later as a result of what is believed to have been a painful stomach ulcer.

The association between Jansenism and Calvinism is only misleading because the former does not put any very special sadistic emphasis on the damnation side of the equation, as Calvin certainly did. It could be called revived Augustinism. It was pessimistic but without cruelty. It concentrated on the impossibility of men following God's commandments without his "special grace." Hostility to the Jesuits helped to unify the movement, and in this hostility Pascal's own eighteen *Lettres provinciales* of 1656–1657 were crucial. Here Pascal attacks notions that are still taught by the orthodox Catholic Church: that God foresaw human cooperation with his free gift of grace; and that in regard to the sinfulness of an action, the law is to yield to human freedom. Pascal, like his fellow-Jansenists, opposed such doctrines with the strict moral rigor and austerity of the early Church. It was what they perceived as Jesuit laxity and casuistry that gave the Jansenists most of their energy and vitality; but they did not dwell on the sufferings of human beings in Hell, or advocate persecution. So much is implied in Pascal's famous "wager," which is to be found in his posthumous *Pensées* (variously arranged from notebooks after his death).

This—and it is typical of a mathematician obsessed by chance—concedes that there is no evidence for the existence of God. Therefore our human predicament is that of a gambler on the result of any game. "Reason can decide nothing here." Therefore we must, Pascal insists, bet on the chance that Roman Catholicism is true. If we win, we have before us a life of eternal bliss. If we lose, well, then, we lose nothing that we will ever know about. However, if we bet against, then we might have to suffer a life of eternal torment (what Calvin prescribed for the mass of us, himself excluded of course).

The force of this is irresistible, emotionally. But only until we recognize its fatal weakness: Pascal unfortunately offers us Roman Catholicism or nothing. However, in the agnostic spirit of the first premise, he quite certainly ought to have offered us Islam, Buddhism, Greek religion—and an actual infinity of other possible universal truths! Indeed, the original idea of the wager itself came, not from Pascal, but from Islam! Alas for his logic, he would not gamble on even that. It causes his wager to be, in strictly scientific terms, positively shoddy.

However, the *Pensées* themselves as a whole are greatly superior to this particular piece of false reasoning. But even that is important: It is an attempt to offer a prudential and not an evidential reason for our being religious— and because in practical terms it can turn the heart toward the dialogue with God that Pascal, more rationally in the light of human hunger for religion, recommends. WILLIAM JAMES's defense of it depends on there being various reasons why in certain cases it might, pragmatically, be "a good idea." Thus, while this famous argument is worthless in terms of logic, it may not be so in its likely emotional effects.

Pascal was arrogant, rather overbearing in manner, and, as well as being a scientific genius, tormented not only by illness and pain but by religious doubt. He had in his time gambled and lived a wild life (we do not really know quite how wild, but this period of his life in any case did not extend much beyond two years). His notebooks (for that is what the *Pensées* amount to, although they have been arranged and presented in differing ways) give an inner account of a man who knew quite as much about life in all its forms as did NIETZSCHE or Kierkegaard. That he was well aware of what he was up against is made clear from the third of the nine hundred or so sections into which the work has been divided. He writes:

> Those who are accustomed to judge by feeling do not understand the process of reasoning, for they would understand at first sight and are not used to seek for principles. And others, on the contrary, who are accustomed to reason from principles, do not at all understand matters of feeling, seeking principles and being unable to see at a glance.

But later he appeals to how people actually do feel:

> What will [the puzzled man] do then, but perceive the appearance of the middle of things, in an eternal despair of knowing either their beginning or their end. All things proceed from the Nothing, and are borne toward the Infinite. Who will follow these marvelous processes? The Author of these wonders understands them. None other can do so. Through failure to contemplate these Infinites, men have rashly rushed into the examination of nature,

as though they bore some proportion to her. It is strange that they have wished to understand the beginnings of things, and thence to arrive at the knowledge of the whole, with a presumption as infinite as their object. For surely this design cannot be formed without presumption or without a capacity infinite like nature.

It is hard to refute this. Indeed, to read Pascal is often to find anew religious feelings that we have deliberately submerged, concealed, or repressed. For, notwithstanding his own Jansenist brand of Roman Catholicism, which was in very large part the result of the excesses of his upbringing and of the laxity and lack of true seriousness of the powerful and favored Jesuits of his time, Pascal may be read as a very highly intelligent guide to the perplexed religious spirit. He took the question *Why are we here?* (mocked as absurd by positivists and atheists), with the utmost seriousness—and it is no mere gamble to assert that every person, whether he will admit it or no, is wracked by that question. Pascal asks it in a peculiarly lucid manner, which has had enormous influence. His paradoxes abound and continue to stimulate: "Man is but a reed, the weakest in nature, but he is a thinking reed." "Man is neither angel nor beast; and the misfortune is that he who would act the angel acts the beast."

Ethics

BARUCH DE SPINOZA

1677

Although his voluminous letters made no immediate impact on the world, no one who wants to understand Spinoza (1632–1677) and thus be enlightened—for thinking has seldom risen to such heights in the interest of what Plato called "the good"—could manage without the *Correspondence* (much of it edited in an English translation by A. Wolf in 1929). Without, for example, the information he gave to his friend Henry Oldenburg (a German diplomat living in London as a secretary to the Royal Society), on many difficult points, his philosophy would be less clear to us. Spinoza did not, like his fellow rationalist LEIBNIZ (a human being much inferior to him, but most others have been, too), give the outlines of his majestic philosophy in his private letters; but those letters do illuminate, and illuminate in a precious manner, his philosophy. They are invaluable. However, his masterpiece, the *Ethics*, upon which he worked for many years—it was published, like almost all his work, after his death—is his chief contribution, and is the natural choice for inclusion here.

Spinoza very thoroughly effaced himself in the interests of his thought: Little is known of the details of his private life (for example, "what he did about sex" is unknown). All that is known is to his credit, which is almost as unusual as his philosophy. It is remarkable, too, that his overall attitude—he wanted, quite above all, to discover a "life of blessedness for man," "a joy continuous and supreme to all eternity"—which, now that he is safely dead, so that his magnanimity may no longer arouse envy except in a mean few, is quite the best loved, or at the very least the most respected, of any philosopher's, arose from a background of prejudice, intolerance, misunderstanding, insensitivity and cruelty.

Of the few score of major philosophers, Spinoza—like PLATO, HUME and KANT—but unlike most of the others, stands out: hardly anyone would dispute that he belongs among the six or so greatest men of all time, or even that he lends a kind of meaning to that dubious term *great*. Beside Spinoza a highly influential as well as gifted thinker as apparently innocuous and even, superficially, as charming as JOHN LOCKE suddenly looks the shifty, brilliant, but ambiguous knave that, at heart, he was. Knavery was just that vice from which Locke most avidly sought to escape.

Spinoza, although his all-embracing philosophy has given rise to wildly varying interpretations (one daft but intellectually plausible school of thought, going along with various zealots of his own times, even claims that he was an atheist), has been found inspiring; the empty-hearted Locke, the ambitious and pious empirical rationalist, has, at best, been found useful—but by both right and left, by BURKE, by that unusually mildly flawed politician the third president of the United States, Thomas Jefferson, by authoritarians disguised as libertarians, and by apostles of freedom such as PAINE and ROUSSEAU—by everyone from the post-Marxists to the Nazis.

Baruch de Spinoza was the son of Portuguese Marranos (forced converts to Christianity clandestinely living as Jews), of Spanish origin, who fled their own country to escape the Inquisition. They settled in Amsterdam, where they enjoyed a degree of tolerance and safety, and where Spinoza's father was able to set up as a successful merchant.

Baruch went to the Jewish school, where (this is a sometimes overlooked aspect of his education) he gained a full knowledge of Jewish mysticism and of theology both Jewish and Arabic. One of his chief teachers was his fellow Marrano, Manassah ben Israel—appointed rabbi at the age of eighteen, and later to play an important part in the return of the Jews to England—a noted liberal of the time. The work of Abraham Herrera introduced him to the KABBALAH, which, although he carefully divorced himself from the misleading mumbo-jumbo always and inevitably associated with it, was a profound influence upon him.

A crisis arose when the Jewish authorities, anxious to assure the Calvinist city fathers of their respectability, tried to persuade Spinoza, by bribery, promise, and then threat, to renounce his "heterodox" and pantheistic opinions. He refused, and was thereupon excommunicated from his community—and cursed by it (with, for good measure, "all the curses of the universe"), an almost sure sign of distinction in a thinker.

He became famous among philosophers and intellectuals before he published anything; but, during his lifetime, so notorious as an "atheist" had he become that he was able to publish only two works: a book on the philosophy of DESCARTES, of whose philosophy he was the first substantial corrector—he wrote this for a pupil, and it may not have conformed to his own views—and then, in 1670, the *Tractatus Theologico-Politicus,* which appeared anonymously and in a disguised binding. This brought him obloquy in full measure, since it was a plea for free thought and full tolerance; it also explained, for the first time, the Scriptures as historical documents. Thus Spinoza is the father of modern rational Bible study. He thought of Jesus as no more than the last of the great Hebrew prophets. But he at the same time pointed to the great moral value of the Bible. In this work he was, too, much influenced by THOMAS HOBBES, whose idea of a social contract, however, he interpreted more liberally and democratically. The immediate occasion of the work was the outbreak of mob violence against the de Witts, enlightened rulers of Holland, after the English navy defeated the Dutch; an event that was blamed on their toleration of "atheism." Spinoza wrote against this madness.

Spinoza made a just adequate living as a lens grinder (the dust generated by this occupation affected his health and contributed to his early death from tuberculosis) and accepted a modicum of financial support from friends; in 1573 he refused an offer of a chair of philosophy at Heidelberg on the characteristic grounds that a philosopher needs to be independent—he wanted, he told the elector palatine who had offered him the job, to pursue his studies "according to his own mind." His whole life was in fact dedicated to discussion, with sympathetic minds, of his and others' ideas for ideas' sake: surely the ideal life for a philosopher. But he paid dearly for his free thinking, being regarded by the majority as an atheist heretic, dangerously committed to secular thought.

Of the three great rationalists (philosophers who, by contrast to the empiricists, believe that the truth may be reached by unaided reason rather than from sense experience—the term used in this way does not imply atheism)—the others were Leibniz and Descartes, Spinoza was the most coherent. He could not accept the splitting, by Descartes, of mind and body into two separate entities, a splitting which had led and would lead to huge difficulties. What was the exact nature of the causal interaction between mental and physical events, or was there (even) an interaction between them at all?

Spinoza rejected the distinction, and replaced it with "substance monism," the view that the universe consists of a single substance that *is* God and is self-dependent. The word *monism* is highly appropriate because whereas Descartes had insisted that there was an infinite number of substances (including each individual mind and body, for a start), Spinoza, arguing in part from the fact that everything is dependent on everything else, asserted that everything "individual" was but a "modification" or "mode," a fragment, of a single reality. Nothing has reality except inasmuch as it is a part of the one substance. We may think of it, conceive it, as physical, or we may think of it as mental; but whatever we do, and however definitive this seems to us, we are in fact viewing the same thing. There is a strong element here of common sense, for (as many still believe today), when, just in an ordinary way, we conceive of an individual, we regard him as being, whether we speak of him psychologically or physically, *a single individual.* For Spinoza a physical event can be explained in mental terms and a mental event can be explained in physical terms. Thought was, for Spinoza, as it is in the Kabbalah, the "higher" mode, because it "knows" "extension" (physical extension in space), whereas extension does not know thought.

Unlike empiricists such as Locke was (in part) Spinoza did not, so to say, think highly of sense perceptions. The pious Locke, so niggardly of praise of those who influenced him, listened to the Psalms being read aloud to him and disingenuously retained rationalist credentials for the belief in God that he found the lack of to be "inconceivable," but in philosophy followed an ambitiously empiricist course. Spinoza, before him, thought sense perceptions to be "inadequate": They are confused because we see the external world, he insisted, imperfectly—as a reflection of our own bodily processes.

However, each entity, each finite thing (the universe itself alone—for Spinoza the equivalent of God, or nature—is infinite), possesses within it an urge toward perfection. This urge or endeavor he called *conatus.* There is a useful physical example of this: If the body takes in a poison, it will try of its own accord to expel it. That is how bodies are made.

Likewise, we may fairly state, the spirit. There is in the spiritual aspect of each individual a natural need to expel ideas and notions and even wishes to perform bad actions. We have built into us a need and even a capacity to understand ourselves truly, and not in a confused or self-deluding manner. The kabbalistic implications of this view have not been properly explored in mainstream philosophy—or even, much, in the English language. But the effort should be made, and made bearing in mind Spinoza's own awareness that pearls inevitably become embedded in slime and dung (as KEPLER memorably said of astrology).

For Spinoza clarity of insight has its own peculiar flavor. And when a human being has experienced this he will know that his or her thinking and perceiving has previously been muddy and clouded. The mind may then abandon its familiar "point of view" in favor of a more rational pursuit of reality. "He who has a true idea knows simultaneously that he has a true idea," he wrote in the *Ethics* (which, like most of Spinoza's other works, was written in Latin).

Spinoza, that most rational of all mystics, believed that the chief obstacle to clarity lay in the poor quality of our emotional life. Our feelings are, ordinarily, imprecise and purely wishful impressions that serve to keep us in a state of confusion—and also make us extremely unhappy. (An obvious and very important corollary is that literature has a high value in that it can demonstrate the exact nature of this, for example in tragedy; equally, the true value of, say, a poem may lie in its degree of clear insight.) "When a man is prey to his emotions, he is not his own master, but lies at the mercy of chance," he wrote. He was not of course denying the power of true and proper emotions, but, rather, denouncing the nature of our own emotions—largely negative or sentimental—as they usually are. The initial remedy lies in discovering their true causes: Do we believe (a familiar enough example) that we "love" a person when in fact we merely lust after them, or want power over them? In that and in other ways Spinoza has been justly seen as a precursor of modern depth psychology. He also reminds us of many ancient movements, such as Orphism, which had in common that they believed that reason in mathematics lifts man toward God. Spinoza carries this much further and maintains that to understand our place in things is to love God. But error, in his always merciful system, is not something meriting the stake or rope: It arises from privation of knowledge: a confusion that is, alas, not seen to be so.

One of Spinoza's main offenses in the eyes of his conventional contemporaries was his pantheism (but the term itself was not used until 1705, by John Toland). This view, that everything is divine and that God and Nature are identical, was grudgingly allowed to poets in the production of their works, but here was an actual philosophy proposing that there is but a single substance, and, furthermore, men may only be granted immortality insofar as they can enter into the "thinking" of God, who is that single substance!

Pantheism is not now of much interest, it being more of a play with words than a real issue—obviously for the religious man in some sense "everything he looks upon is blessed" and (borrowing the words of W. B. Yeats) he is "blessed by everything," and just as obviously for the atheist everything is meaningless but what we make of it; but Spinoza's view upset those who, in the cruel tradition of AUGUSTINE and his followers, required a savage God to judge and punish and reward. Although his philosophy contains in some measure a discussion, or the beginnings of a discussion, of all that has concerned or still concerns philosophers, Spinoza's greatest importance, like that of Plato, lies in his persuasive advocacy of a world of laws in which human beings can find fulfillment.

48

Pilgrim's Progress

John Bunyan

1678–1684

The legacy of Calvinism was not, and could not have been, as hateful as its inventor intended and stated it to be. The root of his own endeavor was too tainted with a personally vindictive malice towards others. However much Calvin had suffered—and we may be sure he did—by the time he gained control of Geneva he was able to feel "reasonably sure of his own salvation."

On others, for example on John Bunyan, the -ism that is named after Calvin has had a different—and often more salutary—effect. The Calvinist notion about election does, after all, act as a compelling dramatic metaphor for many states of mind, not the least of those being that in which people feel cut off, by the banausic or otherwise "non-authentic" nature of their existence, from their essential selves.

Therefore the claim that it is a serious misreading and over-simplification of Puritanism to regard it as wholly repressive, and wholly sexual in origin, is eminently just. Of course as a movement it embraced much that was serious as well as salutary. In actual practice, too, whatever the "theology" involves, the vast majority of "Calvinists" of whatever persuasion did regard salvation as, after all, and however illogically in the light of Calvin's thinking, *attainable*. The worry (as in the case of John Bunyan at the time of his original illness, called his "crisis") was only ostensibly about whether you had been elected; what really happened was that you looked at yourself and tried to persuade yourself that you were really behaving like a saint after all. At the very least, the Puritan could then be fairly sure of his *own* salvation. He thus had only the salvation of others to worry about, and this anxiety he could minimize by telling those others what to do—and by punishing them when they would not, or (better still) *could* not, obey.

After all, it is worth reminding ourselves that if Calvin's (notoriously and significantly feeble) theology is taken literally and logically, then there is no point at all even in having the right kind of faith or "certitude"—everything has already been decided, outside time; the righteousness of it, or otherwise, is put beyond question. Calvin stated that *all* human beings *deserve* damnation; logically, then, it was only by something as vulgar as mere luck that they even possessed the Calvinistic "certitude," let alone that they had actually been elected as God took the names out of a hat. There is no point at all in good works. Hence Calvin's arguments about the necessity of ordered government, because a heaven on earth would (given God's good time) eventually ensue in Geneva, is a false corollary. What might well be called Calvin's grand confidence trick—you were *supposed* to do good works because you were a saint, i.e., elected, but the argument is a circular one—has been treated with remarkable equanimity by historians and theologians. But it has had an enormous influence, despite the fact that its central tenet (of arbitrary damnation by God of most of the human race) has always been carefully ignored. No one can conduct business (and commerce has been particularly important to Calvinists) on such a basis. . . . If it is true, better forget it! A dollar in the hand is worth ten in the bush, especially if the bush is burning in Hell.

The common statement, therefore, that the persecuted Baptist John Bunyan sat down to write a *Calvinist* tract, but succeeded in producing a folk epic, *Pilgrim's Progress,* is an understandable but slightly misleading one. For Bunyan, even if his kind of devout and of course non-Anglican Christianity derived from LUTHER through Calvin, did not *really* believe that most people, apart from himself, were damned. *Pilgrim's Progress* would make no sense at all in such a light. He had only believed that while he was profoundly depressed, from 1648. We must, I think, sympathize with the poet Samuel Taylor Coleridge, who denied the "Calvinism" of the book, and thought that Bunyan's "piety was baffled by his genius." "Bunyan the dreamer," he wrote, "overcame the Bunyan of the conventicle."

But the leading modern editor of *Pilgrim's Progress,* Roger Sharrock, seems to disagree, and writes that Calvinism, despite its evil reputation for "intolerance and bigotry," "provided a powerful and dramatic myth: life was a confrontation between the powers of light and the powers of darkness. . . ."

But what the central tenet of Calvinism in particular did was to provide a quite different metaphor (a perverse lottery in which a few undeserving souls escaped deserved damnation just because God desired to exhibit his own glory), at least for the truly creative and thoughtful—who had perforce either to succumb, or (as Bunyan did) to overcome and thus escape. What counted in Bunyan's case was the sense of earning his salvation—through his way of life *and* through the manner of his faith—a sense that he obtained, apart from his own conscience, from Protestantism's comparatively recent return to the alarmed urgency of early Christianity. This was violent in Luther; in the sadistic Calvin it was pathological. So Coleridge was right: in Bunyan an imagination gained from physical and spiritual experience transcended all forms of dogma. Life, as the novelist George Moore wrote, is after all a "rose that withers in the iron fist of dogma." Men who discover a way, as Bunyan did for himself in his book, must also allow that there are other ways.

Bunyan, as the author of *Pilgrim's Progress,* turned Calvin's vindictiveness on its head. The pathological—we should call it clinical—depression that lies at the heart of Calvinism is, in the first and superior part of *Pilgrim's Progress,* understood, humanized and finally overcome. It may thus be described as an *anti*-Calvinist fable!

John Bunyan was born in Elstow, a village near Bedford, not far north of London, in 1628. His father was an itinerant tinker (or brazier), a devout man in the Puritan mold. John, who deliberately exaggerated the "lowness" of his origins (his father's people had been landowners) was educated at a grammar school—this is sometimes forgotten, and the quality of his mind thus somewhat underestimated on account of his obvious lack of interest in history; but the education at a grammar school at this time was superior to that given at most modern universities. At sixteen (1644) he was pressed by the parliamentary forces into service against King Charles I. After his release from the army he married, in a state of abject poverty. Then (in about 1648) he began to undergo a violent religious crisis. Like so many of those brought up in the Calvinist persuasion, he began to doubt his own salvation.

Grace Abounding to the Chief of Sinners (1666), a spiritual account of this crisis, written while he was in prison for his Puritan preaching, is in part a pathological record—an alarming one—and lacks the dramatic power and wide appeal of his later and more famous work, although it is interesting in its own right. It describes how his "tumultuous thoughts . . . like masterless hellhounds," roared and bellowed and made "a hideous noise" within him. By 1653 he had recovered. From 1655, as one of a flourishing nonconformist group centered in Bedford, he began preaching. When Charles II came to the throne in 1660 he was arrested for his preaching but, offered freedom, he refused to give an undertaking not to stop it. He thus spent the next twelve years in and out of Bedford jail (he was not permanently confined there, as legend used to suggest). Only his own obstinacy—and integrity—denied him his freedom.

In 1672 Bunyan, by then the author of several edifying works, was able to obtain a license to preach under the terms of the Declaration of Indulgence. When he went to London he could attract an audience of at least three thousand. In 1673, when the Declaration was cancelled, Bunyan spent another six months in jail; it was on this occasion—possibly stirred into creativity by a sense of sudden disappointment, quickly followed by despair that he would ever be able to escape persecution—that he began the first part of *Pilgrim's Progress,* which reached its final form (in the first printing there was no Mr Worldly Wiseman) in 1679. It may well be that he had written a first draft of the book many years earlier, during his first and longer imprisonments. (The second part, issued in 1684, about Christian's wife—Bunyan had married again after the death of his first wife—and her journey, is lucubrated and not of quite the same quality.) Later Bunyan was made pastor of the Bedford Separatist Church, and he became famous for his preaching throughout Bedfordshire and the neighboring county of Cambridgeshire.

Bunyan's last book was a violent attack on the Roman Catholic Church, occasioned by the soon-to-be frustrated plans of James II (who nervously tried to bribe him with a "place of public trust," an offer which he refused) for restoring papism to England. Had he lived for just a few more years, he would have been able to see the beginnings of the absorption of dissent into the fabric of society (William of Orange was himself a "Calvinist," though he did not for all that believe that most of his new subjects were damned). Within less than a century many leading nonconformists (including a teacher to WILLIAM GODWIN) were asserting that eternal suffering in hell was not an idea to be taken literally. . . .

Pilgrim's Progress is an allegory, a narrative in which a second meaning is to be read beneath and concurrent with the surface story. Its strength and vigor come mainly from its use of the colloquial, but that is mixed in with what Bunyan had read: the Authorized Version of the Bible (the various contemporary versions, in the ghastly jargon employed by bureaucrats, are but imprudent travesties of this), various popular nonconformist books (one of these, the *Plain Man's Pathway to Heaven,* was brought into his home by his first wife), Foxe's *Book of Martyrs,* the Book of Common Prayer, and, not least, chivalric romances that Bunyan guiltily enjoyed as a young man (Dr. Johnson thought that he had read Spenser's *Faerie Queen,* and the suggestion has been widely accepted). But when Bunyan mixed this rather archaic and often stately language with that of the common people, the result was unique. Scholars spent much time wondering how this nonuniversity man, this (to their snobbish minds) illiterate, could have achieved such a moving tour de force; they ransacked medieval and renaissance literature for models that Bunyan might have used. But they could find nothing.

In 1623 the magnificent Czech, as we would now call him, Jan Amos Komensky (1592–1670)—the educationist and theologian better known to us as Comenius—wrote *The Labyrinth of the World and the Paradise of the Heart,* which was published in 1631. But this learned and pessimistic allegory, in which an honest pilgrim is conducted on a tour of the contemporary world by crooked guides (politicians and ambitious priests) who lie and even distort his vision with deceitful spectacles, and who eventually finds Christ in his own heart, was not translated into English at all until 1901, and there is no way that Bunyan could have heard of it. It is a priceless masterpiece—a most wonderful book—now open to new discovery, but its resemblance to *Pilgrim's Progress* is, stylistically, slight: Bunyan's book is the language of the common man, and uses only personification, whereas Comenius employs all the literary devices that were known to him and convincingly rejects both science and art as practiced in his time (there currently exists a good and more recent translation of this book).

Pilgrim's Progress is an allegorical dream in which Christian travels from the City of Destruction to the Celestial City. Its satire is wholesome, and the fact that it is a shade more "literary" than Bunyan wanted it to be taken to be works in its favor: the persona of simple man (simpler than he in fact was) that the narrator takes up is just right. The influence of the book has been very largely upon individuals, since it is not possible to imitate it. And who can resist the majestic opening, who has not been in such a condition, and why is it even necessary to "interpret" it?

> As I walked through the wilderness of this world, I lighted on a certain place where was a den. And I laid me down in that place to sleep: and as I slept I dreamed a dream. I dreamed, and behold I saw a man clothed with rags, standing in a certain place, with his face from his own house, a book in his hand, and a great burden upon his back. I looked and saw him open the book and read therein; and, as he read, he wept, and trembled; and not being able longer to contain, he brake out with a lamentable cry, saying, What shall I do?

49

Mathematical Principles of Natural Philosophy

ISAAC NEWTON

1687

Isaac Newton (1642–1727), father of the Age of Reason, described by a for once enraptured DAVID HUME as "the greatest and rarest genius that ever arose for the ornament and instruction of the species," was himself far more interested in alchemy, gnosticism, prophecy, the work of the German mystic Jacob Boehme, and theology than in mathematics and physics. This paradox, increasingly embarrassing to the majority of historians of science, has been left unresolved by the tactic of virtually ignoring such works as his million-word *Observations Upon the Prophecies of Daniel*—and, in particular, their implications.

The problem has not been made easier for Christian physicists and mathematicians: Newton was a heretic, an Arian. He believed what Arians postulated: that the Church had taken a wrong turn when it abandoned the belief that God had created Jesus Christ as anything more than an instrument for the creation of the world.

The Newton paradox is deepened by the fact that the cosmology established by his physics favored an interpretation which, on religious grounds, he himself rejected. In that lies a little acknowledged part of his enormous influence. Unlike Thomas Burnet in his fundamentalist *Sacred Theory of the Earth* (1681–89), in which the author rewrote the OLD TESTAMENT in naturalistic terms, Newton in the *Principles* (its full original title is *Philosophiae Naturalis Principia Mathematica*) presented a stoutly scientific picture, elaborating on the discoveries of GALILEO. Yet, at a higher level, he is trying to do the same thing as the now forgotten Burnet whose book was hugely popular in its time.

Like Galileo, Newton believed that the planets of our solar system fell down in straight lines and were then switched, by God, into neat orbits; God also doubled "the attractive powers of the sun." The mechanist drift of his theory, though—so adored by LOCKE—militated against such an odd conclusion. Newton never made a serious attempt to reconcile the two sides of himself: the scientific and the "occult." Thus his work gave decisive help to displacement of God from the center of the universe, even though he himself believed that the order of that universe was so admirable and wonderful as to be attributable only to God.

Newton was born in Woolsthorpe in Lincolnshire on the east coast of England, on Christmas Day 1642. His people were of farming stock. He attended Trinity College, Cambridge, as a poor scholar, and in 1665, while on enforced leave from the university owing to the plague, formed his basic scientific ideas. Probably more believe that the famous apple tree story is true than do not—the minority view, more likely, and that of the mathematician Karl Gauss, is that he used to tell this tale to those stupid enough to ask him how he had discovered gravity. Something, however—even if it was not a falling apple—made him wonder if the same force that affected falling objects affected the moon, too, and made it travel in an elliptical orbit around the earth. He himself wrote that at that time he was "in the prime of my age for invention, and minded mathematics and philosophy more than at any time since." He had not before this showed much aptitude for study, and even been found weak in EUCLID. He was just twenty-three.

In the course of his enforced and solitary study Newton also decomposed white light, and thus discovered that it consisted of primary colors; and created calculus—the subject of an ugly later quarrel with LEIBNIZ from which he emerged with little credit. Newton became a professor of mathematics at Cambridge before he reached thirty. Later (1696) he became warden of the Royal Mint, and then its master. He was president of the Royal Society from 1703 until his death. He was knighted in 1705 not for his scientific achievements, but for his services to the mint. According to his great admirer VOLTAIRE he got the mint job only because the treasurer, Lord Halifax, was in love with his niece. Whether that is so or not, he conscientiously saw through a reform of the currency.

Newton is most generally famous for his discovery of the force of gravitation and for his laws. His laws of motion are: Everything preserves its motion in a straight line unless it is deflected from that course by a force; The rate at which a body travels is in proportion to the force applied to it; and, To every action there is an equal and opposite reaction. His version of how the universe perpetuates itself held sway until EINSTEIN's revision of it. To bring God into the picture Newton wrote (in his *Opticks,* 1704): "For while Comets move in very eccentric Orbs . . . blind fate could never make all the Planets move one and the same way in Orbs concentrick. . . . Such a wonderful Uniformity in the Planetary System must be allowed the effect of Choice." We live, Newton concluded, within the space of God's mind.

But this argument had little effect and has hardly withstood the mechanistic drift of his scientific conclusions. The poet Alexander Pope was able to write, soon after Newton's death: "Nature and Nature's Laws lay hid in Night:/God said, Let Newton be! And all was Light!"

Although the physical world seemed, by Newton's few but immensely powerful laws, to be completely and precisely explained, other disciplines besides science—logic, morals, social organization—were left in complete chaos. The philosophers Locke, Hume, and even (negatively) BERKELEY, who wished to resolve this chaos, were all deeply influenced by Newton. Only Berkeley perhaps was able to see, if dimly, that Newton's universe was not totally correct, and did not mark an end to science—it was just, as he put it, "useful." It was, of course, we are bound to add, very useful indeed, and it still holds approximately good.

It is almost invariably stated that "little connection" can be found between Newton's mechanics and the millions of words he wrote—but did not publish—on the subject of alchemy. We know that he believed in the possibility of the transmutation of base to precious metals—one or two of his biographers have expressed regret that the evidence for this cannot be denied! To exactly what extent Newton was committed to alchemy we cannot tell; all we know is that alchemy, except at a low and ill-informed level, or one dictated by mere greed, was a search not for wealth but for perfection of spirit.

Perhaps Newton privately (and without arrogance) felt himself divinely appointed to announce the nature of the universe to mankind. Or perhaps he was acted upon by powers of which he was aware but could not understand: was like Mozart inasmuch as he bore the burden of an enormous genius. He must well have understood the apparently atheistic and mechanical drift of the celestial mechanics he established, even if he denied it. Indeed, in certain respects his science was not as positivistic as was made out, and he did write:

> To tell us that every species of things is endowed with an occult specific quality by which it acts and produces manifest

effects, is to tell us nothing: *But to derive two or three general principles of motion from phenomena, and afterwards to tell us how the properties and actions of all corporeal things follow from these manifest principles, would be a very great step....*

But such a revelation as he effected—a combination of what KEPLER and GALILEO had between them discovered, and thus a combination of the laws governing both heaven and earth—nonetheless made the deism of men like Voltaire almost inevitable. Yet he himself was most interested in a highly esoteric mysticism! That Newton's writings on esoteric subjects are scarcely known, that he was himself fearful of publishing them, that they have received little attention, is surely odd for so eminent a scientist.

He was as curious a man as one might expect. He was so frail at birth that his life was despaired of; but he lived to eighty-five. He was modest, and declared that

I do not know what I may appear to the world; but to myself I seem to have been only like a boy playing on the seashore, and diverting myself in now and then finding a smoother pebble or a prettier shell than ordinary, whilst the great ocean of truth lay all undiscovered before me.

That the *Principia* was published at all was only due to the financial assistance and the heroic tact of the astronomer Edmund Halley (discoverer of the comet that now bears his name). Nor was it designed to be accessible: it is on the contrary impenetrable to all but those learned in mathematics. *A Ladies' Newton* was published, along with dozens of other popularizations; but few of those were adequate.

Yet Newton could be mean and petty. He was avaricious, although probably not corrupt (allegations of financial corruption have been made but seem unlikely to be true). He despised poetry, art, and music. His behavior over the question of who discovered the calculus *was* corrupt: He himself secretly wrote the Royal Society's supposedly objective report on the matter! The truth is that his discovery was just prior to that of Leibniz in terms of time, that they were independently reached—and that the form in which Leibniz presented his discovery was the more useful. (Leibniz was more generous in the exchange between the two men and their supporters.) Newton, alas, seems to have wanted it to be announced that Leibniz had got wind of his ideas and started working on them. In fact Pierre Fermat, the French mathematician, was also working on the problem presented by this "grasping of the fleeting instant," for it was in the air.

Newton never married. If he ever had feelings of a sexual nature, then these are completely unknown to us. In the summer of 1693 he went temporarily mad, and his character from then onward (he was fifty-one), seems to have steadily deteriorated. Yet his *Opticks* of 1704 is far more generally accessible than the *Principles.* He lived surrounded by the color crimson—and nothing but crimson, the color of fury. Few human beings have had so vast an influence, and few remain so enigmatic, although his obvious successor, Einstein, may seem to us to be easier to understand only because he lived so much closer to us in time. One thing is perhaps sure: Newton's scientific discoveries were not wholly independent of his religious beliefs and speculations. The matter is not even half as simple as that, and reason demands that it be further investigated, and by minds not unscientifically certain that religion in its implications implies no more than "superstitiousness."

Newton's telescope

50

Essay Concerning
Human Understanding

John Locke

1689

The Englishman John Locke (1632–1704) is the most worthy and undistinguished of the indisputably great philosophers. His influence has been enormous—a part of it is quite undeserved. And George Berkeley, his opponent in most respects, would have had more success in his enterprise of demolishing his philosophy had he not been so persistently misunderstood. Technically Locke was not adept. But he was extremely sensible. David Hume is the greater philosopher because his exquisitely ironic style imparts a quality to his thinking that always implies the host of poetic or mystical matters which—with the exception of "sympathy"—his philosophy is so eager to cut out of human affairs. Locke's style is prosaic (if in the very best sense). But Hume owed, as we know, most of all to Locke; so much that he could not bring himself to mention him.

Locke's *Essay* was published in 1689—he was paid twenty-nine pounds, about fifty dollars—but dated 1690. 1689 was the year after the expulsion of King James II from the throne, the year of the "Bloodless Revolution," with whose principles Locke entirely agreed; he had quietly worked for them for many years.

He had been writing and changing the *Essay* for more than twenty years, and when he eventually published it, it was in full awareness of its shortcomings, which consist of repetitions and inconsistencies which would have been disastrous in the case of a lesser philosopher. He had, he said, tried to make it shorter. The work owed much to the French philosopher Pierre Gassendi (1592–1655), a critic of DESCARTES; but Locke never acknowledged this debt.

Locke, unlike SPINOZA or GALILEO, was usually fortunate and comfortable. His thinking flourished in his own times. He was at his peak when English governments were in the process of fundamental reforms: The powers of kings were being systematically cut down, freedom of religious thought was beginning to be established, and all types of authoritarianism were under heavy and continuous fire. BACON and HOBBES in particular had already established—in very different ways—the importance of scientific methods. As Locke flourished, so did the idea of scientific progress.

Locke heads what is fairly known as the British empiricist school of philosophy. British philosophy parted company from the rationalism of Europe when it insisted that knowledge may only be acquired by commonsense experience. Hume elaborated on this, but Locke established it on the heels of Bacon and Hobbes.

This unadventurous man, a lifelong sufferer from asthma, was born in the county of Somerset, the son of a wooden-headed country lawyer who had fought against Charles I in the civil war. His first publication was a bad poem in praise of Oliver Cromwell. Later he wrote equally bad love poetry—but he never married. He attended Oxford, where he hated the by then lifeless scholastic philosophy that he was taught. Yet he was never to free himself from the idea of "substance" derived from Aristotle by the scholastic philosophers of the Middle Ages. There is no sense in going into this notion now, since it is itself hard to grasp and beset by a tangle of different meanings. Suffice it to say that it alludes to "the ultimate subject of properties," to which are attached various "attributes." To Locke, famously, substance was "something-I-know-not-what." In the hands of the great medieval philosophers the term could have profound meaning, but that meaning can only be understood by long study of the contexts in which it is used.

By 1665 Locke had been appointed a teacher at Oxford, of "moral philosophy." He qualified in medicine, and, although his experience was small, accepted a position as physician and secretary in the household of the earl of Shaftesbury, whose grandson—known simply as Shaftesbury (1671–1713)— became an influential philanthropist and philosopher (and critic of Locke) himself. (It was from the philosopher Shaftesbury, among others, that Hume derived his idea of "sympathy.")

Locke supervised (1668), but did not perform, a complex operation on the earl's liver, to remove a cyst which forever afterward required draining by a silver tap. He played some part in diplomacy and politics, and was in exile in Holland—Shaftesbury was in 1683 in some danger of being impeached for treason—for most of the reign of James II. He returned when William of Orange took the throne of Great Britain. The new government awarded him minor posts; he died in the home of a former girlfriend who had married another, and who became, as Lady Masham, his patron. She was reading to him from the Psalms when he died.

As well as being the father of English empiricism, Locke is also fairly regarded as one of the founders of liberal democracy; his ideas are certainly enshrined in the American constitution. His political thinking, although it stems from his philosophy, is contained in two other books he published: the *Two Treatises on Government* and the *Letter on Toleration*.

The *Enquiry* is in four books. In Book I Locke attacks the Platonic and rationalist notion (associated with Spinoza, Descartes, and LEIBNIZ) of innate ideas: there is nothing in human minds, he argues, that is already there, "supplied by nature," upon which to establish doctrines of truth. Hence his famous description of the mind at birth as a blank sheet of paper (*tabula vasa*). He could not bear, it seems, the notion that human beings are born with any "knowledge" within. In Book II he develops his empiricist thesis that we can account for all our ideas by experience—by experience of sensation or reflection (introspection). His account here is so confused that there is still much dispute about what he really meant. In Book III he tries to give an account of the nature of language. He anticipates KANT in pointing out that all our knowledge must be subjective: that we work, not with reality, but with our idea of it. He recommended sitting down "in quiet ignorance" of those matters of which we could know nothing—a far cry, perhaps, from the devotion to God he himself manifested. In Book IV, the least satisfactory but the most suggestive, he seems—or so it is now convincingly advanced—to draw a rationalist conclusion from an empirical basis.

Locke was of too frail health, or lazy, or both, to be a meticulous or truly consistent philosopher. His account of the human mind undoubtedly forms one of the bases of modern psychology, yet there is profound disagreement as to what he really meant. Is his analysis of the mind merely a wonderful piece of common sense, but no more than that? Or is it profound? And is common sense in any case superior to what is usually meant by profundity? Locke, like Hume a few years after him, gave British philosophy a huge dose of common sense—indeed, Isaiah Berlin suggested that he almost invented the concept, and there is much to this claim.

Locke failed to reconcile his intellectual empiricism with his wholly genuine belief in God, just as—perhaps on a higher level—Kant later did. Belief in God (or, to state it more precisely, belief in a supernatural authority) is mainly emotional in origin; but Locke could not combine emotion and intellect, and so pretended that belief in God is based on reason and logic. However, belief in God cannot be "reasonable" unless it is at least preceded by arguments drawn from introspection—arguments that so far have not been produced. But as Bertrand Russell, who was deeply influenced by Locke, said, Locke could not abide paradoxes. His great weakness—it may be a great weakness of empiricism as this is philosophically understood—is that under-lying his commonsense program is an extremely unsystematic metaphysical one. He was confused in that he held two irreconcilable ideas: first, that the world is whatever scientists can reasonably say it is—he seems really to have believed this, being so much under the sway of his friends NEWTON and the chemist Robert Boyle—but, second, although more weakly, that God exists. But scientists, unless they are doing more than just science as it had by then been established, cannot state that God exists. Hence the historians' ten-dency to ignore the mystical bases and inspirations of the thinking of such men as COPERNICUS and KEPLER.

Locke, whatever his own inclinations, thus has some responsibility for the "scientism," or "positivism," the materialism, that is now rapidly destroy-ing the world. Berkeley, who was educated in Ireland on Lockean principles, was surely right in being horrified by the consequences of Locke's work. So has Hume such a responsibility, but in Hume's case he himself added to the literature of the world—and thus defied science in the narrow sense. For sci-ence as it is still conceived—it is a wholly intellectual pursuit bent on the pur-suit of logic—has no room for literature, or for delight, which arises from the imagination. We read Hume with pleasure whether we agree with what he says or not. No one reads more than a passage or two of Locke for pleasure.

Yet Locke cleared away much lumber, and he also championed a degree of freedom, and in so doing inspired such thinkers as PAINE and, of course, Thomas Jefferson. However, those who regard him as a true liberal should first look as his "vicious" proposals for combating poverty (in his position as commissioner for Trade and Plantations, which he held from 1695 until 1700). Often put forward as a "figurehead" of the Enlightenment, he has also been described as a "pre-Enlightenment figure." Some of the confusion is due, in this case, to the self-described "underlaborer" (to the scientists Newton and Robert Boyle) himself. He failed to answer the objection to his views of Leibniz, which he wrongly dismissed as "trivial." No tributes to him as a person, such as were accorded to Hume or Spinoza, exist. He is, though, an enduring monument to what a human being can manage to do without humor, wisdom, or ripeness. Probably he does deserve the famous tribute to him from VOLTAIRE, who regarded him with real awe and great respect:

> Many a philosopher has written the tale of the soul's adven-tures, but now a sage has appeared who has, more modestly, writ-ten its history. Locke has developed human reason before men, as an excellent anatomist unfolds the mechanism of the human body. Aided everywhere by the torch of physics, he dares at times to affirm, but he also dares to doubt. Instead of collecting in one sweeping definition what we do not know, he explores by degrees what we desire to know.

51

The Principles of Human Knowledge

GEORGE BERKELEY

1710, revised 1734

George Berkeley (1685–1753), whose "subjective idealism"—or, as he himself better called it, "immaterialism"—was held by such eminent contemporaries as JONATHAN SWIFT and SAMUEL JOHNSON to be a perverse affront to common sense, made a very early entry in a notebook: "to be continually banishing Metaphysics etc. and Recalling Men to Common Sense." Few have been prepared to swallow whole Berkeley's notion that matter "does not exist." Johnson, refuting and of course (as we shall see) grossly misunderstanding it, famously kicked a rock and exclaimed: "I refute it *thus*." But do we altogether blame him? Should we? Well, we don't blame him—but we should.

Berkeley's philosophy is in fact a remarkable tour de force, and one that is capable of being revised in a new form at any time that fashions (or, as we shall see, what T. S. KUHN calls paradigms) in philosophy, and particularly in the philosophy of science, change. Modern science itself, beginning with the Austrian physicist and philosopher Ernst Mach (1838–1916) and continuing with ALBERT EINSTEIN and then quantum physicists, has confirmed that Berkeley was not the fool certain people have thought him. But those who do think him a fool have not paid sufficient attention to his statement that

> the only thing whose existence we deny is . . . matter or cor-
> poreal substance. . . . If anyone thinks that this detracts from the
> . . . reality of things, he is very far from understanding what has
> been premised. . . . We are not . . . deprived of any one thing in
> Nature.

Thus Berkeley is not saying that everything is an illusion, and that we do not really feel, see, hear, suffer, have pleasure. . . . In his philosophy the rock that Johnson so indignantly kicked is just as hard as he felt it to be; but the hardness is only an *idea* of hardness.

Berkeley's arguments for his "commonsense" view of reality are elegant, lucid, and parsimonious: all, in fact, conducted along lines recommended by the English Franciscan philosopher William of Ockham (1285–1349), who (persecuted of course by his fellow Christians) put forward the principle, called "Ockham's Razor," of *entia non sunt multiplicanda,* "entities ought not to be multiplied"—"plurality is not to be posited without need" as he himself put it. In other words, don't use two or more things where one will properly do.

When we sympathize with Johnson's "refutation"—as with his friend Swift's joking refusal to open the door to Berkeley on the grounds that he ought to able to pass through it without difficulty—we ought also to take into consideration the words of another nonphilosopher, the after all very earthy American poet Walt Whitman, who expressed the universal human uncertainty about the nature of reality—the other side of Johnson's certainty—with great poignancy and insight, when he wrote:

> Oh the terrible doubt of appearances
> Of the uncertainty after all that we may be deluded . . .
> Maybe the things I perceive, the animals, plants, men, hills, shining
>   and flowing waters,
> The skies of day and night colors, densities, forms—maybe these are
>   (as doubtless they are) only apparitions, and the real something has
>   yet to be known. . . .

Berkeley, to whose kindness and goodness of nature there are far more genuine tributes than there are to the man whose philosophy he was determined to overthrow, JOHN LOCKE, was born in Kilkenny, Ireland. His grandfather had gone there at the restoration of King Charles II. He entered Trinity College, Dublin, in 1700, and was there educated on generally Lockean principles—for, with the revolution of 1688 and the immediate publication of the *Enquiry,* Locke had quickly become world famous, as no doubt he had always intended (Berkeley was not all ambitious in the way).

By the time Berkeley came to England for the first time, in 1713, he had published his main works: *An Essay Towards a New Theory of Vision* (1709), and still important—some now even believe this to be his most important contribution), the *Principles* (1713), and the *Three Dialogues Between Hylas and Philonus* of the same year, in which he elaborated his views about matter in what he hoped would be a more persuasive form. Like many other philosophers, he formed his main ideas when very young—the seeds of his later work are in notebooks he wrote when in his early twenties (these were not discovered until 1871).

Berkeley married in 1728 and was made bishop of Cloyne in Ireland in 1734. Between his marriage and his appointment as bishop he spent three years in America, mostly in Newport, Rhode Island. His intention was to found a university in Bermuda for the training of men of different races for the ministry. But the money promised by the House of Commons for this venture was not forthcoming, and he returned in 1732. However, he left the (still carefully preserved) house he built for himself in Newport; and the first president of Columbia University, a philosopher called Samuel Johnson (not related to the English Johnson), was a believer in his doctrines, which he thought "would prevail." Most of the rest of Berkeley's life was spent in ministering to the poor of his flock—and in promoting the virtues of "tar-water," which he believed was a panacea for most ills; to that end he published (1744) a strange half-philosophical, half-medicinal work now usually known as *Siris,* which the author of the best short book on him, the English philosopher and poet the late G. J. Warnock, calls "a disorderly mixture of quaint lore and learning."

Berkeley's philosophy was well known; but few in England took serious notice of it in his own times. Essentially it was a reaction against the scientific view that at the time, after the work of Locke—which skillfully courted the utmost popularity—reigned supreme. The view of the majority of educated people was that the world consisted of atoms ("corpuscles") which had been set to work by God in a mechanical way. The *primary* qualities of matter were its weight, shape, size, motion; these inhered in matter itself. The *secondary* qualities, taste and color and so forth, were not in matter at all—but in ourselves.

These notions, taken over too uncritically from Locke (who could be critical—but not critical enough—of what amounted to his own metaphysics) by members of the French Enlightenment such as VOLTAIRE, soon became widely accepted. Berkeley attacked them, surprisingly to most of those who took them as sound common sense (the ideas were, philosophically, confused), on the grounds of common sense. Ironically, then, that the philosopher who most closely anticipated the theoretical nature of modern physics with its predictive theoretical structures did not share Locke's wild and disingenuous enthusiasm for the scientific revolution of his own day. He said that these theories (including NEWTON's) were nonfactual "useful theories"; and that after all is what they have turned out to be. Modern science is continually insisting that it will find the solution to "everything" within a few years—but at its best it is never more than useful and nonfactual, if only in the strictest sense.

What Berkeley concluded was that matter *could* not exist. His grounds for this belief were, too, quite ruthlessly empirical—in a way that not even the determinedly empiricist Locke could manage. His arguments are beautifully stated, in a prose quite different from, but rivaling, HUME's. In *Siris* is to be found the original of Cowper's more famous phrase: tar-water "is of a nature so mild and benign . . . as to warm without heating, to cheer but not inebriate"; may we not, he asked, regard "fluxions" as ghosts of departed quantities?; "He who says there is no such thing as an honest man, you may be sure is himself a knave." Berkeley as a writer of good prose has been badly underrated.

Berkeley was repelled by Locke's horrible and intrinsically godless delight in the universe as a great machine, with engines and pulleys and springs and wheels: He loathed—and any poet must agree with him—the notion that what he was able without the least inconsistency to call the "visible beauty of creation" might be no more than a "false imaginary glare." Locke, for all his piety and God-driven system of ethics, was quite incapable of writing such a phrase. One might easily, if only at certain points, suspect the good although property-worshiping Locke of being an odious hypocrite, although that is probably unjust—emotional stupidity owing to the early frustration of poetic and amorous aspirations is nearer to the mark. (After all, why *did* Locke write poetry? Berkeley's poetry is minor but of a quite different caliber, as even the famous

> Westward the course of empire takes its way;
> The first four acts already past,
> A fifth shall close the drama with the day:
> Time's noblest offspring is the last.

clearly demonstrates.)

Berkeley's solution of the problem that plagued and confused Locke, that things might really be utterly different from how they were perceived, was to deny their existence. "We have first raised a dust," he pointed out, "and then complain we cannot see." No one has proved him wrong, but of course the idea has not caught on. Perhaps it needs further consideration? He did, really, no more than take his premise that all "the choir of heaven and furniture of earth . . . all those bodies which compose the mighty frame of the world—have not any subsistence without a mind" to a logical conclusion.

What Berkeley is saying is this: that to "exist" is no more than to "be perceived." By getting rid of matter he was of course getting rid of all kinds of difficulties. But he could hardly expect to be convincing, and especially not to those who could not bear to think of their wealth and property as no more than a collection of ideas. For him reality is the existence of an infinite and eternal God communicating with finite beings by means of ideas. A thing, an orange or a piece of cake or a piece of money, is simply a collection of ideas. That is by no means appealing to a property owner brought up on Locke's conveniently materialistic principles. Nor, to be fair, does it appeal intuitively—especially when we are suffering pain. But at least the idea is not ignoble. And Isaiah Berlin, sympathetic to Berkeley and rather less so to Locke, with his unexplained "great lumps of matter," wrote that Berkeley was one of the first philosophers to "point out that language is used for many purposes besides that of describing" and that his achievement was "an intellectual service of the first order."

There is a very famous limerick about Berkeley's immaterialism, written by a Roman Catholic theologian and popular writer, Ronald Knox:

> There was a young man who said, "God
> Must think it exceedingly odd
> If he finds that this tree
> Continues to be
> When there's no one about in the Quad."

This was witty but clumsily missed Berkeley's main point. The answer to Knox was accurately made in this riposte:

> Dear Sir:
> Your astonishment's odd:
> I'm always about in the Quad,
> And that's why the tree
> Will continue to be,
> Since observed by
> *Yours faithfully,*
> God.

The New Science

Giambattista Vico

1725, revised 1730, 1744

He was the son of a poor bookseller who inspired him with a thirst for learning. With his usual irony and use of symbolism, he half-seriously ascribed his interest in philosophy to a fall he had from a ladder in his father's shop at the age of seven. But, extraordinary though he was and must have seemed, Giambattista Vico's reputation did not properly flourish until long after his death. He was too bold and too imaginative—his very "modern" mind must have seemed merely eccentric in the generally noncritical and nonskeptical Naples of his age—and even now there is comparatively little on him (as yet) in the English language, although a good translation was made in 1948 of his masterpiece, *The New Science*, which has subsequently been much consulted.

His work had too much of a touch of the personal for it to be fully accepted in the early seventeenth century. Always his primary source was personal experience rather than books, although he was profoundly well read. Just then "the personal" did not fit in. Vico was discovered, or rediscovered, by

251

the German romantics between about 1790 and 1810; then an abridged translation of *The New Science* was made by the French historian Jules Michelet in 1824. Since then his influence has gradually increased. Today few would think of omitting him from any kind of history of Western thought.

His appeal is by no means, in fact, confined to romantics—after all, although he used the history of ancient Rome to illustrate his main thesis, he was among the first thinkers to warn against the glorification of antiquity. He is hardly classifiable. He looked at history in an entirely new way. He saw it as a circular process. He was lawyer, historian, poet—and the first social scientist, the true inventor (if not in a strictly technical sense) of the sociology that COMTE systematized and named. James Joyce based the spiral structure of his novel *Finnegans Wake* on Vico, and he has been called both the "real discoverer of myth" and the first man who put forward a "theory of history in a modern sense." He was also—after MONTAIGNE—for all that he did not have much data at his disposal, one of the first anthropologists—of a depth of understanding quite undreamed of by Comte.

Giambattista Vico's life was one of comparative failure, and, clearly manic-depressive by temperament, he often railed against his poor lot. It is unfortunate that his *Autobiography* is almost devoid of personal information (he does not even mention his own family); instead, it is a record of his intellectual development. Much in it must be read between the lines, just as his special treatment of the Jews can only be understood in the light of his interest in the KABBALAH.

Vico was born in Naples and remained within a radius of sixty miles of that city for the rest of his life. He was a brilliant student of law and even defended his father in a lawsuit before he had qualified. Then his brilliance did seem to be rewarded: He won the post of professor of rhetoric at the University of Naples at the age of thirty-one. He held the chair until forty-two years later, when he resigned. But this appointment held no prestige or even adequate salary; when in 1723 he tried for the coveted professorship of civil law at the same university, he was rudely passed over. In 1699 he entered into a happy marriage with a poor and unlettered woman, who bore him four children. Although the quality of his mind was esteemed in Naples, and his life was externally a quiet one, he was always on the very edge of poverty and even had to give private lessons. His only consolation was that his frustration spurred him to the composition of his masterwork, and, despite the survival of the Inquisition, he could hardly be restrained. He just had to be careful not to seem to be a heretic. It is clear that he believed himself to be quite independent of all establishment orthodoxy. Influenced by MACHIAVELLI, BACON, and HOBBES, but opposed to DESCARTES for his "inconsistency," he was chiefly interested in the origins of society and in language. Above all, though, he was perhaps *the* pioneer of the study of mankind through self-study. ("Judge others by yourself," said GURDJIEFF, in an epigram whose real, and sad, meaning few like to acknowledge, "and you will not be far mistaken.")

Vico "invented," long before the German philosopher Wilhelm Dilthey (1833–1911) and the sociologist Max Weber (1864–1920) introduced the term into common (and very necessary) currency, the notion of *Verstehen.* In that not after all really so modern tradition we are supposed above all to *understand* (this is the meaning of the word *verstehen*) human behavior *from within.* In other words (there are of course various thinkers of a more or less behaviorist variety who oppose the tradition) we judge whatever it is that we have to judge by a use of empathy: by putting ourselves into the positions of others.

Vico challenged Descartes's rationalism. He looked not outside himself for knowledge, but into himself. "The true and the made are identical," he wrote. Yes, mathematics *was* "true"—here he agreed with Descartes and the rationalists—but only because it was created by human beings. It did not just exist out there, in a void. And he therefore, unlike Descartes, put much more emphasis on human activity in general—on society—than on pure science.

But Vico was as scientific as he then could be about his approach to human language and institutions. Many of the germs of modern anthropology, which depends on careful work in the field—with due allowance being made for the fact that an observer's entrance into a field changes the field itself—are to be found in *the New Science.* Vico is also important for his notion that history runs not in a straight line from bad to better to best (as in Comte's naive theory) but in circles: what he called *corsi e ricorsi,* from growth to decay. The German Oswald Spengler introduced a similar theory in his book *The Decline of the West* (1918–1922), and so did Arnold Toynbee in his *A Study of History* (1934–1961). Both, but particularly the former, were highly influential for a short period; but both are now almost forgotten; the influence of neither has persisted—nor is it in their nature that such influence could be permanent. Vico's *New Science,* for all that it was written so much earlier, is in a different category: Spengler and Toynbee both oversimplified Vico, and in their works (the former's is punctuated by genuinely interesting insights; the latter is mainly trash) Vico is divested of his enormous potential.

Vico saw a society as the product of its literature, myth, language, law, art, types of government, religion, and philosophy. He has been called an "evolutionist" and, while that is in one sense correct, it is also misleading, if only because people generally think of that word as implying that the direction will be onward and upward, forever, into something "better." Vico did not believe that. He traces how societies evolve, but he also traces how they decline. He advocates chaos and even oblivion. He was by far the most objective thinker of his age. It is again a little misleading when it is asserted, as it so often is, that because Vico saw Divine Providence at work in human affairs, so was he a "Catholic philosopher." Vico was obliged—if he wanted to keep his wretched job—to cast everything into terms that should not appear heretical to insensitive and ignorant priests. It was then just as it is now with the "politically correct": Sadistic mediocrities, driven by their sense of inadequacy, seek to damage the lives of their superiors. In Vico's youth some of his friends had been penalized by the Inquisition for what was called "Epicureanism"! He wanted to annotate the writings of the great Dutch Hugo Grotius (1583–1645), the founder of international law, but could not do so because Grotius was a "heretic."

But he was religious, and particularly so in his view of what "binds people together" (the word religion itself derives from a verb meaning "to bind together"), he could even be described as Christian after a fashion; but he was no more specifically devoted to Roman Catholicism than he was obliged to be. That is why his position as Italy's greatest philosopher—which everyone knows perfectly well he is—has met with more than a little resistance. Yet Italy's greatest twentieth century philosopher, Benedetto Croce, was devoted to him. Croce understood the idea that underlay all Vico's endeavors: that what human beings can most truly and completely know is, not their existence (as is implied in Descartes's philosophy) but *what they have themselves created.* Experimentation in science is uncertain simply because we can do no more than imitate nature when we test her alleged laws. Experimentation in what men have made is more certain.

The word *empathy* (used above) was in fact coined at the beginning of what we call the modern age, when *Verstehen* (understanding), too, became a requisite in modern thinking. But Vico's work is replete with the desperate human need for empathy and for a terrible degree of self-understanding. Since we are human, he reasoned, we must know best of all what humans have created. He foresaw to what a deadly extent the illusion of a "perfect science" (in the Comtean sense) would take hold of the world when it began to believe that it had lost God. And of course, as NIETZSCHE long afterward showed, in a cultural sense it *had* lost God. There was no meaning to God anymore. Vico was sufficiently enlightened—after all, it was the age of the so-called Enlightenment and of *THE ENCYCLOPEDIA*—to be able, already, to see the difference between a God of culture and a true God, to whose providence he never unsubtly appealed.

Vico was the first *contextualist* (this term is preferable to the increasingly confusing one, *historicist*): He saw that periods of history could not be understood in the terms of contemporary ones without causing serious distortion. And of course it is necessary to exercise imaginative empathy if you are trying to understand the past. Far from being a merely scientific enterprise—a strictly scientific inquiry is certainly needed, but only as a basis for understanding, as distinct from mere knowledge—this must involve the controlled use of the imaginative faculties. Vico was one of the pioneers of defining just what kinds of control we are obliged to use. And—like Nietzsche (to an extent), WITTGENSTEIN, and for that matter the unfashionably religious English philosopher of our own times, Alfred North Whitehead—he was a frustrated poet. If his prose is not always lucid, then this is understandable: He was trying to be as objective as he could (he understood the difficulties) in an age whose beliefs prevented it from reading him aright.

Vico believed that what was known as "the art of memory", as practiced by the great Kabbalist scholar and syncretist Pico della Mirandola (1463–1494), by Giordano Bruno (1548–1600), and by many others—this is an art that is now almost lost to us—gave the key to the lost origins of what humanity itself had first created. He asserted that it was *poetry*, not philosophy, that the ancients had possessed. To summarize in brief (for Vico himself must be read, and struggled with): Each age of mankind had its own kind of arts, laws, and politics. All human endeavor is based in the use of language. A society's use of language can be used to discover the state it is in. And Vico, in a remarkable tour de force, distinguished between various types of language: colloquial, symbolic, and so forth.

As Vico's own poetry (which is interesting) demonstrates, he could not express himself as a poet; but he had the mind of a poet and was therefore a good reader of poetry—something which is quite as important as being a writer of it, for without a writer-reader symbiosis how could poetry exist at all? Vico knew that, too.

Vico believed, perhaps somewhat gloomily, but in any case certainly influentially, that the (divine) fate of all ages, and all historical cycles, was oblivion. To understand why this is, however pessimistic it might be, we can have recourse to the subtleties implicit in Hinduism and its offshoot Buddhism; we need to meditate on the meaning of "nothing."

His work abounds in ironies and anticipations of more or less everything we think of as "modern": psychoanalysis and FREUD, existentialism and SARTRE, language and CHOMSKY, even Marxism and MARX. His vision—of mankind acting under unseen, terribly immediate, and apparently contingent emergencies, and yet all the time fulfilling a divine destiny—needs far wider study than it has yet received.

53

A Treatise
of Human Nature

DAVID HUME

1739–1740

The Scot David Hume (1711–1776), born in Edinburgh to a minor landowner—and strict Presbyterian—was one of the supreme philosophers of the world, and the greatest to write in the English language. Significantly, he was never a professional philosopher. When in 1745 he applied for the chair of Ethics at his old university, Edinburgh, he was unsuccessful.

His chief ambition, he declared, was literary fame. He was, as well as a philosopher and a historian, a man of society, a man of affairs—and a man of passion. But he never married; like EDWARD GIBBON, he became unduly corpulent in his latter years. He resembled, according to his friend the French novelist and philosopher DENIS DIDEROT, a "well-fed Benedictine monk." The unnamed Edinburgh street in which he lived became known, at his death, as St. David's Street; for, although regarded as an unbeliever, he was a notably good man. ADAM SMITH wrote of him that he approached "more nearly to the idea of a perfectly wise and virtuous man as perhaps the nature of human frailty will admit."

Hume attended Edinburgh University, and then studied for a legal career, which he soon abandoned. He began a course of reading in order to satisfy his burning curiosity. It was so intensive that it led to an emotional breakdown.

For, from all this prodigious reading he discovered "little more than endless dispute." He decided to find a "medium by which truth might be established." He had formed his main views by an astonishingly early age.

He went to La Flèche in France, where DESCARTES had studied, and there wrote his masterwork, and now the most highly regarded of all his books, *A Treatise of Human Nature*. He published it in two parts, Books I and II in 1739 and Book III in 1740.

It fell "dead born from the press," he later complained. No real notice was taken of it. He had, he wrote, been "carried away by the heat of youth." He had wanted to do for philosophy, at a stroke, what NEWTON had done for science in *The Principles*.

Hume, the effect of disappointment upon whom has probably been underestimated, restated his case in two shorter works, which came to be known as *An Enquiry Concerning Human Understanding* (1748) and *An Enquiry Concerning the Principles of Morals* (1751). It was upon these that he said he wished to be judged, and it was indeed through the first of them that he attained his enormous and crucial influence as a thinker.

However, as the British philosopher Bertrand Russell wrote, in it he left out the best parts of the *Treatise*, and most of the reasons for his conclusions. Here, therefore, we concentrate upon his best work, the youthful *Treatise*, now once again, and rightfully, the center of philosophical attention.

Hume was a skeptic, but not a thoroughgoing one. To the thoroughgoing skeptic such as Pyrhho (whom we met in SEXTUS EMPIRICUS) nothing whatsoever can be known. Hume saw that this led to something very near to nonsense. He injected the strongest dose of common sense into philosophy that it had yet received. Nothing since has had the same lasting impact. In his lifetime he became famous and financially successful through his *History of England* (1754–59), which is remarkable but nothing like as important as his first book. He lived in France for a time (1763–1766), and while there was the darling of Paris salons. He became friendly with JEAN-JACQUES ROUSSEAU, and brought him back to England with him. Although Rousseau quarreled with him and developed the paranoid notion that Hume was trying to destroy his reputation, he was nevertheless left something in Hume's will.

Although Hume's philosophy does have the virtues of simplicity, it is profound and initially hard to grasp. Here we shall concentrate upon its most important feature: its crucial development of *empiricism* (derived from the Greek word for *experience*). The great seventeenth-century philosophers SPINOZA, LEIBNIZ, and Descartes had all been *rationalists*, that is to say—in the sense in which the word is here used—they based all their thinking on theory. European philosophy has always tended to operate in this way. To the rationalists knowledge may be gained through deductive reason alone; knowledge, moreover, consists of a single system, and all things can on principal be explained in terms of that system because they are part of it.

Anglo-Saxon philosophy, from BACON and HOBBES onward, has resisted this approach. LOCKE (to whom Hume owed most, although he does not mention him) and even the idealist Bishop BERKELEY took an empirical approach. Hume elaborated this the most fully. Empiricism denies that there are any "innate ideas" in the mind of human beings at birth. Only common-sense experience can provide "ideas." Thus, the "ideas" of PLATO are rejected out of hand. There is no "ideal table." There are only a huge number of real, observed tables. Knowledge of the kind alleged by Plato and, later, Spinoza, is not knowledge. Real knowledge is acquired piecemeal; the process is gradual, frustrating, difficult, and always experimental. Hume wrote of the philosophy "transmitted to us by Antiquity," that it was "entirely hypothetical." He felt that everyone "consulted his Fancy . . . without regarding Human Nature." He proposed, with scientific method in mind, to consult human nature itself.

Bishop Berkeley's empiricism had led him to the apparently strange conclusion that matter was inexplicable and therefore existed only in the mind of God. Therefore Hume (wrongly) would not list Berkeley as one of the empiricists. He argued—he had to be careful about offending religious opinion—that the existence of God is not demonstrable (and, in the terms of ordinary logic, it is indeed not; nor is the nonexistence of God demonstrable in such terms). The notion of God, he thought, arises through what he called an *association of ideas*. Thus the ideas behind the systems of Berkeley (or Spinoza or Leibniz) depended on sheer fantasy: They did not rely on actual experience.

Hume was a psychologist inasmuch as he very intelligently (and ironically) analyzed the real nature of moral judgments ("Thou shalt not kill"; "Adultery is wrong," and so on). He delighted in showing that these, too, could not be demonstrated to be true. Such judgments depended, he influentially believed, on feelings of approval or disapproval, and those feelings in their turn depended on pleasant or unpleasant consequences. We forbid killing, for example, ultimately, on the grounds that it would be unpleasant to be killed. Indeed, he finally reduced everything to sensations or pleasure and pain. A person, Hume believed, is "nothing but a bundle or collection of different perceptions, which succeed one another with an inconceivable rapidity, and are in a perpetual flux and movement." This "bundle" theory finds its echo in Buddhist philosophies, and was developed further by WILLIAM JAMES in his epoch-making *The Principles of Psychology.*

Hume's philosophy was for long ignored. Some of it, such as his explanation of why vice and virtue are important to us—that we have a mild preference for the good, based on what he called "sympathy"—is unconvincing and rather feebly pseudoscientific. He was not as strictly scientific as he supposed himself to be.

But it has proved impossible, since his philosophical work (the *Treatise* in particular) was properly understood, to "do metaphysics" in the old manner. KANT was the first important philosopher to be crucially influenced by Hume: Upon reading him, he said, he was awakened "from his dogmatic slumber." Much of Kant's philosophy consists of answers to problems Hume first stated.

Hume's skeptical irony (often called "perverse") has been appreciated mostly by those who have not been, as he was not, professional philosophers. But it is true that he hardly contributed to "the science of human nature" in any direct sense; however, he did demonstrate (to, for example, William James) that an inquiry into human nature could legitimately be conducted. He fails to cast light on religious impulse, since he failed to make a connection (so far as we know) between his playful skepticism and his well-noted goodness as a human being. But there is scarcely an area of human thinking—psychology, anthropology, sociology, history—that has not been greatly influenced by him.

54

The Encyclopedia

Denis Diderot, ed.

1751–1772

The Enlightenment or the Age of Reason are the two names most commonly given to the intellectual movement that, so it is (reasonably, but not quite accurately) alleged, started in the late seventeenth century in England, with the philosophy of John Locke, and culminated in France in the time of such thinkers as Voltaire, Denis Diderot, and Jean le Rond d'Alembert—men who, as long as they are French, and if their names are not gathered together with those of David Hume, Benjamin Franklin, and many others under the rubric of the *philosophes,* are actually referred to as the *Encyclopedists.* For *The Encyclopedia,* edited by Diderot and Jean le Rond d'Alembert (until the latter resigned because he believed that mathematics was a more fundamental science than biology), in seventeen volumes of text and eleven of illustrations, and with contributions from Voltaire and all the other French thinkers of the time, was the most notable of all attempts—to its date—to bring together the fruits of human learning into a single work.

Besides offering a summary of information on all theoretical knowledge, and incidentally challenging (with gleeful irony) the authority of the Catholic Church, it aimed—thus faithfully reflecting the general spirit of the Enlightenment, that all men could improve themselves until perfection would eventually be reached—to give practical advice, and was thus also a sort of do-it-yourself manual. It was intermittently suppressed, by Jesuits and others, but the sheer weight of its learning and its self-evident seriousness as an enterprise—as well as the support of the indecisive Louis XV's mistress Madame de Pompadour, which proved to be crucial in the shorter term—eventually prevailed.

Few of course have read *The Encyclopedia,* or even seen it (but there are now plans to put it on the Internet), and the circulation of its four thousand copies was even in its own time restricted by the high price put upon it (it made a profit). It was seen as an important part of a great (and optimistic) offensive of knowledge against ignorance. It is thus, although rarely seen today, immensely influential. One may see this influence in its successors—only recently have the standards it set begun to decline (as in a recent book of "historical facts" which omits the Franco-Prussian War). It also has historical importance: The articles on philosophy and religion are, as well as "enlightened," amusingly contrived so that the censors should be deceived. Censors, however well meaning, have always managed to represent the last bastion of reaction—only would-be censors can exceed them in this respect. Yet one of the chief censors in this instance, the excellent Chrétien-Guillaume de Lamoigne de Malesherbes (defender of the unfortunate Louis XVI, and a truly enlightened administrator), was on its side!

The prevailing viewpoint throughout *The Encyclopedia* was deist: that God created the universe and gave it fixed laws, but is unresponsive to human need or prayer. Deism, when it was at all elaborated, was derived from the philosophy of the brother of the poet George Herbert, Lord Herbert of Cherbury (himself a very good poet, who was as it happens a religious man and in no way a superficial thinker), who lived between 1583 and 1648. (The duplicitous fraud John Locke himself, who attacked Herbert, by implication though not by name in Book III of his vicious *Essay,* for holding that some ideas are innate, managed to be, himself, both a deist and a *soi-disant* Anglican.)

The Encyclopedia is also often aggressively anti-Christian. A book called *Traité de trois imposteurs* (Treatise on the three imposters, 1719), mischievously admired by Voltaire—possibly it is by Henri, comte de Boulainvilliers—actually compares Christ to Genghis Khan, and presents him as a char-latan; the priest-baiting spirit of this is not absent from *The Encyclopedia*, which like its editor, Diderot, put its main emphasis not on ideas but, rather, on what can be done with them. It has been well described as "a calculated death-blow to the parasites within the aristocracy and the Church"; that it contributed greatly to the forces behind the revolution that erupted in France in 1789 there can be no doubt at all.

The highest and best ideals of the Enlightenment may be found in this ironic, even wistful—and incomparably well written—passage from Hume, every word of which should be weighed:

> The *imagination* of man is naturally sublime, delighted with whatever is remote and extraordinary and running without control into the most distant parts of space and time in order to avoid the objects which custom has rendered too familiar to it. A correct *judgment* observes a contrary method and, avoiding all distant and high enquiries, confines itself to common life and to such subjects as fall under daily practice and experience, leaving the more sub-lime topics to the embellishment of poets and orators or to the arts of priests and politicians.

But the dominant spirit of the age, during which poetry turned toward prose (as in Alexander Pope) rather than toward the sublime (from whose attractions and horrors BURKE shrank, but he wrote eloquently of them in *On the Sublime and Beautiful*, 1757) made various more extreme assump-tions than the meticulous Hume necessarily implies. One might add that even the most "romantic" or "sublime" imaginative writer who could not accept the distinction between two different attitudes, thus stated, and the reason for the need to know the one in order to attain the other, would be unlikely to amount to much. Hume was hardly to know that his prose often approached the sublime—but nor do any writers know very much about their highest qualities, since those are not attained by direct striving, but by their equivalents in character.

The assumptions of the Enlightenment included the following—often enough every one of them, but not always. *Reason* is paramount, and is the key not only to virtuous thought but also to virtuous behavior. Tolerance itself is among the virtues. Human perfection is attainable, and this in itself implies a brotherhood of man (so psychologically aware a writer as WILLIAM GODWIN stated in *Political Justice* that perfectibility was "one of the most unequivocal characteristics of the human species, so that the political, as well as the intel-lectual state of man, may be presumed to be in a state of progressive improvement"). All human beings are born equal and have equal rights (GEORGE ORWELL's "some are born more equal than others" does support the spirit of this, but begins to doubt its reality). Man is naturally virtuous. To believe in miracles is superstitious, since the creator is above all a rational

entity. Taste is more important than "genius" and, thus, correctness, or whatever correctness is held to be, takes precedence (as in Pope) over imagination. The reaction to this, of course—a reaction that absorbed most (or much)
of what was reacted against—was that romanticism which Burke and others
anticipated.

Humanity veers between the reasonable and the sublime in so obstinate
a manner as to suggest that the latter has some irresistible appeal—and that
in fact is exactly what Hume meant. You could not have pure reason and
SHAKESPEARE, and this is why the eighteenth century tried to "correct" him.
But its approach to reason was distinguished by nobility, by hope, by such concern for truth as was possible in so secular an age, and by fraternal feelings.

In fact, as ought to be obvious, there is no "initial year" of the awaken-
ing of this Enlightenment, whose ideals are so appropriately (and deliberately) enshrined in *The Encyclopedia*. Voltaire and Diderot between them
are the two figures who best embody the Enlightenment (Hume is too skeptical altogether). But there have always been those who, within the context of
their times, have been just as "enlightened." The Italian Frenchwoman,
Christine de Pizan (c. 1364–1429), is only one example (alas, she is still
patronized and neglected) of a person whose wide-ranging mind would have
been perfectly at home in the seventeenth century. ERASMUS is another.
Some of the ideas held by members of the Enlightenment were held in the
sixteenth century. Others, for example, ideas of perfectibility, are held by certain so-called humanists and "rationalists" of today. Contempt for dogma
(again Erasmus comes to mind, as well as Buddhism) is not a province only
for deists and atheists. The Roman Catholic Church in France in the
eighteenth century was, indeed, quite self-destructively and peculiarly—
comically, were it not for the consequences—oppressive.

Nor were all of the *philosophes* any better than they should have been.
Diderot was more consistent and conscientious than Voltaire (Diderot was a
thinker of higher quality and more subtlety and delicacy, but not as bold in
attack or as capable of such destructive irony) whose interest in NEWTON
arose from his antipathy to DESCARTES rather than to any true understanding
he had of him. Another of the great Encyclopedists, a cousin to d'Alembert,
the priest Etienne Bonnot de Condillac (1715–1780), translated Locke into
French, but was really less interested in Locke's philosophy (such as this is)
than in its antimetaphysical bias and in its anti-Cartesianism.

Most of the objections to Descartes made by seventeenth-century
thinkers are to be found in the work of the Roman Catholic priest Pierre
Gassendi (1592–1655), a more substantial and more honest philosopher than
Locke, and one to whom the slyly ambiguous Englishman was profoundly
indebted—but he is not yet regarded as such. Indeed, the only indisputably
great Enlightenment *philosopher*, as such, was the German IMMANUEL KANT.
But Diderot and some others anticipated many aspects of other disciplines
not strictly philosophical, particularly psychology.

The Encyclopedia, though, remains a monument of the seventeenth century and an example to this one. Its contents in themselves are hardly valuable to us now, except historically. But taken as what it set out to be in its day, it is exemplary.

Its actual history is interesting. The conception of an encyclopedia dates back to ancient times. But until the eighteenth century it was not possible, for various reasons—availability of knowledge and the state of printing are but two—to produce an encyclopedia resembling our modern ones, which, after a period of proliferation, are just now tending to decline (in certain too frequent cases) into farragoes of misinformation perpetrated by the essentially incurious (lack of curiosity is fatal to encyclopedias).

The first modern one was produced by a Scottish globemaker called Ephraim Chambers, in the form of a two-volume *Cyclopaedia* in 1728. Two French publishers approached Diderot with the wish to have this translated. But he, seeing the opportunity, persuaded them to think again: What about a larger work, he suggested, assembled on lines suggested by FRANCIS BACON? Thus was *The Encyclopedia* born. (Diderot did not have a hand in the extra volumes published between 1776 and 1780.) Diderot's chief helpers in the enterprise, d'Alembert apart, were Voltaire, Jaucourt, and Marmontel. Contributors read like a roll call of the major names of the time: the pioneer naturalist Georges-Louis Leclerc, Comte Buffon, ROUSSEAU, the political philosopher Charles de Secondat, Baron de Montesquieu, and the economist and administrator Anne-Robert-Jacques Turgot (a friend of ADAM SMITH).

The Enlightenment as such was of course "wrong" in many respects: For example, it did not fully understand the scholastic philosophy which, however, it really had to replace (its exponents did not understand it either!), and it was overoptimistic. But its legacy and its main aspirations and the spirit of the many men and women involved in its production remain intact. It soon purged itself of the moral sickliness of Locke. *The Encyclopedia* represents a far nobler, more substantial, and more decent thing.

55

A Dictionary of the English Language

SAMUEL JOHNSON

1755

Few have ever even seen, unless perhaps in a museum or library, the two Bible-size volumes of the original of—to give it just the beginning of its long full title—Doctor Samuel Johnson's famous *A Dictionary of the English Language in which the WORDS are deduced from their ORIGINALS and ILLUSTRATED in their DIFFERENT SIGNIFICATIONS by EXAMPLES from the best WRITERS....*

It was, until a few years ago, fashionable to damn this great work with faint praise. However, although Johnson's influence on grammar and usage was at one time overestimated, the statement that his Dictionary's influence on subsequent lexicography has been "unequaled" (as a modern linguist has recently put it) remains absolutely true. To put it in brief, it was the first decent English dictionary—and it is a one-man job, since the copyists were just that and no more.

The great American lexicographer and linguist Noah Webster claimed that Johnson's contribution to his subject had been equivalent to that of Newton to mathematics. That was something of an exaggeration, but it is easy to see how such a comparison arose. Johnson almost deserves the compliment. His dictionary is the best in English before the great eleven-volume *Oxford English Dictionary,* initially compiled by James Murray (1837–1915), which took from 1864 until 1933 to complete, and which is now being added to all the time. But this has been compiled by the best of all the known methods: In principle everything in the language is read, the usages of words recorded, then sorted, and then defined with examples. This was beyond Johnson's scope. He had only six assistants, and he knew that, for him, it was impossible. It was not until recently that the computer took over.

The nearest that anyone who is not a scholar is likely to have come to Johnson's actual *Dictionary* is either in one of the many selected editions of it published until about 1860, or, more likely, in the form of the good selection from it made in 1963 by E. L. McAdam Jr. and George Milne: *Johnson's Dictionary: A Modern Selection.* But one could almost quarrel with the statement that they make at the beginning of their introduction: "If Shakespeare had wanted to use an English dictionary, he would have had to compile his own." That is true enough, but not *quite* true. From 1604 until he gave up writing, Shakespeare could have made use of the very first single-language English dictionary: Robert Cawdrey's *A Table Alphabetical,* which contained twenty-five hundred entries.

But the history of dictionaries—as they developed from word lists—goes back far longer: to China, Arabia, and Greece. There was a Chinese-Japanese dictionary by the eleventh century. In English before Johnson by far the best was by Nathan Bailey, whose *Universal Etymological English Dictionary* (1721), as substantially revised in 1736, served Johnson as his main base. He acknowledged this, as he acknowledged his other predecessors. How did Johnson work, and what new principles did he add? How has he been superseded—or, indeed, ought he to have been?

Although Johnson had to decide against making a record of *all* written English usage, he refused to make a mere word list. He determined to improve on Nathan Bailey's work by trying to make a scholarly record and by introducing a literary dimension. On the lines laid down by earlier French and Italian dictionaries, he selected a "golden age" from which he would work. For him this was the century that ran from the later sixteenth century (the time of Sir Philip Sidney's *Arcadia*) until the English Restoration of 1660. He was self-consciously and deliberately setting out to make a dictionary from the "best authors," and so he did occasionally break his own rule, and go back to Geoffrey Chaucer.

He disagreed with the French, who had formed an academy in order to permanently "fix" their language. He believed that such stability was needed, but, unlike his older contemporary Jonathan Swift, did not wish to achieve it by means of some government-appointed agency. And, although he did favor stability, he still based his definitions on usage, and he did give examples. In the later editions within his own lifetime he greatly improved the work; for example, he kept up his interest in electricity and in Benjamin Franklin's work on it—for all that he condemned the colonists' protest against taxation. He paid much attention to medicine, and he took care to deflate what he considered to be the superstitious and nonscientific side of it. Here is a part of what he wrote about *amber:*

> A yellow transparent substance of a gummous or bituminous consistence, but a resinous taste, and a smell like oil of turpentine; chiefly found in the Baltick sea, along the coasts of Prussia. . . . *Amber,* when rubbed, draws or attracts bodies to it; and, by friction, is brought to light pretty copiously in the dark.

And here is *fairy:*

> A kind of fabled being supposed to appear in a diminutive human form, and to dance in the meadows, and reward cleanliness in houses; an elf; a fay.

And here, to show that Johnson was not afraid of vulgar expressions (he did omit some obscene words, but these had not often appeared in print), is *fart:*

> **fart.** Wind from behind.
> Love is the *fart*
> Of every heart
> It pains a man when 'tis kept close;
> And others offend, when 'tis let loose—Suckling [John Suckling, seventeenth-century poet]
> **to fart.** To break wind behind.
> As when we a gun discharge,
> Although the bore be ne're so large,
> Before the flame from muzzle burst,
> Just at the breech it flashes first;
> So from my lord his passion broke,
> He farted first, and then he spoke—Swift

And here, lest it ever be forgotten, is the beginning of the famous and ironic "Preface." (Johnson had been working for nine years, since 1746.)

> It is the fate of those who toil at the lower employments of life, to be driven by the fear of evil, than attracted by the prospect of good; to be exposed to censure, without hope of praise; to be disgraced by miscarriage, or punished for neglect, where success would have been without applause, and diligence without reward.
>
> Among these unhappy mortals is the writer of dictionaries; whom mankind have considered, not as the pupil, but the slave of science, the pioneer of literature, doomed only to remove rubbish and clear obstructions from the paths of Learning and Genius, who press forward to conquest and glory, without bestowing a smile on the humble drudge that facilitates their progress. Every other author may aspire to praise; the lexicographer can only hope to escape reproach, and even this negative recompense has been yet granted to very few.
>
> I have, notwithstanding this discouragement, attempted a dictionary of the English language, while it was employed in the cultivation of every species of literature, has itself hitherto been neglected, suffered to spread, under the direction of chance, into wild exuberance, resigned to the tyranny of time and fashion, and exposed to the corruptions of ignorance and caprices of innovation.

This view of language is unfashionable now, and in certain respects plain wrong. That is to say, by his powerful influence, Johnson caused dictionaries in general to become more *authoritative*. That meant that they were appealed to as "standard" and as "correct." Many still take an *Oxford* or a *Webster* definition as the last word. However, from a scientific point of view, a dictionary should be no more than an accurate record of a changing language. It was not that Johnson did not understand that language changed. He did. But he regarded most of the changes as degenerate. That view is now described as an "elitist" one. But do not such "elitist" presumptions help to keep a language better able to do its job? Let us take an example.

For *infer* Johnson has an quotation from LOCKE: "To *infer* is nothing but, by virtue of one proposition laid down as true, to draw in another as true." For *imply* he quotes from the poet John Dryden showing that the word means to suggest something without stating it.

Now it used, until quite recently, to be regarded as serious *error* to use the word *infer* to mean *imply*—it was, too, a common error. We infer *from*. It is a useful word. An editor of an edition of the *Oxford Concise Dictionary*, a brief one-volume version of the great *Oxford*, decided that what used to be an *error* had now been turned, by usage, into a correct use. Was this an odious wretch who cared to rob his own language of a fine distinction in order to gain applause as politically correct and "nonelitist," or was he a brave man? Should he simply have given the "correct" usage, but then added that *infer* was very frequently used "wrongly" or "in another sense." Is there, indeed, a "correct" usage at all? When does "error" turn into "correct usage"?

We know what Johnson would have answered, and in what kind of strong terms. Do we need a few Dr. Johnsons around from time to time, or should they be strung up as "elitist swine" "against the people"? Does it matter how "wrong" Dr. Johnson was, in any case? Can a change toward blurring fine distinctions be slowed up by the Dr. Johnsons of this world? Are "authoritative" (or "authoritarian") dictionaries a bit like the God of whom VOLTAIRE spoke: if they did not exist, would we have had to invent them?

In considering these questions, we must remember that there is a further distinction to be made: There is, we might confidently assert, a difference between *careless* or *vulgar* usage (if, of course, there is such a thing as *vulgarity:* Johnson defined it as "meanness, state of the lowest people" and "mean or gross mode") and *common usage,* that is, the racy, vigorous, *living* language of the common people such as we find in Shakespeare or in such novels as Thomas Hardy's *Far From the Madding Crowd.* Was Johnson oblivious to the energy of this, which is both priceless and precious? Do we excuse his famously "prejudiced" definition of *excise* as a "hateful tax levied upon commodities, and adjudged not by the common judges of property"? Where should we be without this kind of thing? Is there, indeed, we must ask ourselves, one aspect of a *tax official* that, in the midst of so many virtues and a noble indifference to common prejudice, really is (or seems) *hateful?*

However, Johnson's true influence was upon dictionaries, rather than upon the English language. Nothing outside itself and common usage, with some contribution from the "best authors" (who listen to common speech), could do that. It took the historical approach that developed in the nineteenth century to produce a better dictionary than he had produced—and even then there is something unique about his. His definition of *cough* was much sneered at in the nineteenth century, even by his admirers, but it still has something of poetry in its directness: "A convulsion of the lungs, vellicated by some sharp serosity. It is pronounced *coff.*" And Johnson did, by his fairly consistent preferences, influence orthography (spelling).

As to his "unscientific" condemnations (of some eight hundred words, such as *black-guard, glum,* and *ignoramus*): Many have been "proved wrong." He failed to kill them. But we love them, and we love Johnson—and so he continues to influence our thinking in the strongest way that is possible for humankind. Nor is that an appeal to sentiment.

56

Candide

François-Marie de Voltaire

1759

François-Marie Arouet, known as Voltaire, was not an original thinker, but he epitomized the Enlightenment more appropriately than any other writer of his time, with the possible exception of Denis Diderot, the editor of THE ENCY-CLOPEDIA (who was, in fact, though rather less satirically inclined, more curious and more original). But Voltaire had an uncanny and unique knack of reflecting the concerns of the intelligent men of his times, and he is probably the single writer most representative of an age in the whole of world literature—which diminishes him as an original, but adds enormously to his historical importance.

His was a contradictory character in many ways: avaricious and yet generous, vindictive yet humane, quarrelsome yet highly intelligent and magnanimous, contemptuous of the masses (*canaille*, "rabble") and yet in practice (at Ferney on the Swiss border at which he settled in 1759) a democrat, owner of a "lion's heart in the skin of a rabbit," in some rather obvious way deficient in emotional expression (his "serious" verse is very frozen) yet emotionally intense. He never achieved serenity or a truly ripe wisdom, and is thus, a great man—but no Olympian. His greatest weakness was that he had no clue about the psychology of religious feeling—and thus was in other ways emotionally deficient. As a scientist he was enthusiastic but careless and apt to reject evidence that did not fit in with his theories—for example, fossils of fish in the Swiss Alps. His wit ("Louis XIV," he wrote in his still highly readable life of that monarch, "was not the greatest of man, but he was the greatest of kings") may have been equaled but it has never been surpassed. Few have ever acquired the breadth of his interests, either.

Both Diderot and Voltaire, significantly, were profoundly influenced by the philosophy of JOHN LOCKE (although not by his arguments concerning Christianity) and by the scientific discoveries of ISAAC NEWTON; both made translations from Locke, and Voltaire wrote a popular guide to Newton's thought.

Arouet de Voltaire (a very approximate anagram of Arouet le jeune, the name he used to sign his works from 1718 onward) was born in Paris of a wealthy family in 1694, and was educated at the Jesuit Collège Louis-le-Grand. His father was a notary who later became a government official. He attracted attention as a child, with a marked aptitude as a poet. His poetry and drama, admired in his own time, is not, however, more than very talented—his *Henriade,* an epic on Henry IV, was prized in its time—except that he was a gifted writer of light verse.

By his early teens he was associating with a "libertine" group of free-thinking intellectuals, the Société du Temple. His father tried to wean him from this by sending him as a page to the French ambassador in Holland, but he was sent back in disgrace owing to an unsuitable love affair. Forced by his father to work in the law, he started to write bitterly satirical lampoons, as a result of which he was sent away to the country and, finally, to the Bastille, in which he spent eleven months.

While there he wrote his tragedy *Oedipe,* which was successfully produced in 1618. By 1722 he was rich (by means of clever speculation from the profits of his play), in favor with the court, and famous. He was not yet thirty. But this first period of success did not last long. He contracted small-pox (which disfigured him), fell foul of an influential chevalier, and then spent a further couple of weeks in the Bastille before being packed off to exile in England. This was the making of the mature Voltaire; it has been said that he went to England as a poet and returned as a philosopher—and he was indeed, at least, the *philosophe* (the name given, imprecisely, to all those Frenchmen who believed in the primacy of reason—and to some, like ROUSSEAU, who did not) *par excellence.*

Voltaire was in England until 1729. He was received at the court of George I and welcomed by the prime minister (Robert Walpole), mastered the language, thoroughly read and studied the literature (SHAKESPEARE in particular), and associated with such as Jonathan Swift, GEORGE BERKELEY, the poets Alexander Pope and John Gay (of *Beggars' Opera* fame), and the playwright William Congreve.

Since Voltaire was not English, he could all the more easily use England as a foil to all that he disliked about France—which had of course dealt with him unjustly. He doubtless obtained much satisfaction later in life, when he was able to increase his considerable prosperity by acting as moneylender to men spoiled by their riches. Like George Bernard Shaw, who lacked his creative genius but shared not a few qualities with him, he was always an astute businessman in his own behalf.

A few years after his return to France he published his *Lettres Philosophiques* (1734), which was publicly burned, and forced him to retreat to the country estate of his mistress Madame de Châtelet—outside the jurisdiction of Paris—at which he remained until just before her death in childbirth (she was pregnant by a new lover) in 1749. These "philosophical letters" included essays (in the guise of letters) in praise of the Quakers, who had impressed Voltaire in England by their devotion to actual religion rather than to its mere show, and others on the Anglican Church, the English governmental system, and English literature. The book was really an attack on the *ancien régime,* the name given to the system of France before the revolution that occurred there eleven years after Voltaire's death in 1778: it was, wrote a historian of French literature, the "first bomb" thrown directly at at the *ancien régime.*

After spending three years at the court of Frederick the Great of Prussia—a period immortalized by Lord Macaulay's exemplary essay on the subject—and after living for a time in Switzerland, he settled at Ferney. He came to Paris in 1778 to attend a performance of his last (feeble) tragedy, *Irène,* and received an unprecedented triumph there—but he was too ill to return to his home, and he died in Paris. The Church refused him burial, but he had prepared for that and so was buried surreptitiously in consecrated ground (probably for the convenience of the heirs to his huge fortune); in 1791 his remains were transferred, in triumph, to the Panthéon.

Voltaire had as huge a capacity for work as he did for acquiring money, and his writings are voluminous. There are poems, essays, tragedies, comedies, many *contes* (tales) just such as *Candide* is, not to speak of the volumes of history and science, and the *Dictionnaire philosophique portatif* (1764), which was burned (in Geneva) and condemned elsewhere for its attacks on religious dogma.

Those who in the main are merely aware of Voltaire have almost certainly read *Candide*—or mean to do so. As in the case of so many of the writers represented in this book, it is the man, and all his writings, which exerted the real influence; in the case of Voltaire this was enormous. And in *Candide* he managed to express and perhaps even to reconcile the two opposing sides of his nature: his personal optimism and his historical pessimism, the latter of which undoubtedly deepened as he grew older. He epitomized his age, and *Candide* epitomized him. This little book, often called a "miracle," expresses his refusal to accept any kind of explanation of existence (Diderot, although an avowed atheist, was more curious about the explanation, and far more fruitfully interested in individual human psychology) and yet expresses, too, his desire to do something with this refusal: to "cultivate his garden."

Candide is in a genre that Voltaire largely invented, and certainly perfected, for himself: the philosophical *conte*. In his *contes* wit compresses his brilliant gift of mockery of absurd matters (he said of established Christianity that those who could ask us to believe absurdities were likely to be guilty of atrocities) with his need to convey a message for unreasonable humanity to heed, and his superb skill at fast-moving narrative.

Candide is in essence Voltaire's spiritual autobiography, and it brings home his lesson that man is better off to cultivate his garden: meaning, do what he can with his own life rather than interfere with others, or get involved with too grand schemes. But he does say "our" garden, thus making it quite clear that he is not recommending selfishness, but, on the other contrary, cooperation. Candide himself possesses what has been called his creator's rather *insouciant* courage; but beneath this lies a "lost and desperate soul."

It is appropriate to compare the work to another, not for its similarities but for its remarkable differences: the *Pilgrim's Progress* of BUNYAN. Bunyan's pilgrim wants to put off this earth for the glories of Heaven; Candide wants to reach a heaven-on-earth. Voltaire, though a deist, had no use for any theories of survival in any form. He believed in the perfectibility of man—but only by the use of reason. Thus he poured scorn (unfairly in fact, because he missed the philosophical point) on LEIBNIZ's idea of "the best of all possible worlds" (had Leibniz used a word other than "best," which he could have, he would not have made himself thus vulnerable). Voltaire's character Pangloss says "all is well." The fantastic story itself—which needs to be read, and resists summary—illustrates Voltaire's thesis that unless men use reason, the world is random and without plan; there is no hidden pattern upon which we may rely. The chief message, though, is that metaphysical speculation must take second place to practical work. However, *Candide* transcends its polemical message by its own ironic perfection and delight in its inventiveness. It contains enough of this for it to satisfy anyone, religious or otherwise.

57

Common Sense

THOMAS PAINE

1776

Most readers might reasonably expect to find here, among the most influential books, not Thomas Paine's *Common Sense*, but his *Rights of Man* (1791). However, *Common Sense* was an undoubtedly important English trigger for American revolt against its colonial status and had a more direct influence on the course of events than did *The Rights of Man*, a reply to

BURKE's attack on the French Revolution which has since been read more widely.

Paine was born at Thetford in Norfolk in early 1737, the son of a Quaker. His early life was singularly unpromising and marked by failure. The steadfast Whig Robert Walpole was still prime minister. Paine worked for his father, a master corsetmaker, for a time. But his father was a stern man. Thomas later wrote:

> Though I reverence their philanthropy, I can't help smiling at the conceit that if the taste of a Quaker had been consulted at the creation, what a silent and drab-colored creation it would have been.

He did not hold any job for long, and his appointment as an officer of the hated excise at Lewes, near Brighton in Sussex, was unsuccessful and ended in dismissal by men even more zealous than their modern counterparts in the collection of duties allegedly due—and because Paine, characteristically, campaigned for higher wages.

But when in London Paine got to know such writers as Oliver Goldsmith, author of *The Vicar of Wakefield* and the play *She Stoops to Conquer*, and, above all, the American Benjamin Franklin. Franklin gave him a letter of introduction to his son-in-law Richard Bache in Philadelphia, and there (November 1774), he settled. Bache found him work on the *Philadelphia Magazine*, whose circulation he soon tripled.

In England Paine had been like a fish out of water—now, at the age of thirty-seven, he found himself thriving and back in his native element. In his first year in Philadelphia he published a bold article against slavery, "African Slavery in America." Soon he was being consulted by all and sundry on just about every subject under the sun, including new inventions judged to be of use to mankind, and against not only slavery but dueling, cruelty to animals, and for women's rights. His approach was the exact opposite to that "drabness" which he had so disliked in his parents: vivid, plain, and based brightly upon simple facts in which he had supreme confidence.

Common Sense went much further than the more elegant, more literary, and more subtle Burke had ever gone in the direction of the colonists among whom Paine now lived. He was not worried, as Burke was, about the rights to revolt. *Common Sense* boldly advocates independence, on the simple and surely irrefutable grounds that it was bound to come anyway. Half a million copies were sold, and the influence on the Declaration of Independence itself was paramount. Many initially believed it to be written either by Franklin himself or by John Adams. And it was the latter who said, without much exaggeration, that "without the pen of Paine, the sword of Washington would have been wielded in vain."

There were certainly few men around who were prepared to be as bold, and yet were as able, as Paine. The cautious George Washington soon gave it his tacit approval when he told someone that a few more battles and "the sound doctrine and unanswerable reasoning contained in the pamphlet *Common Sense,* will not leave numbers at a loss to decide upon the propriety of separation."

Common Sense has all the virtues of having been proved right by events. Sometimes such virtues are dubious (as in the case of Hitler's *Mein Kampf*); but Paine was certainly here prophesying what was inevitable. He summed up the prevailing feelings in America when he wrote, in one of the political articles that comprise *The American Crisis* (1776–83), the famous words (December 19, 1776) "These are the times that try men's souls" (coinciding with Washington's retreat across the Delaware).

Paine had been careful—insofar as such a passionate man can be called careful—to express his general political feelings in *Common Sense.* He begins:

> Some writers have so confounded society with government, as to leave little or no distinctions between them; whereas they are not only different, but have different origins. Society is produced by our wants and government by our wickedness; the former promotes our happiness *positively by* uniting our affection, the latter *negatively* by restraining our vices. The one encourages intercourse, the other creates distinctions. The first is a patron, the last a punisher.

In other words, government—Paine used these very words—is a necessary evil, a lesson that has not been lost on many Americans, especially, ironically enough, on parties to the right of center. But later, in *The Rights of Man,* Paine made it clear that he regarded as "natural" the rights of a people to obtain from their governments old-age pensions, medical welfare, and education.

Paine, despite his profoundly radical views, has been disliked by only a very few. This is because of his possession of that quality which inspired him to the title of his most influential work: *Common Sense.* Too much of what he said is simply humane. William Pitt the Younger, Great Britain's prime minister from 1784 until 1801, who could (if contentiously) be said to have abandoned a program of reform in the interests of the rich and privileged, said privately of *The Rights of Man,* "Tom Paine is quite in the right, but what am I to do? As things are, if I were to encourage Tom Paine's opinions we should have a bloody revolution."

But despite this he lived to be execrated beyond his time (President Theodore Roosevelt referred to him as a "dirty little atheist," despite Paine's having attributed his survival to "divine providence"), and by some of the very people who had previously so admired him. Given a house in New Rochelle, New York, he could just have settled down and become a rich man. Instead, he wanted to build an iron bridge across the Schuylkill River. No one would put up money for it, and so in 1787 he decided to return to Europe. He went to Paris to show the designs for his bridge, and then he went back home to see his old mother. He was able to spend time with Burke, and more with enthusiasts for the French Revolution. At this point Burke was divided between admiration and fear for the cherished English institutions with which he was by now seduced. When Paine read his *Reflections,* he wrote that he had previously considered him to be a "friend to mankind"; now, though, he felt that he must answer this "flagrant . . . abuse" of the revolution. Soon, although a copy of his bridge was built in Derbyshire, he thought it prudent to take himself off to France. But there he did not long prosper: he was almost executed for having openly tried to save the life of Louis XVI. He failed there, but he succeeded in saving many other lives before he returned to America in 1802.

There, although he composed some of the most vital and interesting of his writings, he was unhappy. He was called an infidel by almost everyone, and Jefferson was attacked for having afforded him passage back to America. The old revolutionaries had by now become conservatives. His obituary (1809) stated that *he had lived long, did some good and much harm.* But he is still read, and, although of course Americans did not owe their inevitable independence to him, he might well have speeded up the process.

58

An Enquiry Into the Nature and Causes of the Wealth of Nations

ADAM SMITH

1776

The Scot Adam Smith (1723–1790) certainly laid the foundations of the "science" of economics. Yet a very influential economist of the twentieth century, Joseph Schumpeter, wrote of Smith's masterwork, that it "does not contain a single idea, principle, or method that was entirely new in 1776." That is probably true but only goes to show that great innovators and proponents of new ideas are seldom entirely original; what they do is to collect together and coherently present new ideas at a time when they are just about acceptable. Without Adam Smith economics would not be discussed as it is even today. Anyway, is "economics"—"political economy," something rulers of countries have to try to look after if they want to retain power—really a science at all?

To answer the last question first, no, it is not. People have tried to be scientific about it, but it is too closely connected to the irrational elements in human behavior to yield to scientific method. Beyond sheer common sense, none of the supposedly immutable "laws of economics" really quite works.

Besides which, Marxists would not like to give up their ideas about how economics works any more than thoughtful usurers (if there are any) would like to part from the notion that they benefit people by bleeding them as dry as they dare. That is, alas, and notwithstanding much sincere effort, the plain truth behind the learned panoply of "economic science," theories of which have been applied both to greed and to impracticable Utopianism.

Adam Smith, son of a judge, born in Kircaldy, was educated at the universities of Glasgow and Oxford. He began as a professor of logic and moral philosophy at Glasgow, and published, in 1759, *The Theory of the Moral Sentiments.* Far less well known than its successor, *An Enquiry,* this attracted the patronage of a rich aristocrat and enabled Smith to retire from teaching and thus to devote himself to his most famous work. This, long worked over, is still one of the bibles of classical economics—once called individualist economics.

Adam Smith's predecessors were such thinkers as Bernard de Mandeville (1670–1733), whom he called "vicious," and, at a less technical level, DR. SAMUEL JOHNSON. Mandeville's thesis, presented as satire in *The Fable of the Bees,* was, in a nutshell, "private vices, public benefits." As Dr. Johnson put it, "you cannot spend money without doing good to the poor. . . . Luxury produces much good." Tell that to your local moneylender when he is creating work by constructing a third swimming pool for the exclusive use of his sharks, and his normal dance of pleasure just might become a little philosophically as well as commercially tinged—but it is not his well-being that economists care about. What Mandeville and Johnson said is, on the face of it, true. Only the extent to which it ought to be exploited by governments, or how far it works in everyone's interests, are in question.

Many of Adam Smith's leading ideas, almost invariably in the interests of decency of behavior, came from his friend DAVID HUME, in particular his notion of the "sympathy" that Hume detected in human beings which caused them to be rationally interested in the welfare of their fellows. This indeed is the central plank of Smith's ethical system, which was also influenced by the thinking of his and Hume's teacher, Francis Hutcheson (1694–1746), the first utilitarian (see JOHN STUART MILL) in that he believed that the touchstone of political life should be the achievement of the greatest happiness (judged in economic terms).

But Smith was also himself influenced by the doctrines of the Stoics (represented here by the *Meditations* of MARCUS AURELIUS). Thus, in a spirit more fervent than that of Hume, Smith's "man of perfect virtue" has "perfect command" of both his good and his bad feelings, and is devoted to the "original and sympathetic feelings of others."

Adam Smith is therefore an apostle of freedom and, on unfortunate occasion, an alleged one of unbridled greed—but disguised as reluctant cynicism. He deserves the first reputation, but hardly the second. Schumpeter's hostility to him was perhaps justified, but then Schumpeter believed, unlike MARX, that capitalism would eventually yield to socialism not because of its failures, but because of its success. In the 1930s and 1940s an Adam Smith appraised of contemporary developments just might have been persuaded to agree with this.

However, Schumpeter's reservations notwithstanding, the *Enquiry* changed the way economics is looked at; and it introduced most, if not all, of the conceptions that still lie at its heart. Smith most influentially and reasonably advocated the notion that selfish behavior has altruistic consequences. In his hands it was softly advocated. Yet, put at its most extreme, this can mean that a rich man's enjoyment of the services of a prostitute has a social benefit. Smith, a gentle moralist for himself, disapproved of such behavior and merely pointed out the fact, which is in the short term undeniable unless, of course, one is of the opinion that individual "immorality" taints society itself.

The *Enquiry* is cast in the form of a study of the creation of wealth. The so-called mercantalists of his time, merchants and statesmen, believed that wealth arose from a favorable trade balance, which ought, moreover, to be manipulated by the government. The French school of physiocrats, which was formed in the wake of the mercantalist school, believed, on the other hand, that wealth derived from land, and so advocated laissez-faire, the removal of obstacles.

Smith's influence was at its greatest when he insisted that wealth depends, not on what either the mercantalists or the physiocrats suggested, but on what is called the *division of labour.* This, already defined in Plato's *Republic,* is simply the process by which labor is allocated to the activity in which it is most productive—i.e., it is identical with the specialization of labor: you make chairs, I make books, we exchange them according to need, and so on. In the overoptimistic Book IV of the *Enquiry* Smith set forth the virtues of the free market, which—despite selfishness—he thought operates to the good of all. Thus, a selfish producer of goods would, in order to be as selfish as possible, for forced to produce goods ("good": hence the term) that people like at a price they like to pay. The central thesis is put forth thus:

> The natural effort everyone is continually making to better his own condition, is a principle of preservation capable of preventing and correcting, in many respects, the bad effects of political economy, in some degree both partial and oppressive. Such a political economy . . . is not always capable of stopping altogether the natural progress of a nation towards wealth and prosperity.

Adam Smith's greatest claim to originality lies in this emphasis on the division of labor in the creation of wealth. Fortunately for his reputation, he did not himself direct economic policy. But he did influence the manner in which economic policy was conducted for at least a century after his death. He was wrong (overoptimistic) about the "free market," if only because the market has never really been free in his kindly sense. Perhaps his well-bred distaste for capitalism, which emerged despite his pragmatism, was his most attractive quality.

59

The Decline and Fall of the Roman Empire

Edward Gibbon

1776–1787

"A puny child, neglected by my mother, starved by my nurse, and of whose being very little care or expectation was entertained," wrote Edward Gibbon of himself in his posthumously published *Autobiography* (1796). Born at Putney in South London, he was the delicate son of a wealthy Tory member of Parliament who went into seclusion and left him to the care of an aunt. Educated at Westminster School and then, briefly, at Magdalen College, Oxford ("steeped in port and prejudice"), he was converted to Catholicism and so sent to Lausanne in Switzerland with a Calvinist minister in order to "cure" him. He met VOLTAIRE at Ferney, fell in love with a young lady there, renounced this as a filial duty ("sighed as a lover but obeyed as a

281

son"), and started to read voraciously. He was reconciled with his father (himself somewhat mellowed) and became attached to his stepmother—and he remained a close friend to the woman he had loved as a young man, who had become the mother of the sage Madame de Staël.

After a spell in the Hampshire militia he went on to write what most still consider to be the most majestic history ever written, a book that, despite the huge amount of work that has since been done on the period, must be consulted both as history and as literature: *The History of The Decline and Fall of the Roman Empire.* This magnificently dramatic work can no more be disposed of than can SHAKESPEARE's wildly inaccurate cycle of history plays; but, unlike Shakespeare, Gibbon is largely accurate, despite all the later research that corrects him. Every effort was made by his friends to distract him from the impossible project.

In 1737, the year of Gibbon's birth, the situation of what we may call the attempt to write history of as objective a nature as possible—a history independent of faction and dogma—was not good, not as good as it had been even in the time of the great Greek and Roman historians, THUCYDIDES and TACITUS ("I know of no one except Tacitus who has quite come up to my idea of a philosophic historian," Gibbon wrote). The fault, if it may thus be described, had not been that of Christianity itself, but rather that of Christian orthodoxy, determined at all costs to suppress every kind of open-minded inquiry.

Gibbon was the first to write an indisputably great history of a whole long period. But he had predecessors, and without in particular the Frenchman, "the father of sociology," Charles de Secondat, Baron de la Brède et de Montesquieu (1689–1755), the *Decline* could not have been written. His masterpiece, the first all-embracing book on its subject since the *Politics* of ARISTOTLE, at least twenty years in the making, *De l'Esprit des Lois,* was published in 1748, when Gibbon was eleven years old. In it Montesquieu tried to trace what principles were discoverable behind the amazing diversity of human existence. He wished to discover the "nature of things," to discover if the universe has laws and, if so, what these laws are. He paid immense attention to the effects of clime, and was the first to do so systematically. Is there, he asked, one great natural law that lies behind all manmade laws? He answers that there is, and he concludes that by understanding this, man can make his own destiny.

Montesquieu's chief influence was not exercised either in his native France (of course the *Esprit* was soon anathema to Roman Catholics) nor even, at first, in England, but in Scotland—upon DAVID HUME (the unbeliever loved by all believers), whose own now neglected, but very remarkable, *History of England* was at least half inspired by it. *The Wealth of Nations* by ADAM SMITH was yet another work that could hardly have existed without Montesquieu's example of "universal history." Montesquieu, like Voltaire, had lived in England, and—as behooved those sufficiently enlightened to foresee an explosion in France—was a great admirer of the English constitution.

Before that, the secular interpretation of history had begun with MACHI-

AVELLI and others. Meanwhile, the orthodoxists of both the Catholic and the Protestant camps had not been able to do much about sheer accumulations of facts; they could hardly call them heretical, especially if the compilers were careful not to draw "wrong" conclusions. Gibbon himself was grateful to Jean Mabillon (1632–1707) and Bernard Montfaucon (1655–1741) for their collections of facts and documents, and even more so to Ludovico Muratori (1672–1741). And there had been interpreters besides the wise and affable Montesquieu—most notable among them was Voltaire.

Voltaire and Montesquieu had much in common, but were in fact and essence at opposite ends of the Enlightenment spectrum. Montesquieu, although ultimately a more intelligent and less fearful man, resembled BURKE in that he held the belief, which lies at the heart of true conservatism (as well as the madness of its extremes), in the innate wisdom of institutions such as the church, the law, constitutions. He was a reformer who did not like reform and could only countenance it as very gradual—even as a process of institutions "acquiring wisdom." Voltaire was more of a revolutionary (though he would never have approved the horrible excesses of the revolution that was to come in his own country). That meant, in the apt terms of the historian Hugh Trevor-Roper, that there could be in the Encyclopedists, a ruthlessness toward humanity and an indifference to truth. Thus D'Alembert, the coeditor of the great ENCYCLOPEDIA, actually suggested that at the end of each century that part of its knowledge deemed unworthy of usefulness ought to be destroyed! This odious and preposterous suggestion, so alien to the thinking of Montesquieu, was one of the inspirations for Gibbon's first published work, of 1761, the *Essay on the Study of Literature*, in which he came down on the side of the author of the *Esprit*. From even the meanest *fact*, he rightly decided, a Montesquieu might deduce "consequences undreamed by ordinary men."

Before 1763 Gibbon had considered various subjects as worthy of the type of philosophical analysis that now he wished to apply to history: the life of Sir Walter Raleigh, the history of Switzerland, and others. But in that year he was released from military duties, and so undertook a journey to Italy. There while he "sat musing amidst the ruins . . . the idea of writing the decline and fall of the city first started to my mind." The first volume appeared thirteen years later. Praised by fellow historians, including Hume (who was seldom wrong in his judgments), it was jumped upon by establishment clergymen, one of whom accused Gibbon of dishonesty and plagiarism. Thereupon, in 1779, he composed his *Vindication*, perhaps the most crushing rejoinder in all literature. Of the most vicious and in fact himself dishonest of his critics, a Davis of Balliol at Oxford, he wrote:

> It was the misfortune of Mr. Davis to *write* before he had *read*. He set out with the stock of authorities which he had found in my quotations, and boldly ventured to play his reputation against mine.

And he proceeded to demolish Davis and his other adversaries, who could have done him more damage had he not been so eloquent.

The work reached its completion in Lausanne, to which Gibbon had returned in 1783, much to his friends' surprise. He might have gone to London had he taken advantage of a certain job offer, but he displayed his humanity and genius when he responded with: "A commissioner of the Excise! The idea makes me sick."

Because Gibbon *is* "literary," but in the best sense, he has thus been accused. But the accusation is not a telling one. True, he did his history from his study; but he did it from the vast accumulations of facts which were at his disposal owing to the labors of those historiographers who had not been inclined to, or had been afraid to, draw conclusions. He was always properly grateful, which Voltaire was not, to the work of such supposed dullards. The opening passage makes clear what his attitude was to Rome before it reached decline:

> In the second century of the Christian era, the Empire of Rome comprehended the fairest part of the earth, and the most civilized portion of mankind. The frontiers of that extensive monarchy were guarded by ancient renown and disciplined valor. The gentle but powerful influence of laws and manners had gradually cemented the union of the provinces. Their peaceful inhabitants enjoyed and abused the advantages of wealth and luxury. The image of a free constitution was preserved with decent reverence: the Roman senate appeared to possess the sovereign authority, and devolved on the emperors all the executive powers of government. During a happy period (A.D. 98–180) of more than fourscore years, the public administration was conducted by the virtue and abilities of Nerva, Trajan, Hadrian, and the two Antonines. It is the design of this, and of the two succeeding chapters, to describe the prosperous condition of their empire; and afterwards, from the death of Marcus Antoninus, to deduce the most important circumstances of its decline and fall; a revolution which will ever be remembered, and is still felt by the nations of the earth.

He shocked even his admiring contemporaries, though, by his attitude toward Christianity. Like his despised Voltaire, Gibbon was himself a deist who had little native appreciation of the genuine side of religion. But in his case, as in that of Voltaire at his best, this was to the readers' advantage. For he was thus able, unprejudiced, to see what we may now fairly call the secular side of religion as a social phenomenon like any other. Judging history as it was (one, he said early on in the *Decline*, largely of crime), he saw religion as having no special privileges. It could be said—though this would be disingenuous, since Gibbon did not have much insight into the inward reasons for religion—that he gave religion its deserts; but he certainly gave the institution of religion its deserts. He regarded the great dogmatic religions as generated by merely local cults, and spread by accidental and not spiritual circumstances. He thus saw Islam, which came within the scope of his 1,300-year subject-matter. The poet Thomas Hardy, who knew and loved his *Decline and Fall*, was only echoing him in his drama *The Dynasts* when he so famously referred to Christianity as "a little local cult."

Trevor-Roper (who has performed incomparably the best abridgment of the *Decline and Fall*) believed that, although Gibbon—who became a member of Parliament—was as a politician "the loyal placeman of Lord North" (i.e., among the bunglers of the American War of Independence), humanity "and reason combined to make him into a radical." This is a fair judgment. *The Decline and Fall* is among the most humane of great works. Its irony, partly called forth by the necessities of an age of such ignorant hypocrites as Gibbon's enemy the Balliol clergyman Davis, is incomparable in any work of history to that date. And never does it fall into cruelty. It has its faults, some not of Gibbon's making but simply owing to the lack of tools available to him at the time, but at no time do these amount to dishonest handling of the evidence. Its chief deficiency is its insensitivity to religious feeling; but the reader is largely compensated for this by its fair-minded account of what atrocities can be performed in the name of religion.

60

Critique of Pure Reason

IMMANUEL KANT

1781, revised 1787

"It is much easier," wrote ARTHUR SCHOPENHAUER, Kant's admirer, "to point out the faults and errors in the work of a great mind, than to give a distinct and full exposition of its value." Some have thought of Kant as the greatest philosopher of modern times, the equal of PLATO or ARISTOTLE, though that is now probably a minority view—and in any case it is an artificial statement, a gesture toward the useless habit of trying to grade people into a hierarchy instead of understanding them. What is certain is this: that, in one important sense, any educated person is, or is not, a Kantian. Clearly that is in itself a great achievement. What, then, is generally meant by a Kantian—in the sense that, say, MARTIN BUBER was a Kantian, and Bertrand Russell was not?

Kant made many contributions not only to philosophy but also to cosmology and even to astronomy. He predicted the existence of the planet

Uranus some years before it was seen by the English astronomer William Herschel (it was for some time called "Herschel"). His early work *The General History of Nature and Theory of the Heavens* (1755) was the first real attempt to give, within a Newtonian framework, an evolutionary account of the cosmos, which Kant saw as still coming into existence.

Later, with his three *Critiques* (*Pure Reason* [*Die Kritik der Reinen Vernunft,* 1781, revised 1787] was the most important; it was followed by *Practical Reason,* 1788, and *Judgment,* 1790), he would assert that his efforts amounted to a "Copernican Revolution" in philosophy. COPERNICUS, too, had lived and worked in East Prussia. Kant, whose work in science has tended to be obscured by his philosophy, has been important in ethics and in religion.

Here, however, we shall concentrate on his single most notable contribution to philosophy: his account, as it may briefly be put, of "how much we can know." Before Kant, most philosophers had assumed that all our knowledge of the world must conform to the objects in it. This is implicit in Kant's great predecessors LOCKE, BERKELEY, and HUME. Kant turned this on its head. He had been anticipated, but no one had previously been so bold.

"Let us make trial," he wrote, "whether we may not . . . suppose that objects must conform to our knowledge." Thus, he supposed, the world as it really is, consisting of "things-in-themselves," is quite simply *not knowable.* (Like Berkeley, he had no time for thoroughgoing skepticism, and wrote of it that it was "a euthanasia of pure reason.") Locke and even Hume had worried about the true nature of the world; Kant did away with all that worry. He wrote:

> All our intuition is nothing but the representation of appearance . . . the things we intuit are not in themselves what we intuit them as being. . . . As appearances they cannot exist in themselves, but only in us. *What objects may be in themselves . . . remains completely unknown to us* [my italics].

Kant called the unknown thing-in-itself a "noumenon" or "transcendental object"—and he has consequently been known as a "transcendental idealist." But he cannot be called a thinker who, like Berkeley, is convinced that matter does not exist. Thus he criticized Berkeley for degrading "matter to mere illusion." Kant described what he called a "transcendent idealist" (without the *al*) as one who would claim knowledge of things-in-themselves.

The above account greatly simplifies Kant's philosophy, which, although written in tedious and clotted prose, is (unlike that of Locke), technically brilliant; but the outline I have given does at least explain clearly enough what being a "Kantian" in the very general sense entails. Bertrand Russell granted Kant his enormous importance, but denied him the supreme position most contemporaries allowed him because, first, he thought the thing-in-itself was an awkward element, and, secondly, he held him responsible for the generally idealistic direction German philosophy took after his death.

Russell also mentions, pertinently, what he called Kant's "mystical side," which, he pointed out where many do not wish to do so, "existed, though it did not appear much in his writings." One of the chief exceptions is the curiously ambiguous *Dreams of a Ghost-Seer*, which is about the Swedish visionary and mining engineer Emmanuel Swedenborg. Kant calls Swedenborg's system "fantastic" but "very sublime."

The truth is that Kant, like so many philosophers before him (there were not so many of his weight after him) was divided in his allegiances. On the one hand, in such works as *Critique of Pure Reason,* he demonstrated that the usual "proofs" for the existence of God were philosophically unsound. But he then concluded that, since virtue exists, so must God. This is a fair argument, but it is not really philosophy. Kant's influence on theology has been incalculable.

Not even a brief discussion of Kant could be complete without mention of his contributions to epistemology (theory of knowledge) and ethics ("the categorical imperative"). The first belongs to the *Critique,* and is indeed one of its central concerns. Hume had turned metaphysics into a wry study of metaphysicians and what was wrong with them—he famously said that all books of metaphysics contained in a library ought to be "consigned to the flames": They "can contain nothing but sophistry and illusion."

Kant, less literary and less ironic, took the question more seriously. Although Hume awoke him from his "dogmatic slumbers" his solution to the problem was not at all Humean. Hume believed in mathematical or empirical (from the senses) knowledge, but in no other sort of knowledge. Kant wanted to find out if there was any other kind of knowledge. He therefore made a distinction between types of a priori proposition. An a priori proposition—if it exists, since some philosophers such as Locke deny that it does— is one that can be known without experience of the actual course of events in the world. Trivial ones such as "All bears are four-footed," in which the conclusion is contained in the subject, he called *analytical.* More interesting and useful ones, whose predicates contain *more than may be inferred from their subject* [my italics] he called *synthetic* (Kant insisted that 5 + 7 = 12—and therefore all mathematical propositions—was synthetic; "Every event has a cause" is also synthetic). This distinction has been hugely important to philosophers, whether they agree with it or not, largely because it is so valuable a formulation of a problem that cannot be evaded.

The categorical imperative is a formal law invented by Kant in the course of his ethics. Again, it functions as a very useful formulation of a profound question: What are moral actions? Kant's ethics are based on an idea of duty: to be moral we must act from duty. But how can we tell what our duty is? Is there a test? Kant invented one, which he called the categorical imperative. A common form of this is: *Every action must be judged in the light of how it would appear if it were to be a universal law of behavior.* Clearly, then, robbing a bank does not pass the test. According to Kant, also, "solitary sex" does not pass it!

The concept has been heavily criticized, and it hardly works. We are told by a philosopher that, technically, although Kant clearly would have thought it wrong, the promise *I shall smother all infants who keep me awake by crying at night* does pass the test! On the other hand, *I shall play tennis on Sunday mornings since everyone else is at church* does not pass it! There has been endless controversy and argument about this ever since, which only, perhaps, demonstrates that the question of what is good behavior and what is bad is far more complicated than even Kant thought. Perhaps he ruined his enterprise here by injecting into it too much of the Lutheran morality in which he had been brought up.

Kant himself was an interesting character. He had no ear for music and was not much interested in art. Literature on the other hand he loved, and he especially liked the English poet Alexander Pope. He remained in Königsberg, where he was born (as the son of a saddler), for the whole of his life. But he was no recluse: he liked company (but not being contradicted), and he had two English friends—living in his town for business reasons—whom he used to visit almost daily for as long as they were there. At the university he studied theology, physics, and mathematics as well as philosophy; he began as a follower of LEIBNIZ. From 1770 onward he was a professor at Königsberg University. He never married, and must—if we are to follow a hint given by Bertrand Russell—many times have acted without the benefit of his imperative, for we can hardly suppose that it would have been safe in the local brothels, since he was so well known (after about 1780) and so punctual that people set their watches by his appearances in the streets.

On one occasion, though, on his own admission, he became so excited that he forgot to be punctual. This was when he was reading the novel *Emile*, by JEAN-JACQUES ROUSSEAU, who was, perhaps a little unexpectedly in view of the latter's hardly having been a philosopher in any technical sense, a powerful influence on him. Rousseau above all affected the idea of liberty of which Kant's work is so redolent. It was largely from his enthusiastic reading of Rousseau that he derived his support for both the American and the French revolutions. Yet his categorical imperative certainly forbade disobedience of the laws of the ruling government. . . .

Kant provides a fine example of the virtues and limitations of the philosopher: against himself but determined not to appear to be. He ought to have been (and probably wanted to be) a poet, but he was hamstrung by his formidable intellect. Himself devout and even mystical, he is (among other things) one of the fathers of a modern theological movement that pronounced God to be dead. Yet the limitations he put on our knowledge of the world also helped to inspire the Kantian Martin Buber in perhaps the most fruitful of all modern religious books. Possibly he has come into his own there. For such is his grandeur as a philosopher that few Kantians agree with Kant.

61

Confessions

JEAN-JACQUES ROUSSEAU

1781

Whether the muddled, quarrelsome Swiss egoist and egotist Jean-Jacques Rousseau really deserves the influence he has wielded must ultimately be a subjective matter. He was, throughout his life, frequently not in his right mind; in his last years he was in the grip of paranoia. But what can never be in question, and cannot be diminished either, is the enormous extent of that influence.

Few sentences have been quoted more often than the opening one of his *Du contrat social:* "Man is born free, yet everywhere he is in chains." But this work—exploited by Robespierre during the French Revolution in the own interests of his own power—argues that man ought to welcome such chains, or, alternatively, that because they express what he called the general will, to which Rousseau gave a mystical significance, they thus guarantee his freedom. In other words, there is no doubt about it, human beings can be "forced to be free." No one has been able to determine to what extent Rousseau really meant that; he did not resolve the paradox.

Although he contributed to THE ENCYCLOPEDIA, you will not find

Rousseau in many dictionaries of philosophers: His thought is not sufficiently consistent to warrant the title of philosopher. Yet, when he is included in such compilations, it scandalizes neither reviewers nor readers. Nor is that surprising or wrong. In discussions of political philosophy, moreover, which (necessarily) range from PLATO through ARISTOTLE, to HOBBES and then of course to LOCKE, and onward to MARX, his *Du contrat social* (1762) is as often as not skated over; he sometimes goes unmentioned in this connection. True, his *Social Contract* adds little, perhaps nothing, to the intellectual argument: one can excuse the omission. But it had quite as much influence as any of the chosen texts: It was, after all, several years before its time in that it was the first work whose author tried to translate what would soon become familiar romantic principles into political doctrine.

The effect of Rousseau upon not only KANT but also HEGEL—whose quieter but more malevolent egoism could match that of the Swiss—was very considerable.

> But he was frenzied,—wherefore, who may know?
> Since cause might be which skill could never find;
> But he was frenzied by disease or woe
> To that worst pitch of all, which wears a reasoning show.

wrote Byron (who was sympathetic to him), in his poem "Childe Harold"; he added that the life of the "self-torturing sophist" was

> one long war with self-fought foes,
> Or friends by him self-banished; for his mind
> Had grown Suspicion's sanctuary, and chose,
> For its own cruel sacrifice, the kind,
> 'Gainst whom he raged with fury strange and blind.

There is certainly a case for choosing, here, either the *Social Contract* or the educational novel *Emile* of the same year. The brilliant and perverse novel *Julie, ou La Nouvelle Héloïse*, hardly qualifies: it made a sensation in its time, but is now regarded as more important to the understanding of its author than of history.

But since, essentially, it was Rousseau, the man himself as represented by both his personality and all his writings, who exerted the everlasting influence, the *Confessions* must take precedence. It is the natural choice. No one who wrote a serious autobiography after 1768 (I do not allude to political memoirs, from which by definition candor is excluded) has been uninfluenced by it, since it almost immediately affected the expectations of the enlightened public. No one had tried to tell the naked and direct truth about themselves before; possibly Rousseau had to be half mad to attempt it. But attempt it he did. And the *Confessions* does—with what has proved, after many years of scholarly investigation into the matter, remarkable accuracy—

go a long way toward describing the man. It is the first "romantic" autobiography, although FREUD believed that (of all pre-Freudians, of course) NIETZSCHE had showed the most extraordinary degree of self-insight.

But did Rousseau pave the way for Nietzsche? Could Nietzsche have written (as he did) that "one's own self is well hidden from oneself: of all mines of treasure one's own is the last to be dug up" had Rousseau not lived before him? Nietzsche in fact reviled Rousseau, since he regarded his "return to nature" as exceedingly dangerous, and thought that in the hands of the masses it could only unleash destructive forces; but he never minimized his importance.

To what degree did Rousseau—and Goethe—"invent" romanticism? Rousseau is after all, given his dates (1712–1778; Goethe was not born until 1749) *the* arch romantic or preromantic (depending on what view is taken of the advent of the romantic "movement," which is really no more than an irresistible tendency); yet on the topical questions of his day he could be empirical enough when it suited him.

He was born in Geneva into a family of French refugees. His mother died within a few days of his birth, and his father's care of him was, although not unloving, eccentric. His upbringing was Calvinist. In 1728 he left Geneva to travel and study. He met many interesting people, to whom he was soon able to demonstrate his unusual gifts, one of the most marked of which was musical.

In 1828, at sixteen, he met his chief benefactress, the Vaudois Madame de Warens. Twelve years his senior, she not only eventually became his mistress (perhaps mainly for maternal reasons, since she had other lovers who may well have pleased her more than Rousseau ever did) but also instilled into him new religious views: Under her tutelage he became a Roman Catholic. She had been converted from Protestant pietism, and she retained the influence. Hell and Original Sin were thus banished from Rousseau's as yet unformed mind. After various periods of study, including a spell at a seminary at which he discovered that he had no vocation for the priesthood, Rousseau lived with Madame de Warens from 1731 until 1740; the effect she had on his self-education of those years was as profound as it was maternal. He read voraciously, and in his own inimitable way grasped the great philosophers, from LEIBNIZ to Locke.

In 1741 he met Thérèse Le Vasseur, a hotel servant girl with whom he stayed for the rest of his life; he married her in 1768. He had five children by her, all of whom he placed, to—as we read in the *Confessions* and elsewhere—his eternal and bitter regret, in the orphanage of the Enfants-Trouvés. This, although quite a common practice of the time, became something of an obsession with him.

Through Denis Diderot Rousseau was introduced to the Encyclopedists. His own contributions to *The Encyclopedia* were mostly on musical subjects, although he wrote one on political economy. He was unknown to the general public until, in 1750, he won a prize (again by the good offices of Diderot) from the University of Dijon for a paradoxical essay attacking the

idea that the arts and sciences were good for human morals. Suddenly he found himself, like the poet Byron after him, famous overnight. Previously he had been appreciated by only a few, particularly for his charming opera *Le Devin du village,* given at court in 1745. His argument in the essay, known as the first *Discourse,* was that the arts and the sciences were pernicious because they lacked primitive purity and promoted luxury. The brilliant essay, one of the cleverest academic exercises of all time, was instantly taken up, although with utter superficiality, by high society.

But Rousseau, though now successful and much discussed, was unhappy. He had while very young served as a lackey; now he felt uneasy with socially exalted people, and his liaison with a servant girl (whom, however, he would not give up) inhibited his social progress. Those who dislike him have often asserted that he always had the mind of a lackey. He returned in 1754 to

Geneva—and (officially) to the Calvinist faith of his childhood. But he remained a divided man, worried by the fact that, although he advocated the banning of opera and theater, he wrote both (his plays are of little interest or account). Rousseau was brilliant always; but his vanity and egoism forbade him much sense of irony as well as robust humor—and that made it difficult for him, and may have contributed to his final paranoia, in which he was even convinced that the friendly and kind DAVID HUME was circulating libels about him and wanted to destroy him.

Around 1750 Rousseau began to promulgate the idea of the noble—or innocent—savage: our ancestor, a man uncorrupted by civilization and untainted by the sin of property. This line of thinking led to *Emile* and the *Social Contract* (both 1762). The first describes, in the form of a novel, the ideal education of the innocent child so that he shall not become tainted by society. Instead of his natural instincts being curbed in schools by moral instruction, the child should be encouraged to develop his individuality in the bosom of his family; religion should be nondogmatic and depend not on the head but the heart; experience should come not from books but from life. Thus, in an important sense, all liberal modern educational experiments derive from Rousseau. He set himself, in *Emile*, against all the traditional methods of education, and the book has understandably and fairly been taken to heart by genuine libertarians, and must have influenced the practice of education insofar as this has gradually if often reluctantly allowed (except in military establishments) more open expression of individuality.

In the *Social Contract* Rousseau illustrated what kind of state the properly educated child should emerge into. The result was an eloquent muddle, and the work itself relies too much on rhetoric and paradox for it to be clear. But its muddle is a rich one. People have argued about whether it is a celebration of liberty or a blueprint for totalitarianism; but it is both. Its value, perhaps like that of HOBBES's more clearly argued and elaborately ironic *Leviathan*, lies in the manner in which it draws attention to the very real difficulties involved in political theory.

Rousseau, despite his early Calvinism, did not believe in original sin; on the contrary, he believed that man was by nature good, but that the social arrangements—notably the institution of the ownership of property—he had somehow (but how, if he is naturally good?) entered into were bad. He owes much to Hobbes, but of course differs from him in thinking of man as good rather than bad.

Rousseau is not an anarchist. He thinks that humanity requires individuals to realize their full individuality by a form of surrender to what he calls the general will—not at all just a crude and unsubtle aggregate of opinion and self-interest, but a kind of collective spirit, which Rousseau equates with the common good. Only by this surrender, this social contract, can an individual (paradoxically) find his fullest freedom. A man who is against the general will is thus against himself. Rousseau really wanted to think of the state as a kind of person with a mysteriously superior and infallible will of its own.

Thus his *Social Contract* can justifiably be taken as a defense of democracy *or* of totalitarianism. Many, remembering the rhetoric of Nazis and communists, have thus rejected Rousseau. It is clear enough that he himself was no totalitarian, but the device he invented to overcome tyranny, what he called the Legislator, was nevertheless a sort of benign (or so Rousseau hoped) dictator. Viewed retrospectively, the Legislator's semidivine character has all too many features in common with those of Hitler and Stalin; and clearly he must often be "cruel to be kind" as well as merely kind.

The *Confessions*, though, is Rousseau's most exemplary work. He opened it thus:

> I have entered on a performance which is without example, whose accomplishment will have no imitator. I mean to present my fellow-mortals with a man in all the integrity of nature; and this man shall be myself.
>
> I alone. I know my heart, and have studied mankind; I am not made like anyone I have been acquainted with, perhaps like no one in existence; if not better, I at least claim originality, and whether Nature did wisely in breaking the mold in which she formed me can only be determined after having read this work.

Not many pages pass before he is admitting that chastisement from a Mademoiselle Lambercier gave him so much pleasure that he offended deliberately in order to merit it—until she gave it up on the grounds that it was too tiring. Thus, famously, he was "long"

> tormented, without knowing by what, I gazed on every handsome woman with ardor; imagination incessantly brought their charms to my remembrance, only to transform them into so many demoiselles Lambercier.
>
> Even after I had attained to manhood, this strange fancy, always persistent, and carried to the length of depravity, even of madness, preserved in me a morality which seems its very opposite.

Throughout the *Confessions* Rousseau examined himself thus, with immense vanity but without kindness. The vanity was perhaps inevitable: How, otherwise, could he have been so interested in himself? Whether he served Christianity by preserving its essential truths in a skeptical age, or whether he undermined it by doing away with original sin—both views have been put forward, and both have merit—he at least laid the foundations for the process of self-examination. The survival of orthodox Christianity is not after all any more important than whatever equally dishonest orthodoxy replaces it. He was not so egoistic that readers of the *Confessions* could not find much of themselves (and much unwelcome at that) in the work; in that way perhaps he did much, therefore, to reinforce the notion of original sin.

62

Reflections on the Revolution in France

EDMUND BURKE

1790

It is often assumed that Edmund Burke, acknowledged as one of the most powerful stylists in the English language, was as great an orator. He was not. He was nothing, for example, in comparison to his sometime ally, the Whig Charles James Fox, who, without ever having much following in the country as a whole, maintained what little political power he managed to attain by his oratory alone.

Some of Burke's speeches which are still read and pondered upon emptied the British House of Commons. He was eloquent, but his delivery was poor. Nonetheless, increasing attention was paid to his views, and he ultimately, despite being a Whig, became one of the most influential of all the spokesmen for conservatism.

It must be explained at this point that the Whigs in Great Britain, among whom Burke was prominent, were those who, from the end of the seventeenth century, upheld popular rights against the power exercised by the king. The English Whigs, like the American advocates of independence, found their creed in the constitutional writings of JOHN LOCKE, although they differed in their interpretations of them. English Whigs—divided into factions although they were—were in power more or less continuously from 1718 until 1761. Then they were (apart from the government formed by Grenville and Fox in 1806) mostly out of office until 1830. They eventually, in the course of the nineteenth century, turned into the Liberals. (In the United States the history of the term *Whig* was quite different—and the Republican Party was formed (1854) by men who thought of themselves as Whigs.)

There is something appropriate in the very fact that Burke was a far greater writer than he was orator. For Burke, who is alive to us now as a political thinker, if not as a theorist, was never quite what he seemed to be. He loved most what he feared most. He was to a large extent like the Milton of *Paradise Lost*—of Satan's party, on the side of the enemy, as William Blake put it. The war against sexual pleasure and the erotic has usually been waged by such puritans as JOHN CALVIN or his Scottish follower John Knox; it is not so often, or so sincerely, waged by devotees; certainly it is not often seen in the form of revolutionary politics. However, if the explanation of Burke's allegiances is to be found in his sexuality, they cannot for that reason be dismissed. Politics can often rather more easily be reduced to sex than it can to decency or principle. In Burke's case the path to a fundamental kind of conservatism lay through fear of but zealous interest in sexual emotions.

Burke, the son of a Protestant lawyer, was born and educated in Dublin, Ireland. His mother was a Roman Catholic, and he was always sympathetic to Catholics, although content with his own Anglicanism. He studied law and went to London to read for the bar, but he soon showed a greater interest in political journalism. He established himself as a writer to be reckoned with in 1756, with *A Vindication of Natural Society*. He had a political career but was never in high office. He entered politics in 1759 and was employed in Ireland; in 1765 he joined the faction called the Rockingham Whigs and became a member of Parliament. In 1770 he published *Thoughts on the Cause of the Present Discontent*, in which he argued for the value of political parties: "[bodies] of men united on public principle, which could act as a constitutional link between king and parliament, providing consistency and strength in administration, or principled criticism in opposition." His speeches in Parliament were sympathetic to the rights of the American colonists. Later he allied himself temporarily with Fox, in order to oppose the administration of Lord North, which was all for keeping the American colonies, and which dealt with their grievances in an inept manner.

But when Lord Rockingham, more sympathetic to his ideas, came into office in 1782 he was excluded from the cabinet; he was awarded the disappointing office of paymaster of the forces. Yet his Acts while in government were the most important. First, he tried and to a large extent succeeded in making his own office fraud-proof, by separating the paymaster's personal accounts from his official ones. Secondly, he (Whiggishly) tried to strike simultaneously at royal influence and at wastage in the royal economy by his Civil List Act. This is worth mentioning because, as many historians have agreed, it was, significantly, too theoretical: It "came fully fledged from Burke's fertile brain [and] had not been tested and tried practically." It was in fact based on Burke's mistaken insistance that George III had wasted huge sums of money in the support of his own political machine.

Indeed, Burke was a complex character, full of both humane common sense and a peculiar vituperativeness that could cause him to act with a ferociously passionate viciousness. Thus, in 1783, he had devised an India Bill which was vigorously opposed by the then governor-general of India, Warren Hastings. It was a bold bill of good intentions, but (significantly) it proposed the hopelessly impractical measure of giving bureaucrats in England control over men in India (who, however corrupt, knew something about the country).

Burke waited for many years to have his revenge. Then he, with the playwright Sheridan and with Charles James Fox, opened impeachment proceedings against Hastings (1787–1794). Hastings was ruined by the long ordeal but eventually acquitted; however, by that time even London high society had become bored and disgusted by the unscrupulous methods of his prosecutors.

Certainly Burke's most important, if not most directly influential, work was his early *A Philosophical Enquiry Into the Origins of Our Idea of the Sublime and Beautiful* (1757, revised two years later), a masterpiece, and an anticipation not only of the romantic movement that was soon to come but also of FREUD. In this work lie the seeds of both Burke's passion for reform (in which he was a trifle unrealistic at times), and his (later developed) terror of its consequences. It has recently been widely recognized that this book has as one of its true subjects something that is as avoided in public discussion as it is ubiquitous in life: the nature of male eroticism. Its subject is much greater than the erotic, however—whether or not Freud was right and the erotic lies behind almost everything. Whenever anyone thinks of the sublime, then they are bound to think of, among other things, sexual pleasure. But Burke, whose descriptions of the sublime in the form of various kinds of landscapes and weather are so subtle and justly famous, equated it with a "disordering": He found that not only his Sublime but also Beauty itself were unmanageable. Our passions, he recognized while still a young man, "have springs that we are utterly unacquainted with."

When the French Revolution broke out in 1789 Burke was alarmed, especially because he feared the consequences of what would happen in England, where it was widely supported. He broke away from Fox and other friends and soon wrote the *Reflections*.

This was originally intended as a letter to a young friend in France; but Burke was swept away by his fear and expanded it into an alarmist treatise.

He favored "manly, moral, regulated" liberty, he explained. He insisted that the English revolution of 1688 had involved no break with the past, but was rather a return to the constitutional practice of an earlier time (this is hardly even arguable). The French Revolution, on the other hand, involved a people's repudiation of their past: The bonds that made society possible would be dissolved: Burke prophesied, correctly, that the only possible consequence could be a military dictatorship.

Clearly Burke found the spectacle "sublime," and as clearly he was therefore appalled by it. Against it, and against his prophetic powers, he opposed a more dubious argument, but one which has had enormous influence ever since. The argument is that society is "organic," and that constitutional monarchy follows "nature" in a manner that is wise "without reflection." Perhaps he was driven to this mystical view, at the heart of certain kinds of modern conservatism, by a feeling that he had expressed in the *Enquiry,* a book on the whole more descriptive than prescriptive: "Uncertainty is so terrible that we often seek to be rid of it, at the hazard of a certain mischief." The book is in many ways badly organized and trivial, but in others—as in the descriptions of the French mobs—it is very powerful. However, it does not make clear, and Burke never did make clear, just how necessary reforms are to be undertaken in the teeth of reactionary opposition to them. He gave excellent warnings about the dangers of revolutions, and he rightly preferred peaceful ones.

But Burke falls down, as do his contemporary followers, on the question of what ought to happen when a people run out of peaceful means.

63

Vindication of the Rights of Woman

MARY WOLLSTONECRAFT

1792

> Strengthen the female mind by enlarging it, and there will be an end to blind obedience; but, as blind obedience is ever sought for by power, tyrants and sensualists are in the right when they endeavor to keep women in the dark, because the former only want slaves, and the latter a play-thing.

This and much else in the *Vindication of the Rights of Woman*, was the first time it had been so forthrightly said. Mary Wollstonecraft had many precursors, but she was the first to have the courage to come out with it.

She was able to do so because of the prevailing conditions; the Revolution proceeding on the other side of the Channel had not yet become universally unpopular on account of its sheer bloodthirstiness. In 1791, the previous year, her friend THOMAS PAINE had published, as a riposte to

BURKE's frightened and eloquent defense of the status quo, *Reflections on the Revolution in France*, his *Rights of Man*. She had preceded Paine with her own *Vindication of the Rights of Men* in 1790—an inferior work, and one which had much irritated William Godwin, who had specifically determined to avoid its abusive and emotional style. Now she, too, wished to reply again to Burke—but this time on behalf of women. Her book was ultimately influential because so much of it is just plain common sense, irresistible—in the long run—to decent and rational inquiry, but running against the grain of male wishes and expectations. It was a very long run.

William Godwin, who became Mary's loving husband—she lost her life after giving birth to their daughter, who became Mary Shelley—devoted much of his time to the memory of her and to the printing of her writings (including her letters to him in the candid and explicit *Memoirs of the Author of A Vindication of the Rights of Woman*); but for many years she was known as a "prostitute" and her ideas rejected on such grounds, or grounds like it— "lascivious," "disgusting," "shameless," "advocate of priapism" (this from a Rev. Polwhele, horrified by the discussion of the "organs of generation" in one of her books). Even those who agreed with her were forced, for a time, to distance themselves from her. But as her reputation as a scarlet woman faded, the arguments of the *Vindication* remained, and in the end most of these have triumphed. The tale of certain men's vulgar and outrageous resistance to this book, as to the first wave of feminism, is a sorry one indeed. Some men still do not accept Wollstonecraft's main thesis—but at least they have to pretend they do.

Mary herself was not—as one might guess—a conventional but rather a rebellious, physically passionate, and even jealous woman, and had had a hard life until she met Godwin. And then their life together was cut cruelly short by puerperal disease. Neither believed in the institution of marriage, but, aware of the unfair stigma carried by illegitimacy, they had married for the sake of their child.

Mary Wollstonecraft was born in London, the second of six children, in 1859. Her father, a weaver turned farmer but without success, was a violent man who ultimately turned to alcohol. In the course of her life she turned her hand to more or less every profession or task that was then open to women: paid companion, governess (she was sacked because the children preferred her to their mother), school-keeper and teacher, social commentator, and writer of novels. Her first publication, *Thoughts on the Education of Daughters* (1787), advocated the education of women on pragmatic grounds, and provided the basis of the *Vindication*; her first novel, *Mary: A Fiction*— inspired by the death of a dear friend—of the following year, is not particularly outstanding except in the light of her later work.

After she had lost her job as governess, Mary returned to London, to the publisher of her books, Joseph Johnson, at whose home she was introduced to most of the important radicals of the time: Godwin, Paine, the painter Henry Fuseli, with whom she was in love for a time (he was later unhelpful to her, and to Godwin), and William Blake (who provided the engravings for an edition of one of her books, *Original Stories From Real Life*).

Ever incautious and passionate, Mary Wollstonecraft met (1793) in London a "Captain" Gilbert Imlay, a shady but doubtless appealing character (he had written a not inferior novel called *The Emigrants*), and fell in love with him. He almost ruined her for good. She lived with him in the Paris of the Revolution as "Mrs. Imlay" and bore him a daughter, Fanny (1794). Then, suddenly, he abandoned her. Twice she tried to kill herself. Then in 1795 she met with Godwin, and the rest of her short life became tolerable. Her novel *The Wrongs of Women* was unfinished and appeared posthumously.

Godwin was right to value his wife's intellect for its knowledge of truths that he himself had not understood before encountering her writings. She is not famous by a mere accident, and her thinking clearly rose far above her propensity to precipitate herself into desperate situations. She wrote to Imlay, the man who eventually betrayed her—but with whom she was ready to share another woman, as she had been with Fuseli—as follows:

> With ninety-nine men out of a hundred, a very sufficient dash of folly is necessary to render a woman *piquant*, a soft word for desirable; and beyond these casual ebullitions of sympathy, few look for enjoyment by fostering a passion in their hearts. One reason, in short, why I wish my whole sex to become wiser, is, that the foolish ones, by their pretty folly, rob those whose sensibility keeps down their vanity, of the few roses that afford them some solace in the thorny road of life.

This is somewhat subtler and more self-critical than the avowed thesis of the *Vindication*, which has been accused by modern feminists of being "misogynist." Mary, they point out, did not much like being a woman, and even seemed to claim, at times, that outstanding women were males in some way imprisoned in female bodies. (But she thought NEWTON, by virtue of his genius, to be only accidentally entrapped in a human frame.) And it is true that her thinking was in some ways confused. It was led to be so by her hatred of what society really did do to women. What are usually called "Victorian" values were actually well in place by her times (expurgated Shakespeares along the lines of Dr. Bowdler's were on their way) , so that women were on the one hand enshrined as "pure" ("Why are girls," she asked, "to be told that they resemble angels; but to sink them below women?"), but on the other con-signed to be chattels, the literal property of men.

However, it has to be recognized that the *Vindication* was polemical: That is to say, it missed out some arguments in the interests of getting itself listened to—and, after the first long reaction against it, it did get listened to, and it did inspire active feminists of later generations all over the world. Godwin did not labor in vain. At no point in the work is it suggested that

women should do anything but struggle against the false psychological categories assigned to them by men. Her critique of woman-as-property anticipates MARX and is still cogent: If a woman knows that she is the legal property of a man, she will even unconsciously regard herself as that—this, perhaps, is what Wollstonecraft meant by advocating that women should be "taught to think."

Her portrayal of most of her female contemporaries as coquettish and manipulative has understandably annoyed many modern feminists but could be taken as simply descriptive, the inevitable result of male domination. Nor is it lacking in descriptive power, for in part it is self-critical—and Wollstonecraft was fascinated by both her own powers of attractiveness to men and by the nature of their sexual curiosity. Some modern feminists repudiate or even deny such inquiries, since they do not like to be self-critical in that way. This does not help them to take the *Vindication* in its context. But, salutary though it was, it does not amount to a full working out of Mary Wollstonecraft's thinking about gender and gender differences. Had she lived later, at a time when women were beginning to obtain education, she would have been more than capable of contributing to the discussion.

An Enquiry Concerning Political Justice

WILLIAM GODWIN

1793

It is always interesting when a law-abiding man, respected as deeply serious, as even rather loftily overmoralistic, by those who know him personally, attracts the shocked odium of a substantial section of society—and that section, moreover, which fancies itself to be "the establishment."

After the initial success of *Political Justice* in the decade of its publication, this is just what happened to William Godwin, political theorist, novelist, verse playwright, and historian, who also wrote and published books for the edification of the young. By his early middle age he was, probably because his book was the first to present the case for the abolition of the state, regularly accused of advocating unlimited sexual promiscuity, abortion-on-demand, atheism, treachery, civil disorder, and infanticide; he was compared to the legendary Indian plant, the tall upas tree, which poisoned everything that lay within its shadow. Nothing was too bad to say about Godwin, and to decry him became a means of entering into society.

Godwin's novel *Caleb Williams* (1794)—the imaginative expression of the state of mind that produced *Political Justice,* and written immediately after it—despite its ponderousness and the fact that it is initially hard to get into, crops up so regularly —in reissues and critical discussions—as to suggest that it has managed to earn itself, by its very persistence, the status of "major" or even "great."

An Enquiry Concerning Political Justice, still probably the anarchist's best and least confused guide to his subject (there are no smoking bombs in it, and Godwin's enemies—puzzled by its author's unmistakably high principles—have had to invent them), is, of course, the book by this stooped, harmless, debt-harassed, persistent, grave, dedicated man that has exercised the greatest direct influence: first, on the generation still excited by the French Revolution—it was only when the fashion for this event died out that this became anathema—on Godwin's son-in-law the poet Percy Bysshe Shelley, on the younger Wordsworth, on the younger *and* the older Coleridge (who maintained his respect for Godwin's decency and goodness of heart and mind long after his own views had become conservative), on MALTHUS—so aptly described as "unadmirable"—on, for that not unimportant matter, his own daughter by MARY WOLLSTONECRAFT, Mary Shelley, the seventeen-year-old author, after all, of that essentially Godwinian novel *Frankenstein,* on most if not all socialists, and on all anarchists, and, last but not least, on the very authorities whose good faith he challenged. But *Caleb Williams* offers an invaluable key to *Political Justice.*

Godwin had faults, but few people (even those who, as ungratefully irresponsible humorists are wont to say, "make Genghis Khan look like a pinko") have been able to question Godwin's innate decency as a person, or the quality of his intellectual powers. If only he had been a rapist or a murderer, so as to prove that the enemies of law and order must be monsters! True, his sexual appetite and his pained sincerity about it have been sneered at—it is all too easy to laugh at him—but only by those who have forgotten their own. For all Godwin's earnestness, then, there is much that is lovable in him. He truly deplored the fundamental vices (greed, injustice, unreflectingness, scoundrelish patriotism) but he did not self-righteously suppose himself to be immune from them. He was also unfortunate: His formidable first wife, Mary Wollstonecraft—generously described by many of his contemporaries as a "prostitute"—died in giving birth to Mary, and then, later in life when he was up against hard times, and much deprecated, Percy Shelley, not the most unselfish of men, came along, claimed to be the heir to his ideas, and ran off with Mary and with other daughters and stepdaughters. On the whole Godwin dealt with Shelley with admirable sincerity and fairness, and if his manner of adhering to his principles (chiefly, that money was the common property of all men) sometimes seems genuinely amusing, he still did stick to them. He did count on money from other people, Shelley among them; but his friends in need, fellow radicals, could also always count on what he had.

Caleb Williams, a work of the morbid imagination if there ever was one, tells the highly imaginative story of the emotional price that must be paid for a desire—originally unsophisticated and simply conceived—for freedom of thought, justice for everyone, a quiet life, peace, and love of truth. This tale of a young man's obsession with the strange secrets of his older and mysterious benefactor—who turns upon him and pursues him with all the awful panoply of the law—is essentially one of "surveillance": of just how that sinister and unnatural entity, the state, intrudes into the life of and ultimately oppresses and destroys the individual. It is *the* book of the eighteenth and nineteenth centuries about the individual's inescapably paranoid state of mind, and it worthily anticipates the great twentieth-century Czech comitragic satirist of bureaucracy and penology FRANZ KAFKA.

But Kafka's books have an ironically neurasthenic lightness of touch, whereas *Caleb Williams* is somewhat stifling. Godwin could not have written, as Kafka did (in his *Diary*), "Dance on, you pigs; what concern is it of mine?" but he experienced the same feelings. His novel offers an explanation, irresistible to an honest and unprejudiced reader, of just how clearly he discerned the real, and inevitable, horrors of government organized for the loving care of its subjects. By Kafka's time bureaucracy had already grown senselessly oppressive, and his account of this madness remains the classic one; Godwin, writing at a time when bureaucracy as we know it had hardly been invented, was only protesting against the main reasons for which HOBBES had offered his contract:

The nonanarchist would claim that *Caleb Williams* is itself clinically paranoid—a diseased work by a man who has failed to grasp, as Hobbes did gleefully grasp, the need for terror, overcomplicated bureaucracy, oppressive law buttressed by chain-clanking penology, and perpetually bubbling resentment and violence. To any nonpolitical individual, on the other hand, it demonstrates the manner in which the practice of politics as we know it has invented a humanity whose individual members must be poisoned by paranoia because their decency is frustrated.

Caleb is, in any case—as might be expected from one who was brought up as a strict Calvinist and who was very early admonished for picking up a cat on the holy Sabbath—as surely on the subject of original sin as any novel ever written. Original sin was, for Godwin, government. For the man who had entirely repudiated the Calvinist belief that had been forced upon him as a child, original sin became the oppressive state, whose metaphysical effects on the individual he examined in this terrifying novel. It is a tribute to the power and relevance of *Caleb Williams* that it continues to attract readers. All of us, even conservatives, may read within it our autobiographies as loyal servants of the state who have no means of contracting out of its demands.

That is the alarming state of mind from which *Political Justice* itself arose. Perhaps the state of mind is not to be wondered at: Its author, born in Wisbech, in the Cambridgeshire fens in 1756, was the son of a Calvinist minister, a member of the Sandemanian sect, and therefore a person who could be described (without undue lack of fairness) as one who felt it necessary to cut down on the already miserably few elect of the too genial JOHN CALVIN. Godwin received a good education from the only institutions then available to dissenters, the dissenting academies—which were excellent institutions, and Calvinist much more in word than deed—and in time, after serving as a minister himself and quarreling with his flock, came to abhor Calvinism. But he retained much of its strictness, and the humor perhaps natural to him was always well tempered—cheerfulness found it hard to break through.

He read prodigiously in Latin, Greek, and English, and became, as a London journalist, one of the more learned men of his time. He met and became friendly with TOM PAINE—and carried his dislike of government a step further. He sat in at Paine's trial for sedition (after the latter had fled to France), and heard the attorney general famously inform the court that the "glorious and incomparable constitution" of Great Britain had been "recognized by Julius Caesar." He published the *Political Justice* as a deliberate (and very courageous) act of defiance—and just got away with it. The prime minister William Pitt the Younger thought it unlikely to do much harm because of its high price.

Godwin offered *Political Justice* to the public, with great scrupulosity, not as the last word on its subject, but as something for their consideration. What Godwin wished to do was to make an inquiry into the philosophical basis for having a government at all. He changed his mind on some matters (he told Shelley that a thinking man's life must be a series of retractions), and he incorporated the changes as best he could in the two subsequent editions of the book, in 1796 and 1798. But his anarchism remained intact, and did so until the end of his long and hard life in 1836.

Godwin's prose is lucid and his tone polite: He writes here, as one of his biographers has well put it, as "the calm friend of truth." This has helped his thousand-page book to survive and to receive respect even from its opponents. The book was set up in type even as he wrote it, and it suffers from the speed with which he had to compose it; but Godwin had no money to give himself leisure—and perhaps this pressure helped him, too, by giving a sense of urgency.

The main argument is that all human beings are naturally equal, and that therefore government corrupts governors and their subjects, and creates inequalities. Only if society is nonpolitical can it produce that natural benevolence from which justice and equality results. Godwin wrote:

> Man is a work of nature and is subject to the laws of nature. Instead of vainly looking outside the world for supernatural beings to bring him the happiness which he cannot find on earth, man should study nature, should learn her laws, and submit to her mandates. God is a meaningless term. Religion arose from man's primitive fears, which priests then exploited to enslave their minds.

But Godwin was not quite an atheist: While he did write that such notions as life-after-death were "foreign" to his mind, he repudiated absolute materialism, and appealed always to a Platonic idea of an "omnipresent and eternal volume of truth." Against such a background there can be no excuse for inequality or slavery. Man he thought, is certainly perfectible by the use of reason. Vice is "nothing more than error and mistake reduced into practice."

Godwin's early utilitarianism (he was a contemporary of Jeremy Bentham, whom he knew slightly, and who formulated the classic case for this philosophy, later elaborated by JOHN STUART MILL), the doctrine by which men aim to bring the greatest happiness to the greatest number, got him into some difficulties. He believed that we have some rights over our present property, even though the distribution of property in general does not tend to the greatest good.

It is obvious, indeed, that Godwin was too much of an optimist, so that it is to *Caleb* that we have to look for the counterweight to this excess. Parts of the arguments contained in this, alas, hastily composed book have, of course, been contested; the drift of the argument as a whole has never been answered—partly, no doubt, because Godwin makes such embarrassing assumptions, such as that war can never be glorious, or that it is wrong for one man to take advantage of another for gain. Things would be far worse, however, if Godwin had not presented the case for anarchism (he did not call himself an anarchist, as did, however, the Frenchman Pierre Joseph Proudhon, who lived from 1809 until 1865) nor is that case, in his hands (he deplored all violence, including that of the French soon after their revolution), ever vicious or bad hearted.

65

An Essay on the Principle of Population

THOMAS ROBERT MALTHUS

1798, revised 1803

Thomas Robert Malthus (1766–1834)—in at least the popular estimation of today and yesterday—is the gloomy clergyman who insisted that only sexual ("moral") restraint could (and has continued to) save the world from starvation and all its atrocious consequences. It will surprise many, and no doubt particularly those who believe in continued filial piety, to know that his father was a well-to-do country gentleman who was a devotee of the French

Marquis de Condorcet

Enlightenment thinker, the Marquis de Condorcet (1743–1794: Condorcet coined the word "*perfectibilité*" in respect to man, and his optimistic and progressive *Esquisse d'un Tableau historique des progrés de l'esprit humain*, of 1794, translated in the following year as *Outlines of an Historical View of the Progress of the Human Mind* after his death by suicide in a French prison, was Thomas Malthus's special target in his own *Essay*. Malthus's father it was who had brought his friends DAVID HUME and JEAN-JACQUES ROUSSEAU together. Malthus *père* was also convinced by the arguments of WILLIAM GODWIN, in his *Political Justice*.

So the genesis of the Rev. T. R. Malthus's most famous work could well be viewed as his resentment of his father's morally lax injudiciousness at propagating him—or, of course, had Freudian theory then been invented, as an attempt to castrate him. "Malthusianism" is often, even usually, regarded as an erroneous interpretation of Malthus; but Malthus rapidly became as "Malthusian" as he could, that is to say, he fell in love with his own reputation.

Malthus at first wrote of tendencies rather than of established facts, and his famous argument remains uncomfortably opposed to welfare, charity, and even to helping less fortunate people at all. But this partly depends on what version one reads of his *Essay*, which by 1817 had reached five volumes and had given up argument for mere statement of fact. Fate, and Malthus himself unwitting, have conspired to make "Malthusianism" an all too frequent instrument of extreme right-wing thinking. But of course it is more than that. And it so happened that the mild-mannered CHARLES DARWIN was eventually triggered into his conception of natural selection by a reading of the *Essay*, which was at least a sincerely felt and perhaps salutory objection to Enlightenment optimism.

The man Malthus was not much, certainly in no way a great thinker; his basic idea was not original—he actually got it from Condorcet, who had a partial answer to it, which he did not mention directly, namely birth-control.

Malthus was born near Dorking, in Surrey, just south of London. At eighteen, having "survived" a series of tutors appointed by his father, he entered Jesus College, Cambridge (the place that Coleridge would soon join the army to escape from). He graduated, was elected to a fellowship, was ordained in 1798, and married in 1804. By then he had formed his main views, and even revised them somewhat.

Soon after the publication of the first edition of the *Essay* he met Godwin, and he continued to get on with him very well until Godwin published a reply to him in 1820. The hostility, however, began with him and not with Godwin. He traveled in Europe extensively over the run of the century, and his second edition of 1803 contains much material based on observations that he made there.

In 1805 Malthus became professor of political economy—the first Englishman to hold such a position—at the new training college at Haileybury for would-be employees of the East India Company. He was there until his sudden death from a heart attack.

The essence of the *Essay*, in all its forms, is this: Population grows in geometric progression, subsistence in arithmetical. Population, Malthus added direly, would, unchecked, double itself in twenty-five years. It is only war, famine, and pestilence (he wrote in 1798) that prevent this catastrophe. (In a geometric progression, e.g., 1, 2, 4, 8, 16, 32, . . . the number increases by a single *multiplying* factor, in arithmetic, e.g., 1, 2, 4, 6, 8, 10, . . . only by an additional factor.) Obviously, therefore, there will arise situations in which, in the absence of useful wars, famines and pestilences, starvation will prevail (as will various forms of violence against the better-off, who took note).

It was the first edition rather than the somewhat modified second of 1803 that was seized upon by the wealthier classes. A tract against the perfectibility of Man, it seemed to argue that the only remedy for the poor lay with themselves. Economics got itself called "the dismal science" because of Malthus's bald statement that "[While] food is necessary to the existence of man. . . . The passion between the sexes is necessary and will remain nearly in its present state." Thus future history will demonstrate that there is no perfection of Man in sight: it will continue, Malthus insisted, in its old cycles of misery.

Neither Malthus nor Godwin—in his hardly heeded 1820 reply, *Of Population*, to the fifth edition of Malthus's *Essay*—put much store by birth control. For Malthus this was "vice," and Godwin, who had practiced "natural" methods with his wife MARY WOLLSTONECRAFT with marked lack of success, probably—he had this at least in common with the majority of the popes—did not like condoms. Birth control had been, in fact, one of the more obvious factors interfering with Malthus's predictions, which held good for the colonialist population of North America of his time but not for the "primitive" Indian natives of that continent. And since his death they have not held good, although some of the reasons for this did lie beyond the scope of his times. Malthus greatly undervalued technical progress, and his models only hold very approximately good for underdeveloped societies. But to a certain extent they did hold good.

Malthus's fame and influence went to his head. He became the leading acknowledged authority on population and thus (quite certainly) helped to prevent the promotion of an effective overseas settlement policy. By 1817 with his fifth edition he was arguing that unemployment and poverty were due *only* to overpopulation, that poor relief should be cut back, and that the already severe penalties against illegitimacy should be stepped up—and he dropped his previously kindly references to Godwin and began to cut him when he came across him at social gatherings.

Godwin's *Of Population* fell flat, and Malthus was able (anonymously) to call *Of Population* a "poor old-womanish performance." For nothing did the literary critic and friend to Godwin William Hazlitt refer to Malthus's notion—added since his first edition—of "moral restraint" as a "sniveling interpolation."

Jeremy Bentham had taken up Condorcet's mention of birth control (for the first time in a serious British book), but Malthus (1817) would hear nothing of this: He believed sexual emission to be weakening and wrote that such vice would "remove a tendency to industry." He had won the day. Thus, the main contribution of his school, as a modern historian has noted, was that "the essence of social policy is that there should be no social policy." Malthusianism was used by some politicians in the early nineteenth century to keep wages down to subsistence level on the grounds that increase in population would force them down again anyway. But, alas for this thesis, the increase in population in the nineteenth century was due, not to any rise in birthrate, but to a decrease in the death rate.

The great fallacy committed by Malthusians and by Malthus himself was to apply a static economic "law" over a period of time; in fact technical progress enables *more* people to live off the *same* piece of land. But the so-called eco-doomsters can point out that this apparent reversal of Malthus's prophecies cannot properly be applied to the future. . . . For example, the importing of the medicines of developed countries by undeveloped countries causes a fall in their death rates, while their birthrates should be rising at the same rate. . . . But are they? At present, not in most cases. But the problem is still with us, rather perhaps as a matter of common sense than any "law." Contemporary China has adopted a partially Malthusian policy. But the problem may need solving in a different manner. The use of Malthusian theory as an argument for ill treatment and lack of charity now seems slowly to be receding.

66

Phenomenology of Spirit

GEORGE WILHELM FRIEDRICH HEGEL

1807

In George Eliot's *Middlemarch* there is an unforgettable character called Edward Casaubon, a clergyman who is engaged in writing, or rather, in preparing to write, a book called *The Key to All Mythologies*. But the book is no more than an idea: It not only never gets finished, but also it never gets started. Would that the unspeakable Prussian, G. W. F. Hegel, had been equally feeble, and that his key to all knowledge had never seen the light of day! But for every ten thousand pathetic Casaubons there is, alas, one Hegel, who actually does write a key to all knowledge. As it is, we are burdened with Hegel's *Phenomenology of Spirit*. Hegel is not without insights and, no doubt at all about it, profundities. His work resembles the "black wall" monument to all those who fell in the Vietnam War in this respect: we should rather do without it, we deplore it, but it must be respected; Hegel's work, however, differs in that it need not, even if it is admired, be honored. Later editions of Hegel's complete works—the 1832–1840 edition brought him great fame and influence—run to many more than the nineteen volumes of that one. It might even be said that whenever the unified Germans are not arranging to dominate the world they are filling in time by extending their Hegel.

In a certain very powerful sense, Hegel deserves the bad reputation he has acquired among the many unfaithful: As a writer he is not merely, like KANT, poor; he is disgusting—murky, so pretentious that he does not even know that he is pretentious—muddled, sometimes almost demonic in the manner by which he conceals his meaning but then works up the consequent vagueness into something that suggests be-all-and-end-all-ness and that Hegel is indeed God, and that the real goal of human history is to learn Hegel's system and then come forever to a blessed and thankful rest.

ARTHUR SCHOPENHAUER reviled Hegel as a charlatan and meretricious scribbler. Many have sympathized with this judgment; and there is much cogency in Schopenhauer's footnote attacks (mixed, unfortunately, with too much abuse) on Hegel in the course of his own masterpiece, which is—as everyone admits—like a glass of clear water after the bleak fog and mud of Hegel. The attack was made not just because Schopenhauer was jealous. He was genuinely affronted by the disingenuous manner by which Hegel—as we shall see—bypassed Kant. He was, too, genuinely offended by Hegel's nationalistic philosophy.

Yet in tracing the progress of world history—even if this was to a large extent no more than the progress of his own blandly optimistic thinking, which took place as if in a hermetically sealed tube protected only by the severe glories of the Prussian monarchy of which he happened to be a loyal subject—Hegel stumbled upon some irresistibly interesting truths and half truths. That he was an ignoble megalomaniac and near-paranoiac, as well as a grim paradigm of the Prussian mentality at its worst, should not deter us from recognizing this.

Hegel was born in Stuttgart in 1770, the son of a petty official all of whose most odious characteristics he, with his superior intellect, dutifully transformed into Higher Things. At the University of Tübingen he studied to become a Lutheran priest—he adhered, officially, to the Lutheran religion for the rest of his life, but the implications of his system reject it quite decisively—but gave this up for philosophy. While at the university he became friendly with the romantic philosopher Friedrich Schelling (1775–1854), and with the poet—one of Germany's indisputably greatest—Friedrich Hölderlin. When he graduated (1793) his certificate remarked on his excellent moral character—and on his inadequate knowledge of philosophy. Upon this judgment Hegel, who was in his way a spiteful man, took horrible revenge, becoming, in Germanic lands, and within his lifetime, the most famous philosopher and, for too many, the one who had invented philosophy anew.

His friend Schelling, it should be noted, was more famous at first—but for the last forty years of his life became a recluse.

Hegel's life was mostly uneventful. In 1801 he took up a position at the University of Jena, where he wrote the *Phenomenology of Spirit* (or *Mind*— *Geist* is conveniently both "mind" and "spirit" in the German language, and hence there are endless quarrels among Hegelians as to what Hegel really meant, the answer to this question still being a flourishing industry). He had the *Phenomenology* in proof form before him on the very eve of the Battle of Jena (1806), Napoleon's victory at which led to the closure of the university and Hegel's departure for Nuremburg. He was for a time, after editing a magazine, the headmaster of the Nuremburg Gymnasium for Boys. He is supposed to have taught its cowed pupils his bizarre system. What the more intelligent of these cowed pupils really thought of the system and of him would be well worth knowing.

Hegel was at the University of Berlin from 1818 until his death in the cholera epidemic of 1831 (from which Schopenhauer escaped). In his lifetime he published four main works: the *Phenomenology*, the *Logic* (1812–1815), the *Encyclopedia* (1817 and subsequent revisions), which is a summary of his system, and the *Philosophy of Right* (1821). The matter of his texts and of the reconstruction of some of the posthumous ones from his lecture notes is problematical—his legacy among his critics was war; but almost all that he wrote has now been put into English, much of which has been the cause of bad feeling, especially over the spirit/mind question. While at Berlin he was extremely famous, as he had always above all wished to be: His overweening ambition and arrogance is, to a disquieting degree, a part of his philosophy. He married in 1816; there were two children of the marriage, one of whom, Karl, became a historian and did much of the editing of the first posthumous *Works*.

Here only an outline can be given of what is most important in Hegel's notoriously complete and perfect system—"perfect" because it amounts to an explanation, if an obviously cooked-up one, of everything.

Kant had denied the possibility of knowledge of the *Ding an sich*, the thing-in-itself. Hegel, as the ambitious explainer of all phenomena, could not remain content with this, and so—rationalist as he was, in the old sense of believing that all knowledge could be derived from the use of reason— became a temporary Berkeleyan empiricist: As an expositor of his philosophy has put it, he argued that "the only grounds for claiming the existence of anything are to be found in consciousness itself." His argument, or so it has seemed to most, is badly flawed (in a technical sense that is beyond the scope of this book); but without it Hegel could not have proceeded, since his philosophy is precisely—this is its only precise feature—an account of the unknowable. To claim that it is uninteresting (especially if you do not have to read it in Hegel's own prose, in which he struggled in vain with a lack of literary technique) would be silly as well as dishonest. But then such a thoroughgoing investigation on the part of anyone could hardly fail to be interesting. We may legitimately sympathize with Schopenhauer:

that a miserable fellow . . . whose entire philosophy is nothing but a monstrous amplification of the ontological explanation [i.e., the proof that God exists, rejected by Protestantism, which replaced it with revelation—and famously demolished by Kant], should desire to defend this proof against Kant . . . is an alliance which the ontological proof itself, little as it knows of shame, might well feel ashamed.

But Hegel did not have the wit or adroitness to appreciate this kind of criticism. There is no laughter in him, and, alas, no laughter in those who still defend his philosophy as a whole. This is a deficiency as grave as he was throughout his days. The greatest influence upon him, undoubtedly, outside philosophy proper, was GOETHE, whose theory of colors he (like Schopenhauer in this) preferred to that of NEWTON. Like many German thinkers of that time, when the sheer genius of Goethe had put such a stranglehold on German literature, his own creative impulses were forced into noncreative channels. But what he made of Goethe's salacious and humorous *Römische Elegian* (*Roman Elegies*, 1795) is anybody's guess. To be sure he did not later read them to the woman who was to become his wife, Marie von Tucher: beat her rigorously he might, so that his sexuality should thus, like the Idea, become conscious of itself (there is no evidence that he did so, of course), but not that. It is a fruitful speculation, hotly relevant; but such levity too often tenses the facial muscles of Hegel's fellow-professors in their public capacity—it is the kind of thing from which they mince away.

The core of his philosophy is that history is mind (or spirit, or God—it is unclear) becoming conscious of itself. The universe is no more nor less than the revelation or unfolding of an absolute idea—or, more simply—for short, absolute. Hegel's idealism does not entail the Berkeleyan notion of matter as nonexistent; that seems to be irrelevant. But how does this absolute work?

Hegel dispensed with traditional logic and substituted for it a logic of dialectic. *Dialectic* derives from the Greek for "argument" or "discourse," and was regarded by Socrates, PLATO, ARISTOTLE, and the Stoic philosophers as a question-and-answer method of elucidating the truth. Sometimes it had been used as a vague synonym for "logic"; but Kant, more precisely, called it "the logic of illusion"—he attacked it as a process of false reasoning which resulted from a vain attempt to understand the unknowable. Hegel, building on post-Kantian work done by Schelling and, in particular, Johann Gottlieb Fichte (1762–1814) raised dialectic to the status of a supreme tool. History itself works by or through it. Mind or the absolute reaches full consciousness of itself by a process of thesis-antithesis-synthesis. But each synthesis becomes a new thesis until we reach Hegel. And so on until we reach the latest development, or synthesis, in Hegel's thinking (which he too often emphasised as "final," as in "final solution"). At the first *being* is the thesis, whose *antithesis* is of course *nothing*. The synthesis is *becoming*. And so, we are told by most commentators, it goes on. In the ancient Orient only one, the ruler, was "free"; in Greece and Rome some were "free"; in Hegel's Prussia all were "free" (but not, it must be added, specifically not, to annoy policeman or to print "seditious material"). Hegel's "freedom" is not the freedom of ordinary people.

Alas! At this point, just as things were becoming clearer, the murk—or so we are informed by some neo-Hegelians—again descends, and dark-yellowish it is. Hegel's "dialectic in general can[not] be reduced to any such three-step"! And it is true that Hegel himself did not employ the terms *thesis, antithesis, synthesis.* But Fichte and Schelling did, and to Fichte in particular Hegel owed a great debt—indeed, most usually his philosophy is explicated in terms used by Fichte (and Schelling) but not by him!

Fichte's "subjective idealism" envisages the universe itself as the outpouring of a fundamental substance, the ego. There are two entities: the self that I am aware of, and the non-ego–everything that I do not regard as myself. The ego is not just me, but a creative agency from which each individual mind derives. Possibly Hegel, envious of Fichte's influence, did not like to employ his terms, and so in adapting his philosophy skated around them. In English versions he does seem often actually to have used these terms, but it appears that his translators were mistaken in rendering such words as "other" or "opposite" as "antithesis". . . . Whether or not these are trivial points is not clear, and remains unresolved. So does what Hegel really meant—if, that is, Hegel really meant anything that can be grasped.

Yet Hegel, like his charlatanic twentieth-century successor Martin Heidegger, is forever circling around and above matters of vital interest: of how ideas develop in minds, of thinking processes, of how (as a famous example) the "master" recognizes himself in his "slave" (and victim), and of how the two eventually switch roles. There is no doubt that some of his insights, when these can be recovered from the sheer muck of his prose, are profound. But his neat notion that the State embodies the reality of Mind's Progress toward Unity with Reason (this is deliberately capitalized, German style), is sinister and is not in accord with reality (with a non-German small *r*). Nor is his idea that "heroes," such as Alexander, Julius Caesar (or Hitler?), who by the dubious virtue of being aware of how to behave violently but with political effectiveness, are immune from Hegel's usually very repressive and Prussian notion of "morality."

Perhaps, on the contrary, the Idea becomes aware of itself in more secret kinds of history: that of the thinking and striving of less determinedly public men, who renounce the Hegelian world. . . . To say, as is so often said by Hegelians, that it is "unfair" to link Hegel's thought to such figures as Stalin or Hitler on the grounds that he would have "hated" their regimes is to say nothing. Doubtless Hegel was a professor of philosophy who really did not have time, in the construction of his grand system, to take note of the sufferings of ordinary people. But he was just that: a professor of philosophy. The nonprofessor SPINOZA's in some (very limited) ways similar solution to the problem of evil is not only more profound. It is more humane, if humanity matters. Evil mattered to Spinoza more than it did to the overexcited, self-absorbed, systematizing Prussian. It shines out in his prose. Yet his "God" is no less "terrible" than Hegel's Idea.

MARX, as we shall see, turned Hegel's philosophy upside down. He simply substituted *matter* for Hegel's *mind* or *spirit*. That this simple substitution could be made (and remember that Spinoza's universe is all matter), is testimony to something wrong in it. Thus, and not only in respect of its contribution to dialectical materialism, Hegel's influence was immense. His grip on philosophy was so tight that even Bertrand Russell (who came to loathe him) began as a Hegelian. The so-called "old," or, better, "right" Hegelians used him to reinforce Protestantism (he had started, in the relatively clear-prosed era of his youth, by proposing a rational alternative to Christianity); the "young," or "left" Hegelians—of whom Marx was one—used his philosophy to try to change the world.

Exported, his absolute idealism became the starting point for the British philosophers A. C. Bradley and J. M. E. McTaggart, and for Josiah Royce in America. The last word, though, should be left to Hegel himself (from *The Philosophy of History*). Of one of his own arguments he wrote: "A result which happens to be known to me, because I have traversed the entire field." That, perhaps, is the true spirit that pervades his philosophy. It may not include concentration camp for those who differ—but it does not exclude it.

67

The World as Will and Idea

ARTHUR SCHOPENHAUER

1819

Arthur Schopenhauer (1788–1860) was supposed to be born in England, but just missed his mother's intentions and was instead born in the port of Danzig, where at that time his father Heinrich had a banking and trading business. His mother was a novelist and writer; from 1806 she ran a salon which Goethe sometimes visited; when her *Collected Works* was published in 1831–32 it ran to twenty-four volumes; she was not a good writer but not a completely bad one, and, although a culture snob, was shrewd and good-humored. She wrote in her posthumously published *My Youthful Life* that a child born in England, though of foreign parents, "becomes thereby an Englishman . . . entitled to all the unpurchasable immunities . . . so valuable to a merchant." But she "wanted to travel," and so her son was born at home. Schopenhauer was angry with his mother, it seems, from birth, and from 1814 until her death in 1838 he never saw her; he thought her frivolous, and she thought him morose—the truth, though, is that they were too fond of each other, and too jealous (he of her success, she of his genius), to get along. There was a younger sister, born in 1796.

In 1793 the free port of Danzig was annexed by the Prussians, and Heinrich—an Anglophile, well educated, and broad-minded, of recognizably Dutch origin—moved to Hamburg. This was the family home until his death, probably by suicide, in 1805. He assumed that Arthur would follow him in commerce but was always enlightened about this wish: In exchange, so to say, for his son's agreement, he allowed him to travel. Arthur was thus in Paris for two years, and in England long enough to attend a school at Wimbledon, on the outskirts of London, for a few months. The key to much of Schopenhauer's truculence, especially against HEGEL, is to be found in his well-educated disdain for that Prussian nationalism and expansionism which would be the main cause of two world wars—a vice from which he was wholly free.

After his father's death Schopenhauer loyally continued in a wretched job as apprentice to a merchant; but in 1807, with his mother's notable agreement, he entered the University at Göttingen, at first to study medicine (to satisfy an impulse to relieve suffering?), but later to learn philosophy. He received his doctorate at Berlin for his first work, *The Fourfold Root of the Principle of Sufficient Reason* (1813). (His mother teased him by supposing that it had been written for herbalists.) The first version of his masterpiece, *The World as Will and Idea* (*Die Welt als Wille Und Vorstellung*, the last word is sometimes translated as *Representation*), followed with remarkable speed in 1818. No one took notice of it at the time, nor did they when it was reissued in considerably amplified form in 1844. But Schopenhauer was given an assistant's post at Berlin. He set himself up as a challenge to Hegel by choosing in 1820 to lecture at the same time and was humiliated; however, he was of a temperament indisposed to see the matter in that light, and, like the French novelist Stendhal, similarly neglected in his time, chose to wait for humanity to wake up to him—which it did in the last decade of his life; nor was he made a prime villain of the twentieth century, as Hegel has very properly been. After the cholera epidemic of 1831 which swept Hegel off, Schopenhauer settled in Frankfurt-am-Main, where he lived for the rest of his life, which—with the exception of his varied erotic life, a splendidly vigorous one which he much regretted when he was not partaking of it—was as ordered as that of his beloved KANT. He read the London *Times* every day and took a regular walk.

The philosophy of Schopenhauer was formed very early in his life; the 1844 edition of his masterwork, while it is certainly the one to use, is essentially an amplification. He gained nothing from either edition in terms of the literary popularity that he desperately if unwillingly craved, but, when the two volumes of his aphoristic essays, *Parega und Pariliponem (Comments and Omissions)* appeared in 1851, he found himself suddenly famous. Attention to, and translations of, *The World as Will and Idea* soon followed, and in the decade before he died he was as famous, if not as philosophically influential, as Hegel.

Like any decent pessimist, he lived a robustly enjoyable life, eating well, amusing others, and slaking his considerable sexual appetite—and, of course, afflicted by anxieties and feelings of unworthiness. His failure to achieve a rapprochement with his beloved mother while she lived became traumatic for him—although it is seldom put in that way—and so it seems that he could never commit himself to a thoroughgoing love, except for his dogs (especially the poodle Atma, "world-soul"), dogs as vital in history as Thomas Hardy's supreme (and overexecrated) dog Wessex.

Schopenhauer starts, essentially, from two premises. One is philosophical; the other is best described as stemming from an emotional conviction that had not been—openly anyway—acknowledged by many other philosophers (unless by HOBBES, whom Schopenhauer admired). Schopenhauer's philosophical premise is from Kant: that there is a difference between the knowable world of phenomena and the unknowable one (noumena). The thing-in-itself Schopenhauer identifies with the *will*, but, as we shall shortly see, his use of this word is a special one.

His other premise is based, truly, in his hatred and fear of cruelty: man's "first and foremost quality," he wrote in his essay on ethics, is "a colossal egoism ready and eager to overstep the bounds of justice"; its "worst trait" is *Schadenfreude* (the untranslatable German word for "pleasure in the misfortunes of others"), which arises when justice would demand compassion in its stead. (EDMUND BURKE gave an English definition of *Schadenfreude* when he wrote, in *On the Sublime and Beautiful:* "I am convinced that we have a degree of delight, and that no small one, in the real misfortunes and pains of others.") Schopenhauer shrewdly saw this as a further perversion of envy. He could not bear to contemplate the state in himself or in others (his tone is often sarcastic, even truculent, and he often sets his opinions above those of others; himself he never sets above others).

Schopenhauer's way into the unknowable is no more nor less than the living body. By being our introspective selves, he believes, we can see into the thing-in-itself. We do experience our bodies in a merely phenomenal way; but, as well, we experience them as expressions of the thing-in-itself. That is, we can experience our actions in two ways: outwardly and inwardly. You can see me eating a piece of bread because I am hungry, and I can see myself doing this; but only I can be actually aware of eating the piece of bread. In this way, I have a special knowledge of my "own willing." Will, then, for

Schopenhauer, is *will to live* and *motivation.* Its end is in its beginning, since all its urge is to relieve itself of its suffering (that is Schopenhauer's definition of pleasure). It thus really seeks its own extinction. (The nature of his influence on FREUD is obvious.)

Schopenhauer had been introduced to Indian philosophy by Goethe (who thought for a time that his philosophy might aid his theory of colors); and then by the romantic critic F. W. Schlegel (who published a bookabout it in 1814); he also read an inadequate but helpful translation of the UPANISHADS (by way of the Persian) by Antéquil du Perron. Hinduism and Buddhism (Hegel had declared that Buddhism "probably" had come first!) much influenced his philosophy, since he regarded the individual will as a part of the will of the entire universe. He recommended, Buddha-like, that we resign ourselves to true extinction, a Nirvana-like quiet. He was thus as "atheist" as Buddha was atheist; but no more. He quotes the Spanish dramatist Calderón with approval: "Man's greatest offense/Is that he everwas born."

Schopenhauer's world, like the Buddhist, is blind and irrational. Art, music above all, is a great consolation; but it is not sufficient. Even forgetting is stupefaction. Renunciation is the only way. That Schopenhauer was not able to perform this renunciation was never a part of his philosophy.

An anticipator of depth psychology, Schopenhauer gave more open attention to sex than any philosopher had before him. He remained obstinate (but amusing) in refusing to ascribe more to "love" than lust ("it may pose as ethereal," but "is rooted in the sexual impulse alone"); he made a profound point when he described how "the sexual impulse," a "subjective need," had the "knack of skillfully assuming the role of objective admiration and hereby deceiving our consciousness." One is here reminded of PARETO, whose influence, although rather more subterranean and more recent, has also been very great. But in the midst of all this pre-Freudian intelligence and welcome plain-speaking Schopenhauer did miss the possibility that sexual activity could contain, for all its usual seat in mere lust—the will at its most rampant, raging, so he claimed, to perpetuate the sorrow of life by creating more of it—another element: a unique enhancement of life.

Schopenhauer might, indeed, have taken a completely different direction as soon as he had found his way into Kant's unknowable. But the dogs he loved were not women. As it is, his pessimism often seems forced as well as glamourized: it is as if he is almost willfully taking the gloomy direction, ignoring the yearning in the will for the divine. His appeal has been mostly to writers—he himself wrote as well as any philosopher has ever written—rather than to professional philosophers; but a few of the latter accept that he made a potent point when he declared that the body was the way into the otherwise unknowable. He denied that suicide was a valid way to achieve renunciation on the grounds that it was itself an assertion of the will. Yet he did not, it seems, accept the Buddhist doctrine of the transmigration of souls (he does, however, discuss this briefly, and not unsympathetically—it may be that he did believe in it, but could not bring himself to say so). Yet really, one thinks, he denied the efficacy of suicide because he so enjoyed his career as a pessimist (like Thomas Hardy, his reader, whose compassion for animals is so often linked with his name).

The many European failed revolutions of 1848 spread much disillusion, and made pessimism both popular and fashionable. This may be one of the reasons why readers suddenly took up Schopenhauer. It is a great irony that he should now give us so much pleasure, intelligent food for thought, and relief from our own pain; but perhaps that was what he had intended all along.

He is often said to have been singularly lacking in compassion for other people. But that is not true. He could not keep away from those of that sex which he is supposed to have "loathed" and which he amusingly and provocatively attacked in his deliberately preposterous essay upon women; he left his fortune to the relief of suffering; he loved his dogs; and his inner compassion was his own.

Course in the
Positivist Philosophy

AUGUSTE COMTE

1830–1842

Auguste Comte (full name Isidore-Auguste-Marie-François-Xavier Comte) had a huge influence—some of it exercised by way of the Englishwoman Harriet Martineau's 1853 translation of his book—but in himself did not amount to much. It is initially surprising, though, to find just how seriously he was taken in his own century: by MARX (upon whom he was a seminal influence), JOHN STUART MILL, George Eliot, her partner George Henry Lewes, Thomas Hardy, and by many more French, English, and American thinkers and writers. These, no doubt, were people who had lost their faith, in varying degrees, in Christianity, but did not wish to forgo what they thought might be its genuine advantages.

The Comtean endeavor to form a "secular church" might now be seen as doomed from the start, since an atheist or at least agnostic position can hardly, in an individual, give rise to a logically religious one. A belief in the sacredness of humanity alone cannot replace one in something that is outside or above humanity. But, largely owing to the work of Durkheim, not a few have tried to find in what he called the "collective conscience" of mankind some sort of valid substitute for God. It was a necessary experiment. Durkheim, though an unbeliever—a rationalist in the newer sense of the word—did not despise what he called the Sacred: On the contrary, he wished to discover its true sources. It could even be said that he found that a form of religion was not, after all, wanting—but that he could not bear to admit this.

Comte, however, a lesser man in every sense, is nonetheless of very great historical importance—and Durkheim, like Mill, took him seriously. Comte's English translator and condenser, Harriet Martineau (1802–1876), was a novelist who began as a devout Unitarian and then became influenced by Jeremy Bentham and John Stuart Mill; eventually she became a British reformist celebrity.

Both Comte's immediate predecessor and erstwhile employer, the Comte Claude-Henri de Rouvroy Saint-Simon (1760–1825), and, as we have seen, the chief of his successors (still a great man by any standards) Emile Durkheim (1858–1917), were intrinsically more important and original— Comte himself was hardly original at all, unless in his genius for classification. Yet he did coin the word *sociology* (on an analogy with "biology"), and he certainly is fairly regarded as, for all that he does not deserve to be (or anything else, much), the founding father of empirical and "positivist" sociology. He thought that people could be dealt with on as scientific a basis as can snails or the movements of planets. For him the word *positive* was synonymous with *scientific*. And it is through him that we usually have to approach the more valuable ideas of VICO, Montesquieu, and Saint-Simon. Only sociologists, probably, value sociology very highly; they have given Comte a rather better press than he deserves, and many of them are still hoping that society can come under a purely scientific microscope—one employing, that is, essentially the same methodology used in experiments with inorganic chemicals and so forth.

It is instructive that the notoriously exact and rational systematizer Comte led the most miserable of lives. As the meticulous enemy of his own interests, he relentlessly caused his own misery. Egocentric to a pathological degree, sentimental and without consideration for the feelings of others, and of an emotional naiveté astonishing in so genuinely gifted a systematizer, he was also an extremely bold and relentlessly logical academician—sufficiently bold to be quite oblivious to any form of psychological reality. That gave him his temporary strength and power to influence. His mean mind lined up the more fecund ideas of his predecessors and seemed to many, for a time, to have made logical sense of them. Secular religions on his lines were founded in America, Great Britain and elsewhere.

Born in Montpellier in 1798, Comte had as disastrous a start as a human being can: His father was a senior tax collector. He survived this, and, precocious in his studies at his Paris school, managed to effect its temporary closure when he led a student uprising. Soon afterward he became a secretary to and associate of Saint-Simon. It was Saint-Simon, a utopian socialist of conservative leanings and progressive beliefs, who generated—but in a piecemeal form—most of the ideas that Comte later elaborated and systematized. Saint-Simon, who had fought in the American Revolution and been threatened in the French (for all that he was a sympathizer), saw society as evolving through three stages: "theological" (fictitious), "metaphysical" (abstract), and "positivist" (scientific and therefore true). He based his thinking on the single case of the rise of modern industrial society from the feudalism of the Middle Ages. He did not believe that traditional Christianity was devoid of virtue, but he did believe that a Christian society bore within it the seeds of its own decay; it failed to cater to the needs of those dominant in the economic field. Hence his influence on Marx. But what Saint-Simon wrote about his belief in a spiritual as well as temporal mode of conduct demonstrates that he was not quite as simpleminded as his disciple—who quarreled with him, however, in 1824, over the matter of the publication of a jointly written book.

In Comte's hands, although deriving in essence from Saint-Simon—and with notions taken from one or two other thinkers, such as Condorcet (The *Sketch for a Historical Picture of the Human Mind*) and the French economist Anne Turgot—the theological-metaphysical-positivist cycle was thus represented: At the theological stage man relies on supernatural agencies to explain what he can't explain otherwise; at the metaphysical stage he attributes effects to abstract but insufficiently understood causes. It is only at the positive stage that he at last understands the purely scientific laws which control the world. Thus super- or preternatural causes are thrown out; Durkheim also thought he had thrown these out, but his investigation of what they might mean was more profound. Comte, though, believed that man, in the spirit of science, could himself control the world; the way is open to Utopia. This scheme was so simple, as presented by Comte in his enormous work— which was impressive and seemed, and even in a sense was, erudite—that it appealed, too widely, to both Victorian optimism and (badly premature, as it turned out) confidence in the all-encompassing powers of scientific method. Eventually the Marxian direction would dominate. But for the time being Comte triumphed, perhaps mainly because of his very lack of subtlety and his ignorance of the actual ways of the world. For science has notably failed to solve problems of human conflict, famine and plagues and, though its methodology remains necessary in certain investigations, is inadequate in itself—either to control or to explain the world.

It was the next stage in Comte's thinking, again deriving from Saint-

Simon, that particularly influenced Durkheim. Comte set out to found a positivist, i.e., a nonreligious, "church." The English Darwinist T. H. Huxley accurately defined it as "Catholicism without Christianity." Comte's *Positivist Calendar* (1849) lists the great secular saints: Frederick the Great, ADAM SMITH, and so on. This was in the interests of the "Religion of Humanity," in which Humanity instead of God was worshiped, and in which men would be prompted by Love and Altruism in just that manner in which Comte himself was specifically not—there has to be some significance in this. Saint-Simon's *industriels*, captains of industry, would be the rulers, and the "priests" would be newly enlightened Comtean philosophers. In a bizarre development, the love of Comte's life (he and his wife separated, he being unlivable with), Clothide Devaux, became on her early death the high priestess of the Religion of Humanity. Meanwhile he quarreled with his chief French disciple, Emile Littré, and with John Stuart Mill—who went on trying to help him financially until he, too, had to give up in the face of Comte's ill-natured greed.

To his credit, Comte was not reductionist; he remained strongly evolutionist in his views. Thus, each branch of knowledge cannot make true progress until it has evolved from a "primitive" state. He was meticulous, possibly too meticulous, in his observation of this. He understood everything so perfectly that perhaps in reality he understood nothing at all. He was far too confident, too, that everything that was not what he called scientific was pure nonsense.

69

On War

CARL MARIE VON CLAUSEWITZ

1832

Carl von Clausewitz (1780–1831) was not a philosopher, although military historians such as Ernest and Trevor Dupuy, in their invaluable but perhaps slightly naive *Encyclopedia of Military History,* have described him as "the greatest philosopher of war." That is not, perhaps, to strain too unduly the meaning of *philosophy;* but it is to expose, unwittingly, the general emotional poverty, the inhumanity, of grand-scale military thinkers. For it is unhappily arguable that this dour Prussian exercised as much influence as many true philosophers—and, what's more, possibly, stopped thousands more from ever needing to think about philosophy or anything else.

Or is that fair? Hardly. Clausewitz's career in the army was distinguished but not outstanding. He was of higher servant, not leader, mentality. Has he been more discussed than actually influential? Well, no one who wants to talk about strategy can or is even allowed to ignore him; his name is well known in every military college in the world. Is it his avid reader the Prussian field marshal Helmuth Karl Bernhard, Graf von Moltke (1800–1891), who deserves the blame—if, of course, we feel that any blame is to be apportioned? Why should it? War is a fact of life.

Clausewitz is most celebrated and most widely quoted outside military circles for his impeccable but chilling and bureaucratic definition, "War is only a continuation of state policy by other means." It is more or less received thinking, especially among professors unacquainted with the inconveniences associated with wars, to hasten to remind us that his doctrine is no more than a "logical deduction from existing conditions." But there is little doubt that Clausewitz well deserves his reputation as a warmonger, even if he did not actually have the capacity to be one: his essentially Prussian nature did not appreciate the lazy and often even downright unpatriotic conditions of peacetime existence. For example, he wrote, again of war, that it was "an act of violence intended to compel our opponent to fulfill our will." This has a ring all too familiar in the twentieth century.

He also wrote: "To introduce into the philosophy of war a principle of moderation would be absurd"; "Let us not hear about generals who conquer without bloodshed"; "Rather than compare war to art, we should more precisely compare it to commerce, which is also a conflict of interests and activities; and it is closer still to politics, which, in its turn, is a kind of commerce, but on a larger scale." It is hardly surprising that there are schools of American businessmen who swear, almost lubriciously, by Clausewitz. An Internet magazine called the *Crisis Manager* refers to Vince Lombardi, the famous coach of the Green Bay Packers, as being a sort of Clausewitz of football: "You gotta go out there and beat the other guy"—and, the *Crisis Manager* sums up, "That is, football=war=politics=business." It is a delicate and cultured group, with many debts to Clausewitz, and it no doubt benevolently controls some of whatever money you or I have left after compulsory deductions and debts to usurers and zealous tax officials.

Clausewitz's only rivals are, from the distant past, the Chinese general and military writer Sun Tzu (about 500 B.C.E.), author of *The Art of War (Ping-fa)*, and, from his own times, his almost exact contemporary, the Swiss-born Antoine Henri Jomini. The first could be as ferociously pragmatic as Clausewitz, but possessed a mellowness he entirely lacked; he wrote in a genuinely philosophical vein, and has had little influence outside China—but recently the men (unless it could be women?) who run the *Crisis Manager* and its like have praised his *Art of War* as "outstanding." It has given them new ideas: "Treat conquered people benevolently, *and they will join you*" (my italics); and "You need popular commitment to wage war" (there are techniques to arrange this). Sun Tzu believed that people should be treated benevolently *anyway* and has recently persuaded the *Crisis Manager* that this *can pay*, too. But Sun Tzu recognized a "moral law" simply not in evidence in Clausewitz. Modern military strategists always begin with Clausewitz.

Ought they perhaps to begin with Jomini? A protégé of Marshal Ney, he had served as a junior officer under Napoleon, but later was treated so unfairly that he offered his services to the Russians in 1813. Thereafter, until he was ninety, he served as a general officer in the Russian army. His *Summary of the Art of War* is said to have presented, for the first time in writing, "the fundamental principles of warfare which today are taken for granted by all military men"—but he is not quoted as often as Clausewitz, or as well known as the Prussian clerk.

Clausewitz has been defended as a brilliant pragmatist who was by no means a militarist. His Kantian purpose, it is claimed, was not to glorify war, but to put it into proper perspective. That, however, might be a little too generous: in awarding him an interest in the humdrum life experienced in peacetime that he just did not possess. Isolated quotations from *On War* can make him sound a little like MACHIAVELLI; but, left unrevised at his death, it is a confused and inconsistently written work—his other writings, all painstakingly tedious, are histories of campaigns, and took up ten volumes as *Hinterlassene Werke* (*Remains*, 1832–1837), in which *On War* first appeared. They, like *On War,* are undistinguished by lucidity, style, wit, or any trace of irony. Clausewitz was not a good writer. However, he might have expressed his disagreement with the words of Genghis Khan (probably the finest military genius the world has yet known, and certainly more successful than Napoleon): "The greatest joy is to vanquish enemies, chase them, tear their wealth from them, watch those who love them weep, and sexually enjoy their wives and daughters."

Clausewitz was born at Burg near Magdeburg, and enrolled in the German army as an ensign at the age of twenty-two. He fought with the Prussians in all the campaigns against his hero Napoleon, from the disaster at Jena (at which he was taken prisoner) to the victory at Waterloo. He spent much of the 1790s on garrison duty, which gave him the opportunity to study what he thought of, ambitiously and Prussian-style, as "the art of war." He soon attracted the attention of General Scharnhorst, and had been, through Scharnhorst, military instructor to the Prussian crown prince for two years when, in common with other Prussian patriots, he resigned his commission on the eve of Napoleon's adventure in Russia. Between 1812 and 1814 he served as a staff officer in the Russian army—did he then meet Jomini?—and returned to the Prussian service and was chief of staff at Waterloo. From 1818 until 1830 he was the director of the War Academy in Berlin, which he had himself attended. He was a victim of the 1831 cholera epidemic at Breslau.

But Clausewitz, though not an admirable stylist—he is like a drill sergeant writing in barracks under orders—was sensible and logical enough when launched upon the subject that obsessed him: war. A central feature of his "absolute-war" theory, which culminated in Hitlerism, is his concept of "military genius": "What genius does is the best rule, and theory can do no better than show why and how this ought to be the case." The key quality to be possessed by the military genius, who is of course brave, bold, capable of endurance and a high degree of self-control, is "understanding of human nature," which amounts, for Clausewitz, in recognizing that everyone longs for honor, renown and advancement.

"No wonder," he woodenly remarks, to the delight of military experts and their businessmen followers, "that war, though it may appear to be uncomplicated, cannot be waged with distinction except by men of out-standing intellect." To be the possessor of an "outstanding intellect" is a prize much desired by businessmen of this type, and they have enough money to announce that they have attained it. Clausewitz indulges himself in much similarly meticulous but exceedingly obvious analysis of the military genius, who is an "expert" who can "make sense out of chaos" and who quickly recognizes truths and knows when to make exceptions. Some military genius, one feels, was known and understood by Clausewitz—and indeed he was, for he was none other than his enemy, Napoleon. And *On War* is not much more than a series of stilted observations of Bonapartism.

Clausewitz's know-how is sourly acknowledged by one James Shanteau in his *Psychological Characteristics of Expert Decision Makers,* published, appropriately, in Berlin (1987). War is now making a comeback where it may have been absent for far too long. Nor is there yet much recognition of the pronouncement made by no less an authority than Lucky Luciano some sixty years back: "We can do all this without killing so many people." Missing from Clausewitz is, of course, any sense of what might be humane or otherwise. "Eternal peace is a dream, and not even a pleasant one," wrote Clausewitz's admirer Moltke; and, the *Crisis Manager* tells us, Armand Felgenbaum, "father of Total Quality Control," "stresses the same idea." The crudity, obvi-ousness, and solemn philistinism of all this might well be traced back to, among other writings, Clausewitz's *On War,* unredeemed as it is by grace, charm, or humanity. One wonders what his reading might have been; if Goethe was included among it, as almost certainly he must have been, then this emphasizes the plain fact that a nation can entirely ignore the spirit of the writer they themselves claim to cherish.

The Dupuys point out in their *Encyclopedia of Military History* that Clausewitz's ideas have strongly influenced every army, and, they add, even "his critics—discarding his basic theories mostly because these theories have been so distorted by German military men in the twentieth century—still repeat many of his observations." The fact is, though, that his "theories," a series of abstracts from accounts of successful military practice, lent them-selves to such "distortion" because they were conceived outside the bound-aries of what is called morality. His treatise has all the indifferent obscurity of the instructions on a can of beans on how to open it. And his analytical qual-ity is low. He never, for example, tries to tell us in any detail what really con-stitutes a military genius: He is just a fortunate product of Prussian education, a man who, in the words of Shanteau, "extracts the essence from the phe-nomena of life, as a bee sucks honey from a flower." "Bonaparte rightly said . . . that many of the decisions faced by the commander in chief resem-ble mathematical problems worthy of the gifts of a *Newton,* . . ." wrote Clausewitz. So, if he was not a warmonger, he was nevertheless full of hyper-bolic praise for those who were. That is really the same as being one.

Full of a very common kind of common sense though it is, *On War* is not without bland idealism: The military genius must, thinks the author, be intimately acquainted with politics and policy, otherwise he might wage a war that could not be won. (The notion of waging a war because war, in general, is wrong, is not dealt with.) But the conduct of a war, he insists, must be firmly in civilian hands. Yet Clausewitz was a disciple of KANT. He took absolute war as a "thing-in-itself" and studied a model of it. It was a gross violation of that usually gentle philosopher.

Clausewitz failed to see, or did not want to see, that the Bonapartism that he admired above all would lead to Hitlerism—or his imagination was too limited for this to be an issue at all with him. So far as influence itself is concerned, he certainly played his part in the unification of Germany, since Bismarck's claim never to have read him is quite irrelevant—Moltke had. His ideas seemed outmoded by the end of World War I, but Hitler's *blitzkrieg* is essentially Clausewitzian; Henry Kissinger belonged to a school that was actually referred to as "neo-Clausewitzian." Now, however, it is asserted (and not only by the *Crisis Manager*) that "Clausewitz . . . told Lyndon B. Johnson why he would lose the Vietnam War: 'Wearing down the enemy in a conflict means *using the duration of the war to bring about a gradual exhaustion of his physical and moral resistance . . .*' " Likewise, "The same lessons apply to marketing, e.g., fighting a protracted campaign for a mature or declining market." It seems as though Clausewitz, with his nice habit of ignoring the costs of war altogether, will be looked to for some time to come—in the nuclear as well as in the business field.

70

Either/Or

SØREN KIERKEGAARD

1843

Either an intense and absolute subjectivity, *or* a false and dingy objectivity that is not even, really, objectivity at all. The Danish theologian, satirist, and philosopher Søren Kierkegaard, archenemy of the HEGEL, who so influenced him in his student days—he did more salutary damage to Hegel than to any other writer, especially when writing as "Johannes Climacus," essentially by showing him up as, an ultimately inert systematizer and therefore a man almost as spiritually dangerous as a cherished institution—is among the half dozen or so nineteenth-century thinkers who has been decisive to twentieth-century thought.

Like NIETZSCHE, he was an unhappy, neurotic, and terribly suffering man—even the proverbial "pain in the neck"—but also one endowed with a faculty for producing aphorisms of great power and wisdom. He has been attacked for being overmorbid; few have suggested that he has nothing of value to say. Some prefer his less ambiguous message to the high-pitched one of Nietzsche: The real direction of his thinking, which is nonpolitical, is not as hard to follow, he was not as near to sheer craziness (after all, Nietzsche did become mad), not as indignant, and he was not as formidably learned and, therefore, as cluttered up with historical knowledge.

He was born in 1813 in Copenhagen, of parents already middle-aged. His mother Ane had been a household servant during her husband's Michael's first marriage, and was already pregnant when she married him. Michael had become so successful in the wool trade and with a fortunate investment that he had been able to retire at age forty (he was fifty-six at Søren's birth). But once, in his poverty-stricken youth, he had cursed God; now, a man subject to pathological fits of melancholy, he marked this incident off as the first in a series, all of which were to demonstrate his fate: to be cursed of God, and have his also cursed progeny disappear without trace.

Michael left an indelible mark on his son. He dwelled continually upon the sufferings of Christ rather than upon his redeeming qualities. Søren said that "humanly speaking," he had been "insanely brought up." As susceptible to melancholy as his father, he was infinitely more flexible, witty, and sophisticated. It might be said that he paid the price of his father's depression, but that he transformed it into wisdom. He remained dedicated to him and to his memory.

In 1830 Søren entered the university, and remained there, indecisively, for a decade. He studied theology and philosophy, and for the priesthood, enthused over and then reacted against Hegel, went through a period of drinking and debauchery, got into debt, and in 1834 began to keep his famous *Journal*. He had decided by 1835 that first of all he must know himself, before he could know what to do with his life. Apart from being a journalist and a very productive writer he never really did "do," in the conventional sense, any more "with" his life. He had adequate means: they ran out on the very day of his death in 1855.

He became engaged to an understanding girl named Regine when she was eighteen, but he broke off the engagement on the grounds that he was "a scoundrel of the first water" and a "seducer": he said, with the terrible and self-destructive irony that became increasingly his hallmark, "Well, in about ten years, when I have sown my wild oats, I must have a pretty young miss to rejuvenate me!" Such a man knew too much, and he could not forget it. He was an—as Arthur Koestler said the Jews as a race were *the*—"exposed nerve of humanity." He had had by the time of his crisis with Regine a profound religious experience, (May 19, 1838) which can only be called mystical: "*Half-past ten in the morning*. There is an indescribable joy which kindles us as the apostle's outburst comes gratuitously: 'Rejoice, I say unto you, and again I say unto you rejoice.'" When his father died in that August he felt that he had "*died for me* in order that if possible I might turn into something."

Kierkegaard turned "respectable" theology upon its head by insisting that subjectivity is the only sort of truth worth knowing. He recognized that he was himself constituted of a number of different and even warring selves. Thus his use of a number of pseudonyms, none of whom "agreed" with one another. Always he was in search of a unifying "I." (This idea, that human beings consist of a number of different I's, not all in concordance—indeed, in disarray—would be an essential feature of the teachings of GURDJIEFF.)

Kierkegaard was well known in Copenhagen as an actively polemical enemy of the established (Lutheran) church. He came to feel that the popular monarchy and the so-called people's church established in Denmark as a result of the 1848 revolutions in Europe (he saw these as wholly irrelevant) were mere pretenses: "finite institutions catastrophically usurping the true role of religion." Like the angry, impatient early Christian Tertullian, but for different, more intelligent reasons, he saw the root of Christianity to lie in its "absurdity."

The Christian (he believed) is well aware that no rational inquiry can support his belief: It is from that viewpoint that it is "absurd." What is *unthinkable* is immune from reason which is "crucified" in faith.

What, many have asked, can be the positive element in such a system? The answer is a life lived as Christ's was lived: in love.

Wittgenstein was sufficiently persuaded to pronounce Kierkegaard the "most profound thinker of the last century." But for the positive content in this strange writer it is necessary to go to the works themselves: it is only by measuring Kierkegaard's mastery of the inner psychology of human beings that one can begin to grasp the import of what he says. Naturally, his "absurdity" has been appropriated by both atheists (such as Sartre) and by those more eclectic in their choices of religions—BUBER is unthinkable without Kierkegaard, but he adds to him by taking away Christianity's terrible exclusiveness—that is not assumed in Kierkegaard, but he did not have time to deal with the problem, and he studied PASCAL rather than other religions. It is not that Kierkegaard was himself exclusive, or that he would have regarded people who never knew of Christianity as in any kind of awful spiritual predicament: It is, rather, that the work he did was all done within the framework of official—and, as he saw it, disingenuous—Christianity. He refused to be a priest because he thought it more urgent to oppose a dishonest church. But of course he respected some men inside the church, and there were many who respected him.

Kierkegaard wrote a number of books, all expressing very different points of view: *Purity of Heart Is to Will One Thing* (1847), taking its motto from the NEW TESTAMENT ("purify your hearts, ye double-minded"), characteristically deals with the problem of doing good for good's pure sake, and not for pride's sake or for that of getting reward or avoiding punishment. It is possibly the most enlightening and realistic discussion of this subject ever undertaken.

Either/Or: A Fragment of Life (1843) was Kierkegaard's first substantial work. (The title in Danish is *Euten-Elle*.) I have chosen it here because it has exercised the most fascination of all this author's fascinating works. Why is he so fascinating? Because he knows so much about the inner life, the stream-of-consciousness, because he emphasized *inwardness*. If Kierkegaard is indu-

bitably neurotic, he is as formidably intelligent. He knows far too much to be a moralist, an atheist, or anything else so silly and self-indulgent.

Either/Or is issued by an "editor," Victor Eremita ("victorious seclusion"?), who claims to have come across the papers of which it consists quite serendipitously. This is no clever presentation of arguments pro and con *à la* George Bernard Shaw. On the contrary, the arguers are genuine *dramatis personae,* convinced of their "rightness." Its intention, though, for all its imaginative honesty (it is, after all, not a tract but a work of fiction), is to change its readers' attitudes. Indeed, it has done so remarkably often.

The first volume is devoted to the hedonistic or, as Kierkegaard ironically calls it, the "aesthetic," life—it contains remarks on music, the famous "seducer's diary," and many other essays. It is of course a self-portrait of Kierkegaard, or, rather, of how he often felt. It is quite extraordinarily "knowing" about how such people lived (and live).

The second volume, by a married "Judge William," presents an alternative: the reflective life, yet not so turned in on itself because outwardly considering. Kierkegaard himself wrote (in his *Journals*) that he had shown marriage as "Or," but "it was not my life's Or."

Either/or set up the antithesis that Kierkegaard would explore (and ironize about) in his remaining works. He knew that his behavior toward Regine (at least) had been repulsive (it would be against the spirit of his whole work to defend it). In a sense his *Concept of Dread* (1844) is a result of what he learned from the melancholy guilt that this behavior induced in him. Here he introduced to the world the idea of what, after the Second World War and with the advent of the philosophy of JEAN-PAUL SARTRE, became popular as *angst*.

Kierkegaard, accurately enough, ascribed the feeling of *angst* to every enlightened person. Existence, at least since the collapse of religion as a universal consolation, has to be seen in the light of infinite and terrifying possibilities. In the *Journals* (May 1843) he had discussed the matter in relation to his rejection of Regine:

> But if I had to explain myself, I should have had to initiate her
> into terrible things, my relation with my father, his melancholy,

the eternal darkness that broods deep within, my going astray, pleasures and excesses which in the eyes of God are not perhaps so terrible, for *it was dread which drove me to excess,* and where was I to look for something to hold on to when I knew, or suspected that the one man I revered for his strength and power had wavered.

Dread explains, for Kierkegaard, the need for fulfillment, the need to return to the innocence that (according to him) each man loses in essentially the same way as Adam lost his. In *Either/Or* the semimythical figure of Don Juan is analyzed at some length; in him, his dread *is* his sexual energy.

Kierkegaard, because of his legacy to the century after his own, could be called as witness to the results of the universal loss of faith. But it is not quite as simple as that. For he may also be called as witness to the results of why faith collapsed. Paradoxically, he represents the essence of individualist Protestantism, yet he challenges the good faith of its church. Just possibly his greatest contribution, however, apart from his priceless self-analysis (he reminds one of the terrible saying, "Judge others by yourself: you will not be far mistaken"), is his demonstration that Hegelianism has a profound contempt for the individual. We long above all for a dialogue between him and Nietzsche, on level terms.

71

The Manifesto of the Communist Party

KARL MARX AND FRIEDRICH ENGELS

1848

Some may ask why *The Manifesto of the Communist Party* rather than *Das Kapital* (1867–1893)—Karl Marx's main work, although he wrote a number of others—has been chosen here. Is this cheating? Perhaps. But to have chosen *Das Kapital*, the last two uncompleted volumes of which were edited by Engels and published after Marx's death, would in a way have been cheating, too: did not the late Sir Isaiah Berlin, whose book about Marx (*Karl Marx: His Life and Environment*, 1939, revised subsequently) is the one most frequently recommended as by far the best introduction, declare on the British radio, just before his death in 1997, that he had not himself got beyond the first volume?—thus adding a sort of respectability to an old joke.

The truth is that Marx, like HEGEL, does not make for easy reading, does not achieve "simplicity"; and so most of us—every professional, it seems, *not* apart—have read no more than potted editions of his works in more or less responsibly made selections. In fact, the sheer unreadability of vast tracts of Marx's works (excepting what is in fact aphoristic in nature) raises a quite serious problem, and it might well be that his manifest confusions (no one calls him a philosopher) are reflected in this dogged and Teutonic unreadability. The now sinisterly popular Mark Heidegger, too, is notoriously unreadable, but then he was a keen Nazi until the end, an anti-Semite, an opportunist, and a fraud; Marx was no fraud, and it is of no use whatsoever to blame him for the atrocities that have been committed in his name. True, he did believe that his vision of the future of mankind was so beautiful—and it does have a sort of beauty—that it was well worth indulging in violence, a violence that was inevitable anyhow (he would have said), in order to reach that state. He can most certainly be blamed for that; he should be blamed for it (and for the unconsidered atheism from which such a belief sprung). But he need not, perhaps, be faulted for assuming that the rulers of this world are not going to renounce their advantages without resorting to violence themselves (it is sometimes called "eternal vigilance"). Marx was confused, often naïve, and was actually most gifted at what he most despised: compassionate analysis of individuals' states of mind.

By contrast to *Das Kapital,* the *Manifesto,* although written before Marx had fully elaborated his system of historical materialism (called "dialectical materialism" only after his death, by the Russian Marxist theoretician Georgii Valentinovich Plekhanov, the "father of Russian Marxism"), is written in an especially clear style, calculated to be understood by the workers of the world whom, explicitly, it urges to unite in revolution against their lot. Furthermore, in *The Economical and Philosophical Manuscripts of 1844,* which did not become available until the 1930s, he had already formed his basic ideas.

If that view be challenged, then, surely, he had formed those ideas by which he influenced history. History in itself never observes subtleties, and it may indeed produce—as TOLSTOY believed—both "the influential books" *and* the subsequent events in order to "take its course." (It is important to recognize that the many failed revolutions that took place in the Europe of 1848 were in no way influenced by the *Manifesto:* They were on their way, and that influenced Marx). Besides, the *Manifesto* has been described, very properly, as a "pristine and unmodified summary of Karl Marx's revolutionary views. . . . [It throws] together Marx's hopes and theories in one spontaneous flurry."

Karl Heinrich Marx was born in 1818 in the Rhenish city of Trier, into the family of a successful Jewish lawyer who converted to Christianity (i.e., became "assimilated") in 1817. He was raised as a Protestant but lost his religious beliefs early. He studied law at the universities of Bonn and Berlin, but then, at first under the sway of Hegel, abandoned this for history and philosophy. He married in 1843 and went to France in the following year. In 1848 he settled in London, enduring for many years great poverty (at one point his sole means of sustenance came from an American publication, which paid him at the rate of about four dollars per article); after 1864 Engels was able to relieve his poverty somewhat; he died there in 1883. Engels, although Marx's faithful and efficient collaborator and editor, made only a very marginal contribution to the writings. The *Manifesto* itself was a result of his questions and Marx's answers to them.

The essence of Marxism is contained in the following famous statement (1845) from his writings: "The philosophers have only interpreted the world in various ways, the point is to change it."

This means that, to Marx, all the problems of philosophy—with which in fact he did not have much patience, and in which he thought he ought to have but little real interest—arise because of the manner in which the social world is organized. When this method of organization has been changed then there will be no more philosophical problems. The Heaven of the Christians will exist here, on earth, in properly concrete terms that will make all speculation absurd and unnecessary. This Heaven is communism, which is in any case inevitable. However, that it is inevitable does not mean that we should not hurry it along. As the *Manifesto* has it at its ending:

> The Communists disdain to conceal their views and aims. They openly declare that their ends can be attained only by the forcible overthrow of all existing social conditions. Let the ruling classes tremble at a Communistic revolution. The proletarians have nothing to lose but their chains. They have a world to win.

WORKING MEN OF ALL COUNTRIES, UNITE!

Hegel, a romantic philosophical idealist of immense fecundity who hid his rich and suggestive muddle under an appearance of rigor (and who also managed to revel in the repressive Prussian state), had seen history as spirit becoming aware of itself, by means of a dialectical process. The energy that drove all this came from God, though not from a Christian God (perhaps he resembled Hegel slightly more than that God). In his murky way Hegel did hit on fundamental truths, especially in the realm of how our world *becomes* as it goes along. But he was not able to leave a clear message, and so we are rightly infuriated by him—his philosophy comes so near and yet is so far. Its essence may be found in the poetry of his friend Hölderlin; but Hölderlin became mad.

The so-called "Old Hegelians" were conservatives who admired the Prussian state, and who tried to emphasize the dubiously Christian elements in their master's scheme. The much livelier "Young Hegelians," however, were liberal and left-wing. They deplored the Prussian state as only a nasty moment in the development of history, and so wished to drag the Great Process into what they thought of as the real world. Hegel's student Ludwig

Feuerbach in *Thoughts Regarding Death and Immortality* (1830) and in particular in *The Essence of Christianity* (1841)—this was translated into English by the novelist George Eliot—the single book that most influenced the young Marx (though he went far beyond it), did not quite deny the existence of God, but he did argue against the idea of the Christian God as anything more than a necessary but strictly temporary phenomenon. That God, Feuerbach maintained, in an almost existentialist formulation, was no more than the essence of man himself: abstracted, falsely "objectified," and then worshiped. The next stage must therefore be to replace man's love of God for man's love of Man.

Title page of *The Communist Manifesto*

Thus Hegel's philosophy is reversed—and so for Marx, if not for Feuerbach, it could then be cast aside. As Marx himself wrote (my italics): *"It is not consciousness that determines existence, it is existence that determines consciousness."*

In Marxian theory the individual is nothing—or almost nothing. He is determined by society. Yet many of Marx's most enduring and exquisite insights are into what can only be described as individual experience; and he was certainly himself a compassionate man, driven first and foremost by a wish for justice. He increasingly insisted, however, that his theory was no less than a *science* of human progress. He is a fine example of the humane and imaginative man turned into overenthusiastic positivist scientist—one whose imagination fails him when he finds that he cannot envisage God (the incomprehensible intelligence informing the universe) as "being a scientist."

Marxist-Leninism became the first secular religion. The Soviet version of this—and the Russian empire—collapsed at the end of the twentieth century. But Marxist theory in itself has plenty more life in it, and no doubt especially in that development of it in which Marx's own denial of religion—not, however, that he himself ever underestimated the quality of religious feelings—has been modified by many Christian Marxists of the twentieth century.

For Marx, who was as much influenced by ADAM SMITH as anyone on the right of the political spectrum, the battleground would be the economic one of industrial production. When the battle was won, everyone one would be free. Society would be free of class distinctions. He pointed out that, in the present situation, a man's labor produced a value over and above that which was needed to satisfy its needs. The resulting surplus became capital for the bourgeois owners of production. Marx himself did not in fact believe that noble workers were personally superior to wicked bourgeois owners—he was not so stupid—but of course many others, including intellectuals, came to do so; thus the ideas of a nonsentimental man soon became aggressively sentimentalized. His prophecy was that accumulation of surplus value, together with the competitive struggle for fewer and fewer markets, would bring capitalism down.

But this has not happened; nor did it happen like that in Russia in 1917—there was no capitalist development there at the time.

Part of the prophecy involved the worsening lot of the proletariat (who would explode when their lot became unbearable). In fact there has been a blurring of class distinction in those countries in which there *has* been capitalist development—none of which has known a communist revolution!—as well as a vast improvement in the lot of the proletariat. Such are the facts, although of course these do not make capitalist society into a now acceptable system. There has not yet been such. Men are not, of course, "born equal." But each individual life is of equal importance.

Marx's general diagnosis that the capitalist system is in some way unnatural to human beings remains as convincing as ever. Although his arguments are often tortuous and flawed, we feel that his description of man as *alienated* from both nature and himself have validity. He developed the idea of *alienation,* feeling estranged—feeling cut off from your own values and beliefs—from Hegel and Feuerbach; in Marx the worker feels cut off from his own work because he cannot contribute, with it, to the community. Thus he is cut off from himself.

It is often objected that it is not possible to explain how one can be "alienated from oneself"—but a glance at the concept of I-Thou of BUBER (as just a single example to be found in this book) immediately explains this far more satisfyingly than Marx ever could, subtle and exquisite though Marx often was in specific instances. But Buber is of course a religious thinker—and it is only in accordance with his subordinate place in the universe, and with his duties toward the facts of his origin, that man could recover his position in the universe. Marx's theory does not give a sufficient value to the inner lives of individuals. For it is only in our mutual understandings of these inner lives that we could ever be together.

It is thus interesting that in himself Marx seems to have been so "ordinary"—and yet as "individual" as anyone else. Here are some of his "confessions," given in fun in a parlor game, but highly significant in fact: His favorite general virtue was "simplicity"; and "in man" it was "strength"—but in women "weakness." His favorite authors included SHAKESPEARE, GOETHE, and DIDEROT, an editor of THE ENCYCLOPEDIA; his heroes were KEPLER and the Roman rebel Spartacus. His favorite food was fish. He detested most the vice of servility. His favorite color was red. The vice he found the most excuse for? Gullibility.

72

Civil Disobedience

HENRY DAVID THOREAU

1849

It would be difficult, perhaps impossible, to determine whether *Walden* or the essay (initially a lecture) "Civil Disobedience" has had the greater influence. The man himself, Henry David Thoreau—shy yet outspoken, scornful yet kind, aloof but attendant, with his paradoxically gentle but fierce resentment of authority and his fear of women or of what he would be like with them in intimate situations—has of course been the decisive influence; but then we see this man most clearly in his huge *Journal* (the thirty-two manuscript volumes took up fourteen in the first, inaccurate 1906 edition)—and not many people have had the time to read that from cover to cover. But they should. *Civil Disobedience* is not (technically) a "book," but it is reprinted in many books, and so is justified in its claim here.

Since, although Thoreau was in no way a systematic philosopher, "Civil Disobedience" remains *the* classic defense of conscience against unjust law (hardly an unimportant issue), is so quintessentially American as such—and was successfully taken as a model by both Mahatma Gandhi and Martin

Luther King, it is the logical choice here. Thoreau, himself greatly influenced by his readings of Hindu literature (and, oddly perhaps, of CONFUCIUS), was eventually described by Gandhi, when he was only three years from the victory of his cause, as his "teacher"; he it was who taught the world what "civil disobedience" could be in practice. Since then the manifestation has become almost respectable. Great Britain was slow to listen to and absorb Thoreau, but today "eco-warriors"—who "occupy" sites set aside by business men for purposes of making money, or, at best, by inept planners bent on destroying wildlife "in the public interest"—are everyday news, are interviewed on television, and attract much support.

But that is not to say that the ecological and other implications of *Walden* are not as important in the long run, in particular the ideas that it is possible to live within a natural environment—and that it is "the unquestionable ability of man to elevate his life by conscious endeavor." Thoreau (he liked the pun on "thorough" that could be made from his name) was not an easy man to get along with, being so shy and sensitive; but, although he loved to lecture people, he never arrogantly set himself above others. He was a true adventurer of the benign type, in that he sought to discover what kind of life is best not only for himself but also for others—or he would not have written.

He was born in 1817 in Concord, Massachusetts, where he is still remembered as a "quirky man." That is appropriate for the one who so famously said that most people "lead lives of quiet desperation"—by which he meant above all, perhaps, that the worthwhile part of a human being is almost inevitably frustrated by the mechanical type of life he has to lead. Here he is of course not far from KARL MARX; but he has seemed much nicer to most of us because he was more modest, did not make a special study of HEGEL—and did not, Hegel-like, invent an entire system and thus become its captive and prophet. ("Civil Disobedience" was usually suppressed in communist countries, which cannot be said to have had quite *nothing* to do with Marx.) Instead he became a quiet observer of nature. He was also a pioneer in the improvement of the graphite used in pencils (as we shall see), and a more than merely interesting poet, who wrote on Sir Walter Ralegh, translated an Indian text and *Seven Against Thebes,* the tragedy by Aeschylus.

The family was originally French (from the channel island of Jersey). Thoreau's father was a storekeeper who went through hard times, but then started to make decent pencils; it was through the efforts of his acid-tongued mother, though, that Henry David was able to graduate in classics and languages at Harvard. During his time at the university he read prodigiously, amassing five thousand pages of notes on his reading. Shy and a "misfit," he (with his elder brother Tom) ran a school until it was closed down because they would not maintain sufficiently severe discipline—Thoreau's last act before resigning was to whip six boys at random. Then they went on a river trip up the Concord and Merrimack, and their diaries became Henry's first book (published in 1849), *A Week on the Concord and Merrimack Rivers.* For Tom had died of tetanus poisoning in 1842, dealing Henry a blow from which he never fully recovered.

For some long time he lived in the household of the sage Ralph Waldo Emerson, with whose wife he uneasily, and with much blushing but successfully, "transcendentalized" his relations. When in 1845 Emerson bought some wooded land on Walden Pond, he offered Thoreau the opportunity to build a cabin on it (it cost him $28.13). For two years, two months, and two days (from 1845 until 1847, when he had, in his words, "exhausted the advantages of solitude," and thought he might have yet another sort of life to live) Thoreau "chose to be rich by making his wants few":

> I went to the woods because I wished to live deliberately, to front only the essential facts of life, and see if I could not learn what it had to teach, and not, when I came to die, to discover that I had not lived. I did not wish to live what was not life, living is so dear; nor did I wish to practice resignation.

This wish Thoreau faithfully carried out, and carried it out well enough to set an example forever—it is an example that those convinced of the excellence of urban greed and "enlightened egoism" can only ignore. Better for them that he never comes their way.

Walden (1854), which took almost a decade to complete, was at its date at once the most original and the most "American" book yet published in its country. Its incomparable and beautiful descriptions of nature aside, it contained a scathing indictment of "progress"—usually by implication but also, and especially in the conclusion, with a candid directness plainly learned from the experience that Thoreau had so "deliberately" wished to have.

After the refusal to pay his poll tax (with which he was in any case overdue) in 1847, Thoreau's life was less eventful. His friendship with Emerson cooled down a little, he became famously indignant at the fate of Captain John Brown (his oration on this subject he insisted the whole village should hear, and he repeated it in Boston), and he wrote in his *Journal* until his premature death from tuberculosis. His family was now prospering owing to his own perfection of the process for producing graphite. He walked, worked as a surveyor, and lectured to everyone as often as he could—this was, it seems, his ruling passion. If that implies a love of fame or of getting attention, then it must be remembered that his personal integrity always came first.

One evening soon after he had left his cabin in the woods by Walden Pond, he was asked for his poll tax. He refused to pay it, on the grounds that it would be spent on an unjust war (in this instance, it was the Mexican War). A shocked aunt paid the tax for him immediately, but, because the official had taken his boots off, he did not release Thoreau until the next day—hence the famous night in prison, which, like most real events that become legends, was not quite what it later seems to be, in this case because he ought not to have been in prison at all. He chose his martyrdom, if such can really be called martyrdom, on principle; it was typical of him.

But "Civil Disobedience," first called "Resistance to Civil Government," is a different matter. It is not only eloquent and heartfelt. It is also good enough, reasonable enough, true enough to an irresistible aspect of human nature, to exercise the influence it has exercised. We have had much of the case for civil *obedience,* from the now strange notion of the "divine right of kings" onward. Here is the case for the opposite, and could it be better put? For example:

> But, to speak practically and as a citizen, unlike those who call themselves no-government men, I ask for, not at once no government, but at once a better government. Let every man make known what kind of government would command his respect, and that will be one step toward obtaining it. After all, the practical reason why, when the power is once in the hands of the people, a majority are permitted, and for a long period continue, to rule is not because they are most likely to be in the right, nor because this seems fairest to the minority, but because they are physically the strongest. But a government in which the majority rule in all cases cannot be based on justice, even as far as men understand it. Can there not be a government in which majorities do not virtually decide right and wrong, but conscience?—in which majorities decide only those questions to which the rule of expediency is applicable? Must the citizen ever for a moment, or in the least degree, resign his conscience to the legislation? Why has every man a conscience, then? I think that we should be men first, and subjects afterward. It is not desirable to cultivate a respect for the law, so much as for the right.

This is hard to answer, but in no way negative; it puts Thoreau into the position of many intelligent people: He is an anarchist, but he cannot but think that anarchism must fail—so he wants governments to be invisible. And it is interesting that we never find such genuinely warm sentiments expressed in the works of the too often so-called right-wing anarchists or libertarians such as HAYEK. "Liberty" for them is a matter of the "rights" of ownership— and, alas, they can draw on LOCKE because of the lack of any similar warmth of feeling or nobility in that pusillanimous writer, who actually made the famously feeble statement that it was possible to "contract out" of a society one did not like!

Thoreau was both a part of and yet aloof from the Transcendentalist movement with which, when his intimacy with Emerson began, he inevitably became associated. Transcendentalism nurtured him, but he did not rise out of it, although his Unitarianism may have been profoundly influenced by William Ellery Channing, one of his transcendentaly-inclined teachers at Harvard.

New England Transcendentalism (some of the leading members of the Transcendentalist Club were Emerson, Bronson Alcott, George Ripley, Margaret Fuller, and Orestes Brownson) has been called a "very diluted variety of philosophical thought." It was notably anti-Calvinist—finding this creed, in which many of them had been brought up, both ignoble and ungenerous—romantic, and mystical, and it drew mainly upon the philosophies and beliefs of PLATO, PLOTINUS, Boehme, the English poet Samuel Taylor Coleridge, and upon Indian thought. There arose from it notable experiments in communal living, including that of Brook Farm (1841–1847) at Roxbury, nine miles from Boston. But Thoreau was a solitary, although never the recluse he was once made out to be, and he was not cut out for community living.

It is what have been called his "quizzical nudgings toward truths" that distinguishes him above all. And no one after BURKE until Thoreau could express so well the qualities by which various forms of landscape could affect the mind. Of "wildness" he was as afraid as Burke, but, instead of equating it with revolution, or giving institutions a false quality of "wisdom," he added that in it is "the preservation of the world."

73

The Origin of Species by Means of Natural Selection

CHARLES DARWIN

1859

It is now commonplace to point out that evolutionary thinking was fairly widespread in the century before Charles Darwin (1805–1882), and that it was a "child of the Enlightenment." Even this is not quite strictly true, although most people in most cultures before the eighteenth century tended to think of origins in a directly "miraculous" way. But Darwin himself quoted the

pre-Socratic philosopher Empedocles, and the even earlier Anaximander of Miletus said that "the source of coming-to-be for existing things is that which destruction, too, happens according to necessity. . . ." The Chinese, too, had a theory of descent: transformism.

It was Darwin, though, who made the most thorough synthesis and who substantiated the theory of transformism. All he lacked, in the *Origin,* was a theory of inheritance—ironically, only seven years after the publication of *The Origin of Species,* one was worked out by GREGOR MENDEL in Brno, in then Austrian Czechoslovakia; but that was not generally known about until the turn of the century.

Darwin, intended for medicine and then for the church, was essentially a naturalist—the most observant and persistent one of his time. In more than one respect he resembled his great predecessor Gilbert White (1720–1793), the naturalist of Selbourne, in Hampshire; like White, he thought of nature as "so full," and he desired to explore it with enthusiasm and curiosity. But he also possessed a passion, quiet, sincere, unprejudiced, and unhobbled by quaint theology, to explain it. Born in Shrewsbury in Shropshire, near England's border with Wales, he was the grandson of the physician and scientist Erasmus Darwin, one of the many who anticipated him. When Charles Darwin entered Cambridge University in 1828 he soon turned to botany and zoology. He graduated in 1831, and at the end of that year set out on the H.M.S. *Beagle* as the naturalist on a voyage of scientific discovery.

He returned five years later, his mind well stocked with what he had seen in Tenerife, the Cape Verde Islands, Brazil, the Galapagos Islands, and elsewhere. He had also contracted a tropical illness—its exact nature is not known—which made him a semi-invalid for the rest of his long life. When he became tired he resorted to a wheelchair. He published the delightfully readable and informative diary of his voyage as *Journal of Researches Into the Geology and Natural History of the Various Countries Visited by H.M.S. Beagle* in 1839.

From what he had seen in so many different places, Darwin began to conclude, although he was deeply anxious about the direction his mind was taking, that species might share a common ancestor. He had been brought up on the prevailing but really highly unconvincing idea that God had created each species separately. But his keenness of observation, his very love of nature and consequent curiosity about it, caused him to doubt that this was the case. Was he deluded or mad, he wondered. Although not himself a very devout Christian—he ended up as a gentle agnostic—he was deeply unhappy about the pain he caused to his wife Emma and to friends who took his theory as a challenge to Christianity. It was not, of course, a challenge to Christianity, or to any other religion, at all; but it did correct the biblical accounts of creation if those were to be taken literally. It would not, allowing for the passing of several eras, have worried MAIMONIDES unduly! But it did destroy notions of man as God's special creature, although allegedly only some six thousand years old! It was, therefore, momentous. Clearly those who wished to retain their Christian faith would have to revise some of the assumptions that went along with it. And even those wiser people who could see that natural selection might well be "a law of God" were still forced to defend their faith against extreme and triumphalist claims.

Before Darwin the French anatomist and botanist Jean-Baptiste de Lamarck (1744–1829) had stressed the variations in species, and had given in his books an account of human development that was plainly evolutionary in spirit. The term *Lamarckianism*—for the doctrine that individual learning may be inherited by offspring—is now usually one of opprobrium; but it should not be. First, because inheritance of acquired characteristics is still—just—a possibility; the notion is not dead. Secondly, because Lamarck was in any case a pioneer, and his idea was by no means a ridiculous one. Thirdly, because although the term *Lamarckianism* is often used in contradistinction to *Darwinism,* Darwin was in fact himself a Lamarckian! Darwin wrote in a letter of 1844 to his friend Hooker: "the conclusions I am led to are not widely different from [Lamarck's], though the means of change are wholly so." But Darwin did, after all, advise mothers-to-be to acquire "manly" skills before giving birth!

It was, however, a reading not of Lamarck but of the *Essay* by MALTHUS that triggered Darwin's great insight: That natural selection, that is, selection of favorable (i.e., in the interests of survival in a given environment) characteristics operated among randomly occurring variations in offspring. All species (he reasoned) produce far too many offspring for them all to survive, and therefore those with favorable variations—owing to chance—are selected. What he got from Malthus was the principle of the *struggle for existence.* Most unfortunately he borrowed, from HERBERT SPENCER, the phrase "the survival of the fittest" as a synonym for his own "natural selection."

"Fit" in Darwin's sense means "best equipped to survive and thrive in a given environment"; but in Spencer's sense it meant "most perfect"—and soon came to mean "strongest" and much more. Darwin wrote that he used "the term *struggle for existence* in a large and metaphorical sense," but to much of his audience this "struggle" was interpreted as "fight," and seemed to apply to society itself, as well as to "species." Although "Social Darwinism" is now entirely discredited, since it confuses the ethical with the biological sphere, it is still influential; this fallacy, however, is dealt with more fully in its place, under the *First Principles* of Spencer. Darwin himself was hardly responsible for it—or for much else of what was popularly advanced in his name.

Throughout the 1840s and most of the 1850s Darwin was planning an enormous work on species. It is unlikely that it would ever have been completed, since he had all the doubts and modesty of a decent man about the conclusions he wished to express. But he received a severe shock—one from which he recovered with remarkable poise and gentlemanliness. The naturalist Alfred Russel Wallace (1823–1913), who had made an extensive natural history collection from the Amazon Basin and from the Malay Archipelago (some of it was destroyed by fire on the ship that was carrying it), also read the grim tract of Malthus on population. On June 18, 1858, Darwin received a letter from him, enclosing a paper he had written. Darwin told a friend: ". . . If Wallace had my sketch written out in 1842, he would not have made a better abstract! Even his terms stand as the heads of my chapters." The two men presented a joint paper to the Linnean Society on July 1, 1858—and Darwin's *Origin of Species* appeared in the following year. Thus was the "question of priority" decided, and in far more gentlemanly fashion than that between NEWTON and LEIBNIZ—when Newton behaved so abjectly—over the matter of the calculus.

Nowadays the orthodoxy, which is frequently challenged from the periphery, is known as neo-Darwinism; it of course takes into account the advances made in genetics since Darwin's times. The notion of life as an accidental excrescence, a byproduct of "selfish" DNA, leads nowhere, and, although propounded in popular books by modish dunces, makes no sense (as it is presented) philosophically or otherwise. For the notion of life on earth as a senseless product of blind chance one must turn, not to pseudoscientists, but to imaginative writers.

Darwin's own contribution, in the *Origin*, was the concept of natural selection (although he had been antici-

Charles Darwin as a young man

pated by Wallace). The extent of the role of this in heredity is now subject to debate; but that something like it exists is no longer open to question. The problem, now, is to define it exactly. Abstractions such as "gene-pool" have been appealed to, but there is actually no such entity. All this has become formidably complex, but obvious examples of selection are widely available: rats that are impervious to rat poison, bacteria that are resistant to antibiotics. . . .

Just how central Darwin's contribution was to the history of evolution is not decided. It was not greater than that of Wallace except that it was Darwin who wrote *The Origin of Species,* which, within a couple of decades, had persuaded most readers of its central thesis. It was this readable and modest book that caused the revolution, or change of paradigm. Darwin went on, in *The Descent of Man* (1871) and *The Expression of Emotions in Man and Animals* (1872), to elaborate on his interests. He deserves his preeminence: *The Origin* admits of obstacles and deals with them fairly; it opposed the older concept of God as benevolent watchmaker with courage, courtesy, and firmness. As for "disposing of God": It did not do that, but it did dismantle a singularly deficient notion of God.

74

On Liberty

JOHN STUART MILL

1859

John Stuart Mill wrote of the ethical system known as *utilitarianism* thus:

> The creed which accepts as the foundation of morals, Utility or
> the Greatest Happiness Principle, holds that actions are right in
> proportion as they tend to promote happiness, wrong as they tend
> to produce the reverse of happiness. By happiness is intended
> pleasure and the absence of pain; by unhappiness, pain, and the
> privation of pleasure.

Thus utilitarianism is the best-known form of the philosophy called
consequentialism, in which an action is judged solely in terms of its consequences. For example, on the question of capital punishment (which Mill
himself reluctantly, and it seems for the time being, supported when he was
a member of Parliament), we do not judge whether it is intrinsically *right* or
wrong to execute a criminal, but only whether this will be socially useful and
a true deterrent. (But there are many other versions of consequentialism,

including those that hold that well-being [a form of "happiness"] must consist of feelings of inner virtue, and also including those that hold that the "good" has precedence over the "right.")

The heyday of utilitarianism as an idea was the nineteenth century, beginning with the philosophy of Jeremy Bentham (1748–1832), which was modified and carried on, most notably, by John Stuart Mill himself and by Henry Sidgwick (1838–1900), that most typical of all the English Victorian academic philosophers. In various developed and elaborated forms, it is still influential and widely held. It had its roots, of course, in many of the philosophies of the past.

It could be argued that utilitarianism, or something very like it, lies behind much (although not all) of twentieth-century democratic political practice since at least the end of the World War I. Both the interwar governments in Britain and Roosevelt's in America could reasonably be described as, very broadly, utilitarian in intention—and so could their successors. The Soviets could also have claimed to be utilitarian, at least in the sense that they believed that they were helping along the inevitable. What has not been utilitarian about the (Western) governments, and much has not, has been influenced by conservative public opinion. But that is not to say that John Stuart Mill himself, the quintessential liberal, would have been satisfied. *On Liberty* is his most influential book, but *The Principles of Political Philosophy* (1848) and *The Subjection of Women* (1861, the most vehement feminist tract in English after the *Vindication* of MARY WOLLSTONECRAFT) have also had their sway. The pamphlet *Utilitarianism* (1861), first published in a magazine, was less successful because more polemical, and has always provided critics of Mill with their chief target. However, in the history of philosophy proper, it is Mill's *System of Logic* (1843) that has been most important as an influence; it may well be that the best of his thinking went into this. His *best* book is undoubtedly his justly famous *Autobiography*, although he could not declare himself in it fully.

Mill was the son of James Mill (1773–1836), a Scottish philosopher, economist, and journalist who was a close friend to Bentham and a prominent—and overidealistic and overrigorous—exponent of the utilitarian philosophy. Jeremy Bentham it was who invented the "greatest happiness" principle, and who tried to demonstrate that government could be conducted under the notion of what he called a hedonic, or felicific, calculus, i.e., a sort of device for quantifying what he thought was for the greatest happiness, which, for him, consisted of *pleasure*. Bentham was a truly distinguished thinker, still consulted, and his intentions were always humanitarian; but eventually he tended, in his enthusiasm, toward a somewhat mechanical interpretation of existence, to every problem presented by which his felicific calculus, he came to believe, could provide the solution. There was something slightly utopian about his (and James Mill's) type of radicalism.

James Mill's upbringing of his son was excessive, and undesirably accelerated, in its utilitarian zeal. It was admirable in all but practice. John was brought up to be a genius—and is possibly unique in that he actually became one, although undoubtedly a damaged one. He was forced to learn Greek at three, logic at twelve, and economics at thirteen. On the one "recreational" daily walk that he was allowed he was extensively quizzed and examined by his father. The result was that at the age of twenty he broke down emotionally and went through a period in which he could only be consoled by poetry, and by the poetry of Wordsworth in particular. He could have become an important and illuminating literary critic and general essayist, but duty called.

After he recovered he devoted much more of his time to the promotion of utilitarianism than, to one of his mental qualities, this philosophy was perhaps worth. As it was, he devoted himself to trying to adapt Benthamism, which he found essentially right, but somewhat rigid, to the more complex demands of his own times. His intention always tended to the promotion of what, in common sense—and in the absence of moral fanaticism—most of us would call decency, fairness, justice, liberty, the notion that the individual should be free of any moral tyranny exercised by others; but his efforts to justify the difficult positions into which his arguments led him, at times rather paltry by his own standards, were unworthy of him. Still the greatest British philosopher of his century, he could have achieved the world-wide stature of a KANT.

Nevertheless, *On Liberty* remains the classic statement of the liberal political position, and it usually (with *Utilitarianism*) provides the departure point for those who oppose its philosophy. Mill weakened (and in fact rather muddied) Bentham's happiness principle. His argument, which has been much criticized, runs like this: If anything at all is ultimately desired, then, if it is not sought for a selfish reason, it may indeed be thought of as a proper end of conduct, and if it is an end of conduct then that is good for the person concerned. Then Mill argues that pleasure *is* such a proper end, because that is what everyone really wants.

What Mill really wanted, above all, in *On Liberty* was that people should be allowed to live as they please within only this one set of limits: that others should not be harmed. But his arguments fail in a manner that is surprising when one considers his work on logic. Everyone agrees that what everyone wants (whether it be a life of self-sacrifice or of selfish pleasure) must be called his own idea of "happiness," even if he seeks unhappiness (for the sake, say, of learning the truth about the universe—it is his pleasure to be unhappy in the course of such a search, if he thinks it must make him so). That is common sense. But his argument seems to be that, from the fact that "each person's happiness is good for that person," so it must follow that *the happiness of everyone* is good for each person." This is an obvious logical fallacy, and it may be that Mill got himself into such a muddle because he was not dealing with subjects of which he was himself convinced were strictly relevant to ethics.

The essence of what we call decency is after all one of what PASCAL would have called the reasons of the heart. Can such matters ever be resolved by logic alone? Are modern utilitarians, like a large number of contemporary professional philosophers, mostly people who have become logic-choppers: Have they separated themselves from life as it really is because they just cannot face the task of accounting for the reasons of the heart? Utilitarianism was always a valiant attempt to move from a purely egoistic position to a moral one, and thus to improve the quality of life for everyone. But were its purely logical means ever adequate? Is there maybe a kind of "logic of the heart" that does not resemble the logic of reason?

We say of Mill as of Bentham or of Sidgwick and others that they were "decent chaps," enemies of reaction and cruelty—and so indeed they were. But we only know this from the general emotional direction that we see their arguments taking. One might even ask, is philosophy itself adequate as anything more than a *means* to an "emotional" (heartfelt) end? Or, can beauty ever be transformed into an analysis of beauty (a "happy" society, in which no one's pleasures interfered with anyone else's pleasures, might well be regarded as beautiful) without being destroyed in the process? We thus suspect that Mill, in his liberal eagerness to argue that the "sole end for which mankind are warranted, individually or collectively, in interfering with the liberty of any of their number, is self-protection," trespassed uselessly on to nonphilosophical grounds which he tried, vainly, to pretend were philosophical—or, at least, were more philosophical than they are.

But that is putting it as strongly as it can be put. Mill himself thought that his tendencies toward libertarianism had been partially corrected by his studies of the later, conservative ideas of the poet Samuel Taylor Coleridge. And it is impossible to determine the exact nature of the influence upon him of the woman, Harriet Taylor, who became his wife after her husband died, and with whom he had maintained a close relationship before that. His work on the rights of women has been exemplary in helping to get common rights granted. His influence has obviously been strong in matters of sexual morality—on the liberal side—but that, unfortunately, was something he could not, in his own age, talk openly about. He famously wrote, to underline his belief that what he meant by "pleasure" was not merely animal, but rational, "Better a Socrates dissatisfied than a pig satisfied." But that—to underline my point made above—is really an appeal to emotion. It makes sense, but there is no *logic* in it.

However, Mill and other utilitarians have done their best, and done it influentially, to keep governments from too much resembling that of CALVIN in Geneva, which prescribed inner as well as outward conformity. It will be significant to some that Hegelians violently object to utilitarianism because it is far too individualistic. One might therefore comment that, however weak it is in terms of philosophy, utilitarianism has nonetheless helped more human beings than it has hindered—or has it, perhaps, hindered any? That there may well be a moral to be drawn—from this philosophical inadequacy—is worth considering.

75

First Principles

HERBERT SPENCER

1862

In his famous short story, "The Duel," the Russian writer Anton Chekhov has the narrator describe a youthful romance thus: "At first we had kisses and calm evenings, and vows, and Spencer, and ideals and interests in common." That was in 1891, and offers an apt demonstration of the enormous influence of the British "philosopher of evolution" Herbert Spencer (1820–1903). Spencer was not only influential in his own country and throughout Europe; he was even more so in America. The rapid rise of this influence, and its scope and width, only makes his fall—or is it only an apparent fall?—all the more dramatic. He is hardly read now, let alone discussed; but can we really deny him his status as the "father of sociology"? And are his ideas really dead?

He was born in the Midlands town of Derby, of nonconformist parents. His father was a schoolmaster. As befits a polymath, his education was so sporadic that ultimately he had to teach himself. Yet, paradoxically, he hated "book-learning." He was a radical journalist in London in the 1840s, working for the *Economist*. In 1857, having published a number of libertarian books— extended essays, really—he planned a vast synthetic philosophy, which was to explain not less than everything in terms of *evolution*, a word he coined some years before DARWIN.

First Principles, his first statement of this philosophy, was followed by further volumes explaining the "principles" of biology, education, history, sociology, psychology, and so on. It and all its successors, until 1893, were taken together and called Spencer's *System of Synthetic Philosophy*. He was regarded in America and elsewhere as a man of "towering intellect." But was he really this?

Spencer's great strength lay in the fact that he ignored books by other writers to the greatest possible extent. He explained that these gave him (literally) a headache. Another paradox: He was notably a man of little experience of life, so that whatever he knew he could only know from books; there is in his work no subtext in which he refers to or relies upon personal experience; he is a remarkably naive writer. "All along," he wrote in a letter to a friend, "I have looked at things through my own eyes and not through the eyes of others." Today, as the inept suitor of the novelist George Eliot, the eccentric who wore earplugs so that chatter should not distract him, and who deliberately and provocatively walked against the traffic going toward the church on Sundays, he strikes a slightly comic note.

Yet his influence at its height was enormous. He was especially popular among working-class readers who aspired to knowledge. The revolution in education was triggered by him. He was independent, self-confident, and hated any kind of coercion. In the 1860s and 1870s he seemed to embody all the virtues of his century; the American publisher Henry Holt spoke for tens of thousands when he recalled that, when he got hold of *First Principles* in about 1865, he had his eyes opened "to a new heaven and a new earth." The scientist T. H. Huxley, Darwin's great exponent and publicist, wrote that before 1859 and *The Origin of Species* the "only person known to me whose knowledge and capacity compelled respect and who was at the same time a thoroughgoing evolutionist, was Mr. Herbert Spencer. . . ." Later, though, Huxley made fun of, and anxiously criticized, Spencer.

Spencer had written two books on evolution before Darwin published *The Origin of Species: The Development Hypothesis* (1952), and *Progress: Its Law and Cause* (1857). Yet, well aware though Darwin was of him—he borrowed from Spencer, with unfortunate results from his own point of view, the phrase "the survival of the fittest"—his own interest in evolution was essentially quite different.

Darwin's interest in evolution was cautious and scientific; Spencer's was overbold and uninterested in true scientific methodology. Having early rejected the "special creation" hypothesis (that God created each species separately) as ludicrous, Spencer overconfidently decided to present every-thing—stars, the universe, civilizations, individuals, countries, ideas, systems of government—as in the process of an inevitable development *upward*. Everything was in a state of continual improvement. It was an example of Victorian over-optimism, and this over-optimism was one of the factors that caused the First World War.

This is the doctrine, or rather the fallacy, of *social Darwinism*. The slow development of species, a matter entirely devoid of morals, wholly divorced from ethics—just a fact deduced and systematized by Darwin—becomes *improvement*, not just of species, but of everything else.

Spencer's original inspiration had not of course been Darwin, but rather those German biologists of his time, or just before it, who pointed out that in complex organisms there was increased specialization and function. Increased complexity, however, was wrongly interpreted as implying "higher."

In these circumstances it is clearly wisest to leave everything as it is, so that it may "develop" in a "natural" manner. Free competition is the best state of affairs. Conditions in which the state does not intervene or plan are the "most natural," since society is seen as being exactly the same as nature. The "fittest" will come out on top "naturally"—for "fittest" implies, or is taken to imply, "best in all circumstances." The strongest rule, and everything is for the best. The emphasis is rather upon strength or power than ability, especially unobtrusive ability. There is actually not much place for a bache-lor who has failed to propagate his kind in a "strong" manner.

The line of argument is almost irresistible; superficially it seems to be so "obvious" that, say, an ape is "superior" to a bird. Thus it soon became a sort of religion, to the extent that the agnostic T. H. Huxley himself—he coined the very word *agnostic*—was eventually explicit in opposing it, in 1893 when in a prominent lecture he declared that man "must combat the cosmic process." Yet it swept the world to the degree that Chekhov, as we have seen, satirized it when he equated it with the idealistic foolishness of young love.

For Spencer evolution was a unifying concept. He described his "law of evolution" thus: "An integration of matter and concomitant dissipation of motion, during which the matter passes from an indefinite incoherent homo-geneity to a coherent heterogeneity." He was once again thinking of the com-plex animals; but his statement is not only obscure but also meaningless, just like his definition of progress as a "beneficent necessity."

In Spencer's philosophy—really an apology for a philosophy—all sci-ence can demonstrate is that nothing whatsoever is knowable. He misunder-stood science to that extent. Therefore in his scheme the Unknowable becomes an Incomprehensible Power (the initial capitals are his, and are typical of him). He then proceeds to generalize, even to the extent that, as Darwin told a friend, we cannot "understand [his] general doctrine." As a contemporary historian of philosophy has remarked, he is "the nineteenth-century publicist *par excellence*." JOHN STUART MILL wrote of him that he threw himself "with deliberate impetuosity into the last new theory that chime[d] with his general way of thinking."

For his general way of thinking is in fact *the* prime example, above all others, of what the Cambridge philosopher G. E. Moore called the "naturalistic fallacy." This fallacy, perhaps the most famous fallacy of all, consists of deducing conclusions about what *ought* to be, from what *is;* it was earlier, and classically, stated by HUME, although not of course under the name Moore gave it. Spencer—thus attracting Mussolini and Hitler, as well as the less extreme Theodore Roosevelt—deduced that since the fittest in a given environment survived in biological terms, so the strongest and most morally ruthless would and *ought to* survive in social terms.

But human beings, to a very large and increasing extent, construct their own environments; what science describes or tries to describe as happening in nature is factual; it has nothing whatsoever to do with "good" or with "bad." A person might dwell in or simply observe slums, and might want to change them (for all sorts of reasons, some selfish, some possibly unselfish). Spencer misconstrued the workings of nature by misinterpreting them in a mechanistic way, and he then applied them to the workings of everything. He wrote:

> The ultimate development of the ideal man is logically certain— as certain as any conclusion in which we place the most implicit faith; for instance that all men will die. Progress, therefore, is not an accident, but a necessity. Instead of civilization being artificial, it is a part of nature; all of a piece with the development of the embryo or the unfolding of a flower.

What Spencer actually did—it is why he is now ignored as a thinker— was to apply to the concept of evolution a set of eighteenth-century ideas. He looks back as much as he looks forward. A year after his death the American pragmatist (or instrumentalist, as he came to call himself) philosopher John Dewey pointed out that Spencer was merely a transitional figure. WILLIAM JAMES as a very young man was carried away by *First Principles;* but the mature James spoke of "the hurdy-gurdy monotony of him . . . his whole system wooden, as if knocked together out of cracked hemlock boards."

What harm did social Darwinism do? At its worst it can emerge as something like this, which is from Hitler's *Table Talk:*

> If we did not respect the law of nature, imposing our will by the right of the stronger, a day would come when the wild animals

would again devour us—then the insects would eat the wild animals, and finally nothing would exist except the microbes. . . . By means of the struggle the élites are continually renewed. The law of selection justifies this incessant struggle by allowing the survival of the fittest. Christianity is a rebellion against natural law, a protest against nature.

Hitler was not an educated man, but, alas, he was a powerful one. If his idea of the "survival of the fittest" was a correct one, then of course all delicate butterflies and flowers and other "weak" creatures and plants and Darwins and Spencers with their headaches and maladies, all Goebbels with their club feet, would soon have been "overpowered" in the course of the "struggle." Spencer must therefore be held partly responsible for such views gaining prevalence.

But Spencer himself was hardly a Spencerian, any more than Theodore Roosevelt really was. Spencer, in fact, was rather more of a kindly fool (by the standards of real philosophy), who could not stomach the consequences of what he self-indulgently believed was his own "philosophy." The British philosophers whom we respect now never did take him seriously.

Thus Spencer criticized HOBBES for being unduly pessimistic and mitigated his message by pointing out that the "stern discipline" of "nature" was only a "little cruel," and then only to be "very kind." The "harsh fatalities" of his philosophy (starving artisans and their widows unprovided for, malformed children, lack of nourishment, war, famine, and so on) were in fact "full of beneficence—the same beneficence which brings to early graves the children of diseased parents, and singles out the intemperate and debilitated as the victims of an epidemic." Those who could not understand this "beneficence" were "spurious philanthropists."

Peter Gay in the third volume of his seminal *The Bourgeois Experience: The Cultivation of Hatred* (1994), rightly calls this simply an "alibi for aggression." Gay also points out that Spencer "violently objected" to the "indiscriminate application of his iron-fisted evolutionary laws": He encouraged private charities and compassionate activities—despite this being totally inconsistent. In other words, he denied his own repulsive philosophy. He was a democrat (why?), and he attacked the Salvation Army for its militancy! He found the Kiplingesque ardor for the Boer War hateful! He wanted better justice and better education—and in this latter field some of his efforts are said to be still with us. If only some of his disciples, even his post-Hitlerian disciples, most of whom do not refer to him and probably have not read him, had shared Spencer's own tacit objections to the cruel silliness of his ideas.

76

"Experiments With Plant Hybrids"

Gregor Mendel

1866

*T*he *Proceedings of the Brno Society for the Study of Natural Science* was never an internationally well-known journal (it certainly, though, qualifies as a "book"), and the article it carried in its 1866 number, based on two lectures given by an obscure Augustinian monk, although sent by its author to Charles Darwin (who never read it), was virtually ignored outside Brno, then in Czechoslovakia (and then, of course, therefore a part of the Austro-Hungarian Empire).

In 1868, two years after his paper had been published, Gregor Johann Mendel—born near Odrau in Silesia in 1822, ordained in 1847, after which he studied science in Vienna (1851–1853)—became abbot of his Brno monastery. Not long after that, perhaps frustrated but perhaps just too busy, he gave up his research into plant breeding altogether. No one seems to have gone very deeply into what his own feelings may have been, although there has been debate about how he understood his own work. His paper was not rediscovered until 1900, thirty-four years after it had been published, and sixteen years after his death. The discovery was made by Hugo de Vries, a Dutch biologist then in his fifties, and by two others independently. Yet, fearsomely complex though the modern science of genetics is, Mendel's findings have on the whole stood up so remarkably well that he is universally regarded as its father. It was not until his paper, with its clearly expressed mathematical arguments, was rediscovered that progress could be made in what was to become genetics.

Darwin, as we know, had been forced to declare that "the laws governing inheritance are for the most part unknown." He therefore believed in both the "blending" of characteristics (which does not occur: the genes are handed on unchanged) and in the inheritance of acquired characteristics. People, especially farmers, had known from time immemorial that offspring tended to display characteristics of parents or grandparents. In 1875 Francis Galton (born in the same year as Mendel—he died in 1911), a cousin to Charles Darwin, published his pioneer investigations into identical and non-identical twins (the difference between them was known); but he did not know of Mendel's work, and so was not able, either, to put forward any satisfactory explanation of the mechanism of inheritance.

Nine years earlier Mendel had, calling what we today call genes (the word itself was first coined by a Danish biologist, William Johannsen, (1857–1927), as a shortening of De Vries's term "pangene"), "factors," found through experimentation with peas—carried out in a strip of the monastery garden—that two tall plants gave tall offspring, and that two short ones gave short; when, however, he bred from tall and short, he found that two tall offspring from these gave, first, all tall, but subsequently, in the second generation, gave three tall to one short; the short plants, though, gave all short. Thus, he concluded, the shortness characteristic was masked by the tallness characteristic in the first generation, but reappeared unchanged in the next. The tallness factor he called "dominant"; the shortness one, "recessive."

He evolved two laws: The Law of Segregation states that the two factors for any characteristic are always separated from each other; the Law of Assortment states that the maternal and paternal factors are arranged so that each "germ cell" gets a random collection of factors from each of the parents. (It is now known that the second of these laws holds good only under certain circumstances.) The matter—especially so in the light of the retrospection of later geneticists—has now become far more complex; but only a brief summary is possible in short compass. However, a modern geneticist, using no more than the terms that were available to Mendel himself, would be hard pressed to express himself with a clarity comparable to that achieved by him.

How Mendel understood the implications of his own work is not certainly known, and there is now much controversy about this. One biologist, quite recently, has gone so far as to accuse him of fraud: His results were not obtained from his garden at all, but cooked up in notebooks! This suggestion, however, has met with little or no approval; it is unlikely, and it does not accord with what is known of Mendel's temperament. It may even stem from an envious feeling that a mere monk—an unscientific believer in God to boot!—with a silly kitchen garden could not possibly achieve what a grand modern scientist can achieve in an expensive laboratory. There was very much discussion of breeding experiments—especially in the matter of sheep—in the Brno of Mendel's time, and his predecessor Abbot Napp was another keen investigator. When Mendel's work finally was rediscovered, it was continued in good faith, in America and particularly by William Bateson (1861–1926) in England.

But modern Mendelism (and rightly called that—one often feels that it is the only honor accorded to Mendel outside Brno) stems from work of the American Thomas Hunt Morgan (1866–1945) started in 1910. It was he, with coworkers, who first successfully identified Mendel's "factors" with parts of rodlike bodies called chromosomes. Lengths of these consist of two forms of nucleic acid—deoxyribonucleic acid (DNA) and ribonucleic acid (RNA). Their division and replication had already been studied, and Johannsen had already named the gene; but he had put forward the name thus formed (1909) as "completely free from hypothesis." It was Morgan who began to clarify the relationship between chromosomes and genes and to demonstrate that the latter were a segment of the former. The history of genetics, now merged into the unifying discipline of molecular biology, is often rather scant with the name of Mendel; this is understandable—but then he did start it. It was not until 1953 that Crick, Watson, and others were able to establish what all this looked like in molecular terms.

At the time of the rediscovery of Mendel's work in 1900, Morgan was coming to the conclusion that internal factors, as distinct from environmental ones, were of greater importance in the determination of the development of embryos. *The Mechanism of Mendelian Heredity* (1915), written with others, at least gives—in its very title—credit to the founder of the subject. It was based on extensive research into the quickly breeding animal called "the vinegar fruit fly," *Drosophila malanoguster.* This work, and later developments of it, was to have important consequences in the 1930s, when the Russian geneticist Theodosius Dobzhansky (1900–1975) "married" Darwinism to genetics in his *Genetics and the Origin of Species* (1937, later much revised until it reached its final form in 1951).

As we have already seen, Darwin lacked a coherent theory of heredity.

His concept of natural selection postulated that the existence of heritable variations within a species, taken together with the fact that more offspring were produced than could possibly survive, provided conditions in which "favorable variations" were preserved. But the work of Morgan and his team made this seem redundant: They believed, and the scientific community tended to agree, that genetic change came about spontaneously and caused new features to come into existence.

Dobzhansky worked with Morgan on the vinegar fly, and he was able to demonstrate that "large changes"—"macroevolution"—were in reality no more than summations of myriads of small changes. The degree to which natural selection operates in heredity is still debated, but certainly the "phenomena," in this case natural selection, was, as of old, "saved."

Gregor Mendel, meanwhile, whose simple work in a monastery garden played such an important part in all this, deserves his eponymous fame—and perhaps a little more than the museum at Brno.

77

War and Peace

LEO TOLSTOY

1868–1869

In terms of influence Leo Tolstoy was a giant. Reformers and would-be reformers came to consult him from all over the world. He was probably the chief single influence on LUDWIG WITTGENSTEIN—yet could any two minds be more different in type? Even those who dismiss all talk of justice and decency (wherever—wrote Tolstoy in one of the better moments in his final overdidactic novel, *Resurrection*—anyone is being flogged, there is a picture of Christ), let alone of anarchism, as fuzzy revolutionary jargon respect him. He is widely read and revered as an author and thinker even in the—to use a word coined by the poet Ezra Pound—usurocracies (rule by usurers, not now reckoned to be a polite term for bankers, since, as the *Oxford Dictionary of the Christian Religion* more or less explains it, God changed his mind about usury and saw that money itself could be "productive of wealth") in which we live, and no novel is more read or admired, year in, year out, than *War and Peace*. (*Anna Karenina* comes in a close second. Both books have been filmed on several occasions.)

Tolstoy's ideas are quite well known, too. Biographies of him, good and bad ones, do well with the public. Yet the paradox is that while he is thus revered, his ideas are utter anathema to the vast majority of people. List his precepts to an average banker and he will want to have you flogged before he sends you to Siberia (unless it is a Sunday). One of the most spectacularly successful men of all time, Tolstoy was also one of the most celebrated failures.

He was born in 1828 into an aristocratic family on an estate some 130 miles from Moscow. He had a happy childhood, but lost his mother when he was nine years old. In 1844 he entered the university at Kazan, but he never took a degree—in 1847 he was treated for venereal disease, and for most of the rest of his life was troubled by his tendency to debauch himself on almost as grand a scale as he attempted in the vast canvas (580 characters) of *War and Peace, (Vonya i mir)*. He himself summed all this up in an autobiographical aside: "Tonight drew up precepts and then went to the gypsies." His agonized candor was quite as powerful as any man's has ever been.

The first really decisive influence upon him was JEAN-JACQUES ROUSSEAU, who inspired him to try to reform the lot of the Russian serfs, and caused him to interest himself in new and libertarian educational methods. Like PLATO in at least this, he saw that the secret of changing the world lay in education—and later in his life, on his own estates, he started many schools in which the children were given liberties unprecedented in Russia. After contracting very heavy gambling debts, he joined the army in 1851 and saw active service in the Caucasus and elsewhere. His *Childhood* (1852–1857) and *Tales from Sebastopol* (1855) gained him literary fame and popularity.

To question Tolstoy's sincerity, and the bitterness of his struggles against himself, is impossible. After he left the army in 1855 he traveled throughout Europe to learn more about society and how to reform it. When he married Sonia Behrs in 1862 (she bore him thirteen children) they both at first tried to be completely candid with each other. It was a heroic experiment on both their parts, and they gained some initial happiness from trying it; but the remarkable arrangement broke down—perhaps mainly because it had been far too idealistic. Certainly there is no point in trying to blame his wife for this failure, as some have done. The only comment that can safely be made—and some will fail to understand even this—is that whereas Tolstoy probably recognized the uselessness of having a "point of view," of seeing things in mechanical terms of right and wrong, his wife clung to more conventional notions. But who is to "blame" her for that? As well as bearing him the thirteen children, she acted as his devoted secretary, and she was probably right in preferring his literary to his social and political activities, which made him very unpopular with the tyrannical rulers of Russia, who—understandably enough—resented having a national genius to criticize them.

After Tolstoy had finished *Anna Karenina* (1875–1877) matters came to a head between him and Sonia. The didactic and moralizing part of him, ever in conflict with the creative (and strongly sensual) part, asserted itself. He renounced all his earlier works (including *War and Peace*). He wrote *Conversion* (1879) to explain all this. It was banned but was still widely circulated. He went on, though, with writing fiction and drama, including the long short story "The Death of Ivan Ilyich" (1884–86), which is as good and as free from moralizing elements as anything he ever wrote.

But as a man he became increasingly doctrinaire. He freed, or tried to free, his serfs, who were not grateful to him and did not understand him. He gave up his property (much to the anguish of his wife). He was at this point as heavily influenced by the philosophy of ARTHUR SCHOPENHAUER as he had earlier been by Rousseau. He oversimplified things, and yet his creative conscience would not allow him to get away with this. In 1883 he met with a disciple, Vladimir Chertkov, who was far more interested in the didactic side of Tolstoy than in his imaginative powers—this caused much grief to Tolstoy's wife, from whom in 1910 he ran away (with Chertkov), only to die shortly afterward at a railway station. In his last novel *Resurrection* (1899) he took up the case of the persecuted Doukhobors, a Christian-communist peasant community who, under his influence, had in 1895 buried their weapons and refused to fight—he had helped many of them to emigrate to Canada. *Resurrection* has its moments of power but is almost entirely undermined by didacticism. It, too, though, was filmed.

Tolstoy preached a form of Christianity which was freed from "all superstitious elements"; he was eventually excommunicated by the Russian Orthodox Church (1901), of whose formal elements he became increasingly critical. His form of Christianity boiled down to five leading ideas that he gleaned from the Sermon on the Mount: human beings must suppress their anger, whether warranted or not; no sex outside marriage; no oaths of any sort; renunciation of all resistance to evil (i.e., if your wife or sister is attacked by rapists in your presence, or even threatened with death, you must not retaliate—people have found this peculiarly difficult); love of enemies. Tolstoy believed that the love in individuals released by these practices would soon overwhelm their capacity for evil. He may well have been right, but he was not practical—he even tended at times toward ignorant virtuousness of an unattractive sort. It is, for example, not easy for us to love our enemies even when we try sincerely to enter such a state of mind. Yet, it must be added, it is not impossible. To take a grotesque example, to love Hitler would involve a warm understanding of what first turned him into a psychopath. There is always a plausible side to Tolstoy's preaching.

So, should Leo Tolstoy be honored for his undoubtedly mighty efforts to observe these precepts in his own life? Or should he be condemned as a naive and harmfully idealistic person who caused much misery and concern by his behavior? Or is there yet another way of looking at him?

Since the answer to the first two questions is a discomfortingly plain if paradoxical yes, it is clear that to reach something resembling the truth we need to resort to the third question. Tolstoy's search for truth and justice in his own life is, like almost everything else he perpetrated, compelling, and is possessed of a peculiar kind of exasperating nobility. The world is not a worse place for his having made his extraordinary moral efforts. In 1888 he really was at last able to eschew meat, tobacco, alcohol, and hunting.

But at the same time he did not, as didact, take human nature (about which he knew so much) sufficiently into account. He could not conceal his aristocratic contempt for the peasants he so professed to love; he tended to believe that he was himself like the moralist in himself. It was only in imaginative work (for example in the great story "The Death of Ivan Ilyich") that he came anywhere near to resolving the conflicts in himself. He is impressive—he is almost always impressive—when, in *What Is Art?*, he condemns Shakespeare, Beethoven, and Dante; but he is not really convincing. His grand failure, indeed, lay in his overconscientious lack of confidence in the art at which he so excelled. Art of his sort is a realistic portrayal of the world.

And that is his real achievement. *Anna Karenina* is perhaps a greater novel than *War and Peace*, but nothing on the scale of the latter has been attempted—before or since. No more convincing picture of war has ever been painted in words. Where else can we go for such a vivid account of Napoleon's attempted conquest of Russia? Yes, some of the facts are wrong or even deliberately changed; but then contemporary people's own perceptions of this war, too, were "wrong." If *War and Peace* is not what it is so often called, "the world's greatest novel," then it certainly has claims to be so considered. Its sense of immediacy is unique. It does make its reader reflect upon what Tolstoy wants him or her to reflect upon: that life goes on *despite* novels. This makes a point, creatively, that Tolstoy could not effectively make in his capacity as didact.

Of course *War and Peace* has been all things to all men. To the novelist Henry James it was a "loose baggy monster" of no plot or direction—yet he admired it. If it is not Shakespeare, it is surely Shakespearean. It has its notable weaknesses, yet those weaknesses have all the vividness of life itself. The main weakness, no doubt, is the manner in which it presents Tolstoy's famous (or infamous) view of history. He tells us that all is predestined, but that we cannot live unless we imagine that we have free will. So far so good. But he fails to enumerate the laws of history to which he so often alludes. We may look at history as a series of events manipulated by "great" men, or we may look at it as a series of men manipulated by great events. The latter view is not popular because we do not like to think of history, or of our own lives, as other-directed; besides, initially it seems merely fanciful. Yet *War and Peace*, for all that it fails in a philosophical sense to present "a compatibilist" view (in which free will is reconciled with determinism, as in the philosophies of HOBBES, LEIBNITZ, HUME and even Hume's less honest predecessor, the pallid JOHN LOCKE), does convey (as it means to) a sense of *inevitability*—and it does that in a way that no didactic treatise can manage.

After all, the notion that we are "fated" does occur to people as often as does the notion that we have complete free will—but we like the latter feeling better. Tolstoy's portrait of the Russian general Kutuzov is said, on good authority, not much to resemble the historical Kutuzov. Yet he seems in the book to be more real than the Kutuzov of whom we may read in the histories! Tolstoy's Kutuzov just waits for events to occur and then steps into the breach. His wise intuitions are strangely convincing. What is anyone's view of anyone else more than an impression?

Then again, just how does Tolstoy manage to convey the sense of the threatened Russia of 1812 when he had been born in 1828. He does this better than any historian. How, almost miraculously, does he make his people act "in character"? As in Theodore Dreiser, a far inferior stylist but a writer whose *An American Tragedy* also possesses an uncanny power (much resented by intellectuals, who cannot account for it in so clumsy an author), a great deal is conveyed by descriptions of the characters' physical habits: their smiles, eyes, postures. It is as if Tolstoy saw his characters as you or I see people in "real life." Think of the emphasis on Napoleon's white hands, and how that works in Tolstoy's portrait of him. The battle descriptions have never been bettered.

War and Peace is not and could not have been a complete success. But who has called it a failure? In its utterly humane and convincing portrait of a nation threatened by invasion, of human beings under the impact of violence and war, it did what the didact and moralist Tolstoy could never do as a preacher.

78

Treatise on Electricity and Magnetism

JAMES CLERK MAXWELL

1873

The case of the lowlands Scotsman James Clerk Maxwell (1831–1879) is one of the aptest of all illustrations of the essential rightness of THOMAS KUHN's much-resented description of the disconcertingly nonscientific manner in which scientific views, "paradigms" (such as the heliocentric hypothesis and its predecessor), change. Maxwell himself, for example, did not even live to see what are now known as "Maxwell's equations"! Contemporary scientists were interested in his conclusions, and eagerly studied them; but they could not, despite the models he characteristically offered, believe them; they were not fully accepted until after his premature death.

The treatise was ignored, by all but a smallish group of workers, until a year or two beyond his death, when, in 1884, Oliver Heaviside (1850–1925, after whom an atmospheric layer was named) expressed his equations as we know them today. In 1879 the German scientist Heinrich von Helmholtz

(1821–1894) had offered a prize for their experimental verification. In 1888, when Maxwell had been dead for almost a decade, his wave theory was verified by H. R. Hertz (1857–1894). Two years later it had gained wide acceptance. Now, as it has been phrased, we "write Maxwell's equations as if they had been handed down in stone." There are four of them, and, significantly, they have great elegance because of their astonishing economy and simplicity. As Kuhn showed, older scientists tend to refuse to heed new, obviously superior paradigms (Maxwell cleared up much confusion about the so-called ether, the medium through which light was supposed to travel), and it takes a new generation to accept them.

Today James Maxwell—a pious Victorian with a penchant for writing poor if capably expressed verse, whose boyhood was marked by his persistent asking of the question, "What's the go of that?" because he was filled with an insatiable curiosity about everything—is regarded by physicists as the most influential scientist of his century; it is not rare for him to be ranked with, or at least just below, NEWTON and EINSTEIN. The latter, when the centenary of Maxwell's birth was celebrated, described his work as "the most profound and the most fruitful that physics has experienced since the time of Newton," and evidently felt grateful to him.

From Maxwell's unprecedented marriage of electromagnetism and optics originates the very concept of electromagnetic radiation. From Maxwell's field equations arose Einstein's establishment of the equivalence of mass and energy. It was through consideration of Maxwell's (only ultimately unsatisfactory) theory of heat radiation, too, that Max Planck, in 1900, was inspired to formulate his quantum theory.

After his mother died, Maxwell was abused by his tutors at Edinburgh Academy, who nicknamed him "Dafty." But he overcame this, and by the time he was fifteen he was regarded as a prodigy. Later in his life people were awed by his intuitive powers, and even believed that he could not "think wrongly" on any problem—nor, in fact, did his thinking ever take wrong directions; perhaps this was because his curiosity took precedence over his desire for fame.

He graduated in physics from Trinity College, Cambridge, in 1874, and seventeen years later returned to Cambridge (to Kings), as the first Cavendish Professor there. His first major contribution to science came with his suggestion that the rings of the planet Saturn consisted of solid particles; this has been confirmed beyond doubt by the *Voyager* spacecraft in our own time.

Next Maxwell made an improved statement of the laws of thermodynamics, demonstrating that they needed to be treated in statistical terms. He thus advanced the development of atomic theory. He also did important work on color vision, and incidentally showed that colorblind people lack a color-sensitive receptor. But of course his greatest contribution was his unification of the electrical and the magnetic effects by means of mathematics.

Newton had been so amazed by his own "magical" theory of gravitation that he could hardly believe it himself—that matter acted on matter at a distance. But observations proved it to be the case, and so the principle was soon extended to both electricity and magnetism. Both these were seen to act in a very similar manner. Electrified and magnetized bodies behaved in much the same way in respect to each other (they also, unlike objects under the influence of gravitation, repelled each other). But few believed that the two were related in any way until in 1820 the Dane, Hans Christian Ørsted (1771–1851), discovered (by accident) that an electric current deflected the needle of a compass, which is of course magnetic.

Michael Faraday (1791–1867) then discovered, in collaboration with a New York schoolmaster named Joseph Henry, that if you changed the distance between an electric current and a magnet you could cause a current to flow—thus inventing the principle of the electric motor and the generator. After all, the self-educated Faraday asked himself, if a wire carrying a current sets up a magnetic field, should not a magnetic field induce current in a wire? It was on Faraday's work that Maxwell depended. But Faraday did not possess Maxwell's gift for mathematics, and all he could manage was to suggest that magnets and electric currents gave off "fields of force." We can "see" these when we put iron filings at the end of a magnet.

No one (still) understands electricity; no one can tell us why a magnet has an attracting (and repelling) force. But the impossible-to-understand *can* be expressed in mathematics. So Maxwell, fascinated by the contradictions he encountered, set himself the task of translating this new information into a mathematical form. Faraday and all others believed that the force fields of electrified and magnetic bodies traveled at an infinite speed. Maxwell showed that electromagnetic waves traveled at a constant speed: that of the speed of light (as this was known at the time). Light, he showed, was itself an electromagnetic wave. He said, "We can scarcely avoid the conclusion that light consists in the transverse undulations of the same medium which is the cause of electric and magnetic phenomena."

Soon afterward Hertz detected waves by purely electrical means. And throughout all the arguments between Einstein and Planck, Maxwell's equations remained valid, so that in the end it was Newton's laws that had to be modified. It is to Maxwell's credit, too, that he explained the effects of all types of radiation—X rays, radio waves, and so on—even before these had been discovered. Of all those waves, the ones that would have surprised him most were those of radio and television.

Von Helmholtz wrote: "To the question, 'What is Maxwell's theory?' I know of no shorter or definite answer than the following, 'Maxwell's theory is Maxwell's system of equations.' "

Thus Spake Zarathustra

FRIEDRICH NIETZSCHE

1883–1885

Friedrich Nietzsche is among the most influential thinkers of modern times. But he was virtually ignored until almost the end of the century in which he lived. His vast influence did not begin to manifest itself until his works were popularized (initially in 1888 in lectures given by the Danish critic Georges Brandes, in Copenhagen) just before the end of the sad period when he lay, incurably insane and oblivious to his surroundings, between 1889—in the January of which he became mad on the streets of Turin, when (perhaps it is significant) he saw a man flogging a horse—and his death eleven years later. He never knew that he had become so famous. What is generally taken to be his masterwork, his most popular book, the prose poem *Thus Spake Zarathustra (Also Sprach Zarathustra)*—but it is best described as a "literary-philosophical experiment"—went ignored at the time of its first appearance. (He published the first three parts at his own expense, and then became almost too discouraged to publish the fourth, which, finally, he issued privately in a few copies.)

Whether or not Nietzsche's madness was the result of syphilitic GPI (general paralysis of the insane, then the third stage of the illness), caused by the disease contracted in his youth, while serving as a soldier, his writing style seems to have been increasingly affected by its onset, but to what exact extent one can only speculate. Nevertheless, no thinker of Nietzsche's stature has been quite so susceptible to quotation out of context—Bertrand Russell, and many other thinkers almost as eminent, totally misunderstood him, and hardly took him seriously except as a bad influence. He has been very widely misrepresented as both an anti-Semite and a woman hater (he did make rude remarks about women, but they were essentially about the stifling and provincial-minded women of his own family, who brought him up at Naumburg—mother, aunts, grandmother, not a single male). He was neither; but his irony, upon occasions, became so convoluted that he too easily lent himself to such fatal misunderstandings; his facetiousness on the subject of women displays him at his feeblest, silliest, and weakest. It has to be added that he failed to take up an opportunity to ally himself with one of the most remarkable and understanding women of his time: the great and radiant Lou Andreas Salomé (1861–1937), later the lover of the poet Rilke and the highly valued friend (a few say lover) of Freud. His malevolent sister Elizabeth (among other things, she forged two letters purporting to come from Lou) helped to botch this single relationship that might have saved him, even though Lou was at that time only a girl.

"Self-overcoming" was the essence of Nietzsche's thought, and it must always be remembered that the vast majority of men challenged by his abject health—agonizing migraine headaches, weak eyesight, a susceptibility to attacks of painful vomiting, periods of near-blindness, addiction to the sleeping drug chloral hydrate (he resembled the Anglo-Italian Poet Dante Gabriel Rossetti in this), and all manner of other afflictions—would have accomplished nothing at all. Here is the Austrian writer Stefan Zweig's famous (and in this respect accurately vivid) portrait of Nietzsche in his final years of sanity:

> Carefully the myopic man sits down to a table; carefully, the man with the sensitive stomach considers every item on the menu: whether the tea is not too strong, the food not spiced too much, for every mistake in his diet upsets his sensitive digestion, and every transgression in his nourishment wreaks havoc with his quivering nerves for days. No glass of wine, no glass of beer, no alcohol, no coffee at his place and no cigarette after his meal, nothing that stimulates, refreshes, or rests him; only the short meager meal and a little urbane, unprofound conversation in a soft voice with an occasional neighbor (as a man speaks who for years has been unused to talking and is afraid of being asked too much). . . . And up again into [his] small, narrow . . . coldly furnished *chambre garnie* . . . only books and manuscripts, and on a tray innumerable

bottles . . . against the migraines . . . stomach cramps . . . spasmodic vomiting . . . slothful intestines. . . . A frightful arsenal of poisons and drugs, his only helpers in the empty silence of this strange room in which he never rests. . . . For hours he sits . . . and writes until his eyes burn.

Nietzsche has been most things to most men in any case: Adolf Hitler kept a bust of him and in 1943 gave his works, in a special binding, as some consolation to the temporarily deposed Mussolini (who, although himself a failed novelist, did not read them—nor, however, had Heidegger's great hero, passed much more than a glance over them); yet certain more responsible thinkers have gone so far as to represent Nietzsche as a prince of peace. FREUD believed him to have possessed more self-knowledge than anyone else of whom he was aware.

"That the Nazis misappropriated him . . . was entirely his own fault: He should have had the moral strength to correct the weakness in his own philosophy." So runs a familiar criticism from thirty years ago. But is this fair? Certainly it is now out of date, even unfashionable: the old notion of Nietzsche-as-protofascist has receded. Certainly, too, the word "entirely" displays ignorance as well as unfairness, for Nietzsche's eventually Nazi sister, Elizabeth—the widow of a virulently anti-Semitic confidence man who killed himself when his hand was caught in the till—in her capacity as his executor, distorted (with the help of others equally unscrupulous or misguided) his message, even resorting to forgery and selective quotation in order to do so. On the other hand, Nietzsche, as well as being quite astonishingly acute and wise, probably the greatest aphorist who ever lived, could all too often be— to use a rare word that is, however, simply too apt to avoid—horrisonous ("sounding horrible"). He had humor, irony, and wit; but with tact he dispensed entirely, as quite beneath contempt. Aphorist above all, he was poet and ironist rather than the systematic philosopher that he has rather too often taken to have been—yet he profoundly influenced the direction of much twentieth-century philosophy proper.

Nietzsche cannot be appreciated without an understanding of his faults, the chief of which was that, although not in fact an advocate of violence (he was perfectly and eloquently explicit about the wickedness of war), he all too often both felt and sounded violent. To that extent, and perhaps to that extent only, did he lend his name to the Nazis who seized power thirty-three years after his death. Nietzsche was also too often inordinately and angrily vain, inasmuch as he found it hard to give credit when he well knew it was due, or even to acknowledge the influence of other thinkers. He wanted to tread on the susceptibilities of his contemporaries, and he did so without mercy. He wrote, "One generally mistakes me: I confess it; also I should be done a great service if someone else were to defend and define me against these mistakes."

He has not lacked defenders, especially in more recent years, during which he has become the archpriest of the postmodernists. One of the

Nietzsche at age 20

reasons for which he may be so variously interpreted is that much of his work consists of random notes, which may be "edited" in many ways and in many directions.

Nietzsche was born in 1844, in Röcken in Saxony, Prussia, the son of a Lutheran priest who died—mad—four years later. Whether he inherited any of his father's psychiatric propensities is a moot point, since there is little information about the latter's illness, described at the time as "softening of the brain." Educated at the universities of Bonn and Leipzig, Nietzsche was, at the extraordinarily young age of twenty-four, appointed as professor of classics at the University of Basel in Switzerland. These were the short-lived days of his triumphant success: Although he had not yet been awarded his doctorate from Leipzig, the university soon gladly supplied it. It was at about this time that he became enamored of the philosophy and the writing of SCHOPENHAUER—the pessimistic influence of which he tried to repudiate in his first book in 1872 (*The Birth of Tragedy*) but which, it could be fairly argued, never really left him. A very strong case may be made out for a Nietzsche who was never able to reconcile himself with a temperamental affinity to Schopenhauer's resignation.

Nietzsche had previously (1867) served in the army, but was quickly discharged after suffering a fall from a horse. At Basel he became friendly with the composer Richard Wagner, then in exile at Lucerne, and with the historian Jacob Burkhardt. He would later dramatically repudiate Wagner, on account of what he believed was his sickly Christianity (as expressed in the music-drama *Parsifal*). He wrote some good poems, and some charming and (now unduly neglected) music. In 1870, although by then a Swiss citizen, he volunteered as a medical orderly in the Franco-Prussian War, but soon contracted dysentery and diphtheria, and could therefore stick at it for only a few months.

He was forced to give up his chair at Basel in 1879 and take a modest breakdown pension, owing to his by now almost spectacularly poor health. He had by then published several works beyond *The Birth of Tragedy*. He spent his last decade of sanity at various resorts in France and Switzerland, trying to restore his health. His descent into madness was, as his father's had been, sudden and catastrophic.

Nietzsche's thinking, with which *Thus Spake Zarathustra* (the book has no bearing whatsoever on the Zoroastrian religion) is pervaded, cannot be neatly summarized. The kernel of his philosophy as such may be illustrated by his remark: "Against positivism, which halts at phenomena—'There are only facts'—I would say: No, facts are precisely what there are not, only interpretations."

This view, although never systematically presented, still influences modern thought, and is seen, for example, in the writings of THOMAS KUHN. His apparent perspectivism—the relativistic and philosophically skeptical view that all truth is only truth from a particular perspective—has also inspired (if *inspired* really is an appropriate word in this connection) much of the more nihilistic type of postmodernist thinking (if again *thinking*, as distinct from *complacently resigning*, really is appropriate in that connection).

In *The Birth of Tragedy* Nietzsche tried to rid himself of pessimism. It was here that he introduced his famous distinction between the so-called Dionysian and Apollonian spirits that he found in Greek thinking. Untactfully arranged (it contains a far too long eulogy of Wagner), *The Birth of Tragedy* diagnoses human beings as subject to unconscious, involuntary, overwhelmingly self-destructive Dionysian instincts; against this tendency, in Nietzsche's view, the Greeks erected—actively, positively, and heroically—the sober, rational, and active Apollonian principle. The relevance of this to

Freud's conception of the id and the superego is too obvious to require explanation. The rejection of Schopenhauer is only skin deep, and, significantly, the exuberance—sometimes overexuberance—of *Zarathustra* is specifically Dionysian.

Thus Spake Zarathustra must be ranked as one of the greatest of books. At the same time, though, it is also often all too clearly the work of a sick man. Nietzsche's attempts in it to deal with the subject of Woman are fourth-rate by comparison to his thinking in general. The text quite often descends into sheer hysteria and melodrama. Some of the jokes misfire or are obscure (and are in many cases untranslatable). But that is the price Nietzsche paid for the achievement of a mostly magnificent style, as adumbrated in the majestic opening: "When Zarathustra was thirty years old he left his home and the lake of his home and went into the mountains. Here he enjoyed his spirit and his solitude, and for ten years did not tire of it. But at last a change came over his heart, and one morning he rose with the dawn, stepped before the sun, and spoke to it thus. . . .

There is no doubt that, as one of its better and more modern translators R. J. Hollingsworth, has written, *Zarathustra* "cries out to be blue-penciled"! However, it is also still perhaps the most wonderful "mine of ideas" in existence. Three of these stand out: the notions of, respectively, the Death of God, the "Overman" (a better rendering than the more familiar but misleading "Superman"), and of the Eternal Recurrence.

Nietzsche's announcement of the Death of God—this should not be confused with a short-lived theological movement in North America in the 1960s—was the most influential. What he meant is of course, as always with him, open to various interpretations. But the gist of it was that a sense of the tragedy and meaninglessness of life had demoralized mankind: Christian thought (for which he had a special hatred) had become divorced from reality and was teaching men to seek refuge in an unreal God—a God that Nietzsche pronounced *dead*. This diagnosis of the old Christian God as dead was, strictly speaking, cultural: It has no logical bearing on whether there is a living God. It is obvious that Nietzsche may be interpreted religiously or atheistically.

The remedy lay in a type of man who could *overcome* this supineness, who could think and act for himself: the "Overman" (*Übermensch*). Thus he writes: "You say that you believe in Zarathustra? But what does that matter? I bid you lose me and find yourselves: and not until you have denied me will I return."

Nietzsche was in fact against the Germans of his time, and against—most especially—that type of German who would become Nazi, and who would eventually settle for a semiliterate and clearly psychopathic leader. He was so fanatic a pro-Semite that at times he does sound like—and his irony on such occasions makes it even worse—an anti-Semite. He did not make sufficient allowance for those less intelligently aware than himself—most were. But had he retained his sanity and a bit of good health, Nietzsche would have revised his work so that it became abundantly clear that his

"Overman" was not a "blond beast," but a human being capable of overcoming his own deficiencies, of transcending the tired values of his time, of refusing to conform just for conformity's sake. That capacity to overcome led him to his belief in "the eternal recurrence of the same," an old Stoic idea. The point here is *not* whether Nietzsche regarded this notion as scientifically plausible (he may have done, or he may not, or he may not much have considered it), but, rather, in what manner the Overman could bear it:

> *The greatest stress.* How, if some day or night a demon were to sneak after you into your loneliest loneliness and say to you, "This life as you now live it, you will have to live once more and innumerable times more; and there will be nothing new in it, but every pain and every joy and every thought and sigh and everything immeasurably small or great in your life must return to you—all in the same succession and sequence—even this spider and this moonlight between the trees and even this moment and I myself. . . ." Would you not throw yourself down and gnash your teeth and curse the demon who spoke thus? Or did you once experience a tremendous moment when you would have answered him, "You are a God, and never have I heard anything more godly."

Nietzsche turns out, too, on careful reading, to have been a prophet of Nazidom and what followed it. The charge that he was in any way a proto-Nazi is therefore unjust. However, he could often sound like one, and his utter disdain for conformist thinking (always dangerous: You can fool some of the people all of the time, all of the people some of the time, but not all the people all the time) was reprehensible in that it showed a somewhat grand disregard for those things that *do,* or at least *can,* bind people together, as well as for that little bit of all of us which does *not* conform. Those who understand Nietzsche can and should make allowances; but what of those who do not? There is certainly enough in him to refute all the worst charges that can be made against him; but proto-Nazis do not have the time or the inclination to seek for truth. They want only to confirm their own savage prejudices. They do not want to hear that Nietzsche wrote "When races are mixed, there is the source of great cultures" or (in a letter) "just now I am having all anti-Semites shot." But, after all, he was distinctly unlucky in his hateful and dishonest sister—and he remains the best aphorist of all time. An anthology called *The Humane Nietzsche* would not be a short book.

80

The Interpretation of Dreams

SIGMUND FREUD

1900

Without consideration of Sigmund Freud (1856–1939), little progress could be made in any account of the twentieth century. In the year 2000 he will be as central a figure as LOCKE or NEWTON in 1700, VOLTAIRE in 1800, or HEGEL or SCHOPENHAUER in 1900.

It is often asserted that Freud "discovered" the unconscious mind. However, the notion of an unconscious goes right back to the beginning: in HOMER, for example, we find men sent by the gods to instill ideas into the minds of unwitting sleepers. And what, in any case, are the *Ajax* of Sophocles or the *Hamlet* of SHAKESPEARE if they are not, among many other things, explorations of unconscious motivation? What did people of all times and in all places mean when they spoke of a person being "overtaken by passion"? The concept of the unconscious mind is implicit, too, in the work of many philosophers, particularly KANT: It is in the unconscious that, for him, our structuring of the world takes place. It plays, as the title suggests, a prominent part in the (for a time) popularly influential work *The Philosophy of the Unconscious* (*Die Philosophie des Unbewussten*, first published in 1886, later revised and extended), by Schopenhauer's disciple Eduard von Hartmann. This is an attempted synthesis of the philosophies of Hegel and Schopenhauer. The book, not a bad one, but not convincing, either, is now unimportant except—and this is significant—as part of the backcloth for the establishment of "Freudianism." But for all that, Freud did—if one may so phrase it—put the unconscious mind on the map as a coherent and (apparently) scientific entity. His work has been adored, hated, confirmed, and dysconfirmed; it will never go away.

The crux of the matter is not so much the existence of the unconscious, of a part of the mind that is hidden from awareness, which few now deny, but of its proper definition—even, indeed, of its "location." In this respect, because Freud had one of the greatest synthesizing minds of all time, he became one of the clearest voices of the twentieth century. The uneven fate of the discipline he founded, that of psychoanalysis, is quite a different matter. This, although interesting, is perhaps the least truly important thing about Freud.

Freud was born into a Jewish family in Freiburg, Moravia, but grew up from the age of four in Vienna, in which city he spent his life until 1938, when he took refuge in London, where he died in the following year. A brilliant pupil at school, he completed his doctorate in neurology in 1881 at the University of Vienna. He went to Paris in 1885 to study under Jean Martin Charcot at the Salpetrière Hospital in Paris. Charcot was famous as the physician and hypnotist in charge of people, mostly but not all women, who suffered from the medical state that became known as "hysteria" (from the Greek for *womb*—the state was for long believed to be unique to women, until Charcot himself demonstrated "virile hysteria"). In this state patients would suffer from disabilities, such as paralyses, which were not caused by known neural damage of any kind. It was "hysteria" that first led Freud to take an interest in psychiatry. Before his time with Charcot, his chief interest had been in biology. He had worked for some years in the laboratory of Professor Ernst Brücke, a close associate of Hermann Helmholtz, the leading German scientist of the era.

After his return from Paris Freud worked as a general physician at the Vienna General Hospital. He wanted a university post, but these were not available to Jews—then, as alas now, Austria was a hive of anti-Semitism. Freud married in 1886 (there were six children of this marriage), and in that same year set up as a specialist in nervous disorders. He lived in the same house until the Nazis drove him out of Vienna. He presided over the psychoanalytical movement he founded with just about as much decent scrupulosity as any leader of any such movement could manage. He was jealous of his position, patriarchal, and occasionally manipulative and petty; but it has not been convincingly shown that he did anything actually wicked. He was, throughout his life, a decent, moderate liberal—something that in some ways has been seen as rather oddly at variance with his revolutionary stance. But he needed to be of such conservative temperament in order to succeed.

Freud's invention of his own form of psychoanalysis as treatment for neurotic illness (if neurosis is now an illness rather than just a general way of life) is hardly the issue here, since although of course psychoanalysis has had some (rather limited) influence in medicine, it has not been even a tenth as influential as the model of the human mind upon which it is based. This amounts to a *Weltanschauung* ("worldview"), and offers a complete theory of human nature on a par with those of PLATO, the Church Fathers' (as distinct from that of Jesus Christ, whose teachings they misappropriated for their own purposes—self-righteous, secular or otherwise) or Hegel or, at a level both more alarming and intellectually tawdry, the pitiful American behaviorist B. F. SKINNER.

What is here required is a brief account of this model, together with some explanation as to why it was invented when it was. It must always be remembered, though, that the chief reason for its formation was the synthetic genius of Freud himself: Freud was a man of almost extreme probity—he did not much like, although he was amused by, the French literary movement upon which he was the leading influence, surrealism—and, although increasingly driven to reductionism by the hostility his ideas aroused in "respectable" people (even the intelligent Finnish anthropologist Edward Westermark complained, exhibiting great emotion, that the notion of his little son wishing to castrate him in order to possess his mother was too horrible for him to contemplate), was too richly endowed imaginatively, and too generous, ever to be a true reductionist.

Freudianism was the product of an almost grotesque contradiction between antivitalist, almost pathologically reductionist positivism, and Hegelianism. Freud's profound and fully acknowledged debt to Schopenhauer was more personal, since it was the latter's pessimism that was influential (perhaps through Hartmann)—and Freud's pessimism was not, as it happens, derived from Schopenhauer, but from his own knowledge of human nature.

Vitalism had from the start insisted that that the world depends on a life-giving force extra to and "above" or outside the material in it. Hegelianism was generally interpreted in a vitalistic manner (this may be arguable, but then Hegel is all things to all men). In Freud vitalism is contained, even by implication denied; but the spirit of it nonetheless exists—in the ceaseless and primitive strivings of the id.

Here, briefly, are the barest bones of Freud's perfectly Darwinian view of the mind. Any summary does little justice indeed to the subtlety of Freud's own mind as it is expressed in his writings; but Freudianism is no less different from its propounder than is any other similar -ism. Freud's writings can hardly be the issue here—what was made of them is.

It should be explained at the outset, since the confusion is a common one, that the *un*conscious is to be distinguished from the *sub*conscious. The former is a part of the mind genuinely hidden from awareness; the latter is better called the *pre*conscious, a threshold within which are held recent memories not actually in consciousness but readily accessible to it. The contents of the preconscious are generally trivial.

Freudian theory, then, although it need not be interpreted in—and often has not been interpreted in—a rigidly mechanistic or Darwinian fashion, depends on a number of instinctual drives, all of whose aim is to ensure survival (but later there was added a death wish, which represents Freud's direct and well-acknowledged debt to Schopenhauer) and, in particular, pleasure, or the achievement of gratification. The height of pleasure, Freud maintained—he has not been alone in this, but it still pains many to discuss it openly—is heterosexual sexual intercourse. He had good evidence for so supposing, although (ironically) the man who became his greatest rival, on the grounds that Freud exaggerated the importance of sex over spirituality, CARL GUSTAV JUNG, had a good deal more varied experience of it as an extramarital activity. Indeed, Jung is a neater case for enraged Freudians than Freud has ever been for pious Jungians.

The human individual in his or her progress to maturity (if that state is ever reached—clearly Freud doubted if it was) goes through the following stages of development: oral, anal, genital, and phallic. The driving force is *libido,* an undoubtedly vitalistic conception; this libido is the striving of the most "primitive" part of the human being, the *id,* a dustbin which (allegedly) holds only murderous, incestuous, and always selfish impulses. This somewhat Hobbesian picture (there is no room for Humean "sympathy" here) is mitigated however, if mitigated it is at all, by a sort of civilizing process. Thus, parents, the police, the authorities, teachers, help to form the *superego,* or "conscience" (there is no "God-given" conscience in Freudianism, since God is an illusion); this superego ought and usually does cause the individual to seek to slake his horrible gratifications by socially acceptable means.

The self of which we are all immediately aware, and which is an uneasy compromise between the id and the superego, Freud called the *ego.* The obstacles to the "normal" process that Freudianism described are many: They consist of traumas, caused by all sorts of failures to resolve tensions. The severest trauma is caused by the necessity to shift sexual attention from the mother to another "socially acceptable" "object," as, concomitantly, by the need to remove the threat of castration by the father. Freud did not really believe that the so-called Oedipus Complex had been resolved in many cases (Oedipus unknowingly killed his father and married his mother). The process in females is slightly different, and cannot be said to have been dealt with very satisfactorily by Freud. "What does a woman want?" he famously asked; his wife's comment was that such matters ought to be "kept out of the nursery!"

One of the chief features of the Freudian account of the mind, as this gradually emerged, is its sheerly mechanistic outlook. (But it cannot be repeated often enough that this is hardly the impression given by Freud's own nonprogrammatic writings.) At the beginning, when he was still interested in "hysteria," (which, while sometimes genuine, also involved much playacting and approval-seeking), he and his associates thought of *energy* as being moved about like a substance, one that could be *discharged*. Yet, when *The Interpretation of Dreams* appeared in 1900, all this served as a perfectly useful metaphor for more subtle and less reductionist purposes, and the unconscious was no longer quite the crudely dynamic engine it had seemed to be in theory. It was this book above all that drew attention to Freud outside Germany and Austria. But at the same time Freud, jealously guarding his new movement, became increasingly anxious about defending the scientific basis of his ideas. The degree of hostility shown to these was later much exaggerated by him; but they were not welcomed, partly—although not wholly—on account of the anti-Semitism of the Austrians and the Germans.

However, it has not been for its scientific correctness (this is hardly demonstrable) that Freud's theory of the mind has been so influential. Although vulnerable to conventional scientific method, Freud revolutionized the way we look at ourselves (or, conversely, refuse to look at ourselves). Nor would many like to assert that his model of the mind lacks any grain of truth, although POPPER—without much effect in this instance—attacked it on the grounds that it was not falsifiable.

As the year 2000 approaches—a perfectly ordinary year, no doubt, but one understandably invested with all sorts of artificial significance—Freud's idea of the mind retains its influence more securely than most of the systems of the past century and a half. The fate of psychoanalysis itself is more dubious; but in that respect it is worth mentioning that Freud himself was of the opinion that physical causes for mental states would eventually be discovered—thus tending to make what is all too often a form of brain-washing obsolete.

81

Pragmatism

WILLIAM JAMES

1908

The Principles of Psychology (1890) is probably William James's greatest book, and it is arguable that it contains at least the germs of all his future books, which include *The Will to Believe* (1897), *The Varieties of Religious Experience: A Study in Human Nature* (1902), and *The Meaning of Truth* (1909). But it is the philosophy of pragmatism for which he is best known, even though he did not invent it.

William James was born in 1842, into an extraordinarily enlightened New York family, whose head, Henry James Sr., was a Swedenborgian theologian (a follower of the Swedish engineer, founder of crystallography, and mystical visionary Emanuel Swedenborg, who also inspired the English poet William Blake). The senior James was a remarkable man (he was an alcoholic while still a boy but was cured of it before he reached maturity) in his own right, who took his family around Europe in order to educate them in the best artistic, humanitarian, and liberal traditions. William's younger (by one year) brother Henry was as famous a novelist—but not as influential in the wider world—as he himself was as a psychologist and philosopher.

By the time William entered Harvard Medical School in 1863 he had already studied to be a painter but had given it up because he did not believe he had the necessary gift—others, possibly significantly, did not agree. This experience at least gave him an invaluable insight into creativity. He graduated as a physician six years later, having in the meantime traveled (again) to Europe and gone on a naturalist expedition to Brazil. He never practiced as a doctor, however; in 1872 he entered Harvard as an instructor in physiology. He stayed there for thirty-two years, becoming first a psychologist—in which capacity he revolutionized the science—and finally a philosopher.

James, although he married, raised a family, and wrote so many major books, was a manic-depressive by type who suffered throughout his life from depression and overexcitement. His brother, Henry, was more neurotic but was spared the bouts of clinical depression and mania that William suffered; however, he was on balance a less happy or realized man because of his necessarily undeclared passion for young men. Henry was also a more envious man.

It is by no means unusual to claim that William has been the best-loved person, of all the philosophers, after SPINOZA. And this despite the fact that he had a well-known and unfortunate habit of overstating his case in brilliant but not always subtle aphorisms. This was unfortunate because men like Mussolini, the Italian dictator, were able to state with some plausibility that they were followers of pragmatism. They were not, but this is not quite as easy to explain as we should like. It was William who, in a letter to the writer H. G. Wells, coined the famous phrase "the great bitch-goddess success." But he was not himself (any more than Wells) completely immune from her spell. However, his good nature was boundless, and everything he wrote (particularly his correspondence with his family and with many others) is worth reading—could well be called essential reading.

James's achievements as a psychologist are manifold. In the *Principles* he is a pioneer of both introspectionism and of the elements of the behavoristic approach (though not of the now at last discredited behaviorism, held by Watson and then SKINNER, which held itself to be the only scientific psychology), of what—it could be put—was useful in behaviorism. For him consciousness could be known by introspection. In *Principles* he pioneered the notion of the *stream-of-consciousness*, which he presented—in this case—with great subtlety. The other great pioneer student of stream-of-consciousness was the French philosopher Henri Bergson—the two men met and admired each other, but their work was independent. This work led directly to the phenomenology of Edmund Husserl (the teacher of Heidegger, who thereupon, when the time was ripe, denounced him to his fellow-Nazis as "non-Aryan") and to certain elements in the so-called "process" philosophy of Alfred North Whitehead, which has influenced two generations of American theologians. Since Husserl's phenomenology stands behind the existentialism of SARTRE, James could well be claimed as an anticipator of existentialism, although whether he would have liked to be so classed is another matter altogether.

But there is always too much to say about James, whatever limitations of space have been imposed: he is behind or relevant to most of the important ideas of the twentieth century. Here we must concentrate on his pragmatism, which he had fully formulated by about 1898, when he was fifty-six.

By the time of James's birth American philosophy as such had become almost entirely divorced from the practical experience of the American people, who had after all been *doing*: building a nation. This people had been forced to *make use* (a keynote in James's philosophy) of every resource at hand.

When William edited his father's *Literary Remains* in 1884, he was undoubtedly impressed with the way in which mysticism could be combined with the practical—Henry Sr. had himself been opposed to academic American philosophy. William began to feel that the idealism of his contemporaries was sterile and useless. As a philosopher he wanted to emphasize, as had SCHOPENHAUER, the importance of the *Will* in experience. As a psychologist he wanted philosophy to be useful to people—or nothing. Always bearing in mind his own now properly famous, if alas unheeded, motto that when people think they are thinking they are merely "rearranging their prejudices," he wished to make a definition of truth that would be above all *useful* in that it would be *usable*.

In brief, pragmatism amounts to this: "The ultimate test for us of what a truth means is the conduct it dictates or inspires." In other words, there is no such thing (as there was for PLATO) as a disinterested truth, an entity divorced from human experience. Everything is seen in terms of the consequences that will flow from it. We must ask ourselves: "How will this or that of my beliefs or convictions *function* in the real world?"

James took his pragmatism from a man who had, perhaps not even arguably, a greater mind—a greater philosophical mind—than his own: Charles Sanders Peirce, a fellow American (1839–1914) whose philosophical thinking lies behind or anticipates, like James's own, much of that of the twentieth century. Peirce was a very difficult man, but he understandably became so frustrated by James that he called his own pragmatism *pragmaticism* to distinguish it from James's more successful version. He truthfully declared that James had taken over his theory of *meaning*—"our idea of anything is our idea of its sensible effects"—and had transformed it into a theory of *truth*. He also admitted, however, that James was "so concrete, so living," whereas he, Peirce, was "a mere table of contents, so abstract, a very snarl of twine."

James treated Peirce well, arranging for him to deliver lectures when no one else would (he had been sacked from Johns Hopkins University for alleged "immorality"), but his important ideas only began to become available in the 1930s, and are still being published. He could not write clearly for long at a time, and some of what he wrote is impenetrable—James therefore cannot and should not be blamed for exploiting his ideas. James's very geniality gives him greater relevance than Peirce; and, after all, like WITTGENSTEIN or NIETZSCHE, he aimed to give philosophy relevance to human life, and therefore to extend it. On the other hand, pragmatism is of course open to the objection that it deliberately limits the truth by its very definition of it.

However, James could argue back that by such a limitation he afforded many non-philosophical people the capacity to hope and to lead better and more fruitful lives.

James denied, very much against the spirit of those American Hegelians who were his contemporaries, that absolute truth was knowable. However, he also argued against skepticism, since it represented negation. He would have argued just as vehemently against modern nihilists and self-styled "post-modernists" such as Jacques Derrida, on the grounds that, like their ultimate master the envious and ambitious Nazi Heidegger, they are barbarians whose overriding wish is to destroy human hope and thus drown their own disappointment.

Therefore he insisted that, even though absolute truth was indeed unknowable except in strictly subjective terms, "our nonintellectual nature does influence our convictions." Thus we *must* and we *do* go "beyond the evidence." He might even have allowed Hegelians or followers of MARX their proneness to this vice—if indeed it is a vice, since we cannot help it. He did not press his personal version of gnosticism—that there was a creator engaged in a fight against evil—upon others, but he did characteristically point out, into what one may well call the very heart of tolerance, that some "tough-minded" people did not need religion, while other "tender-minded" ones did.

But since James was judged on short remarks taken out of context, remarks such as "truth is in its results," he was therefore accused, and with some justification, of constructing a do-it-yourself kit which could be used to justify the Inquisition, aversion therapy, or the crude sadistic "psychology" of now properly marginalized modern "thinkers" such as Jensen or the Anglicized German, Hans Eysenck (tyrants of the "intelligence test," the "results" of which may be and have been interpreted along racist lines). That he was himself a kindly and decent man, who would have had no difficulty in rejecting fascism, is not a complete answer. However, his own notion of what he called a "pluralistic universe" (*A Pluralist Universe,* 1909) makes it perfectly clear that he was no advocate of violence or injustice.

How are we to judge what "works" (i.e. what in this system is "true") if we cannot go to pragmatism for guidance of a moral or ethical kind? And, strictly speaking, we cannot do the latter, because all it will give us is the purely subjective. "But," replied James, "experience is not simply an object: It is the whole sum of the relationship between concrete experiences of solving problems, and that is a process that never finishes, that is, indeed, always in process of becoming." That is what he called a pluralistic universe, and in it—he urged—we must continually try to discover, with open minds, what *does* work in an ethical sense. This is a universe which rejects (for example) Saint AUGUSTINE's "apology for evil" and allows for the pragmatic avoidance of it. But James never fully developed this side of his philosophy.

82

Relativity

Albert Einstein

1916

If (strictly between ourselves) we can only pretend to understand Einstein's theory of relativity we have at least this excuse: It is so hard to grasp—so in its way uncanny—that it took some years before resistance to it faded out among ordinary run-of-the-mill physicists. *Relativity* is the title of the book Einstein himself wrote to explain both his theories to the general public: the theory of *Special Relativity* (1905), and then the theory of *General Relativity* with which, after much struggle, stress, and strain, he completed it. This book went through sixteen editions and is still widely held to be incomparably the best introduction to its subject. But it is, inevitably, very technical—especially so its pivotal notion, the coordinate system; it cannot be said to be as "simple" as Einstein liked to claim.

The classical laws of physics had been formulated by NEWTON in his *Principles* in 1687. They assume that anything that is not subject to external forces will move at a constant velocity in a straight line. They also assume that *space, time,* and *mass* are absolute qualities. (In the Newtonian universe time, too, is, if only in principle, reversible.) Two tiny objects at an enormous distance exert the force of gravity upon each other; the equation needed to measure the force between them is the product of their masses multiplied by the constant of gravity, called G (a tiny amount) divided by the square of the distance. (One problem here was how could these two objects "know" each other.)

There seemed no reason to challenge Newton's laws until, in the terms of thermodynamics, Rudolf Clausius (1822–1888), following on work by Carnot and others, invented the term *entropy* (1859), and formulated the first two laws of thermodynamics—the second states that, in the real world, disorder (entropy) increases. In other words, kettles do not boil themselves.

On a different level, the new discoveries about magnetism and electricity by Faraday, MAXWELL, Hertz, and others, began to raise certain other fundamental difficulties.

Greek ideas about what they observed as the force of gravity were simple enough, and were based in a common sense vitiated (possibly) by their contempt for experimentation (a menial task fit only for slaves). Motion and standing-still (inertia) were absolute concepts. Bodies "respected" the center of the universe, which was the center of the earth, and they were attracted to it. Later, in Aristotelian scholastic philosophy, a body was said to become "jubilant" (an excellent example of anthropomorphism) as it neared its goal, and so to speed up: to accelerate. In the Newtonian universe all motion was seen as taking place against an absolute inertial "frame." This frame amounted to an infinite space that was at rest relative to everything else. Newton could assume that God had ordered things thus: that space consisted of points, time of instants. How he conceived the matter as a mystic (which, after all, he was) has not really been studied, or is not known.

The Victorians, in the face of their new difficulties, postulated the existence of some thing or things which they called the *ether* or *aether;* this provided a sort of artificial medium in which light waves, magnetic waves, and other sorts of waves could perform their functions. It is hard to imagine that when mathematicians and philosophers such as Bertrand Russell and Alfred North Whitehead were doing their earlier work, around 1900, these difficulties were persisting—that these men would have had no option but to consider "the ether." The term was still being used in the 1930s, although by then it did not mean anything. Only the philosopher William Clifford seems to have intuited the theory of relativity.

As the first decade of the twentieth century passed, things became increasingly puzzling and controversial, and the president of the American Society for the Advancement of Science, speaking in awareness of Einstein's Special Theory and of the work of the French mathematician Henri Poincaré (who nearly anticipated Einstein in 1898) and many others working in this field, probably best summed up how the run-of-the-mill scientists felt: "I do not believe that there is any man now living who can assert with truth that he can conceive of time which is a function of velocity or is willing to go to the stake for the conviction that his 'now' is another man's future or still another man's past."

For some years now, since 1945, though, scientists, using atomic clocks, have been able to measure the tiny difference between a clock on the top floor of a tall office

Einstein before the publication of his Theory of Relativity.

building, and one on its ground floor! The implications are obvious—and at least these can be clearly understood. As Einstein had himself written in 1905 in *On the Electrodynamics of Moving Bodies:* "Thence we concede that a balance clock at the equator must go more slowly, by a very small amount, than a precisely similar clock situated at one of the poles under otherwise identical conditions."

Now it is a measurable matter that your upstairs clocks run faster than your downstairs ones.

Einstein was born in Ulm, Germany, in 1879, into a Jewish family. His father was a successful businessman; his mother was more cultured and played the piano. He took up Swiss nationality in 1894 and became an American in 1940. Such of his books as the Nazis could get hold of were, of course, burned in Berlin, in 1933. (The Nazis also tried out a 300-degree circle, and made out that Shakespeare originated in Germany.)

Einstein's great discoveries were accomplished when he was young, and while he was living in comparative isolation from his fellow-scientists. When the article stating the Special Theory was published in 1905, he was employed in Berne, Switzerland, as an examiner of patents for technical flaws—he had failed to land any job as a physicist. He was a mere Swiss civil servant, third class. But he had known, if only vaguely, what he wanted to say since the age of about sixteen: yet another odd case of an undoubted genius seeming to "remember" his fate. Since he was not a particularly bright pupil at the Munich gymnasium where he received much of his education, and since he had been slow to talk—nicknamed by his nurse "Father Bore" on account of his dreaminess and uncommunicativeness—his genius is hard to account for in ordinary terms. The other great interest in his life was classical music, and this—in the 1930s—he played together with two of his closest friends, the king and queen of Belgium.

The scientific revolution he effected—although it must be emphasized that, while he was himself a solitary, similar work was always proceeding elsewhere along the lines he was pursuing—was as absolute in its way as those effected by COPERNICUS, GALILEO, KEPLER (who was able to rescue Galileo's theories from the scientifically damaging assumption of circular motion), and Newton himself.

Because Einstein's theory was *called* "relativity," it influenced historians and writers in every possible direction that this word could imply. Readers of Lawrence Durrell's pretentious but once widely admired *Alexandria Quartet* of the 1960s will recall that it was supposedly composed on "Einstein's principles." So were scores of other works. Such was Einstein's sway—whether, strictly speaking, it was really *his* sway or not.

I make no attempt here to give a full technical description of Einstein's progress from the Special Theory to the General Theory. This is no more than a brief summary of the difference that relativity has made, or in some cases ought (had it been understood) to have made, to "ordinary life." It is hardly even necessary, though, beyond emboldening its text, to point out the effect of Einstein's equivalence of mass and energy in the equation e = mc² (that is to say, energy is equivalent to mass multiplied by the speed of light, which is a constant—very approximately 186,320 miles per second—and which nothing that we know of can exceed). . . . It is not yet fully known how that will influence us. . . . This, though, was the most painful and drastic consequence of his thinking. Nor perhaps is it necessary to point out that all objects (but most noticably very heavy ones such as the sun) bend light. It was in this way that Einstein's theory was experimentally confirmed.

For ARISTOTLE and for the scientists of several centuries after him, the center of the earth was a special place, which was also the center of the universe. Einstein, on the contrary, argued that there was no special place in the universe: The laws of physics must be the same for every observer, wherever he may be. Motion is always relative: A given speed, to be meaningful, must depend on who makes the measurement—and from where and to where. In other words, distance and mass became relative, and both depend on the particular frame of reference of the observer. Einstein found that Newton's laws worked well enough up to certain speeds; but when these became really high (the true speed at which some far galaxies of our universe are receding from us add up to high proportions of the speed of light) then measuring rulers shrank and became heavier, and clocks ran slower. These effects hold with all motion, but most are simply not detectable.

For Newton's old absolute frame, Einstein substituted another and real constant: the speed of light. All these things have been shown to be true by a variety of increasingly sophisticated instruments, and it is still the fact that nothing has been found that can travel faster than light (particles called *tachyons* which can—as they accelerate they are supposed to lose energy—have been postulated, but none have been detected, and no one now seems to believe in them).

That was as far as Einstein had got in 1905, and it presented him with problems. Until then gravity had been looked upon as a force acting instantaneously. His solution tells us why the theory of relativity is really a theory of gravity. But how could the force of gravity travel "faster" than the speed of light? How could it act instantaneously? Essentially what Einstein did was to substitute spacetime, or space-time, for the hitherto separate concepts of space *and* time. By this means he could cease to regard the ubiquitous gravity as, precisely, a *force;* instead, he redefined it as a property of spacetime—which is curved because of it. Or, put another way, matter shapes the geometry of what is around it.

Although there is little doubt that Einstein's theory of relativity will eventually be displaced by another theory, one even more explanatory of all the features of the universe—this is expected by most scientists—it has so far been favored by experiments over the Newtonian account. In the bang-up-to-date terms of an efficient popular science writer, his theories "work equally well when applied to the Universe as a whole. . . . The Universe can be pictured as an inside-out black hole"—a black hole, or singularity, being, of course, a region of spacetime that has been bent back on itself by its very high (indeed, unimaginably high) density. If the "big bang" theory of the universe is correct—it is almost universally accepted now, but that does not mean that it will prove to be right, any more than Ptolemy was right when he explained the manner in which the sun and planets orbited the earth—then in the first few seconds of creation matter was at its densest. The best account of this event outside physics is the *Tzimtzum,* an element in the later thinking of the KABBALAH—although perhaps picked up from a first-century hint.

Einstein in his later life could never come to terms with the Uncertainty Principle formulated in 1927 by Werner Heisenberg (1901–1976) and arising from quantum physics. In the subatomic world of quantum physics—to a nonphysicist, and perhaps to an honest physicist too, it appears to be a crazy Alice in Wonderland world—the velocity of a particle may be measured, and so may its position—but not both. (Many science-fiction writers profitably fail to distinguish between the subatomic world and the ordinary "sane" one.) Heisenberg admitted that he owed his formulation of this famous principle to a conversation he had with Einstein in 1926—but Einstein could never reconcile himself with the notion that it was now necessary to give up a deterministic view of nature, and so famously said that while quantum mechanics demanded "special attention" it was not the "true Jacob": "He [God, in a figurative sense] does not play dice."

For some years Einstein worked with positive interest on the quantum theory, but in about 1925, in the words of his most useful and scrupulous expositor, Jeremy Bernstein, writing in his *Einstein* in 1973, "he turned against it. Perhaps some future generation of physicists will, somehow, discover that Einstein's critical intuitions were really right, though this does not now seem likely."

It seems now even less likely than it did twenty-five years ago. Yet in this field, now torn apart as much by metaphysics as by physics (one particularly absurd proposal is that a certain version of quantum mechanics could explain "creation from nothing"), paradigms (in the sense used by KUHN) can change. We do need to respect scientific methodology, and even to insist on it; but we should not be misled as to its scope. We are fairly sure that black holes exist, but we cannot know for certain what is in one unless we should be contained within it. Einstein himself was a kind of deist: On the imaginative level he was quite a simple man, all of whose nonscientific passions went into music.

Stephen Hawking—Einstein's successor in the eyes of many—is, at that level, an even simpler man, quite without Einstein's gifts (or perhaps wish) for lucidity. *A Brief History of Time* does not make sense as it stands, whereas *Relativity* makes a fair stab at doing so. Hawking's cosmology is very muddled indeed, and he is pretentious when he tries to write about it in nonscientific terms, whatever the future will say about his status as just a scientist—and this will not be as enthusiastic about him as the general public is now.

What is needed is a physicist who is also a real Kabbalist—not a man who is flattered to be asked to talk about "god" but who is quite incapable of doing so to any serious effect. But physicists and Kabbalists don't usually come together.

83

The Mind and Society

Vilfredo Pareto

1916

The art or science, or art/science—or whatever it may or may not be—of sociology began with Auguste Comte, who named it and was overconfident about its potential. Granted, then, Comte's influence, that of Franco-Italian Vilfredo Pareto was far more decisive, and of much greater depth. Pareto was, in essence, a twentieth-century heir of Machiavelli—of whom Bacon wrote that he tells of "what men do and not what they ought to do"—and his reputation suffered just as Machiavelli's preposterously did, and still does. (It cannot go unmentioned that he also owed much to another formidable Italian politician and thinker, Gaetano Mosca, 1858–1941.) But you do not have to like a person, or to approve of the mask he chooses to wear, to acknowledge his value as a thinker. Sociologists, while they did not much like Pareto's undoubted fascist connections, could hardly ignore him. With the German Max Weber and the Frenchman Emile Durkheim (the latter is mentioned in more than passing in the section on Comte), he is one of the three founding fathers of modern sociology. Within that mixture, seldom in any case bland, Pareto represents the bitterest factor of all—and he enjoyed being like that. No trace whatsoever of sentimentality—not even that modicum that makes people "human"—can be found within his vast works. Nor was he important and influential only as a sociologist.

He was born in Paris, of a Genoese father who had been exiled from his country by the ruling House of Savoy, and a French mother. The family returned to Italy when he was ten years old, and he received his education in Turin. He qualified as an engineer and worked on the railways and then as manager of an iron mine. It was his belief in free trade, the necessity of which he preached in alliance with the liberals, that cost him his political and academic career in his own country. But in 1893 he was appointed professor of political economy at the University of Lausanne. In this period, until 1898, he became an economist highly influential in France and Italy (he wrote fluently in French as well as in Italian). His view that an economy reaches maximum efficiency ("Pareto optimality") only when it is impossible to improve one individual's position without damaging another's, and that this happens only when the largest proportion of the people—"Eighty—twenty," "the trivial many—the critical few," as some laconically put it—are (to put it bluntly) badly off, was as unpopular as it was influential. Much of his bad reputation has stemmed from the refusal of his critics to recognize that as a thinker, though a sour misanthropist, he was essentially *descriptive* rather than *prescriptive*. He would have been even more useful had it been recognized that he directed himself always to how-things-are as distinct from how-they-ought-to-be. His reputation rose temporarily when his early prophecy against Marx (with many of whose economic analyses he agreed), that in any Marxist system the wicked old elites would soon be replaced by equally wicked new ones, was proved right in the years after 1917.

Pareto made an enormous contribution to thinking about the nature and function of sexuality in society with his *La Mythe vertuiste et la littérature immorale* (1911), in which he analyzed to devastating effect the hypocrisy of governments and their advisers toward "indecent" literature. But that book, untranslated into English, in which he applied his fundamental insights to the single most vexing subject known to man (and woman), has hardly been influential, rather it has been virtually ignored. It is, as Pareto always was, hard on all parties. But it will have its day yet. His description of the ways in which Western societies "dissemble" their concerns with sex has classical power and force, and he can hardly be ignored for much longer.

One strategy employed to cause ignorance of what he tried to say has been to dismiss him as a cynical fascist—but this will no longer do. He was no more a true fascist than many other early supporters of Mussolini, and Italy abounded in these and included many who later became socialists and communists, who opposed him with great bitterness and determination. Pareto died before Mussolini had long been in power, and in any case would even during his own lifetime have endorsed Churchill's famous wartime dismissal of Il Duce as "a tattered lackey." Pareto never believed anything of this world was *much* good. And Italy itself has retained Mussolini's legal system, and already neofascists have virtually participated, in government. . . .

After 1898 Pareto became a recluse. He inherited money and so was able to retire to Céligny, in Switzerland, to devote himself to writing. He reemerged in 1922 when he praised Mussolini (who had just seized power in Italy) in an ambiguously half-ironic article—but while praising Mussolini's "achievements" he also later made a plea for free speech, academic freedom, and the avoidance of an agreement (which was later reached, if that is the word) between the Italian government and the Vatican!—and was appointed senator. Mussolini had once arranged to take one of his courses in Switzerland, and was quite infatuated with him—as he also was with WILLIAM JAMES.

That certainly was a mistaken lapse into vanity by a man who had been neglected by his own country for far too long. It is also right to recall that Pareto turned his back, with ostensible thoroughness, upon his own past, during which he had sheltered refugees, passionately taken the side of Dreyfus in the notorious affair (in which a loyal Jew had been convicted of an act of treason committed by another), and had been a hot-blooded liberal. But to call him "the Marx of fascism" because of all this, as the left-wing critic Franz Borkenau did, was a worse and more misleading mistake. Pareto was already doubting the wisdom of his action before he died in August of 1923, less than a year later. After all, Mussolini was not then quite the dictator he became, and he had the support of many others beside (for example) George Bernard Shaw and Winston Churchill.

Although the connection is never made—and is hardly ever even mentioned, on the bizarre grounds (invented by thin-blooded academics, or ones who copulate and express their romantic urges in painless trance) that personal affairs cannot influence ideas—something else, as well as disillusion with crooked Italian liberal politicians, had happened to such optimism as poor Pareto had once possessed. It was this, and not the fortune he inherited, that caused him to turn part-recluse (he suffered from heart disease, but did occasionally give lectures until 1907).

In 1889 he had married Alessandra Bakunin. One day he returned from a Paris trip to find that she had absconded with the cook and a considerable amount of property. It is hardly a wonder that he turned to a passionately selective and careful use of wines—in which he became an expert—and hedonistic liqueurs (his collection was renowned), and to the denunciation of all emotional expression in all circumstances. No doubt he went too far, but this excess did not prevent him from exercising his mind in an extraordinarily useful and salutary manner. He wrote: "My sentiments lead me to favor freedom; therefore I have taken pains to react against them. But I may have gone too far." That at least was corrosively intelligent. So no matter, then, that it was his younger self that he was angrily lambasting in his prose, which is self-parodyingly and professorially dull, but relieved by quite substantial patches of lucid and playful irony. He built his luxurious house in the canton of Switzerland that charged the lowest taxes. Roman Catholic laws prevented him from divorcing Alessandra, but he was fortunate in finding a French girl, Jean Regis, who lived with him and looked after him. By obtaining technical citizenship of Fiume he managed at last to marry her just a few months before his death. She alone knew the "human" side of him, which was far more genial and humane than he ever allowed the public to suspect. Even his detractors admit that he would never have tolerated Mussolini for long: He liked too much to be able to say "I told you so"—and that had been his comment when Mussolini marched on Rome. But his influence, like that of Machiavelli, has been abrasive in the extreme, and he meant it to be.

Pareto's main points, cast in more everyday terms than he liked to employ, are that, besides the fact that any definition of the word *sociology* is worse than useless, human nature does not really change; and that while men actually live according to what he called *sentiment* (the word has a peculiar force with him), they pretend to do so according to *reason*. One instantly recalls the far more dry-as-dust KUHN, and the rage he caused when he suggested that the too-hallowed scientists were not only more ingenious but also as nonrational as the rest of us.

In what is one of the most unobtrusively psychological examinations of human behavior made in the twentieth century, Pareto in his *Mind and Society (Trattato de Sociologica Generale)* relentlessly demonstrates that societies, like the people of whom they consist, do not behave according to reason. He does not use Freudian terminology, and would not even had he carefully read FREUD, but the Freudian influence has been adduced more than once.

Without going into the question of whether he used Freud's work or not (he must have known of him), *The Mind and Society* can confidently be described as evincing a sociology that is thoroughgoingly Freudian in spirit. He studies the nonlogical actions of men (not their *illogical* actions so much: he takes those for granted), and states that they provide the foundation of the social system. They arise from his *sentiments*.

Pareto then introduces what he calls *residues*. These, which he cautiously classifies, are (he claims) the product of "certain instincts in human beings" (i.e., the sentiments). The liking for sugar would not be a residue. But *a belief in sugar* would be a residue. The sentiments are stable, but the residues are not: They are variable. We might call some of them (but with less deadly accuracy than Pareto achieves) *prejudices, monstrosities,* or *insanities*.

It was an astute and subtle analysis, and it remains a formidable way of explaining many social absurdities. For example, some believe that the works of SHAKESPEARE as explicitly acknowledged by his publishers and by the Elizabethan public and his personal friends, were not by him. This error arises from a combination of a number of instincts or Paretian sentiments: from *paranoia* and *suspicion*, from *snobbishness* (those who did not attend universities cannot be great poets or playwrights), from *vanity* (*I* know better), and so on and so forth. It is *nonlogical* even though, for all I know, it may not be *illogical*. Such harmful monstrosities as the invention of "satanic child-abuse," or "alien invasions," for which there is no hard evidence whatsoever, can to this day best be explained by recourse to Paretian methodology. But we cannot pretend to understand all the basic instincts or sentiments. For Pareto shrewdly added: "We can only have found those instincts [here he means *sentiments*] which give rise to rationalization; we cannot have encountered those which are not concealed by rationalizations."

Pareto has been called a "positivist" and an adherent of "scientism." This is seriously misleading, but understandable. His work does seem cold, and especially so to those who would really like to improve the world. But such an improvement is not within the grasp of the kind of inquiries he was set upon making. You cannot make a silk purse out of sow's ear, and Pareto, like Machiavelli (and Mosca) was concerned with the nature of the sow's ear. Also, it is true that at the outset of his career he wished to be as detached as was possible in his work and to be able to draw the same conclusions from his material as physicists drew from theirs. But there is an important difference. Pareto's own disclaimer at the beginning of the *The Mind and Society* that it is impossible to define sociology, and indeed the whole spirit of his work—especially his rapturous and sometimes Swiftian irony—makes it clear that he was no positivist. He enjoys annoying people, perhaps mainly because his wife ran off with his cook, but he keeps what he is saying in his work, as perhaps distinct from how he sometimes presents it, quite free from his anger, his hatred, and his disappointment with his own youthful ideals.

T. S. Eliot, a very minor poet and plagiarist once taken as "great" (which he wanted to be), once memorably expressed the near-commonplace notion that reality is unpleasant: "Mankind cannot bear much reality." So Pareto is unpleasant to have around. He is probably not in paradise. But his account of how *not* to reach paradise is inimitable and even precious—and it is often very funny. It remains to add that he was, personally, always a generous and considerate man.

84

Psychological Types

Carl Gustav Jung

1921

In psychology and therefore in our understanding of the way the human mind works (of which the degree of our knowledge, though considerable, could be compared to the visible tip of the proverbial iceberg), the Swiss Carl Gustav Jung (1875–1961) has been only less influential than Sigmund Freud, from whom he took some—though not quite all—of his basic ideas. Neither of these men, to the considerable irritation of some psychologists, were qualified psychologists.

It is Jung's outlook as a whole that has been so influential, and much of this is embodied in *Psychological Types*. But if Freud is (inevitably) controversial, then Jung is perhaps doubly so. Unlike Freud, so far as we can certainly know, Jung is now known to have, on occasion, faked evidence; he also did what no physician or analyst is supposed to do: slept with his (female) patients—and more than once. Yet he coined the term *complex* (as in such phrases as "inferiority complex" or "Oedipus complex"), and he developed a form of word-association test by which patients' hidden concerns may often be traced. His faking was not so much deceitful as done in the exasperation of his own certainty.

He was the son of a Protestant pastor in Keswil, in Canton Thurgau. By 1905 he was lecturing on psychiatry at the University of Zürich, after qualifying as a doctor and doing practical work in a mental hospital. Between 1907 and 1913 he collaborated with Freud, who thought very highly of him. But in 1913 he broke away from Freud: He did not like to be the subservient partner, and, perhaps more important, he believed (to put this in its simplest terms) that Freud put too much emphasis on sexuality. Much later, in opportunistic papers published in Nazi Germany, he would meanly attack Freud for his Jewishness. Jung's anti-Semitism is now well established, although his supporters claim that he has been misunderstood—otherwise there are two views of this matter, that he was an anti-Semite ("the Jew," he wrote in a Nazi journal, "is like the woman"), or that he was simply an opportunist. Eventually Freud modified his own theory of sexuality, so that it became more or less indistinguishable from Jung's; but the men differed in their attitude to religion, Freud, like the philosopher Ludwig Feuerbach, seeing it as an illusion, Jung as a reality.

Jung had more experience of, and was more interested in, actual madness—psychosis—than was Freud. His first notable book (1906) was a study of schizophrenia. However, he made little or no eventual contribution to the treatment of this illness, since all the real progress that has been made, as also in the case of manic-depressive illness, has depended on the use of drugs—and of that branch of medicine, pharmacology, Jung had little knowledge. Real insanity, it is now well realized, cannot be cured by talking to—or being brainwashed by—analysts of any persuasion. That it cannot be prevented through the same procedure is not yet quite so well established.

However, what Jung had to say about the origins of schizophrenic psychosis was later reinterpreted in the light of what he called analytic psychology (to distinguish it from Freud's psychoanalysis), and so, in this sense, as a theory of the human psyche, it *was* influential. Jung's notion of psychosis was that the delusional symptoms suffered by the patient were in fact explanatory devices which in themselves tried to make sense of his or her situation. These symptoms also drew on myth in a manner that led Jung to postulate an actual entity, which he called the "collective unconscious," a deeper layer of the mind which lay beneath the merely personal.

To take but one notorious example of the differences that developed between Jung and Freud: Freud of course "invented" and defined the so-called Oedipus Complex in males, as a repressed wish to have sexual intercourse with the mother and to kill the father (the process in girls was, he alleged, more complicated). Jung, taking what seemed to be a far more common sense view (but in fact he had less commonsense than Freud) asserted, on the contrary, that in either sex there existed a powerful need to possess, exclusively, the mother, the most protective and comforting being known. Freud's account, which bears about it a preposterous whiff of truth—though the notion of "sexual intercourse" needs to be modified—would account much more satisfactorily for that mysterious and still incompletely explained factor, the taboo on incest; but Jung's is easier to work with and yields its own wider insight.

Jung's best and most important book is *Psychological Types* (1921). This is based on work he began in 1913, just after he had broken with Freud. Little of it is really original, but Jung was one of those (like Freud himself in psychology or ADAM SMITH and KEYNES in economics) who can sum up the concerns of an era at a stroke, and in a convincing manner. Here Jung made his famous distinction (the first to be made) between "extroverts" and "introverts." This is undoubtedly his greatest contribution to psychology—not because such types necessarily exist, but because the theory has excellent explanatory potential. A similarly intelligent and thoughtful distinction, between so-called Shame Cultures and Guilt Cultures, made by the American anthropologist Ruth Benedict, failed only because it was not thought to possess such potential.

The extrovert is one who is interested mostly in the external world; the introvert is interested in what goes on in his own mind. Jung elaborated on this by distinguishing among four types of approach: thinking, feeling, sensation, and intuition—two pairs of opposites. By nature human beings sought to achieve balance, equilibrium, but they were also one-sided: hence their neuroses. Jung encouraged his own patients to try to achieve equilibrium by a process he called "individuation": In the course of this they were to make use of not only dreams but also of waking fantasies (free reveries); these latter were reminiscent of his earlier word-association tests. Above all patients (but Jung, increasingly a Wise Old Man, came to conceive of the whole of humanity as his patient) were urged to make full use of their creative faculties, and in particular to write out or paint their inner experiences. He found that people, although different, tended to draw upon remarkably similar experiences or "landmarks." These "primordial images" he christened, using an existing word, "archetypes." Jung believed in the real existence of these archetypes, although he seemed little interested in any philosophical precedents upon which he might have drawn for such an assertion.

Jung drew on much "occult" and religious material, although never in a really scholarly manner: gnosticism (some of the findings at Nag Hammadi were called the "Jung Codex" in his honor), alchemy (originally a complex attempt to achieve individuation, not one to obtain riches by the transmutation of base metals to gold), and Oriental books such as the I CHING. He also developed—from earlier thinking— the notion of "synchronicity," or "significant coincidence." A moment, he insisted, possessed—beyond mere cause and effect—a quality of its own. Thus he explained astrology and supernatural phenomena. His book on this subject, *Synchronicity: An Acausal Connecting Principle* (1952), has proved very influential. In it he claimed that if "natural law were an absolute truth, then . . . there could not possibly be any processes that deviate from it. But since causality is a *statistical* truth, it holds good only on average . . . . By synchronicity I mean the occurrence of a *meaningful coincidence in time.*"

Where Freud tended to mechanistic explanations, Jung was devoted to a more religious approach, in which the human being has a place in the universe. But Jung was far less systematic than Freud and was a much less effective, less lucid writer. Furthermore, his own system has been seen, not at all unconvincingly, as largely a romantic elaboration of Freud's. Jung's midlife crisis, about which he wrote, was more severe than Freud's. *Answer to Job* (1952), the book he wrote under the influence of various gnostic and kabbalistic works which he had never even studied systematically or with real scholarly care, lacks the lucidity to be found in the work of Gershom Scholem and MARTIN BUBER. But his "dark impressiveness" has been enormously influential, and the various always semiwarring factions of analytical psychology continue to flourish—nor are these factions lacking in sinister manipulative personalities, men, some of them ex-priests or charlatans of the first order, who have gained great power—power which they do not exercise with decency, care, or responsibility. True, such men (and occasionally women) exist in all persuasions—but more exist within what calls itself the Jungian fold than elsewhere.

Jung affected the lives or at least the views of personalities as diverse as the novelist and playwright J. B. Priestley, the critic and poet Herbert Read (an editor of his *Collected Works* in English), the now unjustly neglected novelist P. H. Newby (a critic wrote an article about him entitled "Portrait of the Artist as a Jung Man") and, possibly more significantly, the physicist Wolfgang Pauli. At the present time, however, as the century draws to its close, his reputation as an honest or even as a completely sane man has begun to sink quite rapidly. The final verdict way well be that, as a necessary counterpart to Freud as an advocate of the spiritual, he was a profound disappointment.

However, even those who cannot admire him must concede that he did much to maintain, as against overconfident atheist-positivists, that religious feeling existed naturally in human beings, and could not be reduced to mere superstition or wishful thinking. In this respect he owed much to a superior thinker who is now in some danger of being forgotten: the German Lutheran Rudolf Otto (1869–1937) who, in his 1917 book *Das Heilige (The Holy)*, coined the word "numinous" (from the Latin *numen*, "spiritual"). Otto, who founded the Religious League of Mankind and who did much invaluable work on Hinduism and Zen Buddhism, insisted, and convincingly so, that numinous experience was one of a "feeling of createdness," which prompted both awe and wonder: A creator is experienced not only as a *mysterium tremendum*, "totally other" but also as a *Fascinans*, something that fills with blissful exaltation. The affinities with Martin Buber are obvious, and the latter's—as distinct from Jung's—more cogent elaborations on this experience may eventually attract more readers, even though they do anything but provide a convenient system. Already one faction in analytical psychology works with a combination of Jungian and Kleinian ideas—the latter based on the thinking of the post-Freudian Melanie Klein—and it seems likely that Jung's own system will become increasingly thus diffused.

85

I and Thou

Martin Buber

1923

Martin Buber exercised his most immediate influence with his retelling of the Hasidic Jewish stories, published throughout his lifetime and eventually collected in translation as *Tales of the Hasidim* (1962). Hasidism was an eighteenth-century European Jewish movement—Buber became aware of it in 1904—which drew its inspiration and its vitality directly from the KABBALAH; and Buber himself, although he notably acknowledged other traditions, can hardly be called other than a thoroughgoing Kabbalist. His own doctrines, which will ultimately have a greater influence even than his retelling of the *Tales,* are set forth in his mystical work, and his masterpiece, *I and Thou (Ich und Du).*

Buber, born in Vienna in 1878, was brought up by his grandfather Solomon Buber (a noted Hebrew scholar) in Galicia in Poland from the age of three, when his parents' marriage broke up. He studied philosophy at various universities, married Paula Winkler (a novelist) in 1902, and became an ardent Zionist. From the beginning, however, his Zionism was cultural rather than political. He even opposed Theodore Herzl's leadership of the Zionist movement. The essence of Zionism is that the Jews are a nation as well as a people; but Buber advocated a Palestine that would be as open to Arabs as to Jews, and at the 1921 Zionist Congress he forcefully put forward this idea. From this time onward Buber became unpopular with a certain sizable section of Jewry; he still was, and for the same reasons, when he died in Jerusalem, in 1965 at the age of eighty-seven. He had settled there in 1938, after defying the Nazis for as long as he could in Germany. Particularly resented by his opponents was his very high international standing.

Buber also distinguished himself, with his friend Franz Rosenweig, as the translator of the Bible into German. This version and its interpretations were themselves highly influential on theology, although Buber was not really any more a theologian than he was a socialist or a philosopher—he was above all a mystic. But perhaps that is not to say any more than that he tried to explain his almost inexpressible vision of life as it should be lived.

Most famous and crucial in the Bible translation was the Buber-Rosenweig interpretation of Exodus 3:14, in which God speaks to Moses. This is usually rendered as "I am that I am," but Buber-Rosenweig changed it to "I will be there such as I will be there," which implies that salvation is by no means inevitable, but requires a special sort of spiritual worth on the part of human beings, whose task is to "redeem God"—in just that sense which the Lurianic KABBALAH insists upon *tikkun* (restoration).

I and Thou appeared in 1923. It represented Buber's "new answer to everything," and saw life as, essentially, a form of dialogue. The book elaborates on the teachings of the founder of Hasidism, the Ba'al Shem Tov (Israel ben Eliezer), a mystic who lived during the first sixty years of the eighteenth century. Israel, who wrote nothing down, brought Jewish mysticism to the common people by giving what had previously lapsed into an elitist and over-learned tradition an emotional and colloquial fervor: Prayer had to be, not ritual and simply by rote, but wholly and truly meant.

In *I and Thou* two kinds of dialogue are discussed. There is the ordinary common one, which we use in everyday life, of I-It, and there is the religious one, of I-Thou. The latter Buber presented, although not explicitly, as a practical means of achieving, or helping to achieve, *tikkun*. His great hero, the Ba'al Shem Tov, had founded Hasidism in the direct wake of the Lurianic Kabbalah. But *I and Thou* was often taken up as a form of existentialism, which is itself a kind of modern and usually secular expression of gnosticism.

Buber had for himself found early support for his speculations in an important aspect of the philosophy of KANT, who insisted that full objectivity was impossible because we can know the world only through the categories, such as space and time, which we are bound to impose upon it. Whereas Kant repudiated mysticism as unnecessary, however, Buber took the other direction. He was a pantheist, too, inasmuch as, like SPINOZA, he saw what we call God not as a separate and special entity, but present in everything. Everything therefore, conversely, was to be found in God.

Buber imposed dialogue, and therefore a spirit of profound tolerance, on the rift between Judaism and Christianity. The Jew "knows" that there has not yet been a messiah. The Christian also "knows" that Jesus Christ was the messiah. These two "knowledges" appear to be wholly irreconcilable. The atheistic approach is to sneer and dismiss both notions as fantasies arising from "ignorance of science." But science, besides being unable to explain the fact of creation, blandly ignores the existence of the mysterious inner life that forms, for everyone, the background of everyday existence.

The nature of this inner life, Buber—unlike most existentialists—insisted, is essentially religious. The psychological details of his establishment of this fact are convincing and profound. On those reconciliatory grounds he stated that the "inner certainties" of the Jew and the Christian (and, indeed, as he made clear, the Hindu, Sufi, Buddhist, or any other nonpathological religion)—he was, essentially, speaking of the inner certainties of *other people*—were themselves mysteries.

For the Kantian Buber we *cannot* know God as an objective entity. But we *can* know our own relationships with her or him (his own particular *Thou* was his wife). Thus he wrote: "The religious essence of every religion is found in the certainty that the meaning of existence is open and accessible in the actual lived concrete, not above the struggle with reality but in it. A human being can enter into an I-Thou type of relationship even with a dog or a meadow." This was close to the thinking of the unrepentant Nazi Heidegger, although in the case of the latter the expression of it is entirely devoid of loving expression, being replaced by a ghastly, barely coherent, and pretentious jargon—yet it is Heidegger who has gained the following of so many postwar philosophers, and who is the malevolent inspirer of the current nihilism called "postmodernism."

The I-It relationship, Buber (good Kabbalist as he was) fully understood, is necessary—just as, in similar types of thinking, the personality that forms over the true character is necessary for the building up of a soul—and people get their living through it. It is not possible to be other than "partial" in business or trade relationships. But we cannot be real and completely ourselves (Buber claimed) in such relationships, and may well be unable to *listen* or *receive* properly. *Listening* and *receiving* are an essential part of the I-Thou relationship. Indeed, as he conceded, every I-Thou relationship is actually fated to turn into and I-It relationship. But the I-Thou can be renewed.

The point is that those who live in the I-It relationship recommended by atheists and even atheist-humanists are *not fully human*. There is more than a mere echo of MARX here, in his writing about the dehumanization involved in economic life; but Buber is against all theory, and with a vengeance. For him we learn to become human through being "called into" an I-Thou relationship—a relationship in which one speaks with "total open-ness" to the other. (The part sexual intimacy plays in this is hardly to be neglected.) Because of the intense difficulty of such relationships, Buber drew heavily on what he called "the holy insecurity" of Hasidism, a kind of tolerant part-skepticism in whose essence he "excelled."

Buber wrote, edited, or translated more than eighty books, including a novel. Most of these were on the subject of Hasidism. He fruitfully applied I-Thou thinking to such activities as education as well as to Jewish-Arab understanding. He is best approached through his retelling of the Hasidic tales, and then through *I and Thou*, which was first translated into English in 1937. Its influence for good, however subterranean and individual, has been incalculable, although politicians and merchants, masters of I-It, never read or speak of it.

86

The Trial

Franz Kafka

1925

"But I'm not guilty. It's a mistake. How can a person be guilty
at all? Surely we are all human beings here, the one like the
other."

"That is right, but that is the way the guilty are wont to talk."

Franz Kafka's novel *The Trial* (*Der Prozess,* written 1914–15) was
published—against his express wishes that all his work (including some stories that he had already published) be "destroyed unread and in their
entirety"—soon after his premature death from tuberculosis of the larynx:
But his close friend, the gifted novelist and critic Max Brod, rightly decided
that all his work was far too vital to suppress under any circumstances.

Posterity has not blamed Brod, who was in any case well aware that
Kafka had been ambivalent on the subject—possibly he had felt, too despair-
ingly, that his "message" was simply too negative. By 1930, when *The Trial*

appeared in the pioneer English translation made by the Scottish poet Edwin Muir and his novelist wife Willa, its fame had already spread far and wide; by today, some seventy years later, the general public knows of it through almost countless movie, radio, and television adaptations.

Combined sales of *The Trial* do not nearly equal those of the perennially popular *Gone With the Wind,* but its *influence* has been incomparably greater. Whereas the one has entertained millions, and is merely read, but hardly remembered, the other has affected some, even many, of the ways in which people think. There has been a slow but sure "trickle-down" effect (if, indeed, such an effect is properly described as *downward*): Kafka was initially most appreciated by "intellectuals," but it is has become increasingly clear that he, although himself very much an intellectual, wrote about how "ordinary people" feel, too. *The Trial* could well be, among other things, a blueprint for members of city councils anywhere; but these are the only people who remain unaware of it—unless of course they vaguely think of it as an Andrew Lloyd Webber musical (Lloyd Webber is the "composer" of a fanfare for the now thriving British Conservative Party), which it will surely become.

The scholar and critic the late J. P. Stern, wrote, in introducing a new, more accurate (although not better accomplished) translation of *The Trial* in 1977:

> "Kafkaesque" is the only word in common English use [he meant "American" as well, of course] which derives from German literature. Its meanings range from "weird," "mysterious," "tortuously bureaucratic" to "nightmarish" and "horrible," yet we do not associate it with the horror machines of science fiction or of Edgar Allan Poe. Inseparable from the "Kafkaesque" effect is its *everyday quality.* It involves, not outlandish gadgets or inhabitants from Mars, but a process in the course of which the *humdrum elements of our experience* are estranged from us. [The italics are mine.]

Franz Kafka was born in Prague, Czechoslovakia—then part of the Austro-Hungarian Empire—into a Jewish family in 1883. His father, Hermann, was a quite prosperous merchant, the owner of a haberdashery warehouse. He was also dominating, mercenary, healthy, philistine, vulgar, and irascible. Franz had three sisters, all of whom perished in Hitler's camps. He was afraid of his father, and, although he mocked and derided himself for it, irresistibly sought an approval from him that he was by no means equipped to give; Franz was quite unable to express, directly, his feelings of extreme hostility toward him. After a strict schooling, Franz Kafka studied law, in which he took his degree, and literature at the German University in Prague (1901–06). He began writing in about 1904, at just about the same time that he contracted the disease that killed him.

In 1908 he took up a post at the Workers' Accident Insurance Institute, a government-sponsored organization. He worked there—always highly conscientiously—for fourteen years, until his health obliged him to retire. He died in a sanatorium near Vienna in June 1924 at only forty-one. During his life he had many girlfriends, many affairs, and a number of always eventually broken engagements. (He did, however, finally settle down with one girl, a Pole, Dora Dymant, from July 1923 until his death in the following June.)

In his short lifetime he published several small volumes of stories, which were much admired but did not make him famous. He did, though, receive the coveted Fontane Prize in 1915 for "The Stoker," which later became the first chapter of his novel *Amerika*. His most substantial novel, *Das Schloss* (*The Castle; Schloss*, however, also means "lock")—it lacks an ending, and *The Trial*, as finished as any long piece Kafka wrote, has exercised more influence—was issued in 1926, followed by *Amerika* in 1927. Editions of the complete works came after that. Also came many editions of his letters—all translated—and of his *diary;* there is even a completely spurious record of "conversations" with him by an amusing Prague literary confidence-man called Gustave Janouch. There are by now at least fifty biographies, as well as Max Brod's own invaluable and in certain respects still unsurpassed account.

There is now a massive literature on Kafka, who is subject to wildly varying interpretations. He has been described as a satirist of bureaucracy, a prophet, a sick pessimist, an allegorist both Christian and Jewish, a surrealist, an atheist, and a symbolist. He is most of these things (but certainly not a Christian in the usual sense, an atheist, or a surrealist), and, in addition, he is a supremely *comic* writer on subjects either tragic or potentially tragic. The Czechs have always been able to see this, as the majority of Russians have been able to see the same thing in Dostoyevsky. Other readers have had difficulties, and some of them invest him with a wholly inappropriate air of solemnity. But of course the adjective *comic* does not imply either "lacking in seriousness" or "unaccompanied by other qualities." If that were the case then RABELAIS, just for one, would have to be written off as unserious.

It is well to see, initially, the comic side of Kafka's writing: of, for example, the fact that a feeble man is transformed into a kind of beetle, at which his father throws an apple core which then rots ("Metamorphosis"). And of the fact that none of us as we read *The Trial* could possibly imagine "anything like that could happen to us"—when the very subject of the novel is that this is a bleak metaphor for what is already happening to us, right now. For are we not the servants of nameless masters who themselves have no purpose?

The protagonist of *The Castle*, Kafka's greatest masterpiece, presents himself as a land surveyor, but he is actually a confidence man without qualifications—nor is there any real castle in the book, for all that a castle is its central subject. It is absolutely essential, then, to see the humor in Kafka.

Kafka was "modernist," but belongs quite as much to the past as he does to the present or the future. He wrote in a serene, "everyday" kind of prose, which is blandly ironic and yet beautiful at the same time; even the letters he wrote in his job capacity are utterly characteristic of him, and are in a sense a part of his work. Modestly doubtful of the extent of his creative gift—sometimes tormented by his doubts—Kafka is the writer *par excellence:* He lived out his doomed life as creator above all, skeptical, devout, questioning, and always able to see the funny side of things, even of the illness that took him at such a tragically young age—"I have no literary interests," he once told a girlfriend, "but I consist of literature, it is the only thing I am and can ever be."

It is worth saying that he was well and loyally served by his friend Brod—who has been the victim of much jealousy and patronage. It is also worth saying that too much emphasis has been put, by literary critics, upon Kafka as "tortured artist." He was a tortured artist. But he was also very much an ordinary man, although highly sexed because the illness from which he suffered often has that effect; he was also though as "fun-loving" as anyone has ever been.

Kafka's relevance to our own times is aptly pinpointed by a remark he made in his diary in 1918: "I have immensely absorbed the negative aspect of my time." He added that he considered himself (and therefore most of all his writings) to "represent" his times, which (with the exquisitely sensitive irony that was a part of his nature) he did not feel able to "challenge." This "negativity" of which he was thinking could be summed up—with again characteristic Kafkaesque serenity—as the continuing and inevitably increasing indifference of human beings for one another's welfare.

Kafka could record such preposterous matters (they lead, after all, to mass violence, torture, starvation, victimization, and slaughter on an unprecedented scale, and to exploitation and crass injustice as well) in the blandest and therefore the most ironic and humorous manner possible. Remember, too, that this "negative aspect," this capacity of men, many of them timid and uncertain in themselves, to sit around tables furnished with soft drinks and quietly discuss the killing of millions—is all the time necessarily and ceaselessly bureaucratized. Everything, however monstrous, is processed by bland clerks who themselves, as individuals, lead lives of quite a degree of "quiet desperation" as those of their victims. Kafka remains the most effective and humane of all the recorders of this (which he effortlessly foresaw), because he just lays it all out before us, and does so without histrionics.

So what is surprising, one might suddenly wonder, about the opening chapter of *The Trial?* What is disturbing to whatever sense of calm its reader might think he possesses, as he awaits the dawn and the postman's arrival. There are the usual forms to fill in, the official letters written in a more ugly and inert version of his own language, whatever that is, than any mere devil could have invented—the new edition of the Bible that he ordered, now rendered in the malevolently stagnant and utterly inactive language used by his internal revenue in its annual raid upon his hard-earned income?

Only that the inevitable sense of surprise, outrage indeed, upon learning that he has been arrested, that *must* have been experienced by the unfortunate Josef K. goes completely unrecorded, and is no more assumed than the average bureaucrat would assume it: It is so glaringly *not* there, that it *is* there far more obtrusively than it would have been had it been recorded. Or *must* it? Is it that, despite his mechanical protests and his bourgeois indignation, Josef K. is in some way *supine* ("more taken aback than annoyed," writes the narrator)—as, of course, Hannah Arendt so controversially accused her fellow-Jews of being in the face of the Nazis?

But then who is Josef K.? Well, he is no more than an individual, a bank clerk. What, therefore, does he matter in the modern world? Such are some of the questions that might be asked. The book begins:

> Someone must have been spreading lies about Josef K., for without having done anything wrong he was arrested one morning. His landlady's cook, who brought him his breakfast every morning at about eight o'clock, did not come on that particular day. This had never happened before. K. waited a little while, watching from his pillow the old woman who lived opposite and who was observing him with a quite uncharacteristic curiosity; but then, feeling both hungry and disturbed, he rang. At once there was a knock on the door and a man he had never seen in the flat before came in. He was slim and yet strongly built; he wore a well-fitting black suit which was like a traveling outfit in that it had various pleats, pockets, buckles, buttons, and a belt, and as a result (although one could not quite see what it was for) it seemed eminently practical.

There it is, stated quite plainly: the bank official Josef K. has not "done anything wrong." But hasn't he? Kafka works at many levels. Yes, this is a satire on the state, even (for a German-speaking writer or reader) on the specifically Hegelian state, that Prussian thing that *is* truth.

But what else is it? For K. is never *forced* to attend the court, and he never even knows what charges have been laid against him. But despite that he is, like some Jewish or homosexual or gypsy victim of the Nazis, marched off and executed (on the very eve of his thirty-first birthday). Kafka is doing something more than just drawing attention to the awfulness of modern life, "immense" though his delineation of its "negative aspect" is. "Looking at you," says a relative of Josef K. to him, "one's tempted to believe the proverb 'To be prosecuted in a case like this means that one has already lost it.'" And of course Josef K. does *feel guilty*.

J. P. Stern, always a sensitive critic of Kafka, pointed out that "a religious interpretation . . . is unavoidable." Kafka, who studied NIETZSCHE carefully, went further than he in the matter of religion—but he, too, knew of the cultural "death of God." He was also aware of the terrible force of Dostoyevsky's question (Dostoyevsky, like Knut Hamsun and the French poet Jules Lafourge, was a writer very important to Kafka) to the effect that if there is no God then why is *everything not permitted*. Josef K., like K. in *The Castle*, is guilty for, as might be said, religious reasons. Kafka himself was on the edge of much speculation of a generally gnostic and kabbalistic sort that was going on in Prague in his time (there was even a contemporary Czech movement called *Marcionism,* referring to one of the earliest gnostic thinkers). He wrote: "There is nothing but a spiritual world, and what we call the world of the senses is the Evil in the spiritual world . . . the fact that there is nothing but a spiritual world deprives us of hope and gives us certainty."

Kafka's concern with this world is more explicit (as explicit as he ever became) in his more complex novel *The Castle*. But in *The Trial* it is at least as evident. *The Castle,* wrote the late Erich Heller, is "the heavily fortified garrison of a company of gnostic demons." In *The Trial* these demons are the hindrances, the obstacles, to Josef K.'s progress. His desire to understand the legal process in which he stands trapped recalls nothing so much as the Kabbalist's quest for God, which is characterized by the paradox that although it is absurd to try to think rationally about God, that premise is itself rational—knowledge of God can only be transmitted by reason! *That* is Josef K.'s real predicament. And thus, to end with Stern's words, in "deep darkness, his creative intelligence is still an illumination."

87

The Logic of
Scientific Discovery

KARL POPPER

1934

The Austrian philosopher Karl Popper was not always a popular figure—although his whole philosophy was based on the absolute necessity of being permanently unsure that scientific views are *right,* he himself reacted very unhappily, even sourly, indeed to any criticism—but he made sure, by his meticulously aggressive rigor, of one thing: that he would be a thinker with whom every responsible person ought to come to terms. His influence has reached beyond those of just science and the history of science: He was, and still is, among the most discussed men of his era. Some might hold that his most influential books of all are *The Open Society and Its Enemies* (1945, revised 1950) and *The Poverty of Historicism* (1957), but, widely influential though these were, their arguments have not stood up quite so well—in part because of *The Structure of Scientific Revolutions,* by THOMAS KUHN—as those of *The Logic of Scientific Discovery (Logik der Forschung)*, which was his first book, and is usually referred to as his masterpiece. A reader may dislike this, even vehemently, and dislike Popper, but he needs to be able to explain why. That is a remarkable achievement in itself. Further to that, of all those questions that become empty and simply fashionable to ask, Popper's "Is this falsifiable?" does have some cogency even if not as much as he believed.

Popper was born in Vienna in 1902, of Jewish parents who had converted to the Lutheran faith and who were therefore, in the quaintly sinister fashion of those times, "assimilated." (As a point of fact, Vienna has always been, at any given time, including the present, the most anti-Semitic city in the world—the Austrian people quite recently elected a president because they knew and liked the fact that he had been a keen, if not himself murderous, Nazi.) Popper was from the outset interested in philosophy, psychology, science—and music, of which he had a great knowledge (of literature and poetry, however, by contrast, he knew little and cared less). In his late teens he was an enthusiastic Marxist, but he soon outgrew this—and in time became one of the fiercest and most effective twentieth-century critics of KARL MARX.

Popper was close to, but not of, the Vienna Circle of logical positivists; in his first book, though, he subjected them to heavy criticism. Much later, not long after the end of the Second World War, he met WITTGENSTEIN, who had been rather closer than he to the logical positivists: they are widely supposed to have had a fight, both armed with pokers. That is not of course strictly true, although Popper does seem to have produced a poker (Popper's own account of the episode has been challenged by some of the others present); but it does illustrate the extreme antipathy that existed between them.

Before Hitler marched into Austria Popper left Vienna with his wife for employment in New Zealand. There he worked on *The Open Society and Its Enemies*. It was that book, rather than its predecessor, which first made him well known.

This is a large-scale attack on totalitarianism of the left and right. (*The Poverty of Historicism* carries on the argument.) Popper's open society is one in which ideas develop freely but responsibly. Popper may very well have been somewhat overoptimistic about how wonderful this type of society actually is: It has often been convincingly postulated, since, that it is by no means as free—or as responsible—as it looks. The closed society, by contrast, is not composed of individuals: It operates "organically," as a single force, a tribe, an essentially primitive mass of people who, since they are devoted to collectivism, are unable to confront or accept new and progressive thinking. What (undeniably!) actually does happen in an open society is the best thing: what Popper called "piecemeal social engineering," by which he meant that progress should be conducted on practical and not theoretical lines.

However, the line of demarcation between these two alleged types of society is hard to draw, and Popper ignored many existing subtleties and distinctions in his description. He did not deal well with the undoubted fact that in an open society the collective aspect does exist—he seems, for example, to have entirely ignored the thinking of the French sociologist Emile Durkheim, who, although he made errors, has written most fruitfully about the way the collective really operates. Throughout his career, in fact, and most especially in the long last phase of it, Popper was notably, sometimes perhaps willfully, unsubtle.

More controversially, Popper chose to attack, as the chief proponents of the latter type of society, PLATO, HEGEL, and Marx. His interpretation of Plato was controversial because Plato, although his notion of justice in *Republic* is certainly collectivist, was so many different things, and it is clear that Popper simply could not appreciate him and, in particular, the poetry in him. He underrated Marx as a thinker. Popper was also criticized for inventing an idea of historicism that did not exist—and then shooting it down. It was complained that his philosophy of progress would not even allow for scholars practicing what in effect is simply *contextualism*, i.e., trying to understand historical phenomena in terms of the times at which they took place. This was plainly absurd—and unimaginative. Like the literary nihilist Jacques Derrida, he confused "ought by my lights" with "is." (Derrida is jealous of authors and so uses certain partial facts about them to pretend that they do not have significance, thus cutting out an aspect of reality which makes him feel uneasy and angry.)

Associated with all this, of course, and in particular with Popper's hatred of Marx (whose genuine insights he tended to ignore), was his view that there are no fundamental laws of history. It is perhaps now generally conceded, except by his devotees, that in his examinations of the thinking of his antiheroes (FREUD was another of these) he did scant justice to *their* own. He ended (*Objective Knowledge,* 1972) by propounding an altogether (so far) less influential philosophy, although there is still a minority interest in it, one that he developed out of his earlier work. He began to compare what he saw as scientific progress to evolution by natural selection, and he even invented a "real" category that he called *World 3.* But he never developed this into a coherent philosophy, and his rather mystical World 3 does not explain anything very fruitfully and is seldom heard from. Though when all is said and done, and Popper's lack of humor and rather intolerant style have been allowed for, it remains true that readers have been well stimulated by these books.

The *Logic of Scientific Discovery* is more fundamentally important. In this Popper attacked the notion of scientific progress by means of the inductive method. He would not have it that it was proper to infer universal laws from a finite number of particular observations. It was not (as HUME and others had pointed out) logical. That you see the sun rise every morning does not prove that there is a law that the sun rises—and, indeed, it is pertinent to add, there really is none, since, in the past, no sun did rise, nor could it eventually continue to do so. Some things that seem obvious are not obvious at all. The inductive method, Popper argued, just was not relevant to science.

So Popper boldly turned the whole process on its head. It was important to proceed by means of what *could* be proved logically. And what could? Why, that certain propositions were *false!* So arose the famous *falsification principle.* Popper's old acquaintances the logical positivists had tried to found a *verification principle.* Vienna in the 1930s had been an exciting period, and much bad metaphysics, at least, was outlawed for a time. But the logical positivists failed, ultimately rather miserably, because they could not provide a logic for their own scientific verification principle. So, for Popper, the only science that was true science proceeded by means of a certain risk: That is to say, only propositions that could be falsified—that were capable of being falsified, that were framed so that they could be falsified—had validity. A properly scientific statement was one that actually denied that it could *not* have an exception made to it. This was Popper meticulously rejecting his own dogmatic nature! The Popperian method is called the hypothetical-inductive method. Freud's ideas consisted of pseudoscience, since (claimed Popper) the propositions he made were incapable of falsification: They were wrongly framed. Many working scientists were delighted and felt free to go ahead with risky theories that could be falsified without incurring shame.

But did Popper give a true account of how science had proceeded or should proceed (clearly Kuhn thought not), and was his falsification principle as simple as all that? Is every proposition that cannot immediately be falsified really fit only for the scrapheap, or could this be an oversimplification, and even a dangerous one?

It is important to recognize that Popper never did in fact deny that *non-scientific* activities could be useful. To him the enemy was pseudoscience. What critics of Popper have pointed to, though, is, first, his overrigorous exclusion of such activities as, say, psychoanalysis, and, more important, his own *lack of rigor* (by standards he wished to set) when he said that certain theories could be accepted if they had been very severely tested. Is this really so different, his critics asked, from the ordinary inductive process that he so vigorously rejected? Clearly it was not. His triumph was short-lived: His falsification principle, clearly, has its own severe limitations.

But it always remains an at least *useful* and interesting question to ask: Does this or that or the other proposition at least allow itself to be falsified? On such questions as those asked by, say, a SHAKESPEARE in his nonscientific sonnets, Popper is a quite useless philosopher—whereas SPINOZA or even Hume are clearly useful. Popper thus operates under quite severe restrictions, and even his talk of music reflects his ignorance of literature. He is not quite a great philosopher, but he is one who immediately recognized his own dogmatic tendencies, and fought in his philosophy to rectify these failings. Alas, Freud's analysis of him, falsifiable or not, would have been very *interesting. . . .*

88

The General Theory
of Employment,
Interest, and Money

JOHN MAYNARD KEYNES

1936

The English economist and mathematician John Maynard Keynes (1883–1946) shares two features with his near contemporary ALBERT EINSTEIN: few among the general public—even the educated general public—understand his writings; the influence of both was very great, and cannot yet be fully assessed.

However, in the case of Keynes, it has been fortunate for those who put themselves forward as fit to rule countries that the public is as ignorant as it is; thus governments find it that much easier to steal more of people's money and then waste it. For these self-appointed people are in truth no better at looking after public finance than you or I are at looking after our private finances after they have been plundered. And how good is that? Sometimes effective, often ineffective, but at least not "expert." The proper course of objects traveling at just below the speed of light can perhaps better look after themselves.

One of Keynes's tutors at Cambridge said of him that he "was beyond doubt or challenge, the most interesting, the most influential, and most important economist of his time." Few would challenge this view, for the revolt against Keynes of the mid-1970s, partly already spent after a quarter of a century, was at least largely couched in Keynsian terms. A whole era, that of the so-called postwar boom, a period of rapid economic expansion, is, for all that Keynes died in 1946, rightly enough called the Keynsian era.

John Maynard Keynes was the son of John Neville Keynes, a Cambridge logician and economist. Although he married a famous ballerina, Lydia Lopokova, in 1925, and had a happy life with her, he was a lifelong homosexual, being especially attached to the Scottish painter Duncan Grant. Keynes, Grant, the novelists E. M. Forster, and Virginia Woolf, and many others connected with art and literature, made up what was called, not too misleadingly, the "Bloomsbury Group." These people had in common that they were liberal, humane, cultured, not too often short of money, and highly intelligent. Many but not all were homosexual. The angry poet and novelist D. H. Lawrence, seeing Keynes in his pajamas one morning while with Bertrand Russell in Cambridge in 1915, wrote angrily to a friend who was himself attached to the group:

> It is foolish of you to say that it doesn't matter—the men loving men. . . . It is like a blow of triumphant decay. . . . We went into [Keynes's] room at midday. . . . As he stood there, gradually a knowledge passed into me, which has been like a little madness to me ever since. . . .

That Lawrence himself had homosexual inclinations is now generally accepted; but it is interesting that Keynes, to some at least an economic savior of the common man, should have seemed so repulsive to such as Lawrence, who envied their couthness, elegance, and learning.

Keynes was at first a civil servant, but in 1908 became a lecturer in economics at Cambridge. His dissertation was refused at the time, but, polished in 1921 and published as *A Treatise on Probability*, it is now recognized as an important contribution to the subject—if it is not a classic then that is no doubt owing to the fact that too few of us still possess an adequate understanding of probability. Keynes was also important, in his later life, as a patron of the arts, and was responsible for the formation of the British Arts Council.

Repelled by many aspects of capitalism, Keynes realized at the same time that it had enormous expansionary powers. Had he pointed to any evils implicit in such expansionism, he would have been regarded as an anarchist or an eccentric, and he would have had no influence at all on government policy. Yet he may often have had his doubts. Anyhow, he has been praised, by those who regard capitalism as a God-given system, both as its savior and as its tentative destroyer. He himself ironically said, with the effete combination of brilliance and timidity that tended to characterize members of the Bloomsbury Group, that as an "immoralist," in the event of a "class war," he would take the side of the bourgeois. But he never took MARX seriously, and, astonishingly, demonstrated no deep knowledge of his writings. Keynes was a liberal with a conscience who loathed both violence and poverty, and yet, to quote the words of another distinguished economist, Joan Robinson, he saw that "the misery of being exploited by capitalists is nothing to the misery of not being exploited at all." That recognition has stood in the way of a great deal of intended revolutionary action as well as given many a capitalist a happy feeling that he is a savior of others.

Marx had pronounced that long-drawn-out cycles of boom and bust would eventually help to destroy capitalism. What he called "classical economics" had revolved, he insisted, around Say's Law. Jean-Baptiste Say (1767–1832) was a Frenchman whose business career was interrupted when he read ADAM SMITH; he became an economist. His so-called "law" stated that supply created an equivalent demand. Keynes was, like MALTHUS, highly critical of this and turned it on its head: Demand, he asserted, created its own supply.

This viewpoint generated what came to be called "demand management," which involved much more government intervention than many "classical" economists thought proper. But between 1940 and about 1975 it was the order of the day. While Keynes was writing the *General Theory* he forecast, to George Bernard Shaw, that it would, "in the course of the next ten years largely revolutionize . . . the way the world thinks about economic problems." He was right, although many more than he contributed to his philosophy of money and to its setting in motion.

To what extent he caused this revolution, and to what extent he merely prophesied it, is still a matter of contention. Already, certainly, Franklin Roosevelt had realized that the state should itself invest; Keynes demonstrated the logic of this, although those to the right of him have vigorously argued that he was mistaken. The real implication of *The General Theory* is that the state has a duty to maintain full employment, which, Keynes's opponents have always argued, leads to unacceptably high levels of inflation. These opponents, it should be noticed, seldom regret lack of employment—which, if it is not yet an established fact, is still true enough to pose a serious threat—since it fits in with their general and too vague philosophy of what is good for the sort of people who might get unemployed.

Keynes first attracted wide attention when, after attending the 1919 Peace Conference at Versailles as the representative of the British Treasury, he published *The Economic Consequences of the Peace* (1919), in which he pointed out the dangers of the too heavy reparations demanded of the Germans. Since events soon made it clear that he had been right, he remained anathema in official circles for almost twenty years. His career was not too unlike that of Winston Churchill in this respect, inasmuch as his rightness about what he warned against was proved so dramatically.

Another way of putting Keynes's thesis—which is inevitably extremely complicated—is that he preached that, in times of prosperity, governments should raise taxes and lower spending power; in recessions, though, they should do the opposite. He hated waste, but hung on to capitalism for the sake of what he believed were its expansionary powers.

As a man, Keynes was "always right"; he could also be ridiculous, as when he said that earthquakes are beneficial because they caused reconstruction booms (but he might have been making a "Bloomsbury joke" here), or that the genius of SHAKESPEARE could only have flourished in an age of inflation (this is simply foolish). He was often thoughtless (more so than his great predecessor Adam Smith), and the label of "bulldozer" with which he has been saddled is a fair one. Yet he was, for many, the father of most that has been humane in the economics of the twentieth century. When he was brutal it was usually because he was lazy, exasperated, trying to be literary— or dealing with obtuse treasury clerks.

All serious economists would like, or have to pretend that they would like, full employment and minimum inflation. What they argue about is how this may be achieved. Keynes, at a time of recession when unemployment never fell below about 5 percent, argued that governments ought to stimulate demand by spending money on public works and welfare—seen by some as "socialism"—and by lowering interest rates.

After a period of rapid postwar expansion, economies began to get into trouble, especially over high inflation. Then arose the Chicago School of economists, of whom the most influential was undoubtedly Milton Friedman (born in 1912). Right-wing in their general political views (Keynes had been, in effect, left of center), these economists argued against interventionism. The only way in which inflation could be controlled, they insisted, was by strict control of the supply of money. Thus "monetarism" was transformed, in America, Great Britain, and elsewhere, into pure laissez-faire—to the degree that Friedman himself criticized it. These developments coincided with the swing to the political right that occurred in the late 1970s.

Few if any economists have endorsed the 1981 British budget—non-Keynsian if anything ever was—which increased taxes in a mistaken attempt to combat the worst recession since the late 1920s. Since then, in both America and Britain, governments have been more ready to intervene, though control of inflation remains the main target. It could be said, and has been said, that things are going back in Keynes's favor; at least it may be argued that the practice of a too crude monetarism will be responsible for the demise of the right as we have known it. But left-wing parties retain at least enough monetarism to make the future of economic policies uncertain.

Political considerations ought not, of course, to determine these policies at all; that they do so is less the fault of Keynes than of the monetarists.

89

Being and Nothingness

JEAN-PAUL SARTRE

1943

Of all philosophers regarded as major only Jean-Paul Sartre has been equally distinguished in his own time as playwright, novelist, political activist, and literary critic. He is or was therefore, as he is usually called, "a unique phenomenon."

Will posterity look upon him as a figure of undoubted historical importance but little intrinsic value? As a great novelist but poor philosopher? As vice versa? Was the mark he left on his native country as indelible as those left by VOLTAIRE or DIDEROT or even Bergson (whom he admired)?

He was the undoubted spearhead of the immediately postwar vogue for existentialism—this, as a craze, had an unusually long life, of about fifteen or even twenty years, and it spread over the Western World—which in its turn has been overtaken by structuralism, deconstructionism, and now by (the hopefully so-called) postmodernism. What will they call the next step? Postpostmodernism?

The contemporary French thinkers now fashionable are probably sufficiently insulated from real life to indulge themselves in such a christening. After all, it may be hard to recognize the fact, but all this is not much more relevant than what a few disappointed people may say to each other in a bar after a day's teaching in a *lycée*. Contemporary French thinking is distinguished neither by its humor (rather, indeed, by its literally deadly earnestness and reliance upon direly phrased gobbledygook) nor by its immediate intelligibility. Sartre was notoriously "difficult," and his prose is not always what an Anglo-Saxon reader would call lucid; but there is no doubt at all of the real emotional impact he had on his contemporaries. The emotional impact of, say—to take a leading but remarkably insubstantial figure—Jacques Derrida, is absolutely nil by comparison. The latter has all the appeal of a bluebottle; only a conspiracy of insecure, inert, and inferior minds keeps him in place at all. Sartre was something quite different—and he could tell stories.

Have latter-day developments—including in particular the depressing cult of the messy and unhappy Michel Foucault—really eclipsed the figure of Sartre, at whose funeral in 1980 more than fifty thousand people turned up, spontaneously, as a sign of respect for him? (That did not happen for Foucault.) Furthermore, throughout the period of changes of fashion during his lifetime (Claude Lévi-Strauss's anthropological structuralism was an exception, inasmuch as it was a completely serious development) Sartre, dangerously intelligible, continued to dominate the intellectual scene.

Sartre's most widely read books are undoubtedly his novels: the brilliant philosophical novel *La Nausée*, translated into English as *Nausea*—his best single work, and one that will survive regardless—and the four-volume *Les Chemins de Liberté*, translated as *The Roads to Freedom* (which was made into a successful television series). But his most *famous* book, and the one containing the existentialist philosophy that *Nausea* anticipated and *The Roads to Freedom* embodied, was *Being and Nothingness* (*L'Être et le Néant*). This philosophy also informs the plays, the best of which are *Les Mains sales* (*Dirty Hands*), a political thriller that transcends categories, and the incomparable *Huis-Clos* (*No Exit*), in which a Woman I loves a Man who loves a Woman II who loves Woman I and so on forever, in hell—and in which occurs the famous phrase, "L'enfer, c'est les Autres" (Hell is other people)! They aren't great plays, and in common with all Sartre's other creative work they never come near to telling us how a person can become "authentic"; but they are good.

Existentialism was the culmination and coming-together of several strands of thinking. It was as much a media phenomenon as it was a philosophy proper. It is a trend, or tendency—not a philosophy. It held as much against academic philosophy as it drew from it. Sartre himself called it *humanism*. It had elements of theology in it, but these Sartre, an aggressive atheist, firmly secularized.

There were "Christian existentialists," the best known of whom was probably Gabriel Marcel. Existentalism had existed, too, in an almost fully blown form, in the brilliant philosophy of the Spanish writer José Ortega de Gasset before it became world famous. Ortega had studied in Germany, though, and long before Sartre briefly (1934–35) did so. There is a version of existentialism in the philosophy of the psychiatrist Karl Jaspers—whose sources are almost identical to those of Ortega.

The main sources of existentialism are: KIERKEGAARD, NIETZSCHE, Husserl, and Heidegger. The yet earlier sources can be traced through others names: some of these, not given chronologically, are Heraclitus, AUGUSTINE, AQUINAS (because he insisted that *being* was prior to *essence*), the neglected Max Scheler (from whom Heidegger dishonestly borrowed so much), aspects of KANT, Dostoyevsky, PASCAL, TOLSTOY. . . . Ironically for what was in the main an atheist movement, existentialism was rooted far more markedly in theological than in secular thinking. But it needed to borrow its fervor from theology. God was always very much in it, because so prominently absent. The general tendency, always more important in existentialism than any tedious detail, is *against* abstraction, and all *for* rough ordinariness. Thus Sartre's *Being and Nothingness* can begin with a (famous) elementary howler about BERKELEY; this worries no one inside existentialism, but causes many outside it to despise it as totally lacking in rigor.

Here, then—and with due reference to the entries on Kierkegaard, Nietzsche, and others who helped create it—existentialism will not be described as a philosophy, but as a climate of thought of which Sartre was the most typical, and for long the leader. The contribution of Kierkegaard and Nietzsche—not to speak of Heidegger—to existentialism was mainly emotional; the intellectual element came almost solely from the Austrian philosopher and mathematician Edmund Husserl (1859–1938), who was far more important, as a thinker, than Sartre. The reason that Husserl's *Ideas: General Introduction to Pure Phenomenology* (1913) is not included in the present book is solely because its influence was entirely indirect: it is accessible only to well-trained philosophers. (That Heidegger's *Being and Time* is not accessible to *anyone* at all, other than the self-deluded, and is unworthy of respect from anyone at all, has not of course prevented *it* from being eagerly "read": The reader can put into it whatever he likes, only provided that it is unpleasant, suitably vague, possesses a forbidding *air* of "rigor," and is devoid of humor or human warmth.) But existentialism cannot be understood without reference to Husserl, a man of decency and probity, and quite unlike his treacherous pupil Heidegger.

Husserl was first a mathematician. Then he came to study under Franz Brentano (1838–1916). Brentano, who *was* truly rigorous, maintained (in a book of 1874) that the world consisted of two sorts of objects: physical and "psychical"—objects like tables and chairs, but also more subtle yet to him no less "real" objects like *hope*. Refusing to yield to romantic temptations and thus to ruin his philosophical enterprise (the later existentialists would do that for him), Brentano went on to define his psychical objects by demonstrating that they were all the subjects of what he called, drawing on scholastic philosophy, *intentionality*. "No hearing," he said, "without something heard, no hoping without something hoped." And, if we think, we do realize that our hopes (lusts, wishes, dreams, internal adventures) are indeed worthy of being elevated to a category. There is an intuition, Brentano suggested, that causes us to know that in such mental activity we have an *inner perception*. This insight was absolutely crucial to twentieth-century philosophy, and Husserl elaborated it into what he called phenomenology.

Unlike Sartre, neither Brentano nor Husserl were attracted by the phenomenological possibilities of black stockings, garter belts, or what goes on in cinemas when no one at all is in them. (What is known as *Sex* would come under Sartre's exceedingly acute phenomenological scrutiny, and *Woman* would be defined as *the Thing With a Hole*—but this more in the interests of honesty of self-observation than of dislike.) One might (perhaps unkindly and unfairly) say that Husserl developed a philosophy of consciousness, an enquiry into the philosophical nature and status of meaning-bearing thinking—but left out all that was interesting to the ordinary man or woman. He studied whatever mental acts had objects in Brentano's sense, and was not so interested in such states as moods (which seem to have no objects and so to be unintentional). He went into the differences between (it is my example) *President Clinton, Bill Clinton on the sax, Bill and Hillary watching Shakespeare with Tony Blair and Cherie and Carving up Europe and the American and British Post Offices, Bill Clinton hearing what Tony really feels about Peter Mandelson, Bill Clinton allegedly asking Madame X for such-and-such an immediate service*, and so on. In this cluster of phrases (some of them could well be untrue, fellatio may not be a "service," maybe she said he said, *Could you kindly do this?* and so on and so forth: in phenomenology we are allowed to "bracket off" all such considerations in the interests of the status of what we are investigating) the object *meant* is identical, but the object *as meant* is not. In what way, if at all, Husserl asked, could we be justified in asserting that we have been referring to the same object?

At this point we have to leave Husserl, and the abiding importance, for example, of such questions as What is the structure of religious belief in consciousness? which his philosophy caused to be asked. But what excited the young Sartre about Husserl was his summing-up of his project: *Go back to things themselves!* because by *things* Husserl at least *could have meant* stockings, garter belts, and things-with-holes. . . . It was left to Sartre's friend the philosopher Maurice Merleau-Ponty to become the true French heir to Husserl—and, as simply a philosopher, despite the overdensity of some of his prose (it is not a fake density, as characterizes much of the self-indulgent trash perpetrated by Lacan or Foucault, but a Gallic curse, something like the Maginot Line), Merleau-Ponty is far more serious than Sartre.

The existential (pertaining to our actual day-to-day existence) and psychological possibilities inherent in Husserl's philosophy are quite obviously as infinite as they are exciting. As Raymond Aron shrewdly told Sartre, in the early 1930s after he had returned from studying Husserl in Berlin, in a nightclub, holding up an apricot cocktail and pointing to it: *You see, my little comrade, if you are a phenomenologist, you can talk about this cocktail and it will be philosophy*. This Sartre, as a creative man at heart, loved. We might say that he asked himself: *Why not drag philosophy into this? I'm French!* He soon got rid of phenomenology's "bracketing out" and its attempt to be scientific: this was impossible, he recklessly said, because each person can only give the truth of his or her own existence.

The writer Sartre most resembles is Kierkegaard, but whereas Kierkegaard was a melancholy Dane trapped in a severe family neurosis, Sartre was a fairly ordinary (but gifted) Frenchman trapped in little more than what we are all trapped in—the difficulty of making sense of our lives. And he really was gifted. He could certainly drum you up a whole system.

Being and Nothingness is philosophically undistinguished, but it does, as its English translator Hazel Barnes claimed, have the courage to present us with a whole system. I do not think that any trained philosopher has ever taken it very seriously, as philosophy, but what it tries to say informs Sartre's best works, which are his first novel *Nausea* and his autobiographies and a few of his really generous obituaries of the friends with whom he fell out (for example, Camus and Merleau-Ponty).

The main thrust of *Being and Nothingness*, as has many times been pointed out, is the gnostic (and kabbalistic) notion of *nothingness*. Sartre was quite unconscious of gnosticism, he simply didn't know about it; but, unwittingly, he reiterated its chief concern for his own times. Sartre wanted the individual's life to mean something in what he took to be a godless world: he called this being-in-freedom-and-with-meaning, after Heidegger, *authenticity*. He saw the mechanical and awful life of most individuals as being *inauthentic*. And to make the transference from inauthenticity to authenticity, he saw, involved the recognition that "an existent can always be revealed as *nothing*": "Man presents himself at least in this instance as a being who introduces nothingness into the world, inasmuch as he is affected with nonbeing for this purpose."

There is a quite moving section in *Being and Nothingness* about how we fail to discern or perceive people in themselves—Sartre uses a hypothetical person called Peter for this purpose. The book is really a series of stimulating notes, mentioning all sorts of unlikely people (for example the American Charles Peirce, from whom WILLIAM JAMES derived his pragmatism) in an illuminating manner, and often moving in its descriptions of Kierkegaardian *dread* and the reasons for it. The best embodiment of this system, not worth much now as such, is to be found in the novel *Nausea*, which manages to sum up, with accuracy and humor and pathos, just how intelligent people felt in France in the 1930s. And then again, Sartre may have looked foolish in his old age handing out student newspapers in the street, and he may have been mistaken in his fellow-traveling—but he cared enough to be there. Is his ridiculousness (if it is even that) more contemptible than the "dignity" of the "patriot"?

90

The Road to Serfdom

FRIEDRICH VON HAYEK

1944

The Austrian economist and would-be philosopher and psychologist Friedrich August von Hayek was born into a family of intellectuals—his father was a physician and botanist—in Vienna in 1899. After reaching a first peak of fame, as an economist in the service of the Austrian government, in the early 1930s he became employed at the London School of Economics, the University of London, and then later (postwar) at the University of Chicago (where Milton Friedman was one of his students). Although the atmosphere at the London School of Economics was virulently anti-KEYNES—Hayek was always an anti-Keynsian—Keynes's ideas eventually got the upper hand, and Hayek's name faded into obscurity for many years.

Although he had taken British citizenship in 1938 and disliked the Nazis (as "socialists"—they called themselves, after all, *National* Socialists), it is unlikely that his (then) odd ideas could have had much influence in time of war. The war may have interfered with his plans in somewhat the same way as history occasionally interfered with those of HEGEL. The only people to whom his ideas were not so strange were Austrians and some Germans, and these two countries were at that time the enemies of Great Britain and America.

Then in 1974 Hayek began an abrupt rise to another and higher peak of fame (his recreation was mountaineering, the only activity in which, he declared, he felt "thoroughly at home") when he received the Nobel Prize in Economics (jointly with the more openly humane Swede Gunnar Myrdal). This was for the pioneering (and meticulous) work he had done on economic fluctuations, which was at all times (contrary to what is sometimes suggested) taken with a degree of seriousness by all economists, including Keynes.

By that time the so-called libertarian or right anarchist movement in Great Britain, but more particularly (in that form, and especially associated with such names as Murray Rothbard) in America, had reached the peak of its influence; in his grand old age the overdignified Hayek (you had, it was no doubt half-jokingly said, to know him for fifty years before you could use his Christian name) was the acknowledged guru of both Prime Minister Thatcher and of President Reagan (or his advisers). But it was always the earlier *Road to Serfdom,* his least muddled book, and a bestseller, that exercised the most influence. His new eminence revived the reputation of this work, and such as Thatcher claimed that it had been their "midnight reading" (Thatcher even referred to candles).

The Road to Serfdom had the advantage of being a critique of fascism and communism as well as of the democratic socialism which, by Hayek's sinister implication, resembled it. In it and subsequent books Hayek sees socialism as leading to all kinds of repulsive tyranny. From Austria, whence he had returned after retiring from his American post, he wrote to newspapers such as the London *Times* congratulating Thatcher, and never seeing in her *dirigiste* policies the least trace of tyranny. If he was aware that she and her governments had increased the overall burden of taxation, especially in the notorious 1981 budget—criticized as excessive even by the monetarist Milton Friedman—then he did not comment on it.

The Road to Serfdom, mainly an attack on fascist and communist, i.e., totalitarian, economies, has as its main argument that no single person, or group of planners, can possibly know enough to direct an economy. This is a "pretense to knowledge." So of course it is. But, to use a term made famous by KARL POPPER when he advocated unplanned but "piecemeal social engineering," it is pretty piecemeal in itself. Hayek himself was only theoretically committed to democracy, since he believed (with an exquisite muddle-headedness that is not disguised by his high and certain tone) that it interfered with true "collective choice." It was to be inferred from *The Road to Serfdom* that any country planning a socialist postwar welfare state would be taking a road to tyranny. As Hayek himself afterward (c. 1950) put it, he was determined to

> trace the sources of the moral and intellectual confusion which
> threatens to destroy our civilization and whose most respectable

and dangerous manifestation I still see in socialism. As this seemed to me to be due more and more to certain mistaken conclusions derived from our present scientific approach to all problems, it drew me more and more into philosophical and psychological problems.

As a young man back from army service, Hayek had been for a year or so a "social democrat"; but this did not last for long, and it is possible that the hatred he developed for the Austrian Social Democrats of his youth—and then for the terrible inflation that he experienced in Austria—remained too obsessively with him. Many of his admirers, even while pleading for him to be considered, have admitted that his writing is both "esoteric" and "incomplete." It is also repulsive in its unfriendly loftiness.

It may well be that Hayek's latter-day fame, a feature of which has been the high praise of him by rulers renowned for their superstitiousness (electrified bath water in the case of Mrs. Thatcher and popular astrology in the case of President Reagan and his wife), but hardly for their intellectuality (even the late British "taxi driver" novelist and reactionary Kingsley Amis, a rapturous disciple, conceded that Mrs. Thatcher had "no ideas"), has been largely undeserved. That is not, however, to say that the detail of his work in economics itself is worthless or that his arguments are wholly without point: one of the translators of his 1933 *Monetary Theory and the Trade Cycle* was Nicholas Kaldor, a prominent economic adviser to the hatefully socialist government of Harold Wilson; and the loathsome Keynes himself remarked his "broad agreement" with much of *The Road to Serfdom*. But Hayek's may not have been an at all distinguished, even though a powerfully pontifical, mind. It is significant that only few not on the extreme right had much interest in him, as a "philosopher," before he became a household name as one of the prophets of "monetarism." As a thinker he is not essential reading: even if it is necessary to know about the fallacy of social Darwinism, that can more easily be learned from HERBERT SPENCER, who, after all, openly advocated it.

After all, is not a muddled and dishonestly disguised social Darwinism all we truly—outside the detail of the undoubtedly significant economic analysis—meet in this dour and humorless Austrian, who was as a man so profoundly unrewarding? And is not his "philosophy"—his fellow Austrian Popper, in some ways much in sympathy with him, refers to him pointedly in his autobiography *Unended Quest* as "not a philosopher"—for all the pomposity of his expression of it (it appeals to the nonintellectuals because it sounds so intellectual), a sort of highbrow (and admittedly far better educated) equivalent to the so-called "objectivism" of the notoriously ill-informed Russian "radical egoist" Ayn Rand, whose work has never been, and could not be (as her perverse and ridiculous book on Nietzsche demonstrates) taken seriously by any professional philosopher, and the style of whose tedious romances is no more than an example of how not to write decently? Yet Rand is very often associated by Americans of extreme right-wing tendencies with Hayek—which was possibly, and if so reasonably, something of an embarrassment to him.

Hayek's economic theories arise from the Austrian School, which was founded in the latter half of the nineteenth century. In the twentieth century it was at first associated with the work of Carl Menger (who died in 1920)—and then with Ludwig von Mises, another Austrian, a teacher of Hayek, who came to America and died there in 1970. Followers of von Mises have often condemned Hayek himself for dangerously leftist tendencies.

Mainstream economists were as cavalier and even hysterically defensive about the Austrian School as mainstream scientists (with the exception of EINSTEIN, who was decent and polite) were about the strange theories of Immanuel Velikovsky, the man who postulated, in *Worlds in Collision* (1950), that great catastrophes had taken place on earth and that the Old Testament gave a fairly accurate record of them. Velikovsky, although he made a few good guesses, and certainly was badly treated, was essentially a paranoid crank but, so far as economics alone was concerned, the Austrian School was not by any means of this order of eccentricity, even if it overemphasized certain factors and if the "philosophy" that underlay it was vulgar and nasty; but that did not prevent even an eminent American economist (winner of the 1970 Nobel Prize), noted for his empirical approach, Paul A. Samuelson, from remarking of it, in a textbook: "I tremble for the reputation of my subject."

The jury is still out, no doubt, on "monetarism" and on the detail of Hayek's own economics. These are highly technical matters in a field in which, in reality, all governments have to, and do, intervene. Hayek himself, never in a position to influence policy directly, claimed that his own job was to make possible what was politically impossible (whatever this really means). He ventured into both philosophy and psychology. He vastly and disingenuously exaggerated the degree to which experience affected I.Q., an idea he derived from the simpleminded but honorable and capable Canadian psychologist D. O. Hebb, who once "proved" the nonexistence of an unconscious mind!—it has been asserted that he came upon the idea "independently"; but it is unlikely that he will ever be taken as the great all-around thinker that a few on the extreme right still take him to have been.

He was originally trained as a lawyer, then as an economist; his excursions into philosophy and psychology were in effect attempts to justify his views about the sacredness of the free market, which was treated in his work with a religious zeal that only just fell short (at times) of fanaticism. The monetarism of Milton Friedman—which, wrong or right, had so great a direct effect during the 1970s and 1980s—was, as an overall policy, far more realistic, sophisticated, and pragmatic than anything Hayek ever came up with. The main thesis of everything Hayek wrote is, essentially, that the state is not, as PAINE so famously claimed, a "necessary evil," but that it really was an *unnecessary* evil—except in the form of policemen and anything else Hayek liked—the interventionist and meddling enemy of individualism. For Hayek and others of the Austrian School, "objectivity" is not possible, and therefore only the subjective is accorded attention. The British philosopher Anthony Quinton, not notably left-wing, called Hayek's *The Constitution of Liberty* (1960)—an exhaustive and extremely muddled and undistinguished, but nonetheless magisterially written, attempt to give legal and even constitutional justification to a right-wing-anarchist (but see below) program—a "magnificent dinosaur." And so, in view of what governments (while they last) have to be, it certainly was and is. People still purchase it, or rather, carry it about: an unread and unreadable bible.

Much of what Hayek has had to say incidentally is of interest, although it has been all been said before, and often more lucidly. Just like Popper, whose dourness and studied lack of interest in poetry he fully and happily shared, he regarded progress as a "piecemeal" affair. Seen retrospectively, no doubt it is—and very reprehensible at that. Economics for him was like science for Popper: a process of discovery in which (although Hayek never invented an economic "falsification" principle) progress is made only by trial and error.

Furthermore, the state (hence his and Popper's common hatred of Hegel), or the state as it is, tainted by socialism, by false wisdom, the "pretense to knowledge," is the enemy of such progress. But he could quite never bring himself to own up to his version of anarchism; this was left to his American disciples, who took little heed, in practice, to the legalistic chicanery of his so-called "constitutional" thinking.

Hayek took to an extreme the notions of BURKE (and the French extreme right as exemplified in the persons of Maurice Barrès and the Vichyist traitor Charles Maurras—yet his ideas about the built-in "wisdom" of institutions are usually quoted as if they were original. An institution was (if he liked it), just as his beloved "free market" was (but all markets are rigged by someone), invested with an authority that transcended the merely human. And, to do him justice— since he is so often referred to as an "anarchist"—he did undoubtedly love the notion of authority, and in a manner that could be described as peculiarly Austrian. But the authority he loved had to be nonsocialistic, of another color—and in his own case this color was never truly clarified.

There is supposedly left anarchism and right anarchism. Left anarchism, like that of GODWIN, carries Paine's view that the state is a "necessary evil" one step further: it wants to get rid of it altogether. Right anarchism is not really anarchism, though it is often thus called, at all. Like Rothbard or Robert Nozick in his notorious and disingenuous *Anarchy, the State and Utopia* of 1974, it postulates, with shamelessly dishonest reference to KANT's view of rights (Kant was after all by way of being a decent human being), that there is only one real political entity: the individual. Rights to private property, private armies, being better off (being worse off does not figure so prominently in this philosophy), must not be denied, and so the only desirable state is what Nozick calls, without much reference to reality, a "minimal" one.

All such arguments, as in the case of another (this time British) darling of the so-called liberal right, those of Michael Oakeshott, use philosophy and Kantian notions of rights, to defend a ferocious kind of disorder from which good will and sense of community are wholly absent except as voluntary exercises of individual's rights to be, if they wish, "charitable" or sentimental or otherwise foolish. They are in favor of that kind of anarchy that allows warlords to battle it out between themselves while ordinary people suffer. They ignore the human quality that HUME and ADAM SMITH after him called "sympathy." If this "sympathy" was not ever well defined in a philosophical sense it was at least well meant. If we must have philosophy of this "right anarchist" sort (and Hayek was of that ilk), then it is better not to have philosophy at all.

91

The Second Sex

SIMONE DE BEAUVOIR

1948

Simone de Beauvoir's long pioneer feminist essay was originally issued in
Paris in two volumes. In 1953 it appeared in its influential English translation
in a substantial single volume. It was, up to its date, the most sheerly distinguished—and philosophically well balanced—book on the liberation of
women since JOHN STUART MILL's *The Subjection of Women* (1861, published
in 1869). De Beauvoir praises both Mill and WOLLSTONECRAFT, but points
out of the latter's *Vindication* that it "lacked concrete bases."

The Second Sex remains the twentieth century's best argued—as well as
most entertaining—feminist book. Not as immediately and explosively influ-
ential, even in its own country, as *The Feminine Mystique*, the polemic by
BETTY FRIEDAN, it was well in advance of it in intellectual scope and depth.
De Beauvoir has even been described by one of her (female) biographers,
Deidre Bair, as "the mother of us all."

She was born in Paris, into a Catholic family, in 1908. She had a
Catholic upbringing and education. She began her lifelong relationship with

JEAN-PAUL SARTRE while she was still a student, in 1929. For a time she was a schoolteacher. She was Sartre's coeditor on the once hugely powerful magazine *Le Temps Modernes* from 1945 onward. Some have suggested that the existentialist philosophy of Sartre, in her hands, was presented both more cogently and more consistently. But she frequently declared that she had never wished, as a writer, to convey "a body of knowledge": Her purpose, rather, was to communicate a sense of how it was to be alive as a thoughtful and reflective woman in her era.

She has lately been much criticized, with great impertinence, by pseudofeminists, for apparently bowing and scraping to Sartre; but that was her affair, and does not in any way affect the arguments of *The Second Sex*. In her novel *The Mandarins* (1954) she gave a full account, albeit fictionalized, of her long affair with the American novelist Nelson Algren. It is clear that, unlike her pseudofeminist critics, she, like her English counterpart the novelist George Eliot, did not know how "to behave as a woman"—i.e., maybe not to have the affair at all, or to have exercised a "courageous homosexual choice" notwithstanding her biological inclinations. However, unlike these critics, who do of course know exactly how to conform to their theory of female behavior (for all that there are so many versions of it), she was interested in reality. After writing several more novels (many of them highly thought of) and plays (not so successful), a tetralogy of memoirs (her finest works, and classics of autobiography by any standards), and *La Viellesse,* a moving study of old age in the modern world (*Old Age,* 1970) she died in 1986, having survived Sartre by six years and endured much conflict with his adopted daughter.

The Second Sex, however, is still de Beauvoir's most influential work, and is still in some not unimportant ways her century's most complete presentation of feminism. The manner in which it has affected society has been far less direct than that in which Friedan's book affected America, but is more fundamental, better researched, and has greater depth. The critique of FREUD's "phallocentricity" has never been better, more amusingly, or more fairly conducted. She had the acuity to observe that making oneself passive "was different" from being a "passive object."

Of course de Beauvoir's approach was "existentialist": that is to say, she assumed that human beings as a whole must *choose,* in a contingent universe, to become what they are. She wholeheartedly agreed with Sartre's atheism, and with his graphic categorization of the "bourgeois" (and to a certain extent himself) as being "filthy swine"(*salauds*). She was just a little less zestful about it. This notion, perhaps better known as the way in which to achieve *authenticity* in a purposeless universe, is peculiarly applicable to women as a whole because many men force them to "play at being themselves." De Beauvoir accused women of being just as "inauthentic" as men because they played a male game:

> In truth women have never set up female values in opposition
> to male values; it is man who, desirous of maintaining masculine

prerogatives, has invented that divergence. Men have presumed to create a feminine domain—the kingdom of life, of immanence—only in order to lock up women therein.

Simone de Beauvoir then went on to characterize women as "the *Other*" (one recollects Sartre's own petrified phenomenological description of Woman as "the thing with the hole," not of course a description that might please all even post-Friedanesque American women; but these should at the same time note that Sartre was being self-critical, and also that one of the psychological aspects of existentialist *angst,* and certainly of Sartre's own, is the desire to fill in holes of all kinds).

Men cannot (de Beauvoir well argued) escape woman: therefore he has "invented" her. She cogently suggested that even homosexual males cannot evade women, and suggested that males invested the same-sex objects of their desires with vaginal magic. (She suggested, too, that while the male tended to move, emotionally, in the "soft" feminine world of his imagination, the woman tended to dwell in the "hard" masculine world.) Woman, she thought, was at best the victim of man's false mysticism, at worst of his sadism. She wrote influentially and sympathetically, too, of lesbianism and the explanations for it. The sexuality of lesbians, she wrote

> is in no way determined by any "anatomical" fate. . . . The truth is that homosexuality is no more than a perversion deliberately indulged in than it is a course of fate. It is an attitude *chosen in a certain situation*—that is, at once motivated and freely adopted. No one of the factors that mark the subject in connection with this choice—physiological conditions, psychological history, social circumstances—is the determining element, though they all contribute. . . . It is one way, among others, in which women solve the problems posed by her condition in general, by her erotic situation in particular. Like all human behavior, homosexuality leads to make-believe, disequilibrium, frustration, lies, or, on the contrary, it becomes the source of rewarding experiences, in accordance with its manner of expression—whether in bad faith [the vice of *les salauds*], laziness, and falsity, or in lucidity, generosity, and freedom.

This, whatever any reader may think about existentialist atheism, is plain and tolerant good sense, and avoids praising homosexuality just as a good thing per se.

In such a sensible spirit de Beauvoir brilliantly and acutely analyzed what had by her time in France become a pervasive myth, referred to almost ubiquitously, under one name or another, as "woman's suffering." The truly eminent French historian and thinker Jules Michelet (quoted by her in other contexts) had once actually stated that

Jean-Paul Sartre and Simone de Beauvoir under arrest in Paris in 1968

woman is continuously suffering from the cicatrisation of an inner wound which is the cause of a whole drama. . . . For fifteen or twenty days out of twenty-eight—one might almost say always—woman is not only made into an invalid but wounded. She suffers incessantly the eternal wound of love.

And this was with good, romantic intentions! That kind of thing does not, de Beauvoir insists, help Woman to become her human self. She was, controversially, scornful of "female mysticism" on the grounds that the female mystic "[put] herself into relation with an unreality." She advocated—here under the direct influence of MARX—that the only way for a woman to become "authentic" was to "employ her labor authentically," that is, to "project it through positive action into human society." The only serious weakness of *The Second Sex* is that it fails entirely to explain—let alone dismiss—religious feeling. Thus: "Only women who have a political faith" and who "take militant action in the unions . . . can give ethical meaning to thankless daily labor."

Events that took place after the publication of *The Second Sex* (the communist takeover in Czechoslovakia, the Russian invasion of Hungary in 1956) forced both Sartre and the other quasi-Marxist existentialists into a sort of wilderness: They could see that only in very small ways indeed could Soviet Russia claim to be a genuine "Marxist" state. This isolation in which such thinkers found themselves tended to highlight the limitations and weaknesses of her book.

But of one weakness de Beauvoir could never be fairly accused, although many latter-day overeager feminists so accused her. It consisted of denying that there were any really decisive differences, even physiological ones, between males and females. But, even of that rare woman whom de Beauvoir considered to have emancipated herself, she wrote that this woman

> is not for all that in a moral, social, and psychological situation identical with that of man. . . . For when she begins her adult life she does not have behind her the same past as does a boy . . . the universe presents itself to her in a different perspective. . . . She refuses to confine herself to her role as female, because it would involve mutilation; *but it would also be a mutilation to repudiate her sex* [my italics].

This implies beyond doubt that Simone de Beauvoir never seriously considered that woman could quite simply "become men," or doubted that there was an ineluctable difference between the two sexes. Indeed, as if to palliate somehow what she must sometimes have realized was the chief defect of her book—that it was overpolitical—she ended by saying that men and women could only affirm what she contentiously called their "brotherhood" "by and through their natural differentiation."

> "Woman is lost. Where are the women? The women of today are not women at all!" We have seen what these mysterious slogans mean. In men's eyes—and for the legion of women who see through men's eyes—it is not enough to have a woman's body nor to assume the female function as mistress or mother in order to be a "true woman." In sexuality and maternity a woman can claim autonomy; but to be a "true woman" she must accept herself as the "Other."

Yet are not the "mysterious slogans" still uttered?

Cybernetics

Norbert Wiener

1948, revised 1961

Considering his importance, the name of the mathematician Norbert Wiener is not heard much nowadays except among specialists. He is most famous as the coiner (or, some say, co-coiner) of the word *cybernetics* (from the Greek word *kybernetes*, for governor or steersman). But that word (compare the closely related *cyberspace*, now a buzzword) is far better known than the mathematician and polymath who first used it. Reputable dictionaries and encyclopedias of philosophy or ideas that define the word *cybernetics* now seldom mention Wiener himself; the fundamental humanism by which he would above all have preferred to be remembered is an embarrassment to more than a few contemporary philosophers of science, who never like to have to doubt—as Wiener always did—the human benefits of their work.

This neglect of Wiener is unfortunate, but not altogether surprising:

438

His achievements are often not at all easy to explain, except to specialists. A list of just a few of these, taken from a book about him, makes this clear:

> To an electrical engineer he might be primarily known as the founder of the modern (statistical) theory of communication and control, to a theoretical physicist for his introduction of the (functional) integral over paths, and to a biologist as the person who had done the most to introduce the fruitful concepts of positive and negative feedback, cybernetic system, message, and noise into biology. To opponents of hypermilitarisation he is an example of one who renounced weapons work on principle after having engaged in it actively. . . .

Norbert Wiener was one of the most remarkable prodigies of his century, and doubtless he paid in psychological terms for being one, just as Mozart and Mendelssohn had done before him. He gave a memorable account of all this in his autobiographies: *Ex-Prodigy: My Childhood and Youth* (1953) and *I Am a Mathematician: The Later Life of a Prodigy* (1956). These well-written books help give a rare insight into the nature of what most people call undisputed geniuses of a scientific sort; they have not been sufficiently widely read.

The son of Leo Wiener, a Russian, professor of Slavonic languages and literature at Harvard University (who helped and guided him greatly), Norbert was born in Columbia, Missouri. He graduated from Tufts University in 1909, when he was fourteen. Later he switched from biology to philosophy, but finally became a mathematician. Nothing scientific was too difficult for him. He was a Harvard Traveling Fellow at only nineteen, and was studying under Bertrand Russell at Cambridge University in England at twenty. He then understood Russell's and Whitehead's pioneer work in mathematics, *Principia Mathematica* (1910–13), as well as anyone. Russell, deeply impressed with him, advised him to stick to mathematics. After that he went on to Göttingen in Germany, where he studied for a while with another one of the greatest mathematicians: David Hilbert. He was a professor at the Massachusetts Institute of Technology from 1919 (he was just twenty-five when he became assistant professor there) until his death in 1964.

A key quotation to Wiener's own attitude to his various insights comes from his second volume of autobiography, and is crucial to an understanding of him. A man such as he was, working in the fields of science and logic, might very well and happily have attached himself to Bertrand Russell's analytical type of philosophizing, or, even more likely, to the Vienna circle of logical positivists who held sway for many years in midcentury, temporarily devastated metaphysics, and devised the so-called law of verifiability (which itself, alas, could not be verified).

But Wiener, instead of that, was more interested in KIERKEGAARD, the Dane who did more than any other thinker toward the establishment of the philosophy of existentialism (though he transcends the label), and in the religious aspects of science (*God and Golem, Inc: A Comment on Certain Points Where Cybernetics Impinges on Religion* was published the year of his death). One might say that he went more in the religious direction taken by Russell's senior collaborator in the *Principia Mathematica*, Alfred North Whitehead. He was not as unhappy as were most other mathematicians when the eccentric (and eventually paranoid) Czech-American Kurt Gödel demonstrated in his epoch-making 1931 theorem that mathematics was not "complete," that is, that it was not, or not provably, consistent. Wiener wrote, in *I Am a Mathematician:*

> To me, logic and learning and all other mental activity have always been incomprehensible as a complete and closed picture and have been understandable only as a process by which man outs himself *en rapport* with his environment. . . .We are swimming upstream against a great torrent of disorganization. . . .It is the greatest possible victory to be, to continue to be, and to have been. . . . No defeat can deprive us of the success of having existed for some moment of time in a universe that seems indifferent to us.

In other words, he did not, as so many scientists have, rejoice in the apparently doom-ridden notion of the Second Law of Thermodynamics, the law that in a closed system entropy (disorder) increases, called in the nineteenth century, "the heat-death of the universe." However, he did accept the full consequences of the fact that, in closed systems (it is not known if the universe is a closed system or not), energy turns into disorder, things run down, and that therefore chaos will hold good.

It is not altogether fanciful to see Wiener's work as a whole as an effort to defeat chaos, or, rather, to limit its influence. His own philosophy, considering who and what he was, has been somewhat neglected. For, although he was not a philosopher, his work continually impinged upon what philosophy at least ought to be.

Such in fact was Wiener's fear and even hatred of what he sometimes worked at that he could be guilty, when he was led to see inescapably dreadful consequences, of what has been called a "half-facetiousness." At first cybernetics was applied willy nilly to more or less everything, and Wiener wrote (not facetiously) of the attempt to apply it to management in capitalism:

> I mention this matter because of the considerable, and I think false, hopes which some of my friends have built for the social efficacy of whatever new ways of thinking this book *[Cybernetics]* may contain. . . . In this, I maintain, they show an excessive optimism and a misunderstanding of the nature of all scientific achievement.

Since he had stated that he believed that "no person, by virtue of the strength of his position, shall enforce a sharp bargain by duress," he disapproved of usury, and therefore, surely, of capitalism itself, since usury, an example of sheer taking advantage ("I've got it: you have not!"), is one of its bases. Wiener wanted, and said he wanted, a "society based on human values." He was not a Marxist (he was as critical of the Soviet Union as he was of capitalism), but he saw that corporate capitalism could not be a just system, but only, even at its best, one that did not deprive its victims of *too much*.

During the war Wiener worked, among other things, on the efficiency of antiaircraft fire. If, he reasoned, this was to be accurate, then it would have to take into account the evasive action of pilots—and that evasive action would include an element of randomness. An absolutely regular, for example, zigzag on their part would be too predictable. His ability to anticipate this degree of randomness—which he treated as if it came from a machine—led him to create the science of cybernetics, which he defined as "the science of control and communication in the animal and machine." He did not advocate the replacement of human beings by machines; and he did not advocate, either, as the monster B. F. SKINNER did, the turning of human beings into machines under the control of a single master (in this case Skinner himself, of course) who knew better than they did what was best for them. Human beings in fact have the capacity not to be machines, but to a great extent do behave like machines; it was in this fact that Wiener was interested, although inevitably he was much misunderstood. He even believed at one point that cybernetics might help mentally ill people by treating their illnesses as informational malfunctions.

American publishers had not at first been much interested in a book about the subject of how mathematical principles could be used to aid our understanding of human beings, but *Cybernetics* caught on, and was for a time applied to every conceivable subject, including psychology, biology, and sociology. Such terms as *feedback, negative feedback, positive feedback, input, information control, output,* and *filtering* (as in filtering out noise when receiving a telephone signal) began to be used almost indiscriminately. Negative feedback occurs when a machine (or human being) dampens its own performance in the interests of its task; positive feedback is employed in stimulating performance. Machines therefore, largely because of Wiener, now perform better. Perhaps his even more vital ideas, such as his belief in good will and justice, have not yet been sufficiently influential. At least his nonscientific work, his autobiographies, and his book *The Tempter* (1959) ought to be read along with his scientific ones.

93

Nineteen Eighty-Four

GEORGE ORWELL

1949

George Orwell's dystopia (the exact opposite of a utopia), a place in which everything is horrible, *Nineteen Eighty-Four* was planned in 1943 under the title *The Last Man in Europe*. It was thus certainly not a bitter and frenzied reaction to his final collapse as a result of the tuberculosis of the lungs that finished Orwell off in January 1950, before he had reached fifty. The work is of Swiftian proportions and quite transcends personal despair. It depicts the wretchedness of individual life under an imagined state, reminiscent of the Soviet Union, of the future. It shows that under heartless socialism individuality is not diminished, but destroyed.

Orwell, always fruitfully confused, retained his generosity and his humility. He did, however, complete the novel under conditions of desperate illness, the symptoms of which he regarded with a remarkably clinical detachment; but it was not at all—as it is too often taken to be—the revengeful prophecy of a dying man. On the contrary, it is a satirical, but hopeful, reminder of what could happen: As well as representing Orwell's view of all that he found most detestable, it was intended as a warning, not an account of a state of affairs that was to come.

Nineteen Eighty-Four has been highly influential; so much so that many have even gone so far as to say that it "prevented what it prophesied." The truth is more nearly stated if we accept that, because it has had such wide currency—not just as a book, but also as a television play and, more recently, as a movie—it may have kept some not uninfluential people in better heart than they might have been had it not existed. "Big Brother" and many other terms from it have, after all, entered the language. And who, after all, needs to be reminded of the "plot"? As well as satirizing Stalinist "purity" and deceit, it anticipates the almost exactly parallel development of the equally drab and tyrannical "political correctness" of our own times—a phenomenon so horrible that no single person will even admit to being "politically correct"—but not yet a phenomenon that has "taken over," since after all it does make a final surrender to the dehumanization process. *Nineteen Eighty-Four* was bound to be resisted at first, and by polite and even intelligent critics it immediately was: "Fantastically irrelevant!" the able and useful Scottish critic David Daiches dismayedly gasped, as one dedicated throughout his career to what might well be described as extreme orthodoxy. However, as the more astute and adventurous American Irving Howe pointed out, it had been bound to set up resistance because it would have been much better "made away with."

Orwell was born in 1903, as Eric Arthur Blair, in Bengal, where his father was in the service of the Indian government; he went to the exclusive public school of Eton (which has never quite been able to cast off its exclusiveness, or its devotion to old-fashioned British flogging) where he was much flogged and always an odd man out. He failed to win a scholarship to university, and started adult life as a member of the Imperial Indian Police, serving in Burma, and then as schoolmaster and journalist. In his earlier days he described himself as a "Tory Anarchist," but during the 1930s he became an always grudging partisan of socialism. Orwell has been claimed both by the left, and, because of his famous satire on Soviet Russia, *Animal Farm,* by the right. But, although indubitably "a man of the left" on account of his general attitude—pacifist, anticapitalist, ashamed of what he called his "lower-upper-middle-classness," and eager to share the simple values of workingmen—in essence he became a Tory-and-politician-hating anarchist.

Above all he was a writer, and he spent much of his time explicitly trying to work out how he could pursue humanitarian and reformist political ideas without losing his independence as a writer. He need not have worried—but had he not recognized the necessity of such conflict, he would not of course have been the writer he was. The shift in his attitude, not untypical of any left-thinking Englishman of the times, is nowhere better illustrated than in two remarks he made, one from 1943:

> The dreary world which the American millionaires and their British hangers-on intend to impose upon us begins to take shape. The British people, in the mass, don't want such a world. . . . Sentimentally, the majority of people in this country would rather be in a tie-up with Russia than with America.

And one from 1947:

> "If you *had* to choose between Russia and America, which would you choose?" . . . We are no longer strong enough to stand alone, and if we fail to bring a western union into being [no one should call the European Community a "union"], we shall be obliged, in the long run, to subordinate our policy to that of one Great Power or the other. And in spite of all the fashionable chatter of the moment, everyone knows in his heart that we should choose America.

But that did not mean, as some anticommunist Americans have taken it to mean, that Orwell had become an admirer of America. For as long as he lived, he was, for example, an enemy of the atomic (as it then was) bomb: "Either we renounce it or it destroys us."

Orwell gave up everything to go to Spain to fight against Franco in the Spanish Civil War. It was during this conflict, in which he was wounded, that he first learned of the Stalinist methods which he would later satirize and condemn in *Animal Farm*. By the end he had retreated into what many take to be the most common British position: uneasy independence of all parties, with a dislike of all totalitarian manifestations. He voted Labour, but it may confidently be said that he did so only because he felt that working people voted Labour. One of his rather comic and harmless weaknesses was his eagerness to share what he felt were the habits of the working classes: He would thus refuse a half-pint of beer in favor of a pint. In retrospect, we can see that he was most firmly committed to decency as distinct from any single party.

Animal Farm brought him some fame, but *Nineteen Eighty-Four* made him world-famous. This, as Orwell himself implicitly acknowledged, owes much to another and—in the West—far less well known dystopia, Zamyatin's *We*. As a so-called rival to *Nineteen Eighty-Four*, it is not *We*, though, that immediately springs to mind in connection with Orwell's: It is, instead, *Brave New World* (1933), by the British novelist Aldous Huxley, who lived much of his life in America (and died there).

Huxley's book *was* prophetic in intent. And as prophecy, rather than as a work of the imagination, it was largely successful. In it Huxley expressed, chiefly, his own cold disgust with the trends of his times toward general mental shallowness and sensual self-indulgence. He, too, owed a great deal—in his case almost everything—to Orwell's Russian source: the novel *We* (in Russian, *My*) by the great dissident writer Evgeny Zamyatin (1884–1937), who came from Lebedyan on the River Don and who died in exile in Paris. But Huxley, for some unnecessary reason best known to himself—probably vanity, a besetting sin of most authors—refused to acknowledge Zamyatin's book and pretended that he had never read it. It is, however, perfectly obvious that he did so, and no serious critic has ever doubted it.

We, written in 1920, first saw the light in a poorish English version in 1924; then it appeared in a wretchedly garbled version in Czech in 1926—the Communists would have nothing to do with it, although the author was then a famous writer living unhappily in Soviet Russia. Another translation was published in 1970, but even this has not met with praise—a really good one is badly needed. Had this existed, because *We* is far above even *Nineteen Eighty-Four* at an imaginative level, then I should have had to include it in this book. As it is, it is enough here to draw attention to it as perhaps the greatest dystopia ever written in modern times, and to point out that Orwell's book, though no mere plagiarism, could not have existed without it.

As Orwell told Gleb Struve, the American critic who drew his attention to *We* in 1944, "I am interested in that kind of book, and even keep making notes for one myself that may get written sooner or later" (at that point he hardly had his *Last Men in Europe* notes in mind). Zamyatin has been consistently underrated by Orwell's biographers and critics, none of whom seems to have had a knowledge of Russian literature: while it is true that he did not "plagiarize" *We*, it is no means true that he "transcended" it or "improved" it. Nor would he have thus claimed. He took over, as well as fully understanding, Zamyatin's majestically subtle and poetic portrayal of how sexuality would function under a robot state (how it was actually beginning to function under many conformist subjects of the Soviets); and he made it a thoroughly English affair; but he could not equal it and did not try to do so. Orwell's leading female character, Julia, is drab compared with Zamyatin's astonishing "E-330."

So *We* does lie squarely behind Orwell's *Nineteen Eighty-Four*. But that does not diminish the latter. Certain music of Mozart lies just as squarely behind Tchaikovsky's *Mozartiania*, and the plays of SHAKESPEARE frequently borrow plots from other works. But Orwell's novel, although not prophetic or meant to be, is perhaps more of a political—in the best sense—than a literary phenomenon. *We* is among the one hundred or so best novels of any time. *Nineteen Eighty-Four* is a myth of England, and an inspired commentary on the fact that the thin crust of "Etonianism" (with which of course Orwell was intimately acquainted) was about to crack. The Eton regime as it was in his days there relied on ritual terror, but it was a gentlemanly terror:

a terror disguised as benevolence in the interests of the individual. It was "fascist" only inasmuch as its theology (one had better call it that) relied on fear in its own turn—the kind of fear found in Kiplingesque imperialism. (Orwell was deeply interested in Kipling.) Orwell was both amused and disgusted by it. But he saw it as giving way to something altogether more sinister: something not *English*. Essentially it is a satire about the unacknowledged, not understood, viciously unintelligent need in certain people— the "critical few" in the view of PARETO, with the "trivial many" too acquiescent?—to exercise power. Thus Orwell's character O'Brien tells his "ordinary hero" Winston Smith:

> The Party seeks power entirely for its own sake. We are not interested in the good of others; we are interested solely in power. What pure power is you will understand presently. . . . The German Nazis and the Russian Communists came very close to us in their methods, but they never had the courage to recognize their own motives. . . . Power is not a means, it is an end. . . . The object of persecution is persecution. . . .

If the world, or rather some part of it, has grown a little less horrified by such passages, then that is to an appreciable extent owing to Orwell. That he was inspired by Zamyatin, who did all that and something more beside, is no matter, so long as credit goes where it is due. What remains disturbing is the fact that *Nineteen Eighty-Four* is still studied at places like Eton. This is "fantastic," but not "fantastically irrelevant."

94

Beelzebub's Tales to His Grandson

GEORGE IVANOVITCH GURDJIEFF

1950

Thirty years ago twelve of us spent many years in central Asia, and we reconstructed the Doctrine by oral traditions, the study of ancient costumes, popular songs, and certain books. The Doctrine has always existed, but the tradition has been interrupted. In antiquity some groups and castes knew it, but it was incomplete. The ancients put too much stress on metaphysics; their doctrine was too abstract.

Gurdjieff said this in 1923 to a questioner into the origins of the doctrine that, about a decade earlier, he had started to teach. The influence of *Beelzebub's Tales to His Grandson,* which contains the essence of the doctrine, has been profound but generally unobtrusive. It contains, although in sometimes deliberately obscure form, the gist of that peculiar teaching which is expounded by P. D. Ouspensky in his more immediately lucid and accessible *In Search of the Miraculous: Fragments of an Unknown Teaching*—a book that, since its publication in 1949, just after Ouspensky's death, has been read by millions. Furthermore, at the end of his life, Gurdjieff—despite the differences between the two men that had developed—gratefully acknowledged (in his always broken English) Ouspensky's book with the words: *"This what I said."*

Why, then, not choose *In Search of the Miraculous* here, instead of *Beelzebub's Tales?* The reason is simple: without the "system" or doctrine taught by Gurdjieff, there would be no *In Search of the Miraculous*. And *Beelzebub's Tales to His Grandson* is Gurdjieff's own "science-fiction"–style exposition of the teaching that he, in collaboration with others, synthesized and evolved. Thus he started a movement, known among its participants as "The Work," which influenced a multitude, sometimes publicly but more often privately. Kipling, J. B. Priestley, and Aldous Huxley are just some of the better-known writers who were influenced by the doctrine; but many more American senators, British members of Parliament (not, however, holders of high office), businessmen, bankers, and others have been involved—either with Gurdjieff himself, or with Ouspensky, who taught his methods, from the early 1920s onward. The doctrine is the most convincing fusion of Eastern and Western thought that has yet been seen. It makes Blavatskyism or Transcendental Meditation look simpleminded or even exploitative; but, just as KEPLER acknowledged in the popular astrology of his day a "pearl in a heap of dung," so "The Work" grants something precious at the heart of those and other more popular movements.

Elements of Zoroastrianism, Buddhism, Christianity (especially Eastern Orthodox), the KABBALAH, Sufism, Pythagorianism, and other religions and systems are present in the doctrine. Ouspensky's invaluable book, much of which quotes Gurdjieff ("G") speaking in the first person, is earnest, obsessed with various ideas about reincarnation (Gurdjieff called this notion "near the truth, but only approximate"), and at first acquaintance rather more in line with the popular "mysterious East" than otherwise. No one could accuse *Beelzebub's Tales* of being earnest; yet all those who have persevered with it have acknowledged a tragic masterpiece. Gurdjieff believed that his reconstructed doctrine contained much of the truth about human existence; he thought truth difficult; he therefore made intense difficulties and created many obstacles for anyone who wished to discover it.

George Ivanovitch Gurdjieff (or Giorgiades, to give the Greek version of his name), the product of a marriage between a Greek father and an Armenian mother, was born at Kars in (then) Russian Armenia in 1866. His father, Ionnas Giorgiades, was, significantly, a grazier by necessity but an *askokh*, a bardic poet such as those who once recited HOMER in ancient Greece, by true profession. After a plague (1873) had exterminated his cattle, he turned to the timber business. From his earliest years Gurdjieff had heard his father recite folkloristic and mythological poems, and also stories of the famous

Turkic "wise fool," Mullah Nassr Eddin, who became one of Gurdjieff's comic role models, and whose pithy and paradoxical style he adapted in such sayings as "as irritable as a man who has undergone full treatment by a famous European nerve specialist." The boy was brought up to be a priest. There were six other children.

Gurdjieff liked to strain people's credulity as well as to shock them—he was a great believer in shocks: these, usually very temporarily, make people become what they really are. Beings, he would earnestly state, live on the surface of the sun—which is icy cold. Apes are descended from men.

His style was deliberately opaque, colloquial, jocular, almost light. The book in question, his main work, was scribbled in pencil in Gurdjieff's native Armenian, then put into Russian by Russian pupils; for the English version we are mainly indebted to the English editor and writer Alfred Orage, who worked on it in close consultation with Gurdjieff. Orage had given up his highly successful career as editor of the *New Age* in the early 1920s, in order to study with Gurdjieff.

Of all this century's spiritual teachers Gurdjieff was unique in that he determinedly sought to undermine his pupils' devotion to him personally—to the extent of renouncing their genuine love for him—in order to make them think and act for themselves.

For some twenty or thirty adventurous years Gurdjieff sought knowledge and wisdom in the company of others, men and women, who wanted to answer fundamental questions—such questions as: *Why am I here? Why are we here? Is there a purpose to life? In what way, if in any at all, are men capable of immortality? What are the laws of nature, and how much can we know of them?* He gave a fictionalized account of those years in his simplest and most immediately accessible book: *Meetings With Remarkable Men*. It was made into a film by Peter Brook under the same title in 1979; the screenplay was written by Brook himself, under the close guidance of Gurdjieff's own appointed successor, Jeanne de Salzmann, who died in 1990 at the age of 101.

The best-known period of Gurdjieff's life came in the early 1920s. After opening his school, which he always referred to as for "the harmonious development of man," in various cities—he had to move frequently owing to the Russian Revolution and the subsequent European political situation—he set up at an old priory, the Prieuré, at Fontainebleau. Here he obtained some newspaper publicity, the vast majority of which was footling and wildly inaccurate. But he did not repudiate it: He wanted to attract the right kind of pupil, and he also did not scruple to soak rich Americans or others for the money he needed.

His wheeler-dealer methods repelled Ouspensky, who, a Russian, was more secretive and earnest than Gurdjieff, part of whose method of teaching used humor and shocks to impart the lesson. Many distinguished people such as Orage and Dr. Maurice Nicoll (hitherto a devoted Jungian) came to him; some such as Orage and Nicoll lasted the course, but many, such as the then well-known doctor James Carruthers Young, did not. Rich men did not like to submit to the indignity of having their cherished opinions challenged as worthless, or being set to dig ditches only to be told to fill them in again—or, perhaps even worse, to be told, when they had performed a task well and quickly: "*Must be done in half the time.*" But those who stayed were eventually encouraged.

Then, in late 1922, Gurdjieff received the New Zealand story writer Katherine Mansfield at the Prieuré. Then at the height of her fame, and there because she valued the system as taught to her by Ouspensky and, chiefly, by her publisher Orage, she was already riddled with tuberculosis. Medical treatments had worsened her condition. Gurdjieff looked after her, made her feel welcome, and gave her a spiritual peace which she would have lacked anywhere else. By the time of her sudden but inevitable death in January 1923 she had expressed her gratitude to Gurdjieff and to the doctrine. But this did not prevent Gurdjieff becoming known as the "charlatan who killed Katherine Mansfield." However, no student of Mansfield, however reluctant, has been able to do less than defend him in this matter. He made her past days radiant; and himself lies buried near her.

In 1924 Gurdjieff had a near-fatal car accident. He seems to have foreseen it, even to the extent of forbidding a woman who had regularly traveled with him on like occasions from doing so on this one. Miraculously, he recovered. But he gave up all hope of continuing at Fontainebleau in the old style, with plenty of pupils. Instead he decided, although quite determinedly not a "*bon ton* writer," to leave his own record of the doctrine. He had finished by the end of the 1930s, although the final volume of what is collectively known as *All and Everything* (*Meetings With Remarkable Men* is the first of the trilogy), the essays of *Life Is Real Only Then, When "I Am,"* were never completed. The books circulated among pupils during the rest of Gurdjieff's life, which ended in Paris in late 1949. *Beelzebub* was published in 1950, the other two books later. Gurdjieff always had a few pupils around him after his accident, but never a "school" in the sense that the Prieuré had been.

Some of the more advanced psychological parts of the doctrine have never been given in writing; a few books have been written by those who never met Gurdjieff or studied with his groups, and who have simply tried to take over his mantle. But there is a core of reliable literature to help to elucidate *Beelzebub*, and among this Ouspensky's *In Search of the Miraculous* is still paramount, although many English-speaking people have preferred the long and detailed *Commentaries on the Teaching of G. I. Gurdjieff and P. D. Ouspensky* by Maurice Nicoll. "The Work," however, was supposed to be taught in a "school"; it insists that its essence can only be learned in a school, and not from books. It is assumed that there is an almost relentless resistance to self-knowledge built into man: that human beings can only survive—and that in no "personal" sense—by help from one another.

The problem for the post-Gurdjieffian student, though, is *which school?* There are many, some following directly on Gurdjieff; but others follow on Ouspensky, and are markedly aggressive toward Gurdjieff—who is said to have given out the ideas, but in an incoherent form. Others believe that this piecemeal and teasing method of Gurdjieff himself is the only way to keep the student awake and to teach him to work things out for himself. Those, therefore, who now discover the ideas for themselves—usually through books—must make their own decisions. There are many Gurdjieff pages on the Internet, some of them useful—they give salutary warnings about spurious schools, of which there are many.

The first important thing to note about this doctrine is that there is, explicitly, no room at all for anyone in it who does not approach it itself in a truly critical and skeptical spirit. It has a cosmology and a psychological system—and a method, often harsh or comic but in any case entirely in the hands of the teacher, of helping people to *become conscious.* But a complete sincerity is required, a sincerity that goes quite beyond devotion or faith as those are ordinarily understood.

For The Work teaches that men and women as they generally exist are, for most of the time, *asleep.* As Gurdjieff's great predecessor the Persian poet Rumi put it:

Your life in this world is like a sleeper who dreams he has gone to sleep.
He thinks, "Now I sleep," not knowing that he is already in a second sleep.

We are—as we normally exist—machines whose workings depend entirely upon external stimuli. When we wake from natural sleep we are not in fact in a state of full consciousness, though we imagine that we are. Thus pupils were told to "remember themselves" as a constant exercise: to try to be aware of their real circumstances, to treat what they had believed to be their real selves as mechanical, to try to discover their chief faults ("chief feature") which might give them a notion of what they had to put right in themselves. The *personality* of a person was carefully distinguished from his or her *essence,* which could be immortal but which had to educate itself, and to do that by learning to subdue the personality that had been formed around it by external circumstances; yet to form a personality was an indispensable part of the process. The ultimate secret lies in transforming the immediate impressions that are received: these are, literally, food, but not of the grosser physical kind. The process of transforming can only be described as miraculous.

In 1923 Gurdjieff told Professor Denis Saurat that he had come to Europe because

> I want to add the mystical spirit of the East to the scientific spirit of the West. The Oriental spirit is right, but only in its trends and general ideas. The Western spirit is right in its methods and techniques. Western methods alone are effective in history. I want to create a type of sage who will unite the spirit of the East with Western techniques.

The "human machine" presented by Watson, SKINNER, and other behavioristic psychologists seems to have much in common with what Gurdjieff taught. But Gurdjieffian psychology is in fact quite different. Man is indeed a machine, *as he ordinarily is*. But even in the ordinary case he is occasionally awakened by shocks. He reacts as a machine but he has the capacity within himself not to do so. Behavioristic psychologists (and adherents of the notion that conventional scientific methodology by itself can plumb the mystery of a godless universe) do not thus acknowledge any exterior spiritual authority, or any need for a feeling of gratitude that we have been granted existence. And man contains within himself, as indeed has been taught by mystical doctrines from time immemorial, all the attributes of the cosmos. In the brain exist, in addition to an intellectual, an emotional, and an instinctive center, a "higher" emotional and a higher intellectual center. But none of our centers work at their full potential; of the higher centers we have only distorted hints in dreams and visions. The sex center, which should be directly in connection with the higher emotional center, works wrongly, through other centers and not as itself; the intellectual and emotional centers should work in harmony, but do not do so. We are, as we are, incapable of anything even approaching "objective" thinking. As PARETO and so many others have insisted, we are irrational creatures pretending to be rational.

Beelzebub's Tales gives a mythological account of how all this, and wars and misunderstandings and poverty and the other human ills arose, and of how it may be possible to amend the current state. The doctrine it inimitably expounds is gnostic and kabbalistic in at least the sense that it presents not an utterly perfect God-creator such as SAINT AUGUSTINE presents, but an unknowable, material "Absolute" whose powers become gradually diminished in an elaborate (and grandly poetic and imaginative) cosmology of inevitable diffusion of energy. This process still serves what we call "Nature," but, the doctrine goes on to explain, something went very wrong with the situation of the people of this planet, which as a consequence is in a very bad part of the universe (which teems with life). Nowhere has the myth of "original sin," the notion of Man having "fallen" from a state of bliss, been more vividly or imaginatively stated than in *Beelzebub's Tales to His Grandson*, which, read with an open mind, can (and has) transformed lives and given them true meaning.

95

Philosophical Investigations

Ludwig Wittgenstein

1953

The Austrian philosopher and mathematician Ludwig Wittgenstein (1889–1951)—who gave away a fortune after his wealthy father's death, which occurred just before the First World War, who valued poetry and religion above his own subject, and who told all those of his students whose minds he most admired, or whom he liked or loved as people, to avoid "doing philosophy" at a university at all costs (get an honest job, he would tell them)—revolutionized twentieth-century philosophy. In this subject he is a figure resembling Goethe in German literature or W. B. Yeats in Irish: he exercised a similar kind of stranglehold, so that even those hardly influenced by him (that is, however, very rare) are discussed as if they were.

Yet few British or American philosophers would, even now, agree with his view of philosophy. It was, he said, a discipline to banish puzzlement—or nothing. In other words, it had no use in itself whatsoever. (That, of course, would put many people out of work.) All this despite the undeniable fact that Wittgenstein's second major work, the *Philosophical Investigations*—

published soon after his death, but (unlike many other posthumous works) more or less substantially as he left it—undermines or seems to undermine his first, the only book he published in his lifetime, the short, sixty-page treatise *Tractatus Logico-Philosophicus* (1921) known simply as the *Tractatus.*

Of all the undisputedly great philosophers, Wittgenstein had read by far the least philosophy. He had little use for it. The British behaviorist philosopher Gilbert Ryle, characteristically disgusted by his mysticism, but respectful because always notably fair-minded, convincingly allowed him a little knowledge—but not much. However, what philosophy Wittgenstein did read, he very well understood. It is almost as if it were all too easy for him. Some of the decisive influences upon him were SCHOPENHAUER, the shabby and half-mad, self-hating Jew Otto Weininger—Wittgenstein was Jewish— the great Austrian satirist, poet, and editor Karl Kraus, TOLSTOY, Dostoyevsky, Bertrand Russell (in matters of technique, and because he was the first to recognize his genius), the English and Cambridge contemporary of Russell, and the most notable proponent of common sense in modern philosophy G. E. Moore (an influence sometimes too minimized), FREUD—and, last but not least, poetry and the Christian tradition.

The most decisive of all of these was certainly Tolstoy, a reading of whose study of the Gospels during the First World War caused Wittgenstein to become a mystic. The influence of Otto Weininger should not be taken too seriously: it was just that he all too often felt just as this morbid suicide— Hitler's only "good Jew," because he had recognized how foul Jewishness was, and so killed himself—had felt: he was a man from whom Wittgenstein could not, emotionally, escape, rather than a true influence.

What relationship Wittgenstein's homosexuality had with his philosophical attitudes and with his frequently suicidal depressions is a controversial issue: A state of high sensuality always accompanied mental (in fact almost certainly manic) speed in him; but he also seems to have believed that the actual exercise of sensuality—as masturbation, or with women, or with men— undermined love. This is the kind of thing that poets rather than philosophers feel (male professors of ethics always, by some odd but demonstrable coincidence—I do not think there is an exception in this century, but perhaps there is—always run off, very ethically of course, with other men's wives). He owned to a sexual relationship with one woman (but this was probably a Viennese prostitute and was transitory).

There is no really hard evidence, however, that he thought of homosexuality as "inferior (or "superior") to heterosexuality, or that he blamed himself in particular for being a homosexual. On the other hand he was brought up in a tradition that forbade homosexuality, and it can very reasonably be speculated that this orientation did make him unhappier than he might otherwise have been. Anyhow, the matter of how he felt about this cannot profitably be discussed in terms of fashionable attitudes, and he above all would have despised any such effort.

His brother Paul, the concert pianist, lost his right arm in the First

World War, and so developed the most formidable left-hand technique in pianistic history. He commissioned piano works for the left hand from Richard Strauss, Ravel, Prokofiev, and, later, Benjamin Britten. He was quite as neurotic and as difficult as Ludwig, and sometimes refused to give the first performances of the works he commissioned. If we think of Ludwig's right hand as philosophical orthodoxy, conventionality, and tact—not lost but entirely wanting—then his own "left-hand technique" offers us an apt parallel. Another Wittgenstein brother, also an army officer, shot himself at the end of the First World War when his men (by then mostly no longer "Austrians," but Czechs, Hungarians, or Poles) refused to obey his orders.

After he had finished the *Tractatus*, which he completed while fighting in the Austrian army (he was repeatedly mentioned for bravery), Wittgenstein renounced philosophy for a job of teaching in Austrian elementary schools: He believed that he had solved all the major problems connected with philosophy. As a teacher he was not altogether successful—especially with his less gifted students. Despite the admirably liberal tradition in which he was trained in Vienna after the war, two of his less attractive methods involved tearing out his pupils' hair (boys' and girls') and soundly boxing their ears. Long afterward, when they had become adults, he returned to apologize to some of them, individually, for these sadistic habits. Most were puzzled and one or two scornful. The behaviour is repulsive; the attempt at apology moving. But he became a sort of father figure to some of his boys.

He was always regarded as being exceedingly difficult to deal with at any level. Yet he was also something of a saint, and one of his sisters complained of this. However, this was a saint of the kind unforgettably portrayed by the French writer Georges Duhamel, in his now far too neglected novel *Salavin:* a pain in the neck. The only difference between him and Duhamel's too-little-heeded Salavin, though, is that he was self-aware. His various male lovers, all of whose lives he made difficult, suffered intensely from his sulks and apologies and self-castigations as a "swine." This he was; but certainly a holy one, as they all knew.

By 1926 he had decided that, after all, he had not solved all the problems of philosophy, and so, after building a house for his sister, went back to Cambridge, at which, in 1939, he was at last elected professor in succession to Moore. During the Second World War, though, he worked as a (rather privileged, and always extremely inventive) porter at a London hospital, and then as a laboratory assistant in Newcastle. By the time he returned to Cambridge for a couple of years after 1945, he was regarded with awe, as by far the greatest philosophical mind of the century. This brought him no satisfaction whatever. It had been his original teacher, Bertrand Russell, who had seen to the publication of the *Tractatus*, which had been refused by many publishers in Austria, Germany, and Great Britain; by as early as 1913 Russell had come to believe that Wittgenstein was *the* man of the future, from whom he and everyone else could learn. Both he and Alfred North Whitehead, his collaborator on the then epoch-making three-volume work on mathematics, *Principia Mathematica,* just completed, had for a time believed that only Wittgenstein was capable of correcting certain sections of this book, or of adding anything to it. Both men certainly regarded his mind as equal to theirs, although Whitehead was oddly silent about him in his own published writings.

Russell, too, returned (from America) to Cambridge after the 1939–45 war—and found his own reputation quite eclipsed by his former pupil's. By then, though, he considered him to have taken a wrong turning. He thought he had become far too mystical—and most do concede that Wittgenstein did, indeed, bring logic and mysticism to the point where they meet (if, of course, they meet at all). Russell was an aggressively atheist humanist; Wittgenstein was one of the most religious-minded of all philosophers, although he was never a member of any church and was not, like Tolstoy (who denied Christ's divinity), interested in the problems set up by the historical Jesus or by the various falsified, legendary (or confused) accounts of him.

Although he was never one of them, the still important 1920s and 1930s work of the Vienna Circle of logical positivists (prominent among them Schlick, Carnap, Waismann, and Gödel), who arrayed themselves against metaphysics and who wished to verify all statements in a far more strictly logical form than had been known before in philosophy (they failed, but set a memorable example), was largely based on Wittgenstein. Yet Wittgenstein has also inspired many religious or quasi-mystical philosophers, whose necessarily metaphysical beliefs were—according to the Vienna Circle, although they were seldom so rude as to say so directly—"nonsense" and even, as Carnap so unforgettably and somehow aptly said of the writings of the Nazi and Hitler-worshipper Martin Heidegger, *"literal nonsense."*

And indeed, it must be stated, by the side of that shabby charlatan and avowed anti-Semite, Wittgenstein's essential nobility is brought out into the clearest possible relief. Heidegger sought—and failed, because even his Nazi friends could not comprehend his murky and crazed babble—to use his muddy substitute for religion to enhance his own standing in the Third Reich; Wittgenstein on the other hand gave some of his money (1914) to Rainer Maria Rilke, whose poetic work he admired more than his own, and never sought to make religion easy by turning it into what he once called "transcendental muck," by which he meant not honest contemplation but Nazi psychobabble of the sort perpetrated by Heidegger.

Wittgenstein was certainly subject to the "fascination of what's difficult," but also to that of "what's simple" (rather than merely easy). His own religious trials and stated wish to be reconciled with God (just before his death of prostate cancer in Cambridge he said, "God may say to me, 'I am judging you out of your own mouth. Your own actions have made you to shudder with disgust when you have seen other people do them'") give the key to his devoutly religious life, one which, significantly, was not stained by intolerant dogma— he would have agreed well with the Irish novelist George Moore, who so memorably wrote: "Life is a rose that withers in the iron fist of dogma."

Wittgenstein's work presents formidable and much disputed technical difficulties, which are quite impossible to deal with in a brief space. Here therefore I concentrate on the change, or development (as it is more appropriately regarded) in his mind and heart between his first masterpiece and his second (just) uncompleted one. Both works had almost equal influence, but *Philosophical Investigations* has had rather more, and in any case it is clearly proper to represent him by the later book, since this expresses the last thoughts that he was able to put down.

In the *Tractatus* language is seen as giving a "picture" of reality. "Picture" is used here in the sense of "model," just as a model may be made of, say, a road accident (it was a French one of these, done by police, that first led Wittgenstein thus to view the problem). A sentence, by this theory, is related to what it says just as a map is related to the landscape it shows. Another feature of the *Tractatus* is that it emphasizes an important difference between *showing* (demonstrating), and talking nonsense. He thus finally denounced the *Tractatus* as nonsense, but as all nonsense perhaps *showing* what is nonsense and what is not nonsense.

The rest of his life's work, as collected in the *Philosophical Investigations*—always carried out in the undoubtedly religious wish that he could be a "better man"—was devoted to an elaboration of this, which also, finally, undermined it. "Meaning" in language was now regarded (Wittgenstein reached this conclusion by 1933) as no more than a contextual affair: It was simply a function of whatever it was in any particular discourse, and it was therefore socially determined. (Wittgenstein had already begun the *Tractatus* with the sentence: "The world is everything that is the case," and was always obsessed—if obsessed is really the word—with just what the American writer Gertrude Stein, also homosexual, was trying to *show*, demonstrate, when she said "a rose is a rose is a rose is a rose"—the final "rose" is usually omitted from quotations, as if the quoter could not quite take it any more). Language, Wittgenstein thought, was used in an almost infinite number of what he ironically called language games. ("Language games" became almost as popular as "geometry" became in Sicily at the time PLATO was there.) There were language games pertaining to engineering, to praying, to making love to men or women, to asking, to hoping, to ordering, to begging, to wishing, to writing poetry—and to, of course, anything else you like to think of. Talking to cats, dogs, goats, peasants, Russell, lovers, and even to Heidegger (who really was a peasant and who had the cunning of an unpleasant one), although Wittgenstein himself did not. We played some of these games well, Wittgenstein thought, but we tended to become over-impressed with certain of the games. In that process we get puzzled, yet, there is no puzzle to us when we speak unreflectingly, when we are not "doing special thinking." All in all, Wittgenstein was above all a brilliant aphorist, probably the greatest of all time. His greatness arises from the fact that, like most of us, he lacked the capacity to make poetic language (his admired Rilke was just the opposite), so he set out to do his best in that full understanding.

96

Syntactic Structures

NOAM CHOMSKY

1957

Noam Chomsky is famous in America for three reasons, and, while he has never much encouraged the making of connections between any of these three leading aspects of his thinking, the temptation to do so has proved irresistible.

In the world outside academe Chomsky is best known as "a kind of socialist anarchist" (his term): an anarchosyndicalist (one who believes, to put it in only the mildest way, that the workers in a corporation ought to have a say in its policies) who is a scourge of General Motors and of all corporations, of media-manipulators, of politicians, and of "the establishment" as a whole. Real anarchism, he claims, is, or would be, "highly structured"; but it differs from corporate capitalism, the present system, because it would "begin from the bottom up." Whether he really believes that anarchosyndicalism can ever come into being is not clear; but this is because he devotes his time to promoting it by means of his critique of the present system.

He has discomfortingly said, of the way in which this system is set up: "There is virtually nothing people can do anyway, without a degree of organization that's far beyond anything that exists now, to influence the real world." Perhaps, although pessimistic (events such as the Falklands War, the Gulf War, or the wars in Yugoslavia tend to cause pessimism), he just feels that it is his human and humane duty that he should make himself, with his influence as a scholar and his obviously very high intelligence, available: It can happen one day. Until recently—when he found that he no longer had the time—he spent a full twenty hours a week answering all the personal letters that reached him by E-mail. His political writings are now ignored by mainstream publishers—but the world of the small presses (he says) is the only milieu he wants to be a part of.

Possibly, too, he believes in the value of a rich inner life—but does not talk about this. He has enraged many left-wing thinkers by his lack of "a theory which might give rise to debate." Possibly, however, he prefers effective direct action to debate—and it is likely, though he is not given to moralizing (he does not commit the notorious "naturalistic fallacy" of confusing "ought" with "is"), that he does not want anyone to kill anyone else using his name as an excuse.

His detractors on the respectable ("mainstream") left, since they do not think that his admittedly "remorseless" accounts of the mendacity of governments and corporations are sufficient, have so far neglected the question that might be thus posed: "Why is there no *prominent* and *popular* theory of the necessity of lying on the part of governments and corporations?" To put the bare facts about lying on the record—after all, why lie if all is really to the good?—is of course a piece of direct action, but (says a Yale professor of comparative literature well satisfied with things as they are), this is "tedious" and "messianic"—and, as many public relations men from many corporations might very well ask: "Why bother?"

Chomsky gives interviews in which he makes statements that cause discomfort and anger: They are not always easy to answer. He stated, to give a famous example, that if the Nuremberg laws (by which the Nazi war criminals were judged) were still in force today then every postwar American president would have had to be hanged. This may be so on strictly logical grounds—but he has (disconcertingly) never advocated that those presidents who have survived *should* be hanged, since he does not believe in violence.

A Frenchman called Robert Faurisson wrote a book in which he claimed that the Holocaust is a Jewish myth. Chomsky—a Jew who is highly critical, as are many Israelis as well, of Israel's policies—without bothering to read the book, wrote a preface to it, advocating, not indeed that there had not been a Holocaust, but that Faurisson had the right to express his opinion. Nor has he asked that Faurisson be beaten up or even imprisoned. Such matters are important to him; but Faurisson's own views do not interest him and ought not to interest anyone else. It would be important in a good society, he seems to think, that everyone should have a right to say whatever he liked without being manhandled. After all, Faurisson's views would be demonstrably self-refuting in a reasonable society. Does ganging up on idiots really do credit to people who call themselves intellectuals? People ganged up on Hitler and had "debate" about him, which seems understandable—but suppose they had just *ignored* him?

Chomsky, although he has drawn upon ideas to be found in the works of MARX, the anarchist Bakunin, and ROUSSEAU, is not a "Marxist," and has been as critical of Marxist governments as he has of others; he could even be seen as a man devoted to making unrhetorical observations, some of which have testable content; but these observations, testable or not, are usually of the sort that anti-Marxists do not like, and his assumptions—such as that General Motors is not completely devoted to the welfare of the people of the world—are shocking. His manner of speech when dealing with topical issues is distinctly unprofessorial, so much so that it might be wondered (by the proverbial Martian) if he is not a humane man given to drawing attention to current injustices in a language that can be readily understood by all; but it is on the whole safer to regard him as a misguided radical driven insane by his immersion in the study of linguistics, in which discipline he caused a revolution. How did he do that? Here we come to the second, but less widely understood, reason for his fame. (The third is really an offshoot of this one.)

Syntactic Structures does not contain the whole of Chomskian linguistic theory (the book coming closest to this is probably James Peck's *A Chomsky Reader* (1987), but has been chosen to represent him here because it marked a very great turning point in linguistics. Since then his linguistic theory has been the basis for almost all research into the nature of the language and therefore of how the "mind," whatever that means, interacts with the brain. That does not, of course, mean that much of this research has not been directed *against* his theory; but the fact of his importance remains. At present there is no way to confirm or to refute the theory—but, as science has often proceeded along intuitive lines or "leaps of faith," Chomsky still dominates.

Linguistics is the study of the general nature (and even the origin, although that mysterious aspect of it is usually ignored) of language. Language is what distinguishes human beings from all other known species, and it is therefore crucial to our understanding. We communicate by means of language, and, although we do not (apparently) always do this very well, we shall continue to do it. One of the cruces is this question: How do we learn language?

Chomsky's early studies in linguistics, like everyone else's at that time, were dominated by the thinking of Leonard Bloomfield (1887–1949), a philologist (in his extreme youth he had translated a fiery socialistic play by the German playwright Gerhart Hauptmann, a future winner of the Nobel Prize). Bloomfield caused linguistics to emerge in America as a separate discipline, and, after being a fanatic "mentalist" or introspectionist for a time, turned to linguistic behaviorism—something which, as we shall see, Chomsky was able to refute in the form advocated by B. F. SKINNER (his review of a book by Skinner—*Verbal Behavior*—was one of the most devastating of the twentieth century).

When we say that Bloomfield became a linguistic behaviorist we mean that he endorsed a new method of viewing language influenced by "advances" in psychology. The psychologist J. B. Watson, a cruel, irresponsible, and unimaginative man—an inspirer of the more scientifically accomplished Skinner—had decided that, since in his view introspectionism could yield no scientific data, it should be ignored along with everything else that was not just purely external, and immediately observable, *behavior*. Introspection, since you could do nothing with it, did not exist. For Watson *thinking = speech without musculature*.

Bloomfield was a capable man, but, over-excited, he saw no fallacy in this argument: He stated that the meanings of linguistic forms could only be interpreted in terms of whatever stimuli caused them to be uttered in the first place—and then in terms of the response-behavior they elicited. As a method of investigating language, without getting confused about the meanings it might or might not have, this was useful, perhaps invaluable—but only if it were realized that it was just a working method, and not *the* truth about language. It simply provided a way of looking at language.

Chomsky's teacher at the University of Pennsylvania—which he entered at sixteen—Zellig Harris, was a Bloomfieldian (he also influenced his pupil politically, as he was a leader of Avukah, a group which believed in Jewish-Arab collaboration in Israel), and all Chomsky's earlier work was done under Bloomfieldian structuralist assumptions; when with *Syntactic Structures* he started to break away from this school, he was still convinced that a language could legitimately be studied without semantic considerations (considerations of meaning). Later, he became more critical altogether. In *Semantic Structures*, however, he was already emphasizing the creative potential of language and its *open-ended* nature. It might be put like this: Already Chomsky was more inspired by the notion of language as a *wonderful* or even a *miraculous* thing than were his Bloomfieldian mentors. Wonder and the miraculous, though, are not in the province of science—and Chomsky the scientist had much to offer.

To put it necessarily briefly, Chomsky tried to answer a question (he calls it "Plato's problem"), in the field of linguistics, that Bertrand Russell had already posed for our own times, and which I have italicized: "*How comes it that human beings, whose contacts with the world are brief and personal and limited, are able to know as much as they do know?*"

Chomsky translated this into the question: "*How comes it that by the age of five or six children are able to produce and understand an infinitely large number of utterances that they have not previously encountered?*" His answer was that human beings possess an innate faculty (that idea goes directly against the empiricist view that the mind, whatever it may be, is a *tabula rasa*, a blank page, at birth), an innate *creativity* (certainly a key word in Chomsky), for language.

Skinner's *Verbal Behavior* was published in the same year as *Syntactic Structures*, and in it Skinner attempted to demonstrate that human beings pick up their linguistic competence by experience alone. In his famously mordant review of this book Chomsky made clear that he believed that human beings are endowed at birth with specific faculties which enable them to act as free agents: They *are* affected by stimuli (he never sought to deny this) from the environment, but they also retain their native ability. This is a proposition that offers more "hope" than behaviorism; but hope is not in the province of science, either—unless in the purely phenomenological sense that people (gamblers such as PASCAL?) can be shown to exhibit it.

The details of Chomsky's theory are complicated, and can here only be stated as follows: stimulus-response theory cannot alone account for linguistic competence. One important point here is that Chomsky was able to deal the pure behaviorism of Skinner and others a blow—a blow from which it has not since recovered. For Skinner, society could be controlled adequately if people were, like his rats and pigeons, "conditioned" to behave "properly" (what was "proper" was never adequately defined).

This brings us to the third important aspect of Chomsky's thinking. When he found that experience alone could not account for linguistic competence, he struck another blow—an incidental one, if you like—this one against philosophical empiricism; it was a blow for the rationalism of PLATO, DESCARTES, LEIBNIZ, and SPINOZA, all of whom claimed that there was something already within us at birth from which adequate philosophical arguments could be made. For if learning experience alone were responsible for linguistic competence, then how could children know such complex rules of grammar as they do? He provides abundant examples. Thus he can write:

> Turning to the human mind, we also find structures of marvelous intricacy developing in a uniform way with limited and unstructured experience. Language is a case in point, but not the only one. . . . Capacities are no doubt unlearned in their essentials, deriving from biological endowment. . . . We are fortunate to have this rich innate endowment. Otherwise we would grow into "mental amoeboids."

It seems to be sufficiently obvious, without Chomsky's needing to draw further attention to it, that there is a connection between his political and linguistic activities.

97

The Structure of Scientific Revolutions

T. S. KUHN

1962, revised 1970

T[homas] S[amuel] Kuhn's *The Structure of Scientific Revolutions*, together with its successor (selected essays defending or modifying his views, or replying to his critics) *The Essential Tension* (1977), has been one of the most influential academic books of the twentieth century. It has even been alleged that it may also have been its own, or Kuhn's, worst enemy. This is because, like his affronted critic KARL POPPER, Kuhn was himself a quite old-fashioned science historian who believed, at heart, in "scientific progress": He believed, that is, that the "advancements" of science were, on the whole, of great benefit to mankind, an entity that is going onward and upward: one which is evolving toward perfection, as evidenced (arms manufacturers will tell you) in the two massive wars of this century.

Yet Kuhn accused science of proceeding, not in the manner that we tend to idealize it as so doing—by an always rational and noble rigor—but in leaps and bounds that have little to do with its own faith in reason. That (some assert) so stung scientists that they have been making sure, ever since his book appeared, that they were *not* "irrational." Therefore, it is suggested, they now tend to resist anything that might seem irrational—and so scientific "progress" suffers accordingly, since the Kuhnian account (it is alleged) is not after all really a hostile but a merely descriptive one!

What is then asserted, though, seems, in retrospect, not yet to have been the case. However, the notion that science "progresses" has recently been challenged on a number of grounds. For example, at a fairly primitive level, what is the use of discoveries about nuclear physics if men cannot control their harmful results? There is not only the cost of Hiroshima and Nagasaki to consider, but also the inability of scientists to exercise full control of nuclear power stations, which are quite obviously not "one-hundred-percent safe"—despite the claims of nuclear bureaucrats, who are not physicists but highly paid public-relations clerks whose chief interest lies in their performance-related pay. Nor, it is becoming increasingly clear, can the nuclear industry dispose of its waste safely. At a more subtle, or at least at a less blindingly obvious level, do we not lose some of the wisdom (wisdom, after all, is a sort of information) implicit in an "old" scientific worldview (what Kuhn called a paradigm) when we abandon it for a new one? Yet there is no common ground between paradigms: only hostility. Kuhn's message might be thus translated for the absolute laymen: The vast majority of scientists do, yes, perform their isolated experiments with true rigor and often brilliant ingenuity. But, contrary to expectations and to their own complacent general claims, they are far from being scientific about the reasons for which they hold their views. They are all too like the rest of humanity!

Thomas Kuhn was born in 1922, the son of an industrialist of Cincinnati, Ohio. He trained at Harvard as a physicist, but after a spell in a radio laboratory went on to become a philosopher and historian of science. He was a member of the faculty of the History of Science at Harvard from 1951 until 1961, then went to Berkeley, then to Princeton; finally in 1979 he moved to MIT. He died in 1996 at the age of seventy-three. Kuhn's style was not elegant (his titles do not suggest that he was very sensitive to the sounds of words), and he may not have been any more interested in poetry than was his chief critic Popper.

The interesting point is that Kuhn was not, by nature, a revolutionary or a heretic, but rather an honest man who was drawn toward the expression of the truth whenever he thought he recognized it. When the Hungarian philosopher Imre Lakatos declared (injudiciously in the circumstances) that Kuhn's ideas equated scientific progress with "mob psychology," Kuhn was surprisingly mild in his reply: "Look, I think that's nonsense, and I'm prepared to argue that." He did not, for example, as some might (just as injudiciously) have done, trash Lakatos as an ex-communist fanatic turned fascist. He was a mild man who did not relish the trouble he received from his opponents, some of whom became exceedingly bad-tempered and "unscientific."

Kuhn's theory (but perhaps it is really more of a description of *one* of the more important ways in which scientists, whether they like it or not, work), allowing for his modifications of it, and for the fact that he became rather more relativistic in his outlook as he grew older, amounts to a major tour de force. Previous to Kuhn, and with the exception of a few historians of science who influenced him (Alexandre Koyré, the iconoclastic and "intolerable" and alas late Paul Feyerabend, Michael Polanyi, Gaston Bachelard, and Stephen Toulmin come to mind), scientists had believed in science as a rather smooth, noble, and rational enterprise. According to Popper, for example, it carried on a process of progressive falsifications of its paradigms in a more or less irreproachable manner. But from Kuhn we learned that scientists worked quite as irrationally as everyone else.

The concept central to Kuhn's view is a *paradigm* (he did not, of course, invent the word) by which in this context he means, roughly, "a model for subsequent scientific activity." Examples of paradigms include NEWTON's *Principia* and DARWIN's *Origin of Species*. A paradigm consists of an open-ended resource—a series of concepts and procedures—which structures the way that scientists work.

Of course this view can be extended—and indeed is often very fruitfully extended—to any field of activity: Thus, to take but two examples, it is a paradigm among the literary community (where, of course, as CHOMSKY has pointed out, you can get away with murder by comparison with scientific communities, to be a member of which you have to know something) that W. H. Auden is a great modern poet, or, among a part of the "musical community" that Lord Andrew Lloyd Webber is a great composer ("better than Beethoven," as one of them put it, "because he has made more money and given pleasure to billions rather than mere millions"). But the "paradigms" of the popular press are part of the history of nonsense, not of sense.

Kuhn held that the environment of what he called *normal science* (which is what goes on for most of the time) consisted of a set of associated beliefs and laws which were simply assumed to be true—they were not questioned. Eventually, however, *anomalies* (I put his other key words or terms into italics) arise. For example, observations are made which just cannot be accounted for in the terms of the old paradigm. Very powerful, even highly irrational, attempts are often made, to force them to fit. Such intelligent men as LUTHER or MONTAIGNE rejected the heliocentric hypothesis. It was strangled at its birth in the third century B.C.E. in the case of Aristarchus, who first postulated it.

When the facts just cannot be fitted into the old paradigm, we then experience, as we did eventually with the acceptance of Copernican theory, a *paradigm shift*. During the period in which this is taking place, the time by which the *anomalies* have put just too much stress on the old paradigm, there is a crisis, followed by a *scientific revolution*. Scientific discipline is then no longer dominated by the old paradigm. But it soon comes under the domination of a new one. The difference between different paradigms, and of

Rabbit-duck

course in particular between an old one and its successor, Kuhn called *incommensurability*. The whole process of passing from one paradigm to another was likened, by Kuhn, not at all to rational discourse, but to a *gestalt switch*, the most famous example of which is the duck-rabbit picture (which so fascinated WITTGENSTEIN): You can see it either as a duck, *or* as a rabbit, but not as both. You might say that scientists were seen for the first time as poor philosophers of their own subject. When one views the rabbit-duck drawing one does not view it either as rabbit or duck for any logical reason: One simply so sees it, and one can switch from rabbit to duck at will. It is disconcerting to a person who thinks that he or she just must be "right." Which is right? And of course in a cogent sense everything has a "duck-rabbit" nature.

To illustrate this, it is perhaps easiest to give an example, allowing for the obvious differences (and for the fact, worth repeating, that in this "discipline," you can get away, as Chomsky said, with murder), from the field of what has been called literary taste. Thus, the late seventeenth-century "metaphysical" poet Abraham Cowley is now very widely, indeed pretty well universally, taken to have been vastly overrated by his own age, in which he got a state funeral and was thought of as greater than Milton. Most modern readers have never heard of him, and only the most fatuously unreadable critics think of writing books about him. There seems (a little more controversially) also to be, just now, at least hints of a switch taking place about the figure of T. S. Eliot, fifty years ago the paradigmatically great poet of the twentieth century, but now becoming, in many eyes, an old-fashioned Jew-baiting cryptofascist whose verse is not really much more than an anthology and an amalgam of other men's flowers. There is already a new game, in which his famous phrases are traced to their original sources. A frantic rearguard action is therefore going on in behalf of his widow and his publishers (who own the rights to the "lyrics" of the greater-than-Beethoven Lord Webber's immortal and high-earning *Cats*).

An enlightening Kuhnian history of literary taste could certainly be written, provided its author was aware of how very (very) much more "open-ended" things can be in that field. In it a George Bernard Shaw can say that SHAKESPEARE was no good. But you cannot quite say, in science, that Newton's laws of gravity are *"no good."* Many have claimed that they understand themselves better as a result of taking a Kuhnian look at their apparent perceptions. Theology, of course, offers another target ripe for Kuhnian analysis.

People could more easily accept such changes of taste in theology or literature, however, because, whatever a theologian or a literary critic does, there is no strictly *scientific* way of "evaluating" a belief or a writer. Attempts to reduce literature to science have always failed, and always quite quickly:

Literary works depend on emotion, which has to be entirely absent in proper scientific experimentation. (Yet at least in the notorious field of statistics, experimenters, it appears, get the results "they want": Over a quarter of a century ago, the malodorous psychologist Hans Eysenck in Great Britain, and Jensen in America, "proved" that blacks were "less intelligent" than "other races"; but others got different results: Does science get more uncertain, less "scientific," as its investigations become more vital?)

Scientists, though, were angry to be told that their discipline as a whole was just as capricious as any other. Kuhn clamed that in normal science, for most of the time, workers did little more than low-pressure puzzle-solving: The dominating paradigm is never rigorously tested, but simply used—rather feebly and routinely—as the resource. Then someone, usually young, often not conventionally qualified, and therefore less constrained (for example, EINSTEIN) comes along and challenges the current paradigm. Kuhn could not find any *logical* reason why paradigms changed, and on the whole this view has now been reluctantly accepted.

Kuhn's view was anathema to Popper, who saw science as being carried out in a soundly logical manner along his lines. On the whole, though, and with some exceptions, Kuhn's view of the history of scientific procedures has prevailed—especially among social scientists, who like to be able to view science itself as an equal—at least in the sense that he could show how often scientists have held views which they have been unable to defend in a scientific manner in public discourse. His books were dryly written, but they had their impact because their content dynamited scientific complacency. In that sense at least they did much good to science.

98

The Feminine Mystique

Betty Friedan

1963

Betty Friedan was born (1921) in the conservative heartland of America, in Peoria, Illinois (population about 100,000). That was highly appropriate for the woman (*née* Goldstein), at first a psychologist by inclination (she studied under the gestalt psychologist Kurt Koffka), who more than any other single person sparked what amounted to a woman's revolution in America—and then, to an extent governed by national differences, elsewhere. The times were ripe for it, but she did it.

It came about in her case because she found her situation as a woman so stifling and so unjust that she could not but rebel against it. She had married a theatrical producer, had three children, read Dr. Spock, did journalism—but then started to feel what she called "the problem that has no name."

Feminist books written after *The Feminine Mystique* have been influential, and the revolution—like all known revolutions—has long since declined into (among, however, many other better things) a silly parody of itself, featuring some women who have distinguished themselves by demonstrating that women can be quite as foolish as men. But men have had—and still for the most part in fact retain—the dominant role for a long time; all that has been proved by the excesses of feminism—that is, pseudofeminism—is that women can be just as human and just as flawed as their counterparts. Most enlightened men, trying to be as feminist as they can be, would probably agree with GURDJIEFF, who said: "Woman knows everything, but has forgotten it." That is not unflattering, especially considering that men in most respects have so much less to forget.

In the history of modern feminism *The Feminine Mystique*, it will in due course be found, was as influential as the writings of MARY WOLLSTONECRAFT and SIMONE DE BEAUVOIR. But as a piece of writing it cannot be compared to the *Vindication*, and the thinking in it is nothing like as distinguished as that in *The Second Sex*. However, it is more polemical than philosophical; it will not be much read in the future for its insights. Its criticism of the maleness inherent in Freudian psychology is cogent, but this has been better discussed elsewhere.

But it did a job. It has been fairly criticized for being wrong or not sufficiently specific on many more points than its attack on FREUD. But, with it, Friedan awakened a movement that had lain dormant in the United States for fifty years. It was a fundamentally rational protest. Those American women who are not grateful to her, and to her good sense and ability to restrain herself, ought to be. But what was this thing that she called "the feminine mystique"?

It was the long cherished American myth of woman. The same kinds of myth existed in other countries but took different forms. Reference to the works of Simone de Beauvoir and to similar books from other countries amply demonstrates this. The American form was peculiarly virulent, and as vicious as sentimentality so often is. Friedan had not only suffered her own peculiarly midwestern frustrations but also, before that, had watched her mother's frustration—as both Jew and woman—when she tried to fulfill her human needs.

In order to count as a woman in America you had, then, to be a paradigmatic "housewife-mother." That myth involved, mainly, various sorts of submission—sexual, domestic, political. The form of submission that is demanded of women by males is a good deal more subtle and complicated than, at that time, Friedan was able to present it as being; but she had a very wide audience, and she had to oversimplify matters. Otherwise no one would have taken notice of her. She had to strike a chord in the minds of other women—and she did. Her initial judgment in this respect was impeccable, for her book sold millions and did effect a change in attitudes. Later she was accused of egocentricity—but to bring about such changes people need to be, or at least to seem, egocentric, powerful, unyielding.

The book is a capable analysis of the forms that the myth took in the 1950s: Friedan plundered popular literature, what passed for educational theory, academic psychology, social science—and her own experience. She pictured the average middle-class American woman (she more or less ignored black or working-class women) as leading a life in which she tried to conform to a false image, and thus suffered inevitable unhappiness: "It is not a harmless image. There may be no psychological terms for the harm that it is doing. But what happens when women try to live according to an image that makes them deny their minds? What happens when women grow up in an image that makes them deny the reality of the changing world?"

Had the book been a profound, detailed, or subtle analysis, it could not have worked. But it was not wrong so far as it went—and it may well have helped later, less popular, but deeper analyses to be made by those women who had gained initial liberation from the impact it had. Of course it overstated its case: It had to. But not always. For example, male editors of women's magazines were accused of conspiring to keep women in domesticity by publishing stories that glorified mother-wife roles rather than feminine independence. This was by and large true, and it needed to be stated thus crudely. Friedan could not possibly anticipate that within twenty-five years male-controlled magazines, nominally edited by women, would be publishing psychologically unconvincing and merely fashionable tales of "liberated" women. It would have been fatal for her to have seen that feminism would soon turn into pseudofeminism. Had she been less crude, she would have risked antagonizing her audience. This was an audience which really did feel frustrated.

Friedan did offer an alternative, "a new life plan for women." Her prescription was, again, crude—but then it had to be crude to be effective: "Who knows of the possibilities of love when men and women share not only children, home, and garden, not only the fulfillment of their biological roles, but the responsibilities and passions of the work that creates the future and the full human knowledge of who they are?"

Friedan went on to become the president of NOW (National Organization for Women), and of course to be accused of having been "hopelessly bourgeois." She got into serious trouble among those who had owed so much to her for declaring that "man is not the enemy" and that "female chauvinism is highly dangerous and diversionary." In the words of a popular and conventional account of her, she "softened her image." As polemic, then, *The Feminine Mystique* stands fairly high. Although any indignant author can easily be provoked into stupidity, it is rarely stupid. The charge that it is specifically middle class may be answered by the simple observation that if you do not get such a revolution at the middle-class level, then you are not going to have it at all. Friedan demonstrated to the middle-class American woman what she lacked, and got something as near to a good result as could be expected. No doubt the book is lacking in an original critique of the sociological view of gender roles—but to provide that, in 1963, would have been impossible within a polemic.

99

Quotations From Chairman Mao Tse-tung

MAO ZEDONG

1966

"The Little Red Book" (as in its heyday it was always popularly known, despite the more mundane real title), carried about by millions during China's disastrous "Great Proletarian Cultural Revolution" of 1966, is seldom discussed these days. But its circulation was by no means confined to China in the later 1960s; it caused fights in London's dockland, and helped to cause university students all over the world to rebel. Its influence is not to be denied, especially on the French events of 1968—events that spawned, among other things, a violent right-wing reaction, an outbreak of Burkean terror, and a general distaste for revolutionary activity.

For a few years, along with the Mao button-badges that were issued with it in China (more than five billion were made), it had all the authority that the Bible has for a red-hot fundamentalist. But it was new and secular, and so it had even more impact. The two great questions, in those four or five years of cruelty and insanity ("political reeducation") that gripped China while the Cultural Revolution lasted, were: *Do you have a Little Red Book?*" and "*Can you recite it?*" (A small *Supplement to Quotations from Chairman Mao* was issued in 1969, in Hong Kong.)

As a writer Mao favored, not Marxist-Leninist jargon but classical Chinese exposition. As a poet, although not major in any serious sense, he was both talented and accomplished: He did not indulge himself in the trashy "tractor" idiom used by so many bad Chinese communist "poets" of his own generation; his poetry is much better than the mere "party" verse of, say, the Chilean Pablo Neruda, who *was* a major twentieth-century poet when he was writing for himself.

There is a tradition in China (and Japan, but the Japanese usually write this kind of poetry in Chinese) that educated people ought to compose poetry simply as an accomplishment. Mao's poetry offers a good example of this tradition at its best, and, when it is read in the light of his many cruel acts, is disconcerting because it seems to express genuinely compassionate feeling. But this is no more disconcerting, perhaps, than the conversion of the Japanese perpetrators of appalling crimes to an apparently serene Buddhism—one of the most extraordinary of post–Second World War phenomena—as soon as they were called to reckoning.

Mao's Little Red Book was the truth. People could live or die by it. The students and others who acted as Mao's "Red Guards," and who so ferociously assailed "the Party's errors," lived.

The "book" itself, incidentally, consists of selected quotations from all Mao's writings up to its date, and is thus little more than a series of easily comprehended aphorisms of a (usually) rather direly practical nature. It was edited by Mao's then minister of defense, Lin Piao. But for people who want to win a war it is still distinctly useful. It is drawn from a list of works with such titles as these: *Significance of Agrarian Reforms in China, Strategic Problems of China's Revolutionary War, On the Rectification of Incorrect Ideas in the Party* (how much does Mao now inspire the tyrannical apostles of modern political correctness?), *A Single Spark Can Start a Prairie Fire, On the Correct Handling of Contradictions Among the People,* and so on and so on—and from "unofficial" sources. Another such compendium, also edited by Lin Piao, is entitled *Long Live Mao Tse-Tung Thought.* It is on the whole strictly practical, not theoretical, stuff. (Later Lin Piao betrayed Mao.)

There is much common sense in Maoism, but this easily drifts into platitude: "Be resourceful, look at all sides of a problem, test ideas by experiment, and work hard for the common good." There are also elements from the works of CONFUCIUS in Maoism, especially the notion of compromise; thus at various times Mao worked with Chiang Kai-shek. From MARX himself he learned a simple form of Hegelian dialectic, and this of course has its equivalent in ancient Chinese thinking.

But Maoism deviated in very important respects from the "Marxist-Leninist" line that China officially followed during the years of alliance with Russia, immediately after 1949. The sayings selected in the *Quotations* help to define it. It is the most populist of all forms of Marxism, and one which is more in line with the thinking of the later Trotsky and of Rosa Luxembourg than of Lenin or Stalin. It is also almost the only case of a genuine populism gaining control of a country—and a large country at that. Mao did gain strength, throughout his years of struggle, by being friendly and helpful to the rural population among which his guerrilla forces moved. Some have even suggested that Mao found in official Marxism no more than a "handy weapon to fight the encrusted tradition of Chinese feudalism." Official Marxist-Leninist communism, for its part, while it lasted in Soviet Russia and its empire, loathed and feared Maoism. The current Chinese leadership itself has been trying to eradicate it since Mao, by then not too sound of mind, died in 1976—even before that it was opposed by many: Mao's control of his fellow leaders was never as sure as the West was inclined to believe.

But for all that, the career of Mao, one of only three peasants (the others were the founders of the Han and Ming dynasties) to gain control of his country throughout its long history—Mao, more or less, ruled a quarter of the world's population for a quarter of a century—was epoch-making, despite his terrible mistakes. He is arguably a more important figure in world history than Alexander the Great. Certainly his policies were responsible for more deaths—counting those who died of starvation, as well as those who succumbed to torture or were executed, these deaths amount to something in the region of at least 100 million. Mao's successors have never entirely repudiated him: They think that most of his policies were counterproductive, but that he was essential to their takeover of the country. In this they are probably right. But perhaps he was more of an anarchist than a Marxist.

Mao was born in the inland province of Hunan in 1893, the son of a peasant farmer whom he early learned—against a strong Chinese tradition—to defy. His mother was a gentler person and a devout Buddhist. Mao worked as an assistant in the library at Beijing University, and then trained as a primary school teacher at Changsa. He graduated at the age of eighteen. He was one of the twelve delegates to the First Congress of the Chinese Communist Party (1921), and thus one of its founding members. However, after he gained power, he was always a zealous critic of this party. He could never gain complete control of his cabinet.

Mao was the first leading Communist to recognize the revolutionary potential of the peasantry. Marx in theory and Lenin in practice had seen communism as an urban doctrine. In the later 1920s Mao organized the people of Hunan—first those of his own village—into a powerful force. This highly pragmatic strategy was one of the main influences on Fidel Castro when in 1959 he was able to take over Cuba. Attention to it also enabled the Vietnamese, Laotian, and Cambodian communists to take over their countries. The Communists in China could never have taken over from the rule of Chiang Kai-shek by simply working along classical Marxist-Leninist lines in industrial urban areas.

Mao's actual rule of China began in 1949, after Chiang Kai-shek had been forced to retreat to Taiwan. It was in the years preceding this victory that he did his best work—few now hold Chiang Kai-shek up as any kind of model. His internal policies were not successful, although he was always consistent in his ideal of trying to keep in close touch with the aspirations of the ordinary peasant. Thus, while the Hungarian uprising of 1956 caused the rulers of Russia's empire to enact new repressions, Mao launched the Hundred Flowers movement: he urged citizens to criticize the Party freely. Here he may be defended: He was forced to halt this internal policy by his own colleagues, who were never so eager as he for the state to "wither away."

His next step is less defensible, and his colleagues had more reason behind their decision to force him to bring it to a halt: The Great Leap Forward (1958), which aimed to increase Chinese steel production to a staggering thirty million tons a year, was completely unrealistic. Yet its aim, to create tens of thousands of small local furnaces, was not without a certain good will. Does one quite *blame* Gandhi for his advocacy of domestic spinning? The feeling behind these plans might have pleased HENRY THOREAU. Given a real chance, could they have succeeded?

By 1965 Mao feared that he was losing control. He had said that "it is to the advantage of despots to keep people ignorant; it is to our advantage to make them intelligent"; but not all his colleagues really agreed with him, and he himself could not see beyond the aspirations of the peasantry. He did not trust his colleagues, and he was not always good at choosing allies when it came to the task of putting his policies into effect. He never understood or sympathized with industry—all very well, but China depended on it.

The formation of the radical Red Guards in 1966, and sending them into the countryside to force bureaucrats, professors, technicians, nonpeasants everywhere, into rural work, almost amounted to a declaration of war against his own cabinet: It has been called a populist revolution against the Communist state—and that is what it amounted to. One can understand the passion behind it, but, like so many other movements, it quickly turned into the opposite of itself: Tens of thousands were murdered or forced to give up their jobs and "recant." There was an outburst of hatred and ignorance; a decent scorn for bureaucrats soon grew murderous and vengeful. China's economy suffered, and she lost all her technicians. To what extent Mao's fourth wife was responsible for some of the excesses is not really clear even now, but she and others (the so-called "Gang of Four") were arrested, tried, and convicted after Mao's death.

Maoism, then, as embodied in the Little Red Book, is a distinctly non-intellectual phenomenon. In Soviet Russia Party officials were almost immune from criticism. In Maoism Party officials are almost forbidden in favor of a direct policy of "listening to the people." No authority is acknowledged, so that even an actual expert in his subject (not a media person, called an expert, who is employed by corporations or politicians to endorse and to promote their case—but a person who knows a job) can be repudiated as "elitist." Maoism is far more anarchistic than Soviet Marxism ever was, and it sounds far more attractive than any Soviet pronouncement; but the events it spawned in 1966 act as a clear warning to those who are attracted by its utopian ideals. China in 1966 was not the country in which to launch a sudden experiment in anarchism, and the experiment turned almost immediately into a brutal mob tyranny.

100

Beyond Freedom and Dignity

B. F. Skinner

1971

During the spring term of 1926 the venerable poet Robert Frost conducted a creative writing course at the University of Michigan. One of his pupils was a twenty-two-year-old Mr. Skinner (as he is called in Frost's *Selected Letters*), to whom he wrote, of his youthful short stories, "I ought to say you have the touch of art. This work is clear run. You're worth twice anyone else I've seen in prose this year." Mr. Skinner had made "real niceties of observation," Frost told him, and had "done 'em to a shade." He ended his note: "Belief. Belief. You've got to augment my belief in life or cross it uglily."

Burrhus Frederic Skinner—born in Pennsylvania in 1904—was going to "cross" not only the gloomy Frost's but many other people's "belief in life" all right, and very "uglily" indeed: more reprehensibly, and more plain stupidly, perhaps, than any other man of this century not a straightforward advocate of totalitarianism—after all, he believed more in the virtue of rewards than in that of punishments, which he did not quite rule out.

Skinner, in his simpleminded novel *Walden Two*, wrote: "When a science of behavior has been achieved, there's no alternative to a planned society." In discussing the utilitarianism of JOHN STUART MILL I suggested that this philosophy—like any other thing that was not more than a mere philosophy as we in Great Britain and in America take it to be—might not be able to come to real terms with the "reasons of the heart" made so famous by PASCAL. In other words, I was suggesting, we need a different language in which we could more fruitfully discuss such questions about society, but we have not found it. Those words of Skinner's have been found by many people to be chilling. For although much democratic government (as all must concede) has been influenced by the humane goals of utilitarianism, much government "planning" has also the loathsome mark of "Skinnerian science," Skinner has thus been seen as antihumanitarian. He has also impressed "planners," "managers," and their like.

So Skinner's ugly "crossing" of the pessimistic poet Frost's insistence upon "belief in life" came, not from a writer of stories or verse (at which he also tried his hand), not from a creative writer, but from a psychologist, the foremost behavioristic psychologist of his age, the man who helped to make Watsonian behaviorism respectable. Skinner would become most famous, or infamous, not as the imaginative writer he had once so wished to be, but for his conditioned rats and pigeons, his "mechanical baby-tenders" and his "Skinner Box" in which people claimed (wrongly, as it happens) that he brought up his children, his outrageously dull and silly (but not badly written) novel *Walden Two* (1948), and for his forcefully written but monstrous tract *Beyond Freedom and Dignity*.

What is the point of mentioning his early efforts as a creative writer and a literary critic? Because, certainly, his project to create a "totally integrated" society, in which everyone was conditioned (by him, no other) by his system of "positive reinforcement," arose from his disappointment at his creative failure, his rage that he was not able to be a poet. In his old age he would quote from his youthful verse, regretfully say that he thought it "not bad" (it was not, very—but what could the behaviorist have meant, talking about a record of nonexistent "inner states"?), and whine that we do have useless emotions—but that, oh, we ought not to do so. So the archenemy of FREUD and Freudianism played right into Freudian hands.

Nowadays, with the exception of a few eccentric and dedicated admirers devoted to conditioning the rest of us, he is rapidly fading into a well-deserved obscurity. But did he leave a deadly mark, a mark that KAFKA prophesied, with a frightening calmness, earlier in the century? Skinner's psychological work, as work done in the American behavioristic tradition set up by J. B. Watson earlier in the century, was rigorous and distinguished. He was never a pseudoscientist, and he knew how to conduct interesting and meticulous experiments on behavior modification in animals. The inferences he then drew, however, were as preposterous as they were foolish.

> We study the height at which a pigeon's head is normally held, and select some line on the height scale which is reached only infrequently. Keeping our eye on the scale we begin to open the food tray very quickly whenever the head rises above the line. The result is invariable: we observe an immediate change in the frequency with which the head crosses the line.

Obviously this is useful, and (someone once cogently suggested) a good example of the manner in which pigeons can train human beings like Skinner to provide them with more food.

The influence Skinner exerted has on the whole been against the social direction that he advocated: of a society composed of conditioned zombies, dull, well behaved, excruciatingly boring, and, beyond that (rather than freedom and dignity, which of course he dismissed as notions wholly without merit, rather than as words badly abused by manipulative politicians and "media experts"), sinister in the extreme in its implications. For Skinner had no imagination whatsoever: That failed him early, and he determined to punish the world for it. Yet his deadly sin was not cruelty or desire for power; it was not to see where his ideas could so quickly lead. He was a fine experimental scientist, but humanly a dangerous and coarse oaf, desperate to banish every sign of tenderness in himself. The early verse he quotes in his autobiographies may be derivative and trite, but it demonstrates that he had possessed tenderness—he need not have been ashamed of it.

It had been obvious to such psychologists as WILLIAM JAMES that there was a valid branch of psychology which could scientifically examine and even measure aspects of purely external behavior, as distinct from introspection, which was beset with so many philosophical problems. But it was the Russian scientist Ivan Pavlov (1849–1936) who really gave the impetus to the behavioristic branch of psychology. His famous experiments with dogs showed that they could be conditioned. A hungry dog was subjected to many pairings of feeding and the sounding of a bell; after being thus conditioned it would salivate at the sound of the bell.

This led Watson, who was almost astonishingly insensitive, to write:

> Give me a dozen healthy infants, well-formed, and my own specified world to bring them up in and I'll guarantee to take any one at random and train him to become any kind of specialist I might select—doctor, artist, merchant-chief, and yes even beggarman and thief, regardless of his talents, penchants, abilities, vocations, and the race of his ancestors.

This was the basis of Skinner's program, but his old literary aspirations stood him in good stead: He was vastly more sophisticated—less obviously idiotic. He put his case as well as it can be put (and free of Watson's overconfident ridiculosities) in his 1938 *The Behavior of Organisms,* which can be described as still the fundamental work on conditioning—if that is all we happen to want.

Skinner then became wholly obsessed with his subject. Genetic issues he in effect condemned on the grounds that these could not be manipulated by a psychologist! His arguments always took the following form: "What I am doing cannot allow for certain factors, therefore those factors are meaningless." Since, however, experiments taking into consideration factors, such as inner states, that are not observable, let alone measurable, are falsifiable in the proper Popperian sense—and in other scientific senses as well—Skinner's methodological restrictiveness was quite intolerable, and it is therefore surprising that he was tolerated for as long as he was. Even more surprising was that the utopia presented in *Walden Two* and *Beyond Freedom and Dignity* was ever taken seriously.

Walden Two took the name of THOREAU in vain. In it Professor Burris (compare Skinner's own first name) is introduced to an efficient and self-sufficient community of bloodless, bored, boring, smug individuals; this community "worked" by means of "reinforcement." This brings us to the "Skinner Box." The rat (i.e., for Skinner, the equivalent of a human being) first wanders about in it randomly. But eventually it is bound, accidentally, to press a lever. When it does that, it gets a scrap of food. This is "positive reinforcement." It learns to press the lever. So the rat became, in Skinner's bizarre language, an "operant." Thus the "people" in *Walden Two.* But of course they are not complete people—they are not even people at all, just ciphers.

In *Beyond Freedom* Skinner, building on all this, felt confident to pour scorn on the "romantic" notion of a humanity that acted of its own volition. Freedom from control of the environment was impossible, he asserted, and so the only hope was for a conditioned humanity. Liberty is "maintained and exercised in a way of subjection to authority." Religious faith, he added, throwing it out by implication, arose from environmental factors which had not yet been "analyzed."

Now there was, if only accidentally, more truth in some of this than people—than any of us—like to recognize. The "mechanical" nature of human behavior, especially the violent behavior of mobs—but also day-to-day life—had, years before, been thus "analyzed" in the strange and remarkable book *Beelzebub's Tales to His Grandson* (1950, but written and widely circulated in the 1920s) of G. I. GURDJIEFF—and in the immediately easier-to-understand and more popular account of Gurdjieff's teaching made by P. Ouspensky in his *In Search of the Miraculous.* J. B. Watson had even met Gurdjieff—in America—and had been very cruelly teased by him when parts of *Beelzebub's Tales to His Grandson* were read aloud to him; he had quite failed to understand what Gurdjieff was trying to say.

But Skinner, in essence Watson's disciple, quite failed, too, to recognize what the much maligned Gurdjieff had recognized: That there was a whole submerged side to humanity that was *not* mechanical, that was "religious," that wanted the truth, that yearned for what the existentialists used to call (but they investigated the matter less precisely than had Gurdjieff) "authenticity," that wished to discover why it existed at all.

Skinner also, rather surprisingly, ignored the undoubted effects that religious faith has had—and still has—on human behavior. It has even been reliably shown that the crime rate in particular communities has been substantially improved by the practice of transcendental meditation (and that despite whatever we might think about transcendental meditation). But because the notion of religious faith of any sort quite simply amazed Skinner into a sneeringly uncomprehending attitude, he was unable to discuss such questions—such as, for example, that the best and most helpful people in the Nazi camps were Jehovah's Witnesses—with any degree of objectivity. His attitude of mind, despite polite concessions, was this: "I cannot understand it—*it's out!*" I do not know what he made of the celebrated remark of the deist VOLTAIRE to the effect that if the idea of God did not exist we should have had to invent it.

It is well known that we must not, unless we know exactly what we are doing and allow for it, attribute human feelings to inanimate objects such as stones. Skinner used this in one of his arguments against our referring to human inner states as providing explanations for behavior. The random child killer—to take a horrible example—acts as he does only because of his "defective environment." The flaws in the logic here are strikingly obvious: Human beings themselves *do* have feelings—and not everyone from a similar environment kills children.

Skinner ended up as a somewhat pathetic figure, sometimes almost accepting that he had been wrong and that his attitude was shockingly inadequate. Yet his ideas about punishment and conditioning were put into practice all over the world and are still used. Some people's behavior these methods did *temporarily* "modify"; but others (most) they did not. The methods were, however, taken overall, no more successful than any others. His career above all exemplifies the fact that—because willfully selective—partial solutions to problems are worse than no solution at all.

AUTHORS, TITLES, AND PUBLISHERS OF THE 100 MOST INFLUENTIAL BOOKS EVER WRITTEN

Alighiere, Dante. *The Portable Dante*. Edited by M. Musa. Viking, 1995.

Aquinas, St. Thomas. *Summa Theologiae*. Tabor, 1981.

Aristotle. *Works*. Harvard University Press, 1933.

Augustine of Hippo. *Confessions*. New City, 1996.

Bacon, Francis. *Novum Organum*. Open Court, 1994.

Beauvoir, Simone de. *The Second Sex*. Translated by H. M. Parshley. Knopf, 1993.

Berkeley, George. *Philosophical Works*. Edited by M. R. Ayers. Knopf, 1993.

Buber, Martin. *I and Thou*. Translated by N. Kemp Smith. Scribner, 1974.

Bunyan, John. *Pilgrim's Progress*. Edited by Roger Sharrock. Penguin, 1965.

Burke, Edmund. *Reflections on the Revolution in France*. Viking, 1985.

Calvin, John. *Institutes of the Christian Religion*. Translated by H. Beveridge. Eerdmans, 1990.

Cervantes, Miguel de. *The Portable Cervantes*. Translated by Samuel Putnam. Viking, 1985.

Chomsky, Noam. *Syntactic Structures*. Peter Lang, 1978.

Clausewitz, Carl Marie von. *On War*. Edited by M. Howard and P. Paret. Princeton University Press, 1984.

Comte, Auguste. *The Essential Comte*. Barnes and Noble, 1998.

Confucius. *Analects of Confucius*. Translated by D. C. Lau. Penguin, 1979.

Copernicus, Nicolaus. *On the Revolution of the Celestial Orbs*. Prometheus, 1995.

Darwin, Charles. *On the Origin of Species by Means of Natural Selection*. Viking, 1982.

Descartes, René. *A Discourse on Method*. Translated by John Veitch. Knopf, 1994.

The Dhammapada. Translated by E. Easwaran. Penguin, 1987.

The Diderot Encyclopedia: The Complete Illustrations, 5 vols. H. N. Abrams, 1978.

Einstein, Albert. *Relativity: The Special Theory and the General Theory*. Crown, 1995.

Erasmus, Deisiderius. *In Praise of Folly*. Translated by B. Radice. Penguin, 1994.

The Essential Kabbalah. Edited by D. C. Matt. Harper, 1997.

Euclid. *Elements*. Dover, 1956.

Freud, Sigmund. *The Interpretation of Dreams*. Buccaneer, 1996.

Friedan, Betty. *The Feminine Mystique*. Norton, 1997.

Galilei, Galileo. *Galileo on the World Systems: A New Abridged Translation and Guide*. Edited and translated by Maurice Finocchario. Univeristy of California Press, 1997.

Gibbon, Edward. *The History of the Decline and Fall of the Roman Empire*. Fawcett, 1994.

Godwin, William. *Enquiry Concerning Political Justice and Its Influence on Modern Morals and Happiness*. Viking, 1993.

Gurdjieff, G. I. *Beelzebub's Tales to His Grandson*. Arkana, 1992.

Hayek, Friedrich von. *The Road to Serfdom*. University of Chicago Press, 1994.

Hegel, George Wilhelm Friedrich. *Phenomenology of Spirit*. Oxford University Press, 1979.

Herodotus. *The Histories*. Translated by J. Marincola. Penguin, 1996.

Hippocrates. *Genuine Works of Hippocrates*. Edited by Francis Adams. Krieger, 1972.

Hobbes, Thomas. *Leviathan*. Viking, 1982.

Homer. *The Illiad*. Translated by Robert Fagles. Viking, 1990.

———. *The Odyssey*. Translated by Richmond Lattimore. HarperCollins, 1991.

Hume, David. *An Enquiry Concerning Human Understanding*. Prometheus, 1988.

The I Ching. Translated by James Legge, edited by Raymond Van Over. Signet, 1971.

James, William. *Pragmatism*. Dover, 1995.

Johnson, Samuel. *A Dictionary of the English Language, a Modern Selection*. Edited by G. Milne and E. L. McAdam. Cassell, 1996.

Jung, Carl Gustav. *Psychological Types*. Edited by Gerald Adler. Princeton University Press, 1976.

Kafka, Franz. *The Trial*. Translated by E. Muir and W. Muir, edited by G. Steiner. Shocken, 1995.

Kant, Immanuel. *Critique of Pure Reason*. Edited by Vasilis Politis. Knopf, 1994.

Kepler, Johannes. *The Harmony of the World*. Translated by E. J. Aiton and A. M. Duncan. American Philosophical Library, 1997.

Keynes, John Maynard. *The General Theory of Employment, Interest, and Money*. Prometheus, 1997.

Kierkegaard, Søren. *Either/Or*. Edited by Victor Eremita. Penguin, 1992.

The Koran. Translated by N. J. Dawood. Penguin, 1956.

Kuhn, T. S. *The Structure of Scientific Revolutions*. University of Chicago Press, 1996.

Lao-Tzu. *The Way and Its Power*. Translated by Arthur Waley. Grove Press, 1958.

Leibnitz, Gottfried W. *Selections*. Edited by P. P. Weiner. Macmillan, 1982.

Locke, John. *An Essay Concerning Human Understanding*. Edited by K. Winkler. Prometheus, 1994.

Lucretius. *On the Nature of the Reality*. Translated by R. E. Latham. Penguin, 1994.

Luther, Martin. *Selections*. Edited by J. Dillenberger. Anchor, 1958.

Machiavelli, Niccolò. *The Prince*. Translated by G. Bull. Penguin, 1996.

Maimonides. *Guide for the Perplexed*. Translated by Chaim Rabin. Hackett, 1995.

Malthus, Thomas Robert. *An Essay on the Principle of Population*. Penguin, 1985.

Marcus Aurelius. *Meditations*. Translated by M. Staniforth. Penguin, 1987.

Marx, Karl, and Friedrich Engels. *The Communist Manifesto*. Viking, 1985.

Maxwell, James Clerk. *Treatise on Electricity and Magnetism*, 2 vols. Dover, 1991.

Mendel, Gregor. *Experiments in Plant-Hybridization*. Harvard University Press, 1965.

Mill, John Stuart. *On Liberty and Other Essays*. Edited by J. Gray. Oxford University Press, 1992.

Montaigne, Michel de. *The Complete Essays*. Translated by M. A. Screech. Penguin, 1993.

The Nag Hammadi Library [The Gospel of Truth]. Edited by J. Robinson. Brill, 1984.

Newton, Isaac. *The Principia*. Translated by Andrew Motte. Prometheus, 1995.

Nietzsche, Friedrich. *Thus Spake Zarathustra*. Translated by R. J. Hollingdale. Penguin 1978.

Orwell, George. *Nineteen Eighty-Four*. Penguin, 1989.

The Oxford Annotated Bible. Edited by H. G. May. Oxford University Press, 1965.

Paine, Thomas. *Common Sense*. Dover, 1997.

Pareto, Vilfredo. *The Mind and Society*. Translated by R. Livingstone. Harcourt Brace, 1935.

Pascal, Blaise. *Pensées*. Translated by A. J. Krailsheimer. Penguin, 1995.

Philo of Alexandria. *Works*, 12 vols. Harvard University Press, 1929–1962.

Plato. *The Republic*. Translated by G. M. A. Grube and C. D. C. Reeve. Hackett, 1992.

Plotinus. *The Enneads*. Translated by J. Dillon. Penguin, 1991.

Plutarch. *Lives*. Translated by John Dryden, edited by A. H. Clough. Random House, 1977.

Popper, Karl. *The Logic of Scientific Discovery*. Routledge, 1992.

Rabelais, François. *The Portable Rabelais*. Translated by Samuel Putnam. Viking, 1977.

Rousseau, Jean-Jaques. *Confessions*. Translated by P. N. Furbank. Knopf, 1992.

Sartre, Jean-Paul. *Being and Nothingness*. Translated by Hazel E. Barnes. Washington Square, 1993.

Schopenhauer, Arthur. *The World as Will and Idea*. AMS, 1975.

Sextus Empiricus. *Outlines of Scepticism*. Translated by J. Barnes, edited by J. Annas. Cambridge University Press, 1994.

Shakespeare, William. *Works*, 3 vols. Oxford University Press, 1987.

Skinner, B. F. *Beyond Freedom and Dignity*. Random House, 1971.

Smith, Adam. *An Enquiry Into the Nature and Causes of the Wealth of Nations*. University of Chicago Press, 1977.

Spencer, Herbert. *First Principles*. Greenwood, 1976.

Spinoza, Baruch. *A Spinoza Reader: The Ethics and Other Works*. Edited by E. Curley. Princeton University Press, 1994.

Tacitus. *The Annals of Ancient Rome*. Translated by M. Grant. Viking, 1956.

Thoreau, Henry David. *Civil Disobedience and Other Essays*. Dover, 1993.

Thucydides. *History of the Peloponneisan War*. Translated by R. Warner. Viking 1986.

Tolstoy, Leo. *War and Peace*. Translated by A. L. Maude and L. Maude, edited by G. Gibian. Norton, 1996.

The Upanishads. Translated by Juan Mascaro. Viking, 1965.

Vico, Giambattitsta. *The New Science*. Translated by T. C. Bergin. Cornell University Press, 1984.

Virgil. *The Aeneid*. Translated by David West. Penguin, 1991.

Voltaire, François-Marie de. *Candide*. Translated by Roger Pearson. Oxford University Press, 1990.

Wiener, Norbert. *Cybernetics*. MIT Press, 1965.

Wittgenstein, Ludwig. *Philosophical Investigations*. Prentice-Hall, 1973.

Wollstoncraft, Mary. *Vindication of the Rights of Woman*. Dover, 1996.

Zedong, Mao. *The Writings of Mao Zedong*, 3 vols. 1987.

The Avesta. Translated by J. Darmesteter. Clarendon, 1880–1887.

INDEX

485